Eugene L. Gross, William L. Gross

An Index to all the Laws of the State of Illinois

Eugene L. Gross, William L. Gross

An Index to all the Laws of the State of Illinois

ISBN/EAN: 9783742813909

Manufactured in Europe, USA, Canada, Australia, Japa

Cover: Foto ©Lupo / pixelio.de

Manufactured and distributed by brebook publishing software
(www.brebook.com)

Eugene L. Gross, William L. Gross

An Index to all the Laws of the State of Illinois

INDEX

TO ALL THE

LAWS of THE STATE of IL

BOTH PUBLIC AND PRIVATE,

WHICH ARE

NOT PRINTED AT LARGE IN GROSS' STATUT

Except Private Acts of 1869.

1818 TO 1869.

BY

EUGENE L. GROSS

AND

WILLIAM L. GROSS,

COUNSELORS AT LAW.

SPRINGFIELD

E. L. & W. L. GROSS

1869

INTRODUCTION.

THE DESIGN OF THIS WORK.—No publication of the "Statutes" of Illinois for popular use, can do more than present the general laws of the state which are in force at the time. This has been done in the edition of statutes which we publish, and it is all that can be accomplished within the limits of a single volume. From such a book, a very large number of acts must of necessity be excluded, either as being not in force, or not of general interest. But a large number of those very acts thus excluded, are of the highest importance to those who *are* interested in them, and it often becomes extremely desirable to know exactly where to find them. These pages, then, are intended as a complete guide to all the legislation of the State of Illinois, enacted since 1188, whether public or private, repealed or obsolete, but not including any acts printed in Gross' Statutes of 1869. It is in two parts, the one dealing with the Public acts, the other with the Private acts.

Part I is a classified synopsis of all the Public Statutes which have been enacted in the state of Illinois, since its admission into the Union, in 1818. This synopsis is made to perform the office of an index, by being arranged in chapters, numbered and entitled to correspond with our "Statutes," and will show: 1. A concise statement of the general subject, or subjects, embraced in each act. 2. The date of the approval of the act, and 3. The book or books and the page where it may be found printed at large. This part of the work is brought down to the close of the session of 1869.

Part II is a classified synopsis of all the Private and Local Statutes which have been enacted and printed in the state of Illinois, since its admission into the Union, in 1818. The classification is by counties, with sub-titles for cities and towns. All acts not capable of being assigned to any particular locality, are grouped under general, and it is hoped, convenient titles, and the whole is then alphabetically arranged. A glance at the table of contents will make this plain. The only private acts not comprised in this index, are the private acts of 1869, not yet in print.

To avoid any possible mistake, a further word of explanation should perhaps be added. In some instances, private and local acts have been placed in Part I. This is where there is a chapter in that Part entitled with precisely the subject of the act. For instance: Roads, Courts, Plank roads and Railroads. Some charters of incorporated companies, which contain no allusion to their locality are indexed under Corporations. On the other hand, those classes of public acts, which could not properly be placed under any chapter of the "Statutes," will be found arranged in the second Part.

BOOKS IN WHICH THE STATUTES OF ILLINOIS HAVE BEEN PUBLISHED.—In order to assist in the examination of past Legislation, we have prepared a list of all the books in which the statutes of the state of Illinois have been published. It will be seen that the first book named, is the session laws of 1819, although there was a session of the Legislature commencing 5 Oct. 1818. No laws were enacted at that session, as an examination of its journals will show, and the reason assigned is that the state had not then been admitted into the Union. The formal resolution for the admission of Illinois as a state was not finally passed by congress until 3 Dec. 1818. Hence the first laws enacted by the state of Illinois, were the acts of 1819.

LIST OF ILLINOIS STATUTES—Official.

No. of Assembly.	Session Begun.	Character of Book.	Pages of Statutes.	How Usually Cited.
1	Jan. 1819.	Public and Private acts	3—387.	Laws 1819.
2	4 Dec. 1820.	" " "	3—185.	Laws 1821.
3	2 Dec. 1822.	" " "	45—212.	Laws 1823.
4	15 Nov. 1824.	" " "	3—184.	Laws 1825.
"	2 Jan. 1826.	" " "	3—96.	Laws 1826.
5	4 Dec. 1826.	Revised Statutes	45—384.	R. S. 1827.
"	" " "	Private acts	3—35.	Pr. L. 1827.
6	3 Dec. 1828.	Public acts	5—237.	R. L. 1829.
7	3 Dec. 1830.	Public and Private acts	5—193.	Laws 1831.
8	3 Dec. 1832.	Revised Statutes	59—677.	R. S. 1833.
"	" " "	Private acts	3—212.	Pr. L. 1833.
9	1 Dec. 1834.	Public and Private acts	3—235.	Laws 1835.
"	7 Dec. 1835.	" " "	3—278.	Laws 1836.
10	5 Dec. 1836.	Public acts	3—335.	1 Laws 1837.
"	" " "	Private acts	3—344.	Pr. L. 1837.
"	10 July 1837.	Public and Private acts	3—109.	2 Laws 1837.
11	3 Dec. 1838.	Public acts	3—202.	Laws 1839.
"	" " "	Private acts	3—249.	Pr. L. 1839.
	1839.	Gale's Compilation	45—728.	Gales' Stat.
11	9 Dec. 1839.	Public and Private acts	3—156.	Laws 1840.
12	7 Dec. 1840.	" " "	3—357.	Laws 1841.
13	5 Dec. 1842.	" " "	3—320.	Laws 1843.
14	2 Dec. 1844.	" " "	3—369.	Laws 1845.
"	3 Mar. 1845.	Revised Statutes	43—617.	R. S. 1845.
15	7 Dec. 1847.	Public acts	3—169.	Laws 1847.
"	" " "	Private acts	3—217.	Pr. L. 1847.
16	1 Jan. 1849.	Public acts	27—229.	1 Laws 1849.
"	" " "	Private acts	3—142.	Pr. L. 1849.
"	22 Oct. 1849.	Public and Private acts	3—51.	2 Laws 1849.
17	6 Jan. 1851.	Public acts	5—201.	Laws 1851.
"	" " "	Private acts	3—326.	Pr. L. 1851.
"	7 June 1852.	Public and Private acts	3—268.	Laws 1852.
18	3 Jan. 1853.	Public acts	3—280.	Laws 1853.
"	" " "	Private acts	3—618.	Pr. L. 1853.
"	9 Feb. 1854.	Public acts	3—31.	Laws 1854.
"	" " "	Private acts	35—253.	Pr. L. 1854.
19	1 Jan. 1855.	Public acts	3—200.	Laws 1855.
"	" " "	Private acts	1—737.	Pr. L. 1855.
	1856.	Purple's Compilation	73—1366.	Purple's Stat.
20	5 Jan. 1857.	Public acts	3—303.	Laws 1857.
"	" " "	Private acts	5—1451.	Pr. L. 1857.
	1858.	Scates' Compilation.	81—1238.	Scates' Stat.
21	3 Jan. 1859.	Public acts	9—214.	Laws 1859.
"	" " "	Private acts	9—733.	Pr. L. 1859.
22	7 Jan. 1861.	Public acts	9—276.	1 Laws 1861.
"	" " "	Private acts	9—749.	Pr. L. 1861.
"	23 Apr. "	Public and Private acts	5—29.	2 Laws 1861.
23	5 Jan. 1863.	Public acts	9—86.	Laws 1863.
"	" " "	Private acts	9—278.	Pr. L. 1863.
24	2 Jan. 1865.	Public acts	1—133.	Laws 1865.
"	" " "	Private acts Vol. I.	1—828.	1 Pr. L. 1865.
"	" " "	" " Vol. II.	1—602.	2 Pr. L. 1865.
25	7 Jan. 1867.	Public acts	1—188.	Laws 1867.
"	" " "	Private acts Vol. I.	1—996.	1 Pr. L. 1867.
"	" " "	" " Vol. II.	1—846.	2 Pr. L. 1867.
"	" " "	" " Vol. III.	1—681.	3 Pr. L. 1867.
"	11 June "	Public and Private acts	5—41.	2 Laws 1867.
	1868.	Gross' Compilation 1868	33—828.	Gross' Stat. 1868.
26	4 Jan. 1869.	Public acts	1—411.	Laws 1869.
	1869.	Gross' Compilation 1869	1—831.	Gross' Stat. 1869.

repealing former laws; but at the end or each act is a section, which in terms repeals the former acts on that particular subject. The various acts are separated by titles, most of which are now the titles of chapters. It was printed at Vandalia.

At the next session, in 1829, it was found that the revision of 1827 had omitted a considerable number of very important acts; these were therefore revised and re-enacted, in the same manner as those in the former volume, so that this book is really a supplement to the revision of 1827, and it takes an examination of both volumes to show the condition of the law on a given subject. For this reason probably, the acts of 1829 were entitled "Revised Laws," and have usually been cited as the Revised Laws of 1829. This volume was printed at Cincinnati, for publishers in Shawneetown.

5. The next revision is that of 1833. It contains nothing to show by whom it was prepared. The plan and arrangement is the same as before. There is no division into chapters. Three thousand five hundred copies were printed by the state for distribution. The printing was done at Vandalia. Former acts are in terms repealed, and a list of them is given. It does not contain the militia law, which was printed separately.

6. In 1839, Stephen F. Gale, of Chicago, published a compilation of the statutes, prepared by himself. It was a careful work and for a long time was the chief authority for statute law in Illinois. Many references to it appear in the earlier reports. The plan of arrangement was very simple, being the same which was afterwards pursued by Judge Purple, and in Gross' statutes. That plan is merely this: To give all the acts on each subject together, under a single general title, and to follow the order of time in placing the various amendments. This book, being a compilation, and brought out by private enterprise, without the authority of the legislature, did not attempt to modify any statute—it simply presented them in a convenient form.

7. We come now to the last revision—that of 1845. It was prepared by General Mason Brayman, an eminent lawyer. He has so well described the character of the task he performed that we re-produce his language: "The only object possible of attainment was sought—that of collating and arranging the laws of the state, in accordance with their true spirit and intention, making them plain and intelligible, and relieving them from that smothering load of useless verbiage, contradictions and doubts, which had been accumulating through so many years of changing legislation. The object became, not so much to make new laws, or to depart materially from the spirit and meaning of those already existing, as to plain away excrescences, reconcile contradictions, and condense and arrange in convenient order all that remained in force at the time. Everything that had been repealed or superseded was omitted—conflicting provisions were reconciled, and sections which were obscure, involved or doubtful in their meaning, were re-written, so as to express the evident intention of the legislature, and conform to constructions fixed by the supreme court." The general plan and outline of the statutes remained as before, the book of Mr. Gale being closely followed. This is the last revision that has been made of the laws of Illinois. The work was so well and faithfully done that, although a new constitution was adopted in 1848, the book of statutes in common use remained the same. The changes in the constitution made some changes in the laws necessary, but the revision of 1845 and the session laws were everywhere consulted, and no new publication of statutes was attempted for nearly twelve years. The state published and distributed among the public officers who were required to know and to carry out the law, an edition of ten thousand copies.

8. In 1856, Norman H. Purple, of Peoria, a distinguished lawyer, and formerly a judge of the Supreme court, published a compilation of the statutes of Illinois, in two octavo volumes. The plan was simple. Following the revision of 1845, the new acts were one by one placed next after the chapters to which they were most nearly related. It was annotated with references to many decisions of the supreme court, and has always been a popular book with the lawyers. The state purchased, for distribution, one thousand copies.

9. Two years later a compilation of the statutes, also in two volumes, was published by D. B. Cooke and company of Chicago. The names of Samuel H. Treat, Walter B. Scates and Robert S. Blackwell appear on the title page as the compilers. It is usually cited as Scates' Compilation, and is commonly understood to have been

mainly prepared by Judge Scates. The state purchased two thousand copies.

10. Ten years afterwards—in December, 1868—the first edition of Gross' statutes, one thousand in all, was published. The state purchased five hundred copies, and an act was passed declaring it to be evidence in the courts. A second edition has been prepared, and is now in use, including the acts of 1869.

SESSIONS OF THE TERRITORIAL LEGISLATURE.

No.	*Begun.*	*Where held.*
1	25 Nov. 1812	Kaskaskia.
2	19 Dec. 1814	"
3	2 June, 1815	"
4	9 Dec. 1815	"
5	2 Dec. 1816	"
6*	1 Dec. 1817	"

*Laws 1819, 75 §1.

SESSIONS OF THE GENERAL ASSEMBLY.

No.	*Begun.*	*Where held.*
	[Constitution of 1848.]	
1.	5 Oct. 1818	Kaskaskia.
	Jan. 1819	"
2.	4 Dec. 1820	Vandalia.
3.	2 Dec. 1822	"
4.	15 Nov. 1824	"
	2 Jan. 1826	"
5.	4 Dec. 1826	"
6.	3 Dec. 1828	"
7.	3 Dec. 1830	"
8.	3 Dec. 1832	"
9.	1 Dec. 1834	"
	7 Dec. 1835	"
10.	5 Dec. 1836	"
	10 July 1837	"
11.	3 Dec. 1838	"
	9 Dec. 1839	Springfield.
12.	7 Dec. 1840	"
13.	5 Dec. 1842	"
14.	2 Dec. 1844	"

No.	*Begun.*	*Where held.*
15	7 Dec. 1846	Springfield
	[Constitution of 1848.]	
16.	1 Jan. 1849	Springfield.
	22 Oct. 1849	"
17.	6 Jan. 1851	"
	7 June. 1852	"
18.	3 Jan. 1853	"
	9 Feb. 1854	"
19.	1 Jan. 1855	"
20.	5 Jan. 1857	"
21.	3 Jan. 1859	"
22.	7 Jan. 1861	"
	23 April 1861	"
23.	5 Jan. 1863	"
24.	2 Jan. 1865	"
25.	7 Jan. 1867	"
	11 June 1867	"
	14 June 1867	"
26.	4 Jan. 1869	"

Time when Statutes Take Effect.—Under the constitution of 1848, no public act is in force until the lapse of sixty days from the adjournment of the general assembly, unless otherwise expressly so stated in the act itself. Art. 3 §23. It has long been the practice, in the official publication of the laws of each session, to mark against each act the date when it was supposed to take effect. But this date has almost uniformly been computed as sixty days from the day when the act was *approved*, and not from the close of the session. Many mistakes on this point have therefore crept into the various publications of our statutes. For convenience of reference, a table of the sessions of the general assembly is subjoined, by which the time when any act went into operation can be determined at a glance. It is prepared from a careful examination of the journals of the assembly. Consult on this subject, *Wheeler v. Chubbuck*, 16 Ill. 361.

Sessions of the General Assembly.	*Date of the closing of each session.*	*When the acts took effect.*
1—1840	Feb. 12	April 13.
2—1849	Nov. 7	Jan. 6.
1851	Feb, 17	April 18.
1852	June 23	Aug. 22
1853	Feb. 14	April 15.
1854	March 4	May 3.
1855	Feb. 15	April 16.
1857	Feb. 19	April 20.
1859	Feb. 27	April 28.
1—1861	Feb. 22	April 23.
2—1861	May 3	July 2.
1863	June 10*	Aug. 9.
1865	Feb. 16	April 17.
1—1867	Feb. 28	April 29.
2—1867	June 28	Aug. 27.
1869	April 20	June 19.

*See *The People*, etc., *vs. Hatch*, etc., 33 Ill. 135.

JUDGES OF THE SUPREME COURT.

Judge.	*From*	*To*	*Remarks.*
Joseph Philips,	9 Oct 1818,	4 July, 1822.	Resigned.
Thomas C. Browne,	9 Oct. 1818,	4 Dec. 1848.	Term expired.
John Reynolds,	9 Oct. 1818,	19 Jan. 1825.	" "
William Wilson,	7 Aug. 1819,	4 Dec. 1848.	" "
Thomas Reynolds,	31 Aug. 1822,	19 Jan. 1825.	" "
Samuel D. Lockwood,	19 Jan. 1825,	4 Dec. 1848.	" "
Theophilus W. Smith,	19 Jan. 1825,	26 Dec. 1842.	Died.
Thomas Ford,	13 Feb. 1841,	1 Aug. 1842.	Resigned
Sidney Breese,	13 Feb. 1841,	19 Dec. 1842.	"
Walter B. Scates,	13 Feb. 1841,	11 Jan. 1847.	"
Samuel H. Treat,	13 Feb. 1841,	23 Mar. 1855.	"
Stephen A. Douglas,	1 Mar. 1841,	28 June, 1843.	"
John D. Caton,	20 Aug. 1842,	7 Jan. 1864.	"
James Semple,	16 Jan. 1843,	16 Aug. 1843.	"
Richard M. Young,	4 Feb. 1843,	26 Jan. 1847.	"
John M. Robinson,	6 Mar, 1843,	27 April, 1843.	Died.
James Shields,	16 Aug. 1843,	2 April, 1845.	Resigned.
Jesse B. Thomas,	24 Aug. 1843,	8 Aug. 1845.	"
Gustavus P. Kœrner,	2 Apr. 1845,	4 Dec. 1848.	Term expired.
Norman H. Purple,	8 Aug. 1845,	4 Dec. 1848.	" "
William A. Dening,	19 Jan. 1847,	4 Dec. 1848.	" "
Jesse B. Thomas,	27 Jan. 1847,	4 Dec. 1848.	" "
Lyman Trumbull,	4 Dec. 1848,	4 July, 1853.	Resigned.
Walter B. Scates,	4 July, 1853,	May, 1857.	"
Onias C. Skinner,	28 June, 1855,	19 April, 1858.	"
Sidney Breese,	23 Nov. 1857,		
Pinkney H. Walker,	19 April, 1858,		
Corydon Beckwith,	9 Jan. 1864,	6 June, 1864.	Term expired.
Charles B. Lawrence,	6 June, 1864,		

CIRCUIT JUDGES.

Cir.	*Judge.*	*Post Office.*
1.	Charles D. Hodges,	Carrollton, *Greene Co.*
2.	Silas L. Bryan,	Salem, *Marion Co.*
3.	Monroe C. Crawford,	Jonesboro, *Union Co.*
4.	Hiram B. Decius,	Majority Point, *Cumberland Co.*
5.	Chauncey L Higbee,	Pittsfield, *Pike Co.*
6.	George W. Pleasants,	Rock Island, *Rock Island Co.*
7.	Erastus S. Williams,	Chicago, *Cook Co.*
8.	John M. Scott,	Bloomington, *McLean Co.*
9.	Edwin S. Leland,	Ottawa, *LaSalle Co.*
10.	Arthur A. Smith,	Galesburg, *Knox Co.*
11.	Josiah McRoberts,	Joliet, *Will Co.*
12.	James M. Pollock,	Mt. Vernon, *Jefferson Co.*
13.	Theodore D. Murphy,	Woodstock, *McHenry Co.*
14.	Benjamin R. Sheldon,	Galena, *JoDaviess Co.*
15.	Joseph Sibley,	Quincy, *Adams Co.*
16.	Sabin D. Puterbaugh,	Peoria, *Peoria Co.*
17.	Arthur J. Gallagher,	Decatur, *Macon Co.*
18.	Edward Y. Rice,	Hillsboro, *Montgomery Co.*
19.	David J. Baker,	Cairo, *Alexander Co.*
20.	Charles H. Wood,	Onarga, *Iroquois Co.*
21.	Charles Turner,	Pekin, *Tazewell Co.*
22.	William W. Heaton,	Dixon, *Lee Co.*
23.	Samuel L. Richmond,	Lacon, *Marshall Co.*
24.	Joseph Gillespie,	Edwardsville, *Madison Co.*
25.	Richard S. Canby,	Olney, *Richland Co.*
26.	Andrew D. Duff,	Benton, *Franklin Co.*
27.	James Steele,	Mattoon, *Coles Co.*
28.	Sylvanus Wilcox,	Elgin, *Kane Co.*
29.	(Not created.)	
30.	Benjamin S. Edwards,	Springfield, *Sangamon Co.*

CONTENTS.

PART I. GENERAL LAWS.

PART. II. PRIVATE AND SPECIAL ACTS.

Organization of Counties.—The time when the acts were passed, under which the several counties in this state were organized, are presented in the following table, with a reference to the book and page where the act is printed at large:

County.	Date of act.	Reference.
Adams,	13 Jan. 1825	Laws 1825, 93.
Alexander,	4 Mar. 1819	" 1819, 133.
Bond,		Territorial.
Boone,	4 Mar. 1837	1 Laws 1837, 96.
Brown,	1 Feb. 1839	Laws 1839, 52.
Bureau,	28 " 1837	1 Laws 1837, 93.
Calhoun,	19 Jan. 1825	Laws 1825, 65.
Carroll,	22 Feb. 1839	" 1839, 160.
Cass,	3 Mar. 1837	1 Laws 1837, 101.
Champaign,	20 Feb. 1833	Pr. L. 1833, 28.
Christian,	15 " 1839, 104.	Laws 1840, 80.
Clark,	22 Mar. 1819	" 1819, 166.
Clay,	23 Dec. 1824	" 1825, 18.
Clinton,	27 " "	" " 27.
Coles,	25 " 1830	" 1831, 59.
Cook,	15 Jan. 1831	" " 54.
Crawford,		Territorial.
Cumberland,	2 Mar. 1843	Laws 1843, 94.
DeKalb,	4 " 1837	1 Laws 1837, 96.
DeWitt,	1 " 1839	Laws 1839, 199.
Douglas,	13 Feb. 1857	" 1857, 71.
DuPage,	9 " 1839	" 1839, 73.
Edgar,	3 Jan. 1823	" 1823, 74.
Edwards,	28 Nov. 1814	Pope 85.
Effingham,	15 Feb. 1831	Laws 1831, 50.
Fayette,	14 " 1821	" 1821, 164.
Ford,	17 " 1859	" 1859, 29.
Franklin,		Territorial.
Fulton,	28 Jan. 1823	Laws 1823, 88.
Gallatin,	14 Sept. 1812	MS, 44.
Greene,	20 Jan. 1821	Laws 1821, 26.
Grundy,	17 Feb. 1841	" 1841, 74.
Hamilton,	8 " 1821	" 1821, 113.
Hancock,	13 Jan. 1825	" 1825, 93.
Hardin,	2 Mar. 1839	" 1839, 234.
Henderson,	20 Jan. 1841	" 1841, 67.
Henry,	13 " 1825	" 1825, 94.
Iroquois,	26 Feb. 1833	Pr. L. 1833, 19.
Jackson,		Territorial.
Jasper,	15 Feb. 1831	Laws 1831, 50.
Jefferson,	26 Mar. 1819	" 1819, 267.
Jersey,	28 Feb. 1839	" 1839, 208.
JoDaviess,	17 " 1827	R. S. 1827, 117.
Johnson,	14 Sept. 1812	MS, 44.
Kane,	16 Jan. 1836	Laws 1836, 273.
Kankakee,	11 Feb. 1851	" 1851, 30.
Kendall,	19 " 1841	" 1841, 75.
Knox,	13 Jan. 1825	" 1825, 94.
Lake,	1 Mar. 1839	" 1839, 216.
LaSalle,	15 Jan. 1831	" 1831, 54.
Lawrence,	16 " 1821	" 1821, 16.
Lee	27 Feb. 1839	Laws 1839, 170.
Livingston,	" 1837	1 Laws 1837, 83.
Logan,	15 " 1839	Laws 1839, 104.
Macon,	19 Jan. 1829	" 1829, 28.
Macoupin,	17 " "	" " 26.
Madison,	14 Sept. 1812	MS, 43.
Marion,	24 Jan. 1823	Laws 1823, 49.
Marshall,	19 " 1839	" 1839, 43.
Mason,	20 " 1841	" 1841, 69.
Massac,	8 Feb. 1843	" 1843, 74.
McDonough,	25 Jan. 1826	" 1826, 76.
McHenry,	16 " 1836	" 1836, 273.
McLean,	25 Dec. 1830	" 1831, 57.
Menard,	15 Feb. 1839	" 1839, 104.
Mercer,	13 Jan. 1825	" 1825, 94.
Monroe,		Territorial.
Montgomery,	12 Feb. 1821	Laws 1821, 143.
Morgan,	31 Jan. 1823	" 1823, 108.
Moultrie,	16 Feb. 1843	" 1843, 83.
Ogle,	" Jan. 1836	" 1836, 274.
Peoria,	13 " 1825	" 1825, 85.
Perry,	29 " 1827	R. S. 1827, 110.
Piatt,	27 " 1841	Laws 1841, 71.
Pike,	31 " 1821	" 1821, 59.
Pope,		Territorial.
Pulaski,	3 Mar. 1843	Laws 1843, 99.
Putnam,	13 Jan. 1825	" 1825, 94.
Randolph,		Original.
Richland,	24 Feb. 1841	Laws 1841, 77.
Rock Island,	9 " 1831	" 1831, 52.
Saline,	25 " 1847	Pr. L. 1847, 34.
Sangamon,	30 Jan. 1821	Laws 1821, 45.
Schuyler,	13 " 1825	" 1825, 92.
Scott,	16 Feb. 1839	" 1839, 126.
Shelby,	23 Jan. 1827	R. S. 1827, 115.
Stark,	2 Mar. 1839	Laws 1839, 229.
St. Clair,		Original.
Stephenson,	4 Mar. 1837	1 Laws 1837, 96.
Tazewell,	31 Jan. 1827	R. S. 1827, 113.
Union,		Territorial.
Vermilion,	18 Jan. 1826	Laws 1826, 50.
Wabash,	27 Dec. 1824	" 1825, 25.
Warren,	13 Jan. 1825	" " 93.
Washington,		Territorial.
Wayne,	26 Mar. 1819	Laws 1819, 268.
White,		Territorial.
Whiteside,	16 Jan. 1836	Laws 1836, 274.
Will,	12 " 1836	" " 262.
Williamson,	28 Feb. 1839	" 1839, 110.
Winnebago,	16 Jan. 1836	" 1836, 273.
Woodford,	27 Feb. 1841	" 1841, 84.

PART I.

GENERAL LAWS.

CHAP. 1. ABATEMENT.

Act 6 Feb. 1819; death of the plaintiff or defendant may be suggested on the record; Laws 1819, 6. . . Act 22 Mar. 1819; pleas in abatement to be verified by affidavit; Laws 1819, 140 §§4, 5. . . Act 30 Dec. 1826; relative to pleas in abatement; the foregoing act of 6 Feb. 1819 repealed; R. S. 1827, 45; R. S. 1833, 59. . . Act 2 Mar. 1839; death of the plaintiff not to abate suit for use of another, similar to R. S. 1845 Ch. 1 §13; Laws 1839, 271.

CHAP. 2. ACCOUNT.

Act 11 Jan. 1827; to regulate actions of account; R. S. 1827, 47; R. S. 1833, 61.

CHAP. 3. ADVERTISEMENTS.

Act 28 Dec. 1826; concerning the publication of advertisements; R. S. 1827, 48; R. S. 1833, 62.

CHAP. 4. ALIENS.

Act 6 Feb. 1819; may purchase and hold real estate; Laws 1819, 6. . . Act 7 Feb. 1827; to enable aliens to hold real estate; foregoing act of 6 Feb. 1819 repealed; R. S. 1827, 49.

CHAP. 5. AMENDMENTS AND JEOFAILS.

Act 22 Mar. 1819; enacting substantially §§9, 10 of this chapter; Laws 1819, 143 §§19, 20. . . Act 11 Jan. 1827; concerning amendments and jeofails; R. S. 1827, 49; R. S. 1833, 63.

CHAP. 5*a*. ANIMALS.

Act 16 Jan., no bull to run at large until approved by the board of bull inspectors; Laws 1836, 254. . . Act 24 Dec. 1836; repeal of the act 16 Jan. 1836; 1 Laws 1837, 49. . . Act 16 Feb., levies tax of $2. to $5. on each dog in counties of Henry and Bureau; 2 Pr. Laws 1865, 333. . . Also levies tax of $3. to $5. on each dog in counties of Whiteside and Winnebago; 2 Pr. Laws 1865, 334. . . Resolution for printing the proceedings of the cattle commissioners convention; Laws 1869, 415.

CHAP. 6. APPRENTICES.

Act 6 Feb., indentures of white children; cruelty or ill treatment; Laws 1819, 5. . . Act 30 Dec. 1826; respecting apprentices; R. S. 1827, 54; R. S. 1833, 68. . . Act 16 Feb., to legalize indentures by the managers of the Pennsylvania house of refuge; Laws 1859, 9.

CHAP. 7. ARBITRATIONS AND AWARDS.

Act 25 Feb., authorizing and regulating arbitrations; Laws 1819, 71. . . Act 6 Jan., regulating arbitrations and references; repeal of the foregoing act of 25 Feb. 1819; R. S. 1827, 64; R. S. 1833, 78. . . Act 1 Mar., amending the foregoing act of 6 Jan. 1827; R. S. 1833, 81.

CHAP. 8. ATTACHMENTS BEFORE JUSTICES.

Act 24 Jan., concerning attachments; R. S. 1827, 68 §6. . . Act 12 Feb., concerning attachments; R. S. 1833, 82 §§1—33. . . Act 27 Feb., to regulate proceedings by attachment before justices, consolidating and amending former acts which are repealed; 1 Laws 1837, 12. . . Act 31 Jan., property pursued and brought back by the officer, similar to R. S. 1845 Ch. 8§ 5; Laws 1840, 30. . . Act 23 Feb., attachment against non resident debtor for $50.; Laws 1843, 19.

CHAP. 9. ATTACHMENTS IN CIRCUIT COURTS.

Act 22 Feb., allowing foreign attachment; Laws 1819, 33 §§1—5. . . Act 24 Feb., proceedings against absconding debtors; Laws 1819, 66. . . Act 24 Jan., concerning attachments; R. S. 1827, 66. . . Act 16 Jan., amending the foregoing act of 24 Jan. 1827, so, as to send writs to foreign counties; Laws 1829; 8. . . Act 12 Feb., concerning attachments; R. S. 1833, 82 §§1—33. . . Act. 31 Jan. 1840; in case of debtor being pursued by sheriff; similar to R. S. 1845 Ch. 9 §3; Laws 1840, 30. To include joint debtors, similar to R. S. 1845 Ch. 9 §6; Id. 31.

CHAP. 10. ATTACHMENT OF BOATS AND VESSELS.

Act 13 Feb., when and how such attachments may be levied; R. S. 1833, 95.

CHAP. 11. ATTORNEYS AND COUNSELORS AT LAW.

Act 10 Feb., manner of licensing attorneys, their duties and liabilities; Laws 1819, 9. . . Act 5 Jan., attorneys liable for the costs of suit brought by them; Laws 1821, 11 §8. . . . Act 1 Mar., licensing attorneys, their duties and liabilities; repeal of the act of 1819; R. S. 1833, 99 §§ 1—11. . . Act 4 Mar., striking from the rolls for collecting money and not paying over, similar to R. S. 1845, Ch. 11 §§5, 6; Laws 1843, 19.

CHAP. 12. ATTORNEY GENERAL AND CIRCUIT ATTORNEYS.

Act 23 Mar., appointment of circuit attorneys; their duties and the duties of the attorney general; Laws 1819, 204. . . Act 30 Mar., supplemental to the foregoing, and fixing the salaries of said officers; Laws 1819, 349. . . Act 18 Jan., supplemental to the foregoing act of 23 Mar., 1819; duties of the attorney general, new attorneys nominated and appointed; Laws 1825, 178. . . Act 17 Feb., relating to the attorney general and states' attorneys; former acts repealed; R. S. 1827, 79; R. S. 1833, 97. . . Act 22 Jan. 1829; attorney general and state's attorneys to give bond; Laws 1829, 114, R. S 1833; 504. . . Act 14 Feb., attorney general elected for four years by joint ballot, first election in Dec. 1834; Laws 1831, 18 §5. . . Act 5 Feb., attorney general to reside at the seat of government; R. S. 1833, 99. . . Act 2 Mar., election of the attorney general; R. S. 1833, 103. . . Act 7 Feb., state's attorneys to be elected biennially by the legislature; Laws 1835, 44. . . Act 2 Mar., to settle the accounts of James Turney, late attorney general; Laws 1839, 272. . . Act 25 Feb., powers and duties of the attorney general in revenue cases; Laws 1841, 35.

CHAP. 13. AUDITOR AND TREASURER.

Act 24 Mar., defining the duties of auditor and treasurer; Laws 1819, 240. . . Act 25 Jan., no money to be paid to persons indebted to the state; Laws 1826, 72. . . Act 19 Feb., mode of issuing and redeeming auditor's warrants; when payable in state paper; R. S. 1827, 81. . . Act 19 Jan., persons indebted to the state, or to the state bank not to be paid: Laws 1829, 114. . . Act 3 Jan., duty of the auditor in suits brought by or against the state; Laws 1829, 171. . . Act 14 Feb., election of the auditor, his duties; Laws 1831, 17. . . Act 16 Feb., payments by the bank to the auditor; Laws 1831, 18. . . Act 11 Jan. 1831; bond of the state treasurer; Laws 1831, 186; R. S. 1833, 589. . . Act 2 Mar., consolidating the acts relative to auditor and treasurer; R.S. 1833, 103. . . Act 12 Feb., money not to be paid to persons indebted to the State; R. S. 1833, 588. . . Act 1 Mar., penalty of the treasurer's bond to be $100,000.; 1 Laws 1837, 334. . . Act 1 Mar., treasurer to deposit the public money in the state bank at Springfield; Laws 1839, 212. . . Act 4 Mar., to amend the act 2 Mar. 1833 "to consolidate the acts relative to auditor and treasurer;" Laws 1843, 20.

CHAP. 14. BAIL.

Act 32 Mar., cases in which bail may be required; mode of taking the same; Laws 1819, 139 §§1—3. . . Act 22 Mar., duty of sheriffs and coroners on *capias ad respondendum*; Laws 1819, 146 §§30—36. . . Act 5 Jan., appearance bail not to be required; Laws 1821, 8. . . Act 26 Jan. 1827; concerning special bail; R. S. 1827, 82; R. S. 1833, 107.

CHAP. 15. BANK NOTES.

Act 8 Feb., to prevent the circulation of any paper currency unauthorized by law; Laws 1821, 115. . . Act 4 Dec. 1838; to prohibit the circulation of foreign bank notes less than $5; Laws 1839, 79.

CHAP. 16. BASTARDY.

Act 25 Mar., maintenance and support of illegitimate children; Laws 1819, 261. Act 23 Jan. 1827; to provide for the maintenance of illegitimate children; former acts repealed; R. S. 1827, 244; R. S. 1833, 334.

CHAP. 17. BIRTHS AND DEATHS.

Act 3 Mar., mode of registering births and deaths, similar to the chapter in the revised statutes (of 1845); Laws 1843, 210. Foregoing to take effect 1 Apr. 1843; Laws 1843, 213.

CHAP. 17 *a*. CARRIERS AND INNKEEPERS.

Act 12 Feb., incorporating the American Express Co.; stock not to exceed $2,000,000.; Pr. Laws 1859, 379. . . Act 22 Feb., incorporating the Northwestern Express Co.; Pr. Laws 1861, 309. . . Act 16 Feb., incorporating the Atlantic and Pacific Express Co. 1 Pr. Laws 1865, 557.

CHAP. 18. CASTOR BEANS.

Act 16 Jan., protection of stock, similar to R. S. 1845, Ch. 18; Laws 1836, 232.

CHAP. 19. CENSUS.

Act 23 Mar., to be taken 1 Aug. 1820; Laws 1829, 197. . . Act 30 Mar., payment to commissioners for service between June and December 1818; Laws 1819, 547. . . Act 13 Jan., compensation for taking the census of 1820; Laws 1821, 12. . . Act 27 Dec. 1824; census to be taken on the first Monday in September 1825, and every five years thereafter; Laws 1825, 32. . . Act 23 Jan. 1829; to provide for

the taking of the census; Laws 1825, 18; R. S. 1833, 114. . . Resolution of 1855, census of all deaf and dumb, blind and insane persons residing in the state; names of heads of family with whom they reside; Pr. Laws 1855, 741. . . Act 7 Jan., to extend the time for taking the census, the act of 13 Jan. 1839; Laws 1841, 52. . . Act 15 Feb., manner of taking for 1855; Laws 1855, 151.

CHAP. 21. CHANCERY.

Act 22 Mar., regulating the practice in courts of chancery; Laws 1819, 170. . . Act 5 Jan., regulating the practice at law and in chancery; Laws 1821, 8. . . Act 27 Dec. 1824; courts of chancery to decree a specific performance of agreements for the conveyance of lands; Laws 1825, 30; Laws 1829, 23; R. S. 1833, 136. . . Act 26 Jan., to prescribe the mode of proceeding in chancery; R. S. 1827, 88; also act 13 Feb.; R. S. 1833, 118. . . . Act 11 Feb., masters in chancery to be appointed, their duties defined; Laws 1835, 32. . . . Act 27 Feb., proceedings against parties whose names are unknown, also in dower and partition; 1 Laws 1837, 324. . . Act 24 Jan., to authorize proceedings by creditor's bill for discovery; set off allowed; Laws 1839, 50. . . Act 21 Feb., masters in chancery appointed for four years; Laws 1843, 10.

CHAP. 22. CHARITABLE USES.

Act 1 Feb. 1831; the first four sections of Ch. 22 R. S. 1845; Laws 1831, 73; R. S. 1833, 240. . . Act 18 Feb., concerning lands conveyed to county, similar to §5 in the revised statutes; Laws 1841, 110.

CHAP. 22 *a*. COMMISSIONERS.

Act of 1 Mar., 1845; appointment of commissioners, their duties; R. S. 580. . . Act 24 Feb., supplemental to the preceding; Laws 1847, 32. . . Act 27 Feb. (1 July) 1851; a consolidation of the two preceding acts which are repealed; Laws 1851, 142; Gross' Statutes 1868, 98. . . Act 22 June, acknowledgements before David Rowland, a commissioner in Washington, between 9 Aug. 1851, and 12 May 1862, legalized; Laws 1852, 186. . . Act 16 Feb., amending the act of 17 Feb. 1851 by increasing the number of commissioners; Laws 1865, 23; Gross' Statutes 1868, 100.

CHAP. 23. CONGRESS.

Act 15 Feb. 1831; dividing the state into three representative districts; Laws 1831, 70; R. S. 1833, 235. . . Act 9 Feb., election of a congressman; Laws 1831, 75. . . Act 1 Mar., to establish seven congressional districts; Laws 1843, 71.

CHAP. 24. CONVEYANCES.

Act 19 Feb., manner of taking acknowledgments; when proved by witnesses; conveyances of the estate of the wife; acknowledgments may be taken by county commissioners or justices; Laws 1819, 19 §§8, 9, 11; 12. . . Act 30 Dec. 1822; deeds executed without this state; Laws 1823, 85. . . Act 27 Jan., circuit judges to take acknowledgments; Laws 1826, 88. . . Act 31 Jan. 1827; concerning conveyances of real property; R. S. 1827, 95; R. S. 1833, 129. . . Act 22 Jan. 1829; amending the act of 31 Jan. 1827, "concerning the conveyance of real property;" deeds to be recorded within six months; R. S. 1829, 24; R. S. 1833, 137. . . Act 8 Jan., effect of "grant, bargain and sell;" satisfaction of mortgages; Laws 1829, 116. . . Act 16 Jan., acknowledgment and record of sheriff's deed, similar to R. S. 1845. Ch. 24 §§29 and 30; Laws 1836, 257. . . Act 16 Jan., certificates of purchase of school and canal lands assignable, similar to R. S. 1845 Ch. 24 §27; 1 Laws 1837, 150. . . Act 21 July, record of conveyances to be notice to creditors and subsequent purchasers; 2 Laws 1837, 13. . . Act 21 July, estates in fee simple and of posthumous children, similar to R. S. 1845 Ch. 24 §§13 and 14; 2 Laws 1837, 14. . . Act 27 Feb., release of mortgage by deed witnessed; similar to R. S. 1845 Ch. 24 §37; Laws 1839, 197. . . Act 2 Mar. 1837; seven years possession and payment of taxes, similar to R. S. 1845 Ch. 24 §§8—10; Laws 1839, 266. . . Act 26 Feb., to admit to record deeds made without this state; similar to the act of 1847 (Laws 1847, 37.); Laws 1841, 66.

Conveyances—Special Acts.—Act 4 Mar., authorizing certain lands belonging to the estate of Toussaint Dubois to be conveyed; Laws 1819, 115. . . Act 8 Feb., administrator of Aaron T. Crane to convey certain lands; Laws 1821, 101. . . Act 14 Feb., lands belonging to the estate of William Jones to be sold and conveyed; Laws 1821, 152. . . Act 24 Jan., administrators of William Jones to convey certain real estate; Laws 1823, 45. . . Act 8 Jan., administrators of Thomas Brady, late of St. Louis, to sell certain real estate; Laws 1823, 69. . . Act 11 Jan., supplemental to above act of 8 Feb. 1821 respecting lands of A. T. Crane; Laws 1823, 71. . . Act 3 Jan., governor to convey a lot in Vandalia to John Warnock; Laws 1823, 74. . . Act 29 Dec. 1822; administrators of Thomas F. Herbert, to sell certain lands; Laws 1823, 78. . . Act 19 Dec. 1822; administrators of John Neely to convey certain lands; Laws 1823, 78. . . Act 26 Dec. 1822; administrators of Resen Club to invest in real estate taking the deeds to his heirs; Laws 1823, 81. . . Act 27 Dec. 1822; administrators of Charles Smith to convey certain real estate; Laws 1823, 83. . . Act 5 Feb., governor to convey a certain lot to James Hull; Laws 1823, 112 . . Act 18 Feb., administrators of Ferdinand Ernst to convey certain real estate; Laws 1823, 177. . . Act 14 Dec. 1824, amending act of 19 Dec. 1822, "authorizing the administrators of John Neely to convey certain land;" Laws 1825, 12. . . Act 24 Feb., deeds and conveyances to secure loans from the school fund of Connecticut legalized; Laws 1839, 19.

CHAP. 25. CORPORATIONS.

Div. 1. Towns.—Act 4 Jan., recording town

plats; Laws 1825, 53; Laws 1829, 184. . . Amendatory act of 20 Jan.; Laws 1826, 63. . . Act 12 Feb., incorporation of towns, similar to Div. 1 Ch. 25 R. S. 1845; Laws 1831, 82 §§ 1—12; R. S. 1833, 362. . . Act 27 Feb., providing for the recording of town plats; R. S. 1833, 599. . . Act 31 Jan., Powers and duties of town trustees, similar to §§ 11—15 (R. S. 1845 Ch. 25 Div. 1.) Laws 1835, 175. . . Act 19 Feb., manner of vacating town plats; Laws 1841, 310. . . Act 23 Feb., road tax in towns and cities; Laws 1841, 213. . . Act 23 Feb., to enable incorporated townships to dissolve their incorporations; Laws 1843, 275.

Charters of Springfield and Quincy.—Act 3 Feb., original charter of Springfield; Laws 1840, 6. . . Act 27 Feb., qualifications of officers and voters; Laws 1841, 61. . . Act 26 Feb., limitation of the power to borrow money; Laws 1845, 285. . . Act 26 Jan., of indictments for gaming; Laws 1849, 15.

Act 3 Feb. 1840; original charter of Quincy; Laws 1840, 113. . . Act 7 Jan., qualifications of electors; Laws 1841, 57.

DIV. 2. ACADEMIES.—Act 6 Mar., incorporation of academies and seminaries; Laws 1843, 6.

Special Acts.—Act 16 Feb., to incorporate the Grand College of the state of Illinois of the Workingmen's Relief society; 1 Pr. Laws 1865, 73. . . Act 29 Jan., to incorporate "Shiloh College;" Laws 1840, 37. . . Act 9 Feb., to incorporate colleges at Alton, Jacksonville, Lebanon and Jonesboro; Laws 1835, 177. Foregoing amended by repealing so much of the act of 1835 as prohibited a theological department in colleges, and limited their lands to 640 acres; (Laws 1835, 179 §§ 7, 12.) Laws 1841, 65.

DIV. 3. RELIGIOUS SOCIETIES.—Act 6 Feb., incorporation of religious societies, similar to §§44—48 (R. S. 1845 Ch. 25); Laws 1835, 147. . . Incorporation of a committee to aid in the erection of church edifices; Laws 1845 (12 Feb.) 251.

Special Act.—To incorporate the Illinois Eldership of the churches of God; Pr. Laws 1861, (13 Feb.) 80. . . To incorporate the German United Evangelical Synod of the Northwest; 1 Pr. Laws 1856 (16 Feb.) 237.

Baptist.—To incorporate the Baptist General Association of Illinois; 1 Pr. Laws 1865 (16 Feb.) 235.

Catholic.—Deeds to bishops of the Catholic church declared valid; Laws 1845 (24 Feb.) 321.

Cumberland Presbyterian.—To incorporate the board of foreign and domestic missions of the Cumberland Presbyterian Church; 1 Pr. Laws 1865 (16 Feb.) 240.

Lutheran.—Act 10 Feb., to incorporate the Evangelical Lutheran Synod of Illinois; Pr. Laws 1853, 424. . . Act 14 Feb., to incorporate the Evangelical Lutheran Synod of Northern Illinois; Pr. Laws 1857, 672.

Methodist.—Incorporation of the Preachers' Aid Society of the Rock River Conference of the Methodist Episcopal Church; 1 Pr. Laws 1867 (21 Feb.) 124. . . Incorporation of the Western Methodist Book Concern; 1 Pr. Laws 1867 (14 Feb.) 161.

Presbyterian.—Act 22 Feb. 1861; to incorporate the Presbyterian College of Illinois; Pr. Laws 1861, 22. . . Incorporation of the United Presbyterian Theological Seminary of the Northwest; 1 Pr. Laws 1867 (5 Mar.) 20.

Protestant Episcopal.—Act 10 Feb., to incorporate the Trustees of the Protestant Episcopal church in the diocese of Illinois; Pr. Laws 1849, 78. . . Act 24 Jan., relating to conveyances made to the Protestant Episcopal church; Laws 1853, 482; Gross' Stat. 1868, 97. . . Act 21 Feb., to amend the foregoing act of 1849; further provisions; Pr. Laws 1861, 82.

DIV. 4. LIBRARIES.—Incorporation of Libraries; Laws 1823 (31 Jan.) 201; R. S. 1833, 357. Foregoing amended; Laws 1835 (31 Jan.) 181.

DIV. 5. FIRE COMPANIES.—Incorporation of Fire companies, similar to §§62—65 (R. S. 1845 Ch. 25) Laws 1835 (12 Feb.) 174.

DIV. 8. AGRICULTURAL SOCIETIES.—Incorporating the Union Agricultural society; Pr. Laws 1839 (19 Feb.) 88. Foregoing amended; Laws 1840 (31 Jan.) 33. And again; Laws 1843 (3 Mar.) 157.

DIV. 9. COUNTY AGRICULTURAL SOCIETIES.—A general law for their incorporation; Pr. Laws 1839 (28 Feb.) 126. . . Annual appropriation of $50. from the state treasury; Laws 1855 (14 Feb.) 131. . . Annual appropriation of $100. for 1857 and 1858; Laws 1857 (18 Feb.) 141. Foregoing revived and made perpetual; Laws 1861 (21 Feb.) 11. . . Atlanta and Sandwich societies included; Laws 1869 (10 Mar.) 9. Also Onarga society; Laws 1869 (13 Mar.) 10.

DIV. 11. CEMETERIES.—Incorporation of the Trible family cemetery association; Pr. Laws 1855 (14 Feb.) 445.

DIV. 12. MANUFACTURING.—Incorporation of companies—a general Law; Laws 1825 (16 Dec.) 13. . . Incorporation of the Union manufacturing company; Laws 1841 (3 Feb.) 182. . . Incorporation of the North Western company for manufacturing; to be located north of the mouth of the Illinois; Pr. Laws 1833 (28 Jan.) 44. . . Incorporation of the Illinois paper manufacturing company to be located in the northern part of the state; Pr. Laws 1833 (1 Mar.) 92. . . Incorporation of the Illinois Beet sugar manufacturing company; Pr. Laws 1837 (18 Feb.) 40. . . Incorporation of the Union steam mill company; Pr. Laws 1839 (2 Mar.) 183. . . Incorporation of the Cantine manufacturing company; Pr. Laws 1855 (15 Feb.) 630. . . Incorporation of the Fox river dairy and cheese factory company; 1 Pr. Laws 1867 (5 Mar.) 904. . . Incorporation of the Union Screw and Bolt company; 2 Pr. Laws 1867 (7 Mar.) 311. . . Incorporation of the Mechanics Foundry and manufacturing company; in either Carroll, Stephenson or Winnebago; 2 Pr. Laws 1867 (23 Feb.) 326. . . Incorporation of the Home Flax manufacturing company; 2 Pr. Laws 1867 (21 Feb.) 333. . . Incorporation of the Western White Lead company; 2 Pr. Laws 1867 (23 Feb.) 345.

Agricultural.—Incorporation of the Icarian Community; Pr. Laws 1851 (13 Feb.) 114. .

Incorporation of the Egyptian Wine company; 2 Pr. Laws 1865 (13 Feb.) 691.

Mining.—Incorporation of the Boston and Elizabeth Mining company; in Pope, Hardin and Gallatin; Pr. Laws 1847 (13 Feb.) 77. . . Incorporation of the Union coal and iron company; Pr. Laws 1853 (12 Feb.) 560 . . Incorporation of the Illinois Central iron and coal mining company, corporate powers defined; Pr. Laws 1862 (20 Feb.) 302. . . Act 16 Feb., incorporating the Empire Mining and Oil company; 2 Pr. Laws 1865, 61. . . Act 16 Feb., incorporating the Illinois California Silver Mining company; 2 Pr. Laws 1865, 66. . . Act 16 Feb., incorporating the Illinois Lead Mining and Smelting company; 2 Pr. Laws 1865, 68. . . Act 16 Feb., incorporating the Illinois Petroleum and Mining company; 2 Pr. Laws 1865, 70. . . Act 15 Feb., incorporating the Illinois Valley Coal company; 2 Pr. Laws 1865, 73. . . Act 16 Feb., incorporating the Kankakee Coal company; in Will, Livingston and Grundy counties; 2 Pr. Laws 1865, 74. . . Act 16 Feb., incorporating the Ohio and Mississippi Petroleum and Mining company; 2 Pr. Laws 1865, 78. . . Act 16 Feb., incorporating the National Lead company; 2 Pr. Laws 1865, 81. . . Incorporation of the Georgetown Gold and Silver Mining company; 2 Pr. Laws 1867 (25 Feb.) 420.

Printing and Publishing.—Incorporation of the Religio-Philosophical Publishing association; 2 Pr. Laws 1865 (16 Feb.) 122. Name of the foregoing changed to the Central Publishing House; 2 Pr. Laws 1867 (23 Feb.) 490. . . Incorporation of the Northwestern Associated Press; 2 Pr. Laws 1867 (25 Feb.) 515.

Miscellaneous.—Incorporation of the Union Exporting and Importing company; Laws 1825 (14 Dec. 1824) 9. . . Incorporation of the Industrial League of Illinois for the dissemination of knowledge; Pr. Laws 1853 (10 Feb.) 514. . . Incorporation of the Garden City Building association; Pr. Laws 1857 (11 Feb.) 434. . . Incorporating the Illinois State Horticultural society; 1 Pr. Laws 1865 (16 Feb.) 596. . . Incorporation of the Artesian Water supply company; 2 Pr. Laws 1867 (7 Mar.) 53. . . Incorporation of "La Societe Francaise de Bien faisance de l' Illinois;" 1 Pr. Laws 1867 (8 Mar.) 136. . . Incorporating the Grand Union of the Daughters of Temperance; Laws 1852 (19 June) 34.

CHAP. 26. COSTS.

Act 22 Mar., non-residents to give security for costs; collection of costs from the securities; Laws 1819, 150 §§44, 45. . . Act 5 Jan., non-residents to give security for costs; Laws 1821, 10 §5. . . Act 10 Jan. 1827; concerning costs; R. S. 1827, 102; R. S. 1833, 165.

CHAP. 27. COUNTIES AND COUNTY COURTS.

Act 19 Feb., official seals to be procured; Laws 1819, 16; Laws 1829, 155; R. S. 1833, 569. . . Act 22 Mar., establishing the courts of county commissioners; Laws 1819, 175; Laws 1829, 33; R. S. 1833, 142. . . Act 23 Mar., suits by and against counties; Laws 1819, 184. . . Act 24 Mar., duty of the county commissioners to erect jails in each county; Laws 1819, 237. . . Act 30 Mar., supplement to the acts establishing Wayne, Jefferson, Clark and Alexander counties; Laws 1819, 350. . . Act 19 Jan., compensation of county commissioners; Laws 1826, 56. . . Act 3 Jan. 1827; to incorporate counties; R. S. 1827, 107; R. S. 1833, 139. . . Act 20 Jan., county commissioners may run county lines where necessary; Laws 1829, 31 §4. . . Act 5 Jan., authorizing and requiring the county commissioners to erect court houses and jails in every county; repeal of the foregoing act of 24 Mar. 1819; Laws 1829, 53. . . Act 7 Jan., filling vacancies in the office of commissioner; Laws 1831, 74. . . Act 11 Jan. 1833; to compel the payment of fines and penalties into the county treasury; R. S. 1833, 141. . . Act. 12 Feb., vacancies in the office of county commissioner; fiscal statement of county made at March term; Laws 1835, 34. . . Act 7 Jan., conveyances by county commissioners to be valid; Laws 1835, 46. . .

Act 31 Jan., appeals allowed from the county commissioners to the circuit court; Laws 1835, 152. . . Act 7 Feb., county commissioners' clerks and county treasurers elected by the people; 1 Laws 1837, 49. . . Act 1 Mar., election of county commissioners; former acts amended and repealed; 1 Laws 1837, 103. . . Act 21 July, per diem of county commissioners $2.50; 2 Laws 1837, 16. . . Act 16 Feb., vacant rooms in the court houses in Peoria and four other counties to be leased; Laws 1839, 119. . . Act 2 Mar., of the annual fiscal statement required to be made by the county commissioners; Laws 1839, 270. . . Act 21 Feb., county commissioners to lease rooms in the court house; Laws 1843, 128. . . Act 24 Feb., erection of fire proof offices for the preservation of county records; similar to Ch. 27 §§44, 45 [R. S. 1845]; Laws 1843, 210.

CHAP. 28. COUNTY TREASURERS AND COUNTY FUNDS.

Act 11 Jan. 1831; fines and penalties to be paid into the county treasury; R. S. 1833, 141. Act 22 July, county orders recorded when presented; sheriffs to report revenue collected; 2 Laws 1837, 59. . . Act 25 Feb., to regulate county treasurers and county funds; similar to Ch. 28 R. S. 1845 §§14—28; Laws 1843, 112. . . Act 28 Feb., to regulate county funds, and fix the duties of county treasurers, similar to Ch. 28 R. S. 1845 §§4—14; Laws 1843, 151.

CHAP. 29. COURTS.

Act 30 Mar., suits by and against justices of of the supreme court; clerks not to make a complete record; Laws 1819, 350. . . Act. 31 Mar., regulating and defining the duties of justices of the supreme court; Laws 1819, 373. . . Act 31 Mar., supplemental to the foregoing act; suits pending at the time of its passage; Laws 1819, 384. . . Act 5 Jan., the clerks not to make complete records; Laws

1821, 11 §9. . . Act 29 Dec., 1824; constituting and regulating supreme and circuit courts; Laws 1825, 36. . . Act 17 Jan., sundry provisions concerning judges and clerks; Laws 1825, 170. . . Act 26 Jan., amending the foregoing act of 29 Dec. 1824, in the matter of appeals from circuit courts; Laws 1826, 83 §3. . . Act 27 Jan., when clerks are to make complete records; Laws 1826, 85. . . Act 12 Jan. 1827; amending the foregoing act of 29 Dec. 1824, "regulating supreme and circuit courts;" R. S. 1827, 118. . . Act 12 Jan. 1827; supplemental to the foregoing act, and relating to suits then pending; R. S. 1827, 119. . . Act 17 Feb. 1827; changing the terms of the supreme and circuit courts and for other purposes; several former acts repealed; R. S. 1827 120. . . Act 19 Jan., regulating the supreme and circuit courts; a consolidation of former acts which are repealed; Laws 1829 39; R. S. 1833, 147. . . Act 22 Jan., to provide a suitable place for holding supreme court; Laws 1829, 47; R. S. 1833, 156. . . Act 25 Jan., supplemental to the foregoing act of 19 Jan. 1829, changing the circuits, making sundry amendments, and repealing former acts; Laws 1829, 48; R. S. 1833, 156. . . Act 15 Feb., clerk of the supreme court removed from office; Laws 1931, 187; R. S. 1833, 159. . . Act 26 Feb. 1833; clerks of courts to renew their bonds periodically; R. S. 1833, 128. . . Act 8 Jan. 1829; establishing a circuit court north of the Illinois river; R. S. 1833, 147. . . Act 7 Jan., election of five additional Judges, to act as circuit Judges; Laws 1835, 150. . . Act 13 Feb., time of holding the supreme and circuit courts; salary of circuit judges $750.; interchange of judges; special terms called; special term at the instance of a prisoner; Laws 1835, 167. . . Act 4 Mar., special terms of court, similar to R. S. 1845 Ch. 29 §50; 1 Laws 1837, 112 §5. . . Act 12 Feb., salaries of judges of supreme court; Laws 1839, 102. . . Act 1 Feb., publication and distribution of the reports of the supreme court; Laws 1840, 77. Summer terms of the supreme court, Id. 87. . . Act 10 Feb., to reorganize the judiciary; five additional supreme judges to be elected, making nine in all; former acts relating to the judiciary all repealed; Laws 1841, 173. . . Act 23 Feb., to establish circuit courts; Laws 1841, 103. . . Act 3 Mar., agreed cases taken to the supreme court, similar to R. S. 1845 Ch. 29 §§16–18; Laws 1843, 134.

SUPREME COURT.

Libraries.—Appropriation of $5,000. for a law and miscellaneous library for the legislature and the supreme court; Laws 1839 (22 Feb.) 149. . . For the law library in the 1st and 3rd divisions, $5,000.; Laws 1849 (26 Jan.) 57. . . For the Springfield library $500.; Laws 1849 (8 Feb.) 98. . . For each grand division in 1851 and 1852, $500. annually; Laws 1851 (28 Jan.) 12. Also, a like sum for 1853 and 1854; Pr. Laws 1853 (22 Jan.) 448. Also, a like sum for 1855 and 1856; Laws 1855 (6 Feb.) 153. . . Appropriation of $500. annually in each grand division—length of time not specified; Laws 1857 (28 Feb.) 44. . . Librarian for each grand division, annual compensation $200.; Laws 1857 (10 Feb.) 57.

Court Rooms.—To be obtained and furnished; Pr. Laws 1827 (30 Dec. 1826.) 4. Also, Laws 1849 (31 Jan.) 57.

Clerk Hire.—Judges to prepare amendments to the statutes; allowance to each $1,000. per annum for clerk hire; Laws 1865)8 Feb.) 127. Also, a further allowance of $1,200. each, per annum, for clerk hire; Laws 1869 (11 Feb.) 46

First Division.—Mt. Vernon. Construction of a court room; Pr. Laws 1854 (28 Feb.) 146. . . Time of holding court; Laws 1849 (6 Jan.) 57. Also, Laws 1857 (10 Feb.) 41. Also, Laws 1865 (16 Feb.) 25. Also, Laws 1867 (16 Feb.) 75; and (22 Feb.) Ibid. . . Mt. Vernon Academy to use rooms in the basement of the court house; Laws 1857 (16 Feb.) 211. . . Terms to be held at Cairo upon conditions; Laws 1865 Feb.) 25.

Second Division.—Springfield. Time of holding court; Laws 1849 (6 Jan.) 57. Also, Laws 1857 (10 Feb.) 41. . . Attaching McLean county to said division; Laws 1865 (16 Feb.) 25.

Third Division.—Ottawa. Time of holding court; Laws 1849 (6 Jan.) 57. Also, Laws 1857 (10 Feb.) 41. Also, Laws 1867 (22 Feb.) 75. . . Erection of a court house; Laws 1857 (14 Feb.) 34. Also Laws 1865 (16 Feb.) 25.

CIRCUIT COURTS.

First Circuit.—Act 31 Mar., first circuit to consist of St. Clair, Madison, Bond and Washington counties; John Reynolds, justice of the supreme court to preside therein; Laws 1819, 378 §§19, 20. . . Act 14 Feb., including St. Clair, Madison, Greene, Sangamo, Pike and Montgomery counties; Laws 1821, 157. . . Act 17 Feb., including St. Clair, Madison, Greene, Pike, Morgan, Sangamon and Fulton counties; Laws 1823, 161. . . Act 29 Dec. 1824; including Pike, Fulton, Sangamon, Morgan, Greene and Montgomery counties; Laws 1825, 41 §18. . . Act 17 Jan., changing the time of holding courts; Laws 1825, 170. . . Act 26 Jan., times of holding courts changed; Laws 1826, 81. . . Act 12 Jan. 1827; including Peoria, Fulton, Schuyler, Adams, Pike, Calhoun, Greene, Morgan and Sangamon counties; R. S. 1827, 119 §3. . . Act 17 Feb. 1827; times of holding courts changed; R. S. 1827, 120. . . Act 25 Jan., including Pike, Calhoun, Greene, Macoupin, Morgan, Sangamon, Macon and Tazewell counties; Laws 1829, 48. . . Act 16 Feb., including Pike, Calhoun, Greene, Morgan, Sangamon, Tazewell, Macon, McLean and Macoupin counties; Laws 1831, 45. . . Act 16 Feb. 1830 [1]; including Calhoun and Pike counties; Laws 1831, 48. . . Act 2 Mar. 1833; changing time of holding courts; R. S. 1833, 162. . . Act 17 Jan., including Calhoun, Greene, Morgan, Sangamon, Macoupin, Macon, Tazewell and McLean counties; Laws 1835, 153. . . Act 4 Mar., terms of court; 1 Laws 1837, 112. . . Act 23 Feb., including Morgan, Cass, Pike, Calhoun, Greene, Scott and Macoupin counties; Laws 1839, 155. . . Act 2 Mar., to change the time of holding courts; Laws 1839, 250. . . Act 30 Jan., including Jersey, Cass and Scott counties; Laws 1840, 86. . . Act 3 Feb., to change the time of courts;

Circuit Courts.

Laws 1841, 103. . . Act 23 Feb. 1841; including Morgan, Cass, Scott, Pike, Calhoun, Greene, Jersey and Macoupin; Samuel D. Lockwood, judge; time of holding courts; Laws 1841, 103. . . Act 14 Feb., to change the time of holding courts; Laws 1843, 129. . . Act 27 Feb., including Greene, Pike, Calhoun, Jersey, Macoupin, Scott, Cass, Mason and Morgan counties; Laws 1845, 49. Act 27 Feb., including Morgan, Scott, Greene, Cass, Mason, Menard, Macoupin, Jersey and Calhoun counties; Laws 1847, 26. . . Act 11 Feb., including Menard county; Laws 1847, 31. . . Act 8 Feb., including Morgan, Cass, Menard, Mason, Greene, Macoupin, Jersey, Calhoun and Scott counties; Laws 1849, 57. . . Act 12 Feb., including Morgan, Scott, Greene, Macoupin, Jersey, Calhoun and Menard counties; Laws 1853, 59. . . Act 14 Feb., including Morgan, Greene, Jersey, Calhoun and Scott counties; Laws 1857, 21. . . Act 31 Jan., including the counties of Morgan, Jersey, Greene, Calhoun and Scott; Laws of 1859, 48. . . Act 16 Feb., including the counties of Scott, Morgan, Jersey, Greene and Calhoun; Laws 1861, 89. . . Act 20 Feb., including the counties of Scott, Morgan, Jersey, Greene and Calhoun; Laws 1861, 89. . . Act 9 Feb., including the counties of Greene, Morgan, Jersey, Scott and Calhoun; Laws 1867, 50. . . Act 30 Jan., to change the time of holding courts in Morgan, Greene and Jersey counties; Laws 1869, 69.

Second Circuit.—Act 31 Mar., second circuit to consist of Crawford, Edwards and White counties; William P. Foster, justice of the supreme court to preside therein; Laws 1819, 378 §§19, 20. . . Act 14 Feb., including, Clark, Crawford, Lawrence, Edwards, Wayne, Hamilton and White counties; Laws 1821, 158. . . Act 17 Feb., including White, Edwards, Lawrence, Crawford, Clark, Edgar, Wayne and Hamilton counties; Laws 1823, 161. . . Act 29 Dec. 1824; including Madison, St. Clair, Monroe, Washington, Bond and Fayette counties; Laws 1825, 41 §18. . . Act 17 Jan., changing the time of holding courts, and attaching Montgomery and Clinton counties to the circuit; Laws 1825, 170. . . Act 26 Jan., times of holding courts changed; Laws 1826. 81. . . Act 12 Jan. 1827; including Madison, St.Clair, Monroe, Randolph, Washington, Clinton, Bond, Montgomery and Fayette counties; R. S. 1827, 119 §3. . . Act 17 Feb. 1827; times of holding courts changed; R. S. 1827, 120. . . Act 25 Jan., including Madison, St. Clair, Monroe, Randolph, Washington, Clinton, Bond, Fayette, Montgomery and Shelby counties; Laws 1829, 48. . . Act 16 Feb., including Madison, St.Clair, Monroe, Randolph, Washington, Clinton, Bond, Shelby, Fayette and Montgomery counties; Laws 1831, 45. . . Act 16 Feb. 1830 [1]; including Madison county; Laws 1831, 48. . . Act 2 Mar. 1833; changing time of holding courts; R. S. 1833, 162. . . Act 17 Jan., including Madison, St. Clair, Monroe, Randolph, Washington. Clinton, Bond, Montgomery, Shelby, Effingham and Fayette counties; Laws 1835, 153. . . Act 16 Jan., changing time of holding courts; Laws 1836, 251. . . Act 10 Feb., time of court in Washington county; 1 Laws 1837, 111. . . Act 15 Feb., to change the time of holding courts; Laws 1839, 103. . . Act 3 Feb., to change the time of holding courts in Clinton and Bond; Laws 1840, 130. . . Act 7 Jan., to change the time of holding courts; Laws 1841, 101. . . Act 23 Feb., including Madison, St. Clair, Monroe, Randolph, Washington, Clinton, Bond, Fayette, Montgomery and Effingham counties; Sidney Breese, judge; time of holding courts; Laws 1841, 103. . . Act 21 Feb., to include the county of Perry and to change the time of holding courts; Laws 1843, 130. . . Act 21 Feb., including Perry, Montgomery, Effingham, Fayette, Bond, Clinton, Washington, Randolph, Monroe, St. Clair and Madison counties; Laws 1843, 130. . . Act 21 Feb., including Shelby county; Laws 1845, 47. . . Act 13 Feb., including Madison, St. Clair, Monroe, Randolph, Perry, Washington, Clinton, Bond, Fayette, Effingham and Montgomery counties; Laws of 1847, 29. . . Act 14 Feb., including St. Clair, Madison, Monroe, Randolph, Perry, Washington, Clinton, Bond, Fayette and Montgomery counties; Laws 1851, 93. . . Act 12 Feb., including Clinton, Marion, Washington, Randolph and Monroe counties; Laws 1857, 20. . . Act 16 Feb., including Monroe county; Laws 1857, 302. . . Act 8 Feb., including the counties of Clinton, Marion, Washington, Randolph and Monroe; Laws 1859, 49. . . Act 20 Feb., including the counties of Marion, Monroe, Randolph, Clinton and Washington; Laws 1861, 90. Foregoing repealed; act 25 22 Feb., Laws 1861, 90. . . Act 3 Feb., including the counties of Fayette, Clinton, Marion, Washington, Randolph and Monroe; Laws 1863, 34. . . Act 29 Mar., additional term in Marion county; Laws 1869, 70. . . Act 10 Feb., to fix the time of holding courts; Laws 1869, 70. Amended as to Clinton county by act 16 Apr. 1869; Laws 1869, 71.

Third Circuit.—Act 31 Mar., third circuit to consist of Monroe, Randolph, Jackson and Union counties; Joseph Philips, chief justice of the supreme court to preside therein; Laws 1819, 378 §§19, 20. . . Act 14 Feb., including Monroe, Randolph, Jackson, Jefferson, Washington, Fayette and Bond counties; Laws 1821, 157. . . Act 17 Feb., including Monroe, Randolph, Jefferson, Marion, Washington, Bond, Montgomery and Fayette counties; Laws 1823, 161. . . Act 29 Dec. 1824; including Randolph, Jackson, Franklin, Johnson, Union and Alexander counties; Laws 1825, 42 §18. . . Act 17 Jan., changing the time of holding courts, and attaching Pope county to the circuit; Laws 1825, 170. . . Act 26 Jan., times of holding courts changed; Laws 1826, 81. . . Act 12 Jan. 1827; including Jackson, Union, Alexander, Johnson, Pope, Franklin, Gallatin, Marion, Hamilton and Jefferson counties; R. S. 1827, 19 §3. . . Act 17 Feb. 1827; times of holding courts changed; R. S. 1827, 120. . . Act 25 Jan., including Gallatin, Hamilton, Jefferson, Marion, Franklin, Perry, Jackson, Union, Alexlexander, Johnson and Pope counties; Laws 1829, 48. . . Act 16 Feb., including Gallatin, Pope, Johnson, Alexander, Union, Jackson, Perry, Franklin, Marion, Jefferson and Hamilton counties; Laws 1831, 45. . . Act 2 Mar. 1833; changing time of holding courts; R. S. 1833, 162. . . Act 17 Jan., including Hamilton, Jefferson, Franklin, Gallatin, Pope, Johnson, Alexander,

Union, Jackson, Marion and Perry counties; Laws 1835, 153. . . Act 16, Jan., supplemental to the act of the present session changing the terms in the 3rd circuit; Laws 1836, 228. . . Act 16 Jan., supplemental to the acts regulating circuit courts, and changing the time of holding courts in this circuit; Laws 1836, 257. . . Act 19 Jan., teste of process after the resignation of Judge Jeptha Hardin: 1 Laws 1837, 179. . . Act 2 Mar., to change the time of holding courts; Laws 1839, 289. . .. Act 23 Feb., including Jackson, Perry, Franklin, Union, Williamson, Alexander, Johnson, Pope, Hardin, Gallatin, Hamilton, Jefferson and Marion counties; Walter B. Scates, judge; time of holding courts; Laws 1841, 103. . . Act 26 Feb., to change the time of holding courts; Laws 1841, 109. . . Act 25 Feb., to change the time of holding courts; Laws 1843, 131. . . Act 25 Feb, including Marion, Jefferson, Hamilton, Franklin, Williamson, Jackson, Union, Alexander, Johnson, Massac, Pope, Hardin and Gallatin counties; Laws 1843, 131. . . Act 27 Feb., including Massac and Johnson counties; Laws 1847, 42. . . Act 3 Feb., including Marion, Jefferson, Hamilton, Franklin, Williamson, Jackson, Union, Alexander, Pulaski, Johnson, Massac, Pope, Hardin, Saline and Gallatin counties; Law 1849, 59. . . Act 6 Nov., including Gallatin and Hardin counties; Laws 1849, 16. . . Act 11 Feb., including Hardin, Pope, Johnson, Williamson, Franklin, Jackson, Union, Alexander, Pulaski and Massac counties; Laws 1851, 30. . . Act 14 Feb., including Hardin, Pope, Johnson, Williamson, Franklin, Jackson, Union, Alexander, Pulaski and Massac counties; Laws 1855, 188. . . Act 3 Feb., including the counties of Perry, Jackson, Union and Alexander; Laws 1859, 51. . . Act 10 Feb., to fix the time of holding courts; Laws 1869, 70. . . . Act 11 Mar., time holding courts in Union county; Laws 1869, 84.

Fourth Circuit.—Act 31 Mar., fourth circuit to consist of Gallatin, Franklin, Pope and Johnson counties; Thomas C. Browne justice of the supreme court to preside therein; Laws 1819, 378 §§19, 20. . . Act 14 Feb., including Franklin, Union, Alexander, Johnson, Pope and Gallatin counties; Laws 1821, 158. . . Act 17 Feb., including Gallatin, Franklin, Jackson, Union, Alexander, Johnson, and Pope counties; Laws 1823, 162. . . Act 29 Dec. 1824; including Jefferson, Gallatin, Hamilton, Wayne and Marion counties; Laws 1825, 42 §18. . . Act 17 Jan., changing the time of holding the courts, and attaching Franklin and Clay counties to the circuit; Laws 1825, 170. . . Act 26 Jan., times of holding courts changed; Laws 1826, 81. . . Act 12 Jan. 1827; including Clay, Wayne, White, Edwards, Wabash, Lawrence, Crawford, Clark, Edgar and Vermilion counties; R. S. 1827, 119 §3. Act 17 Feb. 1827; times of holding courts changed; R. S. 1827, 120. . . Act 25 Jan., including White, Edwards, Wabash, Lawrence, Crawford, Clark, Edgar, Vermilion, Clay and Wayne counties; Laws 1829, 48. . . Act 16 Feb., including White, Edwards, Wabash, Lawrence, Wayne, Clark, Crawford, Edgar, Vermilion, Coles and Clay counties; Laws; 1831, 45. . . Act 7 Feb., including Coles county; Laws 1831, 88. . . Act 2 Mar. 1833; changing time of holding courts; R. S. 1833, 162. . . Act 17 Jan., including Wayne, White, Edwards, Wabash, Lawrence, Crawford, Jasper, Clark, Edgar, Vermilion, Champaign, Coles and Clay: Laws 1835, 153. . . Act 19 Dec. 1834; including Jasper county; Laws 1835, 155. . . Act 16 Jan., times of holding court changed; Laws 1836, 239. . . Act 12 Jan, 1835 [1836]; including White county; Laws 1836, 240. . . Act 1 Mar., time of courts changed; 1 Laws 1837, 110. . . Act 29 Jan., to fix the time of holding courts in Coles, Champagn, Vermilion and Edgar counties; Laws 1840, 90. . . Act 23 Feb, including White, Wayne, Wabash, Edwards, Clay, Lawrence, Crawford, Jasper, Clark, Edgar, Coles and Vermilion counties; William Wilson, judge; time of holding courts; Laws 1841, 103. . . Act 1 Mar., to change the time of holding courts; Laws 1843, 133. . . Act of 1 Mar., including Wayne, White, Edwards, Wabash, Lawrence, Crawford, Clark, Edgar, Vermilion, Coles, Jasper, Richland and Clay counties; Laws 1843, 133. . . Act of 21 Feb., including Coles, Cumberland, Jasper, Richland and Clay counties; Laws 1845, 48. . . Act of 16 Feb., including Wayne, White, Edwards, Wabash, Lawrence, Crawford, Clark, Coles, Cumberland, Jasper, Clay and Richland counties; Laws 1847, 30. . . Act 30 Jan., including Wayne, White, Edwards, Wabash, Lawrence. Crawford, Clark, Coles, Cumberland, Jasper, Clay, and Richland counties; Laws 1849, 59. . . . Act of 15 Feb., including Crawford, Lawrence, Richland, Clay, Effingham, Jasper, Cumberland, Coles and Clark counties; Laws 1851, 110. . . Act of 21 June, including Crawford, Lawrence, Richland, Clay, Effingham, Jasper, Cumberland, Coles and Clark counties; Laws 1852, 96. . . Act of 12 Feb., including Edgar, Clark, Crawford, Lawrence, Richland, Clay, Jasper, Cumberland and Coles counties; Laws 1853, 64. . . Act of 12 Feb., including Edgar, Cumberland, Jasper, Clay, Richland, Lawrence, Crawford and Clark counties; Laws 1857, 22. . . Act 1 Feb., including the counties of Coles, Edgar, Clark and Cumberland; Laws 1859, 52. . . Act 14 Feb., including the counties of Clark, Cumberland, Coles, and Edgar; Laws 1861, 90. Supplemental to the foregoing: Act of 18 Feb. 1861; Laws 1861, 91. . . Act of 3 Feb., including the counties of Effingham, Shelby, Clark, Cumberland, Coles and Edgar; Laws 1863, 31. . . Act of 15 Feb., including the counties of Clark and Cumberland; Laws 1865, 26. . . Act of 7 Mar., including the counties of Effingham, Jasper, Crawford, Clark and Cumberland; Laws 1867, 51. . . Act 30 Mar., to change the fall terms; Laws 1869, 71.

Fifth Circuit.—Act 29 Dec. 1824; including the counties of White, Edwards, Lawrence, Crawford, Clark and Edgar; Laws 1825, 42. . . Act 17 Jan., changing the time of holding the courts, and attaching the county of Wabash to the circuit; Laws 1825, 170. . . Act 26 Jan., times of holding court changed; Laws 1826, 81. . . Act 12 Jan. 1827; the counties of White, Edwards, Wabash, Lawrence, Crawford, Clark and Edgar are made part of the fourth circuit; R. S. 1827, 118. . . Act 8 Jan., establishing a circuit court north of the Illinois, river; Laws 1829, 38. . . Act 25 Jan., inclu-

Circuit Courts.

ding Jo Daviess, Peoria, Fulton, Schuyler and Adams counties; Laws 1829, 48. . . Act 16 Feb., including Cook, La Salle, Putnam, Peoria, Fulton, Schuyler, Adams, Hancock, McDonough, Knox, Warren, Jo Daviess, Mercer, Rock Island and Henry counties; Laws 1831, 45. . . Act 2 Mar. 1833; changing time of holding courts; R. S. 1833, 162. . . Act 17 Jan., including Pike, Adams, Hancock, McDonough, Knox, Warren, Fulton and Schuyler counties; Laws 1835, 154. . . Act 4 Mar., including Calhoun county; 1 Laws 1837, 111. . . Act 19 Jan., teste of process after the resignation of Judge R. M. Young; 1 Laws 1837, 179. . . Act 23 Feb., Adams, Hancock, Warren, Mercer, Knox, Fulton, Schuyler, Brown and McDonough counties; Laws 1839, 155. . . Act. 2 Mar., to change the time of holding courts; Laws 1839, 278. . . Act 23 Feb., including Schuyler, Brown, Adams, Hancock, McDonough, Warren, Henderson, Knox and Fulton counties; Stephen A. Douglas, judge; time of holding courts; Laws 1841, 103. . . Act 4 Mar., to change the time of holding courts; Laws 1843, 135. . . Act of 4 Mar., including Fulton, McDonough, Schuyler, Brown, Adams, Hancock, Henderson, Warren and Knox counties; Laws 1843, 135. . . Act of 28 Feb., including Warren county; Laws 1845, 108. . . Act 13 Feb., including Hancock county; Laws 1847, 30. . . Act 5 Feb., including Pike, Fulton, Schuyler, Brown, Hancock, Henderson, Warren, Knox, McDonough and Adams counties; Laws 1847, 43. . . Act 5 Nov, including Pike, Brown, Adams, Schuyler, Hancock, McDonough and Henderson counties; 2 Laws 1849, 12. . . Act 6 Nov., including Schuyler, Brown, Pike, Henderson, Hancock, McDonough and Adams counties; 2 Laws 1849, 16. . . Act 22 June, including Pike, Brown, McDonough, Schuyler, Mason and Cass counties; Laws 1852, 177. . . Act 29 Jan., including Fulton, McDonough, Schuyler, Brown, and Pike counties; Laws 1857, 5. . . Act 8 Feb., including the counties of Fulton, McDonough, Pike, Schuyler and Brown; Laws 1859, 53. . . Act 26 Jan., including the counties of Pike, McDonough, Brown, Schuyler and Fulton; Laws 1865, 27. . . Act 7 Mar., including the counties of Pike, Brown, McDonough, Fulton and Schuyler; Laws 1867, 51. . . Act 9 Feb., to change the time of holding courts; Laws 1869, 72.

Sixth Circuit.—Act 17 Jan., including Jo Daviess, Rock Island, Mercer, Henry, Peoria, Putnam, LaSalle, Cook and Iroquois counties; Laws 1835, 154. . . Act 4 Mar., terms of court changed; 1 Laws 1837, 111. . . Act 12 Feb., payment of $500. to Dan. Stone, judge; Laws 1839, 102. . . Act 23 Feb., including Jo Daviess, Stephenson, Boone, Winnebago, Whiteside, Rock Island and Carroll counties; Laws 1839, 155. . . Act 2 Mar., to change the time of holding courts; Laws 1839, 250. . . Act 15 Jan., including the county of Lee; Laws 1840, 44. . . Act 29 Jan., to change the time of holding courts; Laws 1840, 88. . . Act 20 Jan., to change the time of courts; Laws 1841, 102. . . Act 23 Feb., including Jo Daviess, Stephenson, Winnebago, Boone, Lee, Carroll, Whiteside, Rock Island, Mercer and Henry counties; Thomas C. Browne, judge; time of holding courts; Laws 1841, 103. . . Act 23 Feb., including JoDaviess, Stephenson, Winnebago, Boone, Lee, Whiteside, Henry, Mercer, Rock Island and Carroll counties; Laws 1841. 108. . . Act 27 Feb., including Lee, Whiteside, Henry, Mercer, Rock Island, Carroll and JoDaviess counties; Laws 1847, 27. . . Act 1 Mar., including JoDaviess county; Laws 1847, 42. . . Act 5 Nov., including JoDaviess, Stephenson, Ogle, Lee, Whiteside and Carroll counties; 2 Laws 1849, 12. . . Act 23 June, including Ogle, Lee, Whiteside, Carroll, Henry and Rock Island; Laws 1852, 239. . . Act 14 Feb., including Rock Island, Henry, Whiteside, Lee, Ogle and Carroll counties; Laws 1855, 130. . . Act 5 Feb., including Rock Island and Henry counties; Laws 1855, 7. . . Act 19 Feb., including the counties of Rock Island and Henry; Laws 1859, 54. . . Act 7 Mar., including the county of Henry; Laws 1867, 52. . . Act 31 Mar., to change the times of holding courts in Rock Island and Henry counties; Laws 1869, 73.

Seventh Circuit.—Act 4 Feb., including Cook, Will, McHenry, Kane, LaSalle and Iroquois counties; 1 Laws 1837, 113. . . Act 4 Mar., terms of court fixed; 1 Laws 1837, 112 §3. . . Act 23 Feb., including Cook, Will, Iroquois, McHenry and Du Page counties; Laws 1839, 155. . . Act 2 Mar., to change the time of holding courts; Laws 1839, 251. . . Act 23 Feb., including Cook, Will, Iroquois, Du Page, Grundy, McHenry and Lake counties; Theophilus W. Smith, judge; time of holding courts; Laws 1841, 103. . . Act 28 Jan., to pay Henry Brown, state's attorney, $134.25; Laws 1843, 19. . . Act 6 Feb., to change the time of holding courts; Laws 1843, 128. . . Act 5 Dec. 1842; to change the time of holding courts; Laws 1843, 135. . . Act 3 Mar., including Cook, Lake, McHenry, Du Page, Grundy, Will and Iroquois counties; Laws 1845, 78. . . Act 27 Feb., including Winnebago, Grundy, Lake, McHenry, Du Page, Iroquois, Will, Boone and Cook counties; Laws 1847, 27. . . Act 22 Feb., including Lake, McHenry, Boone, Du Page, Grundy, Will, Iroquois and Cook counties; Laws 1847, 28. . . Act 13 Feb., including Boone county; Laws 1847, 31. . . Interchange between the county judge of Cook county and the judge of the ninth circuit; Pr. Laws 1847 (1 Mar.) 42. . . Act 5 Nov., including Cook county; 2 Laws 1849, 14. . . Act 5 Nov., including Lake county; 2 Laws 1849, 16. . . Act 6 Nov., including Lake county; 2 Laws 1849, 15. . . Regulating the practice in chancery cases in said circuit; act 12 Feb.; Laws 1853, 66. . . Act 12 Feb., including Cook county; practice in the circuit court of said county; Laws 1853, 172. . . Act 14 Jan., including Lake and Cook counties; construction of the act of 12 Feb. 1853, concerning the practice in the circuit court of Cook county; suits in said court, how dismissed; judgments entered in vacation; act 14 Jan. Laws 1857, 10. . . Fees of the state's attorney in the recorder's court; act 24 Feb., Laws 1859, 17. . . Act 9 Mar., including the counties of Lake and Cook; Laws 1867, 53. . . Compensation to the judge of said circuit; act 25 Feb., Laws 1867, 70. . . Fees of the state's attorney in the 7th circuit: Laws 1869 (10 Mar.) 178.

Eighth Circuit.—Act 23 Feb., circuit established, including Sangamon, Macon, McLean, Tazewell, Menard, Logan, Dane and Livingston counties; judge to be elected by the general assembly; Laws 1839, 155. . . Act 2 Mar., to change the time of holding courts; Laws 1839, 251. . . Act 1 Feb., to change the time of holding courts; Laws 1840, 5. . . Act 23 Feb., including Menard, Sangamon, Christian, Logan, Shelby, Macon, DeWitt, McLean, Champaign, Tazewell, Mason, Piatt and Livingston counties; Samuel H. Treat, judge; time of holding courts; Laws 1841, 103. . . Act 28 Feb., to change the time of holding courts; Laws 1843, 132. . . Act 21 Feb., including Sangamon, Tazewell, Woodford, McLean, Livingston, DeWitt, Piatt, Champaign, Vermilion, Edgar, Moultrie, Christian, Logan and Menard counties; Laws 1845, 48. . . Act 25 Feb., including Christian, Logan and Menard counties; Laws 1845, 49. . . Act 11 Feb., including Shelby, Sangamon, Tazewell, Woodford, McLean, Logan, DeWitt, Piatt, Champaign, Vermilion, Edgar, Moultrie, Macon and Christian counties; Laws 1847, 31. . . Act 20 Jan., including Sangamon, Tazewell, Woodford, McLean, Logan, DeWitt, Piatt, Champaign, Vermilion, Edgar, Shelby, Moultrie, Macon and Christian counties; Laws 1849, 60. . . Act 3 Feb., including Sangamon, Logan, McLean, Woodford, Tazewell, DeWitt, Champaign and Vermilion counties; Laws 1853, 63. . . Act 11 Feb., including Logan, McLean, DeWitt, Champaign, and Vermilion counties; Laws 1857, 12. . . Act 24 Feb., including the county of Vermilion; Laws 1859, 55. . . Act 4 Feb., including the counties of McLean, Logan and DeWitt; practice in said circuit; Laws 1861, 100. . . Amending the foregoing; act 22 Feb., Laws 1861, 102. . . Additional terms of court; Laws 1869 (4 Mar.) 73.

Ninth Circuit.—Act 23 Feb., circuit established including Peoria, Putnam, Marshall, Kane, DeKalb, Bureau, Henry Ogle and LaSalle counties; judge elected by the general assembly; Laws 1839, 155. . . Act 2 Mar. 1829 [1839]: to change the time of holding courts; Laws 1839, 251. . . Act 29 Jan., time of holding courts in DeKalb, Kane and Peoria counties; Laws 1840, 92. . . Act 23 Feb., including Peoria, Marshall, Putnam, LaSalle, Kendall, Kane, DeKalb, Ogle, Bureau and Stark counties; Thomas Ford, judge; time of holding courts; Laws 1841, 103. . . Act 26 Feb., time of holding courts in Putnam; Laws 1841, 110. . . Act 20 Feb., to change the time of holding courts; Laws 1843, 120. . . Act 20 Feb., including Marshall, Putnam, LaSalle, Kendall, Kane, DeKalb, Ogle, Bureau, Stark and Peoria counties; Laws 1843, 120. . Act 11 Feb., including Livingston county; Laws 1847, 31. . . Judge of said circuit may interchange with the county judge of Cook county; Pr. Laws 1847 (1 Mar.) 42. . . Act 5 Nov., including LaSalle, Putnam Marshall, Bureau, Kane, DeKalb, Kendall and Livingston counties; 2 Laws 1849, 12. . . Act 6 Nov., including LaSalle, Livingston and Kendall counties; 2 Laws 1849, 15. . . Act 17 Feb., including LaSalle, Livingston, Kendall, Bureau, Putnam and Marshall counties; grand juries not summoned; Laws 1851, 152. . . Act 23 June, including LaSalle, Bureau, Kendall, Marshall Livingston and Putnam counties; Laws 1852, 207. . . Act 12 Feb., including Kendall, Bureau, Marshall, Putnam, Livingston and LaSalle counties; Laws 1853, 62. . . Time of holding courts changed; Laws 1857 (10 Feb.) 19 §6. . . Act 17 Feb., including LaSalle county; Laws 1857, 27. . . Act 11 Feb., including the counties of Bureau and LaSalle; Laws 1859, 56. . . Act 12 Feb., including Bureau county; Laws 1859, 57. . . Act 18 Feb., including Kendall county; practice to be the same as in the thirteenth circuit; Laws 1859, 58. . . Act 22 Feb., including the county of Bureau; Laws 1861, 104. . . Act 2 June, including the county of Kendall; Laws 1863, 34. . . Act 16 Feb., including the county of Kendall; Laws 1865, 34. . . Act 20 Feb., including the county of Kendall; Laws 1867, 63. . . Act 28 Feb., including Bureau county; Laws 1867, 67. . . Act 15 April, confessions of judgment in said circuit during vacation; Laws 1869, 73. . . Act 27 Mar., to change one of the terms in Bureau county; Laws 1869, 74. . . Act 30 Mar., appointment of an official reporter in said circuit; Laws 1869, 348.

Tenth Circuit.—Established by act 5 Nov., including Fulton, Peoria, Stark, Henry, Rock Island, Mercer, Knox and Warren counties; 2 Laws 1849, 12. . . Act 22 June, including Fulton and Peoria counties; Laws 1852, 123. . . Act 11 Feb., including Fulton, Knox, Warren and Mercer counties; Laws 1853, 129. . . Act 14 Feb., including Fulton, Mercer, Henderson, Warren and Knox counties; Laws 1855, 149. . . Act 29 Jan., including Mercer, Henderson, Warren and Knox counties; Laws 1857, 5. . . Act 16 Feb., including the counties of Mercer, Knox, Warren and Henderson; Laws 1859, 58. . . Act 13 Feb., including the county of Warren; Laws 1863, 33. . . Repeal of the foregoing; act 13 June, Laws 1863, 36. . . Act 21 Feb., including the counties of Warren, Knox, Mercer and Henderson; Laws 1867, 53. . . Changing the time of holding courts; Laws 1869 (4 Mar.) 74.

Eleventh Circuit.—Established by act of 12 Feb., including Iroquois, Will, DuPage, McHenry, Boone and Winnebago counties; Laws 1849, 61. . . Act 5 Nov., including Winnebago, Boone, McHenry, DuPage, Will, Grundy and Iroquois counties; 2 Laws 1849, 12. . . Special election for state's attorney in April 1851; act 4 Feb., Laws 1851, 21. . . Act 17 Feb., including Will, Du Page, Iroquois, Grundy and Kankakee counties; Laws 1851, 159. . . Act 21 June, including Will, Iroquois, Grundy and DuPage counties; Laws 1852, 105. . . Act 14 Feb., including Will county; Laws 1857, 28. . . Act 26 Jan., including the counties of Will, Grundy and Du Page; practice in said circuit prescribed; Laws 1859, 59. . . Amending the foregoing; act of 2 Feb., Laws 1859, 61. . . March term in Will county for common law and chancery business only; affidavit of merits in the counties of Will, Du Page or Grundy; act of 18 Feb., Laws 1861, 93. . . Act 12 Feb., including the counties of Will and Grun-

dy; practice in said circuit; acts repealed; Laws 1863, 32. . . Act 12 Feb. 1853, concerning practice in the seventh circuit, extended to the eleventh circuit; act 16 Feb., Laws 1865, 27. . Act of 16 Feb., including the county of Will; Laws 1865, 34. . . Amending the act of 16 Feb. 1865; act 28 Feb., Laws 1867, 66.

Twelfth Circuit.—Established by act of 1 Feb. 1851, including Marion, Jefferson, Hamilton, Wayne, White, Wabash, Edwards, Gallatin and Saline; Laws 1851, 13. . . Act 22 June, including White, Wabash, Edwards, Wayne, Marion, Jefferson, Hamilton, Saline and Gallatin; Laws 1852, 177. . . Act 12 Feb., including Gallatin county; Laws 1855, 128 . . Act 16 Feb., including White, Wabash, Edwards, Wayne, Jefferson and Hamilton counties; Laws 1857, 27. . . Act 22 Feb., including the counties of White, Wabash, Edwards, Wayne, Jefferson and Hamilton; Laws 1859, 61. . . Act 13 Feb., including the counties of White, Wabash, Edwards, Wayne, Jefferson and Hamilton; Laws 1861, 92. . . Act 16 Feb., including the counties of Jefferson, Wayne, Edwards, Wabash, White and Hamilton; Laws 1865, 28.

Thirteenth Circuit.—Established by act of 4 Feb., including Kane, DeKalb, Boone and McHenry counties; Laws 1851, 20. . . Act 17 Feb., including Kane, DeKalb, Boone and McHenry counties; Laws 1851, 152. . . Act 17 Feb., including Boone and McHenry counties; Laws 1851, 159. . . Act 21 June, including Kane, McHenry, Boone and DeKalb counties; Laws 1852, 53. . . Act 11 Feb., including McHenry and Kane counties; Laws 1853, 34. . Act 14 Jan., including Kane, Boone, DeKalb and McHenry counties; fees of clerks in said circuit to be taxed under §§4 and 5 of the act of 6 Feb. 1849, (Laws 1849, 69,) as amended by §17 of the act of 12 Feb. 1853, (Laws 1853, 175) Laws 1857, 10. . . Judgments by default and by confession; action on penal bonds; special summons; practice in said circuit prescribed; act 16 Feb., Laws 1857, 29. . . Repeal of §5 of the act 14 Jan. 1857, concerning the fees of circuit clerks in said circuit; act 16 Feb., Laws 1857, 118. . . Act 4 Feb., including the counties of Kane, Boone, McHenry and DeKalb; Laws 1859, 62. . . Act 16 Feb., including the counties of Boone, DeKalb and McHenry; Laws 1861, 102. . . Act 16 Feb., including the county of DeKalb; Laws 1865, 29.

Fourteenth Circuit.—Established by act 12 Feb., including JoDaviess, Stephenson and Winnebago counties; Laws 1851, 82. . . Act 17 Feb., including Winnebago county; Laws 1851, 159. . . Act 15 Feb., including JoDaviess, Stephenson and Winnebago counties; Laws 1855, 127. . . Act 7 Feb., including JoDaviess, Stephenson and Winnebago counties; Laws 1857, 10. . . Act 24 Feb., including Winnebago county; Laws 1859, 62. . . Assessment of damages upon a judgment by default; judgments by confession; act 21 Feb., Laws 1861, 93. . . Practice in the county of Stephenson; act 20 Feb., Laws 1861, 104. . . Practice in the county of Stephenson; act 12 June; Laws 1863, 34. . . Act 6 Feb., including the county of Winnebago; Laws 1865, 35. . . Act 11 Feb., including the counties of JoDaviess, Stephenson and Winnebago; Laws 1867, 54. . Practice in Stephenson; act 20 Feb., Laws 1867, 64. . . March term in JoDaviess county; act 25 Feb., Laws 1867, 66. . . Act 5 Mar., including JoDaviess county; Laws 1867, 68. . . Act 19 Apr., fix the April term in Stephenson; Laws 1869, 75. . . Act 26 Mar., to change the time of holding courts, and to regulate the practice; Laws 1869, 75.

Fifteenth Circuit.—Established by act 12 Feb., including Adams, Hancock, Henderson and Mercer counties; Laws 1851, 82. . . Act 14 Feb., including McDonough county; Laws 1853, 35. . . Act 19 Feb., including Adams and Hancock counties; Laws 1857, 27. . . Act 5 Feb., including the counties of Adams and Hancock; docket fee in criminal cases; Laws 1867, 55. . . Act 15 Mar., to change the time of holding courts, and to regulate the qualifications of jurors; Laws 1869, 76. . . Act 9 Apr., to amend the foregoing, and to fix the fees of the clerk and sheriff in Adams county; Laws 1869, 77.

Sixteenth Circuit.—Established by act 9 Feb., including Peoria and Stark counties; Laws 1853, 127. . . Act 9 Feb., including Peoria county; practice in said circuit; Laws 1855, 125. . . Act 7 Feb., including the counties of Peoria and Stark; Laws 1859, 94. . . Act 29 Jan., including the counties of Peoria and Stark; Laws 1863, 29. . .. Act 16 Feb., including Peoria county; Laws 1865, 29. . . Act 13 Jan., to change the time of holding courts, and to regulate the practice; Laws 1869, 79.

Seventeenth Circuit.—Established by act 12 Feb., including Bond, Fayette, Montgomery, Christian, Shelby, Effingham, Moultrie, Macon and Piatt counties; Laws 1853, 62. . . Act 14 Feb., including Christian, Montgomery, Bond, Fayette, Effingham, Shelby, Moultrie, Piatt and Macon counties; Laws 1855, 129. . . Act 12 Feb., including Macon, Piatt, Fayette, Effingham, Shelby, Moultrie and Coles counties; Laws 1857, 19. . . Act 4 Feb., including the counties of Macon, Moultrie, Piatt, Fayette, Effingham and Shelby; Laws 1859, 64. . . Act 18 Feb., including the counties of Macon, Moultrie, Piatt, Fayette, Effingham and Shelby; Laws 1861, 95. . . Act 16 Feb., including Shelby, Fayette, Macon, Piatt and Moultrie; notices of publication; Laws 1865, 30. . Act 29 Jan., including the counties of Ford, Champaign, Fayette, Piatt, Macon, Shelby and Moultrie; Laws 1867, 57. . . Act 27 Jan., to change the time of holding courts, to fix the qualifications of jurors and concerning publications; Laws 1869, 81.

Eighteenth Circuit.—Established by act 11 Feb., including Sangamon, Macoupin, Montgomery and Christian counties; Laws 1857, 14. . . Act 12 Feb., including the counties of Montgomery, Macoupin, Christian and Sangamon; Laws 1859, 64. . . Act 14 Feb., including the counties of Montgomery, Macoupin, Christian and Sangamon; Laws 1861, 96. . . Act 21 Feb., including the counties of Montgomery, Macoupin, Christian and Sangamon; Laws 1867, 58. . . Act 19 Apr., to change the time of holding courts; Laws 1869, 83. . . Act 11 Mar., election of a prosecuting attorney; Laws 1869, 91 §4. . . Act 31 Mar., appointment of an official reporter in said circuit, viz: Sangamon, Macoupin, Christian and Montgomery counties; Laws 1869, 349.

Nineteenth Circuit.—Established by act of 7 Feb., including Pulaski, Massac, Pope, Hardin, Gallatin and Saline counties; Laws 1857, 3. . . Act 4 Feb., including the counties of Pulaski, Massac, Pope, Hardin and Gallatin; Laws 1859, 65. . . Act 16 Feb., including the counties of Pulaski, Massac, Pope, Hardin and Gallatin; Laws 1861, 97. . . Act 10 Feb., including the counties of Gallatin, Hardin, Pope, Massac and Pulaski; Laws 1863, 30. . . Act 25 Feb., including the counties of Alexander, Pulaski, Massac and Pope; Laws 1867, 59. . . Act 11 Mar., to attach Johnson county to said circuit; Laws 1869, 83. To fix the time of holding courts in said circuit; Id. 84.

Twentieth Circuit.—Established by act 7 Feb., including Kankakee, Iroquois, Livingston and Holmes counties; practice in said circuit regulated; Laws 1857, 16. . . Act 12 Feb., including the counties of Iroquois and Kankakee; Laws 1859, 66. . . Act of 13 June, including the county of Kankakee; Laws 1863, 36. . Act 23 Feb., including the county of Livingston; Laws 1867, 60. . . Act 19 Feb., time of holding courts in said circuit; official reporter appointed; Laws 1869, 85, 351.

Twenty-first Circuit.—Established by act of 7 Feb., including Woodford, Tazewell, Mason, Cass and Menard counties; Laws 1857, 8. . . Act 15 Jan., including the counties of Tazewell, Mason, Cass, Menard and Woodford; Laws 1859, 68. . . Act 19 Feb., including the counties of Tazewell, Mason, Cass and Menard; Laws 1859, 69.

Twenty-second Circuit.—Established by act 5 Feb., including Lee, Ogle, Whiteside and Carroll counties; Laws 1857, 6. . . Act 8 Feb., including the counties of Whiteside, Lee, Ogle and Carroll; chancery orders, judgment by confession, default; Laws 1859, 69. . . Act 10 Feb., including the county of Lee; Laws 1863, 35. . . Act 28 Jan., including the counties of Lee, Carroll, Whiteside and Ogle; Laws 1867, 61. . . Act 28 Feb., including the counties of Whiteside, Lee and Ogle, Carroll; Laws 1867, 61. . . Act 25 Mar., to extend the powers of the judge in vacation; Laws 1869, 86.

Twenty-third Circuit.—Established by act of 10 Feb., including Bureau, Putnam and Marshall counties; Laws 1857, 18. Repeal of the foregoing; act 11 Feb., including the counties of Marshall, Woodford and Putnam; Laws 1859, 56. . . Act 13 Feb., including the county of Woodford; practice in said circuit; Laws 1861, 98.

Twenty-fourth Circuit.—Established by act of 12 Feb., including the counties of Bond, St. Clair and Madison; Laws 1857, 20. . . Act 11 Feb., including the counties of St. Clair, Bond and Madison; Laws 1859, 70. . . Act 18 Feb., including the counties of Bond, St. Clair and Madison; Laws 1861, 99. . . Act 29 Mar., additional term in St. Clair county; Laws 1869, 87.

Twenty-fifth Circuit.—Established by act of 1 Feb., including the counties of Crawford, Clay, Richland, Jasper and Lawrence; Laws 1859, 52. . . Act 10 Mar., to change the time of holding courts in said circuit; Laws 1869, 88.

Twenty-sixth Circuit.—Established by act of 3 Feb., including the counties of Franklin, Saline, Williamson and Johnson; Laws 1859, 50. . . Act 16 Feb., including the counties of Franklin, Saline, Williamson and Johnson; Laws 1859, 50. . . Act 16 Feb., including the counties of Franklin, Williamson, Johnson and Saline; Laws 1865, 31. . . Act 25 Feb., including the counties of Johnson, Williamson, Saline, Gallatin and Hardin; Laws 1867, 62. . . Act 11 Mar., to change the time of holding courts; Laws 1869, 88. Foregoing repealed; Laws 1869, 89. . . Act 11 Mar., to fix the time of holding courts in said circuit; Laws 1869, 84.

Twenty-seventh Circuit.—Established by act of 4 Feb., including counties of Vermilion, Champaign, Douglas and Ford; Laws 1861, 99. Amending the foregoing; act 22 Feb., Laws 1861, 102. . . Act 10 Feb., including the counties of Douglas, Edgar, Champaign, Coles, Vermilion and Ford; notices for publication; Laws 1865, 32. . . Act 25 Feb., including the counties of Douglas, Vermilion, Edgar and Coles; Laws 1867, 63. . . Act 30 Jan., to change the time of holding circuit courts; Laws 1869, 89.

Twenty-eight Circuit.—Established by act 16 Feb., including the counties of Du Page and Kane; Laws 1861, 102. . . Practice in the circuit courts of Kane county; act of 14 Feb., Laws 1863, 65. . Judgments by confession in DuPage county; act of 16 Feb.; Laws 1865, 33. . . Act 16 Feb., including Du Page county; Laws 1865, 34. . . Amending the act of 14 Feb., 1863, concerning the practice in Kane county; act of 16 Feb., Laws 1865, 36. . Practice in Kane county; act of 16 Feb., Laws 1865, 38. . . Repeal of §§6, 7, 8 and 9 of the foregoing act of 14 Feb. 1863, concerning practice in Kane county; act of 9 Mar., Laws 1867, 69.

Thirtieth Circuit.—Act 11 Mar., circuit established, including the county of Sangamon; times of holding courts; Laws 1869, 90. . . Official reporter appointed; Laws 1869 (31 Mar.) 350.

District Courts.—Established in certain cases for special purposes; Laws 1847 (20 Feb.) 44.

CHAP. 30. CRIMINAL JURISPRUDENCE.

Act 22 Feb., to suppress dueling; Laws 1819, 32 §§1—7. . . Act 27 Feb., to suppress the counterfeiting of bank notes; Laws 1819, 81. . Act 1 Mar., proceedings against vagrants before justices; binding, hiring or whipping of vagrants; Laws 1819, 88. . . Act 5 Mar., to prevent vice and immorality by punishing work or play on Sunday; Laws 1819, 123. . . Act 22 Mar., to compel persons legally commanded to aid in executing process; Laws 1819, 158. . . Act 23 Mar., a general law concerning crimes and punishments; Laws 1819, 212 §§1—28. . . Act 20 Feb., regulating the firing of woods, prairies and other lands; Laws 1819, 384. . . Act 19 Jan., prosecution of county officers for mal-feasance and omission of duty; Laws 1821 20. . . Act 31 Jan., for the prevention of vice and immorality by punishing those who work or play on Sunday; nearly the same as

the act 5 Mar. 1819, which it repeals; Laws 1821 48 §§1—17. . . Act 12 Feb., respecting crimes and punishments; Laws 1821 126§§1—16. . . Act 14 Feb., amending the act of 20 Feb. 1819, "regulating the firing of woods, prairies and other lands;" Laws 1823, 140. . . Act 14 Feb., to prevent the selling of spirituous liquors in this state; Laws 1823, 148. . . Act 14 Feb., amending the laws respecting the counterfeiting of notes and coins; Laws 1823, 149. . . Act 3 Jan., to prevent the disinterment of the dead; Laws 1825, 51. . . Act 10 Jan, supplementary to the act of 31 Jan. 1821, "for the prevention of vice and immorality;" Laws 1825, 61. . . Act 26 Jan., writs of error in criminal cases; Laws 1826, 84 §§5, 6. . . Act 30 Jan. 1827; relative to criminal jurisprudence; consisting of 17 divisions §§1—189; prepared by Judge S. D. Lockwood; repeal of the former acts; R. S. 1827, 124. . . Act 6 Jan. 1827; to regulate the apprehension of offenders, and for other purposes; R. S. 1827, 169; R. S. 1833, 219. . . Act 19 Jan., amending the act of 20 Jan., 1837 in relation to Sabbath breaking; Laws 1829, 138; R. S. 1833, 662. . . Act 15 Feb.; amends all previous acts; Laws 1831, 103 §§1—44. . . Act 26 Feb. 1833; a consolidation of previous acts which are repealed; R. S. 1833, 171 §§1—191. . . Act 1 Mar. 1833; punishment for the disturbance of worshiping congregations; R. S. 1833, 661. . . Act 11 Feb., amending act 6 Jan. 1827 "for the apprehension of offenders;" 1 Laws 1837, 113. . . Act 7 Feb., incest defined and punished, similar to R. S. 1845 Ch. 30 §§124—126; Laws 1843, 155.

CHAP. 31. CUMBERLAND ROAD.

Act 2 Mar., to protect said road, and prevent trespasses; similar to Ch. 31 R. S. 1845 §§1—4; Laws 1839, 245. . . Act 3 Mar., said road to be kept in repair, penalty for injuring; Laws 1843, 265.

CHAP. 32. DETINUE.

When and for what the action will lie; R. S. 1827 (6 Jan.) 179. R. S. 1833, 231.

CHAP. 33. DIVORCES.

Causes for which Divorces may be granted, similar to the chapter in the R. S.; Laws 1819 (22 Feb.) 35. Foregoing amended; Laws 1825 (17 Jan.) 169. Further amendment; Laws 1827 (12 Jan.) 180. R. S. 1833, 232. . . A new act on this subject, repealing all the former acts; R. S. 1827 (31 Jan.) 181. R. S. 1833, 232. Foregoing amended; R. S. 1833 (4 Dec. 1832.) 234.

Special Acts.—John Elkins divorced from Elizabeth Elkins 9 Feb.; Laws 1821, 118. . . Act 24 Jan., divorcing Mary and Archibald Farr; Laws 1823, 52. . . Act 11 Jan., divorcing Elizabeth and John Postlewait; Laws 1823, 70. . . Act 3 Jan., divorcing Joseph T. and Nancy Atchinson; Laws 1823, 76. . . Act 23 Dec. 1822; divorcing Polly and Israel Bozarth; Laws 1823, 79. . . Act 27 Dec. 1822; divorcing Nancy and Andrew Milton; Laws 1823, 84. . . Act 30 Jan., divorcing Samuel and Nancy Atherton; Laws 1823, 96. . . Act 31 Jan., divorcing Patsey and Obadiah Johnson; Laws, 1823 97. . . Act 10 Feb., divorcing John and Fanny Rutherford; Laws 1823, 119. Act 14 Feb., divorcing John H. C. and Catherine Wageman; Laws 1823, 143. . . Act 14 Feb., divorcing Sarah and James Burrows; Laws, 1823, 144. . . Act 17 Feb., divorcing William G. and Enlalie Goforth; Laws 1823, 155. . . Act 15 Jan., divorcing Thomas and Eliza B. Shannon, and Martha and Mathias Drain; Laws 1825, 120. . . Act 15 Feb., divorcing Samuel and Sarah Walker; Joshua and Sally Holm; Thomas and Julia Jones; Elijah and Margaret Price Evans; John and Elizabeth Jarrard; John and Margaret Scott; Nathan and Polly Turner; Legar and Angelina Hebbart; Thomas and Levina Elliott; Arthur and Rebecca Morgan; Laws 1831, 71; Samuel and Elizabeth Nowland; James and Elizabeth Etherton; John and Patience Langley; Green and Mary Coleman; John W. and Elizabeth Doty; William and Cloe Mackelyea; John and — Crawford; Stephen and Sarah Strawn; John and Clarissa Goodman; James and Polly Quarles, and Isaac and — Carson; Laws 1831, 72. James and Sarah Vermilion; William and Eve Robins; John and Annetta Mize; Laws 1831, 72. . . Act 15 Jan., divorcing Richard H. and Elizabeth McGoon; Joshua S. and Fanny Shaw; George and Jane Flower; Laws 1836, 250. . . Act 4 Dec. 1838; to divorce Julia A. and Jeremiah Hull; Laws 1839. 79.

CHAP. 34. DOWER.

Act 12 Feb., how dower may be assigned; Laws 1819, 12. . . Act 6 Feb., 1827; for the speedy assignment of dower and partition of real estate; former acts repealed; R. S. 1827, 183; R. S. 1833, 236.

CHAP. 35. DROVERS.

Act 3 Feb. 1841; to prevent the unlawful driving away of cattle and other stock, similar to Chap. 35 R. S. 1845 §§1—3; Laws 1841, 51.

CHAP. 36. EJECTMENT.

Act 23 Feb., improvements made by occupying claimants of land; this is substantially Ch. 36 §§50—58; Laws 1819, 40; Laws 1829, 98; R. S. 1833, 416. . . Act 23 Feb., tenants secreting declarations; landlords to defend in place of their tenants; Laws 1819, 55 §§8, 9. . Act 13 Jan., to simplify proceedings in ejectment, similar to R. S. 1845 Ch. 37 §57; Laws 1836, 238. . . Act 2 Mar., to define and regulate proceedings in ejectment, similar to this chapter in the revised statutes; Laws 1839, 220.

CHAP. 37. ELECTIONS.

Act 26 Feb., election to fill a vacancy in the office of Governor; Laws 1819, 74. . . Act 1 Mar., general act providing the manner of conducting state and county elections; Laws 1819, 90 §§1—29. . . Act 2 Mar., election of electors of president and vice president of the United States; Laws 1819, 101. . . Act 31 Mar., regulating the time when counties shall be laid off into townships; Laws 1819, 373. . . Act 3 Feb., general act relating to elections; Laws 1821, 74 §§1—16. . . Act 6 Feb., election of officers in new counties formed at this session; Laws 1821, 99. . . Act 3 Jan., a general law on this subject; repeals the act of 1 Mar., 1819 and of 3 Feb. 1821; Laws 1823, 53 §§1—37. . Act 29 Nov. 1824; amending the act of 2 Mar. 1819, "for the election of presidential electors;" Laws 1825, 3. . . Act 7 Dec. 1824; compensation of presidential electors; Laws 1825, 5. . . Act 17 Jan., supplemental to the act regulating elections; Laws 1825, 166. . . Act 9 Feb., to amend the act regulating elections; R. S. 1827, 187 §1—3. . . Act 11 Jan., mode of electing electors of president and vice president; R. S. 1827, 188; R. S. 1833, 242. . . Act 10 Jan., regulating elections; a consolidation of former acts, which are repealed; Laws 1829, 54 §§1—31; R. S. 1833, 243. . . Act 9 Feb., additional poll books opened at county seats; Laws 1831, 75; R. S. 1833, 142. . . Act 25 Feb. 1833; compensation of clerks and other persons for comparing poll books; R. S. 1833, 127. . . Act 28 Feb. 1833; manner of contesting elections; former acts repealed; R. S. 1833, 257. . . Act 29 Jan., counties divided into election precincts by the county commissioners' court; Laws 1835, 141. . . Act 15 Feb., election of members of congress; former act repealed; vacancies in the general assembly; Laws 1839, 109. Also, to prohibit betting on elections, similar to R. S. 1845 Ch. 37 §§52, 53. Ibid. . . Act 20 Feb., to amend and explain the election law of 10 Jan. 1829; Laws 1841, 111. . . Act 20 Dec. 1842; special election of a senator in place of John Pearson; Laws 1843, 137.

County Officers.—The act of 27 Feb. 1845 (R. S. 573; Pur. 288.) fixed the time for the election of county officers on the first Monday in Aug. Section one of this chapter (R. S. 214.) fixed the time of holding the general elections on the first Monday of November. But these acts were both repealed; 1 Laws 1849 (12 Feb.) 71 §2. . Clerks of the county commissioners' courts elected probate justices; Laws 1847 (11 Feb.) 64. . . Elections previously ordered by the governor to fill vacancies in county offices, confirmed; 2 Laws 1849 (6 Nov.) 8.

CHAP. 38. ESCHEATS.

Proceedings in case of escheated property, similar to chapter in revised statutes; R. S. 1833 (1 Mar.) 264.

CHAP. 39. ESTRAYS.

Act 23 Mar., water craft found adrift, and estray animals; Laws 1819, 206. . . Act 17 Feb., amending the foregoing in several particulars; Laws 1823, 167. . . Act 31 Jan. 1827; water craft found adrift, lost goods and estray animals; R. S. 1827, 189; R. S. 1833, 267. . . Act 22 Jan.; amending the act of 10 [31] Jan. 1827, "concerning water craft," etc.; Laws 1829, 73; R. S. 1833, 277. . . Act 14 Feb., amending the act of 10 [31] Jan. 1827, "concerning water craft," etc.; Laws 1831, 189; R. S. 1833, 278. . . Act 9 Feb., a general law amending and consolidating former acts which are repealed; Laws 1835, 229. . . Supplemental act of 4 Mar. 1843; Laws 1843, 139. . . Amendatory act of 6 Mar. 1843; Id. 140.

CHAP. 40. EVIDENCE AND DEPOSITIONS.

Act 19 Feb., deposition of witnesses out of the state or county taken on commission; Laws 1819, 17. . . Act 20 Feb. acts of the legislature of any other state or territory, when authenticated to be received in evidence; Laws 1819, 30. . . Act 25 Feb., perpetuation of testimony concerning lands, etc.; substantially §§26—29 of this chapter; Laws 1819, 69. . . Act 22 Mar., negroes, mulattoes and Indians not to testify; definition of a mulatto; Laws 1819, 143 §§17, 18. . . Act 22 Mar., depositions taken *de bene esse* to be used in court; Laws 1819, 146 §29. . . Act 31 Jan., repeals all acts concerning the taking of depositions, except that of 25 Feb, 1819 for the perpetuation of testimony; general act relating to the taking of depositions; Laws 1821, 54. . . Act 28 Jan., relating to evidence in courts of justice; receivers and registers' certificates, copies of corporation records, exemplifications of the laws of the other states, recorded conveyances; Laws 1823, 94. . . Act 10 Feb., depositions of witnesses in other counties; Laws 1823, 120. . . Act 9 Feb., 1827; regulating the mode of taking depositions, and to provide for the perpetuation of testimony; R. S. 1827, 174; R. S. 1833, 224. . , Act 10 Jan. 1827; what shall be evidence in certain cases; former acts repealed; R. R. 1827, 199; R. S. 1833, 280. . . Act 27 Feb., a patent for land better evidence than a register's certificate, similar to R. S. 1845, Ch. 40 §5; Laws 1839, 196. . . Act 2 Mar., evidence of joint liability, similar to R. S. 1845 Ch. 40 §§7, 8; Laws 1839, 266. . . Act 17 Feb., evidence of copartnership, similar to R. S. 1845 Ch. 40 §7; Laws 1841, 112. . . Act 24 Feb., evidence of corporate action of cities and towns; similar to R. S. 1845 Ch. 40 §9; Laws 1843, 140.

CHAP. 41. FEES AND SALARIES.

Act 25 Mar., salaries of the auditor, treasurer and other state officers; Laws 1819, 253. . Act 29 Mar., a general law fixing the fees and salaries of officers generally; Laws 1819, 321 §§1—16. . . Act 3 Jan., compensation of the electors for president and vice-president; Laws 1821, 4. . . Act 3 Jan., compensation of sheriffs; Laws 1821, 4. . . Act 3 Jan., fees of the attorney general and circuit attorneys; Laws 1821, 7. . . Act 31 Jan., repeals §11 of the foregoing act of 29 Mar. 1819; Laws 1821, 61. . Act 9 Feb., postage of the auditor to be paid; Laws 1821, 118. . . Act 12 Jan., fees of witnesses attending the impeachment trial of Theophilus W. Smith, a Judge of the Supreme Court; Pr. Laws 1833, 212. . . Act 12 Feb.. salaried

officers allowed fifty per cent advance by reason of the depreciation of the paper of the state bank; Laws 1823, 131. . . Act 14 Feb., if officers refuse to take state paper for fees, payment shall be stayed for three years; Laws 1823, 141. . . Act 14 Dec. 1824; attorney general and circuit attorneys allowed fifty per cent under the terms of the foregoing act of 12 Feb. 1823; Laws 1825, 10. . . Act 17 Jan., regulating the fees of the several officers therein mentioned; a general law concerning fees; Laws 1825, 137. . . Act 19 Jan., regulating the fees of certain officers; repeal of former acts; Laws 1826, 54. . . Act 19 Feb. 1827; a general law regulating salaries, fees and compensation of officers; former acts repealed; R. S. 1827, 203 §§1—17; R. S. 1833, 281. . . Act 23 Jan., in addition to the last foregoing act, and repealing §6 thereof; Laws 1829, 140; R. S. 1833, 300. . . Act 1 Mar., salary of the governor $2,000.; Laws 1839, 211. . . Act 24 Feb., fees of circuit clerks for naturalization; Laws 1843, 67. . . Act 6 Mar., duty of clerks where fees are remaining unpaid; similar to R. S. 1845 Ch. 41 §39; Laws 1843, 68. . . Docket fees regulated; Laws 1843, (4 Mar.) 142. . . Act 12 Feb., 1845; salaries of the judges of the supreme court; R. S. 1845, 584. Also, Laws 1847 (25 Feb.) 63. . . Act 16 Jan., per diem of a county commissioner; Laws 1847, 38. . . Act 12 Feb., §10; fees of the successful party at law; Laws 1849, 81; repealed 14 Feb., 1855; Laws 1855, 39. . . Fee of state's attorneys on convictions; 1 Laws 1849 (12 Feb.) 81 §9. Amended; Laws 1855 (14 Feb.) 32 §2. Practically repealed; Laws 1865 (14 Feb.) 65; Ch. 41 §20. . . Per diem of county judges; 1 Laws 1849 (12 Feb.) 63 §4. Also, Laws 1855 (14 Feb.) 181 §2. . . Concerning the fees of the secretary of state; 1 Laws 1849 (2 Feb.) 183. Repealed; 1 Laws 1861 (22 Feb.) 176.

CHAP. 42. FERRIES AND TOLL BRIDGES.

Act 20 Feb., to establish and regulate ferries; Laws 1819, 28 §§1—7. . . Act 27 Mar., county commissioners to grant licenses for the construction of toll bridges and turnpike roads; Laws 1819, 300. . . Act 9 Feb., further time to record ferries; Laws 1821, 117. . . Act 10 Jan., amending the act to establish and regulate ferries; Laws 1825, 64. . . Act 20 Jan., amending the act "to provide for recording town plats and ferry licenses;" Laws 1826, 63. . Act 27 Jan., county commissioners' court to establish ferries and regulate tolls; Laws 1826, 87, §6. . . Act 12 Feb. 1827; to provide for the establishment of Ferries, Toll Bridges and Turnpike roads; former acts repealed; R. S. R. S. 1827, 220; R. S. 1833, 302. . . Act 12 12 Feb., 1827; supplemental to the act 20 Feb., 1819, to "establish and regulate ferries;" R. S. 1827, 227; R. S. 309. . . Act 22 Jan., amending the act of 12 Feb., 1827, "to provide for the establishment of ferries," etc.; Laws 1829, 73; R. S. 1833, 545. . . Act 15 Jan., power of county courts where the legislature has granted to any person a right to build a bridge, and it is not built; Laws 1831, 31 §§4 and 5. . . Act 2 Mar. 1833; repealing so much of the act 12 Feb., 1827 as makes surveyors road viewers; R. S. 1833, 546.

Special Acts.—These will usually be found indexed under the county where situated; a few whose locality appears somewhat uncertain are given here.

Act 10 Jan., Adam Smith to establish a ferry, at Bridgewater and the Mississippi; Laws 1825, 79. . . Act 17 Jan., Hazel Beden to establish a ferry on the Illinois river immediately below the mouth of apple creek; Laws 1825, 137. . . Act 14 Jan., Wm. Kirkpatrick to build a toll bridge across the Winnebago swamps on the Galena and Peoria road; Laws 1836, 213 §5. . Act 3 Mar., W. T. Reed to keep a ferry across the Ohio at Newport; 1 Laws 1837, 119. . . Act 19 Feb., H. W. Cleveland to build a toll bridge across Green river and the Winnebago swamp, on the Peoria and Galena road; Laws 1839, 140. . . Hurst & Smith to keep a ferry across the Big Muddy near Rush Island; Pr. Laws 1833 (25 Feb.) 10. . . John Phelps to keep a ferry across Rock river; Pr. Laws 1833 (25 Feb.) 36. . . Act 18 Feb., amends act authorizing Geo. W. Jones to establish ferry from Jordon's ferry to Dubuque; limit extended to March 1859; Pr. Laws 1847, 45. . . Act 11 Feb., amends act 3 Feb. 1840 incorporating the Madison Ferry Co.; extended 20 years from date; Pr. Laws 1847, 71. . . Act 8 Feb., continues act 18 Jan. 1840, authorizing H. H. Gear to run a ferry across the Mississippi, for 30 years; Pr. Laws 1849, 35. . . Act 17 Feb., amends act 27 Feb. 1847, authorizing school trustees of town 13—10 to establish a ferry across the Illinois; time extended; Pr. Laws 1851, 297. . . Joseph Adkins to keep a ferry across the Sangamon in Cass and Mason counties; Laws 1845 (28 Feb.) 100. . . Amending act 23 Feb. 1843, authorizing Charles G. Eldridge to keep a ferry across the Mississippi; act 26 Feb., Laws 1845, p. 168. . . To R. and W. W. Wells, across the Illinois, at Fredericksville, in township 19—12; act 26 Feb., Laws 1845, p. 291. . . L. F. McCrillis to keep a ferry across the Illinois between Calhoun and Jersey; Laws 1852 (23 June) 238. . . E. Briggs to keep a ferry across crooked creek and the Illinois river in Schuyler, Brown and Cass counties; Laws 1853 (10 Feb.) 196. . . Extending for 15 years an act of 8 Feb. 1859; Laws 1859 (18 Feb.) 114. . . W. & F. Burnett to keep a ferry across the Mississippi opposite Louisiana, Mo.; Laws 1859 (15 Feb.) 116. . . Trimble, Preston and Green to keep a ferry across the Ohio at Brooklyn; Laws 1859 (22 Feb.) 118.

CHAP. 43. FORCIBLE ENTRY AND DETAINER.

Act 23 Feb., proceedings against tenants at will holding over; Laws 1819, 57 §§12—14. . Act 24 Feb., manner of proceeding before two justices; Laws 1819, 61. . . Act 2 Feb 1827; concerning forcible entry and detainer; repeals act 24 Feb. 1819; R. S. 1827, 228. . . Act 28 Feb., jurisdiction of justices in this action; part of the act of 1827 repealed; 1 Laws 1837, 119.

CHAP. 44. FRAUDS AND PERJURIES.

Act 19 Feb., enacting the first three sections of this chapter; Laws 1819, 14. . . Act 16 Feb. 1827, for the prevention of frauds and perjuries; R. S. 1827, 230 §§1—4; R. S. 1833, 313. . . Act 28 Feb. 1833, to prevent fraudulent devises; R. S. 1833, 315.

CHAP. 45. FUGITIVES FROM JUSTICE.

Act 25 Mar., governor to offer a reward for the apprehension of criminals as in §8 of this chapter; Laws 1819, 254. . . Act 6 Jan. 1827; concerning fugitives from justice; former acts repealed; R. S. 1827, 232; R. S. 1833, 317.

CHAP. 45*a*. GAME.

Act 12 Feb., forbids the killing of certain kinds of game from 1 Jan. to 20 July, in 15 specified counties; Laws 1853, 254; Gross' Stat. 1868, 323. . . Act 15 Feb., forbids the killing or trapping of certain kinds of game, from 15 Jan. to 1 Aug., in all except 58 counties which are by name excepted; Laws 1855, 137; Gross' Stat. 1868, 323. . . Act 9 Feb; the act of 1855 extended to Clinton county; Laws 1857, 56; Gross' Stat. 1868, 324. . . Act 16 Feb., amending the acts of 1855 so far as it relates to Edgar county; Pr. Laws 1857, 1123; Gross' Stat. 1868, 324. . . Act 18 Feb., explaining the act of 1855 as to warehousemen and carriers; Laws 1857, 99; Gross' Stat. 1368, 325. . . Act 24 Feb., repeals the act of 1855 so far as relates to Greene county; Laws 1859, 120; Gross' Stat. 1868, 325. . . Act 21 Feb., the act of 1855 extended to Knox county; Laws 1861, 126; Gross' Stat. 1868, 325. . . Act 12 Feb., the Knox co. act extended to four other counties; Laws 1863, 50; Gross' Stat. 1868, 325.

CHAP. 46. GAMING.

Act 16 Jan. 1827, to restrain gaming by declaring gaming contracts void; R. S. 1827, 235; R. S. 1833, 320.

CHAP. 47. GUARDIAN AND WARD.

Act 5 Feb. 1827, concerning minors, orphans and guardians; R. S. 1827, 301; R. S. 1833, 458. . . Act 7 Feb., being §§14 and 15 Ch. 47 R. S. 1845; Laws 1831, 100; R. S. 1833, 456. . . Act 27 Jan., father to dispose of the custody of infant; nearly as in R. S. 1845 Ch. 47 §17—20; Laws 1835, 35. . . Act 4 Mar., guardian appointed in all cases whether there is real estate or not; poor children bound out; 1 Laws 1837, 163.

CHAP. 48. HABEAS CORPUS.

Act 22 Jan. 1827, regulating the proceedings on writs of habeas corpus; R. S. 1827, 236; R. S. 1833, 322.

CHAP. 49. HORSES.

Act 20 Feb., stoned horses may be taken up and gelded; Laws 1819, 26. . . Act 3 Jan., for improving the breed of horses; act of 20 Feb. 1819 repealed; Laws 1829, 75; R. S. 1833, 330.

CHAP. 50. IDIOTS AND LUNATICS.

Act 12 Feb., regulating the estates of idiots, lunatics and persons distracted; Laws 1823, 133; Laws 1829, 77; R. S. 1833, 332. . . Act 19 Jan., sections 8 and 9 Ch. 50 R. S. 1845; Laws 1831, 81; R. S. 1833, 334. . . Ch. 50, R. S. 1845, appointment of conservator for idiot, lunatic or distracted person; his powers and duties; R. S. 276; Gross' Stat. 1868, 345. . . Act 15 Feb., penalty of the bond of a conservator; Laws 1851, 98; Gross' Stat. 1868, 345.

Idiots, Schools for.—To be kept in connection with the institution for the education of the deaf and dumb; Laws 1865 (15 Feb.) 71. . . Appropriations for 1867 and 1868; Laws 1867 (28 Feb.) 9.

CHAP. 50*a*. INSANE HOSPITAL.

Established at Jacksonville; Laws 1847 (1 Mar.) 52. . . Special state tax to be collected for four years; 1 Laws 1849 (3 Feb.) 93. . . *The act of* 1851 *contains some provisions which are included in full in the chapter on this subject, namely, sections* 4, 5, 8, 12 *and* 14. *The remaining sections are:* §1. Special tax for the Hospital Fund. §2. Cost of keeping insane paupers to be paid by the state. §3. Building finished and furnished. §7. Certificate of a county clerk to be authority for arresting and detaining a lunatic; changed by the act of 1853. §9. Notice of the time of opening. §10. Married women and infants detained without the verdict of a jury; repealed by the act of 1867. §13. Compensation of the sheriff and his assistants; changed by the act of 1853. §15. Penalty in conservators' bonds; changed by the act of 1869, Ch. 50. §16. Superintendent not required to perform road labor, serve on juries, or attend court as a witness. §17. Hospital employees also exempt from jury duty and road labor. §18. Printing the trustees' reports; changed by later acts relating to printing. §19. $5,000, borrowed for deficiences. Laws 1851 (15 Feb.) 96. . . *The act of* 1853 *also contains provisions which are given in full in Chap.* 50*a. namely, sections* 6—17. *The remaining sections are:* §1. Nine trustees appointed by the governor, their classification and powers; changed by the act of 1869 Ch. 22. §2. Treasurer and his duties. §3. Semi-annual meetings of trustees. §4. Vacancies in the board of trustees. §5. Treasurer's quarterly settlement; Laws 1853, (12 Feb.) 242. . . Special tax for state institutions repealed; Laws 1855 (14 Feb.) 42 §18. . . Foregoing statutes amended; number of the trustees; Laws 1857 (13 Feb.) 84.

Appropriations.—For completing the building $66,666.66; fifty dangerous patients provided for; Laws 1857 (16 Feb.) 148. Farther appropriations; Laws 1859 (19 Feb.) 18. Also, Id. (21 Feb.) 14. To pay J. M. Higging, superin-

tendent $775.75; Laws 1859 (19 Feb.) 149. For completing unfinished buildings, and for 1861 and 1862; Laws 1861 (21 Feb.) 134. For 1863 and 1864; Laws 1863 (21 Feb.) 16. For 1865 and 1866; Laws 1865 (15 Feb.) 16. For completing the east wing; Laws 1865 (8 Feb.) 17. To pay debts; Laws 1867 (12 Feb.) 4. For 1867 and 1868; Laws 1867 (28 Feb.) 9. For 1869 and 1870; Laws 1869 (24 Mar.) 23; also, to meet deficiencies of appropriation for current expenses; Id. 27.

Asylum for the Insane.—For the location of an Asylum for the insane, erecting the buildings and carrying on the same; Laws 1869 (16 Apr.) 19.

Northern Illinois Hospital and Asylum.—Establishment of and and how located; Laws 1869 (16 Apr) 24.

CHAP. 51. ENCLOSURES AND FENCES.

Act 20 Feb., height and construction of fences; manner of determining damages and enforcing payment; Laws 1819, 23; R. S. 1833, 261. . . Act 23 Feb., enclosure and cultivation of common fields; Laws 1819, 37; Laws 1829, 69; R. S. 1833, 258. . . Act 23 Feb., removal of fences made by mistake on the lands of other persons; Laws 1819, 44; R. S. 1833, 419. . . Act 27 Jan., amending the act "regulating enclosures;" liability of owner where animals break lawful fence, being similar to R. S. 1845, Ch. 51 §§15—18; Laws 1835, 144.

CHAP. 52. INSOLVENT DEBTORS.

Act 27 Mar., for the benefit of insolvent debtors, and providing for their discharge; Laws 1819, 301. . . Act 12 Jan., for the relief of insolvent debtors; former acts repealed; Laws 1829, 78; R. S. 1833, 351.

CHAP. 53. INSPECTIONS.

Act 23 Mar., to establish inspections of articles of exportation; Laws 1819, 199; R. S. 1833, 337. . . Act 12 Jan., regulating the inspection of tobacco; Laws 1829, 174; R. R. 1833, 339. . . Act 2 Mar., supplemental to the act of 1829; Laws 1839, 283.

CHAP. 53a. INSURANCE.

Charters of companies are indexed in the counties where located. This one contains no indication of its location. Incorporation of the Western World Insurance company for fire and tornadoes, etc; 2 Pr. Laws 1867 (7 Mar.) 105.

CHAP. 54. INTEREST.

Act 2 Mar., rate to be six per cent; Laws 1819, 106; Laws 1829, 108; R. S. 1833, 350. . . Act 28 Feb. 1833, nearly the same as Ch. 54, R. S. 1845; R. S. 1833, 348.

CHAP. 55. JAILS AND JAILORS.

Act 22 Mar., jail to be guarded by the militia, upon demand of the sheriff; Laws 1819, 160. . . Act 22 Mar., where there is not a sufficient jail, prisoners may be taken to another county; Laws 1819, 165. . . Act without date, probably about 20 Jan. 1821; safe keeping of United States prisoners; Laws 1851, 30. . . Act 31 Jan., subsistence of prisoners in criminal cases; Laws 1823, 99. . . Act 17 Feb., to abolish imprisonment for debt in certain cases; Laws 1823, 158. . . Act 26 Jan. 1827; concerning jails and jailors; former acts repealed; R. S. 1827, 246; R. S. 1833, 366.

CHAP. 56. JOINT RIGHTS AND OBLIGATIONS.

Act 13 Jan., concerning partitions and joint rights and obligations; Laws 1821, 14; R. S. 1833, 473.

CHAP. 57. JUDGMENTS AND EXECUTIONS.

Act 22 Mar., debtors allowed to give bond and have a stay of execution for 12 months; Laws 1819, 158. . . Act 22 Mar., property which a head of family may hold exempt from execution; Laws 1819, 160. . . Act 22 Mar., subjecting real estate to execution, and fixing the mode in which the same shall be sold; Laws 1819, 177. . . Act 16 Jan., executions suspended until 20 Nov. 1821; Laws 1821, 17. . Act 27 Jan., officers selling under process not to purchase at their own sales; constables to pay over money collected; redemption of property sold on execution; Laws 1821, 37. . . Act 8 Feb., penalty against officers failing to pay over money collected; Laws 1821, 116. . . Act 15 Feb., manner of selling property on execution; not to be sold for less than half its valuation; Laws 1821, 174. . . Act 11 Jan., agricultural premiums exempt from execution, etc.; Laws 1823, 71. . . Act 17 Feb., concerning judgments and executions; repeal of the foregoing acts of 22 Mar. 1819; repeal of the act of 15 Feb. 1821, and of sections of other acts; Laws 1823, 169. . . Act 17 Jan., concerning judgments and executions; a general law; Laws 1825, 151 §§1—24; Laws 1829, 85; R. S. 1833, 370. . . Act 27 Jan., the taking of delivery bonds under §17 of the foregoing act of 17 Jan. 1825; Laws 1826, 85. . . Act 1 Mar. 1833, to regulate the taking of delivery bonds; former acts repealed; R. S. 1833, 223. . . Act 6 Feb., to repeal so much of §9 of act 17 Jan. 1825, as requires property levied on to be appraised; Laws 1839, 56. . . Act 12 Feb., in relation to garnishees, similar to R. S. 1845 Ch. 57 §§38, 39; Laws 1839, 86. . . Act 1 Feb., property exempt from execution; Laws 1840, 89. . . Act 19 Feb., to facilitate the collection of judgments by executors and administrators; similar to Ch. 57 R. S. 1845 §§40—42. Redemptions of land sold on execution; similar to R. S. 1845 Ch. 57 §§14—21; Laws 1841, 168. . . Act 26 Feb., property exempt from execution; former acts repealed; Laws 1841, 171. . . Act 27

Feb., valuation of property levied on by execution; Laws 1841, 172. . . Act 26 Feb., certificates of the levy of attachments to be filed; Laws 1841, 181. . . Act 4 Mar., property exempt from execution; Laws 1843, 141. . . Act 25 Feb., proceedings on the death of the defendant in execution; similar to Ch. 57 (R. S. 1845) §37; Laws 1843, 168. . . Act 6 Jan., to regulate the sale of property on judgments and executions; property levied on to be valued and sold for two-thirds the value; (Consult Smoot vs. Lafferty, 2 Gilm. 383;) Laws 1843, 186.

CHAP. 58. JURORS.

Act 23 Mar., mode of summoning grand jurors; Laws 1819, 201. . . Act 25 Mar., concerning petit jurors; the manner of summoning, their duties, qualifications and fees; Laws 1819, 255. . . Act 9 Feb., all discreet householders competent to serve as grand jurors; Laws 1821, 115. . . Act 17 Feb., extending the right of peremptory challenges; Laws 1823, 154. . . Act 18 Feb., amending the act of 23 Mar. 1819, concerning the "mode of summoning grand jurors;" Laws 1823, 182. . . Act 7 Feb. 1827; mode of summoning grand and petit jurors, their qualifications and duties; former acts repealed; R. S. 1827, 251; R. S. 1833, 378. . . Act 13 Feb., fees of jurors, their certificate, etc; Laws 1835, 37. . . Act 24 Jan., amending the act of 1827, and requiring return to be made to the circuit clerk; Laws 1835, 144. . . Act 1 Feb., grand and petit jurors at special terms; Laws 1843, 169. . . Act 4 Feb. 1843; mileage allowed to grand and petit jurors; Laws 1843, 169.

CHAP. 59. JUSTICES AND CONSTABLES.

Act 19 Feb., manner of appointing justices; Laws 1819, 22. . . Act 22 Mar., appointment of constables, their powers and duties; Laws 1819, 162. . . Act 23 Mar, powers and duties of justices of the peace; Laws 1819, 185. . . Act 30 Mar., continuation and final determination of suits begun before territorial justices; Laws 1819, 353. . . Act 20 Jan., supplemental to the act of 22 Mar. 1819, for the appointment of constables; penalty against constables for a neglect of duty; Laws 1821, 28. . . Act 27 Jan., constables to pay over money collected on execution; Laws 1821, 38, §2. . . Act 12 Feb., appeals from justices; duties of justices further defined; Laws 1821, 130 §§1—23. . . Act 14 Feb., writs of certiorari may be issued by judges of probate, to take up cases from justices; Laws 1821, 185. . . Act 11 Jan., fines and penalties to be paid into the county treasuries; Laws 1823, 69. . . Act 18 Feb., to regulate and define the duties of justices and constables; Laws 1823, 184 §§1—32. . . Act 17 Jan., amending the several acts relating to the duties of justices and constables; concerning executions; Laws 1825, 135. . . Act 23 Jan., regulating the mode of proceeding on writs of certiorari; Laws 1826, 65. . . Act 30 Dec. 1826; to provide for the election of justices of the peace and constables; act 19 Feb. 1819 on the same subject repealed; R. S. 1827, 255; R. S. 1833, 382. . . Act 3 Feb. 1827; a general law specifying the jurisdiction of justices, their powers and duties, and defining the duties of constables; former acts repealed; R. S. 1827, 259 §§1—57; R. S. 1833, 386. . . Act 12 Feb. 1827; supplemental to the above act 3 Feb. 1827, and extending the jurisdiction of justices to trespass and trover; R. S. 1827, 274; R. S. 1833, 401. . . Act 29 Dec. 1826; extending the jurisdiction of justices to assaults and affrays; R. S. 1827, 274; R. S. 1833, 402. . . Act 13 Jan., amending the foregoing act of 30 Dec. 1826; filling vacancies, election of new officers; Laws 1829, 93; R. S 1833, 405. . . Act 23 Jan., amending the foregoing act of 13 Feb. 1829, "concerning justices of the peace and constables;" former laws repealed; Laws 1829, 94; R. S. 1833, 407. . . Act 14 Feb., amends §7 of the foregoing act of 13 Jan. 1829; Laws 1831, 50. . . Act 7 Jan., tenure of office unaffected by alteration of county line; Laws 1831, 88; R. S. 1833, 411. . . Act 1 Mar. 1833; to amend the acts concerning justices of the peace and constables; R. S. 1833, 412. . . Act 2 Mar. 1833; jurisdiction where demand is reduced to $100. by fair credits: R. S. 1833, 415. . . Act 6 Feb., constables to be elected in each justice's district; Laws 1835, 29. . . Act 7 Jan., increase of the number of justices' districts; Laws 1835, 39. . . Act 13 Feb., jurisdiction of justices against officers who fail to pay over money collected; Laws 1835, 32. . . Act 12 Feb., trial by jury to be demanded, and fees advanced, similar to R. S. 1845 Ch. 59 §47: Laws 1839, 87. . . Act 2 Mar., appeal bonds and the trial of appeals; Laws 1839, 291. . . Act 1 Feb., certificate of magistracy on an execution to another county; Laws 1840, 64. Failing to pay over money collected; Id. 78. . . Act 31 Jan. appeals allowed in actions *qui tam* and actions for a penalty; Laws 1835, 153 §3. . . Act 21 July, where the plaintiff wishes to prove his demand by his own oath, summons to issue stating that fact; 2 Laws 1837, 47. . . Act 12 Jan., execution from docket of deceased justice, similar to R. S. 1845 Ch. 59 §110; Laws 1839, 41. . . Act 3 Feb., to amend the former acts in relation to appeals; Laws 1840, 108. . . Act 26 Feb., to amend the several acts in relation to constables; Laws 1841, 176.

CHAP. 60. LANDLORD AND TENANT.

Act 23 Feb., proceedings in case of distress for rent, and tenants at will holding over; Laws 1819, 53. . . Act 13 Feb., 1827; concerning landlords and tenants; repeals the act of 23 Feb. 1819: R. S. 1827, 278. . . Act 4 Jan., enacts §§7, 8 and 9 Ch. 60 R. S. 1845; Laws 1831, 88; R. S. 1833, 420.

CHAP. 61. LANDS.

Act 15 Feb., similar to R. S. 1845 Ch. 61; Laws 1831, 82; R. S. 1833, 420, . . Act 27 Feb., possession in case of settlement on the public lands; similar to R. S. 1845 Ch. 61 §§52—

1 Laws 1837, 154. . . Act 2 Feb., to provide for the collection of demands growing out of contracts for sales of the possession of the public lands; Laws 1839, 47. . . Act 16 Feb., supplemental to the act of 27 Feb., 1837; Laws 1839, 124. . . Resolution concerning pre-emption rights; Laws 1839, 295. For the establishment of a surveyor general's office in Illinois; Id. 296. In relation to unsurveyed lands in Illinois; Id. 298. For the purchase by the state of all unsold lands at 25 cents per acre; Id. 300. . . Act 21 Feb., to provide for settlers on lands purchased by the state; right of pre-emption allowed; Laws 1843, 184. Receipt of the distributive share of the state in the proceeds of the sales of the public lands; Id. 194. . Resolution that congress reduce the price of the public lands to 50 or 75 cents; Laws 1843, 324. Resolution relating to pre-emption rights, and reducing the price of public lands; Id. 334. . Act 21 Feb., 1843, providing for the receipt of the share of Illinois of the proceeds of sales by the United States; R. S. 616. . . State lands suspended from sale; act 7 Feb., Laws 1851, 23 . . Auditor to sell all the lands owned by the state and withheld from sale by the foregoing act; terms of sale; moneys received; pre-emptions; act 14 Feb., Laws 1853, 231. . . Amendment concerning such pre-emptions; act 10 Feb., Laws 1855, 45. . . Amending the previous acts concerning the sale of the public lands, and the right to pre-emptions thereon; act 16 Feb., Laws 1857, 61. . . In Kankakee and Iroquois counties to be sold by the auditor; act 13 Feb., Laws 1857, 89.

CHAP. 62. LAWS.

Act 4 Feb., enacting the common law of England as in Ch. 62 §1 R. S. 1845; Laws 1819 3; Laws 1829, 102; R. S. 1833, 425.

For convenience of reference to the English statutes and law reports, the table of regnal years is here given:

SOVEREIGNS.	Commencement of reign.	Length of reign.
William I	Oct. 14, 1066	21
William II	Sept. 26, 108	13
Henry I	Aug. 5, 11007	36
Stephen	Dec. 26, 1135	19
Henry II	Dec. 19, 1154	35
Richard I	Sept. 23, 1189	10
John	May 27, 1199	18
Henry III	Oct. 28, 1216	57
Edward I	Nov. 20, 1272	35
Edward II	July 8, 1307	20
Edward III	Jan. 25, 1326	51
Richard II	June 22, 1377	23
Henry IV	Sept. 30, 1399	14
Henry V	March 21, 1413	10
Henry VI	Sept. 1, 1422	39
Edward IV	Mar. 4, 1461	23
Edward V	April 9, 1483	—
Richard III	June 26, 1483	3
Henry VII	Aug. 22, 1485	24
Henry VIII	April 22, 1509	38
Edward VI	Jan. 28, 1547	7
Mary	July 6, 1553	6
Elizabeth	Nov. 17, 1558	45
James I	Mar. 24, 1603	23
Charles I	Mar. 27, 1625	24
The Commonwealth	Jan. 30, 1649	11
Charles II	May 29, 1660	37
James II	Feb. 6, 1685	4
William and Mary	Feb. 13, 1689	14
Anne	Mar. 8, 1702	13
George I	Aug. 1, 1714	13
George II	June 11, 1727	34
George III	Oct. 25, 1760	60
George IV	Jan. 29, 1820	11
William IV	June 26, 1830	7
Victoria	June 20, 1837	—

Although Charles II did not ascend the throne until 29th May, 1660, his regnal years were computed from the death of Charles I, January 30, 1649, so that the year of his restoration is styled the twelfth of his reign.

1831, 1 & 2 Wm. IV.		1849	12 & 13 Vic.
1832, 2 & 3	"	1850	13 & 14 "
1833, 3 & 4	"	1851	14 & 15 "
1834, 4 & 5	"	1852	15 & 16 "
1835, 5 & 6	"	1853	16 & 17 "
1836, 6 & 7	"	1854	17 & 18 "
1837, 7 Wm. IV. & 1 Vic.		1855	18 & 19 "
1838, 1 & 2 Vic.		1856	19 & 20 "
1839, 2 & 3	"	1857	20 "
1840, 3 & 4	"	1857	20 & 21 "
1841, 4 & 5	"	1858	21 & 22 "
1841, 5	"	1859	22 "
1842, 5 & 6	"	1859	22 & 23 "
1843, 6 & 7	"	1860	23 & 24 "
1844, 7 & 8	"	1861	24 & 25 "
1845, 8 & 9	"	1862	25 & 26 "
1846, 9 & 10	"	1863	26 & 27 "
1847, 10 & 11	"	1864	27 & 28 "
1848, 11 & 12	"	1865	28 & 29 "

Act 30 Mar., repeal of the territorial laws, some exceptions—private acts; Laws 1819, 351; R. S. 1833, 425. . . Act 2 Mar., acts to be transmitted by the governor to the executives of other states; nearly the same as §§2 and 3 of this chapter; Laws 1819, 105; Laws 1829, 103. . Act without date, probably about 20 Jan. 1821; manner of distributing the laws of the general assembly of this state; Laws 1821, 31. . . Act 26 Dec. 1826; acts may become laws notwithstanding the objections of the council of revision; R. S. 1827, 280; R. S. 1833, 437. . . Act 19 Feb. 1827; publication of the revised laws, and the laws of the session of 1827; manner of distributing the same; R. S. 1827, 281. . . Act 14 Jan., publication and distribution of the laws and journals; Laws 1829, 104; R. S. 1833, 422. . . Act 1 Jan. 1819 [1829]; duty of the governor to transmit laws to other states; former act repealed; R. S. 1829, 103; R. S. 1833, 422. . . Act 2 Mar. 1833; list of acts required to be printed in the revised statutes of 1833; all former public acts repealed, with some exceptions; R. S. 1833, 426. . . Act 22 Feb. 1833; secretary of state to have the U. S. laws and state laws bound; R. S. 1833, 438. . . Act 2 Mar., to reprint laws for justices; Laws 1839, 290. . . Act 29 Jan., laws and journals distributed to recorders and school commissioners; Laws 1840, 65. . . Act 2 Feb., distribution of the laws and documents of congress, similar to §§13, 14 of Ch. 62 (R. S. 1845); Laws 1843, 173. . Resolution for the distribution of Gross' Stat-

utes; Laws 1869, 424; under the act of 10 Mar. 1869; Id. 30. . . Copying of the laws and journals; 1 Laws 1849 (12 Feb.) 95, changed by the act of 1869. This act of 1849 also provided for the distribution of the laws and journals by contract; it was amended by allowing contractors further time to file bonds; Laws 1851 (17 Feb.) 148. But the act of 1867 appears to take the place of all former statutes. . . Publication and distribution of the acts of the session; 2 Laws 1861 (3 May) 28.

Resolutions.—Register and Journal to publish the acts of the session; Pr. Laws 1855, 740. Reports, journals and documents sent to A. Vattemau at Paris; Ibid. . . Distribution of the laws and journals of the session; Pr. Laws 1857, 1453. Laws to be published in the Journal and Register; Id. 1454.

Special Acts.—E. B. Myers to publish the laws of each session on his private account; Laws 1865 (16 Feb.) 100. . . Callaghan & Cutler to publish the Public Laws; Laws 1867 (25 Feb.) 141.

CHAP. 63. STATE LIBRARY.

Act 15 Dec. 1842; concerning the state library, similar to Ch. 63, R. S. 1845; Laws 1843, 290. . . Resolution to preserve the historical essay of Sidney Breese; Laws 1843, 322. . . Librarian to subscribe for periodicals; act 21 Feb. 1845; R. S. 594. . . Duties of the librarian; act 26 Jan., Laws 1847, 160. . . Repair of the library room; act 12 Feb, Laws 1853, 229. . . Certain funds used to purchase books; $500. appropriated annually therefor, in 1855 and 1856; act 15 Feb., Laws 1855, 171. . . Powers and duties of the librarian defined and extended; act 16 Feb., Laws 1865, 87. . . Payment of the librarian; act 5 Mar., Laws 1867, 28. . . Three commissioners appointed to make rules; appropriation of $3,000. for 1867 and for 1868; act 3 Mar., Laws 1867, 28. . . Appropriates $3,000. to purchase miscellaneous books; Laws 1869 (25 Mar.) 47.

CHAP. 64. LICENSES.

Act 27 Feb., to license and regulate taverns; Laws 1819, 77; R. S. 1833, 595. . . Act 16 Feb. 1831; enacts §§1—6, Ch. 64 R. S. 1845; repeals former acts; Laws 1831, 89; R. S. 1833, 438. . . Act 2 Mar. 1833; amending the foregoing act of 1831; R. S. 1833, 441. . . Act 14 Feb. 1833; to prevent the sale of spirituous liquors; R. S. 1833, 594. . . Act 31 Jan., mode of granting license to clock pedlers; Laws 1835, 63. . . Act 12 Feb., amending the act to license taverns, fixing license at $50.; Laws 1835, 154. . . Act 4 Mar., Wm. Armstrong, Benj. Chesney and Wm. Henson to peddle without license, except clocks; 1 Laws 1837, 187. . . Act 10 Feb., cider and beer sold without license; 1 Laws 1837, 326. . . Act 2 Mar., to repeal laws concerning tavern licenses; license to groceries, similar to R. S. 1845, Ch. 64; Laws 1839, 72. . . Act 17 Feb., to amend an act "to regulate tavern and grocery licenses;" Laws 1841, 178. Supplemental to the foregoing; act 18 Feb. 1841; Id. 179. . . Act 27 Feb., licenses to be issued to merchants and pedlars; Laws 1841, 179. Agents of foreign insurance companies to obtain license; Id. 180. . Act 4 Mar., to repeal the act 27 Feb. 1841 "to regulate foreign insurance companies;" other provisions on the same subject; Laws 1843, 165.

Physicians.—Establishment of four medical societies; physicians to be examined and licensed; Laws 1819 (24 Mar.) 233. Foregoing repealed; Laws 1821 (3 Jan.) 3. . . Manner of issuing licenses to physicians; Laws 1825 (15 Jan.) 111. Foregoing repealed; Laws 1826 (25 Jan.) 75.

CHAP. 65. LIENS.

Act 13 Jan., for the benefit of mechanics, etc.; Laws 1825, 101; Laws 1829, 106. . . Act 22 Feb. 1833; lien for the benefit of mechanics, etc.; R. S. 1833, 447. . . Act 10 Dec. 1839; to secure a lien to mechanics and others, similar to the chapter in the revised statutes; Laws 1840, 147. . . Act 14 Feb., allowing lien to sub-contractors, under certain conditions in sixteen counties; Laws 1863, 57; Gross' Stat. 1868, 425. . . Act 19 Feb., provisions of said act extended to Adams county; Laws 1865, 91; Gross' Stat. 1868, 427. . . Act 7 Mar., provisions of the act 1863 extended to seventeen other counties; Laws 1867, 133; Gross' Stat. 1868, 427. . . Act 5 Apr., is a general act on this subject, applicable to the entire state; Ch. 65 §31. By §10 the act of 1863 is in terms repealed; Laws 1869, 255. . . Act 31 Mar., to extend the act of (14 Feb.) 1863, to McLean, Macon and DeWitt counties; said act is repealed (5 Apr. 1869; Laws 1869, 257 §10.) Laws 1869, 258. . . Act 30 Mar., also extending said repealed act to Douglas county; Ibid.

CHAP. 66. LIMITATIONS.

Act 22 Mar., limitations of the different classes of actions; Laws 1819, 141 §§8, 9. . . Act 18 Feb., ejectment only to be brought on ten years previous possession; rights of minors etc.; Laws 1823, 183. . . Act 10 Feb. 1827; for the limitations of actions, and for avoiding vexatious law suits; former acts repealed; R. S. 1827, 284; R. S. 1833, 441. . . Act 17 Jan., amending the act of 1827, being §§11 and 8 R. S. Ch. 66; Laws 1835, 42. . . Act 11 Feb., act of 1827 not to extend to non-residents unless infants; 1 Laws 1837, 160.

CHAP. 67. MANDAMUS.

Act 6 Jan. 1827; to regulate proceedings on writs of mandamus; R. S. 1827, 287; R. S. 1833, 444.

CHAP. 68. MARKS AND BRANDS.

Act 6 Feb., revising so much of the act of 23 Mar. 1829 as relates to marks and brands; Laws 1835, 51. (There does not appear to be any such law among the public printed acts of 1829.)

CHAP. 69. MARRIAGES.

Act 6 Feb., who may be joined in marriage; the ceremony of marriage; Laws 1819, 26. . . Act 27 Jan., circuit judges authorized to marry; Laws 1826, 88. . . Act 14 Feb. 1827; concerning marriages; repeal of the act of 20 Feb. 1819; R. S. 1827, 288; R. S. 133, 445. . . Act 2 Mar., to legitimate marriages by ministers; Laws 1839, 277.

CHAP. 70. MILITIA.

Act 26 Mar., establishing a general system for the state; Laws 1819, 270 §§1—56. . . Act 12 Feb. 1819; persons having conscientious scruples allowed to be exempt from militia duty on annual payment of $6.; Laws 1819, 13. . Act 18 Jan., repeals act 12 Feb. 1819; such persons exempt on payment of $3.; Laws 1821, 13. . . Act 8 Feb., amendment to the general law; Laws 1821, 106, §§1—13. . . Act 24 Jan., persons exempt from duty on payment of $1. or two days work on the highway; Laws 1823, 46. Act 5 Feb., formation of a new brigade; Laws 1823, 113. . . Act 14 Feb., times of holding company musters; Laws 1823, 141. . . Act 15 Feb., incorporating the Invincible Dragoons, of the second division Illinois militia; Pr. Laws 1839, 47. . . Act 15 Jan., amending the act for the organization of the militia; Laws 1825, 117. . . Act 25 Jan., organization and government of the militia; a general law; Laws 1826, 3 §§1—75. . . Act 27 Jan., supplemental to the last foregoing act; Laws 1826, 44. . . Act 9 Feb. 1827; in addition to the act 25 Jan. 1826, "for the organization and government of the militia;" R. S. 1827, 290. . . Act 6 Feb. 1827; relief of persons having conscientious scruples against bearing arms; R. S. 1827, 296. . . Act 19 Jan., amending the former acts; repeal of some former acts; Laws 1829, 107. . . Act 22, Jan., amendatory and supplemental; Laws 1831, 94. . . Act 10 Feb., amends the act amending act 19 Jan. 1829; exemption on payment of 75 cents; Laws 1831, 95. . . Act 1 Mar. 1833; concerning the public arms; R. S. 1833, 499. . . Act 4 Mar., amending the act "for the organization and government of the militia;" 1 Laws 1837, 163. Act 2 Mar., encouraging volunteer companies; 1 Laws 1837, 165. . Act 26 Feb., brigade inspector for the first brigade and third division; Laws 1839, 189. . . Act 24 Feb., to legalize the military acts of Reese Bayless; Laws 1843, 218. . . General act 3 Mar. 1845; R. S. 355. Regulating the pay of brigade majors; act 12 Feb., Laws 1849, 41. organizing six regiments of volunteers; act 25 Apr., Ex. Laws 1861, 5. . . Confirming elections of officers held 25 April 1861; act 29 Apr.. Ex. Laws 1861, 7. . . *Compensation to the board of medical examiners; act 1 May, Ex. Laws* 1861, 7. . . Appointment of chaplains in active service; act 2 May, Ex. Laws 1861, 12. . Payment of discharged volunteers; act 2 May, Ex. Laws 1861, 13. . . *Organization of ten regiments; act 2 May, Ex. Laws* 1861, 13. . . *Amendment to Ch. 70 in R. S. concerning militia; act 3 May, Ex. Laws* 1861, 17. . . *Quartermaster general's office; aids to the governor; act May 2, Ex. Laws* 1861, 19. . . For auditing accounts under the call for volunteers; board of commissioners; act 2 May, Ex. Laws 1861, 22. . Formation and equipment of volunteer companies; act 2 May, Ex. Laws 1861, 24. . . *Raising a regiment of cavalry; act 3 May, Ex. Laws* 1861, 27. . . Repeal of the statutes of 1, 2 and 3 May 1861, concerning military affairs; act 14 Feb., Laws 1863, 56. This act repeals those printed above in italic. . . Appointment, rank, pay and duties of the adjutant general; act 2 Feb., Laws 1865, 1. . . To prevent enlistment in this state of substitutes; substitute broker's license; act 16 Feb., Laws 1865, 63. . Chief of ordnance appointed; his duties defined; act 16 Feb., Laws 1865, 92. . . Military state agents appointed; their duties defined; act 16 Feb., Laws 1865, 126. . . War accounts barred by limitation to be paid; act 16 Feb., Laws 1865, 132. . . Act 13 Feb., Allen C. Fuller allowed from 14 Feb., 1863 to 1 Jan. 1865 same per diem allowed the Adjutant General by act of 2 May 1861; 2 Pr. Laws 1865, 240. . . Act 15 Feb., Jeremiah M. Wardwell allowed $14,133. balance due for 4000 Enfield Rifles; 2 Pr. Laws 1865, 251. . . Act 10 Mar., to repeal former acts and define the duties of the adjutant general; Laws 1869, 5. . . Act 19 Apr., repairs on the state arsenal; Laws 1869, 6. . . Act 29 Mar., to prevent loaning flags and trophies of war; Laws 1869, 6. . . Act 31 Mar., distribution of the reports of the adjutant general; Laws 1869, 5. Also, a resolution to the same effect; Id. 413. Also, to regimental officers; Ibid. Also, to clerks and pension officers; Ibid. For the packing and shipping; Ibid. Further distribution to members; Id. 414. State arsenal to be used as the adjutant general's office; Id. 415.

CHAP. 71. MILLS AND MILLERS.

Act 25 Mar., regulation of grist mills and millers; Laws 1819, 264 §§1—10. . . Act 9 Feb. 1827; regulating mills and millers; repeal of the foregoing act of 25 Mar. 1819; R. S. 1827, 297; R. S. 1833, 449. . . Act 3 Mar., penalties under the act of 1827 may be sued for before a justice; Laws 1843, 179.

CHAP. 71*b*. NAMES.

Act 10 Feb., Clayborn Elder changed to Clayborn Elder Bell; Laws 1835, 80. . . Act 21 July, T. J. Sanders changed to T. J. McDowell; Francis Hood to Francis Thornbury; 2 Laws 1837, 52. . . Act 24 Jan., Lavina Joliff changed to Lavina Phelps; Laws 1843, 179. . Act 3 Feb., Lucy Robinson changed to Lucy Sullivan; Laws 1843, 179. . . Act 3 Mar., W. C. Asky changed to W. C. Mitchell; P. and J. McLean, to P. and J. McLean Clark; Laws 1843, 180. . . David Findley to David Mitchell Findley; Edward Hand Fitch to Edward Fitch Evans, and made him heir of H. B. Evans; Bryant Durand Chamberlain to Bryant Durand Beach; William Asberry Kingman to William Asberry Kenyon; John Berry to John Stout; Henry Lehmon and Peter Franklin Lehmon confirmed in their names; act of 3 Mar., Laws 1845, 178. . . Nathan Kingsberry Hinman changed to John E. Hinman; act 31 Dec. 1844;

Laws 1845, 188. . . Joseph Lewis Breese changed to Samuel Livingston Breese; act of 22 June, Laws 1852, 176. . . Katherine Early to Katherine West; act of 8 Feb., Laws 1853, 92. . . Frank to Frank Childs; act of 12 Feb., Laws 1853, 94. . . Elizabeth Hart to Elizabeth Hord; act of 12 Feb., Laws 1853, 94. . . Ensley Moore Goudy to Ensley Moore, to have the same rights as if he were the son of Joshua Moore; act of 12 Feb., Laws 1853, 94. . . Thomas Rockwood to Justice Beston; act of 10 Feb., Laws 1853, 95. . . David and R. W. Hengst to David and and R. W. Hent; act of 26 Jan., Laws 1859, 127. . . Act 27 Feb., Jonas Reeves changed to Jonas Rhodes. Pr. Laws 1847, 21. . . Act 27 Feb., Hezekiah Bryant changed to Hezekiah Sams. Pr. Laws 1833, 121. . . Act 17 Feb.. Elizabeth Dennis changed to Elizabeth Curry, Pr. Laws 1851, 202. . Act 26 Jan., Mary Ann Burns changed to Mary Ann Merrell. Pr. Laws 1853, 479. . . Act 8 Feb., John A. Smith changed to John A. Rhone; and his children Weston, Ray W., and Mary M. to the same. Pr. Laws 1853, 490. . , Act 9 Feb., James Helmantoller changed to James Helman. Pr. Laws 1855, 686. . . Act 9 Feb., surnames of Catharine, Rosetta, Frederick, Silas D., Napoleon B., Josephine, Thomas J. and David Leibsheitz changed to Lasier. Pr. Laws 1855, 687. . . Act 9 Feb., Mary Jones changed to Elizabeth Jones Totten; heir of James M. Totten. Pr. Laws 1855, 691. . . Act 15 Feb., James and William Peets changed to James and William Eads; heirs of James Eads; Pr. Laws 1855, 716. . . Act 14 Feb., Catharine Chute changed to Kate Analine Elizabeth Allen; heir of Nathan Allen and wife. Pr. Laws 1855, 726. . . Act 9 Feb., Emeline Bowen changed to Emeline Sampson; heir of Dariands Sampson. Pr. Laws 1855, 730. . . Act 19 Jan., Mina Stebins changed to Mina R. Baldwin. Pr. Laws 1857, 23. . . Act 31 Jan., Mary Ann, Bernard John and John B. Tocking changed to Bennett. Pr. Laws 1857, 228. . Act 13 Feb., Amanda E. and James L. Baker changed to Hammack. Pr. Laws 1857, 512. . Act 13 Feb., Charlie Grannis changed to Charlie Foster; heir of Cephas Foster. Pr. Laws 1857, 551. . . Act 18 Feb., Emily F. Wallham changed to Emily F. North; heir of John J. North. Pr. Laws 1857, 1242. . . Act 22 Feb., James and William Peets changed to Eads; heirs of James Adair Eads. Pr. Laws 1861, 477. . . Act 14 Feb., Roxy L. Morton changed to Roxy L. Kennedy. Pr. Laws 1863, 216. . . Act 16 Feb., Sarah E. Keplin changed to Sarah E. Cameron; heir of James Cameron. 2 Pr. Laws 1865, 94. . . Act 16 Feb., Jane Thomson Singleton changed to Minnie Jane Van Veghten; heir of Thomas S. Van Veghten. 2 Pr. Laws 1865, 96. . . Act 20 Feb., Lucilla Deen changed to Mary Ann Scurlock; heir of Wm. R. Scurlock and wife. 1 Pr. Laws 1867, 232. . . Act 11 Mar., John W. Semon changed to John W. Lee; heir of John W. and Mary F. Lee. 1 Pr. Laws 1867, 234. . Act 28 Feb., Emma and Anna [unknown] changed to Emma and Anna Collar. 1 Pr. Laws 1867, 235. . . Act 27 Feb., Thos. Griffith changed to Thomas J. Wilson; heir of Harry S. Wilson and wife. 1 Pr. Laws 1867, 235. . . Act 7 Mar., Augustus Ernestien Kurth changed to Retzloff; heir of John Retzloff. 1 Pr. Laws 1867, 236. . . Act 9 Mar., Minnie McMahon changed to Mather; heir of Frederick H. Mather. 1 Pr. Laws 1867, 238. . . Act 8 Mar., Mary Alice Waters changed to Williamson; heir of Eli Williamson. 1 Pr. Laws 1867, 238. . Act 9 Mar., Anna M. Houston changed to Littleton; heir of Jacob Littleton. 1 Pr. Laws 1867, 239. . . Act 8 Mar., George W. Goodman changed to Wm. Felt. 1 Pr. Laws 1867, 239. . Act 8 Mar, Emma Lucas or Driscol changed to Emma Linda Crarcy; heir of Alfred A. Crarey and wife. 1 Pr. Laws 1867, 240. . . Act 9 Mar., Jennie May Allen made heir of Harvey E. Allen. 2 Pr. Laws 1867, 85. . . Act 9 Mar., Rachel Paul changed to Mary V. Munson; heir of Franklin Munson. 2 Pr. Laws 1867, 846. . . Act 2 Mar., changing the name of Jane Coombs to Jane Patterson; Laws 1869, 263. . . Act 30 Mar., changing the name of L. A. Denning to L. A. Rhodes; Laws 1869, 264. . . Act 24 Mar., changing the name of John Kelley to John Riffey; Laws 1869, 264. . . Act 27 Mar., to change the name of Albert King to Albert Griffin; Laws 1869, 265. . . Act 31 Mar., change the name of Chas. Muthank to Chas. Munt; Laws 1869, 267. . . Act 31 Mar., changing the name of J. A. Rogers to J. A. Seass; Laws 1869, 267.

CHAP. 71*c*. NAVIGATION.

Under this head it has been found most convenient to classify the various acts relating to the improvement of navigable streams, the removal of obstructions, and in some few instances, bridge and ferry acts not readily to be located in the proper county.

General Acts.—Improvement of the navigation of the Saline Creek, Little Wabash, Great Wabash and Big Muddy; bridges across Fox and Bon Pass Rivers; R. S. 1827 (15 Feb.) 358. . . Appropriations from the proceeds of the Salines for the improvement of rivers; Little Wabash $10,000.; Kaskaskia $2,000.; Sangamon $1,000.; Macoupin $800.; Big Vermilion $2,000.; Embarrass $300.; former acts for the sale of Salines repealed; Laws 1829 (19 Jan.) 146. . . Lusk Creek navigable to Cowen's Mill; Grand Pier Creek to Chip's Mill; Big Creek to Twitchel's Mill; Laws 1837 (1 Mar.) 167. . . Resolution for the survey of the northern and western lakes; Laws 1839, 299. . Jurisdiction of the counties on the Mississippi and Wabash; Laws 1843 (4 Mar.) 100. . . Resolution that Congress should improve the navigation of western rivers; Laws 1843, 328. Also that congress improve the navigation of the Mississippi; Id. 337. Also, the Des Moines and Rock river rapids; Id. 339. . . For canal and river improvements; Laws 1867 (28 Feb.) 81. Foregoing amended; Laws 1869 (25 Feb.) 60.

Slack water navigation.—Formation of navigation and manufacturing companies on the Little Wabash and Saline rivers, and other navigable streams; 2 Laws 1849 (6 Nov.) 35.

Beaucoup River.—John Flock to bridge and take toll; Laws 1819 (24 Feb.) 60. Navigable to the shoal; Id. (26 Feb.) 73. Bridges to be built by J. Smith; Id. (1 Mar.) 86.

Navigation.

Big Bay.—Navigable to the St. Louis and Golconda road; apron to Green's dam; Pr. Laws 1833 (22 Feb.) 128.

Big Muddy.—Navigable up to the intersection of the East and West Forks; Laws 1835 (31 Jan.) 56. Wm. Drummond to build a dam at Shallow Ford; 1 Laws 1837 (3 Mar.) 161. Dam of Hillon Mason; Laws 1839 (28 Feb.) 203. Navigable to Watertown; Id. 208. To improve the navigation; Id. (2 Mar.) 99. Navigation company incorporated; Pr. Laws 1851 (15 Feb.) 185.

Big Vermilion.—Navigable—part, penalty for obstructing; Laws 1831 (5 Feb.) 127.

Bon Pas.—Declared navigable; Laws 1831 (1 Jan.) 126. Declared a highway; navigation to be improved; Laws 1845 (21 Feb.) 343.

Cache River.—Navigable to its main fork in town 13—3; Laws 1819 (24 Feb.) 69. Not navigable; concurrent jurisdiction of Alexander and Pulaski counties; Laws 1867 (21 Feb.) 79. Foregoing repealed, former act re-enacted; Laws 1869 (9 Mar.) 261. And also, Id. (25 Mar.) 161.

Des Plaines.—Declared navigable; Laws 1839 (28 Feb.) 208. Toll bridge by G. W. Smith; Laws 1831 (19 Feb.) 132.

Embarrass River.—Bridge by John Small in town 3—11; Laws 1819 (23 Feb.) 44. Time to C. Taylor to complete his toll bridge; Laws 1821 (19 Jan.) 13. Declared navigable; Laws 1831 (1 Jan.) 126. Time to J. Nabb to complete his toll bridge; Laws 1835 (29 Jan.) 80. To improve navigation; L. 1839 (28 Feb.) 97. Resolution for the donation of town 5—14 to improve navigation; Laws 1839, 299. To improve navigation; Laws 1845 (26 Feb.) 195. Also, Laws 1847 (27 Feb.) 85. Repeal of the act of 1847 as to Lawrence, Crawford and Jasper; Laws 1855 (15 Feb.) 142. Incorporation of the Embarrass navigation company; Pr. Laws 1851 (15 Feb.) 198.

Fox River.—Navigable to the Wisconsin line; Laws 1840 (15 Jan.) 98. Incorporating the Fox River Valley navigation company; Pr. Laws 1855 (15 Feb.) 639. Incorporating the Fox River Navigation and Manufacturing company; 2 Pr. Laws 1867 (9 Mar.) 460.

Illinois River.—Toll bridge by S. Lapsley in town 33—1; Laws 1831 (9 Feb.) 30. Incorporation of the Illinois river improvement company; Laws 1857 (14 Feb.) 212.

Kankakee.—Incorporation of the Kankakee and Iroquois navigation and manufacturing company; Pr. L. 1847 (15 Feb.) 91. Foregoing amended; Pr. Laws 1851 (15 Feb.) 212. Further amended; Pr. L. 1857 (16 Feb.) 1047. Name changed to "Kankakee Company," and charter amended; Pr. Laws 1859 (24 Feb.) 411. Corporate powers extended; 2 Pr. L. 1865 (16 Feb.) 96.

Kaskaskia.—Declared navigable to the north line of town 7; Laws 1819 (20 Feb.) 25. Herbert and Slade to build a dam in town 2—2; Laws 1819 (23 Mar.) 209. Charter of a company to build a bridge in one mile of Kaskaskia village; Laws 1819 (30 Mar.) 364. C. Slade to have the benefit of the act of 23 Mar. (1819); Laws 1823 (31 Jan.) 96. Further time to A. H. Mitchell for completing bridge at Vandalia; Laws 1823 (7 Feb.) 116. Toll bridge by Chas. Slade; Laws 1823 (12 Feb.) 135. Also by S. Wiggins; Laws 1831 (14 Feb.) 22. Repeal of an act of 1833 (28 Jan.) authorizing Beeler's ferry; Laws 1835 (12 Feb.) 66 . . Incorporation of a board of commissioners to improve the navigation; Laws 1829 (23 Jan.) 124. Settlement of their accounts; Laws 1836 (16 Jan.) 244. Resolution for improving the navigation; 1 Laws 1837 (6 Jan.) 337. . . Incorporating the Kaskaskia river navigation company; Laws 1841 (27 Feb.) 215. And also, Pr. Laws 1851 (15 Feb.) 185. And also, Pr. Laws 1855 (8 Feb.) 556. . . Act of 1853 amended; Pr. Laws 1855, 633. Revival of the act of 1853; 2 Pr. Laws 1867 (12 June) 455.

Macoupin Creek.—Mill dam of J. L. Evans; Laws 1823 (27 Dec. '22.) 83. Navigable to the Carrollton and Alton road; Laws 1837 (2 Mar.) 168.

Piasa.—Navigable in Jersey and Madison counties; Laws 1861 (18 Feb.) 150.

Rock Creek.—Channel changed by A. Brown and others; Laws 1843 (3 Mar.) 244.

Rock River.—Incorporation of Rock river bridge company at Grand De Tour; Laws 1843 (3 Mar.) 48. Foregoing amended; Laws 1845 (26 Mar.) 163. . . Incorporation of the Rock river navigation company; Laws 1841 (27 Feb.) 141. . . Incorporation of the dam and bridge company, and to improve navigation; Laws 1845 (1 Mar.) 139. . . Incorporation of the Board of commissioners to improve the navigation; Laws 1845 (25 Feb.) 279. . . System of slackwater navigation; 1 Laws 1849 (5 Feb.) 136. Foregoing amended; Pr. Laws 1855 (13 Feb.) 663. . . Charter of the Rock River Navigation and Water power Co.; 2 Pr. Laws 1867 (25 Feb.) 455. . . To preserve the fish in Rock river; Laws 1869 (21 Feb.) 161.

Saline Creek.—Toll bridge of J. A. Richardson; Laws 1825 (23 Dec. '24) 24.

Sangamon.—Navigable to the 3rd principal meridian; Laws 1823 (26 Dec. 1822) 81. Navigable on the North Fork to Champaign county; Laws 1845 (3 Mar.) 261.

Shoal Creek.—Lambert and Provines to build a toll bridge; Laws 1819 (27 Mar.) 298.

Snycarty.—Declared navigable; Laws 1843 (4 Mar.) 244. Navigable in Pike and Adams; Laws 1859 (24 Feb.) 189.

Spoon River.—Navigable up to Cameron's Mill; Laws 1835 (12 Feb.) 143. Foregoing amended; Laws 1843 (28 Feb.) 240. To improve the navigation; Laws 1839 (2 Mar.) 285. . Incorporation of the Spoon river navigation Co.; Pr. L. 1847 (3 Mar.) 259. Foregoing amended; Pr. Laws 1837 (19 Feb.) 176. Further amendment; Pr. Laws 1851 (15 Feb.) 177, and Laws 1845 (28 Feb.) 136. In aid of said company; L. 1852 (23 June) 223. Amending said act of 1852; Pr. Laws 1853 (3 Feb.) 577.

Wabash River.—Improvement of the navigation; Laws 1823 (30 Dec. 1822) 72. Baker's Mill dam at Coffee Island; Laws 1835 (31 Jan. 1831) 47. Improvement of navigation; R. S. 1833 (12 Feb.) 609. Resolution for improvement of the navigation; 1 Laws 1837 (2 Mar.) 338. Also S. Munday to pay certain moneys to fund commissioners; 1 Laws 1837 (4 Mar.) 120. Time for Baker's dam extended; Laws 1839 (19 Feb.) 131. Levee and other improvements; Laws 1847 (18 Feb.) 86. Supplemental act, levee extended;

Laws 1851 (15 Feb.) 103. Repeal §3 of the act of 1847; Id. 142.

Wabash Navigation Company.—Incorporation; Laws 1825 (13 Jan.) 96, amendment; Laws 1835 (12 Feb.) 173. Supplemental to the act of 1825 and extending it 40 years; Pr. L. 1833 (25 Feb.) 53. Reviving the acts of 1825, 1833 and 1835; Laws 1845 (1 Mar.) 126. . . Another act of incorporation; Pr. Laws 1847 (30 Jan.) 63.

Little Wabash.—Incorporation of the Little Wabash Navigation company; river a highway to McCawley's bridge; Laws 1826 (23 Jan.) 68. Settlements of the accounts of J. Groves for a lock at Robinson's Mill; Laws 1835 (20 Jan.) 69. Navigable to the north line of Clay county; Laws 1836 (18 Jan.) 212. Navigable to the National road; Laws 1837 (2 Mar.) 168. Navigation improved up to Ewington; Laws 1839 (2 Mar.) 288. Navigation improved; Laws 1841 (27 Feb.) 219. Appropriating $3,500. to improve the navigation; Laws 1869 (12 Mar.) 56. *Bridges and Dams.*—Toll bridge at Carmi; Laws 1819 (2 Mar.) 103. E. W. Jones' mill dam at Harris' shoals; Laws 1831 (1 Jan.) 98. Dams at New Haven and Carmi; Laws 1845 (1 Mar.) 99.

Skillet Fork.—Navigable to Ridgway's mills; Laws 1826 (23 Jan.) 68. Bridge on the Vandalia and Carmi road; Laws 1829 (20 Jan.) 13 §6. Navigable to Slocum's Mill; Laws 1837 (2 Mar.) 168. Relating to Witter's toll bridge; Laws 1840 (1 Feb.) 70.

CHAP. 72. NE EXEAT AND INJUNCTIONS.

Act 22 Jan. 1827; regulating the issue of writs of *ne exeat* and injunction; R. S. 1827, 304; R. S. 1833, 466.

CHAP. 73. NEGOTIABLE INSTRUMENTS.

Enactments of §§8—9; Laws 1819 (6 Feb.) 3. . . Failure of consideration, similar to §10; Laws 1819 (24 Feb.) 59. . . Act 24 Mar., concerning bills of exchange, manner of protesting; Laws 1819, 247 §§1—5. . . Act 14 Feb., regulating bills of exchange; Laws 1821, 169. . . Act 28 Dec. 1826; concerning bills of exchange; repeal of the above act of 14 Feb. 1821; R. S. 1827, 87; R. S. 1833, 112. . . Act 3 Jan. 1827; relative to promissory notes, bonds, due bills and other instruments in writing, and making them assignable; former acts repealed; R. S. 1827, 320; R. S. 1833, 482.

CHAP. 74. NEGROES AND MULATTOES.

Act 30 Mar., respecting free negroes, mulattoes, servants and slaves; Laws 1819, 354; R. S. 1833, 457. . . Act 8 Jan., amending the foregoing; L. 1825, 50. . . Act 17 Jan., to more effectually prevent kidnapping; Laws 1825, 149. . . Act 17 Jan., free negroes and mulattoes, servants and slaves; Laws 1829, 109; R. S. 1833; 463. . . Act 1 Feb., no negro or mulatto to reside in this state without giving bond; Laws 1831, 101; R. S. 1833, 462. . . Act 1 Mar. 1833; persons failing to comply with §3 of the act 1819; R. S. 1833, 466. . . Act 19 Feb., native blacks may record their names and the evidence of their freedom; Laws 1841, 189.

CHAP. 75. NOTARIES PUBLIC.

Act 22 Feb., appointment of notaries, their duties; Laws 1819, 31 §§1—3. . . Act 10 Feb., foregoing amended; Laws 1823, 121. . . Act 30 Dec. 1828; appointment of notaries public; former acts repealed; Laws 1829, 112; R. S. 1833, 470. . . Act 9 Feb., oaths before notaries, if false to be perjury; Laws 1831, 102; R. S. 1833, 472. . . Act 12 Jan. 1833; amending act 1819, and providing additional notaries; R. S. 1833, 471. . . Act 1 Feb., additional notaries in Morgan, Greene, Pike, Randolph, Calhoun, Cass, Will, Cook and Madison counties; Laws 1839, 55. . . Act 22 Feb., for the appointment of notaries on petition; Laws 1839, 148. Act 29 Jan., appointment of additional notaries; Laws 1840, 66. . . Act 21 Feb., notaries appointed for four years; Laws 1843, 10.

CHAP. 76. OATHS AND AFFIRMATIONS.

Act 30 Mar., authorizing certain persons to administer oaths; Laws 1819, 348. Act 26 Dec. 1826; concerning oaths and affirmations; R. S. 1827, 308; R. S. 1833, 472. . . Act 18 Jan. 1833; oaths on the trial of impeachments; R. S. 1833, 337. . . Act 7 Jan., oaths to witnesses before committees, similar to R. S. 1845, Ch. 76 §4; Laws 1839, 39.

CHAP. 77. OFFICERS.

Act 23 Feb., defective laws to be reported; Laws 1819, 46; R. S. 1833, 504. . . Act 23 Mar., auditor to bring suits for the state; his duty to pay judgments against the state; Laws 1819, 184. . . Act 11 Jan., clerks of courts to reside at the county seats; Laws 1823, 70; Laws 1829, 35; R. S. 1833, 144. . . Act 22 Jan., certain county offices vacated by non-residence: Laws 1829, 115 §3. . . Act 3 Jan., mode of bringing suits by or against the state; duty of the auditor; Laws 1829, 171; R. S. 1833, 593. . Act 9 Feb., clerk to appoint deputies; residence of clerks; Laws 1831, 49; R. S. 1833, 126.

CHAP. 78. OFFICIAL BONDS.

Act 26 Jan., in relation to official bonds; similar to this chapter in R. S. 1845; Laws 1843, 40. . . Act 5 Dec. 1842; for the relief of securities on official bonds, similar to Ch. 78 §§7—15 (R. S. 1845) Laws 1843, 222.

CHAP. 79. PARTITIONS.

Act 20 Feb., regulating the partition of lands; Laws 1819, 385. . . Act 13 Jan., concerning partitions, joint rights and obligations; Laws 1821, 14; R. S. 1833, 473. . . Act 6 Feb. 1827; for the speedy assignment of dower, and the partition of real estate; former acts repealed; R. S. 1827, 183; R. S. 1833, 236.

CHAP. 80. PAUPERS.

Act 5 Mar., general act to provide for the relief of the poor; Laws 1819, 127. . . Act 6 Feb., board, nursing, medical aid, and burial of poor persons not paupers; Laws 1821, 100; Laws 1829, 113. . . Act 2 Feb. 1827: for the maintenance of the poor: repeal of the act of 5 Mar. 1819; R. S. 1827, 309. . . Act 1 Mar. 1833; for the relief of the poor; former acts repealed; R. S. 1833, 480 §§1—7. . . Act 13 Feb., amending the act of 1833, and requiring proof of 12 months residence; Laws 1835, 66. . . Act 21 Feb., to amend still further the act of 1833; act of 1835 repealed; Laws 1839, 138. . Act 20 Feb., residence of paupers defined; pauper chargeable at residence; Laws 1841, 190. . Act 20 Feb., county authorized to appropriate $2,500. for poor farm and poor house, similar to Ch. 80 §23 (R. S. 1845); Laws 1843, 184.

CHAP. 81. PENITENTIARY.

Alton.—Act 15 Feb. 1827; Shadrach Bond, William P. McKee and Gersham Jayne commissioners to purchase a site at or near Alton, and erect suitable penitentiary buildings; R. S. 1827, 357 §18. . . Act 15 Feb., regulation and government of the Alton penitentiary; Laws 1831, 103; R. S. 1833, 474. . . Act 19 Feb. 1833; to regulate the penitentiary—appointment of inspectors; R. S. 1833, 477. . . Act 9 Feb., amending the act of 1833; election of warden, sale of lots; Laws 1835, 52. . . Act 24 Jan., warrant to L. J. Clawson for $223. for building wall; Laws 1835, 77. . . Act 16 Jan., salary of the warden to be $600.; Laws 1836, 238. . . Act 18 Jan., amending former acts; deposits in the state bank; Laws 1836, 250. . . Act 21 July, power of the inspectors increased; 2 Laws 1837, 47. . . Act 19 Jan., to make an appropriation of $2,300.; Laws 1839, 46. . . Act 18 Jan., to pay the late warden $200.; Laws 1839, 46. . . Act 2 Mar., compensation of sheriffs for conveying convicts to; former provisions repealed; Laws 1839, 274. . Act 2 Mar., repeal of former acts; inspectors to appoint warden and watchmen; Laws 1839, 278. . . Act 4 Mar., payment of $555.67 to Dorsey & Greathouse, contractors; depreciated paper disposed of; Laws 1843, 180. . . Act 2 Mar., a general statute amending and consolidating former acts, some of which are repealed; Laws 1843, 181. . . Leasing of the penitentiary; R. S. 1845 (1 Mar.) 582. . . Additional cells and improvements; duty of inspectors; duty of chaplain; landing at Alton; $3,000. for a warden's house; Laws 1847, 64. . . Purchase of five lots in Alton; walls to be built; lease to be extended; chaplain to be appointed; letters; act 8 Feb., Laws 1849, 101. . . Buckmaster's lease extended for five years upon conditions; act 31 Jan., Laws 1851, 13. . . Inspectors to settle with the lessee, improvements authorized; guards exempt from road labor; act 10 Feb., Laws 1851, 25. . . Additional cells to be built; burial ground to be purchased; act 14 Feb., Laws 1855, 146. . . Payment of $11,056.45 to S. A. Buckmaster; act 14 Feb., Laws 1857, 54. . . Lease to S. K. Casey for five years; act 16 Feb., Laws 1857, 120. . . Appropriations therefor; act 24 Feb., Laws 1859, 16.

Joliet.—Location of the penitentiary, erection of buildings; Laws 1857 (19 Feb.) 131. . . Further appropriations; removal of convicts from Alton; act 21 Feb., Laws 1857, 14. . . Additional provisions and appropriations; act 19 Feb., Laws 1861, 149. . . Additional appropriations; act 14 Feb., Laws 1863, 61. . . Lease of James M. Pitman; act 14 Feb., Laws 1863, 62. . . Sundry appropriations; act 12 Feb., Laws 1867, 4. . . Sundry appropriations; act 28 Feb., Laws 1867, 22. . . Warden appointed, his duties defined; act 6 Mar., Laws 1867, 32. . . Lease to M. M. Bane and others; act 27 Feb., Laws 1867, 137. . . Supplemental to the foregoing; act 5 Mar., Laws 1867, 139. . . Act 11 Mar., appropriations for maintaining and carrying on; Laws 1869, 31. . . Act 15 Mar., to pay for work done by the late lessees; Laws 1869, 31. . . Act 11 Mar., to pay George P. Adams $1,708.75; Laws 1869, 51. . . Act 31 Mar., to pay John R. Casey $480.; Laws 1869, 53. . . Act 10 Mar., to pay D. Kriegh & Co.' $7,177.58; Laws 1869, 53. . . Act 11 Mar., to pay Fox & Baxter $2,606.35; Laws 1869, 54. . . Act 30 Mar., fixing the salary of the commissioners at $2,000.; Laws 1869, 304. . . Act 31 Mar., salary of the chaplain $1,800.; Laws 1869, 304. . . Resolution relating to the Joliet stone; Laws 1869, 421.

Southern.—Location, construction and carrying on; Laws 1867 (28 Feb.) 11.

CHAP. 82. PETITONS.

Act 30 Jan., notice to be given of the formation of a new county; Laws 1821, 47. . . Act 26 Dec. 1826; notice of petition for a new county; R. S. 1827, 110; R. S. 1833, 479. . . Act 27 Feb., county line ten miles from the county seat—area 400 square miles, similar to §§1 and 2 of this chapter of the revised statutes; Laws 1841, 98.

CHAP. 82*a*. PLANK ROADS.

Albion and Grayville.—To charge tolls under the general law; Pr. Laws 1861 (21 Feb.) 478.

Alexander and Pulaski.—Chartered; Laws 1852 (21 June) 91. Chartered again; Pr. Laws 1863 (21 Apr.) 218. Last named act amended; 1 Pr. Laws 1867 (15 Feb.) 167.

Alton and Jerseyville.—Chartered; Laws 1852 (18 June) 15.

Alton and Woodburn.—Chartered; Pr. Laws 1853 (12 Feb.) 322. Charter amended: Pr. Laws 1857 (18 Feb.) 1400. Further amended; Pr. Laws 1859 (22 Feb.) 414.

American Bottom.—Provisions of the general law extended to it; Pr. Laws 1851 (17 Feb.) 273. May borrow money and mortgage road; Pr. Laws 1853 (12 Feb.) 159.

Aurora and Chicago.—Chartered; Laws 1845 (3 Mar.) 239. Amendment; Pr. Laws 1847 (19 Feb.) 106.

Belleville and Mascoutah.—Organization under

the general law confirmed; Pr. Laws 1854 (1 Mar.) 204.

Belleville and Richmond.—Chartered; Pr. Laws 1853 (10 Feb.) 288.

Burlington and Warren.—Right of way and ferry privileges; Laws 1852 (23 June) 220.

Cairo, Mound City and Metropolis.—Chartered; Pr. Laws 1857 (18 Feb.) 1857.

Canton and Liverpool.—Articles of association amended; capital increased; Laws 1852 (15 June) 11. Charter amended; Pr. Laws 1854 (1 Mar.) 205.

Carbondale and Marion. — Chartered; Pr. Laws 1857 (18 Feb.) 1310.

Carlinville and Chesterfield.—Chartered; Laws 1852 (21 June) 103.

Chicago and Calumet.—Chartered; Pr. Laws 1853 (14 Feb.) 9.

Chicago and Rock River.—Chartered; Laws 1845 (21 Jan.) 334. Amendment; Pr. Laws 1847 (23 Feb.) 113.

Chicago Southwestern.—Chartered; the Chicago and DesPlaines P. R. may transfer to; Pr. Laws 1849 (10 Feb.) 70. Amendment; Pr. Laws 1853 (20 Jan.) 484.

Collinsville.—May be sold and relocated; Pr. Laws 1861 (20 Feb.) 477.

Danville and Perryville.—Chartered; Pr. Laws 1849 (12 Feb.) 61.

Elgin and Genoa.—Released from building east of Elgin; Pr. Laws 1851 (12 Feb.) 105.

Elizabethtown and Benton.—Chartered; Pr. Laws 1853 (12 Feb.) 292. Amendment; Pr. Laws 1854 (4 Mar.) 154.

Franklin and Perry County.—Chartered; Pr. Laws 1853 (3 Feb.) 317.

Grundy and Kendall.—Organization under the general law confirmed; Pr. Laws 1853 (10 Feb.) 343. Amendment; Pr. Laws 1854 (28 Feb.) 177.

Henry, Caledonia, Magnolia and Central.—Chartered; Pr. Laws 1853 (12 Feb.) 185.

Jonesboro.—How inspected; Pr. Laws 1851 (13 Feb.) 112.

Lacon, Wyoming and Toulon.—Chartered; Laws 1852 (22 June) 125.

Lake and McHenry.—Corporate powers extended; Pr. Laws 1851 (15 Feb.) 241. Powers of any plank road co. extended to this; Pr. Laws 1857 (7 Feb.) 301.

Lake Shore.—May substitute gravel or stone; Pr. Laws 1857 (16 Feb.) 926.

Lockport, Plainfield and Yorkville.—Corporate powers extended; Pr. Laws 1854 (28 Feb.) 130.

Madison and St. Clair.—Chartered; Pr. Laws 1847 (30 Jan.) 58.

Metropolis City, Vienna and Marion.—Chartered; Pr. Laws 1851 (17 Feb.) 317.

Monmouth and Oquawka.—Chartered; Pr. Laws 1849 (12 Feb.) 69.

Murphysboro and Grand Tower.—Chartered; Pr. Laws 1853 (12 Feb.) 243.

Northwestern.—Chartered; Pr. Laws 1854 (1 Mar.) 224.

Okaw Bottom.—Chartered; Pr. Laws 1851 (17 Feb.) 293. Tolls on foreign travel; Laws 1852 (23 June) 212.

Olney, Lawrenceville and Wabash.—Name changed to Lawrenceville and Wabash; Pr. Laws 1853 (8 Feb.) 600. Charter amended; Pr. Laws 1855 (12 Feb.) 466.

Oswego and Indiana.—Chartered; Pr. Laws 1849 (12 Feb.) 57. Stockholders may organize under the general law; Pr. Laws 1857 (12 Feb.) 505.

Ottawa and Vermilion.—Chartered; Pr. Laws 1857 (14 Feb.) 669.

Ottawa Northern.—Chartered, by confirming the organization; Laws 1852 (15 June) 8. Assessments to pay debts; Pr. Laws 1854 (22 Feb.) 84.

Pekin and Fairview.—Chartered; Pr. Laws 1853 (12 Feb.) 310.

Peoria and Farmington.—Time of completion extended; Pr. Laws 1854 (28 Feb.) 131.

Peru and Grand de Tour.—Chartered; Pr. Laws 1857 (13 Feb.) 513.

Pittsfield and Florence.—Stockholders competent witnesses for and against the company; Pr. Laws 1854 (28 Feb.) 157. Said company may repair with gravel; Pr. Laws 1857 (13 Feb.) 587.

Princeton and West Hennepin.—Chartered; Laws 1852 (21 June) 100.

Salisbury.—Chartered; Pr. Laws 1849 (12 Feb.) 65. Amendment; Pr. Laws (14 Feb.) 129.

Shawneetown and Equality.—Chartered; Pr. Laws 1851 (17 Feb.) 294. Again; Laws 1852 (21 June) 110. Last charter amended; Pr. Laws 1853 (27 Jan.) 573. Further amendment; Pr. Laws 1857 (13 Feb.) 512.

Springfield and Taylorville.—Chartered; Pr. Laws 1853. (12 Feb.) 294.

Springfield, Athens and Havanna.—Chartered; Pr. Laws 1853 (12 Feb.) 284.

St. Charles and Warrenville.—Incorporation legalized and stock increased; Laws 1852 (23 June) 199.

Sycamore and Chicago.—Chartered; Pr. Laws 1849 (12 Feb.) 67.

Vandalia and State Line.—Chartered; Pr. Laws 1854 (3 Mar.) 133.

Winchester and Illinois River.—Branch to Chili; also to LaHarpe, and to any other point in McDonough county; Pr. Laws 1853 (10 Feb.) 535. Double tolls over Illinois bottom; Pr. Laws 1854 (28 Feb.) 203. Repairing with gravel; Pr. Laws 1857 (13 Feb.) 587.

CHAP. 83. PRACTICE.

Regulation of the practice in the supreme and circuit courts; Laws 1819 (22 Mar.) 130; R. S. 1833, 485 and also 434 §2. Amendment; Laws 1826 (26 Jan.) 83 §3. Suits by and against corporations; Laws 1819 (23 Mar.) 184. Repealed; Laws 1829 (3 Jan.) 171. . . Regulating practice; Laws 1821 (5 Jan.) 8. . . Act 29 Jan., concerning practice in courts of law; former acts repealed; R. S. 1827, 310; R. S. 1833, 486. .

Act 2 Feb. 1827; scrawls; proceedings in supreme court; evidence of negroes; R. S. 1827, 320; R. S. 1833, 496. . . Act 30 Dec. 1828; defendant sued only in the county where he resides or is found; Laws 1829, 36; R. S. 1833, 145. . . Act 9 Feb., amends the foregoing act of 29 Jan. 1827; Laws 1831, 113; R. S. 1833, 496. . . Act 1 Mar 1833; amending the act of 29 Jan. 1727 [1827] concerning practice in courts of law; R. S. 1833, 497. . . Act 25 Feb. 1833; proceedings by petition and summons; R. S. 1833, 499. . . Act 7 Feb., damages assessed by the clerk; Laws 1835, 152. . . Act 6 Dec. 1836; where judgment is affirmed on appeal and writ of error: similar to R. S. 1845 Ch. 83 §50; 1 Laws 1837, 12. . . Act 25 Feb., process to be tested in the name of the clerk and not the judge; former acts repealed; 1 Laws 1837, 178. . . Act 20 July, process tested in the name of the judge to be valid; 2 Laws 1837, 51. To the same effect is the act of 21 of July 1837; Id. §1. . . Act 21 July 1837; concerning exceptions, similar to R. S. 1845, Ch. 83 §§22, 23; 2 Laws 1837, 109. . . Act 19 Feb., service of process against corporations, similar to R. S. 1845, Ch. 83 §4; Laws 1839, 160. . . Act 2 Mar., proof of assignments, similar to R. S. 1845, Ch. 83 §59; damages on appeal to the supreme court, similar to §57, Ibid; damages on appeal from justices, similar to §58, Ibid; Laws 1839, 271. . . Act 23 Feb., manner of docketing suits, order of trial: Laws 1841, 191.

CHAP. 84. PRINTING AND BINDING.

Resolutions for copying and indexing the acts of the session; Laws 1823, 213. . . Printing of the private acts of 1833; R. S. 1833 (27 Feb.) 436. . . Act 24 Jan., defining the duties of the public printer, and fixing the time and manner of performing the same; Laws 1835, 163. . . Act 16 Jan., printing and binding of the laws and journals; Laws 1836, 236. . . Act 4 Mar., forty days for printing journals; 1 Laws 1837, 179. . . Act 31 Jan., for the binding of the laws and journals; Laws 1840, 34. . Act 23 Feb., supplemental to the act "defining the duties of public printer;" Laws 1841, 192. . Act 23 Feb., to amend the act 31 Jan. 1840 "for binding the laws and journals;" Laws 1843, 173. . . Act 14 Mar., supplemental to the several acts defined the duties of the public printer; part of the act of 23 Feb. 1841 repealed; Laws Laws 1843, 194. . . General act of 1845 revising and consolidating former laws; R. S. 1845 (3 Mar.) 422. . . Printing the messages of Gov. French and Gov. Ford in German; Pr. Laws 1847 (19 Feb.) 212. . . Secretary of state to advertise for proposals for printing; act 8 Feb., Laws 1849, 104. Reports of the secretary, auditor and treasurer, when to be printed; binding of the acts of 1849; act of 12 Feb., Laws 1849, 106. . . Binding to be let to the lowest bidder; act 12 Feb., Laws 1849, 97 §9. . . Proposals for printing advertised for; 1,000 reports to be printed; act 17 Feb., Laws 1851, 148. . . Reprint of the session laws of 1849; extra copies of session laws to be printed and sold; act of 14 Feb., Laws 1853, 230. . . Binding the private laws; act 21 Feb., Laws 1861, 137. . . Publication of the laws and reports of the session; act of 22 Feb., Laws 1861, 137. . . Resolutions for settlement of the accounts for printing and binding the Adjutant General's report; Laws 1869, 414. Relating to the paper contract of G. W. Chatterton, Id. 415, 416. For printing the Governor's message; Id. 418. Relating to Howlett and Adair's manual; Id. 419. Printing evidence relating to the state institutions; Id. 419. Newspapers for the officers and members of the General Assembly; Id. 420, 421.

CHAP. 85. PROBATE COURT.

Act 10 Feb., to establish courts of probate, manner of proceeding therein; Laws 1821, 119. . . Act 12 Feb., amending the foregoing; repeal of §1, and repealing the salary of $50.; judges of probate to be elected; Laws 1823, 132 . Act 12 Jan., amending the act of 10 Feb. 1821, "establishing courts of probate;" Laws 1825, 87. . . Act 2 Jan., relating to courts of probate; consolidating former acts which are repealed; Laws 1829, 37; R. S. 1833, 145. . . Act 4 Mar., repeal of the act of 1829; election and duties of Probate Justices of the peace; 1 Laws 1837, 176. . . Act 21 July, probate justices to be elected at the same time as county clerks; 2 Laws 1837, 46. . . Act 7 Jan., to legalize process issued by probate judges and justices under private seal; Laws 1839, 39. . . Act 1 Feb., resignation of probate justice; manner of filling vacancies; Laws 1843, 185.

CHAP. 86. QUO WARRANTO.

Act 28 Dec. 1826; to regulate proceedings upon information in the nature of a *quo warranto;* R. S. 1827, 347; R. S. 1833, 506.

CHAP. 86*a*. RAILROADS.

Generally.—Resolution for the extension of Illinois railroads into Indiana; Laws 1839, 300. . . Board of public works to survey and construct the continuation of certain Indiana railroads; Laws 1839 (28 Feb.) 96. . . Rock Island, Mercer, Warren, McDonough, Schuyler, Cass, Scott and Greene counties, and the towns in said counties to subscribe to R. R. stock; Laws 1869 (25 Mar.) 322.

Alton and Sangamon.—Charter; Pr. Laws 1847 (27 Feb.) 144. Amendment; Pr. Laws 1851 (29 Jan.) 35. Extended to Bloomington; Pr. Laws 1851 (11 Feb.) 75. Amending the act of 1847; Pr. Laws 1851 (17 Feb.) 279. Said act further amended; name changed to Chicago and Mississippi; Laws 1852 (19 June) 46.

Alton and Shawneetown.—Chartered; Laws 1836 (18 Jan.) 51.

Alton and St. Louis.—Charter; Pr. Laws 1859 (4 Feb.) 422.

Alton, Mt. Carmel and New Albany.—Formed by consolidation; Pr. Laws 1849 (12 Feb.) 92.—Charter confirmed; Pr. Laws 1851 (17 Feb.) 259. Consolidated as St. Louis and Louisville; Pr. Laws 1861 (22 Feb.) 480.

Railroads.

Alton, Wabash and Erie.—Chartered; Laws 1836 (16 Jan.) 16.

American Central.—Formerly Western Air Line; Pr. Laws 1859 (21 Feb.) 526.

Arenzville, Virginia and Bloomington.—Charter; 1 Pr. Laws 1867 (7 Mar.) 976.

Ashley and Mt. Vernon.—Charter; Pr. Laws 1861 (21 Feb.) 483.

Ashley and St. Louis.—Charter; Pr. Laws 1859 (19 Feb.) 424.

Atlantic and Pacific.—Charter; 2 Pr. Laws 1865 (16 Feb.) 129.

Aurora Branch.—Charter: Pr. Laws 1849 (12 Feb.) 96. Amendment—name changed to Chicago and Aurora; Laws 1852 (22 June) 170.

Beardstown and Springfield.—Formerly the Beardstown and Petersburg; Pr. Laws 1854 (4 Mar.) 141.

Beardstown and Petersburg.—Charter; Pr. Laws 1853 (12 Feb.) 31. Changed to Beardstown and Springfield; Pr. Laws 1854 (2 Mar.) 141.

Belleville and Eldorado.—Charter; Pr. Laws 1861, (22 Feb.) 485.

Belleville and Fairfield.—Charter; Pr. Laws 1855 (15 Feb.) 296. Changed to St. Louis and Louisville; Pr. Laws 1857 (11 Feb.) 432.

Belleville and Illinoistown.—Charter; Pr. Laws 1849 (12 Feb.) 93. Chartered again; Laws 1852 (21 June) 114.

Belleville and Mississippi.—Chartered; Laws 1836 (28 Dec. 1835) 3.

Belleville and Murphysboro.—Charter; Pr. Laws 1853 (8 Feb.) 115. Amendment; Pr. Laws 1854 (8 Feb.) 74. Further amendment; Pr. Laws 1854 (2 Mar.) 204. Amendment; Pr. Laws 1857 (17 Feb.) 1175.

Belleville and Southern Illinois—Charter; Pr. Laws 1857 (14 Feb.) 707. Amended; Pr. Laws 1859 (4 Feb.) 427. Amendment; Pr. Laws 1861 (14 Feb.) 487. Amendment; 2 Pr. Laws 1865 (16 Feb.) 155. Also, Id. (16 Feb.) 155. Further amendment; 2 Pr. Laws 1867 (14 Feb.) 680.

Belleville and Tamaroa.—Charter; Pr. Laws 1859 (14 Feb.) 427.

Belleville Eastern Extension.—Charter: Pr. Laws 1853 (10 Feb.) 108. Foregoing revived; Pr. Laws 1859 (24 Feb.) 426.

Belleville, Red Bud and Murphysboro.—Charter; Pr. Laws 1857 (12 Feb.) 493.

Belvidere and Illinois River.—Charter; 2 Pr. Laws 1865 (28 Feb.) 599.

Belvidere and La Salle.—Charter; Pr. Laws 1855 (14 Feb.) 313. Chartered again; Pr. Laws 1857 (7 Feb.) 282.

Belvidere and Ottawa.—Charter; 2 Pr. Laws 1867. (8 Mar.) 628.

Bloomington and Pekin.—Charter; Pr. Laws 1853 (10 Feb.) 58.

Bloomington and Wabash Valley.—Charter; Pr. Laws 1853 (20 Jan.) 170. Amendment; Id. (10 Feb.) 175.

Bloomington, Kankakee and Indiana State Line.—Charter; Pr. Laws 1855 (14 Feb.) 342. Foregoing revived; 2 Pr. Laws 1865 (16 Feb.) 155.

Bureau and Fort Wayne.—Charter; Pr. Laws 1857 (17 Feb.) 1159.

Cairo and St. Louis.—Charter; 2 Pr. Laws 1865 (16 Feb.) 135.

Cairo and Vincennes.—Charter; 2 Pr. Laws 1867 (6 Mar.) 558.

Caledonia.—Chartered; 2 Laws 1837 (21 July) 36. Amendment; Pr. Laws 1839 (6 Feb.) 3.

Camanche, Albany and Mendota.—Construction authorized; Pr. Laws 1857 (30 Jan.) 109.

Camp Point and White Hall.—Charter; 2 Pr. Laws 1867 (28 Feb.) 591.

Canton and Piketon.—Chartered; Pr. Laws 1837 (3 Mar.) 255. New charter; Pr. Laws 1839 (26 Feb.) 120.

Carthage and Burlington.—Charter; 2 Pr Laws 1867 (8 Mar.) 622.

Central Branch Wabash.—Chartered; Laws 1836 (16 Jan.) 21. Amended; Pr. Laws 1837 (4 Mar.) 202.

Central Military Tract.—Charter; Pr. Laws 1851 (15 Feb.) 191. Chartered again; Laws 1852 (10 June) 36. Supplemental act; Pr. Laws 1853 (11 Feb.) 535. Amendment; Pr. Laws 1855 (14 Feb.) 275. Joint operating contracts; Pr. Laws 1855 (16 Jan.) 288.

Chester and Centralia.—Charter; 2 Pr. Laws 1867 (5 Mar.) 609.

Chester Branch.—Charter; Pr. Laws 1851 (15 Feb.) 243.

Chester, Mississippi and Chicago branch.—Formerly the Southern Illinois; Pr. Laws 1853 (11 Feb.) 15.

Chester, Nashville and Pinckneyville.—Chartered; Pr. Laws 1837 (4 Mar.) 292.

Chicago, Alton and St. Louis.—Formerly the Chicago and Mississippi; joint operating contracts; Pr. Laws 1855 (14 Feb.) 322. Changed to the St. Louis, Alton and Chicago; Pr. Laws 1857 (21 Jan.) 5.

Chicago, Amboy and Upper Mississippi.—Charter; Pr. Laws 1857 (13 Feb.) 559. Cities, etc. to take stock; Laws 1857 (18 Feb.) 225. Foregoing revived and amended; 2 Pr. Laws 1857 (9 Mar.) 636.

Chicago and Alton.—Formerly St. Louis, Alton and Chicago; Pr. Laws 1861 (18 Feb.) 489. Amendment; 2 Pr. Laws 1865 (16 Feb.) 137.

Chicago and Aurora.—Formerly the Aurora Branch; Laws 1852 (22 June) 170. Amendment; Pr. Laws 1853 (26 Jan.) 465. Amendment—name changed to Chicago and South Western; consolidation authorized; Pr. Laws 1854 (28 Feb.) 143. Name changed to Chicago Burlington and Quincy; Pr. Laws 1855 (14 Feb.) 287. Joint operating contracts; Pr. Laws 1855 (16 Jan.) 288.

Chicago and DesPlaines.—Charter; Pr. Laws 1855 (15 Feb.) 277.

Chicago and Great Eastern.—Charter; 2 Pr. Laws 1865 (16 Feb.) 147.

Chicago and Illinois River.—Charter; 2 Pr. Laws 1867 (28 Feb.) 756.

Railroads.

Chicago and Indiana.—Charter; 2 Pr. Laws 1867 (5 Mar.) 538.

Chicago and Vincennes.—Chartered; Laws 1835 (17 Jan.) 88. Supplemental act; Pr. Laws 1837 (27 Feb.) 118.

Chicago and Milwaukie.—Formerly the Illinois Parallel; Pr. Laws 1853 (5 Feb.) 90. Amendment; Pr. Laws 1855 (14 Feb.) 288. Amendment; Pr. Laws 1857 (11 Feb.) 464.

Chicago and Mississippi—Formerly the Alton and Sangamon; Laws 1852 (19 June) 46. Capital increased; Pr. Laws 1853 (11 Feb.) 574. Amendment; Pr. Laws 1854 (28 Feb.) 200. Changed to Chicago, Alton and St. Louis; Pr. Laws 1855 (14 Feb.) 322. Changed to Alton, Chicago and St. Louis; Pr. Laws 1859 (16 Feb.) 429.

Chicago and North Western.—Formerly Chicago, St. Paul and Fon du Lac; Pr. Laws 1859 (19 Feb.) 433. Preferred stock; Pr. Laws 1863 (13 Feb.) 235. Powers extended; 2 Pr. Laws 1865 (15 Feb.) 148.

Chicago and Plainfield.—Charter; Pr. Laws 1859 (24 Feb.) 432. Amendment; 2 Pr. Laws 1867 (25 Feb.) 786.

Chicago and Rock Island.—Formerly Rock Island and LaSalle; Pr. Laws 1851 (7 Feb.) 47. Foregoing amended; Laws 1852 (22 June) 146. Amendment; Pr. Laws 1854 (27 Feb.) 83. Amendment; Pr. Laws 1855 (14 Feb.) 324.

Chicago and Southwestern.—Formerly the Chicago and Aurora; Pr. Laws 1854 (28 Feb.) 143. Afterwards Chicago, Burlington and Quincy; Pr. Laws 1855 (14 Feb.) 287.

Chicago, Burlington and Quincy.—Formerly Chicago and Aurora; Pr. Laws 1855 (14 Feb.) 287. Relocation between Batavia and Batavia Junction; 2 Pr. Laws 1865 (15 Feb.) 145. Also, Id. (16 Feb.) 145. Line from Aurora to Morris; Id. (16 Feb.) 146.

Chicago, Danville and Vincennes.—Charter; 2 Pr. Laws 1865 (16 Feb.) 140. Cities, ect. to take stock; 2 Pr. Laws 1867 (7 Mar.) 842.

Chicago, St. Charles and Mississippi.—Formerly the St. Charles Branch; Pr. Laws 1853 (31 Jan.) 128. Right of way from Savanna to Galena; Laws 1853 (10 Feb.) 182.

Chicago, St. Paul and Fon du Lac.—Sale authorized; Pr. Laws 1859 (19 Feb.) 433.

Chicago, Sterling and Mississippi—Charter; Pr. Laws 1853 (7 Feb.) 101.

Chicago, Sterling and Warsaw.—Charter; 2 Pr. Laws 1865 (16 Feb.) 149.

Clayton and Rushville.—Charter; 2 Pr. Laws 1865 (16 Feb.) 150.

Clayton and White Hall.—Charter; 2 Pr. Laws 1867 (5 Mar.) 553.

Court Creek.—Charter; 2 Pr. Laws 1867 (7 Mar.) 585.

Danville and Bloomington—Charter; Pr. Laws 1857 (11 Feb.) 438.

Danville and Covington.—Chartered; Pr. Laws 1837 (1 Mar.) 156.

Danville and Mattoon.—Charter; 2 Pr. Laws 1865 (16 Feb.) 156.

Danville, Urbana, Bloomington and Pekin.—Charter; 2 Pr. Laws 1867 (28 Feb.) 758.

Decatur and Danville.—Charter; Pr. Laws 1853 (12 Feb.) 93.

Decatur and East St. Louis.—Charter; 2 Pr. Laws 1867 (26 Feb.) 770.

Decatur and Galena.—Charter; Pr. Laws 1857 (16 Feb.) 927.

Decatur and Indianapolis.—Charter; Pr. Laws 1853 (8 Feb.) 127. Amendment—consolidation confirmed; Pr. Laws 1854 (20 Feb.) 86.

Decatur and Pekin.—Charter; Pr. Laws 1853 (11 Feb.) 134.

Des Moines Rapids.—Chartered; Pr. Laws 1839 (19 Feb.) 75. Supplemental act; Laws 1841 (27 Feb.) 197.

Dixon, Peoria and Hannibal.—Charter; 2 Pr. Laws 1867 (5 Mar.) 604.

Edwardsville and Chippewa.—Chartered; Pr. Laws 1837 (1 Mar.) 168.

Elgin and State Line.—Charter; Pr. Laws 1859 (12 Feb.) 436.

Elizabethtown and Benton.—Charter; Pr. Laws 1857 (11 Feb.) 443.

Elmwood and Mississippi.—Charter; Pr. Laws 1857 (19 Feb.) 1433.

El Paso, Pontiac and Kankakee.—Charter; 2 Pr. Laws 1867 (6 Mar.) 580.

Evansville and St. Louis.—Charter; Pr. Laws 1863 (7 Jan.) 256.

Fairbury, Pontiac and North Western.—Charter; 2 Pr. Laws 1867 (7 Mar.) 575.

Forreston and Chicago.—Charter; 2 Pr. Laws 1867 (26 Feb.) 775.

Fort Wayne and Chicago.—Charter; Pr. Laws 1853 (5 Feb.) 105. Amendment; Pr. Laws 1854 (22 Feb.) 80.

Fox River Valley.—Charter; Laws 1851 (18 June.) 29.

Fulton.—Charter; Pr. Laws 1863 (21 Feb.) 248. Amendment; 2 Pr. Laws 1865 (16 Feb.) 160.

Fulton City, Mt. Carroll and Freeport.—Charter; Pr. Laws 1861 (20 Feb.) 493.

Freeport and Richland Valley.—Charter; Pr. Laws 1857 (19 Feb.) 1427.

Freeport and State Line.—Charter; Pr. Laws 1857 (14 Feb.) 761. Amendment; 2 Pr. Laws 1867 (5 Mar.) 553.

Galena.—Chartered; Pr. Laws 1837 (30 Mar.) 273.

Galena and Chicago Union.—Chartered; Laws 1836 (16 Jan.) 24. Amendment; Pr. Laws 1837 (4 Mar.) 291. Further amendment; Pr. Laws 1847 (24 Feb.) 118. Further amendment; Pr. Laws 1849 (12 Feb.) 86. Constructed at the expense of property benefited; Id. (9 Feb.) 87. Act of 1836 amended; Pr. Laws 1853 (11 Feb.) 92. Same again amended; Pr. Laws 1854 (25 Feb.) 165. Consolidated with the Rock River Junction; Pr. Laws 1855 (15 Feb.) 287. Charter amended; Id. (15 Feb.) 284.

Galena and Illinois River.—Charter; Pr. Laws 1857 (18 Feb.) 1400.

Galena and Rock Island.—Charter; Pr. Laws 1857 (18 Feb.) 1210.

Galena and Southern Wisconsin.—Charter; Pr.

Railroads.

Laws 1853 (26 Jan.) 189. Supplemental act; Id. (10 Feb.) 175.

Galesburg and Muscatine.—Charter; Pr. Laws 1857 (16 Feb.) 1437.

Galesburg and Rock Island.—Charter; Pr. Laws 1857 (18 Feb.) 1312.

Gilman, Clinton and Springfield.—Charter; 2 Pr. Laws 1867 (4 Mar.) 534.

Grafton and Alton.—Charter; 2 Pr. Laws 1867 (7 Mar.) 667.

Grayville and Mattoon.—Charter; Pr. Laws 1857 (6 Feb.) 268. Amendment; 2 Pr. Laws 1867 (1 Mar.) 736.

Great Western.—Chartered to build a road from Cairo to the Illinois, *via* Decatur and Bloomington; Laws 1843 (6 Mar.) 199. Foregoing repealed; Laws 1845 (21 Feb.) 333. Again repealed; Id. (3 Mar.) 253. And again; Laws 1851 (17 Feb.) 192. Amendment to the act of 1843 (6 Mar.); Pr. Laws 1849 (10 Feb.) 89. Same repealed; Laws 1851 (17 Feb.) 192. *See Illinois Central.* Release by Holbrook, president accepted by the state; Laws 1851 (17 Feb.) 192.

Great Western.—Formerly Sangamon and Morgan; Pr. Laws 1853 (12 Feb.) 130. Charter amended; Pr. Laws 1855 (13 Feb.) 347. Amended with reference to the Quincy and Toledo; Pr. Laws 1857 (31 Jan.) 229. Consolidation; Laws 1857 (16 Feb.) 127. Changed to Great Western of 1859; Pr. Laws 1859 (29 Jan.) 439.

Great Western of 1859.—Formerly Great Western; Pr. Laws 1859 (29 Jan) 439. Stock increased; 2 Pr. Laws 1865 (16 Feb.) 160.

Hamilton, Lacon and Eastern.—Charter; 2 Pr. Laws 1867 (7 Mar.) 654. Cities, etc. to take stock; Laws 1869 (5 Mar.) 325.

Hannibal and Naples.—Formerly Pike county; Pr. Laws 1863 (12 Feb.) 232. May consolidate; 2 Pr. Laws 1867 (7 Mar.) 567.

Havana and Macomb.—Charter; 2 Pr. Laws 1867 (5 Mar.) 551.

Havana Lincoln and Champaign.—Charter; 2 Pr. Laws 1867 (9 Mar.) 637.

Illinois and Fox River.—Charter; 2 Pr. Laws 1865 (16 Feb.) 161.

Illinois and Mississippi.—Charter; 2 Pr. Laws 1867 (8 Mar.) 642.

Illinois and Rock River.—Time of completion extended; Laws 1843 (6 Mar.) 199. Foregoing revived; Pr. Laws 1841 (27 Feb.) 96.

Illinois and Southern Iowa.—Charter; Pr. Laws 1857 (12 Feb.) 524.

Illinois and Wisconsin.—Charter; Pr. Laws 1851 (12 Feb.) 108. Supplemental act; Id. (17 Feb.) 274. Supplemental act—northern terminus; Pr. Laws 1853 (14 Feb.) 287. Foreclosure and sale; Pr. Laws 1855 (14 Feb.) 268.

Illinois Central.—*See Great Western.*—Chartered; Laws 1836 (16 Jan.) 129. Route surveyed; Laws 1839 (2 Mar.) 242. Termination in Galena; Id. (4 Mar.) 99. Repeal of the act of 1836; Laws 1851 (17 Feb.) 192. Act of congress granting lands in aid accepted; Laws 1851 (17 Feb.) 192. . . Chartered again; Pr. Laws 1851 (10 Feb.) 61. Supplemental act; Pr. Laws 1851 (17 Feb.) 276. Amendment; Laws 1852 (22 June) 130. Time of completion extended; Id. (23 June) 208. Time of completing the first 50 miles; Laws 1853 (12 Feb.) 221. Time of completion extended; Pr. Laws 1854 (27 Feb.) 192. May lay out towns; Pr. Laws 1855 (14 Feb.) 283. Assessments; Laws 1859 (21 Feb.) 206. Shawneetown branch; 2 Pr. Laws 1865 (16 Feb.) 216. And also, Id. (16 Feb.) 218. To amend the constitution as to tax, etc.; Laws 1869 (30 Mar.) 96.

Illinois Central Cross.—Charter; Pr. Laws 1855 (15 Feb.) 312. Amendment; Pr. Laws 1857 (11 Feb.) 367.

Illinois Cross.—Charter; 2 Pr. Laws 1867 (18 Feb.) 685.

Illinois Farmer's.—Charter; Pr. Laws 1859 (23 Feb.) 449. And again; 2 Pr. Laws 1867 (28 Feb.) 737.

Illinois Grand Trunk.—Charter; 2 Pr. Laws 1867 (28 Feb.) 595.

Illinois Parallel.—Charter; Pr. Laws 1851 (17 Feb.) 266. Changed to the Chicago and Milwaukie; Pr. Laws 1853 (5 Feb.) 90.

Illinois River.—Charter; road from Jacksonville to LaSalle; Pr. Laws 1853 (11 Feb.) 53. Amendment; Pr. Laws 1854 (1 Mar.) 207. Further amendment; Pr. Laws 1857 (29 Jan.) 105. Amendment; Id. (16 Feb.) 838. Amendment; Pr. Laws 1859 (14 Feb.) 457. Changed to Peoria, Pekin and Jacksonville; Pr. Laws 1863 (11 June) 234.

Illinois River and Pana.—Charter; 2 Pr. Laws 1865 (16 Feb.) 163.

Illinois River Valley.—Charter; 2 Pr. Laws 1867 (11 Mar.) 733.

Illinois Southern.—Charter; Pr. Laws 1857 (31 Jan.) 183. Amendment; Pr. Laws 1861 (22 Feb.) 496. Amendment; Pr. Laws 1863 (14 Feb.) 239.

Illinois Southern and Chicago.—Organization under general law confirmed; Pr. Laws 1854 (27 Feb.) 193. Supplemental act; Id. (28 Feb.) 185.

Illinois South Eastern.—Charter; 2 Pr. Laws 1867 (25 Feb.) 750.

Illinois Transportation.—Chartered to build a road from Alton to Chicago; Pr. Laws 1847 (27 Feb.) 128. Amendment; Pr. Laws 1849 (26 Jan.) 41.

Indiana and Illinois Central.—Line extended; Pr. Laws 1855 (14 Feb.) 311. Termination at St. Louis; Pr. Laws 1857 (14 Feb.) 772. Time of completion extended; Pr. Laws 1861 (22 Feb.) 499.

Jacksonville, Alton and St. Louis.—Formerly Jacksonville and Carrollton; Pr. Laws 1857 (7 Feb.) 287. Further amendment; Pr. Laws 1859 (14 Feb) 460. Right of way in Alton and Upper Alton; Laws 1859 (21 Feb) 134. Amendment; Pr. Laws 1861 (20 Feb.) 498. Consolidated as St. Louis, Jacksonville and Chicago; Pr. Laws 1863 (13 Feb.) 245.

Jacksonville and Beardstown.—Charter; Pr. Laws 1857 (18 Feb.) 1261.

Jacksonville and Carrollton.—Charter; Pr. Laws 1851 (18 Feb.) 193. Amendment; Pr. Laws 1853 (11 Feb.) 132. Amendment; Pr. Laws 1854 (27 Feb.) 85. Changed to Jacksonville,

Railroads.

Alton and St. Louis; Pr. Laws 1857 (7 Feb.) 287.

Jacksonville and Meredosia.—Chartered; Laws 1835 (5 Feb.) 197. Supplemental act; Id. (13 Feb.) 185. Amendment; Laws 1836 (18 Jan.) 95.

Jackson 'lle and Naples.— Chartered; Pr. Laws 1837 (18 Feb.) 47.

Jacksonville and Savanna. — Charter; Pr Laws 1855 (14 Feb.) 356. To have part of the track of the Peoria and Warsaw; Pr. Laws 1857 (9 Feb.) 304. Line extended to Galena; Id. (16 Feb.) 859. Amendment; Pr. Laws 1859 (21 Feb.) 466.

Jacksonville, North Western and South Eastern. —Charter; 2 Pr. Laws 1867 (28 Feb.) 709.

JoDaviess and Stephenson Central.—Charter; Pr. Laws 1855 (15 Feb.) 337. Amendment; Pr. Laws 1857 (15 Feb.) 808.

Joliet and Aurora.—Charter; 2 Pr. Laws 1867 (28 Feb.) 723.

Joliet and Chicago.—Charter; Pr. Laws 1855 (15 Feb.) 263. Amendment; Pr. Laws 1861 (15 Feb.) 497.

Joliet and Elgin.—Charter; Pr. Laws 1855 (15 Feb.) 348.

Joliet and Oswego.—Charter; Pr. Laws 1857 (17 Feb.) 1177.

Joliet and Terre Haute.—Charter; Laws 1852 (23 June) 223. Amendment; Pr. Laws 1854 (28 Feb.) 139. Amendment; Pr. Laws 1854 (23 Feb.) 183. Cities, etc., to take stock; Laws 1857 (18 Feb.) 225. Name changed to Joliet Newark and Mendota; Pr. Laws 1859 (24 Feb.) 469.

Joliet, Newark and Mendota.—Formerly Joliet and Terre Haute; Pr. Laws 1859 (24 Feb.) 469.

Jonesboro and Mississippi.—Chartered; Pr. Laws 1837 (3 Mar.) 262. Amendment; Pr. Laws 1854. (1 Mar.) 215. Amendment; Pr. Laws 1857 (7 Feb.) 273.

Kankakee Valley.—Charter; Pr. Laws 1859 (21 Feb.) 469.

Kaskaskia. — Chartered; Pr. Laws 1837 (1 Mar.) 180. Amendment; Laws 1843 (3 Mar.) 195.

Kenosha and Rockford.—Chartered; Pr. Laws 1857 (20 Jan.) 16. Amended (probably); Pr. Laws 1861 (20 Feb.) 500.

LaFayette, Bloomington and Mississippi. — Charter; 2 Pr. Laws 1867 (28 Feb.) 765.

La Salle and Chicago.—Charter; 2 Pr. Laws 1867 (28 Feb.) 728.

La Salle and LaFayette.—Charter; Pr. Laws 1855 (15 Feb.) 251. Amendment; Pr. Laws 1859 (21 Feb.) 473.

Lewiston and Liverpool.—Chartered; Pr. Laws 1837 (2 Mar.) 245.

Liberty and Pinckneyville.— Chartered; Pr. Laws 1837 (1 Mar.) 175.

Lisbon Branch.—Chartered; 2 Pr. Laws 1867 (19 Feb.) 695.

Liverpool, Canton and Knoxville.—Chartered; Pr. Laws 1837 (1 Mar.) 148. Foregoing revived and amended; Pr. Laws 1847 (25 Feb.) 126. Amendment; Pr. Laws 1849 (10 Feb.) 85.

Logansport, Peoria, and Burlington.—Formerly Peoria and Oquawka; Pr. Laws 1861 (21 Feb.) 516. Re-organization; Pr. Laws 1863 (14 Feb.) 225.

Lostant and Kankakee.—Charter; 2 Pr. Laws 1867 (8 Mar.) 527.

Macomb, Vermont and Bath.—Charter; Pr. Laws 1853 (11 Feb.) 20. Amendment; Pr. Laws 1854 (4 Mar.) 175. Further amendment; Id. (24 Feb.) 237.

Madison and Clinton.—Charter; Pr. Laws 1853 (12 Feb.) 122.

Manchester and Bridgeport.—Chartered; Pr. Laws 1837 (2 Mar.) 214.

Marion and Jefferson county.—Chartered; Pr. Laws 1855 (15 Feb.) 228.

Mattoon and Decatur.—Charter; Pr. Laws 1861 (22 Feb.) 501.

Mendota and State Line.—Charter; Pr. Laws 1859 (24 Feb.) 502.

Metropolis and Evansville.—Charter; Pr. Laws 1855. (14 Feb.) 289.

Michigan and Mississippi.—Charter; Pr. Laws 1857 (10 Feb.) 323. Amendment; Pr. Laws 1859 (24 Feb.) 479.

Michigan Southern.—To hold real estate, 2 Pr. Laws 1867 (25 Feb.) 732.

Mineral Point.—[Chartered in Wisconsin.] Extension of road; Pr. Laws 1855 (15 Feb.) 285.

Mississippi.—Charter; 2 Pr. Laws 1865 (15 Feb.) 172.

Mississippi and Atlantic.—Organization under general law confirmed; Pr. Laws 1854 (23 Feb.) 79. Amendment; Pr. Laws 1859 (24 Feb.) 479.

Mississippi and Illinois.—Chartered; Pr. Laws 1837 (24 Feb.) 84.

Mississippi and Rock River Junction.—Charter; Pr. Laws 1851 (15 Feb.) 254. Amendment; Laws 1852 (21 June) 51. Eastern terminus; Pr. Laws 1853 (8 Feb.) 573. Amending the act of 1851; Pr. Laws 1854 (28 Feb.) 177.

Mississippi and Wabash.—Charter; Pr. Laws 1853 (10 Feb.) 73. Amendment; Pr. Laws 1855 (9 Feb.) 283. Three divisions created; Pr. Laws 1857 (14 Feb.) 1053. Amendment; Pr. Laws 1859 (24 Feb.) 479. Amendment; Pr. Laws 1861 (29 Jan.) 500.

Mississippi River and Wisconsin State Line.— Charter; 2 Pr. Laws 1867 (28 Feb.) 745. Amendment; 2 Laws 1867 (13 June) 12.

Mississippi, Springfield and Carrollton.—Chartered; Laws 1836 (16 Jan.) 12.

Mobile and Chicago.—Charter; Pr. Laws 1857 (11 Feb.) 395.

Monticello.—Charter; Pr. Laws 1861 (21 Feb.) 502. Amendment; 2 Pr. Laws 1865 (16 Feb.) 184. Further Amendment; Further Amendment; 2 Pr. Laws 1867 (9 Mar.) 620.

Mt. Carmel and Alton.—Chartered; Laws 1836 (16 Jan.) 54. To construct the "Southern Cross" R. R.; Laws 1841 (27 Feb.) 197. Act of 1841 revived; Pr. Laws 1847 (27 Feb.) 135. Charter continued; state interest sold; Pr. Laws 1849 (12 Feb.) 91. Consolidated and name changed to the Alton, Mt. Carmel and New Albany R. R.; Pr. Laws 1849 (12 Feb.) 92.

Railroads.

Mt. Sterling and Camp Point.—Charter; Pr. Laws 1855 (15 Feb.) 325.

Mt. Sterling and Carrollton.—Charter; Pr. Laws 1855 (13 Feb.) 260.

Mt. Vernon.—Charter; Pr. Laws 1855 (15 Feb.) 240.

Murphysboro and Shawneetown.—Charter; 2 Pr. Laws 1867 (7 Mar.) 648.

Naples and Hannibal Air Line.—Charter; Pr. Laws 1857 (14 Feb.) 642.

Northern.—Charter; 2 Pr. Laws 1865 (15 Feb.) 188. Amendment; 2 Pr. Laws 1867 (8 Mar.) 641. Further amendment; Id. (28 Feb.) 716.

Northern Cross.—Naples branch abandoned; Laws 1839 (2 Mar.) 246. Completion from Springfield to Jacksonville; Laws 1841 (26 Feb.) 194. . . Chartered; Laws 1843 (6 Mar.) 195. Resolutions that congress aid with a grant of land; Id. 349, and that the governor obtain the lease of S. M. Tinsley & Co.; Id. 340. . . Sale of what lies between Springfield and the Illinois river; Laws 1847 (16 Feb.) 109. . . Company Chartered; Pr. Laws 1849 (10 Feb.) 82. Bonds for the completion between Springfield and Jacksonville; 1 Laws 1849 (10 Feb.) 45. Funding of said bonds; Laws 1851 (14 Feb.) 88. Supplemental to the act of 1849 (10 Feb.); Pr. Laws 1851 (1 Feb.) 42. Changing the northern terminus; Pr. Laws 1851 (15 Feb.) 243. Supplementary to the act of 1849 (10 Feb.); Laws 1852 (11 June) 3. Same act amended; Id. (21 June) 108. Construction facilitated; Pr. Laws 1853 (10 Feb.) 93. Re-location in part; Pr. Laws 1854 (28 Feb.) 212. Joint operating contracts; Pr. Laws 1855 (16 Jan.) 288. Changed to Quincy and Chicago; Pr. Laws 1857 (10 Feb. 373.

Northern Illinois.—Charter; Laws 1852 (23 June) 208. New charter; Pr. Laws 1859 (24 Feb.) 484. Ferry across the Mississippi; 2 Pr. 1865 (16 Feb.) 191.

Northern Indiana.—To hold real estate; 2 Pr. Laws 1867 (25 Feb.) 732.

Ogle and Carroll County.—Charter; Pr. Laws 1857 (18 Feb.) 1230. Amendment; Pr. Laws 1859 (24 Feb.) 488.

Ohio and Mississippi.—Charter; Pr. Laws 1851 (12 Feb.) 89. Amendment; Laws 1852 (22 June) 122. Supplemental act; Pr. Laws 1853 (11 Feb.) 92. Amendment; Pr. Laws 1854 (27 Feb.) 78. New charter; Pr. Laws 1861 (5 Feb.) 508.

Ohio River and Alton.—Charter; Pr. Laws 1857 (14 Feb.) 779. Formerly Ohio river, Alton and Benton; Id. (18 Feb) 1412.

Ohio River and Wabash.—Charter; Pr. Laws 1853 (25 Jan.) 466. Supplemental act; Pr. Laws 1853 (12 Feb.) 92. Second Supplemental act; Pr. Laws 1854 (28 Feb.) 175.

Oquawka and Chicago.—Charter; Pr. Laws 1857 (17 Feb) 1162.

Oswego and Aurora.—Charter; Pr. Laws 1851 (17 Feb.) 302.

Ottawa, Oswego and Fox River Valley.—Charter; Laws 1852 (21 June) 56. Amendment; Pr. Laws 1854 (28 Feb.) 158. Amendment; Pr. Laws 1857 (13 Feb.) 578. Cities, etc. to take stock; Laws 1857 (18 Feb.) 225. Termination at Winona; 2 Pr. Laws 1865 (16 Feb.) 192. Further amendment; 2 Pr. Laws 1867 (8 Mar.) 621.

Paducah, Metropolis and St. Louis.—Charter; Pr. Laws 1859 (16 Feb.) 490.

Pana, Springfield and Northwestern.—Charter; 2 Pr. Laws 1865 (16 Feb.) 192.

Paris and Chicago.—Chartered; Pr. Laws 1857 (12 Feb. 488.

Paris and Decatur.—Charter; Pr. Laws 1861 (18 Feb.) 509. Amendment; 2 Pr. Laws 1865 (16 Feb.) 198.

Paris, Urbana and Bloomington.—Charter; Pr. Laws 1857 (31 Jan.) 187.

Pecatonica Valley.—Chartered; Pr. Laws 1857 (14 Feb.) 775.

Pekin and Decatur.—Charter; Pr. Laws 1855 (15 Feb.) 257.

Pekin, Bloomington and Wabash.—Chartered; Laws 1836 (16 Jan.) 8.

Pekin, Canton and Macomb.—Charter; Pr. Laws 1853 (12 Feb.) 94.

Pekin, Lincoln and Decatur.—Charter; Pr. Laws 1861 (21 Feb.) 518. Amendment; 2 Pr. Laws 1865 (16 Feb.) 198. New charter; 2 Pr. Laws 1867 (22 Feb.) 698.

Peoria and Bureau Valley.—Charter; Pr. Laws 1853 (12 Feb.) 48. Amendment; Pr. Laws 1854 (27 Feb.) 131.

Peoria and Hannibal.—May use grade of Peoria and Warsaw; Pr. Laws 1857 (10 Feb.) 352. Stock may equal actual cost of construction; Id. (14 Feb.) 649. Time of completion extended; Pr. Laws 1863 (11 June) 235. Ipava and Havana Branch; 2 Pr. Laws 1865 (16 Feb.) 202.

Peoria and Oquawka.—Charter; Pr. Laws 1849 (12 Feb.) 99. Amendment; Pr. Laws 1851 (12 Feb.) 60. To have the grade of the Peoria and Warsaw without payment; Laws 1852 (21 June) 103. Charter amended; Id. (22 June) 193. Further amendment; Pr. Laws 1853 (8 Feb,) 513. Farmington branch; Pr. Laws 1855 (15 Feb.) 286. Stock increased; Pr. Laws 1855 (14 Feb.) 325. Double track; Pr. Laws 1857 (10 Feb.) 352. Changed to Logansport, Peoria and Burlington; Pr. Laws 1861 (21 Feb.) 516. Purchasers incorporated; Pr. Laws 1863 (10 June) 240.

Peoria and Rock Island.—Charter; 2 Pr. Laws 1867 (7 Mar.) 659.

Peoria and Springfield—Formerly Springfield and Pekin; Pr. Laws 1859 (12 Feb.) 501.

Peoria and Warsaw.—Charter; Pr. Laws 1855 (14 Feb.) 244. Track transferred to the Jacksonville and Savanna; Pr. Laws 1857 (9 Feb.) 304. Grade used by the Peoria and Hannibal; Id. (10 Feb.) 352.

Peoria and Wenona.—Charter; 2 Pr. Laws 1867 (25 Feb.) 522.

Peoria, Monticello and Paris.—Charter; Pr. Laws 1857 (16 Feb.) 993.

Peoria, Pekin and Jacksonville.—Formerly Illinois River; Pr. Laws 1863 (11 June) 234. Supplemental act; 2 Pr. Laws 1865 (16 Feb.) 203. Amendment; 2 Pr. Laws 1867 (19 Feb.) 707.

Petersburg and Springfield.—Charter; Pr. Laws 1853 (8 Feb.) 3. Changed to Sangamon and Northwest; Pr. Laws 1854 (1 Mar.) 165.

Railroads.

Petersburg and Waverly.—Charter; Pr. Laws 1857 (16 Feb.) 827.

Pittsburg, Fort Wayne and Chicago.—Sale confirmed; Pr. Laws 1861 (8 Feb.) 513.

Pittsfield and Mississippi.—Chartered; Pr. Laws 1837 (1 Mar.) 204. Stock increased; 2 Laws 1837 (21 July) 40. Amendment; Pr. Laws 1839 (6 Feb.) 44.

Pittsfield and Shelbyville.—Charter; Pr. Laws 1855 (14 Feb.) 330.

Quincy, Alton and St. Louis.—Charter; 2 Pr. Laws 1867 (8 Mar.) 644.

Quincy and Chicago.—Formerly Northern Cross; Pr. Laws 1857 (10 Feb.) 373.

Quincy and Peoria.—Charter; 2 Pr. Laws 1867 (5 Mar.) 543.

Quincy and Toledo.—Charter; amending charter of the Great Western; Pr. Laws 1857 (31 Jan.) 229. Sale under mortgage; Pr. Laws 1861 (20 Feb.) 520. Line extended to Quincy; 2 Pr. Laws 1865 (16 Feb.) 205.

Quincy and Warsaw.—Charter; 2 Pr. Laws 1865 (16 Feb.) 205.

Quincy, Beardstown and North Eastern.—Charter; 2 Pr. Laws 1867 (7 Mar.) 562.

Quincy, Clinton and Warsaw.—Charter; Pr. Laws 1857 (14 Feb.) 815.

Racine and Mississippi.—Formerly the Rockton and Freeport; Pr. Laws 1855 (14 Feb.) 284. Id. (13 Feb.) 317. Includes the Savanna Branch; other consolidations confirmed; Pr. Laws 1857 (14 Feb.) 648. Purchasers incorporated; Pr. Laws 1863 (21 Feb.) 254.

Rockford and Mississippi.—Charter; Pr. Laws 1857 (28 Jan.) 66.

Rockford and Rock Island.—Charter; Pr. Laws 1851 (12 Feb.) 95. Amendment; Pr. Laws 1854 (1 Mar.) 1863. Further amendment; Pr. Laws 1857 (14 Feb.) 615.

Rockford Central.—Charter; Pr. Laws 1855 (15 Feb.) 269.

Rockford, Rock Island and St. Louis.—Charter; 2 Pr. Laws 1865 (16 Feb.) 209.

Rock Island and Alton.—Charter; Pr. Laws 1855 (14 Feb.) 305. Amendment; Pr. Laws 1857 (14 Feb.) 892. Changed to St. Louis, Alton and Rock Island; Pr. Laws 1859 (24 Feb.) 494. So also, Pr. Laws 1861 (18 Feb.) 522. Time of completion extended; 2 Pr. Laws 1865 (16 Feb.) 214.

Rock Island and Galva.—Charter; 2 Pr. Laws 1867 (28 Feb.) 731.

Rock Island and LaSalle.—Charter; Pr. Laws 1847 (27 Feb.) 139. Name changed to Chicago and Rock Island; Pr. Laws 1851 (7 Feb.) 47.

Rock Island and Peoria.—Charter; Pr. Laws 1855 (14 Feb.) 317. Amendment; 2 Pr. Laws 1867 (7 Mar.) 591.

Rockton and Freeport.—Charter; Pr. Laws 1853 (10 Feb.) 69. Amendment; Pr. Laws 1854 (1 Mar.) 180. Changed to Racine and Mississippi; Pr. Laws 1855 (14 Feb.) 284. Id. (13 Feb.) 317.

Rockton, State Line and Mississippi.—Charter; Pr. Laws 1853 (11 Feb.) 86.

Rushville.—Chartered; Laws 1836 (16 Jan.) 85. Amendment; Pr. Laws 1839 (6 Feb.) 44.

Sangamon and Massac.—Charter; Pr. Laws 1853 (10 Feb.) 177.

Sangamon and Morgan.—Chartered; Laws 1845 (1 Mar.) 150. Supplemental act; Pr. Laws 1847 (28 Feb.) 150. Amendment; Pr. Laws 1851 (23 Mar.) 10. Changed to the Great Western; Pr. Laws 1853 (12 Feb.) 130. Repair of the Northern Cross R. R. to Meredosia; Id. (24 Jan.) 473.

Sangamon and North West.—Formerly Petersburg and Springfield; Pr. Laws 1854 (1 Mar.) 165. Amendment; Pr. Laws 1855 (14 Feb.) 336. Three divisions created; Pr. Laws 1857 (18 Feb.) 1243. Sale of branch between Alton and Bloody Island; Pr. Laws 1859 (4 Feb.) 496.

Sangamon Valley.—Charter; 2 Pr. Laws 1865 (16 Feb.) 214.

Savanna and Wisconsin State Line.—Charter; Pr. Laws 1859 (24 Feb.) 496.

Savanna Branch.—Charter; Pr. Laws 1851 (12 Feb.) 103. Amendment; Pr. Laws 1855 (15 Feb.) 283. Changed to Racine and Mississippi; Pr. Laws 1857 (14 Feb.) 648.

Shawneetown and Alton.—Chartered; Laws 1836 (18 Jan.) 46.

Shawneetown and Chicago Branch.—Charter; Pr. Laws 1857 (18 Feb.) 1394.

Shawneetown and New Haven.—Chartered; Pr. Laws 1839 (2 Mar.) 232.

Shokokon and Rushville.—Chartered; Pr. Laws 1837 (28 Feb.) 138.

South Eastern.—Chartered as an extension of the Pana, Springfield and North Western; 2 Pr. Laws 1867 (5 Mar.) 614.

Southern Illinois.—Charter; Pr. Laws 1851 (17 Feb.) 294. Changed to Chester Mississippi and Chicago Branch; Pr. Laws 1853 (11 Feb.) 15. A new charter; Laws 1852 (23 June) 200. Changed to the Massac and Sangamon; Pr. Laws 1853 (10 Feb.) 177. New Charter; Pr. Laws 1857 (19 Feb.) 1361.

South Western Branch.—Charter; 2 Pr. Laws 1867 (28 Feb.) 717.

Springfield and Beardstown.—Chartered; Pr. Laws 1837 (4 Mar.) 312.

Springfield and Carlyle.—Charter; Pr. Laws 1853 (12 Feb.) 79.

Springfield and Pana.—Charter; Pr. Laws 1857 (16 Feb.) 1024. Amendment; Pr. Laws 1861 (16 Feb.) 528.

Springfield and Pekin.—Charter; Pr. Laws 1853 (12 Feb.) 12. Changed to Peoria and Springfield; Pr. Laws 1859 (12 Feb.) 501.

Springfield and Terre Haute.—Charter; Laws 1852 (22 June) 140. Amendment; Pr. Laws 1854 (1 Mar.) 184.

Springfield, Keokuk and Warsaw.—Charter; Pr. Laws 1857 (13 Feb.) 519. Amendment; 2 Pr. Laws 1865 (16 Feb.) 220.

State Line and Mississippi.—Charter; Pr. Laws 1853 (12 Feb.) 39.

St. Charles and Mississippi.—May condemn property; Pr. Laws 1851 (12 Feb.) 101.

St. Charles Branch.—Charter; Pr. Laws 1849 (31 Jan.) 78. Changed to Chicago, St. Charles and Mississippi; Pr. Laws 1853 (31 Jan.) 128.

Sterling and Rock Island.—Organization legalized; Pr. Laws 1859 (18 Feb.) 512.

St. Louis, Alton and Chicago.—Formerly Chicago, Alton and St. Louis; Pr. Laws 1857 (21 Jan.) 5. Changed to Chicago and Alton; Pr. Laws 1861 (18 Feb.) 480.

St. Louis, Alton and Rock Island.—Formerly Rock Island and Alton; Pr. Laws 1859 (24 Feb.) 494. So also, Pr. Laws 1861 (18 Feb.) 522. Time of completion extended; 2 Pr. Laws 1865 (16 Feb.) 214. Road mortgaged; Id. (16 Feb.) 220. Branch authorized; 2 Pr. Laws 1867 (23 Feb.) 709.

St. Louis, Alton and Terre Haute.—Formerly Terre Haute and Alton; Pr. Laws 1861 (18 Feb.) 530. Line extended; Pr. Laws 1863 (13 Feb.) 237. And again; Id. (20 Feb.) 236.

St. Louis and Louisville.—Formerly Belleville and Fairfield; Pr. Laws 1857 (11 Feb.) 432. Consolidation; Pr. Laws 1861 (22 Feb.) 480.

St. Louis, Jacksonville and Chicago.—Formed by consolidation; Pr. Laws 1863 (13 Feb.) 245

St. Louis, Shelbyville and Detroit.—Formerly St. Louis, Shelbyville and Tolono; 2 Pr. Laws 1867 (9 Mar.) 636.

St. Louis, Shelbyville and Tolono.—Chartered; 2 Pr. Laws 1867 (19 Feb.) 687. Changed to St. Louis, Shelbyville and Detroit; 2 Pr. Laws 1867 (9 Mar.) 636.

St. Louis, Vandalia and Terre Haute.—Charter 2 Pr. Laws 1865 (10 Feb.) 221. Amendment; 2 Pr. Laws 1867 (8 Feb.) 671.

Tamaroa and Mississippi.—Chartered; Pr. Laws 1837 (3 Mar.) 279.

Terre Haute and Alton.—Charter; Pr. Laws 1851 (28 Feb.) 29. Supplemental act; Pr. Laws 1851 (13 Feb.) 113. Amendment; Pr. Laws 1853 (12 Feb.) 133. Amendment; Pr. Laws 1854 (28 Feb.) 159. Changed to St. Louis, Alton and Terre Haute; Pr. Laws 1861 (18 Feb.) 530.

Terre Haute and York.—Charter; Pr. Laws 1853 (12 Feb.) 63. Amendment; Pr. Laws 1854 (28 Feb.) 159. Amendment; Pr. Laws 1855 (14 Feb.) 321. Further Amendment; Pr. Laws 1857 (12 Feb.) 552.

Tolono and Indianapolis.—Charterd; 2 Pr Laws 1865 (16 Feb.) 224.

Tolono and Pana.—Charter; Pr. Laws 1857 (11 Feb.) 455.

Tonica and Petersburg.—Charter; Pr. Laws 1857 (15 Jan.) 9. Supplemental act; Id. (16 Feb.) 1031. Amendment; Pr. Laws 1859 (14 Feb.) 517. Amended; Pr. Laws 1861 (22 Feb.) 512. Consolidated as St. Louis, Jacksonville and Chicago; Pr. Laws 1863 (13 Feb.) 245.

Tuscola, Charleston and Vincennes.—Charter; 2 Pr. Laws 1867 (7 Mar.) 568.

Union.—To make and use a road in Cook county; Laws 1852 (22 June) 129. Amendment; Pr. Laws 1854 (3 Mar.) 215.

Upper and Lower Mississippi.—Charter; road from Jacksonville to Rock Island; Pr. Laws 1853 (11 Feb.) 34.

Vincennes and Decatur.—Charter; Pr. Laws 1857 (13 Feb.) 570. Amendment; 2 Pr. Laws 1865 (16 Feb.) 227.

Vincennes and Pana.—Charter; 2 Pr. Laws 1867 (15 Feb.) 682.

Vincennes and Jonesboro.—Charter; Pr. Laws 1867 (16 Feb.) 938.

Wabash.—Formerly Wabash Valley; Pr. Laws 1857 (17 Feb.) 1155.

Wabash and Indiana.—Chartered; Pr. Laws 1837 (4 Mar.) 326. Amendment; Pr. Laws 1839 (2 Mar.) 208.

Wabash and Mississippi.—Chartered; Laws 1836 (15 Jan.) 36.

Wabash and Mississippi Union.—Chartered; Laws 1836 (18 Jan.) 64.

Wabash Valley.—Charter; Laws 1852 (22 June) 187. Amendment; Pr. Laws 1855 (15 Feb.) 276. Extended to Paris; changed to Wabash; Pr. Laws 1857 (17 Feb.) 1155.

Warsaw.—Chartered; Pr. Laws 1839 (26 Feb.) 98.

Warsaw and Macomb.—Charter; Pr. Laws 1851 (15 Feb.) 173.

Warsaw and Port Byron.—Charter; Pr. Laws 1853 (12 Feb.) 156.

Warsaw and Rockford.—Charter; Pr. Laws 1849 (10 Feb.) 85. Amendment; Laws 1852 (21 June) 88. Directors increased; Pr. Laws 1853 (24 Jan.) 481. Amendment; Pr. Laws 1854 (3 Mar.) 160. Acts consolidated; Pr. Laws 1863 (21 Feb.) 241. Amendment; 2 Pr. Laws 1867 (9 Mar.) 622.

Warsaw, Peoria and Wabash.—Chartered; Laws 1836 (14 Jan.) 76.

Waverly and Auburn.—Charter; Pr. Laws 1853 (12 Feb.) 128.

Waverly and Grand Prairie.—Chartered; Laws 1836 (16 Jan.) 81.

Webster, Ottawa and Kishwakee.—Chartered; Pr. Laws 1837 (4 Mar.) 321.

Western Air Line.—Charter; road from New Boston *via* Lacon, towards Ft. Wayne; Pr. Laws 1853 (9 Feb.) 95. Amendment; Pr. Laws 1857 (14 Feb.) 613. Changed to American Central; Pr. Laws 1859 (21 Feb.) 526.

Western Union.—Organization confirmed; 2 Pr. Laws 1867 (4 Mar.) 603.

Winchester, Lynnville and Jacksonville.—Chartered; Pr. Laws 1837 (18 Jan. 1836) 341. Stock increased; 2 Laws 1837 (21 July) 40. Amendment; Pr. Laws 1839 (6 Feb.) 41.

CHAP. 87. RECORDS AND RECORDERS.

Act 19 Feb., establishing a recorder's office in each county, and fixing the duties of the recorder; Laws 1819, 18. . . Act 17 Jan., amending the foregoing act; Laws 1825, 135. . . Act 22 Jan., deeds may be recorded in the state recorder's office, and must be recorded within six months; Laws 1829, 25 §§3, 4. . . Act 8 Jan., duties of the county recorder defined; former acts repealed; Laws 1829, 116; R. S. 1833, 510. . . Act 30 Jan. 1821; ancient books, pa-

pers and records delivered to the recorder of Randolph county; R. S. 1833. 502. . . Act 15 Feb., recovery of records illegally withheld, as in R. S. 1845 Ch. 87 §§10—12; Laws 1831, 114; R. S. 1833, 502. . . Act 13 Feb., supplemental to the act of 8 Jau. 1829, and explanatory thereof; Laws 1835, 61. . . Act 11 Feb., election of county recorders; Laws 1835, 165. . Act 30 Jan., records in certain counties to be transcribed; Laws 1840, 86.

State Recorder.—Act 12 Feb. 1827; establishing a recorder's office, to record deeds and title papers of non-residents, and titles to bounty lands; R. S. 1827, 378. . . Act 22 Jan., deeds of residents may be recorded by him; Laws 1829, 25 §3. . . Act 18 Jan. 1833; abolishing the office of state recorder; R. S. 1833, 587. . Act 9 Feb., books of the late state recorder removed to the recorder's office in Rushville; Laws 1835, 157.

CHAP. 88. REPLEVIN.

Act 29 Jan. 1827; to regulate the action of replevin; R. S. 1827, 349; R. S. 1833, 508. . . Act 12 Feb., supplemental to the act of 1827, and similar to R. S. 1845 Ch. 88 §§1—3; Laws 1839, 77.

CHAP. 89. REVENUE.

Act 27 Mar., for the valuation of lands and other property, and for laying a tax thereon; Laws 1819, 313. . . Act 30 Mar., authorizing non-resident pedlars to sell goods in this state; Laws 1819, 352. . . Act 19 Jan., sheriffs allowed until 1 March next to pay over the taxes; Laws 1821, 19. . . Act 31 Jan., allowing property sold for taxes, both real and personal, to be redeemed; Laws 1821, 64. . . Act 6 Feb., sheriff's to collect taxes in new counties; sheriffs to have until 1 April 1821 to pay over the taxes of 1819 and 1820; Laws 1821, 100. . Act 15 Feb., amending the act first above; repeal of the triple tax; Laws 1821, 182. . . Act 8 Jan., to remit triple taxes in certain cases; Laws 1823, 68. . . Act 23 Dec., compensation for collecting the taxes of 1821 and 1822; Laws 1823, 80. . . Act 14 Feb., amending the act of 30 Mar. 1819 "authorizing non-resident pedlars to sell;" Laws 1823, 145. . . Act 18 Feb., levying and collecting a tax on land and other property; former acts repealed; Laws 1823, 203 §§1—30. . . Act 3 Jan., postponing the sale of lands by the auditor for taxes until the third Monday of June; Laws 1825, 52. . . Act 14 Jan., further time allowed for redemption from tax sales; Laws 1825, 106. . . Act 17 Jan., amending the above act of 18 Feb., 1823, "for levying and collecting a tax on land and other property;" Laws 1825, 172. . . Act 26 Jan., form of deeds to be made by the auditor for lands sold for taxes; effect thereof; Laws 1826, 78. . . Act 27 Jan., relating to the revenue of Calhoun, Pike, Adams, Schuyler, Fulton and Peoria counties; Laws 1826, 89. . . Act 28 Jan., sundry provisions amending former acts; Laws 1826, 92 §§8—14. Land in incorporated towns liable only to be taxed for corporation purposes; Pr. Laws 1827 (6 Jan.) 5 §2. . . Act 19 Feb. 1827; to provide for raising a revenue, former acts repealed; a general law consolidating all the acts; R. S. 1827, 325 §§1—43; R. S. 1833, 513. . . Act 10 Feb. 1827; to complete the assessment and collection of the land tax of 1826 etc.; R. S. 1827, 338. . . Act 13 Feb. 1827; for the relief of certain persons whose lands have been sold for taxes; R. S. 1827, 339; R. S. 1833, 512. . . Act 19 Jan., supplemental to the act of 19 Feb. 1827, "to provide for raising a revenue;" former acts partly repealed; Laws 1829, 119; R. S. 1833, 523. . . Act 12 Feb., amending the former acts; Laws 1831, 125; R. S. 1833, 527. . . Act 27 Feb. 1833; concerning the public revenue; former acts repealed; R. S. 1833, 528 §§1—18. . . Act 20 Feb. 1833; to extend the time of settlement for the county revenue to certain sheriffs therein named—20 counties; R. S. 1833, 581. . . Act 12 Feb., owner listing lands out of his own county; Laws 1835, 51. . . Act 31 Jan., time of the sheriffs in 9 counties to settle and pay over tax, extended; Laws 1835, 72. . . Act 13 Jan., redemption of land sold for taxes; Laws 1836, 230. . . Act 16 Jan., notes of the state bank received for revenue; Laws 1836, 244. . . Act 17 Dec. 1836; receiving a distributive share of the surplus revenue of the United States on deposit; 1 Laws 1837, 193. . Act 6 Dec. 1836; sheriffs to pay over in December and March, final settlements; 1 Laws 1837, 194 . . Resolution 6 Jan., repeal of the exemption of lands from taxation for five years after they are sold; 1 Laws 1837, 337. . . Act 21 July, county clerk to list lands not returned; 2 Laws 1837, 58. . . Act 26 Feb., concerning the public revenue—previous acts consolidated and amended; Laws 1839, 3 §§1—65. Act 1 Mar., supplemental to the above; Id. 23. . . Act 1 Feb., to amend the foregoing act of 1839; Laws 1840, 3. . . Act 26 Feb., appointment of assessors, their powers and duties; Laws 1841, 34. . . Act 27 Feb., appointment of assessors in certain cases; Laws 1841, 35. . . Act 19 Feb., to prevent collectors from speculating on auditor's warrants; Laws 1841, 63. . Act 27 Feb., tax or interest on the public debt; Laws 1841, 165. . . Act 7 Jan., to legalize the assessment of taxes in Peoria and other counties for the year 1840; Laws 1841, 303. . Act 1 Feb., to legalize the assessment for 1842 in Mercer and other counties; Laws 1843, 14. So also, 1 Mar.; Laws 1843, 15. . . Act 23 Feb., to prohibit the receipt of bank bills for public dues; Laws 1843, 39. . . Act 2 Mar., burying grounds and church grounds exempt from execution, to be certified; Laws 1843, 53. . . Act 6 Mar., suits against delinquent collectors; Laws 1843, 68. To exempt the property of colleges and common schools from taxation; Id. 70. . . Act 20 Feb., collection of the revenue for 1842; parts of former acts repealed; Laws 1843, 228. . . Act 6 Mar., to amend the former act of 1839 "for the collection of the revenue;" Laws 1843, 231. Certificates of purchase assignable; several tracts included in one sheriff's deed; Id. 238. Suits against delinquent collectors; uncurrent money to be disposed of; Id. 239. . . Legalizing and assessment in Moultrie county, and regulating other assessments for 1844; Laws 1845 (15 Jan.) 178. . .

Late collectors to collect taxes due and unpaid: Laws 1845 (10 Feb.) 588. . . The general law of (3 Mar.) 1845 appears to be identical with this chapter of the revised statutes, except that §80 is not found in the latter, and that section was elsewhere expressly repealed; see Laws 1845, 3; and for the repeal R. S. 1845, 585. . . Collectors in Randolph, Monroe, St. Clair, Madison, Jackson, Union, Alexander, Washington, Clinton and Mason counties allowed further time to settle for the revenue of 1844; Laws 1845 (3 Mar.) 267. . . Duty of the clerk of the county commissioners' court with the list of lands and lots forfeited to the state; Laws 1847 (25 Feb.) 83. The act appears to be entirely changed by the revenue laws of 1853; Ch. 89 §§170—174 and §§313—317. . . Amendments to the chapter in the revised statutes; Laws 1847 (27 Feb.) 79. Only a few of its provisions are now in force, as will appear by the following synopsis: §1. Now given as §1 of the chapter on revenue. §2. Amends §8 of this chapter of the revised statutes, and afterwards changed by later acts; see note in place of §8 Ch. 89. §3. Amends §12 of this chapter of the revised statutes, and afterwards changed by later acts; see note in place of §12 Ch. 89. §4. Deputy county assessor; changed in 1853, by what is now §241. §5. Amends §14 of this chapter of the revised statutes, and afterwards changed by later acts; see note in place of §14 Ch. 89. §6. Blanks and books furnished by the auditor; changed in 1853 by what is now §§108 and 269. §7. Time of completing the assessment; changed in 1853 by what is now §§88 and 247; changed again in 1867 by §371. §8. Extension of taxes by the clerk, including back taxes; changed in 1853, §§149, 150 and 287, 288. §9. Person aggrieved by an assessment; an amendment to § 26 Ch. 89; changed in 1847 (79 §9), and again in 1853, by §§89 and 248. Also changed once more in 1861, by Ch. 103*d* Art. 16 §§11—13. §10. Collector's bonds to be sent to the auditor; changed in 1853 by §§144—146, and 284. §11. Penalty against assessors, now §37. §12. Assessment list delivered by the clerk to the collector; changed in 1853, by §§147 and 285. §13. Payment of the school fund; changed in 1853, by §§199—201, and 348—350. §14. Sales of lands and lots forfeited to the state; changed in 1853, by §§173, 174 and 317. *Reference by section only is made to Gross' Stat.* 1869, Ch. 89. . . Owner of land sold for taxes to have a written notice from the county clerk; Laws 1847 (28 Feb.) 78. Repealed; 1 Laws 1849 (12 Feb.) 122 §6. . . Relating to the duty of the auditor: partly special and temporary, and containing other provisions which have been changed by later acts; Laws 1847 (1 Mar.) 19. . . A general act of 1849 (12 Feb.) contains a few sections that are still in force. The rest is merely temporary, or has been changed by later acts, as shown in the following synopsis: §1. Assessments of 1848 and prior years, not made in time and declared valid. §2. Time of completing assessment; changed by §371. §3. Collector's bonds; changed by §§144 and 284. §4. Jurisdiction of county courts in suits by collectors for taxes; changed in 1853, by §§154 and 293. §5. Advertising real estate for taxes; amended at the next session; 2 Laws 1849 (6 Nov.) 46 §7; changed in 1853 by §§157 and 301. §6. Mode of obtaining a tax deed; changed in 1853, by §§158 and 302. §§ 7 and 8. Auditor to obtain list of lands sold by the United States and transmit them to the county clerks; changed in 1853, by §§104 and 265. §9. Clerk to make list of lands for the assessor; changed in 1853, by §§105 and 266; changed in 1855, by §§139 and 278. Changed again in 1861 as to counties under township organization; Ch. 103*d*. Art. 16 §6. Changed again in 1867, by §370. §10. Collector to file in the county court a list of delinquent lands; changed in 1853, by §§164 and 308. §11. Delinquent tax paid before judgment; changed in 1853, by §§165 and 309. §12. Judgment for taxes; changed by §§166 and 310. §13. Appeals to the circuit court; changed by §§167 and 311. §14. County clerk to perform the duties of the circuit clerk; now §39. §15. County clerk to send the auditor a transcript of the tax sales; changed in 1853, by §§169 and 312. County clerk also to send a list of lands forfeited to the state; changed in 1853, by §§171 and 314. §16. Penalty for failure to comply with the foregoing section; now §40. §17. Suits for taxes of 1848 and prior years may be prosecuted either in circuit or county courts. §18. Assessments and collections for 1849. §19. Duty of the collector to demand the taxes on receiving the lists; changed in 1853, by §§ 111, 152 and 290. §20. Distraining personal property for taxes; changed by §§112 and 291. §21 Collection and application of the two mill tax; now §41. §22. County treasurer to be *ex officio* assessor; changed in 1853 by §238; as to counties under township organization consult Ch. 103*d*. Act. 16. §§23, 24. Land records in the office of the auditor to be corrected and transcribed. §25. Land taxed before becoming taxable; now §42. §26. Assessor to give the owner a certificate of assessment; amends R. S. Ch. 89 §16; changed in 1853 by §§50, 51 and 214, 215. §§27, 28. Auditor to furnish books, etc. under this act. §29. Duty of assessor when any person shall refuse to list property; changed by §§54 and 218. §30. Assessor to administer oath to owner listing; changed by §§78 and 245.—1 Laws 1849, 121. . . Auditor to furnish each county with a transcript of all lands sold therein, at the seat of government for taxes; 1 Laws 1849 (12 Feb.) 37. . . Concerning forfeited lands sold or redeemed prior to 1 June 1849; 1 Laws 1849 (12 Feb.) 128. Section 6 authorized the clerk to receive redemption money; it was repealed; 2 Laws 1849 (6 Nov.) 49 §18. . . Act of the second session of 1849, amending and consolidating former acts. Most of its provisions were changed by the acts of 1853, as will appear from the following synopsis: §1. County clerk to deliver to the assessor a list of taxable real estate; changed in 1853, by §§105 and 266; changed again in 1855, by §§139 and 278, and changed again in 1867, by §370. §2. Assessment to be completed and returns make by 1 Oct.; now 1 Aug. by §371. §3. County clerk to deliver tax books to the collector on first Monday in Dec.; changed in 1853, by §§147 and 285. §4. Collector to file his bond at the Dec. term; changed in 1853, by §§143 and 282. §5. Sheriff to attend in the precincts for the collection of taxes; changed in 1853, by §29. As to counties under township organization, con-

sult §§111 and 147. §6. Duty of the sheriff to attend in his office for the collection of taxes; changed by §290. §7. Time of selling land for taxes; changed in 1855, by §§206 and 355. §8 Collector's list of abatements by reason of tax not collected; changed in 1853, by §§153 and 295. §9. County clerk to furnish to the collector, for the auditor, a certified statement of the tax abated; changed by §§153 and 295. Final settlement by collector with the auditor; changed by §§156 and 300; consult also §§169 and 312. §10. Collector to receive a certificate from the auditor on final settlement; now §43. §§11, 12. Manner of proceeding after the death of the collector; changed in 1853 by §§159, 160 and 303, 304. §13. Judgment for taxes, and sale thereon; changed by §§205, 206 and 355. Infants, etc. redeeming from tax sales; changed by §§175 and 318. §14. Penalty against the collector, now §44. §15. Time and manner of applying for judgment for taxes; changed by §§161 and 305. Consult also §§154 and 296. §§16, 17. Fees of the printer for advertising tax sale; changed by §§162, 163 and 306, 307. Consult also §406. §18. Taxes on lands forfeited to the state; changed by §§171 and 314. §19. Overpayment by a collector to the state; changed by §§178 and 321. §20. Disposition of fines; changed by later school laws; Ch. 98 §82. §21. Manner of obtaining a pedlar's license; now §4. §22. Printer's fees paid by the state; changed by §§162, 163 and 306, 307.—2 Laws 1849, 45. *Reference by section only is to Gross' Stat.* 1869. . . Assessments for 1849 legalized; 2 Laws 1849 (6 Nov.) 51. . Time for completing collections extended, in counties under township organization; Laws 1851 (24 Jan.) 7. . . Tax for state or special purposes, levied and collected in 1853 (12 Feb.) 260. . . Time for township collectors to pay over the tax for 1858; Laws 1859 (11 Feb.) 205. . . Collection of taxes for 1860 postponed; 1 Laws 1861 (14 Feb.) 168. Auditor to retain coupons, on bonds deposited by banks, to pay their taxes; Id. (18 Feb.) 38. . . Collection of the revenue for 1862 postponed in certain counties; Laws 1863 (12 Feb.) 69. . . War fund transferred to revenue fund; Laws 1865 (13 Feb.) 132. . . Interest fund transferred to revenue fund; Laws 1867 (14 Feb.) 130. . . Distribution of interest on the school, college and seminary fund; Laws 1865 (21 Feb.) 131.

CHAP. 90. REVISED STATUTES.

Free holder defined as a person who has entered land or holds a bond; Laws 1819 (24 Mar.) 237. . . Act 10 Jan., to provide for digesting the statutes; the work to be done by judges of the supreme court; Laws 1825, 67. . . Resolution that judges may use the books in the secretary's office; Laws 1825, 186. . . Act 19 Jan., effect of repealing acts; Laws 1826, 56; Laws 1829, 103; R. S. 1833, 421. . Act 2 Mar. 1833; list of acts to be published with the revised strtutes of 1833; former acts repealed, with some exceptions; R. S. 1833, 426. . . Act 31 Jan., sheriffs to sell the revised statutes of 1833 for $1.; Laws 1835, 141. . . Act 16 Jan., distribution of the revised statutes of 1833; Laws 1836, 240. . . Revised statutes of 1845 to be copied and certified; R. S. 1845 (3 Mar.) 585 §5. Surplus copies to be distributed and not sold; Laws 1851 (23 Jan.) 5. . . Appointment of commissioners to prepare a revision; Laws 1869 (8 Mar.) 49. Duty of circuit judges in that behalf; Id. (29 Jan.) 49.

REPEALING STATUTES.

NOTE.—This is an attempt to bring together and classify the acts which in terms repeal a former act. It is doubtless incomplete. The general subject of the acts repealed is shown by the side titles in italic; the classification follows the revised statutes of 1845. The different repealing acts are separated by periods. Words expressing the subject of any particular act refer to the repealed and not to the repealing act. Reference is first made to the book and page of the repealing act, and afterwards, in parenthesis, a reference is in many cases made to the book and page of the act repealed. The abbreviation "Ib." if not in parenthesis, cites the last preceding reference which is not in parenthesis. "Ib." in parenthesis, cites the last preceding reference in parenthesis.

Abatement.—R. S. 1827, 46 §7. . R. S. 1845, 455. (R. S. 1827, 30 Dec. 45.) Id. 466. (Laws 1839, 2 Mar. 271.)

Account.—R. S. 1845, 455. (R. S. 1827, 11 Jan. 47.)

Advertisements.—R. S. 1845, 455. (R. S. 1827, 28 Dec. 1826, 48.)

Aliens.—R. S. 1827. 49 §3.

Amendments and Jeofails.—R. S. 1845, 455. (R. S. 1827, 11 Jan. 49.)

Apprentices.—R. S. 1845, 455. (R. S. 1827, 30 Dec. 1826, 54.)

Arbitrations.—R. S. 1827, 66 §8. Arbitrators and referees; R. S. 1845, 455. (R. S. 1827, 6 Jan. 64.) Amendatory act; R. S. 1845, 455. (R. S. 1833, 1 Mar. 81.)

Attachments before Justices.—1 Laws 1837, 17 §14. . R. S. 1845, 455. (R. S. 1833, 12 Feb. 82.) . . R. S. 1845, 455. (1 Laws 1837, 27 Feb. 13.) . R. S. 1845, 468. (Laws 1843, 23 Feb. 19.)

Attachments in Circuit Courts.—R. S. 1845, 455. (R. S. 1833, 12 Feb. 82.) . . R. S. 1845, 467. (Laws 1840, 31 Jan. 30 and 31.)

Attachments of Boats and Vessels.—R. S. 1845, 455. (R. S. 1831, 13 Feb. 95.)

Attorneys.—R. S. 1827, 81 §7. . R. S. 1833, 102 §11. . R. S. 1845, 455. (R. S. 1833, 1 Mar. 99.) . . Money collected; R. S. 1845, 468. (Laws 1843, 4 Mar. 19.)

Attorney General and Circuit Attorneys.—R. S. 1845, 455. (R. S. 1827, 17 Feb. 79.) . . Attorney General; R. S. 1845, 455. (R. S. 1833, 5 Feb. 99.) . . Attorney general and state's attorneys; R. S. 1845, 455. (Laws 1835, 7 Feb. 44.)

Auditor and Treasurer.—R. S. 1845, 455. (R. S. 1833, 2 Mar. 103.) R. S. 1845, 464. (Laws 1831, 11 Jan. 186.) . . Treasurer's bond; R. S. 1845, 465. (1 Laws 1837, 1 Mar. 334.). . . Id. 468. (Laws 1843, 4 Mar. 20.)

Bail.—R. S. 1845, 455; (R. S. 1827, 26 Jan. 82.)

Bank Notes.—R. S. 1845, 465. (Laws 1839, 4 Dec. '38, 79.)

Bastardy.—R. S. 1827, 246 §9. . R. S. 1845. 459. (R. S. 1827, 23 Jan. 244.)

Births and Deaths.—R. S. 1845, 460. (Laws 1843, 3 Mar. 210.)

Castor Beans.—R. S. 1845, 464. (Laws 1836, 16 Jan. 232.)

Census.—R. S. 1845, 455. (R. S. 1829, 13 Jan. 18.)

Chancery.—R. S. 1845, 455. (R. S. 1833, 13 Feb. 118.) . . Id. 465. (Laws 1839, 24 Jan. 50.)

Charitable Uses.—Grants confirmed; R. S. 1845, 458. (Laws 1831, 1 Feb. 73.) . . R. S. 1845, 468. (Laws 1841, 18 Feb. 110.)

Congress.—Division of the state into districts; R. S. 1845, 458. (Laws 1831, 15 Feb. 70.) . . Seven districts; R. S. 1845, 468. (Laws 1843, 1 Mar. 71.)

Conveyances.—R. S. 1845, 456. (R. S. 1827, 31 Jan. 95.) . . Specific performance; Id. (Laws 1825, 27 Dec. 1826, 30.) . . Acknowledgment and recording; Id. (R. L. 1829, 22 Jan. 24.) . Id. (2 Laws 1837, 21 July, 14.) . . Recording conveyances; Id. (Id. 21 July 13.) . . Seven years possession and payment of taxes; R. S. 1845, 461. (Laws 1835, 17 Jan. 42.) . .Amendment; Id. (1 Laws 1837, 11 Feb. 160) . . Release of mortgages; R. S. 1845, 466. (Laws 1839, 27 Feb. 197.) . . Seven years possession, etc.; R. S. 1845, 466. (Laws 1839, 2 Mar. 266.) . . Recording; R. S. 1845, 467. (Laws 1841, 26 Feb. 66.)

Corporations.—Fire companies; R. S. 1845, 458. (Laws 1835, 12 Feb. 174.) . . Libraries; Id. 459. (Laws 1823, 31 Jan. 101.) . . The same; Id. (Laws 1835, 31 Jan. 181.) . . Towns; R. S. 1845, 459. (Laws 1831, 12 Feb. 82.) . . The same; Id. (Laws 1835, 31 Jan. 175.) . . Religious societies; R. S. 1845, 463. (Id. 6 Feb. 147.) . . Recording town plats; R. S. 1845, 464. (R. S. 1833, 27 Feb. 599.) . . Academies; R. S. 1845, 468. (Laws 1843, 6. Mar. 6.)

Costs.—R. S. 1845, 457. (R. S. 1827. 10 Jan. 102.)

Counties and County Courts.—Court houses and jails; Laws 1829, 54 §4. . R. S. 1845, 456. (Laws 1835, 7 Jan. 46.) . . Incorporating counties; Id. (R. S. 1827, 3 Jan. 107.) . . Fines; Id. (R. S. 1833, 11 Jan. 141.) . . Establishing county commissioners' courts; Id. (Laws 1819, 22 Mar. 175.) . . Vacancies; R. S. 1845, 456. (Laws 1835, 12 Feb. 34.) . . County commissioners; Id. (1 Laws 1837, 1 Mar. 103.) . . Pay of county commissioners; Id. (2 Laws 1837, 21 July 16.) . . Court houses and jails; Id. (R. L. 1829, 5 Jan. 53.) . Appeals from county commissioners; R. S. 1845, 457. (Laws 1835, 31 Jan. 152.) . . Annual statement; Id. 466. (Laws 1839, 2 Mar. 270.) . . County seats and county lines; R. S. 1845, 467. (Laws 1841, 27 Feb. 98.) . . Jurisdiction on the Mississippi and Wabash; R. S. 1845, 468. (Laws 1843, 4 Mar. 100.) . . Leasing court houses; Id. (Id., 21 Feb. 128.) . Fire proof offices; R. S. 1845, 469. (Laws 1843, 24 Feb. 210.)

County Treasurers and County Funds.—Money collected; R. S. 1845, 467. (Laws 1840, 1 Feb. 78.) . . Annual settlements; Id. 469. (Laws 1843, 25 Feb. 113.) . . Treasurer's duty; Id. (Id., 28 Feb. 151.)

Courts.—Complete records; Laws 1821, 11 §9. . . Supreme judges, terms of court; Laws 1825, 47 §43. . Courts; R. S. 1827, 124 §13. . Laws 1829, 47 §23; Id. 52 §13. . Circuit courts; Laws 1839, 290 §2. . Judiciary; contracts; Laws 1841, 173 §1. . Circuit north of the Illinois river; R. S. 1845, 456. (R. L. 1829, 8 Jan. 38.) . . Regulating supreme and circuit courts; Id. (Id., 19 Jan. 39.) . . Supplemental to the foregoing; Id. (Id., 23 Jan. 48.) . Place of holding supreme court; Id. (Id., 22 Jan. 47.) . . Clerk of supreme court; R. S. 1845, 456. (Laws 1831, 15 Feb. 187.) . . Courts; Id. (Id., 16 Feb. 44.) . . Courts in Madison and Calhoun; R. S. 1845, 457. (Laws 1831, 16 Feb. 48.) . . Circuit courts; Id. (R. S. 1833, 2 Mar. 162.) . . Uniform mode of holding circuit courts; Id. (Laws 1835, 7 Jan. 150.) . . Dividing the state into circuits; R. S. 1845, 457. (Id. 17 Jan. 153.) . . Time of holding circuit and supreme courts; Id. (Id., 13 Feb. 167.) . . Circuit courts in certain counties; Id. (Laws 1836, 16 Jan. 239.) . . Circuit and supreme courts; R. S. 1845, 457. (Id., 12 Jan. 240.) . . Circuit courts, supplemental; Id. (Id., 16 Jan. 251.) . . The same; Id. (Id. 16 Jan. 257.) . Third circuit; Id. (Id. 16 Jan. 228.) . . In 4th circuit; R. S. 1845, 457. (Laws 1837, 1 Mar. 110.) . . Court in Washington Co.; Id. (Id., 10 Feb. 111.) . . Courts in 1st, 6th and 7th circuits; R. S. 1845, 457. (1 Laws 1837, 4 Mar. 111.) . Forming 7th circuit; Id. (Id. 4 Feb. 113.) . . Courts in 2d circuit; R. S. 1845, 465. (Laws 1839, 15 Feb. 103.) . . Division of the state into circuits; Id., 466. (Id., 23 Feb. 155.) . . Time of supreme and circuit courts; R. S. 1845, 466. (Laws 1839, 2 Mar. 250.) . . Courts in the 5th circuit; Id. (Id., 2 Mar. 278.) . . Courts in 3rd circuit; R. S. 1845, 466. (Laws 1839, 2 Mar. 280.) . . Courts in 8th circuit; Id. (Laws 1840, 1 Feb. 5.) . . Publication of the supreme court reports; R. S. 1845, 467. (Laws 1840, 1 Feb. 77.) . . Courts in 6th circuit; Id. (Id., 29 Jan. 88.) . . Courts in Clinton and Bond; R. S. 1845, 467. (Id., 3 Feb. 130.) . . Jurisdiction of Sangamon circuit court; R. S. 1845, 467. (Laws 1841, 26 Feb. 35.) . . Courts in 2d circuit; Id. (Id., 7 Jan. 101.) . . Courts in 6th circuit; R. S. 1845, 467. (Laws 1841, 20 Jan. 102.) . . Courts in 1st circuit; Id. (Id., 3 Feb. 103.) . . Circuit courts generally; R. S. 1845, 467. (Laws 1841, 23 Feb. 103.) . . Id. (Id., 26 Feb. 110.) . . Judiciary re-organized; R. S. 1845, 468. (Laws 1841, 10 Feb. 173.) . . Supreme court; Id. 469. (Laws 1843, 3 Mar. 134.)

Criminal Code.—Prevention of vice and immorality; Laws 1821, 54 §17. . Killing hogs; Id. 130 §15. . Firing woods' and prairies; Laws 1823, 140 §2. . Crimes and punishments; Id. 198 §30. . R. S. 1827, 168 §189. . Laws 1831, 113. . R. S. 1833, 219 §191. . R. S. 1845, 457. (R. S. 1833, 26 Feb. 171.) . . Apprehension of offenders; Id. (R. S. 1827, 6 Jan. 169.) . . Sabbath breaking; Id. (R. L. 1829, 19 Jan. 138.) . . Apprehension of offenders; R. S. 1845, 457. (1 Laws 1837, 11 Feb. 113.) .

Repealing Statutes.

Marks and brands; R. S. 1845, 461. (Laws 1819, 28 Mar. 217 §§14, 15.) . . Disturbing worshipers; R. S. 1845, 465. (R. S. 1833, 1 Mar. 661.) . . Betting on elections; Id. (Laws 1839, 15 Feb. 109.) . . Incest; R .S. 1845, 469. (Laws 1843, 7 Feb. 155.)

Cumberland Road.—R. S. 1845, 466. (Laws 1839, 2 Mar. 245.)

Detinue.—R. S. 1845, 458. (R. S. 1827, 6 Jan. 179.)

Divorces.—R. S. 1827, 183 §7. . R. S. 1845, 458. (R. S. 1827, 12 Jan. 180.) . . Id. (Id, 31 Jan. 181.) . . Id. (R. S. 1833, 4 Dec. 1833 [2], 234.)

Dower.—R. S. 1827, 187 §17. . R. S. 1845, 458. (R. S. 1827, 6 Feb. 183.) . . Unknown parties; Id. (1 Laws 1837, 27 Feb. 324.)

Drovers.—R. S. 1845, 467. (Laws 1841, 3 Feb. 51.)

Ejectment.—Action simplified; R. S. 1845, 458. (Laws 1836, 13 Jan. 238.) . Occupying claimants; Id. 460. (Laws 1819, 23 Feb. 40.) . R. S. 1845, 466. (Laws 1839, 2 Mar. 220.)

Elections.—Laws 1821, 80 §16. . Laws 1823, 68 §36. . Presidential electors; Laws 1825, 4 §1. . Elections; Id. 169 §12. . Presidential electors; R. S. 1827, 189 §5. . Election of justices; Id. 256 §1. . Elections; Laws 1829, 68 §30. . Contesting elections; R. S. 1833, 258 §4. . Election of county commissioners; 1 Laws 1837, 104 §7. . Comparing poll books; R. S. 1845, 456. (R. S. 1833, 25 Feb. 127.). . Additional polls at county seats; Id. (Laws 1831, 9 Feb. 75.). . R. S. 1845, 458. (R. S. 1827, 9 Feb. 187). . Presidential electors; Id., (Id. 11 Jan. 188.). . Elections; Id. (R. L. 1829, 10 Jan. 54.). . Elections, amendatory; R. S. 1845, 458. (R. S. 1833, 28 Feb. 257.). . Elections, amendatory; Id. (Laws 1835, 29 Jan. 141.). . County clerks and county treasurers elective; Id. (1 Laws 1837, 7 Feb. 49.). . Elections; R. S. 1845, 465. (Laws 1839, 15 Feb. 109.). . Id. 468. (Laws 1841, 20 Feb. 111.). . Tenure of office; R. S. 1845, 468. (Laws 1843, 21 Feb. 10.)

Escheats.—R. S. 1845, 458. (R. S. 1833, 1 Mar. 264.)

Estrays.—Laws 1823, 169 §5. . Water craft and estrays; Laws 1831, 191 §5. . Laws 1835, 235, §11. . Estrays; R. S. 1845, 458. (Laws 1835, 9 Feb. 229.). . Id. 469. (Laws 1843, 4 Mar. 139.). . Id. (Id., 6 Mar. 140.)

Evidence and Depositions.—Depositions; R. S. 1827, 179 §14. . Evidence; Id. 200 §7.—Depositions; R. S. 1845, 457. (R. S. 1827, 9 Feb. 174.) Evidence; Id. 458. (Id., 10 Jan. 199.). . Land patent; R. S. 1845, 466. (Laws 1839, 27 Feb. 196.) Evidence of partnership; R. S. 1845, 468. (Laws 1841, 17 Feb. 112.). . Copies; Id. 469. (Laws 1843, 24 Feb. 140.)

Fees and Salaries.—State's attorneys fees; Laws 1821, 7 §1. . Fees; Id. 61 §1. . Laws 1825, 149 §10. . Laws 1826, 55 §3. . Fees and Salaries; R. S. 1827, 220 §17. . Sheriff's fees; Laws 1829, 141 §4. . Fees and Salaries; R. S. 1845, 458. (R. S. 1827, 19 Feb. 203.). . The same; Id. (R. L. 1829, 23 Jan. 140.). . Salaries supreme judges; R. S. 1845, 465. (Laws 1839, 12 Feb. 102.). . Governor's salary; R. S. 1845, 466. (Id., 1 Mar. 211.). . Naturalization fees; Id. 468. (Laws 1843, 24 Feb. 67.). . Fees of preceeding clerk; R. S. 1845, 468. (Id., 6 Mar. 68.). . Id. 469. (Laws 1843. 4 Mar. 142.)

Ferries and Toll Bridges.—R. S. 1827, 227 §17. R. S. 1845, 458. (R. S. 1827, 12 Feb. 220.). . The same; Id. (Id., 12 Feb. 227.). . Ferries; Id. (R. S. 1833, 19 Jan. 310.). . Ferries, toll bridges and turnpikes; R. S. 1845, 463. (R. L. 1829, 22 Jan. 73.). . R. S. 1845, 469. (Laws 1843, 1 Feb. 1843.)

Forcible entry and Detainer.—R. S. 1827, 230 (R. S. 1827, 2 Feb. 228.). . §6. . (1 Laws 1837, 120 §3.) . R. S. 1845, 459. Amendment; Id. (1 Laws 1837, 28 Feb. 119.)

Frauds and Perjuries.—R. S. 1845, 459. (R. S. 1827, 16 Feb. 230.). . Fraudulent devises; Id. (R. S. 1833, 28 Feb. 315.)

Fugitives from Justice.—R. S. 1827, 234 §8. . R. S. 1845, 459. (R. S. 1827, 6 Jan. 232.)

Gaming.—R. S. 1845, 459. (R. S. 1827, 16 Jan. 235.)

Guardian and Ward.—R. S. 1845, 461. (R. S. 1827, 5 Feb. 301.). . Similar act; Id. (Laws 1831, 7 Feb. 100.). . Similar act; Id. (1 Laws 1837, 4 Mar. 163.)

Habeas Corpus.—R. S. 1845, 455. (Laws 1835, 11 Feb. 32.). . The same; Id. 459. (R. S. 1827, 22 Jan. 236.)

Horses.—Laws 1829, 77 §7. . R. S. 1845, 459. (R. L. 1829, 3 Jan. 75.)

Idiots and Lunatics.—R. S. 1845, 459. (Laws 1823, 12 Feb. 133.) Trading with; Id. (Laws 1831, 19 Jan. 81.)

Inclosures and Fences.—Common fields; R. S. 1845, 458. (Laws 1819, 23 Feb. 37.). . Inclosures; Id. (Id., 20 Feb. 23.). . Foregoing amended; Id. (Laws 1835, 27 Jan. [Feb.] 144.) Fences erected by mistake; R. S. 1845, 460. . (Laws 1819, 23 Feb. 44.)

Insolvent Debtors.—Laws 1821, 125 §23. . Laws 1829, 84 §24. . R. S. 1845, 459. (R. L. 1829, 12 Jan. 78.)

Inspections.—R. S. 1845, 459. (Laws 1819, 23 Mar. 199.). . Tobacco inspection; Id., (R. L. 1829, 12 Jan. 174.). . R. S. 1845, 466. (Laws 1839, 2 Mar. 283.)

Interest.—R. S. 1845, 459. (Laws 1819, 2 Mar. 106, and R. S. 1833, 28 Feb. 348.)

Jails and Jailers.—R. S. 1827, 250 §16. . R. S. 1845, 459. (R. S. 1827, 26 Jan. 246.)

Joint Rights and Obligations.—R. S. 1845, 461. (Laws 1821, 13 Jan. 14.)

Judgments and Executions.—Laws 1821, 39 §4. Laws 1823, 177 §19. . Laws 1825, 160 §24. . Delivery Bonds; R. S. 1833, 224 §3. . Property exempt; Laws 1841, 171 §1. . Judgments and executions; Laws 1843, 188 §7. . Simplifying acknowledgment of sheriff's deeds; R. S. 1845, 456. (1 Laws 1836, 16 Jan. 257.). . Delivery bonds; Id. 457. (R. S. 1833, 1 Mar. 223.). . Judgments and executions; R. S. 1845, 459. (Laws 1825, 17 Jan. 151.) . . Id. 465. (Laws 1839, 6 Feb. 56.). . Garnishees; Id. (Id., 12 Feb. 86.). . Duty of executors, etc.; R. S. 1845, 468. (Laws 1841, 19 Feb. 168.). . Redemptions; Id. (Id., 19 Feb. 168.). . Exemptions; R. S. 1845, 468. (Laws 1841, 26 Feb. 171.). . Property valued;

Repealing Statutes.

Id. (Id., 27 Feb. 172.). . Attachments levied; R. S. 1845, 468. (Laws 1841, 26 Feb. 181.). . Exemptions; Id. 469. (Laws 1843, 4 Mar. 141.) . . Notice to administrators; Id. (Id., 25 Feb. 168.)

Jurors.—Grand Jurors; Laws 1823, 183 §3. Jurors; R. S. 1827, 254 §15. . R. S. 1845, 459. (R. S. 1827, 7 Feb. 251.). . Amendment; Id. (Laws 1835, 24 Jan. 144.). . Same amended; Id. (Id., 13 Feb, 37.). . Mileage; R. S. 1845, 469. (Laws 1843, 4 Mar. 169.) . . Juries at special term; Id. (Id., 1 Feb. 169.)

Justices and Constables.—Justices; Laws 1821 142 §23. . Laws 1823, 200 §32. . Certiorari; Laws 1826, 66 §7. . Justices and constables; R. S. 1827, 274 §57. . Laws 1829, 98 §15. . Election of; R. S. 1845, 458. (Laws 1835, 6 Feb. 29.). . The same; Id. (Id., 7 Jan. 29.). . Election of Id. 459. (R. S. 1827, 30 Dec. '26, 255.). . Powers and duties; R. S. 1845, 459. (Id., 3 Feb. 259.) . . Supplemental; Id. (Id., 12 Feb. 274.). . Extending jurisdiction; Id. (Id., 29 Dec. '26, 274.). . Election of; R. S. 1845, 460. (R. L. 1829, 13 Jan. 93.). . Powers and duties; Id. (Id., 23 Jan. 94.). . New counties; Id. (Laws 1831, 7 Jan. 88.). . Qualifications and duties; R. S. 1845, 460. (R. S. 1833, 1 Mar. 412.). . Jurisdiction; Id. (Id., 2 Mar. 415.). . The same; Id. (Laws 1835, 13 Feb. 32.). . Amendment; R. S. 1845, 460. (2 Laws 1837, 21 July 46.). . Election of; Id. 465. (Laws 1839, 12 Jan. 41.) . . Jury trial; Id. (Id., 12 Feb. 87.). . Appeals and appeal bonds; R. S. 1845, 466. (Laws 1839, 2 Mar. 291.). . Certificate of magistracy; R. S. 1845, 467. (Laws 1840, 1 Feb. 64.). . Appeals; Id. (Id., 3 Feb. 108.). . Constables; R. S. 1845, 468. (Laws 1841, 26 Feb. 176.)

Landlord and Tenant.—R. S. 1827. 280 §7. . R. S. 1845, 460. (R. S. 1827, 13 Feb. 278.). . The same amended; R. S. 1845, 460. (Laws 1831, 4 Jan. 88.)

Lands.—R. S. 1845, 460. (Laws 1831, 15 Feb. 82.). . Extent of possession; Id. (1 Laws 1837, 27 Feb. 154.). . R. S. 1845, 465. (Laws 1839, 16 Feb. 124.)

Laws.—Distribution; R. S. 1833, 422 §3. . Sent to other states; R. S. 1845, 460. (R. L. 1829, 1 Jan. 103.). . Publication and distribution; Id. (R. S. 1827, 14 Jan. 281.). . What laws in force; R. S. 1845, 460. (Laws 1819, 4 Feb. 3.) . . To repeal certain laws; Id. (Laws 1819, 30 Mar. 351.). . Printed with R. S. 1833; R. S. 1845, 460. (R. S. 1833, 2 Mar. 426.). . Acts becoming laws notwithstanding the objections of the council of revision; Id. (R. S. 1827, 26 Dec. '26, 280.). . Distribution; R. S. 1845, 467. (Laws 1840, 29 Jan. 65.). . Distribution of congressional documents; R. S. 1845, 469. (Laws 1843, 2 Feb. 173.)

Library, State.—R. S. 1845, 469. (Laws 1843; 15 Dec. '42, 290.)

Licenses.—Laws 1831, 92 §5. . R. S. 1845, 461. (Laws 1831, 16 Feb. 89.). . The same; Id. (R. S. 1833, 2 Mar. 441.). . Clock Pedlars; Id. (Laws 1835, 31 Jan. 63.). . Liquor sold Indians; accounts for liquor; R. S. 1845, 464. (Laws 1823, 14 Feb. 148.). . Tavern licenses; Id. (Laws 1819, 27 Feb. 77.). . Id. (Laws 1835, 12 Feb. 154.). . Id. (1 Laws 1837, 10 Feb. 326.). . R. S. 1845, 465. (Laws 1839, 2 Mar. 71.). . Id. 468. (Laws 1841, 17 Feb. 178, and also, Id., 18 Feb. 179.). . Pedlars; R. S. 1845, 468. (Laws 1841, 27 Feb. 179.). . Foreign insurance companies; R. S. 1845, 469. (Laws 1843, 4 Mar. 165.)

Liens.—R. S. 1845, 461. (R. S 1833, 22 Feb. 447.). . Id. 467. (Laws 1840, 10 Dec. '36, 147.)

Limitations.—R. S. 1827, 286 §10. . R. S. 1845, 461. (R. S. 1827, 10 Feb. 284.). . The same; Id. (Laws 1835, 17 Jan. 42.). . Limitations; R. S. 1845, 461. (1 Laws 1837, 11 Feb. 160.)

Mandamus.—R. S. 1845, 461. (R. S. 1827, 6 Jan. 287.)

Marks and Brands.—R. S. 1845, 461. (Laws 1835, 6 Feb. 51.). . Marks and brands in the criminal code; Id. (Laws 1819, 23 Mar. 217 §§14, 15.)

Marriages.—R. S. 1827, 290 §7. . R. S. 1845, 461. (R. S. 1827, 14 Feb. 288.). . Id. 466. (Laws 1839, 2 Mar. 277.)

Militia.—Laws 1821, 13 §2. . Id. 112 §13. . Laws 1823, 46 §1. . Laws 1826, 44 §1. . Laws 1829, 108 §5. . R. S. 1845, 461. . Purports to repeal an act of 2 Mar. 1833, "for the organization and government of the militia;" no act of that title *and date*, appears among the printed statutes: an act of that *title* had been previously passed; Laws 1826 (25 Jan.) 3. . Amendment; R. S. 1845, 461. (1 Laws 1837, 4 Mar. 163.). . Encouraging volunteer companies; Id. (1 Laws 1837. 2 Mar. 165.). . Public arms; R. S. 1845, 462. (R. S. 1833, 1 Mar. 499.). . Laws 1869, 5 §1.

Mills and Millers.—R. S. 1827, 300 §15. . R. S. 1845, 461. (R. S. 1827, 9 Feb. 297.). . R. S. 1845, 469. (Laws 1843, 3 Mar. 179.)

Ne Exeat.—R. S. 1845, 455. (Laws 1835, 11 Feb. 32.). . Ne exeat and injunctions; Id. 461. (R. S. 1827, 22 Jan. 304.)

Negotiable Instruments.—Bills of exchange; Laws 1821, 170 §4. . R. S. 1827, 87 §3. . Negotiable instruments; Id., 323 §9. . Bills of exchange; R. S. 1845, 455. (R. S. 1827, 28 Dec. '26, 87.). . Id. 462. (R. S. 1827, 3 Jan. 320.)

Negroes and Mulattoes.—R. S. 1845, 461. (Laws 1819, 30 Mar. 354.). . Id. (Laws 1831, 1 Feb. 101.). . Id. (R. L. 1829, 17 Jan. 109.). . Id. (R. S. 1833, 1 Mar. 466.). . R. S. 1845, 468. (Laws 1841, 19 Feb. 189.)

Notaries Public.—Laws 1829, 113 §6. . R. S. 1845, 461. (R. L. 1829, 30 Dec. '28, 112.). . Id. (R. S. 1833, 12 Jan. 471.). . Oaths by; Id. (Laws 1831, 9 Feb. 102.). . R. S. 1845, 466. (Laws 1839, 22 Feb. 148.)

Oaths and Affirmations.—R. S. 1845, 461. (Laws 1831, 9 Feb. 102.). . Id. (R. S. 1827, 26 Dec. '26 308.). . Witnesses before committees; R. S. 1845, 465. (Laws 1839, 7 Jan. 39.)

Officers.—Deputy clerks appointed; R. S. 1845, 456. (Laws 1831. 9 Feb. 49.). . Residence at county seat; Id. (Laws 1823, 11 Jan. 70.). . Defective laws reported; R. S. 1845, 462. (Laws 1819, 20 Feb. 46.). . Vacancy by non residence; Id. (R. L. 1829, 22 Jan. 115.). . Suits by or against the State; R. S. 1845, 464. (R. L. 1829, 3 Jan. 170.)

Official Bonds.—Renewal by clerks; R. S. 1845, 456. (R. S. 1833, 26 Feb. 128.). . Id. 468. (Laws 1843, 28 Jan. 40.)

Partitions.—R. S. 1827, 187 §17. . R. S. 1845, 458. (R. S. 1827, 6 Feb. 183.). . Unknown parties; Id. (1 Laws 1837, 27 Feb. 324.). . R. S. 1845, 461. (Laws 1821, 13 Jan. 14.)

Paupers.—Laws 1823, 212 §30. . R. S. 1827, 310 §5. . R. S. 1833, 481 §7. . Laws 1839, 140 §16. . R. S. 1845, 462. (R. S. 1833, 1 Mar. 480.). . Id. (Laws 1835, 13 Feb. 66.). . R. S. 1845, 465. (Laws 1839, 21 Feb. 138.). . Id. 468. (Laws 1841, 21 Feb. 190.)

Penitentiary.—Laws 1839. 275 §3; Id. 278 §1. Laws 1843, 183 §8. . . R. S. 1845, 462. (R. S. 1833, 19 Feb. 477.). . Id. (Laws 1835, 9 Feb. 52.) . . Id. (Laws 1836, 18 Jan. 250.). . R. S. 1845, 462. (1 Laws 1837, 21 July 47.). . Id. 466. (Laws 1839, 2 Mar. 278.). . R. S. 1845, 469. (Laws 1843, 2 Mar. 181.)

Petitions.—R. S. 1845, 462. (R. S. 1827, 26 Dec. '26, 110.)

Practice.—R. S. 1827, 319 §38. . Laws 1829, 171 §3. . Testing process; 1 Laws 1837, 179 §2. . R. S. 1845, 456. Purports to repeal an "act of 30 Dec. 1828, amendatory of an act of 29 Jan. 1827;" no such act appears in the laws of '29; it is found in Laws 1831 (9 Feb.) 113. . Process; R. S. 1845, 457. (1 Laws 1837, 25 Feb. 178.). . Process in 3rd and 5th circuits; Id. (Id., 19 Jan. 179.). . . Legalizing process; Id. (2 Laws 1837, 20 July, 51.). . Process; Id. (Id., 21 July, 51.). . R. S. 1845, 462. (Laws 1819, 22 Mar. 139.). . Id. (R. S. 1827, 29 Jan. 310.). . R. S. 1845, 462 purports to repeal an act of 2 Feb. 1837, "concerning practice;" there is no act of this title and date—it should be 1827; (R. S. 1827, 320.). . R. S. 1845, 462. (R. S. 1833, 1 Mar. 497.). . Petition and summons; Id. (Id., 25 Feb. 467.). . Id. (Laws 1835, 7 Feb. 152.). . Appeals and writs of error, R. S. 1845, 462. (1 Laws 1837, 6 Dec '36, 12.). . Practice; Id. (2 Laws 1837, 21 July, 109.). . Process against corporations; R. S. 1845, 466. (Laws 1839, 19 Feb. 160.). . Id. (Id., 2 Mar. 271.). . Docketing; R. S. 1845, 468. (Laws 1841, 23 Feb. 191.)

Printing and Binding.—Printing; Laws 1843, 195 §3. . Printing; Pr. Laws of 1833; R. S. 1845, 460. (R. S. 1833, 27 Jan. 436.). . Binding; Id. (Id., 22 Feb. 438.). . Duties of the printer; R. S. 1845, 462. (Laws 1835, 24 Jan. 163.) . . Laws and journals; Id. (Laws 1836, 16 Jan. 236.). . Printer; Id. (1 Laws 1837, 4 Mar. 179.). . Binding; R. S. 1845, 467. (Laws 1840, 31 Jan. 34.). . Printer; Id. 468. (Laws 1841, 23 Feb. 192.) . . Binding; R. S. 1845, 469. (Laws 1843, 23 Feb. 173.) . Printing; Id. (Id., 4 Mar. 194.)

Probate Court.—Laws 1823, 132 §1. . Laws 1829, 38 §8. . 1 Laws 1837, 176 §1. . R. S. 1845, 456. (R. L. 1829, 2 Jan. 37.). . Election of Probate justices; Id. 460. (1 Laws 1837, 4 Mar. 176.). . Amendment; R. S. 1845, 460. (2 Laws 1837, 21 July 46.). . Process by judges and justices of probate; Id. 465. (Laws 1839, 7 Jan., 39.). . Probate justices; R. S. 1845, 469. (Laws 1843, 1 Feb. 185.)

Quo Warranto.—R. S. 1845, 462. (R. S. 1827, 28 Dec. '26, 347.)

Records and Recorders.—Recording; R. L. 1829, 25 §3. . Records and Recorders; Id. 118 §8. . Ancient books and records; R. S. 1845, 462. (Laws 1821, 30 Jan. 46.). . Recovery of property withheld; Id. (Laws 1831, 15 Feb. 114.) . . Records removed to Rushville; R. S. 1845, 462. (Laws 1835, 9 Feb. 157.). . Transcribing records; Id. (Id., 12 Feb. 158.). . Id. (Laws 1836, 18 Jan. 247.). . Recorders; R. S. 1845, 462. (R. L. 1829, 8 Jan. 116.). . Id. (Laws 1835, 11 Feb. 165.). . Id. 463. (Id., 13 Feb. 61.) . . Abolishing state recorder; R. S. 1845, 464. (R. S. 1833, 18 Jan. 587.). . Deputy recorders; Id. 587.

Replevin.—R. S. 1845, 462. (R. S. 1827, 29 Jan. 349.). . Id. 465. (Laws 1839, 12 Feb. 77.)

Revenue.—Laws 1821, 100 §3. . Id. 184 §6. Laws 1823, 212 §30. . R. S. 1827, 338 §43. . Lands classified for taxation; Laws 1831, 125 §2. . R. S. 1845, 463. (R. S. 1827, 13 Feb. 339.). . Id. (Id., 19 Feb. 325.). . Id. (R. L. 1829, 19 Jan. 119.). . R. S. 1845, 463. (Laws 1831, 12 Feb. 125.). . Id. (R. S. 1833, 27 Feb. 528.). . Id. (Laws 1835, 12 Feb. 51.). . Redemptions; R. S. 1845, 463. (Laws 1836, 13 Jan. 230.). . Revenue; Id. (Id., 15 Jan. 231.). . Surplus revenue; Id. (Laws 1837, 4 Mar. 194.). . Revenue; R. S. 1845, 463. (Id., 6 Dec. '36, 194.). . Id. (2 Laws 1837, 22 July 59.). . Id. (Id. 21 July, 58.). . R. S. 1845, 463. (Id., 21 July 59.) . . Id. 465. (Laws 1839, 26 Feb. 3.). . Id. (Id., 1 Mar. 23.). . R. S. 1845, 466. (Laws 1840, 1 Feb. 3.). . Assessors; R. S. 1845, 467. (Laws 1841, 26 Feb. 34, and also, Id., 27 Feb. 35.). . Speculating in warrants; Id. (Laws 1841, 19 Feb. 63.)

Revised Statutes.—All the territorial laws with some exceptions; Laws 1819, 351 §1. All former public acts; R. S. 1833, 434 §2. . Revival of statutes; R. S. 1845, 460. (Laws 1826, 19 Jan. 56.)

Right of Property.—Laws 1823, 115 §3. . R. S. 1827, 352 §8. . R. S. 1845, 463. (R. S. 1827, 29 Jan. 351.) . . Id. (Laws 1835, 30 Jan. 56.) . . R. S. 1845, 465. (Laws 1839, 12 Feb. 118.) . . Id. 466. (Id., 27 Feb. 193.) . Id. (Laws 1839, 28 Feb. 206.) . . R. S. 1845, 469. (Laws 1843, 2 Feb. 189.)

Right of Way.—R. S. 1845, 463. (R. S. 1833, 28 Feb. 534.)

Roads.—Laws 1821, 169 §6. . Laws 1825, 60 §2. . Laws 1826, 58 §4. . Id. 87 §7. . R. S. 1827, 346 §23. . Laws 1831, 161 §12. . Laws 1835, 139 §34. . R. S. 1845, 463. (R. S. 1827, 12 Feb. 340.) . . Id. (Laws 1835, 3 Feb. 129.) . . Id. (Laws 1836, 16 Jan. 227.) . . R. S. 1845, 463. (Id., 18 Jan. 207.) . . Id. (1 Laws 1837, 3 Mar. 274.) . . Id. (2 Laws 1837, 61.) . . R. S. 1845, 466. (Laws 1839, 27 Feb, 167.) . . Id. (Id., 23 Feb. 183.) . . R. S. 1845, 468. (Laws 1841, 20 Feb. 232.) . . Id. (Laws 1843, 4 Mar. 111.)

Saltpetre Caves.—R. S. 1845, 463. (Laws 1835, 6 Feb. 151.)

Seat of Government.—R. S. 1845, 464. (1 Laws 1837, 25 Feb. 321.) . . Id. (Id., 3 Mar. 322.)

Secretary of State.—Laws 1831, 170 §6. . Care of furniture; R. S. 1845, 462. (R. S. 1827, 15 Feb. 324.) . . Id. (Laws 1831, 14 Feb. 169.) . . Seals; Id. (Laws 1819, 19 Feb. 16.) . . Stationery and firewood; R. S. 1845, 464. (Laws 1825, 6 Jan. 59.) . . Geological specimens; R. S. 1845, 469, (Laws 1843, 4 Mar. 154.)

Securities.—R. S. 1845, 464. (Laws 1819, 24 Mar. 243.) . . R. S. 1845, 469. (Laws 1843, 5 Dec. '42, 222.)

Schools.—School lands; R. S. 1827, 3 70 §16. . Schools; Laws 1829, 149 §§1, 2. . Title of school and canal lands; R. S. 1845, 456. (1 Laws 1837, 16 Jan. 153.) . . R. S. 1845, 463. (R. S. 1827, 17 Feb. 364.) . . Id. (Laws 1825, 15 Jan. 121.)

Sheriffs and Coroners.—R. S. 1827, 375 §16. . R. S. 1845, 464. (R. S. 1827, 12 Feb. 371.) . . Id. (Laws 1831, 7 Feb. 177.) . . Id. (Id., 7 Jan. 178.) . . Coroners; R. S. 1845, 464. (Laws 1819, 20 Jan. 22.) . . Sheriffs and coroners; R. S. 1845, 466. (Laws 1839, 1 Mar. 217.)

Shows and Jugglers.—R. S. 1845, 464. (R. L. 1829, 23 Jan. 162.)

Slander.—R. S. 1845, 464. (Laws 1823, 27 Dec. '22, 82.)

Steamboats.—R. S. 1845, 464. (2 Laws 1837, 21 July 89.)

Surveyors.—Laws 1829, 174 §9. . R. S. 1845, 464. (R. L. 1829, 14 Jan. 172.)

Trespass.—R. S. 1845, 464. (Laws 1819, 27 Feb. 84.) . . Id. (R. S. 1833, 25 Feb. 604.) . . R. S. 1845, 465. (Laws 1839, 12 Jan. 42.)

Venue.—R. S. 1827, 384 §9. . Laws 1841, 214 §1. . R. S. 1845, 464. (R. S. 1827, 23 Jan. 381.) . . Id. 466. (Laws 1839, 28 Feb. 198.) . . R. S. 1845, 467. (Laws 1840, Feb. 36.)

Warrants of Cities and Towns.—R. S. 1845, 468. (Laws 1843, 4 Mar. 67.)

Weights and Measures.—R. S. 1845, 469. (Laws 1843, 4 Mar. 317.)

Wills.—Sale of real estate to pay debts; Laws 1823, 94 §8. . Id. 127 §1. . Sale of real estate to pay debts; R. S. 1827, 202 §11. . Wills; Laws 1829, 236 §140. . Laws 1831, 193 §7. . R. S. 1845, 464. (R. L. 1829, 23 Jan. 191.) . . Id. (Laws 1831, 14 Feb. 191.) . . Id. 465. (R. S. 1833, 25 Feb. 657, and also, Id., 23 Jan. 659.) . . R. S. 1845, 465. (Laws 1835, 27 Jan. 35.) . . Probate of wills; Id. 466. (Laws 1839, 2 Mar. 259.) . . Administration after division of county; R. S 1845, 467. (Laws 1841, 17 Feb. 22.) . . Id. 469. (Laws 1843, 6 Mar. 319.) .

Wolves.—Laws 1825, 117 §5. . Laws 1826, 95 §15. . R. S. 1845, 469. (Laws 1843, 15 Feb. 319.)

CHAP. 91. RIGHT OF PROPERTY.

Act 12 Feb. 1821; mode of trying the right to property taken on execution; Laws 1821, 148. . . Act 7 Feb. 1823; mode of trying the right of property in certain cases; Laws 1823, 114. . . Act 10 Jan. 1825; amending the above act of 7 Feb. 1823; Laws 1825, 68. . . Act 29 Jan. 1827; prescribing the mode of trying the right of property; former acts repealed; R. S. 1827, 351; R. S. 1833, 537. . . Act 30 Jan. 1835; amending the previous acts; Laws 1835, 56. . . Act 27 Feb. 1839; supplemental to former acts; mode of summoning witnesses, similar to R. S. 1845 Ch. 91 §§3—5; Laws 1839, 193. . . Act 28 Feb. 1839; trial of the right to property taken on justices' executions; Laws 1839, 206. . . Act 2 Feb. 1843; jurors before justitices to be six, similar to Ch. 91 §15 (R. S. 1845); Laws 1843, 189.

CHAP. 92. RIGHT OF WAY.

Act 28 Feb. 1833; obtaining the right of way for a road, canal or other public work, nearly as in R. S. 1845 Ch. 92 §§1—6; former act repealed, (which act was never printed); R. S. 1833, 534. . . Act 12 Feb. 1839; appeals by owners allowed; Laws 1839, 118. . . Act 1 Feb. 1840; to allow changes of venue after appeal taken; Laws 1840, 36. . . Act 23 Feb. 1841; damages not allowed when the land is not actually taken; Laws 1841, 214.

CHAP. 93. ROADS.

General Acts.—Repairing, improving and regulating; Laws 1819 (29 Mar.) 333. Foregoing amended; Laws 1821 (15 Feb.) 167. . . Amendatory act; Laws 1825 (15 Jan.) 130. Supplemental act; Laws 1826 (27 Jan.) 86. . . Amending and consolidating former acts which are all repealed; R. S. 1827 (12 Feb.) 340; R. S. 1833, 539. Amendment; Laws 1831 (15 Feb.) 158. . . Amending and consolidating former acts which are all repealed; Laws 1835 (3 Feb.) 129. Amendment; Laws 1836 (18 Jan.) 207. Road tax; Laws 1836 (15 Jan.) 227. . . Act 3 Mar. 1837; to amend the act of 18 Jan. 1836 "concerning public roads;" 1 Laws 1837, 274. . Act 27 Feb. 1839; manner of petitioning the general assembly for locating or altering state roads; Laws 1839, 167. . . Act 23 Feb. 1839. to regulate public carriages and the law of the road, similar to §§1—8, Ch. 93 R. S. 1845; Laws 1839, 183. . . Act 1 Feb. 1840; county commissioners' courts to alter and relocate state roads; Laws 1840, 51. . . Act 30 Jan. 1840; to extend for locating roads under the acts of 1839; Laws 1840, 68. . . Act 20 Feb. 1841; concerning public roads, similar to the chapter in the revised statutes; amending and consolidating former acts which are all repealed; Laws 1841, 232—244. . . Act 4 Mar. 1843; county commissioners to assess a tax for road purposes; Laws 1843, 111.

Local Acts. 1819.—Act 24 Mar., location from Golconda to Kaskaskia; Laws 1819, 239.

1821—Act 12 Feb., the United States road from Shawneetown to Kaskaskia declared a public highway; Laws 1821, 148. . . Act 14 Feb. 1821; toll bridges across the Little Muddy, Big Muddy, Mary's and Beaucoup rivers, on the state road from Kaskaskia to Shawneetown; Laws 1821, 156.

1823.—Act 31 Jan., road from Shawneetown to the Saline in Gallatin county, a public highway; Laws 1823, 98. . . Act 10 Feb., road from Carmi to Bonpas, a public highway; Laws 1823, 120. . . Act 10 Feb., location from Vandalia to Shawneetown; Vandalia to Kaskaskia; Vandalia to Covington, Brownsville, Jonesboro and America; Vandalia to Golconda, *via* Mount Vernon and Frankfort; Vandalia to Palestine; Vandalia to Alton; Vandalia to the town of Illinois; Vandalia to intersect the old road from St. Louis to Vincennes, and from such new road to Fairfield; from John McCal-

la's to Vincennes; Fairfield *via* Albion to opposite Harmony; Fairfield to Carmi; Laws 1823, 123. . . Act 14 Feb., location from Mount Vernon to the Saline tavern in Gallatin county; Laws 1823, 143. . . Act 14 Feb., the road from McCalla's bridge to St. Louis declared a public highway; Laws 1823, 144. . . Act 18 Feb., the old road from Shawneetown to Kaskaskia declared a public highway; Laws 1823, 178.

1825.—Act 16 Dec. 1824; vacation and relocation of that part of the road from Vandalia to Palestine which is in Crawford county; Laws 1825, 15. . . Act 23 Dec. 1824; location from the Gallatin county Saline to Littleton's ferry on the Mississippi; Laws 1825, 22. . . Act 29 Dec. 1824; location from Springfield to Paris; Laws 1825, 35. . . Act 6 Jan., road from Illinoistown to Vandalia a public highway, and $200. spent on it; location from Columbia *via* Cahokia to the town of Illinois; Laws 1825, 60. . . Act 10 Jan., location from Springfield to the Illinois river; Laws 1825, 81. . . Act 13 Jan., re-location from Fairfield to Carmi; Laws 1825, 91. . . Act 14 Jan., locating from Prairie Du Rocher to Cahokia; Laws 1825, 104. . . Act 14 Jan., location from Wakefield's settlement to Paris; Laws 1825, 105. . . Act 14 Jan., location from Vandalia to Atlas *via* Carrollton; Laws 1825, 107. . . Act 15 Jan. location from Carmi to Shawneetown; Laws 1825, 115. . . Act 15 Jan., road commissioners under the act of 10 Feb. 1823, to account; Laws 1825, 128.

1826.—Act 18 Jan., legalizing the survey from Springfield to Paris by Amos Williams; Laws 1826, 49. . . Act 19 Jan., amending the act of 14 Jan. 1825, "establishing a public road from Vandalia to Atlas *via* Carrollton;" road from Troy, *via* Greenville, to Vandalia a public highway; Laws 1826, 57. . . Act 20 Jan., location from Springfield to Quincy; Laws 1826, 61. . . Act 20 Jan., amending the act of 15 Jan., 1825, "requiring certain road commissioners to account;" Laws 1826, 62. . . Act 23 Jan., location from Peoria to the Indiana state line; Laws 1826, 67. . . Act 25 Jan., compensation to the commissioners for laying out a road from Carmi to Shawneetown, Springfield to the Illinois river, and from Paris to Wakefield's settlement; Laws 1826, 73. . . Act 25 Jan., re-location from Fairfield to Vandalia; Laws 1826, 74. . . Act 28 Jan., payment for locating the road from the Gallatin county saline to Littleton's ferry under the act of 23 Dec. 1824; Laws 1826, 91 §4.

1827.—Act 12 Feb. 1827; road from Mt. Vernon to Carlyle a highway; also, road from Equality *via* John Black's and Josiah L. Potts' to Ford's ferry on the Ohio river; also, the road from Carlyle through Bond county to Sangamon county; also, the road from Springfield to Peoria *via* Samuel Musick's and Thomas Dillon's; R. S. 1827, 347. . . Act 23 Jan., from Embarrass river to the Wabash opposite Vincennes; $1,000. to improve; Pr. Laws 1827, 12. . . Act 24 Jan., from W. C. Wiggin's house to the bluffs near George Swiggarts; amending the act authorizing; Pr. Laws 1827, 13. . . Act 31 Jan., from bridge opposite Vandalia through the bottom to east bluff; $1,000. allowed to finish; Pr. Laws 1827, 20.

1829.—Act 20 Jan., location from Illinoistown *via* the French village and Belleville, to Kirkpatrick's on Little Muddy in Franklin county; from Kirkpatrick's to Big Muddy declared a state road; location from Hillsborough to Paris, also from Lawrenceville to Springfield; the main road from Vandalia *via* Hillsborough and Widow Ferrel's to Springfield a state road; location from Curtis' bridge on Shoal creek *via* Joseph Duncan's to Edwardsville; Laws 1829, 121 §§4—11. . . Act 20 Jan., the roads last laid out from Carrollton and from Jacksonville to Thomas Beard's ferry declared public highways; the road from Abraham Irvin's *via* McLeansboro to George McKinzey's declared a state road; location from said McKinzey's to Equality; Laws 1829, 131. . . Act 20 Jan., location from Vandalia *via* Johnson's and Plant's bridge to Shackford's plantation near Lebanon; Laws 1829, 132. . . Act 22 Jan., survey from Beard's ferry *via* Rushville to Quincy; Laws 1829, 133 §2. Repealed; Pr. Laws 1833, 178. . Act 22 Jan., county road from Vincennes through Lawrence, Crawford, Clark, Edgar and Vermilion to Danville declared a state road; Laws 1829. 133. . . Act 22 Jan., location from Georgetown in Washington county *via* Pinckneyville to Dillinger's mill in Jackson county; Laws 1829, 136 §3. . . Act 23 Jan., location from Vincennes *via* Lawrenceville, Salem, Carlisle, Lebanon and Hathaway's to the Mississippi opposite St. Louis; Laws 1829, 136. . . Act 23 Jan., location from Vandalia to Eminence on the Mississippi; Laws 1829, 138. . . Appropriation of $700. road from Vandalia to Galconda; also, $600. road from Vandalia to Palestine; Laws 1829, (19 Jan.) 145 §12. Appropriation for bridges across the Hurricane; also Boaze's, Beck's and Hickory creeks, all on Vandalia roads; Laws 1831, (9 Feb.) 25.

1831.—Act 1 Jan., re-location in part from Paris to Vandalia; Laws 1831, 128. . . Acts 15 Jan., location from Mt. Carmel to Maysville; public road from Fairfield to Maysville; Laws 1831, 129. Location from French creek bridge to Mt. Carmel; Laws 1831, 130. . . Act 22 Jan., location from Hillsboro to Shelbyville; Laws 1831, 131. . . Act 27 Jan., re-location in part from Springfield to Paris; Laws 1831, 132. . . Act 28 Jan., location from Mt. Carmel to Fairfield; Fairfield to Salem; Salem to Vandalia; vacation from Fairfield to the St. Louis and Vincennes road; declared to be state roads—from Ford's ferry to Mt. Vernon; Equality to Mt. Vernon; Golconda to Salem; from . . . to Shelbyville; Laws 1831, 133. . . Act 22 Jan., payment to Abner Eads and others for location of road from Peoria to the Indiana line; re-location east of Danville; Laws 1831, 135. . . Act 15 Jan., location from Vincennes to Chicago; Laws 1831, 137. . . Act 7 Jan. 1831; location from Lawrenceville to Shelbyville; Laws 1831, 139. . . Act 7 Jan., location from Henderson's to Jacksonville; Laws 1831, 140. . . Act 1 Jan., payment for viewing a road from Vandalia to Eminence; Laws 1831, 142. . . Act 28 Jan., location from Shelbyville to Paris; Laws 1831, 142. . . Act 5 Feb., location from Springfield to Rock Island; Laws 1831, 144. . . Act 5 Feb., re-location from Vandalia to Kaskaskia; road from Brownsville to the Golconda and Vandalia, road a state road; Laws 1831, 145. . . Act 9 Feb., location from Carmi to the Wabash river; re-location from Albion to Bon Pass; Laws 1831, 146. . . Act 10 Feb., location from Greenville to Shelbyville; Laws 1831, 148. . . Act 10 Feb., location from Pekin to Big Grove in Vermilion county; Laws 1831, 150. . . Act 14 Feb., re-location from Vandalia *via* Carrollton to Atlas; Laws 1831, 153. . . Acts 15 Feb., location from the Cumberland road to Kaskaskia; New Nashville to Gill's ferry; Lively's ferry to Kirkpatrick's bridge; Tatman's ferry to Belleville; Belleville to Gordon's; Laws 1831, 155. Location from Alton to Beardstown; Galena to Beardstown; Laws 1831, 157.

1833.—Act 27 Feb. 1833; time for commissioners to act under the road laws of 1833 extended; R. S. 1833, 436. . . Act 25 Feb., from Gill's ferry on the Mississippi to Little Muddy bridge in Franklin county; Pr. Laws 1833, 10. . . Act 28 Jan., from Steamboat ferry landing opposite St. Louis to Alton, Jacksonville, Macomb and Galena; Pr. Laws 1833, 33. . . Act 1 Mar., incorporating the Vincennes and Chicago Road Co.; Pr. Laws 1833, 74. . . Act 28 Jan., re-location road from Fairfield Wayne county to Carmi (Will); Pr. Laws 1833, 129. Act 28 Jan., located from Jacksonville to Burnett's ferry opposite Louisiana on the Mississippi, *via* Lynnville and Atlas; Pr. Laws 1833, 130. Act 1 Feb., located from Paris *via* Grand View to the intersection of National road near Embarass river (Coles); Pr. Laws 1833, 132. . . Act 13 Feb., located from New Nashville, (Washington) *via* Pinckneyville to the bridge on the Lumb (Jackson); Pr. Laws 1833, 133. . Act 13 Feb., part of road from Lively's ferry through Pinckneyville to Kirkpatrick's bridge (Franklin) vacated; Pr. Laws 1833, 134. . . Act 15 Feb., located from Hayne's ferry on the Illinois opposite Pekin *via* Knoxville to Denniston's ferry on the Mississippi (Mercer); Pr. Laws 1833, 135. . . Act 12 Feb., located from Golconda *via* Pinckneyville to Belleville; Pr. Laws 1833, 136. . . Act 12 Feb., located from Quincy to Macomb; Pr. Laws 1833, 137. . . Act 19 Feb., located from the mouth of the Ohio river at Trinity to opposite St. Louis, thence to Lower Alton; Pr. Laws 1833, 138. . Act 20 Feb., re locate from Vandalia to Kaskaskia in Clinton and Washington; Pr. Laws 1833, 140. . . Act 20 Feb., located from Golconda to St. Louis; Pr. Laws 1833, 140. . . Act 20 Feb., located from Decatur *via* Boston (Shelby) to the National road near Spring Point; Pr. Laws 1833, 142. . . Act 22 Feb., located from Rushville to the county seat of Hancock; Pr. Laws 1833, 144. . . Act 22 Feb., located from Lebanon to Lower Alton; Pr. Laws 1833, 146. . . Act 22 Feb., located from Greenville to Jacksonville; Pr. Laws 1833, 147. . . Act 25 Feb., located from Decatur *via* Athens to Havana, and made a continuation of road from Paris to Decatur; located from mouth of Spoon river to Macomb; Pr. Laws 1833, 152. . . Act 25 Feb., located from Wilson's (Macon) *via* Bolivar to Springfield; Pr. Laws 1833, 153. . . Act 25 Feb., located from county seat of Hancock *via* the ford on Bear creek to intersect road from Quincy to Macomb; located from Wagle's (Adams) to Phillips' ferry (Pike); Pr. Laws 1833, 153. . . Act 25 Feb., located from Hillsboro to Greenville; Pr. Laws 1833, 155. . . Act 25 Feb., located from Frankfort (Franklin) *via* Jonesborough, to Ledbetter's ferry on the Mississippi; Pr. Laws 1833, 156. . . Act 25 Feb., located from Jacksonville *via* Meredosia to intersect the Quincy and Philips' ferry road near Wagle's (Adams); located from opposite Naples to intersect the last named road between Meredosia and Wagle's; Pr. Laws 1833, 156. . . Act 26 Feb., located from Paris *via* Sugar creek bridge town 14—11, to intersect state line in direction of Clinton, Ind.; vacates all other roads from Paris to Clinton; Pr. Laws 1833, 157. . . Act 26 Feb., located from Salem *via* Israel Jenning's to New Nashville; Pr. Laws 1833, 158. . . Act 26 Feb., located from Albion *via* Sumpter's mill to Salem; vacates that part of road from Mt. Carmel to Fairfield between Albion and Fairfield; Pr. Laws 1833, 159. . . Act 27 Feb., amends act 22 Dec. 1832 locating road from Beard's ferry to Alton [Laws 1833, 195] directing its location from Manchester, the present traveled route, to Alton; Act 2 Jan. 1833, requiring commissioners to meet in Springfield [Laws 1833, 187] extends time of meeting; Pr. Laws 1833, 160. . . Act 27 Feb., located from Mt. Carmel through Lawrence county to intersect National road near Spring Point; Pr. Laws 1833, 160. . . Act 27 Feb., located from a point on the Springfield and Paris road to where it intersects the state road, west of east fork of the Kaskaskia; vacates that part of road changed; Pr. Laws 1833, 161. . . Act 27 Feb., located from the bank of the Mississippi just above the great Cluster of the Dardenne islands *via* Gilead (Calhoun) and the county seat of Pike, to Rushville; Pr. Laws 1833, 162. . . Act 28 Feb., re-locating that part of Vincennes and Chicago road between Aurora and Edgar county so as to pass through Livingston; Pr. Laws 1833, 163. . . Act 28 Feb., located from Blair's ferry on the Ohio (Pope) intersecting McFarland's road near Bradford's, thence to Vandalia; the road from Golconda to Equality viewed; Pr. Laws 1833, 165. . . Act 1 Mar., located from a point on the Cumberland road east of the Kaskaskia, to New Nashville; if commissioners to re-locate from Vandalia to the Hurricane fail or refuse remaining commissioners to appoint others; Pr. Laws 1833, 165. . . Act 1 Mar., commissioners allowed $1.50 per day laying out road from Vandalia to Shawneetown and America, under act 10 Feb. 1823 [Laws 1823, 123]; Pr. Laws 1833, 166. . . Act 1 Mar., located from Young and Alexander's ferry on Rock river *via* Knoxville to Beardstown; located from Lewistown direct to Knoxville; Pr. Laws 1833, 167. . . Act 1 Mar., located from Springfield to Shelbyville; vacates other roads between points named; Pr. Laws 1833, 168. . Act 2 Mar., located from Jacksonville to Carlinville; Pr. Laws 1833, 169. . . Act 2 Mar., located from south line of Tazewell *via* Mackinaw to the mouth of the Vermilion; Pr. Laws 1833, 172. . . Act 28 Jan., located from opposite Ottawa *via* Hennepin, to Wilson's ferry on the Mackinaw; Pr. Laws 1833, 172. . . Act 28 Jan., located from the Ohio river opposite Paducah; to intersect the Belgrade and Pittallo's bluff road, near Campbell's; Pr. Laws 1833, 174.

Roads.

. . Act 18 Jan., located from Vandalia to Hurricane; Pr. Laws 1833, 175. . . Act 18 Jan., located from Danville to Ottawa; Pr. Laws 1833, 175. . . Act 18 Jan., located from Peoria to Galena; Pr. Laws 1833, 176. . . Act 14 Jan., located from Beard's ferry *via* Rushville to Quincy; repeals §2 act 22 Jan. 1829 [Laws 1829, 133]; Pr. Laws 1833, 177. . Act 7 Jan., vacates road between house of Dr. Ezra Baker jr. and Jourdon Cook, and the county road between same points declared state road; vacates road between Ransom Higgins' (Edwards) and Thomas Mason's (Lawrence) and the county road between same points declared state road; Pr. Laws 1833, 178. . . Act 12 Jan., located from Peoria *via* the mouth of Fox river, to Chicago; Pr. Laws 1833, 179. . Act 7 Jan., located from Wilcox's ferry on the Ohio (Johnson) *via* Vienna, to intersect (in Franklin) the Golconda and Vandalia road; Pr. Laws 1833, 180. . . Act 7 Jan., located from Hillsboro to Alton; Pr. Laws 1833, 181. . . Act 7 Jan., part of the road from Johnson's ferry on Fox river to New Harmony Ind., running through the farm of Wm. Witsell changed; Pr. Laws 1833, 182. . . Act 7 Jan., changed a part of the road from Henderson's Grove to Jacksonville; repeals conflicting portion of act 7 Jan. 1831 [Laws 1831, 140]; Pr. Laws 1833, 183. . . Act 7 Jan., located from Chicago to Galena; Pr. Laws 1833, 184. . . Act 7 Jan., located from Maysville (Clay) *via* Ewington to Shelbyville; Pr. Laws 1833, 186. . . Act 2 Jan., located from Springfield *via* county seat of Macoupin, to Alton; Pr. Laws 1833, 187. . . Act 2 Jan., located from Mt. Carmel *via* Lawrenceville to Palestine; from Lawrenceville to intersect road from opposite Vincennes to Chicago at Palestine *via* Lackey's and Wiggins' mill; Pr. Laws 1833, 188. . . Act 2 Jan., located from Springfield to Beardstown; Pr. Laws 1833, 189. . . Act 2 Jan., located from Chicago *via* Ottawa, Bloomington, Springfield, and Carrollton, to Grafton; Pr. Laws 1833, 190. . . Act 2 Jan., located from the Fox river crossing of the Mt. Carmel and Maysville road *via* Bonpas creek to intersect the Mt. Carmel and Maysville road at Gard's (Wabash); Pr. Laws 1833, 191. . . Act 2 Jan., located from Pekin *via* Mackinaw, to intersect the Danville and Big Grove road at post 40; Pr. Laws 1833, 192. . . Act 27 Dec. 1832, located from Beard's ferry to the head of the Des Moines rapids (Hancock); Pr. Laws 1833, 193. . . Act 27 Dec. 1832; located from Danville to Charleston; Pr. Laws 1833, 194. . . Act 22 Dec. 1832; located from Beardstown *via* Jacksonville and Carrollton to Alton; Pr. Laws 1833, 195. . Act 22 Dec. 1832; re-locating part of Vandalia and Atlas road, between Hillsboro and the mouth of Apple creek *via* Carlinville and Carrollton; Pr. Laws 1833, 196.

1835.—Act 6 Feb., amending the act for road from "Peoria to Chicago"; Laws 1835, 94. . . Act 31 Jan. 1835; changing part of road from Jonesboro to the mouth of the Ohio; Laws 1835, 95. . . Act 20 Jan., location from Bloomington to Chicago; Laws 1835, 96. . . Act 12 Feb. 1835; location from Rushville to Monmouth; Laws 1835, 97. Act 10 Feb., location from Crow's (Morgan) to Musick's bridge on Salt creek; Laws 1835, 98. . . Act 9 Feb., location from Rushville to Commerce; Laws 1835, 99. . . Act 6 Feb., road from Mt. Vernon to New Nashville a state road; Laws 1835, 100. . . Act 6 Feb., relocation from Springfield to Carlinville; Laws 1835, 100. . . Act 12 Feb., location from Blair's ferry to Vandalia; Laws 1835, 101. . . Act 10 Feb., relocation of the Peoria and Indiana road from Peoria to the east line of Tazewell county; location from Gilead *via* Pittsfield to Rushville; Laws 1835, 102. . . Act 12 Feb., location from Springfield to Lewistown; Laws 1835, 103. . . Act 7 Feb., vacation and relocation from Meredosia to John Wigle's (Adams); Laws 1835, 103. Location from Shelbyville to Chicago; Laws 1835, 104. Location from Shelbyville to Chicago; Laws 1835, 104. . . Act 13 Feb., location from Knoxville to New Boston; Laws 1835, 105. Location from Knoxville to Rock Island; Id. 106. . . Act 7 Jan., location from Hillsboro to Alton; Laws 1835, 107. Road from Paris to Terre Haute, a state road; Id. 107. . . Act 12 Feb., road from Fairfield to Mt. Vernon, a state road; Laws 1835, 108. . . Act 6 Feb., location from Moses Thomas' to Bloomington; Laws 1835, 108. Act 28 Feb. 1833; "authorizing a relocation from Vincennes to Chicago," revived; Laws 1835, 109. . . Act 27 Jan., changing part of the road from Hillsboro to Shelbyville; Laws 1835, 110. . . Act 13 Feb., location from Frankfort *via* Vienna to Wilcox's ferry on the Ohio; Laws 1835, 110. . . Act 15 Feb., changing part of road from Equality to Mt. Vernon; Laws 1835, 111. . . Act 26 Jan., location from the Wabash to the lower Yellow banks on the Mississippi; Laws 1835, 112. . Act 17 Jan., amending act 12 Feb. 1833 "locating road from Quincy to Macomb;" Laws 1835, 113. . . Act 24 Jan., relocation from Springfield to Peoria in part; relocation from Belgrade *via* Green's mill to Golconda and Vandalia road; Laws 1835, 113. . . Act 27 Jan., road from Danville to the Indiana line a state road; Laws 1835, 115. . . Act 24 Jan., location from Lebanon to Benj. Johnson's (Bond); act 22 Feb. 1833, for locating a road from Lebanon to Lower Alton, revived; Laws 1835, 115. . . Act 7 Jan., location from H. I. Mills' (Edwards) to the road from Palestine to Heath's mills; Laws 1835, 117. Act 6 Feb., location from Shelbyville to Vincennes; Laws 1835, 118. . . Act 13 Feb., location from Golconda to Pinckneyville; road from Pinckneyville *via* Lively's ferry and Belleville to St. Louis a state road; Laws 1835, 120. . . Act 12 Feb., location from Brownville *via* Pinckneyville to New Nashville; Laws 1835, 122. . . Act 7 Feb., location from Greenville to Carlinville; Laws 1835, 123. . . Act 15 Jan., improvement of road from Equality *via* Crenshaw's works to Shawneetown; Laws 1835, 125. . . Act 12 Feb., location from Equality to McLeansboro; Laws 1835, 126. . . Act 10 Feb., location from Chicago to Galena; from Paw Paw Grove *via* Princeton to Rock Island; Laws 1835, 128.

1836.—Act 15 Jan., location from Rushville to Commerce; Laws 1836, 177. . . Act. 13 Jan., location from Equality to McLeansboro; Laws 1836, 186. . . Act 15 Jan., location from Frankfort *via* Vienna to Wilcox's ferry; Laws 1836, 187. . . Act 16 Jan., location from Quincy to Macomb; Laws 1836, 188. . . Act

13 Jan., relocation from Paris to Grandview; Laws 1836, 190. . . Act 18 Jan., location from Kirkpatrick's bridge to St. Louis, also to Pinckneyville; from the town of Illinois to Alton; Laws 1836, 191. . . Act 28 Dec., location from Crow's (Morgan) to Musick's (Sangamon); Laws 1836, 193. . . Act 18 Jan., location from Pittsfield *via* Augusta and Winchester to Lynnville; Laws 1836, 194. . . Act 15 Jan., location from Maysville to Shelbyville; Laws 1836, 195. . . Act 13 Jan., relocation in part from Springfield to Lewistown; Laws 1836, 199. . . Act 16 Jan., location from Wabash *via* Greenup to Shelbyville; Laws 1836, 201. . . Act 7 Jan., location from Gilead to Rushville; Laws 1836, 203. . . Act 18 Jan., location from Peoria to Pekin and the Springfield road; report of location from Pekin and Mackinaw to Danville confirmed; Laws 1836, 206. . . Act 16 Jan., location from Peoria to Chicago; Laws 1836, 209. . . Act 15 Jan., location from Commerce to Peoria; Laws 1836, 210. . . Act 18 Jan., location from Danville to Ottawa; act 18 Jan. 1833 of like tenor repealed; Laws 1836, 211. . . Act 14 Jan., location from Peoria to Galena; Laws 1836, 212. . . Act 15 Jan., location from Quincy to Pittsfield; Laws 1836, 215. . . Act 18 Jan., location from Indiana state line *via* Marseilles to Ottawa; Laws 1836, 216. . . Act 15 Jan., location from Meacham's Grove to Galena; Belvidere to the mouth of the Pekatonica; Laws 1836, 217. . . Act 9 Jan., location from Mt. Carmel to Maysville; Laws 1836, 221. . . Act 13 Jan., location from Bonpas bridge to Bedell's mills; Laws 1836, 223. . . Act 16 Jan., location from Rushville to Warsaw; Laws 1836, 224. . . Act 13 Jan., location from Lebanon to Lower Alton; repeal of act of 24 Jan. 1835; Laws 1836, 225. . . Act 4 Mar., location from Conger's Tavern (Tazewell) to Albany (Sangamon); 1 Laws 1837, 25.

1837—Acts 24 Feb., to change the Hillsboro and Alton road over the lands of Carlew; 1 Laws 1837, 195. Location from Peoria to Princeton, *via* Chillicothe; Id. 196. From Clarksville *via* Fairfield to the Gilead and Pittsfield road; Id. 197. Relocation, in part, from Decatur to Bloomington; Id. 197. Location from Grafton to the Carrollton road, *via* Camden; Id. 198. Changing part of the road from Gilead to Rushville; part of road from Clarksville vacated; Id. 211. Location from Nashville to Equality; Id. 211. . . Act 25 Feb., location from Knoxville to Stephenson; 1 Laws 1837, 199. Relocation near Carpenter's ferry of the Springfield and Peoria road; Id. 200. Location from the Decatur and Springfield road, *via* Buffalo Heart Grove to Waynesville; Id. 201. . . Acts 27 Feb., location from Peoria to Galena *via* Osceola; 1 Laws 1837, 202. Relocation in town 19—7 of the Springfield and Peoria road; Id. 203. In part from Meredosia to Quincy; Id. 204. Location from Pekin *via* Athens, to Springfield; Id. 205. From Thornton *via* Lockport and Plainfield to Dixon's Ferry on Blackberry Creek; Id. 206. From Pinckneyville to Golconda; relocation in part, from Golconda to Frankfort; Id. 207. Location from Darwin towards Terre Haute to the Indiana state line; Id. 209. From Ottawa *via* Dixon's Ferry to Owne's at High Point; Id. 210. From Albion to Maysville; Id. 222. From Chester to Belleville *via* Preston; Id. 306. . . Acts 28 Feb., location from Beardstown to Mt. Sterling; 1 Laws 1837, 203. From Tully in Missouri to the Quincy and Macomb road, *via* McFaddens; Id. 232. From Chester to Waterloo, *via* Evansville; Id. 248. Location from Shawneetown to Golcond; Id. 259. Relocation from Pinckneyville to Grand Coat Prairie; from Shawneetown to Kaskaskia; Id. 286. Location from opposite Burlington to Farmington, *via* Augustine; Id. 298. Location from Monmouth *via* Grandview to Stephenson; Id. 299. . . Act 18 Feb., location from Danville to Ottawa; 1 Laws 1837, 213. . . Acts 15 Feb., location from Orendir's (Marion) to Nelson's (Clay); 1 Laws 1837, 214. From Waterloo to Nashville, via Tamarawa; Id. 215. Road from Peoria to Knoxville a state road; Id. 262. Location from Washington to Columbia; Id. 268. From Equality to Vienna; Id. 268. Location from LaFayette to Ottawa; Id. 285. . . Acts 16 Jan., location from Shelbyville to Danville; 1 Laws 1837, 218. Roads from Carrollton *via* Fayette to the county line, and from Jacksonville to Alton *via* Fayette, declared state roads; Id. 224. Relocation in part from Paris to Decatur; Id. 228. Location from Ottawa to Naperville; Id. 229. . . Acts 1 Mar., location from the Indiana line to Mineral Point *via* Winchester; 1 Laws 1837, 219. From Carlinville to Greenville; a former act repealed; Id. 220. Reviving act 13 Jan. 1836, "to locate a road from Bon Pas Bridge to Bedell's Mills"; Id. 222. Location from Meacham's Ferry to Carlinville, *via* Glasgow; from Bridgeport to the Montezuma and Glasgow road; Id. 225. From Danville to New Castle, *via* Syracuse; Id. 260. Map of the road from Meacham's Grove in Cook county to Galena; Id. 269. Location from Decatur to Carlinville *via* Edinburgh; Id. 270. From Meredosia to Warsaw; Id. 272. From Commerce to Farmington; Id. 287. From Liberty to Pinckneyville; Id. 302. Location from Marshall to Charleston; Id. 258. . . Acts 10 Feb., location from Vandalia to Alton *via* fork of Wood river; 1 Laws 1837, 221. From Atlas to the South line of Adams county, *via* Rockport; Id. 251. From Hennepin to Springfield, *via* Hudson; Id. 252. From Peoria to Hendersonville, *via* Prince's Mill; Id. 267. . . Acts 19 Jan., location from Crow's to Jacksonville, *via* Musick's bridge and Robertson's Mill; 1 Laws 1837, 223. Location from Macomb to opposite Burlington; Id. 236. . . Acts 2 Mar., location from Newton to Decatur, *via* Essex; 1 Laws 1837, 224. From Danville to Decatur; Id. 230. From Enterprise to Knoxville, *via* Kinnorwood, Windsor and Frazier's Grove; Id. 231. From Princeton to Paw Paw Grove; Id. 240. From Jacksonville to Bloomington, *via* Greensburg; Id. 280. From Ellisville to Macomb; Id. 283. From Grand View to Paris; Id. 291. From White Hall to Pittsfield *via* Wilmington; Id. 300. From White Hall to Fayette, *via* Greenfield; Id. 301. From Lake fork bridge to the Dry Fork of the Macoupin; Id. 303. . . Acts 4 Mar., location from Pekin to Paris, *via* Clinton; 1 Laws 1837, 226. Relocation from Chicago to Oregon City; Id. 273. Location from Vandalia to Springfield, *via* Edingburg; Id. 277. From Windsor to Bloomington, *via* Columbia;

Id. 290. From Hardy Foster's to Shelbyville; Id. 293. Relocation, in part, from Frankfort to Jonesboro; Id. 295. From Springfield to Shelbyville; Id. 297. Location from the Peoria and Ottawa road, *via* Hanover, to the Chicago and Vincennes road; Id. 302. Relocation from Jonesboro to the mouth of the Ohio; location from Freeman's ferry to Herralds; Id. 308. . . Acts 3 Mar., Location from Cleveland to Versailles; 1 Laws 1837, 227. From Shawneetown to Equality; Id. 229. From Covington to Nashville; Id. 232. From Griggsville to Joshua Hanks,' *via* Portland; Id. 239. From Anderson's Bridge (Madison), to B. Johnson's (Bond), *via* Marine town; Id. 271. Relocation, in part, from Palestine to Shelbyville; Id. 277. Location from Marshall to Grandview; Id. 282. From Stephenson to the mouth of the Pickatonneka, *via* Dixon; Id. 283. From Jacksonville to Pekin, *via* Havana; Athens to Havana, *via* Greenburg; Id. 288. From Ottawa to the state line, *via* Munson; Id. 289. From Grafton to Wood River; Id. 292. From Wesley City to Bloomington; Id. 294. From McLeansboro to Golconda; Id. 296. . . Acts 31 Jan., location from Peoria to Knoxville; 1 Laws 1837, 235. Also from Peoria to Quincy, *via* Canton; Id. 241. Relocation from Naples to Centreville; Id. 245. Location from Shokokon to Rushville *via* La Harpe; Id. 246. Relocation from Shelbyville to the Wabash; Id. 247. Location from the Indiana line to the Paris and Springfield road; Id. 248. . . Act 11 Feb., location from Galena to Beardstown; 1 Laws 1837, 237. . . Acts 27 Jan., location from Salem to Chester, *via* New Nashville; 1 Laws 1837, 240. Vacation in part from Rushville to Commerce; Id. 243. . . Act 4 Feb., location from Warsaw to Peoria; 1 Laws 1837, 249. . . Acts 7 Feb., location from Utica to Farmington, *via* Aurora; 1 Laws 1837, 251. From Ottawa to Grandature, and thence to the Galena and Peoria road; Id. 254. From Stephenson to Peoria, *via* La Grange and LaFayette; Id. 256. From Quincy to Philip's Ferry; Id. 257. Relocation in part from Gilead to Rushville; Id. 261. Location from Henderson to Morristown, *via* Andover; Id. 261. From Charleston to Springfield; Id. 263. From Shelbyville to the Danville and Chicago road, *via* Urbana; Id. 263. From Fairfield to Monmouth; Id. 264. From Shawneetown to Gill's ferry; Id. 266. Relocation from Liberty to Tremont; Id. 269. Continuing the Shawneetown road to Chicago, *via* Fairfield, Greenup and Charleston; Id. 305. Location from French creek bridge to Bon Pas creek; Id. app. xv. . . Act 28 Feb., location from Hennepin to mouth of Rock river, *via* Windsor; 1 Laws 1837, app. xv. . . Acts 20 July, relocation from Rushville to Carthage; 2 Laws 1837, 60. Time allowed to all the commissioners of 1837; Id. 61. Location from Knoxville to New Boston legalized; Id. 62. From the Indiana state line at the Sac trail towards Madison, *via* Lockport; Id. 64. From Beardstown to Petersburg, *via* Richmond; Id. 65. From Appanoose to the Drowning Fork of Crooked Creek; part of road from Beardstown to Commerce vacated; Id. 67, 68. . . Act 21 July, relocation in part from Vandalia to Jacksonville; 2 Laws 1837, 61. Location from Alton to Gwinn's on the Dry fork of the Macoupin; Id. 70. Relocation from Crow's (Morgan) to Musick's bridge (Sangamon); state road from Springfield to Rochester; location from Lawrenceville to Russellville; Id. 71. Location from Albion to H. I. Mills' (Edwards); Id. 72. From Salem to Charleston, *via* Ewington; Id. 73. Relocation in part from Springfield to Beardstown; location from Cartwright's (Sangamon) to New Virginia; Id. 73 and 80. Location from Munson *via* Paw Paw Grove to the Wisconsin line; Fox river to Oregon; Peru to the Indiana line towards LaFayette; Pontiac to the State line; Juliet to Rock Island, *via* Georgetown; Carlinville to Grafton *via* Jerseyville; Id. 74—76. Location from Canton to Knoxville; Lewistown to Knoxville, *via* Fairview; St. Marion (Ogle) to Savannah; Hennepin to Fulton *via* Prophetstown; Id. 76—79. Location from Bowling Green to Newton *via* Ewington; Vandalia to Carlyle; Id. 79. New commissioners under act 1 Mar. 1837 to locate road from Decatur to Harris Point *via* Edinburg; Id. 83. . . Acts 22 July 1837; relocation from Shelbyville to Vandalia, in part; concerning the location of the road from Vandalia to Springfield, and from Foster's (Marion) to Shelbyville; 2 Laws 1837, 83. Location from Petersburg to Macomb; state road from Salem to Greenville; Martin's Ferry (Clinton) to Alton; Id. 84.

1839.—Act 26 Feb., to legalize the plat and survey from Peoria to Knoxville, and from Peoria to Hendersonville; Laws 1839, 45. . . Act 2 Mar., *Locations:* from Robertson's (Gallatin) to Sarahsville (Franklin); Parkin's Ferry to near Brownville; Laws 1839, 56. McLeansboro to Mt. Vernon; Id. 57. Danville to the Indiana line; Newton to Vandalia and Maysville road; Id. 58. From Four mile Prairie to Louisville; Slocumb's mill (Marion) to Maysville; Louisville to Mt. Carmel road; Clay county line to Charleston; Id. 59. From Carlinville to Greenville; Upper Alton to Greenville; Id. 60. From Lexington (Morgan) to Matanzas *via* Virginia; Pope's creek (Knox) to Stephenson (Rock Island); New Albany to Genesee; Id. 61. From New Boston to Richmond (Henry); Juliet to the Indiana line; Farmington to Richmond; Macomb to opposite Burlington; Clayton to the Rushville and Warsaw road; Id. 62. From Mt. Sterling to Liberty (Adams); Chicago to the Wisconsin line towards Madison; Id. 63. From Crystalville (McHenry) to Round Prairie and towards Mineral Point; Will county line *via* Rockford towards Mineral Point; Winnebago towards the Will county line; LaSalle to State line towards Mineral Point; Beverly (Adams) to west of Perry; Union Grove to Elkhorn Creek; Id. 64. From Ford's ferry to Jacksonville; Appanoose to opposite Burlington; Id. 65. From Columbus to Chambersburg; Quincy to Mt. Sterling; Farmington to Monmouth; Id. 66. From Springfield to Macomb; Vandalia to Springfield; Andover to the Mississippi opposite Port Byron; Id. 67. From Salem to Charleston; Indiana line to Ottawa; Shelbyville to Chicago; Naples to Bloomfield; Hennepin to Victoria; Rockford to Savannah; Id. 68. From Charleston to Shelbyville; Louisville to Onslott's; Id. 70. From Gill's ferry to Shawneetown, Id. 71. *Relocations:* From Golconda to Pinckneyville; Laws 1839, 57. Frankfort to Wilcox's ferry; Id. From Palestine to

Shelbyville; Id. 58. From Vandalia to Carlyle; Id. 59. From Waynesville to Bloomington; Carlinville to Meacham's ferry; Id. 60. From Galena to Phrophet's town; Id. 61. From Quincy to Philip's ferry; Knoxville to New Boston; Rushville to Carthage; LaFayette to Leek's Mill (Knox); Id. 63. From Carlinville to Jacksonville; Hillsboro to Alton; Meredosia to Mt. Sterling; Rushville to Quincy; Id. 65. From Kishwaukee to Freeport; Peoria to Burlington; Decatur to Bloomington; Id. 66. From Warsaw to Canton; Id. 67. From Maysville to Shelbyville; Id. 68. From Dorwin to New Richmond; Union Prairie to Charleston; Atlas to Kinderhook; Douglass to Carlinville; Id. 69. From Peoria to Knoxville; Danville to Shelbyville; Charleston to Springfield; Id. 70. *Vacation:* From Beardstown to Mt. Sterling; Laws 1839, 65. . . Acts 12 Feb., re-location in part from Stephenson to the mouth of the Pickatonica; Laws 1839, 75. Location from Beardstown to Manchester; Ibid. 101. . . Acts 16 Feb., re-location in part from Vandalia to Salem; Laws 1839, 122. Re-location from Thornton to Lockport; Id. 123. Location from Jonesboro to Ryburns (Franklin); Id. 124. Location from Naperville to Indian creek (McHenry); Id. 125. Acts 21 Feb., location of a road through Vermilion and Champaign counties; Laws 1839, 142. Re-location in part from Mt. Carmel to Graysville; state road from Mount Carmel to Lawrenceville; vacation in part from Mt. Carmel to Maysville; Id. 147. . . Act 22 Feb., re-location in part from Peoria to Knoxville; Laws 1839, 153. Location from Mt. Sterling to Macomb; Ibid. Re-location from Calhoun county to Schuyler county; Id. 157. Location from Warsaw to Lima; Id. 158. . . Act 23 Feb., re-location in Crawford and Lawrence counties of the Chicago and Vincennes road; Laws 1839, 170. . . Act 26 Feb., re-location in part from Equality to Vienna; Laws 1839, 172. Location from opposite Pekin to Canton; Id. 174. . . Act 23 Feb., re-location from Monmouth to Illinois City (Rock Island); Laws 1839, 183. . Act 26 Feb., location from Mount Sterling to Springfield; Laws 1839, 187. . . Act 27 Feb., location from Rushville to Pittsfield; Laws 1839, 190. From Shelbyville to Decatur; Ibid. From Chicago to Madison (Wisconsin); Id. 193. From Middle Fork (Franklin) to Maulding's mills (Wayne); Id. 194. Re-location in part from Mt. Vernon to Nashville; Id. 202. . . Act 28 Feb., location from Bainbridge to Jonesboro; Laws 1839, 206. . . Act 1 Mar., relocation from Appanoose (Hancock) to the Drowing Fork of Crooked creek (McDonough); Laws 1839, 238. . . Act 2 Mar., location from Tremont to Josephine (McLean); Laws 1839, 243. Location from Winchester to Wilmington (Greene); Id. 247. From Nashville to Belleville; Id. 248. From Fox river (Kane) to Dixon's ferry (Ogle); Id. 249. From Salem to Pinckneyville; Ibid. From the Vermilion and Iroquois line to Joliet; Id. 254. From Jameson's ferry to opposite Cape Girardeau; Id. 255. From Huey's (Clinton) to the northeast corner of Fayette county; Id. 256. From Charleston to Keller's (Macon); Id. 260 From the Peoria and Galena road *via* Osceola to the Peoria and Knoxville road; Id. 263. From Rochester (Peoria) to Stephenson (Rock Island); Ibid. From Belleville to Brownsville (Jackson); Id. 271. From Shelbyville to Hillsboro; Id. 275. Location from the west line of Will county to the county seat of Winnebago; Id. 290. . . Resolution for the establishment of a mail route from Carlyle to the mouth of the Ohio; Laws 1839, 298.

1840.—Act 18 Jan., to revive an act of 27 Feb. 1839 "to locate a certain state road therein mentioned;" Laws 1840, 22. . . Act 1 Feb., location from Petersburg to Waverly; Laws 1840, 64. Relocation in part from Decatur to Danville; Id. 85. . . Act 3 Feb., location from the Little Muddy to Benton and thence to Galatia; Laws 1840, 105.

1841.—Acts 26 Jan., location from McLeansboro to Pinckneyville; Laws 1841, 220. Relocation in part from Paris toward Clinton, Indiana; also, of several other roads out of Paris; Id. 221. . . Act 27 Jan., location from Shawneetown to Vienna; Laws 1841, 222. . . Act 18 Feb., location from B. Johnson's (Bond) to Lebanon; road from Hickory Grove to Lebanon vacated; Laws 1841, 223. . . Act 19 Feb., from Dutchman's Point to Chicago; Shawneetown to Vienna; Equality to Marion; re-location from Quincy to Macomb, in part; Springfield to Beardstown; Auburn to New Richmond (Clark); Hunt's bridge (McDonough) to Appanoose (Hancock); Greenville to Jacksonville; Jacksonville to Carlinville; McLeansboro to Mt. Vernon; Jacksonville to Springfield; Carlinville to Jacksonville; Jacksonville to Winchester; Laws 1841, 224. Location from Columbus to Brooklyn (Schuyler); Id. 227. Location from Moore's (Bond) to Van Burensburg (Montgomery); Carlinville to Berlin; Id. 228. From Peoria to Fairview; Id. 229. From Columbus to Houston; Id. 230. From Shelbyville to Lawrenceville; Id. 231. . . Acts 26 Feb., location from Urbana to Marion (DeWitt); Laws 1841, 244. State road from Chicago to Sand Ridge; Id. 245. . . Act 26 Feb. 1841; to extend the time for H. W. Cleveland to build a bridge and causeway across the Winnebago swamp; Laws 1841, 44. I. D. Patterson to build a bridge across Salt creek in Menard and Mason counties; Ibid. . Acts 27 Feb., relocation in part from Hillsborough to Jacksonville; Laws 1841, 246. Concerning the toll gates on the Great Western Mail route; Id. 247. Relocation in part from Carlyle to Vandalia; location from Jacksonville to Mauvisterre creek; relocation from Palestine to Vandalia, in part; part from Jacksonville to Griggsville; location from Oliver's Grove (Livingston) to Peoria; from Shelbyville to Chicago; relocation in part from Jonesboro to Cruse's; location from Hillsboro to Shelbyville; relocation in part from Decatur to Sidney; from Carlinville to Hillsboro; location from McLeansboro to Bear creek bridge; relocation in Coles county; state road from LeRoy to Lexington; location from Ottawa to the Wisconsin line; relocation of the Kaskaskia road; location from Decatur to Macoupin Point; from Mt. Vernon to Brownsville; from Geneva to Warrenville; from Lima to Nauvoo; from Four mile prairie to Louisville; Laws 1841, 249—253 §§1—25. Location from York to Watertown (Clay); Id. 253. Relocation in part, from Monmouth to

Illinois city (Rock Island); road from Farmington to Weathersfield confirmed; Id. 255. Location from Richmond (Coles) to the Shelbyville and Vandalia Road; Id. 255.

1843.—Act 21 Jan., relocation in part from Equality to Benton; Laws 1843, 245. Act 24 Jan., location from Harrison's (Monroe) to Prairie Du Pont; Laws 1843, 247. . . Acts 3 Feb., location from Belvidere to Little Fort; Laws 1843, 248. . . Quincy to Augusta; Ibid. Taylorville to Zanesville; Id. 249. . . Act 2 Feb., location from Marion to Jonesboro; Laws 1843, 250. . . Act 8 Feb., location from Lancaster to Peoria; Laws 1843, 251. . . Act 24 Jan., location from Princeton to Pawpaw grove; Laws 1843, 253. . . Acts 23 Feb., location from Chicago to Grand de Tour; Laws 1843, 256. Confirming the survey and location from Charleston to Peoria; Ibid. Location from Petersburg to Macomb; Id. 257. Location from Jemison's ferry to Cape Girardeau; Id. 258. From Fox River to Gary's Mills (Du Page); Ibid. . Act 24 Feb., location from Vandalia to Hickory hill near the Hamilton line; Laws 1843, 259. . Act 1 Mar., location from Lewistown to Monmouth; Laws 1843, 261. Acts 3 Mar., location from Hendersonville to Millersburg; Laws 1843, 262. Location from Chicago to Dixon; from Elgin to the Oregon road; Id. 263. Location from LaSalle to Inlet Grove; Id. 264. . . Acts 4 Mar., location from Josephine (Woodford) to Knoxville; Laws 1843, 266. Location from Frederickville to Macomb; Id. 267. From Wright's (Iroquois) to Portland (Cook); Id. 268. . . Act 6 Mar., location from St. Charles to Rockford; Laws 1843, 268. . . Act 4 Mar., location from Brown's (St. Clair) to Nashville; Laws 1843, 269.

1845.—Located from Mt. Sterling to Springfield *via* Arenzville; Havana to Clinton *via* Big Grove; road from Wright's to McHenry a state road; from St. Charles to Brawdies' Grove, in Ogle county; Naperville to the steam mill bridge in Cook county; Farmington to Monmouth; Golconda to Elizabethtown; from the outlet of Lake Peoria to Bloomington; Olney to Richland; LaSalle to Homer; Dixon to Daysville; David Strain's to Middleport; Postville to Mechanicsburg; Mendon to Carthage; York to Watertown; Fulton City to Oregon; Des Plaines river to Aurora and Dixon road; Toulon *via* La Fayette and Walnut Grove to Oquawka; Charleston and Darwin pike state road; certain roads in Lee county legal; location from Ottawa to Peru; Mount Carmel to Chicago; Peru to Galena; Belvidere and Little Fort; Fredericksville to Virginia; Chester to Murphysboro; Peru to Nathan Pattan's; Nathan Pattan's to Bloomington; Knoxville to Josephine; Clear Creek to Bowle's Farm; Vandalia to the Fairfield road; Mt. Pleasant to Springfield; York to Martinsville; Henry to the Indiana state line; Charleston to Mt. Pleasant *via* Monticello; Massac to Union Point; Bath to Vermont; Equality to Marion; re-location from Chicago to Grand de Tour; Galena to Freeport re-located; located from Springfield to Bath; bridge across Sangamon river; Northampton to Boyd's Grove; part of road from Quincy to Mt. Sterling vacated; Worchester to Carthage; act 1 Mar., Laws 1845, 81. . . Part of the Northern Cross railroad near Naples, declared a state road: Mt. Carmel and Alton railroad, between the Wabash and Albion, declared a state road; location of a road to Western Saratoga, (Union) declared valid; act 28 Feb., Laws 1845, 103. . . Re-location from Amity to Highland; re-location of the St. Louis road out of Amity; act 28 Feb., Laws 1845, 104. . . Location in Union county; act of 1 Mar., Laws 1845, 139. . . Location from Van Burensburg to George Moore's *via* Mulberry Grove; act 26 Feb., Laws 1845, 166. . . Re-location of part of the road from Griggsville to the Mississippi, near Kinderhook: act 1 Jan., Laws 1845, 186. . Location from Columbiana to J. Andrew's cabinet shop; act 27 Feb., Laws 1845, 189. . . Location from St. Mary's to Cumberland; act 21 Jan., Laws 1845, 193. . . Location from Pinckneyville to Liberty *via* Princeton; act 26 Jan., Laws 1845, 196. . . Location from Little Rock to the steam mill bridge in Cook county; act 21 Jan., Laws 1845, 218. Location from Elgin to Sycamore; act establishing a road from Elgin to the Oregon road, 3 Mar. 1843, repealed; act 10 Feb., Laws 1845, 233. . . Location from Mt. Sterling to Griggsville; act of 3 Mar., Laws 1845, 277. . . Legalizing the location from Belvidere to Little Fort; act 3 Mar., Laws 1845, 279. . . Location from Chicago to Miller's Grove; act 26 Feb., Laws 1845, 290. . . Location from Batavia to David Bennett's, in Du Page county; act 11 Feb., Laws 1845, 291. . . Re-location of the Vincennes and St. Louis road, near Salem; act 11 Feb., Laws 1845, 333. . Re-location of part of road from Salem to Vandalia; act 21 Feb., Laws 1845, 348.

1847.—Located from Decatur to Edwardsville; act 1 Mar., Laws 1847, 88. . . Road through Moore's lane (Scott) to Mechanic's ferry on the Illinois river; act 27 Feb., Laws 1847, 91. . . Darwin, Charleston and Springfield turnpike; road from Marshall's grove to Sullivan; act 1 Mar., Laws 1847, 91. . . From Sparta to Thomas Ferrill's (Union); state road located; act 1 Mar., Laws 1847; 93. . . Location from Salem to the Marion line towards Greenville; bridge across the Okaw at Keyes' post (Clinton); act 27 Feb., Laws 1847, 93. . . From Equality to Marion; Rockford to Ottawa; Astoria to Fulton; Bridgeport to Pittsfield; Bridgeport to Wilmington; Harrison's to Prairie de Pont; Chicago to Dixon; LaSalle to Savannah; La Salle to Grand de Tour; Chicago to Rockford; Bloomington to Spring Bay; Kaskaskia to St. Louis; Beardstown to above Rock river on the 4th meridian; Springfield to Liverpool; Liverpool to Canton; from north line of Massac, on the third meridian, to the Illinois in La Salle; Bloomington to Farmington; Lewistown to Petersburg; Peru to Galena; DuPage county to Kane county; part of Wabash and Shelbyville road vacated; from DuPage county to Aurora; Lacon towards Lafayette, Indiana; Main street in Quincy extended from Wood street one mile east; Edwardsville to Decatur; Spring Bay to Hennepin, (repealed 1 Mar. 1847; Laws 1847, p. 89, §5); Havana to Crane creek; expenses of the Darwin and Charleston turnpike through Christian county; Ottawa to Peru; act 1 Mar., Laws 1847, 95. . . From Fox river to Rock river; act 28 Feb., Laws 1847, 102. . . From Batavia to Bennett's (DuPage); act 28 Feb., Laws 1847, 103. . . From Rockford to the state line; act 28 Feb., Laws 1847, 103. . . The Northern Cross railroad in Adams county a state road; act 26 Feb., Laws 1847, 103. . . Bath to Waverly; act 19 Feb., Laws 1847, 104. . . Liverpool to Canton; act 17 Feb., Laws 1847, 105. . . Knoxville to Macomb; act 15 Feb., Laws 1847, 105. Springfield to Alton; act 15 Feb., Laws 1847, 106. . . Vacation of part of the road from Cairo to Jonesboro; from Equality to Marion located; act 15 Feb., Laws 1847, 107. . . From Jacksonville to Alton; act 15 Feb., Laws 1847, 107. . . From Worcester (McDonough) to county line, re-location; act 13 Feb., Laws 1847, 108. . . Repeal of act locating road from Vandalia to McLeansboro; act 16 Jan., Laws 1847, 108.

1849.—Act 12 Feb., Pekin to Decatur; Carrollton to Columbiana; Columbiana to Hamburg; Sycamore to Marengo; Waverly to Miller's ferry; Newton to Martinsville; proviso in §6 of the act 27 Feb. 1847, to locate a road and build a bridge, repealed; Thomas Keys and others to build said bridge; Sullivan to Decatur; Walnut Hill to Okaw Bottom; Petersburg to Lewistown; Marion to Pinckneyville; Peru to Knox's Grove; Monmouth to Keithsburg; Sycamore to Marengo and the state line; a road in Kane county; Ovid A. Knox's Grove to Peru; certain reports under §§2 and 8 of the act 1 Mar. 1847, legalized; Nashville to Chester; vacation of a road through a school section in Morgan county; change of road through Liberty (Morgan); Laws 1849, 146. . . Bradley's house to Gillespie's prairie; act 25 Jan., Laws 1849, 150. Location from Ottawa to Madison, Wisconsin; act 25 Jan., Laws 1849, 150. . . Mulkytown to Chester; act 2 Feb., Laws 1849, 151. . . Wabash and Shelbyville road which was vacated by act 1 Mar. 1847, revived and altered; act 9 Feb., Laws 1849, 151.

1851.—Part of road from Springfield to Beardstown re-located; act 14 Feb., Laws 1851, 91. . . To locate a road in Sangamon, Morgan and Macoupin; act 14 Feb., Laws 1851, 95. . . Brooklyn to Frankfort; act 15 Feb., Laws 1851, 114. . . Lima to Warsaw; act 15 Feb., Laws 1851, 114. . . Springfield to Carrollton; act 15 Feb., Laws 1851, 115. . . Location of part of road from Vandalia to Greenville; act 15 Feb., Laws 1851, 126. . . Chester to Troy; act 17 Feb., Laws 1851, 134. . . Re-location from Athens to Sparta; act 17 Feb., Laws 1851, 136. . . Pipe Stone creek to Tea Cup Knob; Mulkytown to Chester; act 17 Feb., Laws 1851, 137. . . Vacation between Vermont and Macomb; re-location thereof; act 17 Feb., Laws 1851, 138. . . Rushville to Greenbush; act 17 Feb., Laws 1851, 151. . . Farmington to Monmouth re-located; act 17 Feb., Laws 1851, 153. . . Location from Canton to Knoxville; Canton to Ellisville; Algonquin to John Gage's; part of act relating to road in Fulton county repealed; Canton to the mouth of Copperas creek; Urbana to Indiana line; part of act 1 Mar. 1847, repealed; (Laws 1847, 95), so that the road there laid on third meridian may vary; Astoria to Rushville; Albion to Salem; Meredosia to Warsaw; Sparta to Cairo; Palestine to Lawrenceville; act 17 Feb., Laws 1851, 176.

1852.—Union to Genoa; act 21 June, Laws 1852, 90. . . Re-location of part of road from LaSalle to Grand de Tour; re-location of part of road from Ottawa to Madison, Wisconsin; act 23 June, Laws 1852, 204. . . Relocation of part of road from Atlas to Carrollton; act 23 June, Laws 1852, 214. . . Road located from Payson to Quincy, according to notes of the surveyor; act 23 June, Laws 1852, 266.

1853.—Springfield to Mt. Pulaski; act 12 Feb., Laws 1853, 130. . . Pekin to Postville; act 12 Feb., Laws 1853, 131. . . Wabash river to Ewington; act 11 Feb., Laws 1853, 132. . . From the Illinois and Michigan canal to Lake Michigan, in Cook county; act 10 Feb., Laws 1853, 133. . . Macomb to Canton and Liverpool plank road in Fulton; act 12 Feb., Laws 1853, 133. . . Dallas city to Farmington; act 9 Feb., Laws 1853, 134. . . Re-location from Marcelline to the Mississippi; location from Ottawa to Homer; act 14 Feb., Laws 1853, 135. . . Virginia to Vermont *via* Browning and Astoria; act 10 Feb., Laws 1853, 136. . . Freeport to Savannah *via* Cherry Grove; act 14 Feb., Laws 1853, 137. . . Elizabethtown to Mt. Vernon *via* Benton; act 11 Feb., Laws 1853, 138. . . Victoria to Henderson; act 12 Feb., Laws 1853, 139. . . Murphysboro to Marion; act 10 Feb., Laws 1853, 139. . . Hutsonville to Olney *via* Robinson; act 10 Feb., Laws 1853, 140. . . Decatur to New Albany; act 11 Feb., Laws 1853, 142. . . Shelbyville to Mount Auburn; 12 Feb., Laws 1853, 143. . . Winchester to Taylorville *via* Manchester, and Virden; act 11 Feb., Laws 1853, 144. . . Cambridge to Geneseo *via* Red Oak Grove and Cambridge; act 12 Feb., Laws 1853, 145. . . Peoria to Rock Island *via* Princeville, LaFayette, Bishop Hill and Cambridge; act 12 Feb., Laws 1853, 155. . . Mascoutah to Pinckneyville *via* Elkton; act 14 Feb., Laws 1853, 156. . From the mill of William Hutchings, (Perry) to road from Sparta to Nashville; Athens to Sparta *via* Lively's Point; Lebanon to Sparta *via* Jeffersonville; act 12 Feb., Laws 1853, 158. . Taylorville to Springfield; act 12 Feb., Laws 1853, 187. . . Walnut Hill to Pinckneyville *via* Richmond; act 10 Feb., Laws 1853, 193. . Peoria to Rock Island *via* Princeville, LaFayette, Bishop Hill and Cambridge; act 11 Feb., Laws 1853, 194. . . Across the bottom to the Illinois at the mouth of Crooked creek; Elias Briggs to construct a plank road there; act 10 Feb., Laws 1853, 195. . . Shawneetown to Urbana *via* Carmi and Charleston; act 12 Feb., Laws 1853, 196. . . Lisle, (Du Page) to north line of Cook county; act 12 Feb., Laws 1853, 197. . . A certain road in Cook Co.; act 12 Feb., Laws 1853, 199. . . Re-location from Oswego to Little Rock *via* Hadden's bridge; act 10 Feb., Laws 1853, 207. . . Re-location of part of road from Peru to Galena; act 10 Feb., Laws 1853, 207. . . Re-location of part of road from Vincennes to Chicago, north of the Iroquois and south of Bever creek; act 12 Feb., Laws 1853, 205. . . Re-location of part of the Jacksonville and Vandalia road between Waverly and the Macoupin line; act 10 Feb., Laws 1853, 208. . . Re-location of part of road in Will county; act 14 Feb., Laws 1853, 209. . . Vacation of road in Durham (McHenry); act 11 Feb., Laws 1853, 213. . Re-location from

Astoria to Lewistown, in part; act 11 Feb., Laws 1853, 222. . . A road in town 34—1, in LaSalle county, not to be vacated; act 10 Feb., Laws 1853, 266. . . From Rushville to Carthage, changed in Plymouth; act 10 Feb., Laws 1853, 266. . . Re-location in Henderson and Warren counties of part of road from Farmington to Burlington, Iowa; act 14 Feb., Laws 1853, 267. . . Re-location in Tazewell county of part of road from Springfield to Ottawa; act 10 Feb., Laws 1853, 267. . . Location and relocation of certain roads in LaSalle county; Ottawa to Troy Grove; act 11 Feb., Laws 1853, 268. Location of a road from Quincy; Lima to Chili *via* Woodville; road out of Quincy by metes and bounds as specified; Henry to Weathersfield; Lacon to the Illinois Central railroad *via* Crow creek; re-location from Quincy to Clayton; act 12 Feb., Laws 1853, 270. . . Act 26 Jan., from town of Big Rock, Kane county to Little Rock, Kendall county; Pr. Laws 1853, 442. . Act 24 Jan., vacates road from Roscoe to Beloit, laid out under act 28 Feb. 1847; Pr. Laws 1853, 449. . . Act 10 Feb., located from Waverly, Morgan county, to Taylorville, Christian county; Pr. Laws 1853, 608.

1854.—Commissioners under all the acts of the session of 1853, allowed further time; act 1 Mar. Laws 1854, 10. . . Act 27 Feb., repeals act 12 Feb. 1853 locating road in DuPage, Cook and Lake; Pr. Laws 1854, 83. . . Act 28 Feb., vacates so much of road from Peoria to Quincy as runs through lands of Hart and Horton; Pr Laws 1854, 129. . . Act 28 Feb., located from town 25—4 (McLean) *via* Sickles' Grove, etc. to Harrie Gilbert's on the Wabash (Vermilion;) Pr. Laws 1854, 129. . . Act 4 Mar., changes part of road from Chillicothe to Indiantown; Pr. Laws 1854, 136. . . Act 25 Feb., commissioners to re-locate part of road from Peru to Galena; Pr. Laws 1854, 139. . . Act 4 Mar., part of road from Waverly to Vandalia re-located; Pr. Laws 1854, 142. . . Act 4 Mar., located from town 7—7 (Peoria) to Farmington; Pr. Laws 1854, 148. . . Act 4 Mar., re-located from Carlinville to Chatham; Pr. Laws 1854, 149. . . Act 1 Mar., from Algonquin McHenry county *via* Wauconda to Lake and McHenry plank road at Des Plaines river bridge; Pr. Laws 1854, 169. . . Act 28 Feb., re-located from Waverly to Zanesville; Pr. Laws 1854, 172. . . Act 1 Mar., re-locating from Farmington to Burlington, in Fulton county; Pr. Laws 1854, 179. . . Act 1 Mar., located from Clinton county to Central City (Marion); Pr. Laws 1854, 206. . . Act 28 Feb., located from the Iroquois bridge at Vincennes and Chicago road to Myers' mill (Vermilon); from Myers' mill to Covington (Ind.); Pr. Laws 1854, 210. . . Act 1 Mar., re-located from Danville to Ottawa; Pr. Laws 1854, 216. . . Act 1 Mar., located from Waverly, *via* Virden to Macoupin Point; Pr. Laws 1854, 220.

1855.—Re-location in Kendall county of the road from Ottawa to Naperville; act 15 Feb., Laws 1855, 49. . . Location from New Liberty to N. Conmer's in Johnson county; act 15 Feb., Laws 1855, 49. . . Re-location of part of Belleville and Nashville road; act 15 Feb., Laws 1855, 91. . . Re-location in part from Ottawa to Peru; act 15 Feb., Laws 1855, 92. . . Vacation from Shelbyville to Palestine, in part; act 15 Feb., Laws 1855, 93. . . Location from Ottawa to the Fall Creek bridge; act 14 Feb., Laws 1855, 95. . . Re-location in part, from Appenoose to Hunt's bridge; act 15 Feb., Laws 1855, 97. . . Location from Marion to De Soto; act 14 Feb., Laws 1856, 98. . . Re-location in part, from Carthage to Rushville; act 14 Feb., Laws 1855, 99. . . Re-location in part, from Charleston to Danville; act 15 Feb., Laws 1855, 104. Location from McLeansboro to Salem; act 15 Feb., Laws 1855, 105. Time allowed for report of location from Steam Mills (Cook) to the intersection of Aurora and Dixon road; act 15 Feb, Laws 1855, 107. . . Location from Kingston to Moore's (Pike); act 15 Feb., Laws 1855, 109. . . Location out of LaSalle; act 15 Feb., Laws 1855, 118. . . Road to Minunk station; from Lacon to the Lacon and Magnolia road; act 15 Feb., Laws 1855, 119. . . From Hamilton to Marcelline; act 15 Feb., Laws 1855, 123. . . From the Farmington road to the Canton and Liverpool plank road; act 14 Feb., Laws 1855, 136. . . Vacation in part from Shelbyville to Palestine; act 14 Feb., Laws 1855, 137. . . Road from the Ohio (Hardin) a state road; act 13 Feb., Laws 1855, 151. . Location from Centralia to A. McClelland; act 15 Feb., Laws 1855, 152. Location near Quincy; act 15 Feb., Laws 1855, 167. . . Re-location in part from York to Charleston; act 14 Feb., Laws 1855, 159. . . Location from Marion to Carbondale; act 15 Feb., Laws 1855, 160. . . Location from Walnut Grove to Keithsburg; act 15 Feb. Laws 1855, 165. . . Re-location in part from Grayville to Carmi; act 13 Feb., Laws 1855, 166. . . Location from Robinson to Marshall; act 15 Feb., Laws 1855, 167. . . Re-location in part from Grayville to Mt. Carmel; act 14 Feb., Laws 1855, 167. . . Re-location in part of the Fairfield and Monmouth road; also of the Carthage and Nauvoo road; act 14 Feb., Laws 1855, 168. . . Re-location in part of the Wabash and Shelbyville road; act 15 Feb., Laws 1855, 169. . . Location from Pleasant Hill and Burr Oak road to Danville and Ottawa road; act 15 Feb., Laws 1855, 177. . . Vacation and re-location in part from Albion to Salem; act 14 Feb., Laws 1855, 184. . . Part of Northern Cross Railroad, near Quincy, a state road; act 3 Feb., Laws 1855, 185. . . Location from Vienna to Carbondale, *via* Campbell's mills; act 15 Feb., Laws 1855, 187. . . Amending the act 12 Feb., 1853; location from Postville to Lincoln; act 12 Feb., Laws 1855, 193.

1857.—Location from Carlinville to Carrollton; act 4 Feb., Laws 1857, 48. . . Location from Pittsfield to Quincy; act 13 Jan., Laws 1857, 50. . . Vacation in part from Freeport to Savanna; act 15 Jan., Laws 1857, 53. . . Re-location in Ogle county, in part, from Grand de Tour to Chicago; act 10 Feb., Laws 1857, 58. . . Vacation near Waterloo of part of Kaskaskia road; act 16 Feb., Laws 1857, 59. . . Location from Charleston to Olney; act 16 Feb., Laws 1857, 60. . . Re-location in part from Josephine to Knoxville; act 9 Feb, Laws 1857, 62. . . Location by metes and bounds from Ottawa to Dwight; act 16 Feb., Laws 1857, 63. . Location in town 6—11 (Crawford); act 9 Feb., Laws 1857, 65. . . Re-location in Tazewell county, of the Peoria and Springfield road; act 11 Feb., Laws 1857, 67. . . Location from the southwest corner of Sangamon county to the Waverly and Virden road; act 14 Feb., Laws 1857, 68. . . From Littleton to Plymouth; act 13 Feb., Laws 1857, 69. . . Location from Shelbyville *via* Neoga, to Prairie City, and thence five miles east; act 13 Feb., Laws 1857, 70. . . From the Virden and Taylorville road to the southeast corner of Sangamon county; act 14 Feb., Laws 1857, 75. . . From Taylorville to Mt. Pulaski; act 16 Feb., Laws 1857, 76. . . From town 13—7 (Morgan) to the Cummington and Girard road; act 13 Feb., Laws 1857, 77. . . Vacation of a certain road in town 37—10 (Will); act 11 Feb., Laws 1857, 78. . . Location from Jefferson street Springfield, west to Spring creek bridge; act 7 Feb., Laws 1857, 78. . . Location from Beverly (Adams) to the east end of Snycarty road; act 29 Jan., Laws 1857, 81. . . Re-location from Aurora to the west line of Kane county; act 13 Feb., Laws 1857, 83. . . Location from the Fox river bridge at Osage, to Bristol and Plano; act 16 Feb., Laws 1857, 86. . . Re-location in part from Shelbyville to Danville; plat in Edgar county to be filed; act 16 Feb., Laws 1857, 88. . . Vacation of the Knoxville and Enterprise road in town 15—8 (Bureau); act 13 Feb., Laws 1857, 89. . . Vacation in part (Lee) of the road from Peru to Grand de Tour; act 14 Feb., Laws 1857, 89. . . Vacation near Wauconda, of the road from Algonquin; act 18 Feb., Laws 1857, 99. . . Location from North Fifth street in Springfield to the new Sangamon bridge, on the Athens road; act 9 Feb., Laws 1857, 101. . . Location from Marion to Benton; act 13 Feb., Laws 1857, 107. . . Location from Higginsville to the Ottawa road, near Ten Mile Grove; act 18 Feb., Laws 1857, 108. . . Re-location in part from Knoxville to Rock Island; from town 13—1 to Robinson's (Knox); act 19 Feb., Laws 1857, 117. . . Vacation in town 8—2 of the road from Burlington to Peoria; act 16 Feb., Laws 1857, 118. . . Re-location in Hancock of the road from Carthage to Macomb; act 16 Feb., Laws 1857, 120. . . Location from Marion to De Sota; act 18 Feb., Laws 1857, 123. . . Re-location in Vermilion county of the Ottawa and Danville road; act 16 Feb., Laws 1857, 124. . . Location from Bloomington to the Indiana line; act 17 Feb., Laws 1857, 137. . Location from Bear creek (Christian) to the Cummington and Chesterfield road; act 18 Feb., Laws 1857, 140. . . Re-location in Hancock county of the Rushville and Commerce road; act 18 Feb., Laws 1857, 144. . . Location from the Ohio and Mississippi railroad, west line of Clinton county, to Elkton; act 16 Feb., Laws 1857, 145. . . Re-location in part of the Belleville and Nashville road; act 18 Feb., Laws 1857, 146. . . Re-location of the Carthage and Worcester road, between Carthage and Crooked creek bridge; act 18 Feb., Laws 1857, 149. . . Location from town 23—10 (Ford) to Pera: act 16 Feb., Laws 1857, 153. . . Re-location of the Knoxville and Cambridge road from Wataga to Oneida; act 18 Feb., Laws 1857, 154. . . Location from Sarahsville to McLeansboro; act 16 Feb., Laws 1857, 155. . . Location from town 25—4 to town 26—5, in McLean county; act 18 Feb., Laws 1857, 155. . . Re-location in Perry county of the Chester and Pinckneyville road; act 18 Feb., Laws 1867, 156. . . Re-location from the Big Muddy (Union) to the place of John Corgis; act 18 Feb., Laws 1857, 165; see also 178. . . Location from Lacon to Middleport; act 18 Feb., Laws 1857, 167. . . Vacation in Monroe county, of the Waterloo and Harrisonville road; act 13 Feb., Laws 1857, 172. . . Construction across Horse swamp, between Marion and Equality; $777. appropriated; act 17 Feb., Laws 1857, 196. . . Re-location from Warsaw to Carthage; act 16 Jan., Laws 1857, 221.

1859.—Location from Albion to Newton; act 24 Feb., Laws 1859, 195. . . Location from the west bank of the Wabash to Effingham; act 19 Feb., Laws 1859, 196. . . Location from Indian Point to Metropolis; Indian Point road company incorporated; act 24 Feb., Laws 1859, 196. . . Location from Tamaroa to the Mississippi *via* Red Bud; act 24 Feb., Laws 1859, 198.

1861.—Act 18 Feb., located from Jeffersonville to Albion *via* New Massillon; Pr. Laws 1861, 540. . . Act 21 Feb., re-locating part of the road from Murphysboro to Jonesboro; Pr. Laws 1861, 541. . . Act 22 Feb., located from Vincennes and Chicago road to the Paris and Springfield road; Pr. Laws 1861, 541. . . Act 18 Feb., located from Pinckneyville to Liberty; Pr. Laws 1861, 543.

1863.—Location east of Mascoutah in St. Clair county; act 14 Feb., Laws 1863, 80. . . Location from State Line station to Washington; act 13 June, Laws 1863, 81.

1865.—Act 16 Feb., incorporating the Quincy and Pittsfield Macadam or Tilford Road company; 2 Pr. Laws 1865, 261. . . Act 15 Feb., amends act 18 Feb. 1861 locating a road through Perry, Randolph and Jackson; 2 Pr. Laws 1865, 266. . . Act 16 Feb., located from Beardstown to Rushville; 2 Pr. Laws 1865, 268. . . Act 16 Feb., located from Fairfield to Clay City; 2 Pr. Laws 1865, 269.

1867.—Act 9 Feb., located from Fairfield to Clay City; 2 Pr. Laws 1867, 815. . . Act 23 Feb., location from Mattoon westward to the Okaw; 2 Pr. Laws 1867, 817. . . Act 25 Feb., located from Chebanse to Odell; 2 Pr. Laws 1867, 819. . . Act 28 Feb., amends act 15 Feb. 1865 locating a road through Perry, Randolph and Jackson; 2 Pr. Laws 1867, 840. . Act 5 Mar., incorporating the Cumberland Graded Road company; 2 Pr. Laws 1867, 841. . . Act 7 Mar., road on county line between Clinton and St. Clair connecting the St. Louis and Vincennes, and the Belleville and Hanover roads; 2 Pr. Laws 1867, 844.

1869.—Act 26 Mar., to revive the act of 10 Feb. 1853 "to locate a road from Virginia to Vermont;" Laws 1869, 375. . . Act 27 Mar., road on the line between Kankakee and Iroquois counties; Laws 1869, 384. . . Act 29 Mar., location from Chester to Elkville (Jackson); Laws 1869, 385. . . Act 31 Mar., to locate a road from Galesburg to Rochester (Peoria); Laws 1869, 386. . . Act 30 Mar., location from Downey's store to Sparta; Laws 1869, 389. . . Act 8 Mar., location from the south line of Sangamon county, on the line between Macoupin and Montgomery counties to the Hillsboro road; Laws 1869, 391.

CHAP. 94. SALTPETRE CAVES.

Act 6 Feb. enclosing and guarding saltpetre caves, similar to R. S. 1845 Ch. 94; Laws 1835, 151.

CHAP. 95. SEAT OF GOVERNMENT.

Kaskaskia.—Consult Cont. 1818 Art. 8 §13.

Vandalia.—Selection of a site; seat of government to be located there for twenty years; Laws 1819 (30 Mar.) 361. . . Act 15 Dec. 1820; any two commissioners allowed to carry out the foregoing act; Laws 1821, 3. . . Act 27 Jan. acts of the commissioners confirmed; seat of government to be at Vandalia for 20 years from the first Monday of December 1820; Laws 1821, 32. . . Act 31 Jan. compensation to the commissioners for turning over their notes; Laws 1823, 98. . . Act 23 Jan. repairs to the state house in Vandalia; Laws 1829, 170. And again; Laws 1831 (16 Feb.) 185. . . Act 5 Feb. vote to be taken for a place which shall forever remain the seat of government; R. S. 1833, 572. . Act 25 Feb. act 5 Feb. 1833 repealed; vote to be taken by the two houses in joint session, 28 Feb. 1837; erection of public buildings; 1 Laws 1837, 321.

Springfield.—Supplement to the act of 1837 (25 Mar.); public square to be conveyed by Sangamon county; public buildings erected; 1 Laws 1837 (3 Mar.) 322. . . To remove the public offices; Laws 1839 (21 Feb.) 141. . . Deed of the square by Sangamon county confirmed; Laws 1847 (17 Feb.) 36.

State House—1. To complete and furnish; Laws 1839 (12 Jan.) 47. Resolution to obtain the portraits of Washington and Lafayette; Id. 294. . . Payment for work and materials; Laws 1841 (29 Jan.) 31. . . Acconnts of state house commissioners examined; Laws 1841 (26 Feb.) 301. . . Same to be settled; Id. (27 Feb.) 301. . . Care of the public buildings; Laws 1841 (26 Feb.) 302. . . Repair of the roof; Laws 1843 (24 Jan.) 289. . . Finishing the Hall of Representatives and repairing the roof; Laws 1843 (4 Mar.) 290. . . Completing vault; Laws 1843, 322. . . Completion of the state house; 1 Laws 1849 (12 Feb.) 184. Outhouses; Id. (12 Feb.) 104. Improving and ornamenting the grounds; Pr. Laws 1854 (28 Feb.) 182. Lighting with gas; Id. (1 Mar.) 137. Supply of water; Pr. Laws 1861 (22 Feb.) 295. Repair of executive office; Laws 1869 (11 Mar.) 44.

State House—2. To be erected; Laws 1867 (25 Feb.) 6 and 162. Supplemental act; Id. (27 Feb.) 164. Amendment to the acts of 1867, Laws 1869 (11 Mar.) 54. Discharge of J. Weber as secretary of the board of commissioners; Id. (27 Mar.) 401.

Governor's House—Repairs on; Laws 1847 (11 Feb.) 49. . . New house to be built; Laws 1853 (12 Feb.) 220. . . Lighting with gas; Pr. Laws 1854 (1 Mar.) 137.

CHAP. 96. SECRETARY OF STATE.

Act 19 Feb. to provide a state seal; Laws 1819, 16; Laws 1829, 155; R. S. 1833, 569. . . Act 1 Mar. defining and regulating his duties; Laws 1819, 87. . . Act 25 Mar. payment of postage upon official papers; Laws 1819, 254. . . Act 12 Feb. care of the public property in the town of Vandalia; Laws 1823, 128; Laws 1829, 170. . Act 6 Jan. stationery and firewood for the general assembly; Laws 1825, 59; Laws 1829, 74; R. S. 1833, 590. . . Act 18 Jan. care taken of public property in the two houses; Laws 1825, 184 §10. . . Act 28 Jan., sundry duties prescribed; Laws 1826, 91 §§2, 3. . . Act 15 Feb. preservation of the property of the state; former acts repealed; R. S. 1827, 324; R. S. 1833, 505. . Act 14 Feb., defining and regulating his duties; former act repealed; Laws 1831, 169; R. S. 1833, 567. . . Act 4 Mar. to receive and preserve geological specimens, etc., similar to R. S. 1845 Ch. 96 §§9—12; Laws 1843, 154.

CHAP. 97. SECURITIES.

Act 24 Mar. relief of securities in a summary way in certain cases; Laws 1219, 243 §§1—8; Laws 1829, 155; R. S. 1833, 570.

CHAP. 98. SCHOOLS.

Act 25 Mar. college township five north, 1 west to be leased until 1 April 1821; Laws 1819, 252. Act 31 Jan. auditor to lease for not less than ten years; Laws 1821, 60. . . Act 2 Mar. lands reserved for the use of schools; Laws 1819, 107 §§1—11. . . Act 24 Mar. relief of persons settled on school lands; Laws 1819, 236. . Act 18 Feb. amending the foregoing act of 31 Jan. 1821, "authorizing the auditor to lease;" Laws 1823, 179. . . Memorial to the President of the United States that the college township be taken a section in a place; Laws 1823, 214. . . Act 7 Dec. 1824; compensation to the persons who selected the seminary lands; Laws 1825, 5. . . Act 15 Jan. establishing free schools; Laws 1825, 121; R. S. 1833, 556. . Resolution for the appointment of agents to protect seminary lands, and prosecute trespassers; Laws 1825, 185. Resolution authorizing commissioners of the school fund to invest the same in auditor's warrants; Laws 1825, 186. . . Act 26 Jan. payment of the three per cent fund granted by congress; Laws 1826, 79. . . Act 26 Jan. to prevent persons from trespassing on seminary and school lands; Laws 1826, 80. . . Act 28 Jan. school funds kept in banks; Laws 1826, 95 §16. . . Act 17 Feb. amending the act of 15 Jan. 1825, "for the establishment of free schools;" R. S. 1827, 364; R. S. 1833, 554. . Act 17 Feb. relating to school lands; a consolidation of former acts which are repealed; R. S. 1827, 366. . . Act 17 Jan. commissioners of the school and seminary fund authorized to loan the same to the state; Laws 1829, 118. . . Act 22 Jan. sections 15, 16 and 17 of the foregoing act of 15 Jan. 1825, "for the establishment of free schools," repealed; also, repealing the foregoing act of 17 Feb. 1827; Laws 1829, 149. . . Act 22 Jan. sale of the sixteenth section; Laws 1829, 150. . . Act 12 Jan. sale of the seminary lands by the auditor; Laws 1829, 158. . . Act 15 Feb. amending the foregoing act of 12

Jan. 1829 for the sale of seminary lands; Laws 1831, 171. . . Act 15 Jan. amending the act of 22 Jan. 1829 for the sale of the 16th section; Laws 1831, 172 §§1—9. . . Act 1 Mar. application of the interest of the fund arising from the sale of the school lands of the townships; R. R. 1833, 562. . . Act 12 Jan. credit on sales of school land; R. S. 1833, 566. . . Act 22 Feb. confirming certain leases of school lands; R. S. 1833, 566. . . Act 13 Feb. school money to be taken from U. S. bank in St. Louis and deposited in the state treasury; R. S. 1833, 567. . Act 7 Feb. distribution and application of interest on school, college and seminary funds; Laws 1835, 22. . . Act 6 Feb. school money to be taken from U. S. bank at St. Louis and deposited in the state treasury; Laws 1835, 25. . . Act 7 Feb. amending act of 1 Mar. 1833; Laws 1835, 25. . . Act 12 Feb. security of school funds—form of mortgage, etc.; Laws 1835, 27. . Act 6 Feb. repealing so much of the act 15 Feb. 1831, as grants pre-emption rights to settlers on seminary lands; Laws 1835, 151. . . Act 15 Jan. amending the act for the "distribution and application of interest on school, college and seminary funds; Laws 1836, 249. . . Act 4 Mar. school moneys to be used to pay the state subscription to the stock of the state bank, and the bank at Shawneetown; 1 Laws 1837, 104. . Act 4 Mar. amending act 7 Feb. 1837; purchase of school lands by the inhabitants of a township; 1 Laws 1837, 312. . . Act 4 Mar. to amend the several acts in relation to common schools; 1 Laws 1837, 314 §§ 1—26. . . Resolution 18 Jan. selection of other lands in lieu of the 16th section; 1 Laws 1837, 338. . . Act 21 July construction of §3 of the last named act of 4 Mar. 1837; 2 Laws 1837, 89. . . Act 16 Feb. to establish and regulate ferries on school lands; Laws 1839, 120. . . Act 27 Feb. in addition to the several acts for the sale of school lands; Laws 1839, 191. . . Act 1 Feb re-valuation of school lands; Laws 1840, 85. . . Act 31 Jan. school commissioners to distribute school funds at the county seats; Laws 1840, 87. . . Act 18 Jan. to amend the act of 4 Mar. 1837 about the vote on being incorporated; Laws 1840, 90. . . Act 3 Feb. to amend the former acts in relation to payment of teachers; Laws 1840, 96. . . Act 7 Jan. distribution of interest on the school, college and seminary fund; Laws 1841, 166. . . Act 25 Feb. school commissioners to convey land in certain cases; Laws 1841, 257. . . Act 17 Feb. collectors to pay the school fund directly to the school commissioners; Laws 1841, 257. . . Act 26 Feb. to organize and maintain common schools; amending and consolidating the former acts which are all repealed by names and titles; Laws 1841, 259—287. . . Act 28 Feb. distribution of the interest on the school, college and seminary fund to new counties; Laws 1843, 149. . . Amending the act of 1841 (26 Feb.); Laws 1843, (20 Feb.) 281. . . A general act amending and consolidating the former statutes which are all repealed; it was in force from its passage (R. S. 1845, 585 §5.) R. S. Chap. 98, 495. Repealed; Laws 1847. (1 Mar.) 148 §119. . . Trustees exempt from military duty and road labor; R. S. 1845 (1 Mar.) 594. . . General act; Laws 1848 (1 Mar.) 119. Repealed; 1 Laws 1849 (12 Feb.) 179 §90. . . Partial certificates; Laws 1847 (11 Feb.) 149. And again; Laws 1853 (11 Feb.) 246. . . Fines given to school fund; Laws 1847 (28 Feb.) 74. And also; Laws 1853 (10 Feb.) 90. Repealed; Laws 1857 (16 Feb.) 297 §97. . . General act; 1 Laws 1849 (12 Feb.) 153. Repealed; Laws 1857 (16 Feb.) 297 §97. . . Amended; Laws 1851, (15 Feb.) 127. Payment to R. M. Young for services; Laws 1851 (17 Feb. 163. . . State superintendent; Laws 1854 (18 Feb.) 13. . . General act; Laws 1855 (15 Feb.) 51.

State Teachers' Institute.—Chartered; property limited to $25,000.; Pr. Laws 1855 (14 Feb.) 506. To have copy of laws, journals, reports, etc.; Id. 743. . . Changed to "Illinois State Teachers Association;" Pr. Laws 1857 (11 Feb.) 463.

CHAP. 99. SHERIFFS AND CORONERS.

Act 2 Mar. defining the duties of sheriffs and coroners; Laws 1819, 109 §§1—13. . . Act 20 Jan., duties of coroners; Laws 1821, 22; R. S. 1833, 578. . . Act 24 Jan. relief of ex-sheriffs, and especially Ephraim Hubbard, late territorial sheriff; R. S. 1827, 370. . . Act 12 Feb. a consolidation of former acts which are repealed; R. S. 1827, 371; R. S. 1833, 573. . . Act 7 Feb. suits on official bonds; Laws 1831, 177; R. S. 1833, 578. Officer to act until his successor is qualified; Laws 1831, 178; R. S. 1833, 578. . Act 1 Mar. execution issued to the coroner on the failure of the sheriff; Laws 1839, 217. . . Act 1 Feb. failing to pay over money collected; Laws 1840, 78.

CHAP. 100. SHOWS AND JUGGLERS.

Act 23 Jan. to prohibit shows of wax figures, tricks of jugglers, etc.; Laws 1829, 162; R. S. 1833, 582.

CHAP. 101. SLANDER.

Act 27 Dec. 1822; declaring certain words actionable; nearly the same as this chapter; Laws 1823, 82; Laws 1829, 163; R. S. 1833, 583.

CHAP. 102. STEAMBOATS.

Act 21 July to prevent disasters on steamboats, similar to Ch. 102 R. S. 1845; 2 Laws 1837, 89.

CHAP. 103. SURVEYORS.

Act 31 Jan. appointment of surveyors for the several counties of this state; their powers and duties; Laws 1821, 62. . . Act 9 Feb., commissions of surveyors; Laws 1821, 117. . . Act 14 Jan. appointment and duties of county surveyors; foregoing acts both repealed; Laws 1829, 172; R. S. 1833, 591. . . Act 13 Feb. supplemental to the act of 1829 and explanatory thereof; Laws 1835, 61. . . Act 11 Feb. election of county surveyors; Laws 1835, 165.

CHAP. 103*a*. SWAMP LANDS.

Resolution concerning U. S. patents to *bona fide* settlers; Pr. Laws 1855, 742. Resolution asking for law to confirm titles to land donated under act of Congress; Pr. Laws 1857 (16 Feb.) 1456.

CHAP. 103*b*. TELEGRAPHS.

Illinois and Mississippi Telegraph Company; charter amended; Laws 1852 (14 June) 4. Further amendment; Pr. Laws 1857 (6 Feb.) 268.

CHAP. 103*d*. TOWNSHIP ORGANIZATION.

General act; 1 Laws 1849 (12 Feb.) 190. . . General act, amending and repealing the foregoing; Laws 1851 (17 Feb.) 35. Amendment; Laws 1854 (27 Feb.) 27. . . Formation of new towns—boundaries; Laws 1857 (14 Feb.) 46. Altering and laying out roads; Id. (12 Feb.) 55. Vacancies in town offices; Id. (16 Feb.) 183. Highways on state line; Id. (7 Feb.) 62.

CHAP. 104. TRESPASS.

To prevent trespass by cutting timber; similar to this chapter; Laws 1819 (27 Feb.) 84; Laws 1829, 185; R. S. 1833, 602. Repeal of §6; R. S. 1833 (25 Feb.) 604. Jurisdiction of justices under said act; Laws 1839 (12 Jan.) 42. . Trespassing on canal lands; Laws 1835 (9 Feb.) 34.

CHAP. 105. VENUE.

Act 23 Feb. mode of changing the venue in courts of record; Laws 1819, 46. . . Act 8 Feb. notice of an application; duty of the clerk, the expenses; Laws 1821, 113. . . Act 23 Jan. changing the venue in civil and criminal cases; a consolidation of the former acts which are repealed; R. S. 1827, 381; R. S. 1833, 606. . Act 28 Feb. after the first term, similar to R. S. 1845 Ch. 105 §§6, 7, 15; Laws 1839, 198. . . Act 1 Feb. 1840; change of venue after appeal in cases of the right of way, similar to R. S. 1845, Ch. 105 §§2—4; Laws 1840, 36.

CHAP. 107. WARRANTS OF CITIES AND TOWNS.

Act 4 Mar. warrants not to circulate as money, similar to this chapter in the revised statutes; Laws 1843, 67.

CHAP. 108. WEIGHTS AND MEASURES.

Act 22 Mar. standards to be provided and kept in each county; Laws 1819, 169, 190; R. S. 1833, 660. . . Act 4 Mar. to regulate Weights and Measures; similar to Ch. 108 (R. S. 1845.); Laws 1843, 317. . . Weight of various articles; R. S. 1845. 532 §6. . . Weight of coal; Laws 1847 (18 Feb.) 168. . . Indian corn; Laws 1851 (15 Feb.) 112. Castor beans; Id. (17 Feb.) 194. . . General act; Laws 1853 (10 Feb.) 256.

CHAP. 109. WILLS.

Act 23 Mar. administrations, and the descent of intestate estates; Laws 1819, 223, §§1—25. . Act 2 Feb. sale of the real estate of minors in certain cases to pay the debts of their ancestors; Laws 1821, 72. . . Act 28 Jan. executors and administrators to sell real estate to pay debts in certain cases; Laws 1823, 90. . . Act 12 Feb. amending the act of 23 Mar. 1819; Laws 1823, 27 §§1—3. . . Act 10 Jan. register's certificates for land sold and transferred by executors, etc.; Laws 1825, 55. . . Act 10 Jan. appointment of public administrators; Laws 1825, 70. . . Act 7 Feb. executors and administrators to sell real estate to pay debts in certain cases; former acts repealed; R. S. 1827, 200. . . Act 28 Dec. 1826; revival of the above act of 10 Jan. 1825, for the "transfer of register's certificates;" R. S. 1827, 280. . . Act 23 Jan. relative to wills and testaments, executors and administrators and the settlement of estates; a consolidation of the former acts which are repealed; Laws 1829, 191; R. S. 1833, 611. . . Act 14 Feb. amends the former acts in relation to wills; Laws 1831, 191 §§1—7; R. S. 1833, 656. . . Act 25 Feb. supplemental to the act of 1829; R. S. 1833, 656. . . Act 1 Mar. supplemental to the act of 1829; R. S. 1833, 659. . . Act 2 Mar. when the probate justice is himself witness to a will, similar to Ch. 109 R. S. 1845 §5; Laws 1839, 259. . . Act 17 Feb. settlement of estates after the division of counties; Laws 1841, 22. . . Act 21 Feb. public administrators appointed for four years; Laws 1843, 10. . . Act 6 Mar. widow allowed six months to file renunciation under the will; real estate of *feme covert* dying intestate; similar to Ch. 109 (R. S. 1845) §47; Laws 1843, 319.

CHAP. 110. WOLVES.

Act 28 Jan. to encourage the destruction of wolves; Laws 1823, 86. . . Act 15 Jan. to encourage the killing of wolves; repeal of the above act; Laws 1825, 116. . . Act 28 Jan. repeal of the last foregoing act; Laws 1826, 95 §15. . . Act 15 Feb. bounty given to encourage the killing of wolves; 1 Laws 1837, 334. . Act 10 Dec. 1839; to amend the act of 1837; Laws 1840, 155. . . Act 15 Feb. county to offer a bounty; Laws 1843, 319.

PART II.

PRIVATE AND SPECIAL LAWS.

ADAMS COUNTY.

County formed and boundary defined; L. 1825 (13 Jan.) 93 §2. Respecting the county revenue; L. 1826 (27 Jan.) 89. Commissioners to stake out road from Quincy to Springfield; Pr. L. 1827 (11 Jan.) 9. Act 22 Jan., survey of a road from Beard's ferry *via* Rushville to Quincy; L. 1829, 133 §2. Repealed; Pr. L. 1833, 178. Act 15 Feb., W. B. Gooding to convey lands belonging to M. J. McCorkle, an infant; L. 1831, 124. Extends §2 of act 22 Jan. 1831 [L. 1831, 38] to last Monday in October 1833; L. 1833 (22 Feb.) 13. Act 25 Feb., Nancy, widow of Thomas Ross to invest surplus in real estate. Pr. L. 1833, 122. Act 12 Feb., vote on removing the county seat from Quincy; L. 1835, 38. Act 12 Feb., records to be copied, also deeds recorded in Rushville; L. 1835, 159. Act 15 Jan., part of revenue law repealed as to said county; L. 1836, 231. Act 3 Mar., western boundary the middle of the Mississippi; 1 L. 1837, 91. Act 12 Feb., name of Fairfield changed to Mendon; L. 1839, 81. Act 17 Feb., to incorporate the Payson Academy; L. 1841, 10. Act 20 Jan., vote on removing the county seat from Quincy to Columbus; L. 1841, 94. Act 24 Feb., John L. Hunsacker to keep a ferry across the Mississippi between Payson and Marion City, Mo.; L. 1841, 116. Act 1 Mar., tax to pay money to Marquette county; L. 1843, 92. Act 3 Feb., to legalize certain records copied by John H. Holton; L. 1843, 208. Additional justice and constable in Lima precinct; act 27 Feb., L. 1845, 159. Legalizing the sale of school lands in towns 1 N—8, 1 S—8 and 2—7; act 27 Feb., L. 1845, 162. Adelphia Theological seminary, incorporated by act of 26 Feb.; L. 1845, 283. New patents to issue to H. T. Ellis, for land in town 1 N—7; act 21 Feb., L. 1845, 299. Act 16 Feb., Silas Beebe to establish ferry across the Mississippi for 20 years, at Payson. Pr. L. 1847, 46. Act 17 Feb., incorporating the German Catholic Beneficent Brothers Society. Pr. L. 1847, 107. Act 28 Feb., incorporating town of Lima; boundary defined. Pr. L. 1847, 152. Securities on the supersedeas bond of Alonzo Pate, convicted of forgery in said circuit court, released from payment; act 9 Jan., L. 1849, 111. Northern Cross railroad in said county declared a state road; act 26 Feb., L. 1847, 103. Town of Mendon created; election herein, act 15 Feb., L. 1851, 117. Town of Payson to elect an additional justice and constable; act 17 Feb., L. 1851, 185. Act 12 Feb., Daniel Moore granted state peddler's license for life, with conditions. Pr. L. 1851, 85. Act 12 Feb., incorporating the Mendon Branch railroad Co. Pr. L. 1853, 44. Act 3 Feb., vacates town plat of Hartford. Pr. L. 1853, 487. Act 11 Feb., releases judgment rendered 25 Apr. 1843 against Richard Eells for secreting negro slave of Chauncey Durkee of Missouri. Pr. L. 1853, 488. Act 12 Feb., vacates part of town plat of Burton. Pr. L. 1853, 501. Act 12 Feb. 1853, W. Wren and H. Ballard to establish ferry across the Mississippi at mouth of Lima Lake Slough. Pr. Laws 1853, 523. Union school district created from lands in Towns 1—9, 2—9, 1—8 and 2—8; act 8 Feb., L. 1853, 186. Act 4 Mar., part of the Northern Cross R. R. appropriated as public highway. Pr. L. 1854, 213. Act 1 Mar., directors of Union School District to appoint a treasurer. Pr. L. 1854, 221. Swamp lands in said county; act 15 Feb., Laws 1855, 176. County court to be held on first Monday in each month; L. 1855 (14 Feb.) 191. Act 14 Feb., incorporating the Quincy and Mendon plank road; complete in 5 years. Pr. Laws 1855, 479. Act 13 Feb., incorporating town of Camp Point. Pr. Laws 1857, 539. Act 13 Feb., name of John Bliss changed to Chas. Wesley Long. Pr. L. 1857, 550. Constructing a levee from Millville along the Mississippi into Calhoun county; for reclaiming overflowed lands; act 10 Feb., L. 1857, 255. Act 14 Feb., Silas Brown, convicted of larceny, restored to citizenship. Pr. L. 1857, 615. Act 18 Feb., revived act 12 Feb. 1853, incorporating the Mendon Branch R. R. Co.; complete in 10 years, may extend to Warsaw; Pr. L. 1857, 1240. Taxation in district 2 in Melrose, to pay for school property and improvements; act 18 Feb., L. 1859, 179. Town 2—9 south of Bear creek attached to a school district in town 1—9; act 24 Feb., L. 1859, 181. Trustees of schools in town 2—8 to purchase a lot from Marcelline Lodge; act 24 Feb., L. 1859, 181. Act 20 Feb., incorporating the Mississippi Levee Co.; limit 20 years; Pr. L. 1861, 447. Act 22 Feb., for extending road through Ellington to intersect the Quincy and Rushville; Pr. L. 1861, 540. Act 22 Feb., incorporating the Adams County Medical Society. Pr. L. 1861, 546. Act 16 Feb., town of Fall Creek to levy special tax to pay bounties to volunteers and drafted men. 1 Pr. Laws 1865, 157. Act 16 Feb., town of Melrose to pay bounties to volunteers in U. S. service.

2 Pr. L. 1865, 164. Act 14 Feb., town of Payson to pay bounties to persons in U. S. service. 1 Pr. L. 1865, 169. Act 16 Feb., for the erection of a new court house and jail in city of Quincy. 1 Pr. L. 1865, 535. Act 16 Feb., amends act 30 Feb. 1861 incorporating the Mississippi Levee Co.; complete in 15 years; to construct a railroad thereon. 2 Pr. L 1865, 1. Act 16 Feb., incorporating the Adams County R. R. Co. 2 Pr. L. 1865, 127. Act 23 Feb., incorporating the Adams County Agricultural and Horticultural Society. 1 Pr. L. 1867, 44. Act 28 Feb., vacates certain avenues traversing part of sec. 24, Town 1—9 as platted by C. A. Savage. 1 Pr. Laws 1867, 55. Act 21 Feb., for the preservation of game and fish in said county and that of Hancock. 1 Pr. L. 1867, 989. Act 28 Feb., repeals act 16 Feb. 1865 enabling town of Fall Creek to levy a war fund tax. 3 Pr. L. 1867, 128. Act 3 Mar., vacates part of town plat of New Liberty. 3 Pr. L. 1867, 240. Act 5 Mar., incorporating town of Keokuk Junction. 3 Pr. L. 1867, 240. Act 1 Mar., incorporating town of Mendon. 3 Pr. Laws 1867, 617. Allowance to sheriff for dieting prisoners; L. 1867 (7 Mar.) 114. Act 24 Mar., to preserve the fish in said county; L. 1869, 185. Act 9 Apr., the county and Quincy to take stock in two R. R.; L. 1869, 202. Act 10 Mar., to change the name of Wm. Bowles to Wm. Creed and make him heir of Thos. Creed; Laws 1869, 263. Act. 31 Mar., official circuit court reporter; L. 1869, 350. Ballard and Wren to establish a ferry across the Mississippi in said county; L. 1869 (24 Feb.) 114.

Quincy.—Act 22 Feb., incorporating the Quincy Manufacturing Co. Pr. L. 1833, 59. Act 31 Jan., trustees of town to build wharves and establish ferries; L. 1835, 72. Act 15 Jan., incorporating the "Quincy Insurance Co.;" L. 1836, 109. Act 4 Mar., incorporating the Quincy Academy; Pr. L. 1837, 287. Town incorporated; boundary defined; lands within town limits, not laid out, to be taxed no higher than they are under general law; Pr. L. 1839 (21 Feb.) 103. Act 3 Feb. 1840; city incorporated; L. 1840, 113. Foregoing amended; L. 1841 (7 Jan.) 57. Vacation of the plat of lots in Randolph's addition; act 26 Feb., L. 1845, 168. Road bed of the Northern Cross railroad, relinquished by the state to the city; act 1 Mar., L. 4845, 212. Charter amended concerning school tax; vote taken thereon; act 14 Feb., L. 1845, 327. The city erected into a common school district; act 27 Feb., L. 1847, 151. Act 16 Jan., John Wood to lay off a part of N. W. ¼ of sec. 11, Town 2—9 as a cemetery, and attach the same to the city, upon terms agreed. Pr. L. 1847, 19. Act 22 Jan., incorporating the Quincy Lodge No. 12 of the I. O. O. F; John Wood's conveyance of burial lots in Woodland cemetery, declared valid. Pr. Laws 1847, 58. Act 27 Feb., amends act 3 Feb. 1840 incorporating the city of Quincy. Pr. L. 1847, 134. Act 10 Feb., incorporating the Quincy Mutual Fire Insurance Co.; limit 20 years. Pr. L. 1849, 48. Act 26 Jan., the German United Evangelical Protestant Congregation of the Lutheran and Reformed Confessions changed to and incorporated as the Evangelical Lutheran Church of St. John. Pr. L. 1849, 75. Acting members of organized fire companies exempt from serving on all juries; act 12 Feb., L. 1849, 84. Resident members of any fire company exempt from all road and street labor, but not from tax on property; act 12 Feb., L. 1849, 84. City assessor to assess state taxes; city exempt from township organization; act 15 Feb., L. 1851, 121. Special tax to pay interest on bonds under act of 6 Nov. 1849; act 17 Feb., L. 1851, 144. Act 28 Jan., further amends act 3 Feb. 1840 incorporating city; Pr. L. 1851, 19. Act 17 Feb., incorporating the German General Beneficial Association. Pr. L. 1851, 288. Manner of assessing and collecting taxes; L. 1852 (23 June) 236. Foregoing amended; Pr. L. 1853 (24 Jan.) 449. Also, L. 1855 (14 Feb.) 132. Act 9 Feb., amends act incorporating the city; for the improvement of streets. Pr. L. 1853, 339. Act 12 Feb., incorporating the Quincy Savings and Insurance Co. Pr. L. 1853, 389. Act 26 Jan., city to subscribe $100,000. stock in Northern Cross railroad; issue bonds and levy tax to pay. Pr. L. 1853, 471. Act 12 Feb., incorporating the Quincy Gas Light and Coke Co., limit 25 years. Pr. L. 1853, 510. Act 9 Feb., incorporating the St. Aloysius Orphan Society of the St. Bonifacius Congregation of Quincy. Pr. L. 1853, 511. Act 10 Feb., incorporating the Railroad Bridge Co.; across the Mississippi at Quincy; complete in 6 years. Pr. L. 1853, 576. Act 17 Jan., supplemental to act 3 Feb. 1840 incorporating city of Quincy. Pr. L. 1855, 59. Act 5 Feb., incorporating the Quincy English and German Seminary; lands 1000 acres; conference of M. E. Church to appoint board of visitors; Pr. L. 1855, 377. Act 15 Feb., revives act 12 Feb. 1853 incorporating the Quincy Savings and Insurance Co. Pr. L. 1855, 385. Act 15 Feb., amends §2 Art. 5 original city charter; council to appoint clerk, treasurer, assessors, street commissioner, etc. Pr. L. 1855, 491. Act 13 Feb., incorporating the Quincy Water Co.; condemn private property; exclusive privilege of supplying water to city for 50 years; city may take stock in. Pr. L. 1855, 553. Act 15 Feb., incorporating the Quincy Wood and Coal Co; construct plank or railroad from lands. Pr. L. 1855, 626. Act 14 Feb., incorporating the Woodland Home for orphans and friendless. Pr. L. 1855, 668. Act 15 Feb., incorporating the Irish Benevolent Society. Pr. Laws 1855, 722. Act 29 Jan., amends act 16 Jan. 1847, authorizing John Wood to lay off a burying ground and convey same to the city; name of Woodland Cemetery; addition made thereto. Pr. L. 1857, 91. Act 30 Jan., reduces the acts incorporating the city to one act and amends the same. Pr. L. 1857, 156. Act 31 Jan., legalizes said city's subscription to the Northern Cross R. R. Pr. L. 1857, 229. Act 10 Feb., incorporating the German Mutual Aid and Gymnastic Society. Pr. L. 1857, 338. Act 11 Feb., incorporating the Odd Fellows, and Mason's Building Association; Pr. L. 1857, 371. Act 11 Feb., amends act 12 Feb. 1853 incorporating the Quincy Gas Light and Coke Co.; may borrow money and issue bonds. Pr. L. 1857, 433. Act 12 Feb., amends act incorporating the Quincy Wood and Coal Co.; not confined to Adams county. Pr. L. 1857, 482. Act 13 Feb., incorporating the Quincy Academy. Pr. L. 1857, 527. Boundaries of the city extended; schools regulated; vote to be taken thereon; act 16

Feb., L. 1857, 179. Act 16 Feb., supplemental to act 30 Jan. 1857 incorporating said city; may issue $75,000. bonds. Pr. L. 1857, 1052. Act 16 Feb., incorporating the New England Society of Quincy. Pr. L. 1857, 1065. Act 18 Feb., incorporating the Adams Grove No. 2 of the United Ancient Order of Druids. Pr. L. 1857, 1348. Act 18 Feb., amends act 14 Feb. 1855 incorporating the Woodland Home for Orphans and Friendless; control over children surrendered thereto extended; regulations respecting the binding out of such. Pr. L. 1859, 12. Act 26 Jan., confirms act 30 Jan. 1857, to reduce the law incorporating the city of Quincy and the several amendatory acts into one, and amend the same; legalizes the acts of said city in pursuance of said act. Pr. L. 1859, 252. Act 21 Feb., incorporating the German Insurance and Savings Institution. Pr. L. 1859, 386. Act 22 Feb., incorporating the German Evangelical Salem's Church. Pr. L. 1861, 85. Act 20 Feb., incorporating the Hebrew Congregation K. K. Buai Avrohum. Pr. Laws 1861, 87. Act 20 Feb., city to levy a two mill tax to create a sinking fund. Pr. L. 1861. 246. Act 22 Feb., supplemental to act establishing a board of education; appointment and salary of superintendent of public schools. Pr. L. 1861, 247. Act 2 Feb., for the establishment of a sinking fund to reduce the city indebtedness; special election; council to appoint sinking fund commissioners. Pr. L. 1861, 248. Act 20 Feb., providing for negotiation of the city bonds. Pr. L. 1861, 249. Act 20 Feb., incorporating the Board of Education; powers and duties. Pr. L. 1861, 249. Act 22 Feb., incorporating the Farmers' and Merchants' Insurance Co. Pr. L. 1861, 375. Act 22 Feb., corporate name of the Quincy Savings and Insurance Co. changed to the Quincy Savings Bank. Pr. L. 1861, 422. Act 22 Feb., incorporating the Tyler and Greenleaf Sewing Machine Co. Pr. L. 1861, 471. Act 21 Feb., amends act 5 Feb. 1855 incorporating Quincy English and German Seminary; changed to the Quincy English and German College. Pr. L. 1863, 10. Act 14 Feb., said city to constitute one revenue collection district; not to give security for costs; collect gas tax. Pr. L. 1863, 171. Act 13 Feb., amends act 22 Feb. 1861 incorporating the Farmers' and Merchants' Insurance Co.; business divided into two departments, Stock and Mutual; effect life insurance. Pr. L. 1863, 208. Act 15 Feb., incorporating the Quincy Academy. 1 Pr. L. 1865, 5. Act 11 Feb., incorporating the Independent German School Association. 1 Pr. Laws 1865, 34. Act 16 Feb., incorporating the Grand Grove United Ancient Order Druids of the State of Illinois. 1 Pr. L. 1865, 74. Act 16 Feb., incorporating the Home for the Children of Deceased and Disabled Soldiers. 1 Pr. L. 1865, 79. Act 16 Feb., incorporating the Evangelical Protestant Widows' and Orphans' Aid Society. 1 Pr. L. 1865, 86. Act 14 Feb., said city to levy special tax to pay bounties to persons in the U. S. service. 1 Pr. L. 1865, 151. Act 16 Feb., supplemental to the foregoing; question of such special tax to be submitted to legal voters at a special election. 1 Pr. L. 1865, 152. Act 15 Feb., revives act 10 Feb. 1853 incorporating the Quincy Bridge Co. 1 Pr. L. 1865, 194. Act 16 Feb., incorporating the Quincy Board of Trade. 1 Pr. L. 1865, 534. Act 16 Feb., incorporating the Board of Fire Engineers; powers and duties of. 1 Pr. L. 1865, 567. Act 11 Feb., incorporating the Quincy Horse Railway and Carrying Co. for 50 years; 1 Pr. L. 1865, 601. Act 16 Feb., the Farmers' and Merchants' Insurance Co. may take wind and marine risks. 1 Pr. L. 1865, 646. Act 16 Feb., name of Atta Z. Orr changed to Atta Z. Adams; said Atta Z. Adams and George Adams infant made heirs of George and Aargery Ann Adams. 2 Pr. L. 1865, 95. Act 15 Feb., incorporating the Illinois and Missouri Transportation Co. 2 Pr. L. 1865, 671. Charges of the city against rafts of lumber; act 16 Feb., L. 1865, 101. Act 6 Feb., legalizes Quincy Railroad Bridge Co. and facilitate its construction. 1 Pr. L. 1867, 165. Act 5 Mar., I. N. Morris to lay off addition to Woodland Cemetery to be known as the Bluff Cemetery. 1 Pr. L. 1867, 226. Act 9 Feb., amends act 26 Jan. 1849 incorporating the Evangelical Lutheran Church of St. John; part repealed; election of trustees. 1 Pr. L. 1867, 240. Act 21 Feb., amends act 22 Feb. 1861 chartering the German Evangelical Salem's Church; powers extended. Pr. L. 1867, 241. Act 28 Feb., extending corporate limits of said city. 1 Pr. L. 1867, 737. Act 8 Mar., city to pay its proportion of county expenses. 1 Pr. L. 1867, 873. Act 27 Feb., further amends act 20 Feb. 1861 establishing the Board of Education. 1 Pr. L. 1867, 913. Act 18 Feb., amends act 16 Feb. 1865 establishing a board of fire engineers; repeals §8; assessments upon insurance companies. 1 Pr. L. 1867, 949. Act 9 Feb., incorporating the Quincy Hotel Co. 2 Pr. L. 1867, 40. Act 23 Feb., incorporating the Woman's Hospital at Quincy. 2 Pr. L. 1867, 77. Act 7 Mar., incorporating the Illinois Life Insurance Co. 2 Pr. L. 1867, 118. Act 5 Mar., incorporating the Quincy Union Mutual Insurance Co. 2 Pr. L. 1867, 168. Act 9 Mar., incorporating the Valley Insurance Co. 2 Pr. L. 1867, 200. Act 19 Feb., to organize and define the powers of the Quincy Library. 2 Pr. L. 1867, 245. Act 22 Feb., incorporating the Library Hall Co. 2 Pr. L. 1867, 246. Act 7 Mar., incorporating the Excelsior Stove Works. 2 Pr. L. 1867, 306. Act 8 Mar., incorporating the Dexter Manufacturing and Mercantile Co. 2 Pr. L. 1867, 318. Act 22 Feb., amends act 11 Feb. 1857 chartering the Odd Fellows' Building Association; powers extended. 2 Pr. L. 1867, 466. Act 7 Mar., incorporating the Quincy Times Co. 2 Pr. L. 1867, 513. Act 28 Feb., incorporating the St. Louis and Quincy Packet Co. 3 Pr. L. 1867, 86. Act 8 Mar., in relation to streets in East Quincy. 3 Pr. L. 1867, 112.

Quincy House.—Act 1 Mar., incorporates the Quincy House Co. Pr. L. 1839, 209. Act 3 Feb., supplemental to foregoing; L. 1840, 132. Conveyed to the state in settlement of a claim against J. Tillson; act 23 Feb., L. 1847, 67. Sale to be made; act 12 Feb., L. 1849, 107. Affirming the sale to Ash and Diller; act of 7 Feb., L. 1851, 22. Act 13 Jan., confirms the survey and plat of town; L. 1836, 231.

Clayton.—Act 27 Feb., town incorporated under act 12 Feb. 1831 [L. 1831, 82] without reference to number of inhabitants. Pr. L. 1837, 107. Act 16 Feb., incorporating town. 2 Pr. L. 165, 422.

Columbus.—Act 10 Feb., incorporating town. Pr. L. 1849, 129. Act 14 Feb., incorporating town. Pr. L. 1855, 187. Act 13 Feb. 1867, amends foregoing; to regulate the sale of liquors. 3. Pr. L. 1867, 610.

AGRICULTURAL COLLEGES.

Illinois Agricultural College incorporated; distribution of seminary lands; L. 1861 (21 Feb.) 9. Foregoing amended; powers extended; 1 Pr. L. 1867 (12 Feb.) 1. To secure the endowment fund of; L. 1869 (19 Apr.) 8. Indentures of apprentices by the New York Juvenile Asylum legalized; L. 1861 (18 Feb.) 15. Donation of public lands by Congress accepted; L. 1863 (14 Feb.) 64. Industrial University located; L. 1867 (25 Jan.) 122. Organization and maintenance of said university; Id. (28 Feb.) 123. Supplemental to the foregoing; Id. (8 Mar.) 130.

ALEXANDER COUNTY.

County established; commissioners to fix county seat; Laws 1819 (4 Mar.) 113. Wm. M. Alexander to dam Cache river on sec. 30, Town 1—15; Id. (27 Mar.) 296. Same to collect toll for crossing his bridge across the Cache; L. 1823 (12 Feb.) 136. Appropriates $500. to improve road across the Cache bottom; L. 1829 (19 Dec. 1828) 143 §4. Acts locating county seat at America repealed; David Haleman and others commissioners to locate county seat and give it a name; Pr. L. 1833 (18 Jan.) 24. [No acts specially locating county seat at America appear among the printed statutes.] Confirming the county seat at Unity; court house and public property at America sold; L. 1835 (24 Jan.) 142. The Vulcan Foundry chartered; Pr. L. 1837 (1 Mar.) 195. The Unity manufacturing Co. chartered; Id. (2 Mar.) 235. The Cairo City and Canal Co. chartered; Pr. L. 1837 (4 Mar.) 302. Foregoing amended; §12 repealed; Pr. L. 1839 (1 Feb.) 32. Further amended; sell lots in Cairo under territorial act of 9 Jan. 1818 chartering the city and bank of Cairo; Id. (2 Mar.) 237. Supplemental to first foregoing; L. 1841 (17 Feb.) 125. Road from Caledonia to Santa Fee located; L. 1839 (12 Feb.) 100. Also, from Haws' via Caledonia to Trinity; Id. (2 Mar.) 253. Wm. Clapp and John Hodges to collect county taxes for 1839; L. 1845 (1 Mar.) 104. Taxes for 1844 remitted, by reason of loss from high water; Id. (21 Feb.) 353. County to borrow $2,000. to complete public buildings; Pr. L. 1847 (4 Feb.) 26. Surities of Jesse J. McClendon, collector for 1839, released conditionally; Id. (23 Feb.) 180. Pre-emptions granted to D. H. Brush and A. P. Gross; L. 1851 (15 Feb.) 104. Green Massey, late sheriff, allowed $60.; Pr. L. 1851 (15 Feb.) 34. To Wm. R. Kendall, ferry across the Mississippi opposite Cape Girardeau; Id. (17 Feb.) 299. Wm. Whitaker, convicted of larceny, restored to citizenship; Pr. L. 1853 (10 Feb.) 443. Trustees in Town 17—1 to use school fund to erect and furnish school house; L. 1853 (10 Feb.) 180. Acts of school trustees Town 14—3 legalized; Pr. L. 1854 (4 Mar.) 179. To Green P. Garner, ferry across the Cache at Unity; Pr. L. 1855 (15 Feb.) 605. Removal of county seat from Thebes to Cairo; first vote thereon; L. 1859 (18 Feb.) 41. Bridge across the Cache at sec. 1, Town 17—1 legalized; Pr. L. 1859 (24 Feb.) 15. James L. Brown, collector for 1854—5, allowed $110.84 overpaid; Pr. L. 1861 (22 Feb.) 56. Copies of Records "A" and "B" legalized; L. 1861 (18 Feb.) 13. For building court house and jail; issue bonds; L. 1863 (12 Feb.) 23. The Alexander and Pulaski County Plank Road and Bridge Co. chartered; Pr. L. 1863 (21 Feb.) 218. The Cairo and Mound City R. R. Co. chartered; 2 Pr. L. 1865 (15 Feb.) 133. To Green P. Garner, ferry across the Cache for 10 years, at Unity; 1 Pr. Laws 1867 (8 Mar.) 934. The Valley Ferry Co. chartered; Id. (6 Mar.) 937. To Albert High, ferry for 10 years across the Mississippi at Santa Fee; Id. (5 Mar.) 948. State taxes for two years remitted, by reason of great number of criminals; L. 1869 (16 Apr.) 330.

Cairo.—City chartered; Pr. L. 1857 (11 Feb.) 400. Amended; city property exempt from county taxation; Pr. L. 1859 (11 Feb.) 113. Further amended; sections named in the two foregoing acts repealed; Pr. L. 1861 (13 Feb.) 117. Again amended; filling in and grading streets, etc.; Pr. L. 1863 (22 Jan.) 166. Previous acts revised and consolidated; 1 Pr. L. 1867 (18 Feb.) 368. Supplemental to foregoing; construction of; Id. (5 Mar.) 694. The Cairo City Mills chartered; L. 1841 (27 Feb.) 145. The charter of Bank of Cairo repealed; L. 1843 (4 Mar.) 36. B. Shawnessy and P. Smith, ferry across the Ohio; L. 1845 (21 Feb.) 333. To Bryan Shawnessy and others, ferry across the Ohio; Pr. L. 1851 (14 Feb.) 127. Foregoing amended; no other to be run within three miles; Pr. L. 1854 (3 Mar.) 140. Cairo Dock Co. chartered; amended after 20 years; Pr. Laws 1851 (15 Feb.) 221. To provide an additional jail—not at expense of county; Pr. L. 1853 (26 Jan.) 463. The Cairo Cemetery Association chartered; 15 acres exempt from taxation; Id. (3 Feb.) 544. The Cairo Farmer's Tobacco Warehouse Co. chartered; Pr. L. 1855 (14 Feb.) 552. The Franklin Building Association chartered; Id. (15 Feb.) 615. The Cairo Gas Light and Coke Co. chartered; Id. (15 Feb.) 648. Court of Common Pleas established; L. 1855 (6 Feb.) 155. Foregoing amended; L. 1859 (14 Feb.) 80. Fees and percentage of attorney of said court; L. 1865 (14 Feb.) 65. Selection of jurors; L. 1865 (16 Feb.) 41. Terms of court; residence of judge; L. 1867 (7 Mar.) 76. Act establishing and amendments, repealed; L. 1869 (19 Feb.) 127. Register's office established; L. 1857 (17 Feb.) 125. Foregoing repealed; L. 1865 (16 Feb.) 42. The Cairo City Hotel Co. chartered; Pr. L. 1857 (9 Feb.) 327. The Cairo City Ferry Co. chartered; Id. (13 Feb.) 604. License moneys paid to city treasury; Id. (16 Feb.) 1123. The Cairo Hydraulic Co. chartered; Id. (17 Feb.) 1183. Foregoing amended; 1 Pr. L. 1865 (15 Feb.) 612. Jurisdiction over certain lands ceded to the United States for a court house, post office and custom house; L. 1859 (18 Feb.) 123. Restoration of records destroyed by fire; Id. 139. Foregoing extended three years; L. 1861 (21 Feb.) 75. Penalties for injury to the levees; L. 1861 (21 Feb.) 118. The Southern Illinois Mutual Insurance Co. chartered; Pr. L. 1863 (13 Feb.) 199. Foregoing amended; name changed

to the South-western Insurance Co.; 2 Pr. L. 1867 (7 Mar.) 109. The Northwestern Chinese Sugar Manufacturing Co. chartered; Pr. L. 1863 (12 Feb.) 261. The Curators of St. Joseph's Female Seminary chartered; 1 Pr. L. 1865 (16 Feb.) 27. The Chamber of Commerce chartered; Id. (16 Feb.) 524. The Arab Fire Co. chartered; Id. 571. Foregoing amended; for building an engine house; 1 Pr. L. 1867 (25 Feb.) 950. The Cairo City Gas Co. chartered; 1 Pr. L. 1865 (16 Feb.) 580. The Cairo Insurance and Loan Co. chartered; Id. 622. Valley Insurance Co. chartered; Id. 812. Cairo Democrat Co. chartered; 2 Pr. L. 1865 (16 Feb.) 116. River Transportation Co. chartered; Id. (10. Feb.) 676. Dollar Savings Association chartered; 1 Pr. L. 1867 (28 Feb.) 60. Cairo German Banking Institution chartered; Id. (6 Mar.) 72. Free Benevolent Sons of America chartered; Id. (14 Feb.) 140. County and city to take stock in any railroad chartered by Missouri or Kentucky; Id. (5 Mar.) 880. Rough and Ready Fire Co. chartered; Id. (7 Mar.) 950. Construction of a jail and improvement of court house grounds; 2. Pr. L. 1867 (9 Feb.) 238. Valley Iron Co. chartered; Id. (5 Mar.) 300. Bullion Mining Co. chartered; Id. 380. The Orphan Asylum for Southern Illinois chartered; Id. (25 Feb.) 469. Evansville and Cairo Packet Co. chartered; 3 Pr. L. 1867 (9 Feb.) 84. Delta Elevator and Warehouse Co. chartered; Id. (6 Mar.) 676. Taxes used to support the Orphan Asylum; L. 1869 (16. Apr.) 330.

America.—Town trustees chartered; L. 1821 (14 Feb.) 160. Foregoing amended; L. 1823 (14 Feb.) 142. H. L. Webb and H. T. Sloo, ferry across the Ohio; L. 1825 (15 Feb.) 114. Auditor not to sell part of town for taxes; Pr. L. 1827 (6 Jan.) 5. To Geo. Cloud, ferry across the Ohio; Pr. L. 1827 (16 Feb.) 28.

Thebes.—County seat located at, conditionally; L. 1845 (4 Feb.) 222. Town chartered; L. 1852 (23 June) 228. County seat removed to Cairo after vote thereon; L. 1859 (18 Feb.) 41. Thebes Marble Working and Manufacturing Co. chartered Pr. L. 1855 (14 Feb.) 620.

ALLEN COUNTY.

County created, boundary and organization; vote first taken; L. 1841 (27 Feb.) 87.

AMERICAN BOTTOM.

See also Lotteries.

Chartering the Northern Division; includes part of counties of Madison and St. Clair south of Wood river; to drain, reclaim and render heathful; pass ordinances; condemn property; Pr. L. 1839 (2 Mar.) 226. Foregoing repealed; L. 1840 (27 Jan.) 67. Winstanly and Duffey contractors paid $3,000.; L. 1839 (2 Mar.) 236. American Bottom Drainage Co. chartered; Pr. L. 1851 (15 Feb.) 183. American Bottom Board of Improvement chartered; drain lands in Towns 1—9 and 2—10, with general powers; Pr. L. 1853 (10 Feb.) 614. Amended and extended; 1 Pr. L. 1867 (28 Feb.) 153. Supplemental and amending; building and repairing levees; L. 1867 (6 Mar.) 152. Charter and amendatory acts amended; L. 1869 (12 Feb.) 196. American Bottom Levee Co. chartered; L. 1859 (19 Feb.) 106. Amended; Pr. L. 1863 (13 Feb.) 188. Further amended; 2 Pr. L. 1867 (7 Mar.) 808. For the relief of citizens of the American Bottom; 2 Pr. Laws 1867 (4 Mar.) 795.

APPROPRIATIONS.

1819.—To Thos. Sloo $30. for certain land abstracts; L. 1819 (22 Mar.) 158. For general purposes in 1819 and 1820; Id. (29 Mar.) 344.

1821.—In settlement of the account of Blackwell and Berry, late public printers; L. 1821 (31 Jan.) 61. Generally for 1821 and 1822; Id. (15 Feb.) 170. For the officers and members of the general assembly; Id. (1 Jan.) 6.

1823.—To Josias Randle $50. for certain abstracts; L. 1823 (17 Jan.) 72. To Blackwell and Berry $150. for distributing the journals; Id. (23 Dec. 1822) 79. In part payment of the officers and members of the session; Id. (27 Dec. 1822) 84. Expenses for 1823–4; Id. (17 Feb.) 163.

1825.—To John Kain $445.50 in satisfaction of a judgment; L. 1825 (7 Dec. 1824) 4. To Guy W. Smith for erecting a monumental corner on the Wabash, on the line between Illinois and Indiana; Id. (7 Dec. 1824) 6. To rebuild the state house at Vandalia; Id. (8 Dec. 1824) 6. In part payment of the officers and members of the session; Id. (11 Dec. 1824) 9. For laying out a road from Mt. Vernon to the Saline Tavern in Gallatin county; Id. (13 Jan.) 96. Expenses for 1825–6; Id. (18 Jan.) 179.

1826.—For finishing the state house; L. 1826 (19 Jan.) 57. Supplemental to the foregoing; Id. (28 Jan.) 90.

1827.—For 1827–8; R. S. 1827 (17 Feb.) 60. In part payment of the officers and members of the session; Id. (8 Jan.) 62. For building certain bridges on the bounty lands; Id. (23 Jan.) 63.

1829.—Expenses of 1829–30; L. 1829 (23 Jan.) 5.

1831.—Expenses for 1831–2; L. 1831 (16 Feb.) 9. The proceeds of Saline lands appropriated for internal improvements; Id. (16 Feb.) 12. In part payment of the officers and members of the session; Id. (24 Dec. 1830) 16. For bridges in counties of Warren, Knox, Jo Daviess, Pike, McDonough and Adams; Id. (22 Jan.) 37.

1833.—In part payment of the expenses of the session; R. S. 1833 (22 Dec. 1832) 74. Expenses for 1833–4; Id. (2 May) 74.

1835.—In part payment of the expenses of the session; L. 1835 (19 Dec. 1834) 3. Contingent expenses for 1835–6; Id. (13 Feb.) 3. To J. G. McDonald and D. W. Beckwith for a survey and plat of the Chicago and Vincennes road; Id. (12 Feb.) 64.

1836.—In part payment of the expenses of the session; L. 1836 (2 Jan.) 229. To B. W. Brooks for surveying road from Vandalia to America; Id. (9 Jan.) 230. Supplemental to act 13 Feb. 1835; Id. (18 Jan.) 241.

1837.—For the expenses of the session, in part; 1 L. 1837 (24 Dec. 1836) 3. General expenses for 1837–8; Id. (4 Mar.) 3. To Franklin and Jackson counties for internal improvements, being part of the proceeds of the Vermilion Saline; Id. (2 Mar.) 10. To a large number of counties for internal improvements; Id. (4 Mar.) 11. For the labor and materials for the new state house; Id. (11 Feb.) 323. Supplemental appropriations for 1837–8; 2 L. 1837 (21 July) 3.

1839.—For expenses of the session, in part; L. 1839 (19 Dec. 1838) 40. General expenses for 1839–40; Id. (2 Mar.) 113.

1840.—For the expense of witnesses before the house of representatives; L. 1840 (18 Jan.) 46. For expenses of the session in part; Id. (8 Jan.) 80. Additional appropriations for 1839–40; Id. (8 Jan.) 80.

1841.—General expenses for 1841–2; L. 1841 (27 Feb.) 28. For expenses of the session, in part; Id. (18 Dec. 1840) 32. Further for 1841–2; Id. (17 Feb.) 32.

1843.—For expenses of the session, in part; L. 1843 (30 Dec. 1842) 11. General expenses for 1843–4; Id. (3 Mar.) 11.

1845.—To Capt. W. Stephenson and others, for expenses in the Mormon war; L. 1845 (1 Mar.) 121. To Gould, Millen and others, for expenses in the Mormon war; Id. (1 Mar.) 132. To widow and heirs of John Morris, killed in Mormon war, $25. annually; Id. (28 Feb.) 134. Partial expenses of the session; Id. (10 Dec. 1844) 184. All money in the treasury to be used for expenses of the session; Id. (9 Dec. 1844) 188. To mechanics and others for work on the state house; Id. (3 Jan.) 197. For expenses of the session, in part; Id. (6 Feb.) 218. To T. H. Campbell $56. for witness fees; Id. (3 Mar.) 253. For copying the territorial and other state records; Id. (28 Feb.) 270. For expenses of the Mormon war; Id. (26 Feb.) 296. General expenses of 1845–6; Id. (3 Mar.) 364.

1847.—General expenses for 1847–8; L. 1847 (28 Feb.) 5. To complete state house; Id. (16 Feb.) 8. For expenses of troops in 1844–5; for work on the Great Western Mail route; Id. (1 Mar.) 9. For the pay of officers and privates in the Hancock county expedition in 1846; Id. (1 Mar.) 10. For expenses of session, in part; Id. (18 Dec. 1846) 10. For subsistence, clothing, etc., furnished the state militia in 1845–6; Id. (22 Jan.) 11. For expenses of session, in part; Id. (5 Feb.) 13. For storage on railroad iron belonging to the state; Id. (3 Feb.) 14. For the funeral expenses of Hon. Wm. Hendry; Id. (15 Feb.) 15. For expenses of state militia; supplemental act; Id. (26 Feb.) 15. For expenses of state militia under Gen. Hardin and Maj. Warren; Id. (26 Feb.) 16. For the same; Id. (27 Feb.) 17. Increase of $3,000. annually, in aid of the Deaf and Dumb Asylum; Id. (23 Feb.) 47.

1849.—For expenses of the session, in part; L. 1849 (11 Feb.) 27. General expenses until next general assembly; Id. (12 Feb.) 27. For expenses of the session, in part; Id. (12 Feb.) 29. Ordinary and contingent expenses until next regular session; Id. (12 Feb.) 29. For expenses of committee visiting penitentiary; Id. (6 Feb.) 31. To Mason Brayman for revising statutes; Id. (10 Feb.) 31. Binding statutes; Id. (10 Feb.) 32. For distributing the constitutional convention journals 1848; Id. (26 Jan.) 32. For the militia pay roll in the Hancock disturbances; Id. (3 Feb.) 33. To H. G. Reynolds for work in office of secretary of state; Id. (31 Jan.) 34. Amends act 13 Feb. 1847, concerning expenses of state militia; Id. (12 Feb.) 35. To J. R. Parker and others, expenses of state militia; Id. (26 Jan.) 35. To P. Sargent, for powder used in Hancock war; Id. (12 Feb.) 36. Refunding $100. to John Pierson, fine imposed by supreme court; Id. (22 Jan.) 36. To S. M. Tinsley & Co., claims on account Northern Cross R. R.; Id. (29 Jan.) 36. Refunding to Morgan county moneys received on recognizances through mistate; Id. (9 Feb.) 37. For printing Hancock delinquent tax list for 1845; Id. (9 Feb.) 37. To S. A. Buckmaster for services and expenses as fund commissioner's agent; Id. (12 Feb.) 37. To Arch. Job as state house comm'r.; Id. (10 Feb.) 118. To Thos. H. Owen and Thos. Wills, for provisions used in Mormon war; Id. (10 Feb.) 118. For completion of state house; Id. (12 Feb.) 184.

1849. *Special Session.*—Expenses of the session; 2 Laws 1849 (6 Nov.) 3. Payment to Paul Anderson for translating the constitution into Norwegian; Id. (29 Oct.) 4. Payment of claim of George Peabody; Id. (29 Oct.) 5. Payment for swords for officers in the Mexican war; Id. (6 Nov.) 5. Payment of J. S. Roberts postage on the letters to the board of the public works; Id. (6 Nov.) 6.

1851.—For expenses of session, in part; L. 1851 (18 Jan.) 5. To B. C. Cook and D. B. Campbell for professional services in 2nd and 3rd grand divisions; Id. (14 Feb.) 89. Amending general act 12 Feb. 1849; Id. (15 Feb.) 107. For expenses of committee visiting the dykes opposite St. Louis; Id. (15 Feb.) 127. For expenses of session, part; Id. (17 Feb.) 134. For expenses of committee visiting, dykes opposite St. Louis, and Jacksonville; other expenses as in act 15 Feb. 1851, 127; Id. (17 Feb.) 137. For a monument to governor Thos. Ford; Id. (17 Feb.) 155. To Richard M. Young for services relating to the 3 per. cent. school fund due the state; Id. (17 Feb.) 163. For expenses of the session, and until next regular session; Id. (17 Feb.) 189. For general expenses until end of next regular session; Id. 198.

1852.—To Saml. Bacon, a blind man, $600.; L. 1852 (21 June) 92. Expenses of the session; Id. (22 June) 173.

1853.—To the State Agricultural Society $1,000. annually; L. 1853 (11 Feb.) 34. Amending and supplemental to act 17 Feb. 1851. 198, for the ordinary expenses; Id. (12 Feb.) 176. Expenses of the session; and contingent and ordinary expenses until next regular session; Id. (14 Feb.) 177. For the geological survey and maps; Id. (12 Feb.) 237. Ordinary and contingent expenses until next general assembly; Id. (14 Feb.) 237.

1854.—Incidental expenses of session; L. 1854 (28 Feb.) 25.

1855.—Expenses until next regular session; L. 1855 (14 Feb.) 99. Funds in the treasury used to pay expenses of session; Id. (12 Feb.)

103. To the engrossing and enrolling clerks; Id. (15 Feb.) 142. Expenses of session, and of the government until the next regular session; Id. (14 Feb.) 143. Expenses of session, in part; Id. (16 Feb.) 182. For completion of supreme court room at Mt. Vernon $10,000.; Id. (9 Feb.) 187.

1857.—Expenses of session, in part; L. 1857 (22 Jan.) 34. For improvements in the Alton penitentiary $11,056.45; Id. (14 Feb.) 54. For State Agricultural Society premiums, $3000. annually; Id. (17 Feb.) 105. To J. H. Deck $50. for apprehending murderer; Id. (16 Feb.) 195. To P. B. Fouke for legal services, $300.; Id. (10 Feb.) 219. For expenses of session, and ordinary expenses until next session; Id. (18 Feb.) 238. Ordinary expenses until next session; Id. (18 Feb.) 241.

1859.—For expenses of session, in part; L. 1859 (13 Jan.) 10. For expenses investigating the funding of canal scrip; Id. (11 Feb.) 10. Completion of Court room at Ottawa; repairs on Court room at Mt. Vernon; Id. (11 Feb.) 11. For erection of grave stones over deceased members of the legislature at Vandalia; Id. (24 Feb.) 127. To P. P. Hamilton as states attorney for 2nd circuit; Id. (19 Feb.) 149.

1861.—To County Agricultural Societies of $100. annually; L. 1861 (21 Feb.) 11. Contingent expenses of sessions; Id. (11 Jan.) 23. Furnishing and repairing Governor's house; Id. (12 Feb.) 25. Expenses of session, in part; Id. (14 Feb.) 26. Postage and stationery of session; Id. (15 Jan.) 26. Contingent expenses of session; Id. (20 Feb.) 26. For certain expenses of the government; Id. (22 Feb.) 30. Pay of members of the general assembly, and for salaries; Id. (21 Feb.) 33. Ordinary expenses until next regular session; Id. (21 Feb.) 35. Expenses of peace commissioners to Washington; also senate investigating committee; Id. (20 Feb.) 37. For defense of suit in U. S. supreme court, Bank of Republic vs. Hamilton county; Id. (30 Jan.) 37.

1861. *Special Session.*—Expenses of session, in part; 2 L. 1861 (2 May) 9. Expenses of the session; Id. (2 May) 15. For extraordinary expenses of the Executive department; Id. 19. For carrying the mails of session; Id. (3 May) 25.

1863.—For relief of Illinois soldiers wounded at Murfresboro and Vicksburg; L. 1863 (12 Feb.) 9. Postage of the session; Id. (12 Feb.) 10. Expenses of session, in part; Id. (14 Feb.) 10. Payment of committee clerks; Id. (22 Jan.) 11. Expenses constitutional convention 1862; Id. (28 Jan.) 11. Expenses of government not otherwise provided for; Id. (13 Feb.) 12. Ordinary expenses until next regular session; Id. (14 Feb.) 14. For certain expenses of the general assembly; Id. (10 June) 17. Postage of session; Id. (10 June) 21. Pay of officers and members of the general assembly; Id. (12 June) 21.

1865.—Expenses of government not otherwise provided for; L. 1865 (25 Jan.) 4. Ordinary expenses until next session; Id. (16 Feb.) 6. Miscellaneous expenses; Id. (16 Feb.) 9. Pay of officers and members, and salaries; Id. (16 Feb.) 14. For purchasing the grounds in which repose the remains of Stephen A. Douglas; Id. (16 Feb.) 18. Furnishing the governor's house; Id. (9 Feb.) 19. Postage of the session; Id. (6 Jan.) 19. For the National Cemetery at Gettysburg; Id. (16 Feb.) 91.

1867.—Postage of session; L. 1867 (12 Jan.) 1. For the Lincoln Monument Association $50,000.; Id. (29 Jan.) 2. For mileage and per diem of session: Id. (29 Jan.) 2. For the French Exposition $7,000.; Id. (5 Feb.) 3. For the Soldier's College at Fulton; Id. (27 Feb) 14. For the State Horticultural Society $2,000. annually; Id. (28 Feb.) 16. Pay of officers and members of the session, and for salaries; Id. (28 Feb.) 16. Ordinary expenses until next regular session; Id. (28 Feb.) 18. For the Illinois Natural History Society at Normal University; Id. (28 Feb.) 21. Sundry expenses; Id. (27 Feb.) 23. For safe in Treasurer's vault $1,200.: Id. (5 Mar.) 30. For removing the remains of W. H. Bissell to Oakridge; Id. (5 Mar.) 30. For binding; Id. (5 Mar.) 31. For the National Cemetery at Gettysburg; Id. (5 Mar.) 31. For portraits of Lincoln and Douglas; Id. (9 Mar.) 36. For uniforms furnished by H. G. C. Moritz; Id. (28 Feb.) 44. For bibles furnished penitentiary convicts by M. I. Lee; Id. (8 Mar.) 44. To pay claim of S. Stookey; Id. (8 Mar.) 45; To F. B. Roberts for erecting barracks; Id. (9 Mar.) 45. For expenses of W. H. Brockman bringing D. O'Brien to Christian county; Id. (8 Mar.) 45. For corn, wood and hay furnished volunteers at Camp Butler; Id. (8 Mar.) 46. Expenses of first special session; 2 L. 1867 (13 June) 5. Expenses second special session; Id. (28 June) 19.

1869.—For expenses of adjourned session; L. 1869 (17 Apr.) 11. Ordinary expenses until next regular; Id. (30 Mar.) 12. Expenses of session, in part; Id. (14 Jan.) 14. Also, Id. (11 Feb.) 15. Ordinary expenses until next regular session; Id. (11 Mar.) 15. Postage of the session; Id. (11 Jan.) 18. Sundry expenses of session; Id. (24 Mar.) 34. For a portrait of Gov. Palmer; Id. (11 Mar.) 46. To pay certain incidental expenses; Id. 204.

AUDUBON COUNTY.

Act 6 Feb., to establish the county of Audubon, after a favorable vote; L. 1843, 73.

BANKS AND BANKING.

Examination of Bank of Edwardsville; Pr. L. 1827 (13 Feb.) 26. General system established; L. 1851 (15 Feb.) 163. Supplemental to foregoing; L. 1853. (10 Feb.) 30. Supplemental act amended; L. 1855 (10 Jan.) 32. Rock Island Bank to file October quarterly report; L. 1853 (1 Feb.) 228. Clark's Exchange Banks consolidated; Pr. L. 1853 (8 Feb.) 539. Auditor's duty with banks going into liquidation; L. 1855 (14 Feb.) 31. Banks to receive due proportion of payments on stocks deposited; Id. (15 Feb.) 164. Amending all the foregoing; L. 1857 (14 Feb.) 23. Amending act 15 Feb. 1851; Id. (18 Feb.) 220. General law amending all the foregoing; L. 1861 (14 Feb.) 39. Bank commissioners to execute their duties; Id (22 Feb.) 52. Establishing a general system on specie basis; submitted to the people; Id. (20 Feb.) 53. Abolishing office of bank commissioner; L. 1865 (13

Feb.) 20. Auditor's duty with bank note plates and impressions; Id. (16 Feb.) 20. Securities withdrawn in certain cases; L. 1867 (28 Feb.) 48.

BENTON COUNTY.

For the creation of; boundary and organization; L. 1843 (4 Mar.) 104..

BLIND ASYLUM.

Establishment of; L. 1849 (13 Jan.) 39. Foregoing amended; L. 1851 (15 Feb.) 100. Further provisions respecting; L. 1853 (12 Feb.) 90. Foregoing amended; two classes of trustees; L. 1857 (13 Feb.) 84. Appropriations for; L. 1859 (19 Feb.) 12. For 1861—2; L. 1861 (21 Feb.) 129. For 1863—4; L. 1863 (21 Feb.) 15. For 1865—6; L. 1865 (15 Feb.) 16. For 1867—8; L. 1867 (28 Feb.) 9. For 1869—70; L. 1869 (10 Mar.) 28.

BOOKS PURCHASED BY THE STATE.

Governor to subscribe for 40 copies of Smith's Map of Illinois; L. 1821 (12 Feb.) 147. Breese Reports, 150 copies at $3. each; L. 1831 (12 Feb.) 188. Sidney Breese allowed $75. in full for said reports; Pr. L. 1833 (28 Feb.) 116. Purple's Real Estate Statutes, 250 copies at not to exceed $3.; L. 1849 (10 Feb.) 94. Freeman's Digest, 500 copies; L. 1855 (13 Feb.) 174. Haines' Township Organization, 10 copies to each township at 25 cents each; Id. (9 Feb.) 188. In addition, 1300 copies; L. 1857 (14 Feb.) 59. Purple's Statutes, 1000 copies at $4. each; L. 1857, (28 Jan.) 43. Scates' Statutes, 2000 copies at $5. each; Id. (16 Feb.) 158. Beecher's Breese, 500 copies at $4. each; L. 1861 (29 Jan.) 73. Freeman's Digest, 3rd volume, 500 copies at $5.; Id. (12 Feb.) 124. Foregoing amended; L. 1863 (2 Feb.) 51. Henry & Reed's Digest, 500 copies at $7.; L. 1865 (13 Feb.) 82. Reports of the Supreme Court, $6. per copy; Id. (8 Feb.) 103. Wood & Long's Digest, 500 copies at $8. 1st volume and $4. 2d volume; L. 1867 (25 Feb.) 8. Bateman's decisions on the school law, one for each board of trustees and school directors at $1.50 each; Id. (16 Feb.) 160. Gross' Statutes, 500 copies at $8. each; L. 1869 (10 Mar.) 30.

BOND COUNTY.

County formed prior to the organization of the state. Auditor to lease College township not to exceed 10 years; L. 1821 (31 Jan.) 60. Manufacturing Co. of Shoal Creek chartered; L. 1823 (5 Feb.) 113. Land reconveyed to Martin Jones; Id. (17 Feb.) 157 86. Samuel Houston, late sheriff, time to pay the state extended; Pr. L. 1827 (13 Feb.) 27. Montgomery and Gilliard, lessees of Shoal Creek Salines, released from conditions; Id. (5 Feb.) 29. Governor to lease Salines; R. S. 1833 (23 Jan.) 550. Roxana Baker to sell and convey real estate; Pr. L. 1833 (19 Feb.) 118. Willard Twiss, county clerk, released from liability for unlawful issue of marriage license; L. 1835 (31 Jan.) 65. Road from Greenville to Vandalia re-located in part; Id. (29 Jan.) 96. Lands of the estate of James McCracken to be sold; L. 1836 (8 Dec. 1835) 261. County to loan its share of the internal improvement appropriation; L. 1839 (12 Feb.) 76. Sale of Saline lands in said county; Id. (2 Mar.) 212. Foregoing amended; L. 1843 (4 Mar.) 271. Amity Academy chartered; Pr. L. 1839 (2 Mar.) 247. Bond County Academy chartered; L. 1841 (19 Feb.) 9. County limits extended; Id. 80. Payment of county revenue out of the internal improvement fund; Id. (17 Feb.) 213. County limits extended; L. 1843 (2 Mar.) 98. The bonus of said county applied to the county school fund; Id. (21 Feb.) 148. Four justices and constables in Amity; Id. (24 Jan.) 170. Town name of Amity changed to Pocahontas; Pr. L. 1847 (25 Feb.) 205. Borrow money and levy a tax to build a court house; L. 1853 (12 Feb.) 180. Action of the county court under the foregoing, legalized; Pr. L. 1854 (22 Feb.) 76. Town name of Houston changed to Mulberry; additional justice and constable allowed; Pr. L. 1857 (7 Feb.) 272. Jurisdiction of county court extended; practice therein; L. 1859 (19 Feb.) 98. To pay expenses of *posse commitatus* called out by deputy sheriff Wm. N. Stephenson July and August 1864; 1 Pr. L. 1865 (16 Feb.) 541. Bond County Trust and Loan Co. chartered; 1 Pr. L. 1867 (21 Feb.) 56.

Greenville.—Trustees not to keep open state or county roads beyond corporate limits; Pr. L. 1839 (28 Feb.) 158. Greenville Hotel Co. chartered; L. 1841 (23 Feb.) 132. First Presbyterian Society name changed to First Congregational Society; L. 1845 (21 Feb.) 318 Town chartered; Pr. L. 1855 (15 Feb.) 29. Foregoing amended and extended; boundary defined; Pr. L. 1859 (24 Jan.) 618. Greenville Mutual Fire Insurance Co. chartered; Id. (15 Feb.) 418. Name changed to Adams Insurance Co.; office transferred to Freeport; Pr. L. 1863 (21 Feb.) 192. Almira College chartered; Pr. L. 1857 (13 Feb.) 582. Ladies' Library Association chartered; 2 Pr. L. 1867 (23 Feb) 254. Vacates an alley; 3 Pr. L. 1867 (25 Feb.) 102.

BOONE COUNTY.

County created; named in memory of Col. Daniel Boone the first settler of Kentucky; 1 L. 1837 (4 Mar.) 96. Boundaries defined; L. 1839 (2 Mar.) 242. Jefferson Institute chartered; located Town 44—4; Pr. L. 1839 (21 Feb.) 86. County boundaries defined; L. 1843 (28 Feb.) 92. Pre-emption to Alfred Shattuck on lands in Town 43—4; L. 1845 (28 Feb.) 109. Special county tax for 1845—6; Id. 115. Jefferson Lodge No. 7 of the I. O. O. F.; Pr. L. 1847 (19 Feb.) 107. To Albert Alexander state pedler's license for life, conditionally; Pr. L. 1851 (12 Feb.) 85. Jurisdiction of county court extended; Pr. L. 1854 (27 Feb.) 239. Further extended; L. 1857 (18 Feb.) 150. Both foregoing repealed; L. 1863 (12 Feb.) 28. County to borrow $10,000. to build court house and jail; Pr. L. 1854 (4 Mar.) 152. Trustees elected at next annual town meeting to supercede the present school trustees; Id. 155. Special tax to liqui-

date county indebtedness; Pr. L. 1855 (15 Feb.) 713. Roads located and platted in townships of Belvidere and Flora in 1856; L. 1857 (5 Feb.) 82. Asel Merrill convicted of larceny, restored to citizenship; Pr. L. 1857 (14 Feb.) 615. Time of holding county court; L. 1859 (18 Feb.) 100. For the purchase of a poor farm; Id. (24 Feb.) 209. Special tax to pay bounty orders; L. 1863 (14 Feb.) 25. Boone County Agricultural Society chartered; 1 Pr. L. 1867 (30 Jan.) 41. Tax levy to pay county indebtedness incurred in raising troops, legalized; 3 Pr. L. 1867 (28 Feb.) 128. Concerning sales of town lots; L. 1841 (29 Jan.) 326.

Belvidere.—Craig Seminary of Learning chartered; Pr. L. 1839 (2 Mar.) 238. Belvidere Seminary Association chartered; purchase blocks 26 and 27; Pr. L. 1847 (18 Feb.) 104. Vacates part of town plat; Id (26 Feb.) 206. Town chartered; L. 1852 (23 June) 252. Boone County Mutual Insurance Co. chartered; Pr. L. 1853 (27 Jan.) 373. Name changed to the Protection Insurance Co.; Pr. L. 1861 (18 Feb.) 347. Supervisors to vacate part of town plat; Pr. L. 1857 (10 Feb.) 348. Location of roads in 1856 legalized; L. 1857 (5 Feb.) 82. Allen C. Fuller and others to form a Hotel Co.; Pr. L. 1857 (16 Feb.) 933. Town to bridge the Kishwaukee; 1 Pr. L. 1867 (25 Feb.) 838. Boone County Monumental Association chartered; 2 Pr. L. 1867 (25 Feb.) 450. Collection of taxes extended; 3 Pr. L. 1867 (26 Feb.) 121.

BOUNTIES.

Conntics of Boone, Carroll, Stephenson, Jo-Daviess, Kane, Lee, Winnebago, Bureau, Knox, Kendall, DeKalb, McHenry, Lake, Edgar, Du Page, Woodford, Stark, Warren, Marshall, Grundy, Putnam, Kankakee, Ogle, Whiteside, Will and Henry to levy special tax to pay bounties to volunteers; 1 Pr. L. 1865 (18 Jan.) 100. Towns in the counties of Rock Island, Peoria, Cook [except North, West and South Chicago], Sangamon, Kane, DuPage, Grundy, Knox, Warren, Stark, Livingston, Vermilion, Bureau, Putnam, Ogle, Henry, DeKalb, Tazewell and Marshall [act 16 Feb. 1865, Id.] to levy special tax to pay bounties to volunteers; 1 Pr. L. 1865 (2 Feb.) 102. Amends §9 of foregoing; Id. (8 Feb.) 106. Counties of Champaign, Piatt, Macon, and Moultric to levy tax to pay bounties to volunteers; Id. (2 Feb.) 106. Counties of Alexander, Pulaski, Massac, Pope, Hardin, Gallatin, White, Edwards, Wayne, Hamilton, Saline, Johnson, Union, Jackson, Williamson, Franklin, Jefferson, Perry, Randolph, Monroe, Green, Washington, Marion, Fayette, Effingham, Clay, Richland, Lawrence and Wabash to borrow money and levy tax to pay bounties; Id. (6 Feb.) 109. Counties of Jasper, Clark, Cumberland and Crawford to levy special tax to pay bounties; Id. (7 Feb.) 109. Counties of Morgan, Scott, Logan, Calhoun and Jersey to borrow each $100,000., to create a fund for bounties to volunteers; Id. (14 Feb.) 111. Counties of Shelby, Douglas and St. Clair to pay bounties; only $100,000. to be raised in any one year; Id. (9 Feb.) 113.

BROWN COUNTY.

County established out of Schuyler; boundary and organization; L. 1839 (1 Feb.) 53. Mt. Sterling chartered; 1 L. 1837 (10 Feb.) 331. Changing the public square; Id. (2 Mar.) 333. Certain town lots deeded to J. W. Edwards; L. 1857 (14 Feb.) 172. Name of Centreville changed to Ripley; 2 L. 1837 (20 July) 94. Centreville Steam Mill Co. chartered; Id. (21 July) 29. County commissioners to appoint an assessor; L. 1841 (17 Feb.) 34. Thomas S. Brockman, collector, released from judgment; L. 1845 (28 Feb.) 115. Foregoing amended; auditor's duty with his accounts; Pr. L. 1851 (15 Feb.) 229. La Grange plat vacated in part; L. 1845 (3 Mar.) 234. Records of law titles transcribed, certified and considered books of record; L. 1851 (1 Feb.) 18. Act 20 Jan. 1849 (L. 1849, 108) extended to said county; Ibid. Sale of the Versailles public square; L. 1851 (17 Feb.) 188. J. C. Moses, late sheriff, allowed time to pay a judgment; L. 1855 (15 Feb.) 152. Copying the records to be completed; effect of; L. 1857 (28 Jan.) 46. Sale of swamp lands; Id. (13 Feb.) 61. Securities of Jno. C. Moses allowed two years from Feb. 1857 to make settlement; Id. (17 Feb.) 201. County subscription to Northern Cross R. R. legalized; Pr. L. 1857 (13 Jan.) 229. Mt. Sterling Marine and Fire Insurance Co. chartered; Id. (11 Feb.) 435. Townships to support their own paupers; Id. (19 Feb.) 1360. Additional school districts created; L. 1859 (9 Feb.) 182. Versailles chartered; Pr. L. 1861 (21 Feb.) 732. Tax to pay bounties to volunteers; not exceeding $500.; 1 Pr. L. 1865 (9 Feb.) 115. Certain lands attached to school district No. 2 Town 1—4; 2 Pr. L. 1865 (16 Feb.) 300. Versailles Mineral Springs Co. chartered; 2 Pr. L. 1867 (23 Feb.) 440. Election of a county surveyor; L. 1869 (5 Apr.) 162. Duties of county Supt. of schools; Id. (16 Apr.) 395.

BUREAU COUNTY.

County created; boundary and organization; 1 L. 1837 (28 Feb.) 93. Erection of public buildings; L. 1839 (2 Mar.) 228. Greenfield changed to La Moile; L. 1840 (3 Feb.) 107. Plat of Fairmont vacated; Id. 108. Commissioners to sell school lands in Town 14—8; L. 1841 (27 Feb.) 258. La Moille Agricultural and Mechanical Association; L. 1843 (6 Mar.) 16. County to borrow $5,000. to complete court house; Id. (23 Feb.) 110. County confirmed in certain ferry privileges; Id. (3 Feb.) 144. County to extend Hugh Freny's lease of Hennepin ferry for 10 years; P. L. 1847 (17 Feb.) 44. Records in Putnam county to be transcribed; certificate and effect; L. 1849 (10 Feb.) 109. Benj. Newell and heirs to construct a canal from the Illinois to lake Depeau; Id. (12 Feb.) 133. Time to build extended to Feb. 1856; L. 1831 (15 Feb.) 125. Grant renewed; complete in 5 years; Pr. L. 1858 (7 Feb.) 273. Hogs not to run at large; Id. (10 Jan.) 185. Clairon Cemetery Association chartered; Pr. L. 1851 (17 Feb.) 291. Town of Gold created; L. 1853 (12 Feb.) 202. Towns to support their own paupers; vote thereon; Id. (10 Feb.) 261. School tax in district No 1 town of Hall legalized; L. 1855 (6 Feb.) 110. Livingston town plat vacated; Pr. L. 1857 (7 Feb.) 271. Sale of swamp lands confirmed; Id. (18 Feb.) 1206. For transcribing the old records of sales and redemption of land from 1823 to 1854; Id. (18 Feb.) 1377. Jurisdiction of county court extended; L. 1859 (24 Feb.) 96. Dover Academy chartered; Pr. L. 1859 (24 Feb.) 361. Princeton and Bureau Valley R. R. chartered; Id (18 Feb.). 491. Preacher's Aid Society of Northern Illinois District; Pr. L. 1861 (18 Feb.) 52. Supervisors location of a road from Arlington to the east county line legalized; Id. (22 Feb.) 544. Sheffield chartered; Id. (22 Feb.) 718. Foregoing amended; 3 Pr. L. 1867 (9 Feb.) 595. Loan in aid of volunteers legalized; L. 1863 (12 Feb.) 25. Plat of Providence partly vacated; Pr. L. 1863 (13 June) 273. County interest bearing bonds issued in payment of bounties legalized; 1 Pr. L. 1865 (6 Feb.) 116. Organization of First Congregational Church at Neponset legalized; Id. (16 Feb.) 236. Benj. Newell to construct a canal from Negro Creek to lake Depeau; Id. (16 Feb.) 556. Lovejoy Monument Association chartered; erect at Oakland Cemetery or village of Princeton; 2 Pr. L. 1865 (15 Feb.) 91. Chas. L. Kelsey surviving trustee to to re-convey to Francis D. Shugart property held in trust for her; Id. (16 Feb.) 249. Road from Hennepin to mouth of Rock river re-located in part; Id. (15 Feb.) 267. Trenton changed to Sherman; Id. (16 Feb.) 584. Vacates a certain street in Berlin—land sold for school purposes; Id. (16 Feb.) 662. Vacates plat of Kinnowood; Id. 664. Towns of Fairfield, Mineral and Concord to bridge Green river at Gold; 1 Pr. L. 1867 (28 Feb.) 180. Bureau Co. Dairy and Cheese Co. chartered; Id. 5 Mar. 906. Bureau County Concrete Co. chartered; 2 Pr. L. 1867 (5 Mar.) 304. Wyanet and Pond Creek Railway and Carrying Co. chartered; Id. (20 Feb.) 696. Road from Mendota to Arlington located; Id. (23 Feb.) 822. Proceedings of school trustees Town 16—9 legalized; 3 Pr. L. 1867 (29 Jan.) 15. Vacates an alley in Arlington; Id. (5 Mar.) 111. Bourbonnais changed to Lovejoy; Id. 247. Neponset corporate powers extended; Id. (25 Feb.) 455. La Moille chartered; Id. (25 Feb.) 485. Sherman changed to Dupue; Id. (18 Feb.) 607. Annexing for school purposes sections 4 and 5 Town 17—6 to Town 18—6; Id. (7 Mar.) 631. Wiona changed to Walden; L. 1869 (26 Mar.) 297. Geo. S. Emerson, treasurer Town 16—7, released from payment of $907.99 of which he was robbed; Id. (27 Mar.) 335.

Princeton.—Time of levying a tax extended; L. 1841 (25 Feb.) 84. Town chartered; Pr. L. 1849 (8 Feb.) 120. Boundary fixed; construction of plank road to the railroad depot; Pr. L. 1853 (12 Feb.) 607. Further respecting plank road to depot; limits extended; Pr. L. 1854 (28 Feb.) 133. Survey of Elston's, Wiswall's and Flint's additions corrected; part of North street vacated; Pr. L. 1855 (15 Feb.) 197. Vacates alleys in Elston's addition; Pr. L. 1857 (16 Feb.) 801. Corporate powers generally extended; Id. (18 Feb.) 1415. Foregoing amended; opening streets and public grounds; Pr. L. 1859 (24 Feb.) 661. Charter amended; power to license; Pr. L. 1861 (22 Feb.) 715. Powers further extended; 2 Pr. L. 1865 (16 Feb.) 560. And again; 3 Pr. L. 1867 (18 Feb.) 610. Princeton Seminary chartered; in Town 16—9; Pr. L. 1837 (21 Feb.) 61. Part of tax for 1858 in district No. 1, remitted; L. 1859 (15 Jan.) 177. Young Men's Association chartered; 2 Pr. L. 1865 (16 Feb.) 19. Princeton Loan and Trust Co. chartered; Id. 24. Bureau County Fire Insurance Co. chartered; 2 Pr. L. 1867 (7 Mar.) 112. Princeton High School District chartered; 3 Pr. L. 1867 (5 Feb.) 16.

Tiskilwa.—Names of Indiantown and Windsor changed to Tiskilwa; L. 1840 (3 Feb.) 107. Town incorporated; Pr. L. 1855 (14 Feb.) 154. Chartered again; Pr. L. 1857 (16 Feb.) 863. Foregoing amended; 3 Pr. L. 1867 (16 Feb.) 588. Leases executed to Geo. Cattell and Calvin Stephens by town trustees confirmed; Pr. L. 1861 (20 Feb.) 723. Liberty Square vacated; Id. (22 Feb.) 724. People's Coal Co. chartered; 2 Pr. L. 1867 (6 Mar.) 390.

CALHOUN COUNTY.

County formed out of south part of Pike; L. 1825 (10 Jan.) 65. Relating to county revenue; L. 1826 (27 Jan.) 89. Appropriating $300. for roads and bridges; L. 1831 (22 Jan.) 19. County seat removed from Gilead to Guilford; 1 L. 1837 (4 Mar.) 106. Foregoing repealed; vote on its removal from Guilford; 2 L. 1837 (21 July) 14. Temporarily located at Hamburg; vote on permanent location; Pr. L. 1847 (23 Feb.) 32. Mississippi and Illinois Canal Co. chartered; Pr. L. 1837 (20 Feb.) 21. Commissioners to receive subscriptions and carry foregoing into effect; L. 1840 (29 Jan.) 48 §2. Calhoun Coal and Mining Co. chartered; Pr. L. 1837 (2 Mar.) 238. Foregoing amended; L. 1840 (31 Jan.) 49. Share of county in internal improvement fund; L. 1839 (27 Feb.) 198. Wm. Howlett allowed $109.50 for apprehending fugitive; L. 1840 (1 Feb.) 100. Calhoun County Agricultural Co. chartered; Pr. L. 1853 (9 Feb.) 414. Vacates plat of Lower Guilford; Id. (11 Feb.) 516. Geo. W. Sampson, ferry across the Mississippi at Cape-au-Grey Rock; Pr. L. 1855 (14 Feb.) 597. Stephen Farrow, ferry across the Illinois at Columbiana; Id. (15 Feb.) 598. For transcribing certain records in Madison and Pike counties; Id. (6 Feb.) 709. For reclaiming overflowed lands by construction of a levee along the Mississippi; L. 1857 (10 Feb.) 255.

CANALS.

See also Illinois and Michigan Canal.

Beardstown and Sangamon.—Chartered; L. 1836 (28 Dec. 1835) 97. Amended; repeals first proviso in §10; Pr. L. 1837 (4 Mar.) 328. Supplemental to first foregoing; if not begun by 1 Jan. 1841 the state to navigate the Sangamon; Pr. L. 1839 (2 Mar.) 196. Amends the several acts; L. 1841 (24 Feb.) 48.

Chicago and Mississippi.—Chartered; 1 Pr. L. 1865 (15 Feb.) 209.

Rockport and Mississippi.—Chartered; Pr. L. 1837 (21 Feb.) 78. Amended (probably); time extended; Pr. L. 1839 (12 Jan.) 15.

Resolution.—Concerning the connection of

certain canals in Illinois and Indiana; L. 1839, 297.

CARROLL COUNTY.

County created; boundary; vote on locating county seat; L. 1839 (22 Feb.) 160. Boundary extended; L; 1841 (27 Feb.) 90. Removal of county seat from Savanna; vote thereon; L. 1843 (2 Mar.) 126. Town 23-3 attached to 23-4, for school purposes; L. 1851 (15 Feb.) 124. Records in recorder's office indexed; to be kept up; Id. 130. Joseph McKaillips pre-empt part of Sec. 17 Town 25-3; Pr. L. 1855 (12 Feb.) 926. Jurisdiction of county court extended under act 27 Feb. 1854 (Pr. L. 1854, 239); L. 1857 (14 Feb.) 55. Foregoing repealed; L. 1859 (10 Feb.) 102. Re-survey and sale of school lands Town 25-4; Id. 173. Towns 25-2 and 25-3 united for school purposes; Id. (16 Feb.) 179. School land in Mt. Carroll and Town 24-4; Id. (18 Feb.) 302. Carroll County Coal and Mining Co. chartered; Pr. L. 1857 (11 Feb.) 442. Again; Id. (19 Feb.) 1431. Amendment; Pr. L. 1859 (12 Feb.) 356. Amendment; name changed to Carroll County Coal Mining and Petroleum Co.; 2 Pr. L. 1865 (16 Feb.) 56. Special tax for volunteer purposes; L. 1863 (13 June) 40. County indebtedness, $75,000. bonded; 1 Pr. L. 1865 (6 Feb.) 536. Geo. A. Thomson, ferry across the Mississippi at Town 23-3; Id. (15 Feb.) 561. Carroll County Petroleum and Mining Co. chartered; 2 Pr. L. 1865 (16 Feb.) 56. York changed to Thompson; Id. 650.

Mt. Carroll.—Vacates town plat; Pr. L. 1851 (8 Feb.) 56. Boundary altered and defined; Pr. L. 1853 (10 Feb.) 579. Funk's survey in 1852 confirmed; L. 1853 (12 Feb.) 270. City chartered; 1 Pr. L. 1867 (25 Feb.) 581. Mt. Carroll Mutual Manufacturing and Hydraulic Co. chartered; Pr. L. 1851 (11 Feb) 76. Mt. Carroll Seminary chartered; L. 1852 (18 June) 18. Amendment; erection of additional buildings; Pr. L. 1855 (14 Feb.) 363. Again chartered; 1 Pr. L. 1867 (25 Feb.) 13.

Savanna.—Vacates town plat; Pr. L. 1847 (20 Feb.) 204. Re-survey; Pr. L. 1855 (12 Feb.) 196. Vacates part of Commerce street, 2 Pr. L. 1865 (16 Feb.) 660. Savanna Seminary of Learning chartered; Pr. L. 1839 (2 Mar.) 238. C. G. Eldridge, ferry across the Mississippi; L. 1843 (23 Feb.) 145. Wade H. Eldridge, the same; Pr. L. 1851 (1 Feb.) 45. Enoch Chamberlain and others, the same; Pr. L. 1861 (8 Feb.) 327. Savanna Cemetery Association chartered; Pr. L. 1855 (15 Feb.) 441. Lease property for school purposes; L. 1869 (26 Mar.) 397.

Lenark.—Town chartered; 3 Pr. L. 1867 (28 Feb.) 515. Pioneer Insurance Co. chartered; 1 Pr. L. 1865 (16 Feb.) 751. Amendment; office removed to Springfield; 2 Pr. L. 1867 (28 Feb.) 182.

CASS COUNTY.

County created; boundary and organization; 1 L. 1837 (3 Mar.) 101. Foregoing confirmed and an election thereunder, fixing county seat at Beardstown; 2 L. 1837 (21 July) 48. Philadelphia plat legalized; Id. (15 Feb.) 311. Road from Levetts' to Maxwell's changed; L. 1839 (2 Mar.) 59. County seat to be at Virginia; Id. 287. Taxes of 1839, collection of; L. 1841 (16 Feb.) 305. Vote on location of county seat; L. 1843 (4 Mar.) 102. Securities of Lemon Plaster, late collector, to settle with the state; L. 1845 (3 Mar.) 127. Securities may be released; Id. (18 Feb.) 343. School commissioner to appropriate certain funds; Id. (6 Jan.) 185. County limits extended; portion of Morgan county included; vote thereon; Id. (26 Feb. 313. Election of school trustees in Towns 17-8 and 9 legalized; Pr. L. 1847 (15 Feb.) 28. J. M. Ruggles to bridge the Sangamon at the Petersburg and Bath road; Cass and Mason counties to keep in repair; Pr. L. 1849 (12 Feb.) 13. County seat removed from Beardstown to Virginia; election first held thereon; L. 1853 (11 Feb.) 152. For the same; L. 1857 (16 Feb.) 193. And again; 1 Pr. L. 1867 (14 Feb.) 892. Vote to take $50,000. stock in Illinois river R. R. legalized; Pr. L. 1857 (16 Feb.) 838. County Fair Grounds Association chartered; Id. (18 Feb. (1181. Meredosia Bridge and R. R. Co. chartered; Id. (18 Feb.) 1318. Incorporation of Chandlerville legalized; Pr. L. 1861 (21 Feb.) 577. Levy special tax to pay bounties; bounty not over $500.; 1 Pr. L. 1865 (16 Feb.) 117. County to refund city of Beardstown $750. wrongfully collected ferry license; Id. (14 Feb.) 892.

Beardstown.—Incorporation legalized; 2 L. 1837 (21 July) 95. Powers extended; L. 1841 (26 Feb.) 340. Fines and penalties collected go to city treasury; Pr. L. 1857 (31 Jan. 227. Levy special tax to pay bonds issued to Rock Island and Alton R. R.; Id. (4 Feb.) 241. City incorporation legalized; limits defined; Id. (16 Feb.) 1049. Charter amended and extended; 1 Pr. L. 1865 (15 Feb.) 252. An additional notary public; 1 L. 1837 (3 Mar.) 176. Beardstown Improvement Co. chartered; Pr. L. 1837 (27 Feb.) 127. Beardstown Seminary chartered; Id. (1 Mar.) 181. Beardstown Insurance Co. chartered; Id. (3 Mar.) 268. Fund commissioners to give up to Bassett & Taylor, 7 promissory notes, conditionally; Pr. L. 1847 (25 Feb.) 183. Alley vacated; Pr. L. 1851 (17 Feb.) 310. German Literary Association chartered; Pr. L. 1857 (11 Feb.) 421. Oakwoods Cemetery Association chartered; Id. (16 Feb.) 919. Beardstown Gas Light and Coke Co. chartered; Id. (16 Feb.) 934. Illinois Insurance Co. chartered; Pr. L. 1859 (21 Feb.) 390. Transfer of ferry by Nancy Beard to Luther A. Jones and others for 25 years confirmed; 1 Pr. L. 1867 (26 Feb.) 942.

Virginia.—Town chartered; Pr. L. 1857 (19 Feb.) 1443. Foregoing amended; provide town prison; §23 repealed; Pr. L. 1861 (22 Feb.) 831. Virginia Seminary of the Cumberland Presby. Church chartered; L. 1852 (18 June) 25. Name changed to Union College; Pr. L. 1857 (16 Feb.) 1072. Virginia Female Seminary of the Providence Presby. Church chartered; Pr. L. 1857 (17 Feb.) 843. Washington Gas Light Co. chartered; 1. Pr. L. 1867 (8 Mar.) 980. Virginia Oil and Mining Co. chartered; 2 Pr. L. 1867 (9 Mar.) 392.

CHAMPAIGN COUNTY.

County created; boundary and organization; court held in Philip Stanford's house; name of county seat to be Urbanna; Pr. L. 1833 (20 Feb.) 28. Share in proceeds of Gallatin Salines; L 1835 (1 Jan.) 43. Application of; 1 L. 1837 (1 Mar.) 88. Saline appropriation of 100 acres of land; L. 1839 (19 Feb.) 137. Assessment for 1839 legalized; L. 1840 (3 Feb.) 111. School lands in Town 20-9; L. 1845 (3 Mar.) 136. Sale of seminary lands; Id. (26 Feb.) 208. School funds paid directly to commissioners; Id. (3 Mar.) 235. School lands Town 18-11 sold; Id. (21 Feb.) 326. School tax levied Town 19-8 legalized; 3 Pr. L. 1867 (25 Feb.) 113. Vacates part of plat of Sidney; L. 1845 (28 Feb.) 288. Collection of revenue for 1850 extended; L. 1851 (14 Feb.) 94. Champaign and Vermilion Railroad and Coal Mining Co. chartered; Pr. L. 1855 (14 Feb.) 336. Urbanna and Champaign Institute chartered; Pr. L. 1861 (21 Feb.) 24. Amendment; $10 repealed; 1 Pr. L. 1867 (5 Mar.) 27. To pay bounties to volunteers; L. 1863 (14 Feb.) 39. Sisters of Charity of St. Joseph chartered; 1 Pr. L. 1865 (15 Feb.) 93. Funding county indebtedness; Id. 537. Farmers' Association of Homer chartered; 2 Pr. L. 1865 (16 Feb.) 667. County road law; L. 1867 (8 Mar.) 172. Champaign Dairy Co. chartered; 1 Pr. L. 1867 (13 Feb.) 908. Drain certain lands; Id. (6 Mar.) 911. Champaign and Urbana Gas Light and Coke Co. chartered; Id. (18 Feb.) 981. Urbana and Champaign Horse Railway Co. chartered; 2 Pr. L. 1867 (25 Feb.) 2.

Urbana. — City chartered; Pr. L. 1855 (14 Feb.) 135. Amended; Pr. L. 1861 (18 Feb.) 296. Further amendment; 1 Pr. L. 1867 (9 Feb.) 286. Urbana Seminary Society chartered; L. 1845 (26 Feb.) 357. Urbana Male and Female Seminary chartered; Pr. L. 1855 (15 Feb.) 372. Urbana R. R. Co. chartered; Pr. L. 1859 (24 Feb.) 522.

Champaign.—City chartered; Pr. L. 1861 (21 Feb.) 153 Amendment; issue bonds; 1 Pr. L. 1865 (16 Feb.) 256. First Presbyterian Church of Urbana changed to same of Champaign; Id. (15 Feb.) 242.

CHRISTIAN COUNTY.

County of Dane changed to Christian; L. 1840 (1 Feb.) 80. County borrow $2,400. to build court house; L. 1841 (26 Jan.) 93. Depreciated funds disposed of by school commissioners; L. 1843 (4 Mar.) 40. Assessment for 1842 legalized; L. 1845 (21 Feb.) 325. Guardian of James Marion Nelson to sell lands; Pr. L. 1847 (1 Mar.) 171. Cross Main St,. Taylorville, relocated; Id. (15 Feb.) 197. Vote on adding part of Shelby county; L. 1851 (15 Feb.) 118. Vacates plat of Allenton; Pr. L. 1853 (10 Feb.) 503. Sale of swamp lands; L. 1857 (16 Feb.) 122. Stock restrained in Rosemond; Pr. L. 1857 (16 Feb.) 1066. Foregoing repealed; Pr. L. 1863 (31 Jan.) 262. Vacates part of plat of Mt. Auburn; Id. (18 Feb.) 1377. Copying records in other counties; L. 1859 (22 Feb.) 134. Plat of Stonnington vacated Pr. L. 1863 (16 Feb.) 266. Tax to pay bounties to volunteers; bounty not exceed $500.; 1 Pr. L. 1865 (14 Feb.) 117. Vacates alley in Taylorville; 2 Pr. L. 1865 (16 Feb.) 656. Relief of School fund Town 11-3; 2 Pr. L. 1867 (28 Feb.) 804. Regulate publication of legal notices; L. 1869 (31 Mar.) 252.

Pana.—Town chartered; Pr. L. 1857 (16 Feb.) 851. Amended; regulate tippling houses etc.; Pr. L. 1861 (22 Feb.) 715. Further amended; elect two justices and constables; 2 Pr. L. 1865 (16 Feb.) 536. City chartered; 1 Pr. L. 1867 (13 Feb.) 288. Vacates part Hayward's division; Pr. L. 1863 (20 Feb.) 272. Pana Hotel Co. chartered; 2 Pr. L. 1867 (9 Mar.) 70.

CLARK COUNTY.

County established; Smith Shaw, Thomas Gill and James Watts to meet at Charles Neely's house to fix seat of justice; L. 1819 (22 Mar.) 166. Attaching part of Crawford county to Clark; L. 1823 (23 Dec. 1822) 79. Removal of county seat from Aurora to McClure's Bluff; name to be Darwin; Id. (31 Jan.) 107. To bridge Big Creek at Bell's Mill, Stony Creek near Aurora and also Mill Creek; L 1829 (19 Jan.) 147 §12. James Farrington to be administrator of Thos. Bullitt late of Louisville Ky.; Pr. L. 1833 (27 Dec. 1832) 198. Vincennes and Chicago road re located in part; L. 1836 (14 Jan.) 192. Foregoing repealed; 1 L. 1837 (4 Mar.) 279. Road from Darwin to county seat located; Id. 219. Removal of county seat from Darwin to a point to be selected; Id. (7 Jan) 255. After a favorable vote; 1 L. 1837 (1 Mar.) 105. Road from Darwin to New Richmond; Id. (2 Mar.) 238. Road from York to New Richmond located; 1 L. 1837 (31 Jan.) 243. Mill Creek navigable to Hollenbeck'e Mill, and Big Creek to Durell's Mill; L. 1839 (16 Feb.) 123. Calvin Boyd to collect taxes for 1841; L. 1843 (24 Feb.) 230. Unpaid taxes for 1842-3 collected by J. Lawrence and J. B. Anderson; sales to be made by them; L. 1845 (28 Jan.) 188. Taxes refunded on certain school lands; L 1847 (4 Feb.) 117. Wm. P. Bennett, sheriff, time to settle with state for 1846 extended; Pr. L. 1847 (23 Feb.) 180. Vacates plat of Pleasant View; Id. (27 Feb.) 210. Change of county seat, Hillibert's Point to be voted upon; L. 1849 (10 Feb.) 53. Judgment docket kept; L. 1853 (10 Feb.) 260. County to aid construction of plank roads; Pr. L. 1854 (28 Feb.) 157. S. McClure, sheriff, allowed reward for apprehending W. J. Shaw charged with murder; L. 1855 (15 Feb.) 158. Vacates plat of Caryford; Pr. L. 1857 (13 Feb.) 538. Chas Summers, ferry across the Wabash at Darwin; Id. 547. Foregoing amended; Edgar Sommers to succeed; Pr. L. 1861 (7 Feb.) 320. Vacates part of plat of Darwin; Id. (18 Feb.) 1341. Vacates plat of Kœrner; Id. (19 Feb.) 1427. County subscription to the Wabash R. R. Co.; submitted to vote; Pr. L. 1859 (21 Feb.) 523. Westfield College chartered; 1 Pr. L. 1865 (15 Feb.) 17. Alvina Blackman made heir of Jemima Dawson; 2 Pr. L. 1865 (15 Feb.) 239. Benj. F. Flesher, ferry across the Wabash at Bowen's Bluff; 1 Pr. L. 1867 (25 Feb.) 941.

Marshall.—Town chartered; Pr. L. 1853 (10 Feb. 212. City chartered; Pr. L. 1855 (15 Feb.) 232. Foregoing repealed; Pr. L. 1859 (24 Feb.)

214. Marshall Academy chartered; may change to Marshall College; Pr. L. 1839 (2 Mar.) 177. Marshall College chartered; Pr. L. 1857 (16 Feb.) 831. Marshall Female Seminary chartered; Pr. L. 1839 (2 Mar.) 214. Marshall Cemetery Association chartered; Pr. L. 1855 (15 Feb.) 442. Foregoing amended; jurisdiction extended over block 7 in said city; Pr. L. 1857 (13 Feb.) 548. Eagle Insurance Co. chartered; Id. (16 Feb.) 930.

CLAY COUNTY.

County formed and boundary defined; L. 1825 (23 Dec. 1824) 18. Road from McCalla's bridge to Vandalia, relative to; Id. (15 Jan.) 119. Road from McCawley's bridge to Muddy Fork, $300, to improve; L. 1829 (2 Jan.) 127. County to share in proceeds of Gallatin Salines for internal improvements; L. 1831 (16 Feb.) 15 §1. County court to enter land with proceeds of saline sales; L. 1835 (12 Feb.) 117 §7. Toll bridge over Little Wabash on Vandalia and Lawrenceville road, by Sullivan & Green; 1 L. 1837 (4 Mar.) 34. The same, on Albion and Maysville road, by Toller and others; Id. 38. L. D. Hillerman to erect a mill dam over Little Wabash in Town 2—8; L. 1839 (23 Feb.) 169. The same, to S. Husalton; L. 1841 (26 Feb.) 187. Assessment for 1839 legalized; L. 1840 (30 Jan.) 70. Collection of revenue for 1839; L. 1840 (3 Feb.) 111. Removal of county seat from Maysville; L. 1841 (26 Feb.) 96. Louisville Exporting, Importing and Manufacturing Co. chartered; Id. (27 Feb.) 147. Erect mill dams across Little Wabash; J. Ditter and N. Levitt, Town. 4—8; H. Yates, Town 3—8; Id. (27 Feb.) 188 The same, across Raccoon creek Town. 2—7, by B. Vermilion; L. 1843 (1 Feb.) 174. The same, across Little Wabash Town 3—7, by Alex. Johnson; Id. (2 Mar.) 176. School commissioners of said county and that of Richland, to make settlement; Id. (3 Feb.) 272. Collection of taxes 1843; assessment for 1844 legalized; L. 1845 (26 Feb.) 163. Distribution of school fund for 1846; L. 1847 (16 Feb.) 115. The same; Id. (22 Feb.) 154. The same for 1848; L. 1849 (30 Jan.) 153. Strother B. Walker, security for Edmund Jones, collector, released from obligations to the state; Pr. L. 1851 (17 Feb.) 261. Carmi mill, to be approved by county courts of Clay and Wayne; L. 1853 (12 Feb.) 246. County swamp lands; L. 1855 (12 Feb.) 150. Deeds to Daniel Ingrahm for certain swamp lands; Pr. L. 1857 (18 Feb.) 1382. Removal of county seat from Louisville to Flora; election first held; L. 1861 (18 Feb.) 81. Addition of territory from Wayne Co.; L. 1863 (21 Feb.) 84. Vote of Horter township to pay bounties legalized; 1 Pr. L. 1865 (16 Feb.) 162. Vacates an alley in Clay City; 2 Pr. L. 1865 (16 Feb.) 654. Vacates Mead's addition to Maysville; Id. 659. Louisville incorporated; 3 Pr. L. 1867 (1 Mar.) 223. Flora incorporated; Id. (27 Feb.) 421. Allowing Levi Hobbs $200. for returning Johnson and Hudson, charged with robbery; L. 1869 (27 Mar.) 51.

Xenia.—Chartered; 2 Pr. L. 1865 (16 Feb.) 644. Foregoing generally amended; 3 Pr. L. 1867 (7 Mar.) 168. Vacates an alley; 2 Pr. L. 1865 (16 Feb.) 654.

CLINTON COUNTY.

County formed from Washington, Bond and Fayette; L. 1825 (27 Dec. 1824) 27. Road from Vandalia to Kaskaskia relocated through this county; R. S. 1827 (12 Feb.) 347. To share in proceeds of Gallatin Salines, for internal improvements; L. 1831 (16 Feb.) 15 §1. John Kain, toll bridge across Beaver and Shoal Creeks; Id. (9 Feb.) 24. County clerk's office kept in Upper Carlyle; Id. (15 Feb.) 48. Road from Carlyle to Charles Cox's relocated; Id. (10 Feb.) 150. Debts of Washington county divided between said county and Clinton under §10 act 27 Dec. 1824 (L. 1825, 27); Pr. L. 183 (2 Mar.) 16. Respecting road from Carlyle to Shoal Creek; Id. (20 Feb.) 141. Circuit and county clerks keep their offices at Lower Carlyle; L. 1836 (16 Jan.) 248. Respecting public records; Id. (15 Jan.) 258. To open road located by act 1 Mar. 1839; L. 1839 (2 Mar.) 57. Saline appropriation changed; Id. (12 Feb.) 76. Borrow money to build court house and jail; Id. (16 Feb.) 110. Clinton Steam Mill Co. chartered; L. 1840 (8 Jan.) 41. Bridge over Shoal creek on Vincennes and St. Louis road to be free; L. 1843 (23 Feb.) 46. Concerning the 16th section Town 1—5; Id. 276. Certain returns under the School law legalized; Id. (3 Feb.) 280. Thos. Hood to sell certain lands in town 3—2; L. 1845 (3 Mar.) 127. Respecting school section Town 1—5; Id. (26 Feb.) 168. Free Bridge over Shoal creek; Id. (26 Feb.) 181. Bridge across the Okaw at Keysport; L. 1847 (27 Feb.) 93. Proviso in §6 repealed; to be built by Thos. Keys and others; L. 1849 (12 Feb.) 147. Certain school funds paid to commissioner of Washington county; Laws 1847 (28 Feb.) 115. Augustus Martin, grocery store license at Keysport; Pr. L. 1847 (27 Feb.) 187. Henry Sherman name changed to Henry Schwaka; Pr. L. 1851 (15 Feb.) 193. Ferry across the Kaskaskia established by county June 9 1841, legalized; Id. 231. Foregoing amended; Washington county court to regulate rates; Pr. L. 1853 (12 Feb) 605. Extending game law of 1855 to said county; L. 1857 (9 Feb.) 56; Gross' Stat. 1868, 324. Bonds for building wire bridge across the Kaskaskia at Clinton; L. 1861 (6 Feb.) 82. To protect wire bridge across the Kaskaskia near Carlyle; Pr. L. 1861 (18 Feb.) 61. Rebuilding jail; Id. 299. Vacates streets in Western Addition; Pr. L. 1863 (16 Feb.) 266. County borrow $100,000. to pay bounties to volunteers; 1 Pr. L. 1865 (15 Feb.) 115. Also, $10,000. to rebuild jail and repair court house; Id. 538. Trenton chartered; 2 Pr. L. 1865 (16 Feb.) 584. Court records made up; L. 1867 (5 Mar.) 67. Trenton Workman's Mutual Aid Society chartered; 1 Pr. L. 1867 (9 Mar.) 139. Germania Sharpshooters' Society at Breese chartered; 3 Pr. L. 1867 (1 Mar.) 94. Clement chartered; Id. (9 Mar.) 193. Baden changed to New Baden; Id. (28 Feb.) 622.

Carlyle.—Town chartered; 1 L. 1837 (10 Feb.) 531. Lower town resurveyed; L. 1841 (20 Feb.) 311. Foregoing amended; L. 1843 (2 Mar.) 302. Part of town plat vacated; Pr. L. 1851 (8 Feb.) 50. Again chartered; Pr. L. 1853 (12 Feb.) 272. Foregoing amended; effect of failure to hold election; plat resurveyed; Pr. L. 1854 (4 Mar.) 155. Further amendment; acts declared valid; Pr. L. 1855 (13 Feb.) 46. City chartered; Pr. L. 1861 (22 Feb.) 185. Powers extended; 2 Pr. L. 1865 (16 Feb.) 413. Chas. Slade to rebuild his toll bridge; L. 1831 (9 Feb.) 27. Carlyle Bridge Co. chartered; Laws 1836 (16 Jan.) 43. Amends §3; commence from Franklin street; Pr. L. 1837 (27 Feb.) 108. Scott Lodge No. 79, F. and A. Masons chartered; Pr. L. 1853 (12 Feb.) 564. Clinton County Marine Fire Insurance and Hotel Co. chartered; Pr. L. 1857 (18 Feb.) 1406. City Savings Bank chartered; 1 Pr. L. 1867 (7 Mar.) 92.

COLES COUNTY.

County created; county seat located; L. 1831 (25 Dec. 1830) 59. Share in proceeds of sale of Gallatin Salines; Id. (16 Feb.) 16 §1. Coles Manufacturing Co. chartered; Pr. L. 1833 (1 Mar.) 96. Joseph Barbour to highten mill dam on Embarrass; Id. (15 Feb.) 105. Road from Shelbyville to Paris relocated west of Kickapoo creek; Id. (13 Feb.) 133. Shelbyville road relocated near John Waddel's; L. 1836 (16 Jan.) 208. Nathan Ellington late justice, acts legalized; 1 L. 1837 (28 Feb.) 153. Lands of Thos. Gordon's estate conveyed; Id. (6 Dec. 1836) 157. Road from Charleston and Paris partly relocated; Id. (1 Mar.) 234. Upon same subject; Id. 281. Road from Greenup to Paris vacated; Id. (31 Jan.) 241. New Salem changed to New Albany; Id. (3 Mar.) 329 §2. Additional judges of election; L. 1839 (15 Feb.) 120. Embarrass and Kaskaskia Bridge Co. chartered; Pr. L. 1839 (27 Feb.) 30. Certain process issued by circuit clerk legalized; L. 1841 (26 Jan.) 62. Conservator of Daniel Linder to sell lands; Pr. L. 1847 (4 Feb.) 172. Usher F. Linder released from recognizance of Andrew Magee; Pr. L. 1851 (11 Feb.) 79. Records transcribed, compared and certified; affect of; L. 1853 (10 Feb.) 212. Release of John W. Brooks by Gov. French from recognizance legalized; Pr. L. 1853 (26 Jan.) 461. Independence changed to Oakland; Pr. L. 1855 (9 Feb.) 703. New Albany changed to Camargo; public square vacated; Pr. L. 1857 (13 Feb.) 538. Sale of school site in New Albany; L. 1867 (16 Feb.) 258. Redemption of lands in Town 12—9, by Abram Highland; Id. (6 Mar.) 145. Road from Darwin to Charleston vacated in part; L. 1869 (27 Mar.) 876.

Charleston.—Town declared chartered under general act 12 Feb. 1831; Pr. L. 1839 (2 Mar.) 236. City chartered; 1 Pr. L. 1865 (9 Feb.) 263. Charleston Seminary chartered; Pr. L. 1837 (1 Mar.) 182. To regulate; L. 1840 (3 Feb.) 131. Repeals §6 of foregoing; L. 1841 (17 Feb.) 63. Surviving trustee to sell property; Pr. L. 1857 (14 Feb.) 777. Marine and Fire Insurance Co. chartered; Pr. L. 1839 (26 Feb.) 117. Charleston Lodge No. 35, F. and A. Masons; Pr. L. 1853 (12 Feb.) 515. Charleston Academy chartered; Pr. L. 1859 (19 Feb.) 360. Union Graded School established; 2 Pr. L. 1865 (16 Feb.) 323. Charleston Union School District established; 3 Pr. L. 1867 (1 Mar.) 44.

Mattoon.—Town chartered; Pr. L. 1859 (22 Feb.) 638. Foregoing amended; Pr. L. 1861 (22 Feb.) 703. Again amended; 2 Pr. L. 1865 (16 Feb.) 511. City chartered; 1 Pr. L. 1867 (6 Feb.) 252. Mattoon Academy chartered; Pr. L. 1859 (21 Feb.) 367. Mattoon Female Seminary chartered; Pr. L. 1863 (21 Feb.) 12. Mattoon College chartered; Id. 15. Mattoon Gas Light and Coke Co. chartered; 1 Pr. L. 1867 (26 Feb.) 972. Mattoon City Railway Co. chartered; 2 Pr. L. 1867 (23 Feb.) 20. International Insurance Co. chartered; Id. (8 Mar.) 216. Common Pleas Court established; L. 1869 (20 Feb.) 133.

COFFEE COUNTY.

County organized after favorable vote; 1 L. 1837 (1 Mar.) 86.

COOK COUNTY.

County created; county seat at town of Chicago, as laid out and defined by the canal commissioners; L. 1831 (15 Jan.) 54 §1. Michigan county formed from, upon favorable vote; 1 L. 1837 (2 Mar.) 82. Borrow $10,000. for county purposes; L. 1839 (16 Feb.) 110. Indexing public records; L. 1843 (23 Feb.) 209. Acts of Geo. W. Smith, deputy circuit clerk, legalized; Pr. L. 1847 (28 Feb.) 217. Hogs not to run at large; Laws 1849 (10 Jan.) 185. Supervisors to borrow money to buy lots and build a jail; L. 1851 (11 Feb.) 27. Circuit Court to appoint county Port Wardens; term of office, duties, bond and fees; Id. (17 Feb.) 156. Supervisors borrow money to erect and improve public buildings; L. 1852 (15 June) 11. Attaching towns of Hanover, Barrington, Palatine and Schaumberg to Kane county; vote thereon; L. 1853 (12 Feb.) 277. Loaning money to encourage volunteering; L. 1863 (21 Feb.) 40. Time for collecting taxes extended; Id. (12 Feb.) 83. Issue not exceeding $1,000,000. 7 per cent bonds to pay bounties to soldiers; 1 Pr. L. 1865 (2 Feb.) 118. Limit increased to $1,500,000.; Id. (15 Feb.) 120. Coroners' deputies; L. 1867 (7 Mar.) 90. Respecting Juvenile Reform School; Id. (5 Mar.) 44 §26. Purchase the interest of city of Chicago in the court house; 1 Pr. L. 1867 (7 Mar.) 882. County judge may interchange with judges of courts of records; L. 1869 (30 Mar.) 149.

Corporations.—Union Agricultural Society chartered; Pr. L. 1839 (19 Feb.) 88. Lake Michigan and Chicago Canal Co. chartered; Pr. L. 1857 (13 Feb.) 607. Northfield Mutual Fire Insurance Co. chartered; Id. (16 Feb.) 820. An Insane Asylum chartered; corporators select name; Pr. L. 1861 (21 Feb.) 48. Land Improvement Co. chartered; Id. (22 Feb.) 451. Chicago and Evanston R. R. chartered; Id. (16 Feb.) 487. Northwestern Fetilizing Co. chartered; 1 Pr. L. 1867 (8 Mar.) 50. Palatine Mutual Garantee Insurance Association chartered; 2 Pr. L. 1867 (25 Feb.) 137. United States Clock and Brass Co. at Austin chartered; Id. (12 Feb.) 369. Culver Coal Co. chartered; Id. (23 Feb.) 408. Chicago, Blue Island and Indiana R. R. chartered; Id. (7 Mar.) 545. Indiana and Chicago R. R. chartered; Id. (5 Mar.) 548. Wash-

"ook County Court" established Feby 21. 1845.

Amendment Feby. 6. 1849.

Name changed to "Cook County Court of Common Pleas" Nov. 5. 1849

Amendment Jany. 16, 1855

do Jany 14. 1857

Merged in "Superior Court of Chicago" Feby 17. 1859

Amendment Feby. 16. 1865

Name changed to Superior Court of Cook County by Constitution of

County Commissioners Courts established in 1819.

(Amendment Jany 19. 1826)

Probate Courts established in 1821 Feby 10

Amendment in 1823 Feby 12

do Jany 12. 1825

do Jany 2. 1829

Probate Courts abolished & Probate Justices of the Peace provided for Mch. 4,

Amendment Feby 21, 1837

Amendments in 1843

do in 1845

do 1847

County Courts established Feby 12. 1849

Amendments in 1849 & 1851

ington Skating Association chartered; 3 Pr. L. 1867 (21 Feb.) 79.

Drainage.—Of marsh in Gross point precinct; L. 1845 (3 Mar. 1844) 318. Of wet lands about Chicago; L. 1851 (17 Feb) 195. Of Towns 37, 38, 39 & 40 in ranges 12, 13 & 14; repeals §§1—9 in foregoing act; L. 1852 (23 June) 240. Foregoing amended; duty of school trustees; Pr. L. 1861 (22 Feb.) 587. Town 40—13 exempt from foregoing act; commissioners from town of Jefferson; L. 1853 (11 Feb.) 184. Supervisors to control the swamp and overflowed lands; Pr. L. 1854 (4 Mar.) 184. Drainage commissioners chartered; Towns 41—13, 42—14 and 40—13; Pr. L. 1855 (15 Feb.) 576. Cook and Lake County Drainage Co. chartered; Towns 42, 43, 44 and 45 range 12 and 13 east; Id. (12 Feb.) 635. Amends act 21 Feb. 1863 (Pr. L. 1863, 185) chartering the Lake County Drainage Commissioners; provisions extended over Cook county; 1 Pr. L. 1867 (7 Mar.) 910. Drainage law extended to Town 40—13; L. 1869 (19 Apr.) 172.

Institutions of Learning.—Franklin Manual Labor College chartered; located in either Cook or LaSalle counties; L. 1836 (16 Jan.) 160. Northwestern University chartered; Pr. L. 1851 (28 Feb.) 20. Amends foregoing; board of trustees increased; no liquors sold within 4 miles; Pr. L. 1855 (14 Feb.) 483. Further amendment; appointment of trustees; Pr. L. 1861 (16 Feb.) 21. And again; 1 Pr. L. 1867 (19 Feb.) 6. Garrett Biblical Institute chartered; Pr. L. 1855 (15 Feb.) 511. Amendment; 1 Pr. L. 1865 (14 Feb.) 20.

Roads and Bridges.—Timothy R. Hale, toll bridge across the Little Calamic [Calumet]; L. 1835 (11 Feb.) 85. Geo. W. Dole and others, same, across the same; 1 L. 1837 (15 Feb.) 29. Same, across the same, Town 37—14; L. 1841 (17 Feb.) 43. Chicago and Joliet Turnpike Co. chartered; L. 1845 (1 Mar.) 254. Act of county commissioners as to South Western Plank Road Co. confirmed; L. 1851 (13 Feb.) 87. State road from Lake Michigan to I. & M. Canal, through Lake and South Chicago; L. 1853 (10 Feb.) 133. Chicago and Calumet plank road chartered; Pr. L. 1853 (14 Feb.) 9. Northwestern plank road chartered; Pr. L. 1854 (1 Mar.) 224. Amendment; sale authorized; 2 Pr. L. 1865 (15 Feb.) 115. Supervisors appropriate money for roads and bridges; L. 1859. (21 Feb.) 212. Road from Brighton House to sec. 24 town of Palos located; Id. (16 Feb.) 264. Trustees of Lake street and County Line road chartered; 2 Pr. L. 1867 (8 Mar.) 825. Towns to levy a road tax; 3 Pr. L. 1867 (5 Mar.) 122.

Schools and School Lands.—School commissioners to loan $12,000. to county commissioners; L. 1835 (31 Jan. 1831 [1835]) 78. School commissioners pay over school funds to counties of Will, DuPage, McHenry and Lake; L 1841 (17 Feb.) 257. School tax for 1856 Town 41—14 legalized; L. 1857 (6 Feb.) 219. Refunding taxes illegally assessed in 1859, in district 23, Town 39—14; L. 1861 (12 Feb.) 192. Regulating the renting of school lands Town 38—13; 2 Pr. L. 1865 (16 Feb.) 313. Surplus bounty fund in town of Lemont appropriated for school purposes; 3 Pr. L. 1867 (28 Feb.) 42. Dissolves Union school district No. 1 Town of Palestine; Id. (23 Feb.) 65.

Towns—Plat of Cottage Grove vacated; L. 1840 (15 Jan.) 45. S. Forbes to dam the Des Plaines in Towns 38—12 and 39—12; L. 1845 (3 Mar.) 287. Chas. H. Babcock pre-empt part sec. 19, Town 42—10; Pr. L. 1853 (3 Feb.) 582. Town of Jefferson to build town house; Pr. L. 1857 (30 Jan.) 113. Town of Jefferson chartered; 3 Pr. L. 1867 (7 Mar.) 161. Amends general township organization act 17 Feb. 1851; two-thirds of the supervisors elected to appropriate money for roads and bridges; Laws 1859 (21 Feb.) 212. Town officers to be elected in November; Id. (24 Feb.) 213. The two foregoing acts declared not repealed by the general township organization act of 1861; L. 1861 (20 Feb.) 266 §10. Tax voted at town meetings; Id. (21 Feb.) 88. Town house in Maine; L. 1859 (11 Feb.) 211. Special tax in Maine for cemetery purposes; 1 Pr. L. 1865 (16 Feb.) 539. Concerning Evanston, New Friar and Ridgeville; L. 1859 (24 Feb.) 211. Vacation, resubdivision and partition of town of Canalport; 2 Pr. L. 1865 (16 Feb.) 400. Vacates Robinson street in town of Dunton; 3 Pr. L. 1867 (7 Mar.) 100 and 336. Vacates part of street canal trustees subdivision of sec. 33, Town 40—14; Id. (28 Feb.) 106 and 111. Vacates streets in Cleaverville; Id. (5 Mar.) 110. Disposition of surplus bounty fund in town of Cicero; Id. (23 Feb.) 129. Town of Cicero chartered; Id. (28 Feb.) 385. For payment of Niles town orders; Id. (12 Feb.) 141 and 596. Town of Lake chartered; Id. (28 Feb.) 228. Town of Proviso chartered; Id. (28 Feb.) 391. Name of Rand changed to Des Plaines and town chartered; L. 1869 (15 Apr.) 280.

Miscellaneous.—Organization of county militia; two battalions and four to eight companies; officers elected 20 Mar. at David Lorton's on the Des Plaines; governor to deliver to the colonel 200 stand of arms; Pr. L. 1833 (22 Feb.) 109. Sale of land of estate of D. L. W. Jones; 1 L. 1837 (6 Dec. 1836) 159. Sale of the lands of Mary Myot, a minor, by Nich. Boilrin; Id. 191. John Walsh, security of Isaac R. Gavin late sheriff, conditionally discharged from liability; L. 1845 (21 Jan.) 167. Mary Ann Clarkson name changed to Funk; Pr. L. 1847 (27 Feb.) 21. Allows Patrick Ballingall $100. for arresting counterfeiters; Id. (28 Feb.) 214. Pre-emptions granted Stephen Dexter and Ebenezer W. Covey for certain lands; L. 1849 (12 Feb.) 102. A. Gitzler allowed $75. as assistant assessor; Id. (25 Jan.) 112. James Long, late treasurer, allowed $108. for advertising delinquent list for 1851; Pr. L. 1853 (10 Feb.) 439. Warrant to the administrator of J. H. Collins for $1.000. due on lost bond; L. 1857 (25 Feb.) 150. Names of Mary Francis and Frank Clark Runyan changed to McVicker; heirs of James H. McVicker; 1 Pr. L. 1867 (7 Mar.) 237. Name of Thomas M. Francis changed to Thos. F. Sellick; Id. (28 Feb.) 235. Name of George Ludwig Theodore Peterson changed to Christian Graden; Id. 234. Name of M. L. McMaster changed to M. L. Wright; L. 1869 (26 Mar.) 266.

County Court.—Jurisdiction extended; R. S. 1845 (21 Feb.) 574. Terms of; L. 1847 (22 Feb.) 28. Election of judge, clerk and prosecuting attorney; L. 1849 (6 Feb.) 69. Changed to Cook County Court of Common Pleas (which see); 2 L. 1849 (5 Nov.) 14.

Court of Common Pleas.—Created from county court (which see); terms and jurisdiction; 2 L. 1849 (5 Nov.) 14. Regulates practice therein; L. 1853 (12 Feb.) 172. No term on first Monday in March; L. 1855 (16 Jan.) 146. Business at vacation terms; suits dismissed; judgments entered; L. 1857 (14 Jan.) 11. Changed to the Superior Court of Chicago (which see); L. 1859 (17 Feb.) 84.

Superior Court.—Created from Cook County Court of Common Pleas (which see); jurisdiction and practice; L. 1859 (17 Feb.) 84. Election of judge, clerk and his deputy; L. 1861 (22 Feb.) 80. Jurisdiction and practice; Id. 81. Docket fee; L. 1865 (16 Feb.) 36. Salary of judges; L. 1867 (25 Feb.) 70.

Courts.—Practice in the circuit court; L. 1853 (12 Feb.) 172; also, L. 1861 (22 Feb.) 81. Compensation of county judge; L. 1859 (18 Feb.) 103. Concerning the same; Id. (24 Feb.) 104. Custody of property held under legal process; L. 1861 (22 Feb.) 76. Foregoing repealed; L. 1863 (3 Feb.) 42. Docket and jury fee; L. 1863 (15 Jan.) 49. Bailiffs for courts of record; L. 1867 (28 Feb.) 69. Terms of county court; Id. (28 Feb.) 71. Official reporters of the courts of Chicago; Id. (6 Mar.) 146. Foregoing amended; L. 1869 (11 Mar.) 346.

CHICAGO.

The City.—John H. Kinzie, Gordon S. Hubbard, Ebenezer Goodrich, John K. Boyer and John S. C. Hogan incorporated as trustees of the town of Chicago; L. 1835 (11 Feb.) 204. Foregoing amended; L. 1836 (15 Jan.) 180. City chartered; 1 L. 1837 (4 Mar.) 50 §§1—92. Supplemental thereto; Id. 81; also Pr. L. 1847 (16 Feb.) 82. Amendment; L. 1841 (27 Feb.) 58. Repealed in part; Pr. L. 1839 (15 Feb.) 63. Limit of taxation for city and school purposes; L. 1845 (25 Feb.) 285. Act chartering and amendments, reduced to one; Pr. L. 1851 (14 Feb.) 132. Foregoing amended; limits extended: clerk to consolidate taxes levied; Pr. L. 1853 (12 Feb.) 609. Again amended; repealing so much as authorized licenses to sell less than one quart of liquor; L. 1852 (23 June) 219. Foregoing repealed; former provisions re-enacted; L. 1853 (12 Feb.) 91. General amendment to act 14 Feb. 1851; Pr. L. 1854 (28 Feb.) 217. Further amendment; council may establish a reform school; Pr. L. 1857 (14 Feb.) 650. Still further amends; treasurer's department established; also police courts; provides for laying out a public park; Pr. L. 1857 (16 Feb.) 892. Foregoing amended; repeals public park provisions; Pr. L. 1859 (19 Feb.) 25. Charter generally amended; Pr. L. 1861 (18 Feb.) 118. Further amends: commitments to reform school regulated; Pr. L. 1861 (22 Feb.) 149. Acts chartering and amendments, reduced to one and revised; Pr. L. 1863 (13 Feb.) 40. Foregoing amended: corporate powers extended; 1 Pr. L. 1865 (15 Feb.) 274. Further amended; Id. (16 Feb.) 284. Both foregoing amended; 1 Pr. L. 1867 (6 Mar.) 708. Supplemental to act 13 Feb. 1863; general; Id. (9 Mar.) 754. Fines and forfeitures for Penalties incurred, to be paid into city Treasury; L. 1851 (17 Feb.) 156. City limits fixed; L. 1843 (21 Jan.) 64. Straighten Madison street; Id. (8 Feb.) 64. Regulating election precincts; Id. (1 Mar.) 65. Supplemental to an act to open a new street; Id. (4 Mar.) 66. State street extended; L. 1845 (3 Mar.) 272. Council to adjust and settle title to wharfing privileges; widen Chicago river; Pr. L. 1847 (27 Feb.) 214. Foregoing amended; powers further extended; Pr. L. 1853 (11 Feb.) 520. Block 39 original town, dedicated to public use as a public common and square; not to be sold or encumbered; county buildings placed thereon: L. 1851 (4 Feb.) 19. Time for completing collection for 1849 extended to Mar. 1850; L. 1851 (1 Mar.) 7. Board of Water Commissioners chartered; may buy out the Chicago Hydraulic Co. (which see); Pr. L. 1851 (15 Feb.) 213. Licenses for fire insurance agents; L. 1852 (21 June) 68. Wards to be election Precincts; L. 1853 (12 Feb.) 203. Board of Sewerage Commissioners chartered; Pr. L. 1855 (14 Feb.) 93. Foregoing amended; borrow money and issue bonds; Pr. L. 1859 (14 Feb.) 533. Council to vacate streets and alleys; L. 1859 (12 Feb.) 201. Vacates part of Water street in block 2; Pr. L. 1855 (12 Feb.) 731. Vacates part of Water street; Pr. L. 1857 (29 Jan.) 95. Alleys vacated; made to conform to sub-additions; Id. (13 Feb.) 577. E. K. Hubbard's subdivision of school section addition, legalized; Id. (16 Feb.) 1022. Acts of fish inspector defined and confirmed; Id. (18 Feb.) 1203. Their acts defined and confirmed; inspections at Milwaukee and Macinac recognized; Pr. L. 1861 (20 Feb.) 148. Their pay; 1 Pr. L. 1865 (16 Feb.) 580. Board of police established; powers and duties; L. 1861 (21 Feb.) 151. For paying damages caused by building Van Buren street bridge; Pr. L. 1861 (20 Feb.) 59. Additional supervisor for each ward; L. 1861 (20 Feb.) 265 §3. City borrow $12,000. to bridge the river at State street; Pr. L. 1863 (12 Feb.) 169. Establishment of sanitary measures and health regulations; 1 Pr. L. 1865 (16 Feb.) 590. Vacates Michigan Terrace between Maple Avenue and Brook street, in sub-division of Cleaureville; 2 Pr. L. 1865 (16 Feb.) 659. Construction of previous acts respecting Board of Public Works; 1 Pr. L. 1867 (7 Mar.) 160. For the location and improvement of a park in South Chicago, Hyde Park and Lake; 2 Pr. L. 1867 (27 Feb.) 472. Commitments to reform school; privileges of parents; 3 Pr. L. 1867 (5 Mar.) 31. To prevent the delay of public improvements by injunction; L. 1869 (11 Mar.) 201. The submerged lands (Lake Park): Id. (16 Apr.) 245. Resolution that Congress declare Chicago a port of entry; Id. 416.

Municipal Court.—Established by city charter; jurisdiction concurrent with circuit court; 1 L. 1837, 75 §§69—82. Judge exercise all the powers of a circuit judge; 2 L. 1837 (21 July) 15. Court abolished; high constable to make return to circuit court; causes pending tried in circuit court; Pr. L. 1839 (15 Feb.) 63.

Recorder's Court.—Established; L. 1853 (12 Feb.) 147. Foregoing amended; city pay expenses of prisoners held or convicted within the city under jurisdiction of court; Pr. L. 1854 (28 Feb.) 150. Fees of prosecuting attorney; L. 1859 (24 Feb.) 17. Cases therein transferred to other courts; writs from issued on notice; L. 1855 (15 Feb.) 147.

Cemeteries.—A canal lot granted for a cemete-

ry; 1 L. 1837 (10 Feb.) 80. Oak Wooks Cemetery Association; chartered; Pr. L. 1858 (12 Feb.) 550. Amends and extends charter; 1 Pr. L. 1867 (7 Mar.) 227. Douglas Monument Association; charter; Pr. L. 1863 (11 Feb.) 184.

Colleges, Seminaries, etc.—Chicago Seminary; charter; Pr. L. 1837 (1 Mar.) 182. Rush Medical College; chartered; Pr. L. 1837 (2 Mar.) 233. Charter amended; L. 1845 (23 Dec. 1844) 177. Trustees to borrow $50,000. to liquidate indebtedness; Pr. L. 1857 (10 Feb.) 350. To fund its indebtedness; 1 Pr. L. 1865 (13 Feb.) 9. University of St. Mary of the Lake; charter; L. 1845 (23 Dec. 1844) 216. St. Francis Xavier Female Academy; charter; Pr. L. 1847 (27 Feb.) 127. University of Chicago; chartered; Id. 132. And again; Pr. L. 1857 (30 Jan.) 100. Charter amended; establish an astronomical observatory; Pr. L. 1863 (13 Feb.) 9. Chicago Theological Seminary; charter; Pr. L. 1855 (15 Feb.) 875. Charter amended; may loan funds; Pr. L. 1857 (16 Feb.) 918. Hahnemann Medical College; charter; Pr. L. 1855 (14 Feb.) 530. J. Young Scammon and others to establish an institution of learning; doctrines of Swedenborg taught; Pr. L. 1857 (14 Feb.) 807. Presbyterian Theological Seminary of Northwest; Id. (16 Feb.) 845. Charter amended; transfer to general assembly confirmed; Pr. L. 1861 (21 Feb.) 24. Chicago Law Institute; charter; Pr. L. 1857 (18 Feb.) 1186. Fines and penalties imposed and collected by any court in Cook county to be paid to said Institute; 1 Pr. L. 1867 (23 Feb.) 965. Charter amended; effect of nonpayment of assessments upon shares of stock; Pr. L. 1863 (14 Feb.) 9. Dearborn Seminary; charter; Pr. L. 1857 (16 Feb.) 1067. Ministerial Education Society of the Methodist Episcopal Church; charter; Pr. L. 1861 (18 Feb.) 50. Industrial School Association; charter; 1 Pr. L. 1865 (16 Feb.) 37. Baptist Theological Union; for establishment of Baptist Theological Institute; Id. 38. Lincoln Institute; charter; in north division; 1 Pr. L. 1867 (6 Mar.) 27. Ladies' Baptist Education Society; charter; 2 Pr. L. 1867 (7 Mar.) 275.

CHICAGO CORPORATIONS.

Banks, Deposit and Investment Companies.—Marine Banks consolidated; Pr. L. 1853 (8 Feb.) 539. International Mutual Exchange and Investment; charter; 1 Pr. L. 1867)7 Mar.) 106. Guarantee and Investment Association; charter; Id. 848. Safe deposit; charter; Pr. 3 L. 1867 (20 Feb.) 1.

Breweries.—Lill's Chicago; charter; 1 Pr. L. 1865 (10 Feb.) 174. Busch and Brand's; charter; 1 Pr. L. 1867 (15 Feb.) 193. Huck's Chicago; charter; Id. (19 Feb.) 197.

Building Associations and Companies.—Chicago Building; charter; Pr. L. 1851 (1 Feb.) 39. German House; charter; Pr. L. 1857 (12 Feb.) 503. Foregoing amended; verbal alterations; Pr. L. 1861 (20 Feb.) 466. Chicago Permanent Building; charter; Pr. L. 1857 (18 Feb.) 1336. Chicago Building Block; charter; 1 Pr. L. 1867 (5 Mar.) 204. Mercantile Building; charter; Id. 205. Hyde Park Hotel; charter; 2 Pr. L. 1867 (21 Feb.) 50.

City Railway Companies. — Chicago City; charter; Pr. L. 1859 (14 Feb.) 530. Amendment; power of council over; 1 Pr. L. 1865 (6 Feb.) 597. Chicago West Division; charter; same powers conferred as by act 14 Feb. 1859; Pr. L. 1861 (21 Feb.) 340. Chicago and Calumet Horse and Dummy; charter; 2 Pr. L. 1867 (5 Mar.) 30.

Clubs.—Chicago Union House; charter; 1 Pr. L. 1867 (12 Feb.) 245. Chicago Caledonian; charter; Id. (21 Feb.) 248.

Dock Companies.—Cook County Marine Dry; charter; Pr. L. 1851 (17 Feb.) 274. Chicago Dock and Canal; charter; Pr. L. 1857 (12 Feb.) 499. Charter amended; Pr. L. 1861 (22 Feb.) 152. Chicago South Branch; charter; Pr. L. 1859 (19 Feb.) 728. The Chicago; charter; Pr. L. 1863 (13 Feb.) 177. Madison; charter; 1 Pr. L. 1865 (16 Feb.) 553.

Gas Light and Coke Companies.—The Chicago; charter; Pr. L. 1849 (12 Feb.) 41. Amendment; capital increased; Pr. L. 1855 (9 Feb.) 642. The People's; charter; Pr. L. 1855 (12 Feb.) 614. Amendment; powers extended; 1 Pr. L. 1865 (7 Feb.) 589.

Firemen, affecting. — Fireman's Insurance; charter; Pr. L. 1855 (14 Feb.) 422. Charter amended; 1 Pr. L. 1865 (16 Feb.) 624. Firemen's Benevolent Association; charter; Pr. L. 1849 (12 Feb.) 43. Charter amended; §6 repealed; funds distributed to orphan asylums; Pr. L. 1861 (22 Feb.) 47. Further amends; Pr. L. 1863 (13 Feb.) 29. Benevolent Association of the Paid Fire Department; charter; 1 Pr. L. 1867 (5 Mar.) 147.

Hospitals, etc.—Illinois General Hospital of the Lake; charter; 2 L. 1849 (29 Oct.) 40. Mercy Hospital and Asylum; charter; L. 1852 (21 June) 53. St. James Hospital; charter; Pr. L. 1855 (14 Feb.) 586. St. Luke's Hospital; charter; 1 Pr. L. 1865 (20 Jan.) 91. Charitable Eye and Ear Infirmary; charter; Id. (16 Feb.) 68. Aided by state $5,000. annually for two years; L. 1867 (6 Mar.) 37. Appropriations in aid; L. 1869 (25 Mar.) 43.

Hydraulic Companies.—The Chicago; charter; L. 1836 (18 Jan.) 112. May sell and convey their property; Pr. L. 1855 (14 Feb.) 721. Lake Michigan; chartered; L. 1845 (1 Mar.) 315. Amendment; powers extended; Pr. L. 1847 (28 Feb.) 151. Chicago City; chartered; Pr. L. 1851 (15 Feb.) 213. Foregoing amended; L. 1852 (15 June) 12. Supplemental to first foregoing; general powers defined; Pr. L. 1855 (15 Feb.) 564. Act chartering and amendments amended; to affect a loan; Pr. L. 1857 (16 Feb.) 1051.

Insurance Companies.—The Illinois; charter; Pr. L. 1839 (2 Mar.) 221. Phœnix; charter; L. 1841 (26 Feb.) 156. Chicago Savings; receive deposits; charter; Pr. L. 1849 (12 Feb.) 51. Chicago City; charter; Pr. L. 1855 (14 Feb.) 415. Mercantile; charter; Id. (15 Feb.) 387. Garden City; charter; Id. 401. Great Western; charter; Pr. L. 1857 (4 Feb.) 244. Merchants'; charter; Pr. L. 1861 (18 Feb.) 413. Amendment; 2 Pr. L. 1867 (18 Feb.) 186. Further amends; Id. (9 Mar.) 224. Commercial; charter; Pr. L. 1861 (18 Feb.) 348. Equitable; charter; Id. (20 Feb.) 370. Ft. Dearborn; charter; Id. 374. And again; 1 Pr. L. 1865 (15 Feb.) 655. Chicago Merchants'; charter; Pr. L. 1861 (22 Feb.) 366. Island; charter; Id. 400. Business of

ry; 1 L. 1837 (10 Feb.) 80. Oak Wooks Cemetery Association; chartered; Pr. L. 1853 (12 Feb.) 550. Amends and extends charter; 1 Pr. L. 1867 (7 Mar.) 227. Douglas Monument Association; charter; Pr. L. 1863 (11 Feb.) 184.

Colleges, Seminaries, etc.—Chicago Seminary; charter; Pr. L. 1837 (1 Mar.) 182. Rush Medical College; chartered; Pr. L. 1837 (2 Mar.) 233. Charter amended; L. 1845 (23 Dec. 1844) 177. Trustees to borrow $50,000. to liquidate indebtedness; Pr. L 1857 (10 Feb.) 350. To fund its indebtedness; 1 Pr. L. 1865 (13 Feb.) 9. University of St. Mary of the Lake; charter; L. 1845 (23 Dec. 1844) 216. St. Francis Xavier Female Academy; charter; Pr. L. 1847 (27 Feb.) 127. University of Chicago; chartered; Id. 132. And again; Pr. L. 1857 (30 Jan.) 100. Charter amended; establish an astronomical observatory; Pr. L. 1863 (13 Feb.) 9. Chicago Theological Seminary; charter; Pr. L. 1855 (15 Feb.) 375. Charter amended; may loan funds; Pr. L. 1857 (16 Feb.) 918. Hahnemann Medical College; charter; Pr. L. 1855 (14 Feb.) 530. J. Young Scammon and others to establish an institution of learning; doctrines of Swedenborg taught; Pr. L. 1857 (14 Feb.) 807. Presbyterian Theological Seminary of Northwest; Id. (16 Feb.) 845. Charter amended; transfer to general assembly confirmed; Pr. L. 1861 (21 Feb.) 24. Chicago Law Institute; charter; Pr. L. 1857 (18 Feb.) 1186. Fines and penalties imposed and collected by any court in Cook county to be paid to said Institute; 1 Pr. L. 1867 (23 Feb.) 965. Charter amended; effect of nonpayment of assessments upon shares of stock; Pr. L. 1863 (14 Feb.) 9. Dearborn Seminary; charter; Pr. L. 1857 (16 Feb.) 1067. Ministerial Education Society of the Methodist Episcopal Church; charter; Pr. L. 1861 (18 Feb.) 50. Industrial School Association; charter; 1 Pr. L. 1865 (16 Feb.) 37. Baptist Theological Union; for establishment of Baptist Theological Institute; Id. 38. Lincoln Institute: charter; in north division; 1 Pr. L. 1867 (6 Mar.) 27. Ladies' Baptist Education Society; charter; 2 Pr. L. 1867 (7 Mar.) 275.

CHICAGO CORPORATIONS.

Banks, Deposit and Investment Companies.—Marine Banks consolidated; Pr. L. 1853 (8 Feb.) 539. International Mutual Exchange and Investment; charter; 1 Pr. L. 1867)7 Mar.) 106. Guarantee and Investment Association; charter; Id. 848. Safe deposit; charter; Pr. 3 L. 1867 (20 Feb.) 1.

Breweries.—Lill's Chicago; charter; 1 Pr. L. 1865 (10 Feb.) 174. Busch and Brand's; charter; 1 Pr. L. 1867 (15 Feb.) 193. Huck's Chicago; charter; Id. (19 Feb.) 197.

Building Associations and Companies.—Chicago Building; charter; Pr. L. 1851 (1 Feb.) 30. German House; charter; Pr. L. 1857 (12 Feb.) 503. Foregoing amended; verbal alterations; Pr. L. 1861 (20 Feb.) 466. Chicago Permanent Building; charter; Pr. L. 1857 (18 Feb.) 1339. Chicago Building Block; charter; 1 Pr. L. 1867 (5 Mar.) 204. Mercantile Building; charter; Id. 205. Hyde Park Hotel; charter; 2 Pr. L. 1867 (21 Feb.) 50.

City Railway Companies.—Chicago City; charter; Pr. L. 1859 (14 Feb.) 530. Amendment; power of council over; 1 Pr. L. 1865 (6 Feb.) 597. Chicago West Division; charter; same powers conferred as by act 14 Feb. 1859; Pr. L. 1861 (21 Feb.) 340. Chicago and Calumet Horse and Dummy; charter; 2 Pr. L. 1867 (5 Mar.) 30.

Clubs.—Chicago Union House; charter; 1 Pr. L. 1867 (12 Feb.) 245. Chicago Caledonian; charter; Id. (21 Feb.) 248.

Dock Companies.—Cook County Marine Dry; charter; Pr. L. 1851 (17 Feb.) 274. Chicago Dock and Canal; charter; Pr. L. 1857 (12 Feb.) 499. Charter amended; Pr. L. 1861 (22 Feb.) 152. Chicago South Branch; charter; Pr. L. 1859 (19 Feb.) 728. The Chicago; charter; Pr. L. 1863 (13 Feb.) 177. Madison; charter; 1 Pr. L .1865 (16 Feb.) 553.

Gas Light and Coke Companies.—The Chicago; charter; Pr. L. 1849 (12 Feb.) 41. Amendment; capital increased; Pr. L. 1855 (9 Feb.) 642. The People's; charter; Pr. L. 1855 (12 Feb.) 614. Amendment; powers extended; 1 Pr. L. 1865 (7 Feb.) 589.

Firemen, affecting.—Fireman's Insurance; charter; Pr. L. 1855 (14 Feb.) 422. Charter amended; 1 Pr. L. 1865 (16 Feb.) 624. Firemen's Benevolent Association; charter; Pr. L. 1849 (12 Feb.) 43. Charter amended; §6 repealed; funds distributed to orphan asylums; Pr. L. 1861 (22 Feb.) 47. Further amends; Pr. L. 1863 (13 Feb.) 29. Benevolent Association of the Paid Fire Department; charter; 1 Pr. L. 1867 (5 Mar.) 147.

Hospitals, etc.—Illinois General Hospital of the Lake; charter; 2 L. 1849 (29 Oct.) 40. Mercy Hospital and Asylum; charter; L. 1852 (21 June) 53. St. James Hospital; charter; Pr. L. 1855 (14 Feb.) 586. St. Luke's Hospital; charter; 1 Pr. L. 1865 (20 Jan.) 91. Charitable Eye and Ear Infirmary; charter; Id. (16 Feb.) 68. Aided by state $5,000. annually for two years; L. 1867 (6 Mar.) 37. Appropriations in aid; L. 1869 (25 Mar.) 43.

Hydraulic Companies.—The Chicago; charter; L. 1836 (18 Jan.) 112. May sell and convey their property; Pr. L. 1855 (14 Feb.) 721. Lake Michigan; chartered; L. 1845 (1 Mar.) 315. Amendment; powers extended; Pr. L. 1847 (28 Feb.) 151. Chicago City; chartered; Pr. L. 1851 (15 Feb.) 213. Foregoing amended; L. 1852 (15 June) 12. Supplemental to first foregoing; general powers defined; Pr. L. 1855 (15 Feb.) 564. Act chartering and amendments amended; to affect a loan; Pr. L. 1857 (16 Feb.) 1051.

Insurance Companies.—The Illinois; charter; Pr. L. 1839 (2 Mar.) 221. Phœnix; charter; L. 1841 (26 Feb.) 156. Chicago Savings; receive deposits; charter; Pr. L. 1849 (12 Feb.) 51. Chicago City; charter; Pr. L. 1855 (14 Feb.) 415. Mercantile; charter; Id. (15 Feb.) 387. Garden City; charter; Id. 401. Great Western; charter; Pr. L. 1857 (4 Feb.) 244. Merchants'; charter; Pr. L. 1861 (18 Feb.) 413. Amendment; 2 Pr. L. 1867 (18 Feb.) 186. Further amends; Id. (9 Mar.) 224. Commercial; charter; Pr. L. 1861 (18 Feb.) 348. Equitable; charter; Id. (20 Feb.) 370. Ft. Dearborn; charter; Id. 374. And again; 1 Pr. L. 1865 (15 Feb.) 655. Chicago Merchants'; charter; Pr. L. 1861 (22 Feb.) 366. Island; charter; Id. 400. Business of

Union Insurance and Trust Co. transacted in Chicago as well as in Marion county; Id. 433. Branch office of the Columbian established; Pr. L.1863 (13 Feb.) 203. Lumberman's; charter; 1 Pr. L. 1865 (6 Feb.) 708. Commercial; charter; Id. (10 Feb.) 631. Amendment; name changed to Commercial of Chicago; 2 Pr. L. 1867 (20 Feb) 150. Commonwealth; charter; 1 Pr. L. 1865 (13 Feb.) 634. Protection; charter; Id. (14 Feb.) 759. Citizen's; two charters; Id. (15 Feb.) 624, 626. Knickerbocker; charter; Id. 696. Republic; charter; Id. 768. Globe; charter; Id. (16 Feb.) 667. Howard; charter; Id. 671. Lamar; charter; Id. 698. National; charter; Id. 726. And again; 2 Pr. L. 1867 (25 Feb.) 129. Packers and Provision Dealers; charter; 1 Pr. L. 1865 (16 Feb.) 749. Safety; charter; Id. 775. Traders; charter; Id. 788. United States; charter; Id. 804. Western Phœnix; charter; Id. 817. Ætna of Chicago; charter; 2 Pr. L. 1867 (7 Mar.) 115. Home; charter; Id. (5 Mar.) 157. Burglar; charter; Id. (8 Mar.) 207. Vesuvius; charter; Id. (28 Feb.) 230. Western Railroad; charter; office at Chicago, Aurora or Batavia; 2 Pr. L. 1867 (9 Mar.) 209.

Fire, Marine and Life.—Germania; charter; 1 Pr. L. 1865 (16 Feb.) 662. Amendment; name changed to Germania Insurance; 2 Pr. L 1867 (7 Mar.) 107. . . *Life.* Northwestern Mutual; charter; Pr. L. 1857 (18 Feb.) 1368. And again; 1 Pr. L. 1865 (15 Feb.) 744. Foregoing amended; name changed to Mutual Life of Chicago; 2 Pr. L. 1867 (25 Feb.) 140. Illinois; charter; Pr. L. 1861 (18 Feb.) 393. Chicago Mutual; charter; Id. (21 Feb.) 362. Provident Life and Investment; charter; 1 Pr. L. 1865 (13 Feb.) 761. Great Western; charter; Id. (15 Feb.) 665. Empire Mutual; charter; 2 Pr. L. 1867 (25 Feb.) 130. International; charter; Id. (7 Mar.) 98. American Mutual Health; charter; Id. (8 Mar.) 212. . . *Marine and Fire.* The Chicago; chartered; L. 1836 (13 Jan.) 30. Amended; Pr. L. 1849 (12 Feb.) 47. Again amended; stock increased; Pr. L. 1859 (4 Feb.) 384. Further amendment; limit extended 30 years; regulating deposits, loans, etc.; Pr. L. 1861 (21 Feb.) 368. Chicago Marine; charter; Pr L. 1851 (28 Jan.) 25. Western; charter; Pr. L. 1853 (10 Feb) 370. Western Valley; charter; Pr. L. 1857 (4 Feb.) 241. Northern Illinois; charter; Id. (11 Feb.) 456. Eureka; charter; Id. (13 Feb.) 597. Ætna; charter; 1 Pr. L. 1865 (15 Feb.) 614. . . *Mutual.* The Chicago; charter; L. 1852 (19 June) 42. Security; chartered; Pr. L. 1853 (10 Feb.) 393. Foregoing amended; 2 Pr. L. 1867 (7 Mar.) 118. Home, Fire; charter; Pr. L. 1861 (22 Feb.) 382. Mercantile, Fire; chartered; 1 Pr. L. 1865 (16 Feb.) 714. Stock and; charter; Id. 783. German, Fire of North Chicago; charter; 2 Pr. L. 1867 (19 Feb.) 141. . . *Travelers.* The National; chartered; 1 Pr. L. 1865 (15 Feb.) 731. Charter amended, name changed to Chicago National; 2 Pr. L. 1867 (5 Mar.) 166. Security; charter; 1 Pr. L. 1865 (15 Feb.) 793. Northwestern Transit; charter; Id. (16 Feb.) 748. Of Chicago; chartered; Id. 790. Charter amended; name changed to Chicago Life; 2 Pr. L. 1867 (21 Feb.) 153. United States; charter; 1 Pr. L. 1865 (16 Feb.) 809. Northwestern; charter; Id. 825. Shippers; charter; 2 Pr. L. 1867 (5 Mar.) 167.

Manufacturing Companies.—Cabinet Makers' Society; charter; Pr. L. 1855 (12 Feb.) 720. Association of Wagon makers; charter; Pr. L. 1857 (11 Feb.) 372. Amends charter of Chicago Refining (organized under general law); Pr. L. 1861 (21 Feb.) 466. Eagle Works; charter; Id. 467. Northwestern; charter; 2 Pr. L. 1865 (14 Feb.) 42. National Watch; charter; Id. (15 Feb.) 41. Mechanical Bakery; charter; Id. 40. Charter amended; 2 Pr. L. 1867 (22 Feb.) 330. Chicago Stone and Lime; charter; 2 Pr. L. 1865 (15 Feb.) 31. Chicago Cotton; two charters; Id. (16 Feb.) 29, 47. Schenck Concentrated Feed; charter; Id. 47. Ditching and Spading Machine; charter; Id. 30. Fox River; charter; Id. 37. Chicago Fanning; charter; Id. 32. Superior Steel and Iron; charter; Id. 49. Garden City Manuf. and Supply; charter; 2 Pr. L. 1867 (13 Feb.) 371. Union Hide and Leather; charter; Id. (14 Feb.) 367. The Lumber; charter; Id. (18 Feb.) 362. Chicago Truck; charter; 3 Pr. L. 1867 (19 Feb.) 637. Lumber Dressing and; charter; 2 Pr. L. 1867 (19 Feb.) 365. Illinois Cotton; charter; Id. 363. Pioneer; charter; Id. 351. Chicago Union; charter; Id. 284. Secor Hand Stamping; charter; Id. (21 Feb.) 355. Grigg's Excelsior Brick Machine; charter; Id. 357. Mansfield Elastic Frog; charter; Id. 332. Chicago Horse Nail; charter; Id. 353. Illinois Linen; charter; Id. (22 Feb.) 358. Northwestern Silver Ware; charter; Id. 334. Pullman's Palace Car; charter; Id. 337. Chicago Iron Works; charter, Id. 323. Northwestern; charter; 2 Pr. L. 1867 (23 Feb.) 282. Golden City Planing Mill and Lumber; charter; Id. 342. Illinois Grain Drying; charter; 1 Pr. L. 1867 (23 Feb.) 994. American Steam Generator; charter; 2 Pr. L. 1867 (23 Feb.) 336. Illinois Soapstone Stove; charter; Id. 330. Chicago Glass; charter; Id. (25 Feb.) 340. Petroleum Fuel and Light; charter; 1 Pr. L. 1867 (25 Feb.) 967. Hapgood; charter; 2 Pr. L. 1867 (28 Feb.) 297. Beater Cotton and Hay Press; charter; Id. 296. United States Hydro-Caloric Light; charter; Id. 290. White Lead; charter; Id. (9 Mar.) 321. Jessup Supply; charter; Id. 322. Northwestern Chemical; charter; Id. 373. Ætna Peat; charter; Id. 372. Fiber and Paper; charter; Id. (1 Mar.) 295. Soap and Candle; charter; Id. (6 Mar.) 308. Greatwestern Agricultural Tool; charter; Id. 305. Spading, Pulverizing and Seeding Machine; charter; Id. (7 Mar.) 314. Cook County Cement, Tile and Drain; Id. 313. The Illinois; charter; Id. 310. Northwestern Fertilizing; charter; 1 Pr. L. 1867 (8 Mar.) 927.

Mining and Transportation Companies.—Chicago and Danville Coal changed to Chicago and Carbon; Pr. L. 1857 (14 Feb.) 622. Union Stock Yard and Transit; charter; 2 Pr. L. 1865 (13 Feb.) 678. Charter amended; stock increased; 3 Pr. L. 1867 (7 Mar.) 100. Union Warehouse and Transportation; charter; 2 Pr. L. 1865 (15 Feb.) 683. Forsythe Coal Mining; charter; Id. (16 Feb.) 63. Illinois Mining and Oil; charter; Id. 69. Illinois Petroleum and Mining; charter; Id. 71. Chicago and Berrien Shipping; charter; Id. 664. Lake Michigan Warehouse and Transportation; charter; Id. 672. Chicago Artesian Well; charter; 1 Pr. L. 1867 (7 Mar.) 51. Chicago Freight; charter; Id. (21 Feb.) 964. Anti-Incrustation; charter;

Chicago Corporations.

2 Pr. L. 1867 (19 Feb.) 352. Union Mining and Prospecting; charter: Id. 23 Feb.) 410. Commonwealth Mining: charter; Id. 413. Lancaster Coal; charter; Id. (28 Feb.) 402. Colorado Mining and Prospecting; charter; Id. (5 Mar.) 388. Illinois and Montana Mining; charter; Id. (9 Mar.) 397. Chicago Tug; charter; 3 Pr. L 1867 (21 Feb.) 644. City Baggage and Transfer; charter; Id. (25 Feb.) 641. Lake Michigan Steamboat; charter; Id. (7 Mar.) 88. Chicago Stage and Baggage; charter; Id. 636.

Miscellaneous. — Construction and use of Northern Indiana and Chicago Railroad; L. 1852 (16 June) 14. St. George Society of Illinois; charter; Id. (21 June) 55. Illinois St. Andrew Society; charter; Pr. L. 1853 (10 Feb.) 299. Chicago Tunnel; charter: Pr. L. 1855 (15 Feb.) 571. Harbor and Canal Improvement; charter; Pr. L. 1857 (18 Feb.) 1341. Gruetti Society; charter; Id. (19 Feb.) 1360. Sociater Arbeiter Verein of West Chicago; charter; 1 Pr. L. 1865 (15 Feb.) 64. Dania Society; charter; Id. (16 Feb.) 67. Chicago Turn-Gemeinde; charter; Id. 96. Chicago Arbeiter Verein; charter; Id. 63. Sharpshooters Association; charter; 2 Pr. L. 1865 (16 Feb.) 270. Societie Francaise de Seconrs Mutuels; 1 Pr. L. 1867 (22 Feb.) 125. Name of Western Engraving Co. changed to Western Bank Note and Engraving Co.; Id. (23 Feb.) 926. Piscatorial Association; charter; Id. 990. Scandinavian Immigrant Aid Society; charter; Id. (25 Feb.) 132. Guarantee Association; charter; Id. (9 Mar.) 853. The Oconto; charter; 2 Pr. L. 1867 (22 Feb.) 286. Svenska Americanavan; charter; Id. (25 Feb.) 318. Atwater Motor; charter; Id. 443. Land Improvement and Irrigation; charter; Id. (1 Mar.) 241. Concordia Maennerchor; charter; Id. (7 Mar.) 276. Vincennes Square Association; charter; 3 Pr. L. 1867 (1 Mar.) 83.

Moral and Intellectual. — Chicago Lyceum; charter; Pr. L. 1839 (27 Feb.) 125. Young Men's Association; chartered; Pr. L. 1851 (30 Jan.) 33. Amendment; Pr. L. 1855 (9 Feb.) 618. Philharmonic Society; charter; Pr. L. 1853 (11 Feb.) 340. Young Men's Christian Association; charter; Pr. L. 1861 (22 Feb.) 47. Charter amended; repeals §3; powers extended; 2 Pr. L. 1867 (21 Feb.) 269.

Printing and Publishing Companies.—Swedish Lutheran Publication Society in North America; charter; Pr. L. 1859 (21 Feb.) 419. Amendment; repeals §3; 2 Pr. L. 1867 (22 Feb.) 499. Tribune; charter; Pr. L. 1861 (18 Feb.) 740. Chicago Post; charter; Pr. L. 1863 (16 Feb.) 182. Republican; charter; 2 Pr. L. 1865 (13 Feb.) 117. Illinois Staats Zeitung; charter: Id. 119. West Publishing; charter; Id. (16 Feb.) 126. People's Anti-Monopoly Publishing; charter; 2 Pr. L. 1867 (18 Feb.) 497. Republic News; charter; Id. (21 Feb.) 501. National Printing; charter; Id. (23 Feb.) 503. Post Printing; charter; Id. (25 Feb.) 507. Franklin Printing and Publishing; charter; Id. (1 Mar.) 516. Chicago Age; charter; Id. (5 Mar.) 519. Prairie Farmer; charter; Id. (7 Mar.) 510. Legal News; charter; Pr. L. 1869 (27 Feb.) ——. Amendment; Laws therein legal evidence; L. 1869 (11 Mar.) 251. For publishing laws of session for immediate use: prima facie evidence; appropriation for copies of laws furnished; Id. (24 Mar.) 250, 12.

Savings Loan and Trust Companies.—Savings Institution and Trust; charter; Pr. L. 1857 (10 Feb.) 369. Illinois Savings Institution; charter; Id. (16 Feb.) 1006. Merchants Savings Loan and Trust; charter; Id. (28 Feb.) 83. Chicago Loan and Trust; chartered; Pr. L. 1859 (19 Feb.) 401. Charter amended; name changed to Commercial Loan; Pr. L. 1861 (22 Feb.) 452. Real Estate Loan and Trust; charter; Id. (21 Feb.) 463. State Savings Institution; charter; Id. 555. Prairie State Loan and Trust; charter; Id. (22 Feb.) 457. Chicago Loan and Deposit; charter; 2 Pr. L. 1865 (16 Feb.) 20. Chicago Real Estate and Land; charter; 2 Pr. L. 1867 (28 Feb.) 239. Illinois Land and Loan; charter; 1 Pr. L. 1867 (5 Apr.) 120. Mutual Trust Society; charter; Id. (6 Mar.) 75. International Mutual Trust; charter; Id. (7 Mar.) 94. National Loan and Trust; charter; Id. (9 Mar.) 104.

Secret Societies.—Myron Lodge No. 1, Old Free Order of Chaldea; charter; Pr. L. 1857 (17 Feb.) 238. Charter amended; name changed to Myron Lodge No. 1; L. 1852 (21 June) 49. Herman's Sons Lodge No. 27, Free Order of the Grand Lodge of New York; charter; Pr. L. 1855 (14 Feb.) 676. Masonic Temple Association; charter; Id. 696. Oriental Lodge No. 33, F. and A. Masons; 1 Pr. L. 1867 (28 Feb.) 969.

Science and Art.—Mechanics Institute; charter; L. 1843 (2 Jan.) 163. Charter amended; stock increased; Pr. L. 1853 (10 Feb.) 411. Chicago Historical Society; chartered; Pr. L. 1857 (7 Feb.) 329. Charter amended; increase resident membership; 2 Pr. L. 1867 (30 Jan.) 261. Granted 50 copies of all public documents printed by the state; Pr. L. 1861 (22 Feb.) 549. Art Gallery; charter; 2 Pr. L. 1865 (16 Feb.) 12. Academy of Sciences; charter; Id. 14. Northwestern Art and Photograph; charter; 1 Pr. L. 1867 (21 Feb.) 957. American Art Association; charter; Id. (28 Feb.) 953. Fine Art College; charter; Id. (21 Feb.) 956. Astronomical Society; 2 Pr. L. 1867 (19 Feb.) 258.

Trade and Commerce.—Association of Tailors; charter; Pr. L. 1855 (15 Feb.) 612. Merchants Exchange; charter; Pr. L. 1857 (5 Feb.) 245. And again; 1 Pr. L. 1865 (16 Feb.) 529. Board of Trade; charter; Pr. L 1859 (18 Feb.) 13. Merchants Association; charter; Pr. L. 1861 (20 Feb.) 474. Board of Underwriters; charter; Id. (22 Feb.) 297. Ice Co.; charter; Id. 345. Chamber of Commerce; charter; Pr. L. 1863 (14 Feb.) 179. Mercantile Association; charter; 1 Pr. L. 1865 (16 Feb.) 527. Stock exchange; charter; Id. 531. Illinois Fruit; charter; 1 Pr. L. 1867 (7 Mar.) 49. Traders Emporium; charter; Id. 847. Weighing and Measuring; charter; 3 Pr. L. 1867 (28 Feb.) 680.

Religious, Charitable, etc.—Dedication of lot 7 block 38 to the Unitarians, confirmed; L. 1841 (17 Feb.) 48. Chicago Bethel Association; edifice erected in 1844 vested in; Pr. L. 1847, (27 Feb.) 131. Acts of trustees of First Presbyterian Society legalized; Pr. L. 1849 (8 Feb.) 77. Chicago Orphan Asylum; charter; 2 L. 1849 (5 Nov.) 42. North Presbyterian Church to convey certain city lots to Mark Skinner; Pr. L. 1853 (10 Feb.) 608. Kehilath Anshe Magrib;

charter; Pr. L. 1855 (12 Feb.) 584. Hibernian Benevolent Society; Id. (14 Feb.) 706. Methodist Episcopal Church changed to First M. E. Church; Pr. L. 1857 (14 Feb.) 612. Foregoing amended; powers extended; 1 Pr. L. 1865 (13 Feb.) 238. St. James' Church borrow $40,000. to complete edifice; Id. (14 Feb.) 801. Illinois Association of the New Jerusalem; charter; Id. (16 Feb.) 1011. Relief and Aid Society; charter; council may aid with appropriations; Id. 1123. Home for the Friendless; charter; Pr. L. 1859 (12 Feb.) 10. Foregoing amended; surrender upon habeas corpus; 1 Pr. L. 1865 (16 Feb.) 81. Seamen's Mutual Benevolent Society; charter; Pr. L. 1861 (22 Feb.) 46. City Mission and Church Home; charter; Id. 45. General Convention of New Jerusalem; charter; Id. (29 Jan.) 81. Catholic Bishop; charter; Id. (20 Feb.) 78. United Sons of Erin Benevolent Society; Pr. L. 1863 (13 Feb.) 31. Ministry at Large; Id. 34. Roman Catholic Asylum of the Diocese of Catholic Bishop of Chicago; charter; Id. (29 Jan.) 25. Laborers' Benevolent Association; charter; 1 Pr. L. 1865 (13 Feb.) 82. Old Ladies' Home; charter; Id. (14 Feb.) 76. Nursery and Half Orphan Asylum; charter; Id. (15 Feb.) 84. Catholic St. Francis Society; charter; Id. 95. Roman Catholic Total Abstinence and Benevolent Society; Id. (16 Feb.) 89. Redemptorist Fathers; charter; Id 88. Bricklayers' and Masons' Benevolent Association; charter; Id. 65. Operative Plasterers' Protective Benevolent Society; charter; Id. 87. Erring Woman's Refuge for Reform; charter; Id. 98. German Masons' and Bricklayers' Society; charter; 1 Pr. L. 1867 (16 Feb.) 133. Washingtonian Home; charter; Id. 141. Deutscher Roemisch Katholischer St. Peter's Unterstuctzungs Verein; charter; Id. 135. United Hebrew Relief Association; charter; Id. (25 Feb.) 130. Seamen's Benevolent Union; charter; Id. (5 Mar.) 149. House of the Good Shepherd; charter; Id. (7 Mar.) 152. Institution of Protestant Deaconesses; charter; 2 Pr. L. 1867 (7 Mar.) 81. Chicago District Camp Ground Association; charter; Id. 206. German Christian Aid Society; charter; Id. (21 Feb.) 265. Sunday School Union; charter; 3 Pr. L. 1867 (28 Feb.) 51. Soldiers' Home; charter; Id. 81. Father Matthew Total Abstinance and Benevolent Society; charter; Id. (21 Feb.) 130. Illinois Society for the prevention of cruelty to animals; charter; L. 1869 (25 Mar.) 114. Woman's Home (organized under act 25 Feb. 1867 for chartering unitary homes); charter amended; property exempt from taxation; Id. (16 Apr.) 400.

Miscellaneous.—Two additional notaries; 1 L. 1837 (16 Jan.) 175. To relieve purchasers of canal lots in 1836; L. 1841 (27 Feb.) 49. Certificate to Updike and Talcott for a canal lot; L. 1843 (28 Jan.) 213. John Albert Spears name changed to John Albert Foss; Pr. L. 1855 (15 Feb.) 717. Wm. Watson name changed to Wm. Sneed Watson; Pr. L. 1837 (31 Jan.) 228. Emma Frances Rice name changed to Emma Jane Bridges; Id. (9 Feb.) 310. Henry Barkus, convicted of ——, restored to citizenship; Id. (18 Feb.) 1400. Lake View Avenue Co. (organized under general law); powers extended; 2 Pr. L. 1865 (16 Feb.) 258. Mrs. Roxana Scott, widow of Col. Joseph R. Scott, allowed $101.27 back pay; Id. 249. Michigan Central R. R. enabled to hold real estate; Id. 171. Illinois Central, Chicago Burlington and Quincy, Michigan Central and the Chicgao and Northwestern R. R's, enabled jointly to hold certain grounds; Id. 171. Vacates roads named; 2 Pr. L. 1867 (28 Feb.) 841. Frederick Scott restored to citizenship; Id. (7 Mar.) 815. J. R. Steele restored to citizenship; L. 1869 (27 Mar.) 118. Cora Snell name changed to E. M. Sloan; Id. (3 Mar.) 268.

Schools and School Lands.—School inspectors and trustees elected; duties defined; L. 1835 (6 Feb.) 161. Foregoing repealed; 2 L. 1837 (20 July) 80. Vacates Heacock's plat of part of school section and confirms Blanchard's plat thereof; L. 1839 (4 Dec. 1838) 80. Relating to common schools; Id. (1 Mar.) 215. Heacock's sub-division of block 30 School Section addition legalized; Id. (2 Mar.) 160. Recorded plat of School Section addition legalized; L. 1843 (3 Mar.) 65.

United States, jurisdiction ceded to. — For three light houses; L. 1849 (11 Jan.) 99. Part of School Section addition to city; for light house and custom house purposes; L. 1855 (13 Feb.) 139. Foregoing amended; L. 1859 (16 Feb.) 121. For a Marine Hospital; L. 1865 (14 Jan.) 90. For the same; L. 1867 (11 Jan.) 175. Over 20 acres yet unpurchased, for the same; Id. (28 Feb.) 176. Over lands joining custom house; L. 1865 (16 Feb.) 44.

Barrington.—Town chartered; 2 L. 1865 (16 Feb.) 369. Academy chartered; 1 Pr. L. 1865 (16 Feb.) 1. Mutual Guarantee Insurance Co. chartered; Id. 620.

Blue Island.—Portland changed to Blue Island; L. 1843 (24 Feb.) 301. Vacates part of Rexford street; Pr. L. 1857 (10 Feb.) 374. Blue Island Avenue Plank Road may macadamize; Id. (16 Feb.) 859.

Brighton.—Hotel and Stock Yard Co. chartered; Pr. L. 1857 (14 Feb.) 922. Amendment; name changed to Brighton Co.; Pr. L. 1861 (22 Feb.) 63. Further amends; powers extended; 1 Pr. L. 1865 (6 Feb.) 602.

Evanston.—Ridgeville changed to Evanston; L. 1857 (17 Feb.) 206. Northwestern Female College chartered; patronage M. E. Church; Pr. L. 1857 (19 Jan.) 6. Evanston Pier Co. chartered; Id. (16 Feb.) 886. Evanston Seminary chartered; Id. 994. Public grounds and streets vacated; boundary extended; 2 Pr. L. 1865 (16 Feb.) 440. Evanston Academy chartered; 1 Pr. L. 1867 (28 Feb.) 16. Northwestern Gas Light and Coke Co. chartered; Id. (21 Feb.) 982. Evanston Hotel Co. chartered; 2 Pr. L. 1867 (20 Feb.) 47. Evanston Philosophical Association chartered; Id. (28 Feb.) 272. Town school tax abated one-half; Id. (12 Feb.) 800.

Hyde Park.—Hyde Park Seminary chartered; Pr. L. 1857 (28 Jan.) 72. Town boundaries defined; Pr. L. 1861 (20 Feb.) 632. Foregoing amended; powers extended; 2 Pr. L. 1865 (6 Feb.) 481. Library Association chartered; 2 Pr. L. 1867 (25 Feb.) 254. Skating Co. chartered; 3 Pr. L. 1867 (7 Mar.) 80. Town incorporation acts reduced to one and amended; Id. (5 Mar.) 344.

Lake View.—Town established; L. 1857 (17

Feb.) 206. Roschill Cemetery Co. chartered; Pr. L. 1859 (11 Feb.) 29. Graceland Cemetery chartered; Pr. L. 1861 (22 Feb.) 71. Foregoing amended; fund provided for permanent improvement; Pr. L. 1863 (13 Feb.) 174. Further amends; trustees of Graceland Cemetery Improvement fund chartered; 1 Pr. L. 1865 (16 Feb.) 222. Locating a public park; 2 Pr. L. 1865 (16 Feb.) 103. Foregoing generally amended; 2 Pr. L. 1867 (8 Mar.) 479. Board of town trustees chartered; Id. (16 Feb.) 484. Foregoing amended and extended; 1 Pr. L. 1867 (5 Mar.) 157. German Pilgrim's Rest Cemetery Association; Id. (1 Mar.) 214.

CRAWFORD COUNTY.

County formed prior to the organization of the state. Cornelius Taylor, toll bridge across the Embarrass at Yellowbanks; L. 1819 (27 Feb.) 80. John S. Woodworth collect taxes for 1818; Id. (22 Mar.) 164. Part of said county attached to Clark; L. 1823 (23 Dec. 1822) 79. Bridge the Raccoon, Hudson, Sugar and Lamotte creeks; L. 1829 (19 Jan.) 147 §12. Share in proceeds of Gallatin Salines; L. 1831 (16 Feb.) 14 §1. Benj. Myers and others allowed expenses building court house; Pr. L. 1833 (1 Feb.) 28. Road from Vincennes to Chicago changed between Palestine and Hutsonville; L. 1835 (29 Feb.) 127. Same subject; L. 1836 (13 Jan.) 191. Road from Palestine to Howards located; L. 1839 (28 Feb.) 195. Sale of Hudsonville lots; Id. (2 Mar.) 239. Removal of county seat from Palestine; vote thereon; L. 1843 (24 Feb.) 118. Guardian of Lucinda E. Fox to sell real estate; Pr. L. 1847 (4 Feb.) 23. Records of transcripts, etc., to be transcribed into new book; L. 1853 (11 Feb.) 211. Collection of taxes for 1847–8–9; Id. (12 Feb.) 236. Huntsville city charter; Pr. L. 1853 (3 Feb.) 330. Foregoing repealed; Pr. L. 1857 (16 Feb.) 917. Noah Ninnicks, convicted of larceny, restored to citizenship; Id. (26 Jan.) 472. Vacates streets in Robinson; Id. 472. Palestine chartered; Pr. L. 1855 (15 Feb.) 62. And again; Pr. L. 1857 (16 Feb.) 1139. County issue $30,000. bonds in aid of Wabash R. R.; vote thereon; Id. (14 Feb.) 710. Alex. G. Southerland, ferry across the Great Wabash at Merom; Pr. L. 1857 (14 Feb.) 613. Joint erection and occupancy of a building by Huntsville Lodge No. 136 Masons, and directors district No. 3, Town 8—11; Id. (18 Feb.) 1363. Memorializing Congress to remunerate Joseph J. Petri for effecting the deliverance of 70 emigrants in the mountains of California; Pr. L. 1857 (28 Jan.) 1455. Jurisdiction of county court extended; L. 1863 (21 Feb.) 26. Foregoing repealed; L. 1869)27 Mar.) 145. Sale of swamp lands legalized; 1 Pr. L. 1867 (20 Feb.) 858. Chester H. Fesh, ferry across the Wabash at Town 7—10; Id. (19 Feb.) 932.

CUMBERLAND COUNTY.

County created; boundary and organization; Laws 1843 (2 Mar.) 94. Acts of James Ewarts, deputy county clerk, legalized; L. 1845 (27 Feb.) 180. Disposition of school funds; return of scholars in 1844; Id. (7 Feb.) 221. Relocation of county seat; points giving bond to be voted for; conveyance of town of DeKalb to James Gill declared valid; L. 1849 (8 Feb.) 50. Estate and heirs of Thos. Sconce, late collector, released; L. 1849 (9 Feb.) 117. Distribution of school fund for 1848; Id. (30 Jan.) 153. Same for 1850–1; L. 1851 (15 Feb.) 99. Aid in construction of plank road; Pr. L. 1854 (28 Feb.) 157. Greenup chartered; Pr. L. 1855 (15 Feb.) 89. Greenup Lodge No. 125, F. and A. Masons chartered; Pr. Laws 1855 (15 Feb.) 708. Relocation of county seat; vote thereon; Id. (9 Feb.) 712. Location of county seat at Prairie City by county court legalized; Pr. L. 1857 (10 Feb.) 349. Wiley Ross to bridge Muddy creek near Woodbury; Id. (16 Feb.) 1102. A. K. Bosworth to transcribe records in Coles county; Pr. L. 1861 (22 Feb.) 55. Jurisdiction of county court extended; L. 1863 (21 Feb.) 26. J. H. Morgan, surity of J. H. Miller discharged from recognizance; L. 1867 (8 Mar.) 155. To regulate support of paupers; 2 Pr. L. 1867 (5 Mar.) 481. For transcribing certain public records; Id. (23 Feb.) 788. Road from Shelbyville via Neoga and Prairie City to National Road, relocated in part; Id. (23 Feb.) 817. Boundary of certain school districts changed; 3 Pr. L. 1867 (9 Feb.) 22. Special bridge tax; Id. (19 Feb.) 120.

DANE COUNTY.

County created; boundary and organization; L. 1839 (15 Feb.) 104. Supplemental to foregoing; Id. (28 Feb.) 205. County name changed to Christian; L. 1840 (1 Feb.) 80.—*See Christian County.*

DEAF AND DUMB ASYLUM.

Established; L. 1837 (23 Feb.) 162. Appropriates $3,000. annually; L. 1847 (23 Feb) 47. Further concerning; L. 1849 (3 Feb.) 93. Additional fund created; proceeds of farm; act 1847 repealed; L. 1851 (15 Feb.) 102. Further respecting; L. 1853 (12 Feb.) 90. For building north wing $6,508.13; L. 1857 (5 Feb.) 62. Foregoing amended; number and class of directors; Id. (13 Feb.) 84. For lighting with gas; Id. (16 Feb.) 148. For heating and lighting $8,458.12; deficiencies $16,000.; Expenses $4,500.; L. 1859 (19 Feb.) 11. For 1859–60 $27,800. per annum; Id. 12. For 1861–2; L. 1861 (21 Feb.) 120. For 1863–4; L. 1863 (21 Feb.) 15. For 1865–6; L. 1865 (16 Feb.) 16. For 1867–8; L. 1867 (28 Feb.) 9. For 1869–70; L. 1869 (27 Feb.) 29. Also, Id. (19 Apr.) 30.

DE KALB COUNTY.

County created; boundary and organization; 1 L. 1837 (4 Mar.) 97. Removal of county seat from Orange; vote thereon; L. 1839 (2 Mar.) 244. Removal of county seat from Coultonville; vote thereon; L. 1840 (30 Jan.) 68. Coultonville Steam and Hydraulic Manufacturing Co. chartered; L. 1843 (1 Mar.) 159. School directors to raise money to build school houses; L. 1847 (28 Feb.) 158. Cemetery for heirs of Billy Ames, sec. 34 Town 44—4, established; Pr.

L. 1851 (17 Feb.) 281. Hogs not to run at large; L. 1849 (10 Jan.) 185. Town of Pierce created; L. 1853 (11 Feb.) 93. School directors district No. 1, Town 41—5, to borrow money to build school house; Id. (12 Feb.) 192. Town of Victor created; part of Amboy added to Lee Centre; Id. (14 Feb.) 204. County borrow $3,000. to build poor house and jail; Id. (12 Feb.) 235. Commissioners of highways to vacate or relocate state roads; Pr. L. 1854 (1 Mar.) 145. Sycamore and Courtland R. R. chartered; Pr. L. 1859 (10 Feb.) 514. Jurisdiction of county court extended; L. 1863 (12 Feb.) 43. Townships to support their own paupers; vote thereon; Id. (13 Feb.) 46. Terms of county court; qualifications of judge; L. 1865 (16 Feb.) 29. Action of county for payment of bounties to soldiers, legalized; 1 Pr. L. 1865 (16 Feb.) 530. Courtland, town chartered; 2 Pr. L. 1865 (16 Feb.) 431. Repeals §4 of the foregoing; 3 Pr. L. 1867 (8 Mar.) 602. Somonauk, town chartered; Id. 578. Said town attached to Kendall county; Id. 579 Township of Sycamore to take stock in Sycamore and Courtland R. R.; Id. (15 Feb) 223. County court at Sycamore; L. 1867 (25 Feb.) 70. County judge to exchange with any circuit judge; Id. (7 Mar.) 72. Relocation of county seat; 1 Pr. L. 1867 (12 Feb.) 858. Foregoing amended; fixes time of holding circuit court; Id. (8 Mar.) 899. Shabbona Masonic Stock Co. chartered; Id. (18 Feb.) 962.

Sycamore.—Alley in block 13 vacated; L. 1855 (15 Feb.) 112. Vacates certain alleys; Pr. L. 1857 (31 Jan) 227. Town chartered; Pr. L. (15 Feb.) 112. 1859 (21 Feb.) 686. Repeals §4 of the foregoing; 2 Pr. L 1865 (16 Feb.) 583. Town take stock in Sycamore and Courtland R. R.; Pr. L. 1861 (20 Feb.) 524. Foregoing repealed; 2 Pr. L. 1867 (5 Mar.) 534. Elmwood Cemetery Co. chartered; 1 Pr. L. 1865 (16 Feb.) 218. Federal Union Insurance Co. chartered; Id. 650. Kiswaukee Insurance Co. chartered; Id. 693.

Sandwich.—Trustees of Sandwich Academy to sell real estate; Pr. L. 1857 (30 Jan.) 104. Baptist church and society of Somonauk changed to First Baptist Church and Society of Sandwich; Id. (11 Feb.) 422. Town chartered; Pr. L. 1859 (21 Feb.) 686. Section 4 of foregoing repealed; 2 Pr. L. 1865 (16 Feb.) 583. Sandwich Fire Insurance Co. chartered; 2 Pr. L. 1867 (7 Mar.) 194. Provisions of act 18 Feb. (L. 1857, 101) revived by act 21 Feb. (L. 1861, 11) and extended to the Union Agricultural Institute; L. 1869 (10 Mar.) 9.

De Kalb.—Town chartered; Pr. L. 1861 (21 Feb.) 598. Foregoing amended; 3 Pr. L. 1867 (8 Mar.) 102. DeKalb Printing Association chartered; 2 Pr. L. 1867 (23 Feb.) 500.

DE WITT COUNTY.

County created; boundary and organization; vote on location of county seat; L. 1839 (1 Mar.) 199. Acts of John J. McGraw confirmed; L. 1843 (25 Feb.) 170. Part of said county attached to Logan; L. 1845 (26 Feb.) 189. Vacates a street and opens an alley in Waynesville; L. 1855 (14 Feb.) 191. Wm. Walters, convicted of perjury, restored to citizenship; Pr. L. 1855 (15 Feb.) 609. Sale of swamp lands; L. 1857 (16 Feb.) 122. Circuit clerk to transcribe certain records of counties of McLean and Macon; Pr. L. 1857 (18 Feb.) 1190. Leonidas Hamil, name changed to Leonidas Cundiff; Id. (19 Feb.) 1363. Form of judgment entries in circuit court; L. 1861 (22 Feb.) 119 Oliver Lakins' survey of Wapella legalized; Pr. L. 1861 (22 Feb) 734. Bounties to soldiers; apply only to townships petitioning; 1 Pr. L. 1865 (15 Feb) 121. Vacates public square in Post's addition to Waynesville; 3 Pr. L. 1867 (8 Mar.) 201. Mt. Pleasant changed to Farmer City; L. 1869 (27 Mar.) 279.

Clinton.—Town chartered; Pr. L. 1855 (15 Feb.) 175. And again; Pr. L. 1857 (18 Feb.) 1234. Foregoing amended; repeals §9; 2 Pr. L. 1865 (16 Feb.) 420. City chartered; 1 Pr. L. 1867 (8 Mar.) 779. Woodlawn Cemetery Association chartered; 1 Pr. L. 1865 (16 Feb.) 233. Clinton Hotel Co. chartered; Id. 605. De Witt County Seminary chartered; 1 Pr. L. 1867 (8 Mar.) 37. De Witt County Loan and Trust Co. chartered; Id. 101.

DOUGLAS COUNTY.

County established; vote thereon; L. 1857 (13 Feb.) 71. And again; vote thereon; L. 1859 (8 Feb.) 24. Supplemental to foregoing; other territory included; Id. (16 Feb.) 28. Tuscola chartered, Pr. L. 1861 (22 Feb.) 724. Foregoing amended; 2 Pr. L. 1865 (15 Feb.) 580. For completion of court house and jail; 1 Pr. L. 1865 (16 Feb.) 540. For the better chartering of Arcola; 2 Pr. L. 1865 (16 Feb.) 347. Vacates streets in Carmago; Id. 662. Bourbon plat vacated; Id. (15 Feb.) 663. Vacates streets in Johnson's addition to New Albany, now Carmago; 3 Pr. L. 1867 (20 Feb.) 101. Vacates streets in Tuscola; Id. (19 Feb.) 106.

DU PAGE COUNTY.

County created; boundary and organization; location of county seat; L. 1839 (9 Feb.) 73. Road from Naperville to Warrenville relocated; Id. (22 Feb.) 155. Assessment for 1839 legalized; L. 1840 (18 Jan.) 47. Road from Naperville to Indian Creek (McHenry) changed in part; Id. (1 Feb.) 76. County clerks office, place of fixed; L. 1841 (26 Feb.) 62. Asa Dudley to collect unpaid taxes for 1841; L. 1843 (1 Mar.) 221. Warrenville Cemetery Association chartered; L. 1845 (3 Mar.) 132. Warrenville Seminary chartered; Id. 249. Acts of Horace Brooks and Geo. W. Wait, deputy surveyors, legalized; Pr. L. 1847 (28 Feb.) 217. Hogs not to run at large; L. 1849 (10 Jan.) 185. Sarah Ann Wright name changed to Mills; Pr. L. 1849 (10 Feb.) 14. Elizabeth M. Walters changed to Grose; Pr. L. 1851 (17 Feb.) 291. Acts of county court after adopting township organization, legalized; records of circuit court transcribed in part; L. 1851 (17 Feb.) 160. Sheep and swine not to run at large after 1 Mar. '53; L. 1853 (12 Feb.) 152. Addison Farmers Mutual Insurance Co. chartered; Pr. L. 1855 (15 Feb.) 392. Foregoing amended; Pr. L. 1857 (19 Feb.) 1442. Further amends; Pr. L. 1859 (24 Feb.) 383. First amendment amended; take

wind risks; Pr. L. 1861 (21 Feb.) 346. Charter again amended; 2 Pr. L. 1867 (25 Feb.) 230. Towns to support their own paupers; Id. 728. Relocating a road in Wayne; L. 1857 (16 Feb.) 177. Removal of county seat; vote thereon; Id. (7 Feb.) 209. Same subject; 1 Pr. L. 1867 (13 Feb.) 894. County seat to be at Wheaton until otherwise decided by the courts; L. 1869 (10 Mar.) 330. County Agricultural and Mechanical Society chartered; Pr. L. 1857 (12 Feb.) 502. Circuit clerk to transcribe record of judgments and executions; Id. (17 Feb.) 1146. Junction changed to Turners; Pr. L. 1859 (24 Feb.) 728. Cook county records to be copied; L. 1861 (18 Feb.) 87. Evangelical Lutheran Teacher's Seminary chartered; 1 Pr. L. 1865 (16 Feb.) 31. Foregoing amended; 1 Pr. L. 1867 (21 Feb.) 242. Highways in Downer's Grove legalized; 2 Pr. L. 1867 (14 Feb.) 73. Downer's Grove Farmers Mutual Insurance Co. chartered; Id. (7 Mar.) 175. Vacates part of Turner plat; 3 Pr. L. 1867 (25 Feb.) 102. Towns issue bonds to pay bounties; 1 Pr. L. 1865 (16 Feb.) 122. Incorporation of German Evangelical Lutheran School at Addison, legalized; 2 Pr. L. 1865 (10 Feb.) 240. Henry F. Vallette, late collector released from judgment; Id. (16 Feb.) 250. Assessment and collection of tax for 1868; L. 1869 (17 Apr.) 354.

Wheaton.—Streets vacated; Pr. L. 1857 (18 Feb.) 1241. Town chartered; Pr. L. 1859 (24 Feb.) 719. And again; 2 Pr. L. 1865 (13 Feb.) 614. Foregoing amended; 3 Pr. L. 1867 (21 Feb.) 597. Illinois Institute chartered; Pr. L. 1855 (15 Feb.) 507. Wheaton Cemetery Association chartered; Pr. L. 1857 (14 Feb.) 784. Wheaton Mutual Security Insurance Co. chartered; Id. (16 Feb.) 1001. Foregoing amended; take lightning risks; 1 Pr. L. 1865 (16 Feb.) 636. And again; name changed to Illinois State Insurance Co.; 2 Pr. L. 1867 (5 Mar.) 168. Wheaton College chartered; Pr. L. 1861 (22 Feb.) 28. Milton Block Association chartered; 1 Pr. L. 1865 (16 Feb.) 207. Foregoing amended; 1 Pr. L. 1867 (9 Mar.) 202.

Naperville.—Vacates part of the Squaw Lane in Martin's Addition; Pr. L. 1853 (12 Feb.) 502. Village chartered; Pr. L. 1857 (7 Feb.) 290. Charter amended; regulate sale of liquors; Pr. L. 1859 (24 Feb.) 726. County to quitclaim to town its real estate therein; 2 Pr. L. 1867 (7 Mar.) 800. Vacates part of Court street; 3 Pr. L. 1867 (21 Feb.) 109. Naperville Academy chartered; L. 1841 (27 Feb.) 17. And again; Pr. L. 1851 (17 Feb.) 320. Naperville Cemetery Association chartered; L. 1843 (6 Mar.) 18. Additional supervisor; L. 1855 (14 Feb.) 45. Bank of Naperville to withdraw certificate conditionally; L. 1859 (18 Feb.) 87. Directors of Graded School chartered; Pr. L. 1863 (13 June) 21. Section 9 of foregoing repealed; additional district; 2 Pr. L. 1865 (16 Feb.) 279.

Bloomingdale.—Bloomingdale Cemetery Association chartered; Pr. L. 1847 (22 Feb.) 20. Foregoing amended; name changed to Greenwood Cemetery Association; Pr. L. 1861 (13 Feb.) 63. Highway Commissioners acts from 17 Apr. '51 to 12 Feb. '53, legalized; L. 1857 (16 Feb.) 302. Bloomingdale Academy chartered; Pr. L. 1861 (22 Feb.) 9. Baptist church to sell and convey real estate; Id. (13 Feb.) 77.

EDGAR COUNTY.

County formed out of Clark; L. 1823 (3 Jan.) 74. Leasing part of school section, Town 12—10; Laws 1826 (25 Jan.) 75. Road from Paris to Vandalia, relocated in part; L. 1829 (10 Jan.) 128. Same, from Paris to State line in direction of Clinton Ind., located; Id. (22 Jan.) 136. Same, between Redmond's and Paris, relocated; L. 1835 (12 Feb.) 110. Same, Springfield and Paris, partly improved; L. 1836 (16 Jan.) 221. Same, Paris to State line, located; 1 L. 1837 (19 Jan.) 237. Foregoing extended; same in Grandview relocated; also, from Smith's to Grandview; L. 1839 (2 Mar.) 58. Same, Bruce's mill to Paris, located; 1 L. 1837 (31 Jan.) 242. Same, Grandview to Livingston, relocated; 2 L. 1837 (20 July) 64. Same, Paris towards Grandview, changed in part; Id. (21 July) 69. Same, Grandview to Terre Haute, relocation in part; L. 1839 (19 Feb.) 137. Same, for improvement of; Id. (26 Feb.) 173. Same, Hall Syms a commissioner to review those running out of Paris; L. 1841 (24 Feb.) 244. Same, part of Steam Point relocated; L. 1869 (31 Mar.) 383. Bridges across Bruett's and Sugar creeks; L. 1829 (19 Jan.) 147 §12. Share in proceeds of Gallatin Saline lands; L. 1831 (16 Feb.) 14. Lands of the estate of Horace Hotchkiss sold; L. 1836 (8 Dec. 1835) 232. A new justice and constable district; 1 L. 1837 (11 Feb.) 115. Additional election precinct in Embarrass Point; L. 1841 (27 Feb.) 177. Wm. Maloney, minor, to convey certain lands; L. 1843 (28 Jan.) 72. Administrator of F. Boyers to convey certain lands; L. 1845 (3 Dec. '44) 192. Executor of Wm. Wood, the same; Id. (28 Feb.) 270. Widow of Joseph R. Smart, the same; Pr. L. 1847 (1 Mar.) 193. Sam'l A. Lodge, for surveying swamp lands; L. 1853 (12 Feb.) 249. John Chestnutwood name changed to Williams; Pr. L. 1855 (9 Feb.) 665. County Agricultural Society chartered; Id. (15 Feb.) 671. Game law 1855 amended as to said county; Pr. L. 1857 (16 Feb.) 123; Gross' Stat. 324. County Agricultural and Mechanical Association chartered; Pr. L. 1861 (20 Feb.) 34. Apportionment of county school fund; 2 Pr. L. 1865 (16 Feb.) 273. Soldiers Monument, erection of; 1 Pr. L. 1867 (28 Feb.) 889. County Land and Loan Co. chartered; 2 Pr. L. 1867 (8 Mar.) 280. Cherry Point City Woolen Manufacturing Co. chartered; Id. (23 Feb.) 325. Edgar Mining and Oil Co. chartered; Id. (14 Feb.) 431. Governor to appoint a county treasurer in place of J. W. Shanks deceased; L. 1869 (4 Mar.) 331.

Paris.—Town chartered; Pr. L. 1853 (12 Feb.) 199. Foregoing amended; limits reduced; Pr. L. 1857 (16 Feb.) 888. Foregoing amendment repealed; Pr. L. 1859 (19 Feb.) 653. Amends amendment of 1857 (repealed by foregoing); 3 Pr. L. 1867 (5 Mar.) 235. Charter election in Mar. 1853, legalized; Pr. L. 1855 (9 Feb.) 693. To regulate sale of liquor; Pr. L. 1863 (20 Feb.) 271. Paris Seminary chartered; Pr. L. 1837 (1 Mar.) 182. Male and Female Seminary chartered; Pr. L. 1851 (15 Feb.) 211. Pocahontas Tribe No. 1, Imperial Order of Red men chartered; Pr. L. 1855 (14 Feb.) 674. Wabash Valley Fire and Marine Insurance Co. chartered; Pr. L. 1857 (14 Feb.) 616. Supplemental to foregoing; Id. (18 Feb.) 1242. Amends first foregoing; name changed to Wabash Insurance

Co.; 2 Pr. L. 1867 (28 Feb.) 160. Edgar Collegiate Institute chartered; 1 Pr. L. 1867 (8 Mar.) 36. Paris Hotel Co. chartered; 2 Pr. L. 1867 (14 Feb.) 42. Home Insurance Co. chartered; Id. (6 Mar.) 101, 225. Farmers and Mechanics Insurance Co. chartered; Id. (5 Mar.) 164.

Kansas.—Name of Midway changed to Kansas; Pr. L. 1857 (14 Feb.) 713. Town chartered; Pr. L. 1859 (24 Feb.) 628. And again; 3 Pr. L. 1867 (25 Feb.) 305.

EDWARDS COUNTY.

County formed prior to the organization of the state. Four commissioners to remove county seat; L. 1821 (1 Feb.) 68. Build court house and jail; L. 1823 (14 Feb.) 146. Claims against county divided between counties of Edwards and Wabash; L. 1826 (19 Jan.) 53. Same subject; Pr. L. 1827 (16 Jan.) 11. Southern boundary line of Wayne and Edwards defined; L. 1829 (22 Jan.) 32. Foregoing construed; 1 Pr. L. 1867 (28 Feb.) 162. Share of proceeds of Gallatin Salines; L. 1831 (16 Feb.) 15 §1. Borrow money to build court house; L. 1852 (18 June) 22. Borrow $5,000. to buy breadstuffs for the unfortunate; Pr. L. 1855 (14 Feb.) 704. Franklin College chartered; Pr. L. 1827 (9 Jan.) 6. Concerning sale of school section, Town 3—14; 1 L. 1837 (3 Mar.) 314. Sale of school lands; L. 1839 (27 Feb.) 192. Resale of school land in Town 2—14; Id. 204. Payment of interest on school fund in Town 2—14; L. 1843 (3 Mar.) 168. Sheriff to receive $127.70 overpaid; L. 1819 (24 Mar.) 239. Sheriff released from liability for failing to pay over taxes; L. 1826 (19 Jan.) 58. Ransom Higgins, toll bridge across Bon Pas creek; L. 1835 (9 Feb.) 83. Appropriates $100. to bridge Bon Pas creek; Pr. L. 1833 (1 Mar.) 5. Mills and Baker, mill dam on Little Wabash, Town 1—10; L. 1839 (12 Feb.) 117. Road, Mt. Carmel to Maysville, relocated; Id. (16 Feb.) 134. Same, Albion to Maysville; Id. (27 Feb.) 203. Bon Pas creek navigable to Higgins Mill; L. 1843 (4 Mar.) 245. Grayville chartered; Pr. L. 1855 (13 Feb.) 293. New Salem changed to West Salem; Pr. L. 1857 (18 Feb.) 1242. Vacates plat of W. Salem; Pr. L. 1861 (20 Feb.) 718.

EFFINGHAM COUNTY.

County established; county seat located and named by commissioners; Laws 1831 (15 Feb.) 50. Election for county officers at Thos. J. Brocketts house; location of county seat ratified; attached to 4th judicial circuit; Pr. L. 1833. (20 Dec. '32) 23. Towns 9—4, 5 and 6 taken from Shelby and added to this; L. 1845 (26 Feb.) 104. Assessments for 1843 legalized; Id. (4 Feb.) 199. Tax books for 1846–7, 8 and 9 examined and corrected; L. 1851 (17 Feb.) 182. Removal of county seat from Ewington to Effingham; vote thereon; L. 1859 (18 Feb.) 43. Provisions for payment of bounties legalized; 1 Pr. L. 1867 (4 Mar.) 879. Wm. Stevens pre-emption of part sec. 16, Town 7—5 confirmed; same extended to actual settlers on section 16 Town 7—1; Pr. L. 1833 (28 Feb.) 119. Distribution of school fund for 1846; L. 1847 (16 Feb.) 115. Same subject; Id. (22 Feb.) 154. Same subject; L. 1849 (30 Jan.) 158. Sale of school lands in Town 8—7; Id. (6 Feb.) 181. Securities of R. J. Hill, late collector, conditionally discharged from liability; L. 1845 (3 Feb.) 199. Bridge Little Wabash near Ewington; free after 10 years; Pr. L. 1847 (19 Feb.) 13. James Cartright, to dam Little Wabash at sec. 22, Town 7—5; Id. (17 Feb.) 40. Widow of Geo. Morris, sell real estate; Id. (26 Feb.) 185. County issue bonds in aid of construction of plank roads; Pr. L. 1854 (28 Feb.) 157. Granville plat vacated; Pr. L. 1855 (15 Feb.) 194. Harman Faithdrop, to dam Little Wabash at sec. 36, Town 8—5; Id. (13 Feb.) 686. Joseph A. Dunlap, convicted of petit larceny, restored to citizenship; Pr. L. 1861 (18 Feb.) 307. John F. Washford's survey of Teutopolis legalized; Id. (22 Feb.) 723. Town of Mason chartered; 2 Pr. L. 1865 (15 Feb.) 507. Foregoing amended; election of police justice and constable; 3 Pr. L. 1867 (25 Feb.) 600. Isaac Gordon, mill dam on Little Wabash, Town 6—6; L. 1843 (28 Feb.) 175. H. W. Higgs, late collector, sell lands for taxes of 1840; Id. (20 Feb.) 215.

Effingham.—Towns of Effingham and Broughton consolidated; Pr. L. 1859 (14 Feb.) 602. Town chartered; Pr. L. 1861 (20 Feb.) 611. Foregoing amended; Pr. L. 1863 (16 Feb.) 265. City chartered; 1 Pr. L. 1867 (15 Feb.) 308.

Ewington.—Town chartered; Pr. L. 1855 (14 Feb.) 54. Foregoing amended; Pr. L. 1857 (9 Feb.) 311. Steam Mill Co. chartered; Pr. L. 1853 (11 Feb.) 514. Ewington Lodge No. 149, F. and A. Masons chartered; Pr. L. 1857 (16 Feb.) 1051.

FAYETTE COUNTY.

County formed, county seat fixed at Vandalia; L. 1821 (14 Feb.) 164. Repeals §9 of foregoing; L. 1823 (12 Feb.) 128. Lots for county buildings selected; Id. (17 Feb.) 154. To subscribe $10,000. to Okaw Bottom Plank road; L. 1853 (8 Feb.) 279. Issue county bonds in aid of plank roads; Pr. L. 1854 (28 Feb.) 157. For repairing court house; L. 1859 (12 Feb.) 210. County war bonds legalized; 3 Pr. L. 1867 (12 Feb.) 115. Compensation to sheriff for fuel and attendance upon Supreme Court; L. 1823 (31 Jan.) 97. Same subject; L. 1826 (23 Jan.) 71; L. 1829, 35. Same subject; Pr. L. 1833 (1 Mar.) 205. Relief of purchasers of Perryville lots; L. 1823 (17 Feb.) 150. McLaughlin and Townsend to build mill near Vandalia; L. 1825 (14 Dec. '24) 11. Adm'r. of James Kelly to account to probate judge; Pr. L. 1827 (17 Feb.) 30. Four acres state land, opposite Vandalia, granted Harvey and Lemuel Lee, conditioned that they keep running thereon a good grist mill; Id. (12 Feb.) 35. Road from Vandalia to Maysville relocated; L. 1831 (9 Feb.) 27 §2. Same Vandalia to Shelbyville, relocated; Pr. L. 1833 (1 Feb.) 131. Permanently established between same points; L. 1835 (7 Jan.) 87. Same, Vandalia to Daniel Brownings located; Vandalia and Shelbyville road changed near Bowling Green; L. 1836 (18 Jan.) 195. Same, Greenville to

Shelbyville, alteration; L. 1839 (1 Mar.) 212. Relocation of certain state roads; L. 1840 (29 Jan.) 66. Same, Greenville and Shelbyville, relocation in part; Id. (1 Feb.) 133. Stephen T. Breeman, erect mill on college township; L. 1831 (15 Jan.) 97. Supplemental and in limitation of foregoing; Id. (5 Feb.) 98. Lands sold for heirs of John McClure; Id. (15 Feb.) 122. Zela Walwood's, on Boaz creek, a public mill; Pr. L. 1833 (15 Feb.) 106. Robert H. Peebles and others, settle accounts of James Hall, late state treasurer, with state bank; Id. (26 Feb.) 123. Special terms of circuit court; L. 1835 (24 Jan.) 33. John Robb, pardoned of manslaughter, released from $50. fine; L. 1835 (13 Feb.) 68. Fayette Seminary chartered; Pr. L. 1837 (1 Mar.) 182. And again; Pr. L. 1851 (15 Feb) 235. Mary Evans, sell and convey real estate, Town 6—1; L. 1839 (4 Dec. '38) 80. For enclosing the graves of state officers; Id. (12 Feb.) 88. John A. McClenahan and others, build mill dams; Id. (28 Feb.) 197. Fayette Steam Mill Co. chartered; L. 1840 (18 Jan.) 19. Chaffin and Casebeer, mill dam on Kaskaskia, Town 7—1; L. 1841 (24 Feb.) 187. Wm. Forrister and A. Howard, mill dam on Kaskaskia, Town 8—3; L. 1845 (27 Feb.) 181. Adm'r. of James Hankins, late collector, to sell delinquent lands and complete settlement; Pr. L. 1847 (30 Jan.) 172. His securities conditionally released; Pr. L. 1851 (15 Feb.) 228. Additional election precinct east side Kaskaskia; Id. (17 Feb.) 29. Joseph A. Jackson, dam on Kaskaskia sec. 36, Town 8—1; Id. (25 (Feb.) 41. Patent issue to J. D. McGraw for part of school section Town 6—3; L. 1857 (31 Jan.) 197. A. P. N. Doyle allowed $1,401.84, error in settlement; time of redemption extended; L. 1859 (24 Feb.) 147. Pay expenses of posse commitatus, called out by deputy sheriff Wm. N. Stephenson, in July and August 1864; 1 Pr. L. 1865 (16 Feb.) 541. Vacates Robinson street in LaClede; 2 Pr. L. 1865 (16 Feb.) 660. Over tax for 1856—7, remitted to estate of Akin Evans, late collector; L. 1867 (8 Mar.) 155. Limits of Town 7—2 extended; 3 Pr. L. 1867 (28 Feb.) 616. Selling state lands Town 5—1; L. 1869 (2 Mar.) 243. M. E. Askins name changed to H. S. E. Miller; Id. (15 Mar.) 262.

Vandalia.—Town chartered; L. 1821 (15 Feb.) 176. Repeals §9 of foregoing; L. 1823 (12 Feb.) 128. Action of commissioners laying out town, confirmed; to be the capital of state for 20 years; duty of commissioners with the lands, lots, notes, deeds, etc.; L. 1821 (27 Jan.) 32. Town charter amended; L. 1825 (23 Dec. '24) 22. Vacates streets; L. 1835 (6 Feb.) 60. Streets running through out-lots; L. 1843 (2 Mar.) 302. Repeals §5 of foregoing; Pr. L. 1857 (16 Feb.) 1030. Town again chartered; Pr. L. 1857 (14 Feb.) 811. Vacates streets and alleys; Pr. L. 1861 (21 Feb.) 732. Repeals §§1, 2 and 3 of foregoing; 2 Pr. L. 1865 (16 Feb.) 661. Governor to convey to town one and a half acres state lands for a burying ground, and 5 lots for house of worship; L. 1823 (12 Jan.) 131. Also, a lot to Lemuel Lee; Id. (12 Feb.) 130. Auditor to sell town lots; Id. 140. Foregoing amended; L. 1825 (14 Jan.) 113. Foregoing extended; L. 1829 (22 Jan.) 188. Abram Starns and others, released from notes given for lots; L. 1823 (17 Feb.) 156. Securities of James Kelly, the same; L. 1825 (14 Jan.) 103. Relief of purchasers generally; R. S. 1827 (14 Feb.) 380. Lots conveyed to Thos. Redmond conditionally; L. 1831 (10 Feb.) 119. Redmond released from further payment for; L. 1835 (7 Feb.) 69. Unsold town lots; R. S. 1833 (1 Mar. '33) 605. Lots for burying ground, and for burial of members of the legislature; L. 1835 (6 Feb.) 60. Fayette County Mutual Labor Seminary chartered; 2 L. 1837 (11 July) 43. Disposition of public property; L. 1839 (19 Feb.) 134. Foregoing amended; vote on dissolution of the town; L. 1843 (6 Feb.) 189. Heirs of Chas. Prentice to redeem town lots; Pr. L. 1847 (28 Feb.) 189. Sale by the County Seminary to the county of part of the old state house and grounds, legalized; Pr. L. 1857 (16 Feb.) 1030.

FORD COUNTY.

County created; boundary and organization; first election; L. 1859 (17 Feb.) 29. Borrow $15,000. for county buildings; Id. (19 Feb.) 33. Funding 30 per cent of county bounty orders issued Sept. 1864; tax to liquidate; 1 Pr. L 1865 (14 Feb.) 112. Issue of $10,000. county bonds, legalized; 1 Pr. L. 1867 (28 Feb.) 890. Paxton chartered; 2 Pr. L. 1865 (16 Feb.) 537. Scandinavian Evangelical Lutheran Augustana College and Seminary at Paxton, chartered; 1 Pr. L. 1865 (16 Feb.) 21. Paxton Cemetery Association chartered; Id. 225.

FRANKLIN COUNTY.

Commissioners to fix county seat; until buildings are erected court to be held at place designated in territorial act 2 Jan. 1818; L. 1819 (26 Feb.) 74. New election for sheriff by reason of tie vote; Id. (22 Mar.) 167. Five commissioners fix county seat; L. 1821 (1 Feb.) 69. Share in proceeds of Gallatin Salines; L. 1831 (16 Feb.) 13 §1. Line between Franklin and Perry; L. 1835 (6 Feb.) 36. Benton the permanent county seat; L. 1841 (7 Jan.) 93. Restoration of records destroyed by fire; L. 1845 (21 Jan.) 213. Borrow $5,000. to purchase breadstuff for the unfortunate; Pr. L. 1855 (14 Feb.) 704. Circuit clerk to transcribe record book "B"; Pr. L. 1857 (14 Jan.) 26. Sales of real estates under judgments and decrees not of record, legalized; L. 1859 (23 Feb.) 34. Construction of county buildings; L. 1861 (22 Feb.) 124. Bonds for bridges, levees, court house and jail; L. 1863 (13 Jan.) 48. And also; Id. (10 Feb.) 48. For transcribing certain public records; 2 Pr. L. 1867 (28 Feb.) 792. Road from Vandalia to Golconda changed; Pr. L. 1827 (7 Feb.) 25. Same, relocating Frankfort to Vienna in part; 1 L. 1837 (7 Feb.) 265. Same, Goose pond to Whittington's, relocated; L. 1839 (12 Feb.) 87. Same, vacates McFarland road; L. 1843 (21 Feb.) 255. Sheriff released from penalty for failure to pay over taxes; L. 1826 (19 Jan.) 58. W. B. Scates to adjust fee bills of S. M. Hubbard, circuit clerk, in bank cases; L. 1836 (18 Jan.) 246. County clerk to sell for taxes of 1833, and pay over; 1 L. 1837 (27 Feb.) 185. Settlement of balance due the state for taxes of 1843; L. 1845 (1 Mar.) 206. Appropriates $6,000. of swamp land fund to improve roads and bridges; Pr. L.

1855 (15 Feb.) 725. Time for paying $984.14 of which M. D. Hodge, late collector, was robbed, extended; L. 1869 (31 Mar.) 336. Pope and Gasoway, mill dam on Big Muddy, Town 7—2; L. 1840; (18 Jan.) 45. Payment by J. D. Morrison, late collector; L. 1841 (20 Feb.) 208. E. D. Ewing, minor, to convey certain lands; L. 1843 (28 Jan.) 72. Wilson Rea and John Golden, convicted of sending challenge to fight, restored to citizenship; L. 1845 (27 Feb.) 180. Luke Barley granted state pedlar's license for life, with conditions; Pr. L. 1851 (12 Feb.) 85. Bainbridge Academy chartered; Pr. L. 1839 (2 Mar.) 230. Supplemental to foregoing; L. 1840 (1 Feb.) 99. Benton Academy chartered; L. 1841 (7 Jan.) 20. Trustees of, to sell and convey real estate; Pr. L. 1857 (12 Feb.) 492. Fancy Farm College chartered; L. 1841 (24 Feb.) 63.

Frankfort.—Town incorporation, under act 12 Feb. 1831, legalized; Pr. L. 1837 (27 Feb.) 107. Improvements, 10 feet in front of lots; L. 1831 (15 Feb.) 80. Frankfort Institute chartered; L. 1836 (16 Jan.) 182. And again; Pr. L. 1839 (2 Mar.) 168.

FULTON COUNTY.

County formed out of Pike; L. 1823 (28 Jan.) 88. The record in Pike of deeds to land in Fulton legalized; L. 1825 (10 Jan.) 80. County revpenue; L. 1826 (27 Jan.) 89. Resident land tax aid into county treasury; repeals law requiring $450. to be paid by state to county; Pr. L. 1833 (25 Feb.) 26. Taxes from residents paid into county treasury; L. 1835 (13 Feb.) 38. County commissioners to collect money loaned; L. 1843 (1 Mar.) 110. Cannah Jones to collect unpaid taxes for 1839; L. 1841 (26 Feb.) 211. Same subject; L. 1843 (1 Mar.) 202. Lost land, "the gore," attached to Fulton and Peoria Counties; L. 1845 (28 Feb.) 267. Removal of county seat, vote thereon; Id. (3 Mar.) 288. County take stock in Peoria and Hannibal, and Jacksonville and Savanna railroads; Pr. L. 1857 (16 Feb.) 860. Action of Supervisors for paying bounties, legalized; 1 Pr. L. 1865 (16 Feb.) 123. Tax to pay bounties; Id. (9 Feb.) 124. Old public records transcribed; 2 Pr. L. 1865 (16 Feb.) 230. Various townships to take stock in railroads; 1 Pr. L. 1867 (22 Feb.) 856. County to aid Peoria and Hannibal railroad; 2 Pr. L. 1867 (6 Feb.) 670. Division and sale of school lands in Towns 6—3, 5—1, 3—2, 5—4, and 6—4 ratified; 1 L. 1837 (25 Feb.) 312. Management of county school fund; L. 1845 (3 Mar.) 321. Bounty fund of Orion transferred to school fund; 1 Pr. L. 1867 (8 Mar.) 162. Division of school funds in Towns 7 and 8—2; 3 Pr. L. 1867 (28 Feb.) 50. Compensation of sheriff increased; L. 1869 (8 Mar.) 400. Road, relocation of Havanna and Macomb; L. 1836 (18 Jan.) 218. Same, from Canton to Knoxville, located in part; L. 1839 (27 Feb.) 191. Same, between Lewistown and Jackson Grove; L. 1841 (19 Feb.) 224. Same, Utica to Tompkin's, mouth Copperas creek; Id. (26 Feb.) 245. Same, Farmington to Charleston; Id. (27 Feb.) 248. Same, Utica to Killsa's landing; L. 1843 (24 Jan.) 246. Canton and Utica R. R. chartered; may construct a canal instead; Pr. L. 1837 (24 Feb.) 97. Illinois Manufacturing Co. chartered; located either in Fulton or Peoria; Id. (4 Mar.) 331. Lewis Freeman, mill dam on Spoon river, Town 4—3; 1 L. 1837 (4 Mar.) 160. Plat of Utica, mistake corrected; Id. (27 Feb.) 331. Vienna changed to Astoria; L. 1839 (24 Jan.) 52. Fulton Mutual Fire Insurance Co. chartered; Pr. L. 1839 (28 Feb.) 134. Resolution to locate the Peoria and Warsaw R. R. via Farmington; L. 1839, 294. Vacates town plat of Washington; L. 1840 (31 Jan.) 32. A. S. Steele to sell part of estate of O. M. Ross; L. 1841 (26 Feb.) 307. Oliver Parlin, mill dam on Otter creek; L. 1845 (26 Feb.) 166. Sarah, Stephen and George W. Bohannan name changed to Atwood; Pr. L. 1847 (27 Feb.) 21. Cheney and Stockton, ferry across the Illinois, for 5 years, at Liverpool; Id. (15 Feb.) 43. James F. Howarth sell interest of Jas. B. Lovell's heirs to certain Bernadotte town lots; Id. (25 Feb.) 187. Delavan plat vacated; Id. (15 Feb.) 201. Stephen Tracy Doolittle name changed, to Stephen Tracy; Pr. Laws 1849 (8 Feb.) 14. Survey of Independence legalized; Id. (10 Feb.) 132. Astoria Seminary chartered; Pr. L. 1851 (15 Feb.) 171. Oliver Shiple name changed to Oliver Shipley; Id. 242. Aiding Canton and Liverpool plank road; L. 1852 (15 June) 11. Centerville changed to Cuba; Pr. L. 1853 (26 Jan.) 479. Pleasantville changed to Ipava; Id. 479. Byron plat vacated; Pr. L. 1855 (15 Feb.) 201. Vermont chartered; Pr. L. 1857 (13 Feb.) 581. Foregoing amended; foregoing restricted and defined; Pr. L. 1861 (18 Feb.) 730. Farmington chartered; Pr. L. 1857 (18 Feb.) 1223. Foregoing amended; 2 Pr. L. 1865 (16 Feb.) 441. Liverpool Coal Mining Co. chartered; Pr. L. 1857 (18 Feb.) 1372. Fairview chartered; Pr. L. 1859 (24 Feb.) 608. Liverpool chartered; Id. (19 Feb.) 637. O. M. Ross, ferry license across the Illinois at Havanna, legalized; Pr. L. 1861 (22 Feb.) 321. William Phelps and others, ferry across the Illinois at Havanna; Id. 322. Vacates a park and public square in Farmington; 2 Pr. L. 1865 (15 Feb.) 659. Town of Astoria pay bounties to soldiers; 1 Pr. L. 1865 (16 Feb.) 154. Towns of Orion and Astoria, same subject; Id. 155. American Hedge Trimmers Co. chartered; 2 Pr. L. 1867 (5 Mar.) 1. Fairview Lead Mining and Smelting Co. chartered; Id. 381. County Soldiers Monument Association chartered; Id. (21 Feb.) 447. Avon chartered; 3 Pr. L. 1867 (8 Mar.) 442. Wm. D. Lewis restored to citizenship; L. 1869 (2 Mar.) 118. John Salmons restored to citizenship; Id. (30 Mar.) 344.

Lewistown.—Town chartered; Pr. L. 1857 (16 Feb.) 1038. Foregoing amended; limits and powers extended; Pr. L. 1859 (21 Feb.) 635. Further amended; election of justice and constable; Pr. L. 1861 (21 Feb.) 678. Still further amends; regulate sale of liquor; license billiard tables; 2 Pr. L. 1865 (15 Feb.) 492. Lewistown Seminary chartered; Pr. L. 1837 (1 Mar.) 182. Auditor to sell certain town lots; Pr. L. 1849 (26 Jan.) 111. Hiram J. Graham, ferry across the Illinois; Pr. L. 1851 (8 Feb.) 57. Fulton Seminary chartered; Pr. L. 1855 (9 Feb.) 380. Fulton Savings Bank chartered; Pr. L. 1863 (21 Feb.) 38. And again; 1 Pr. L. 1867 (7 Mar.) 90. Town pay bounties to volunteers; 1 Pr. L. 1865 (2 Feb.) 163.

Canton.—Town chartered; Pr. L. 1849 (8 Feb.) 112. Foregoing amended; 2 L. 1849 (8

Nov.) 44. Philo M. Knapp, enclose certain streets and alleys in Little's addition; L. 1841 (26 Feb.) 314. County commissioners appoint judges of election in Canton precinct; Pr. L. 1847 (16 Feb.) 42. Vacating streets; Id. (27 Feb.) 199. City chartered; Pr. L. 1853 (12 Feb.) 574. Foregoing amended; 1 Pr. L. 1867 (28 Feb.) 636. Canton College of Illinois chartered; Pr. L. 1837 (28 Feb.) 136. Amends foregoing; acts of trustees confirmed; Pr. L. 1839 (9 Feb.) 37. Library Association chartered; Pr. L. 1847 (25 Feb.) 126. Canton Cemetery Co. chartered; Pr. L. 1851 (1 Feb.) 43. Foregoing amended; 1 Pr. L. 1867 (25 Feb.) 231. Mechanics Savings Institution chartered; Pr. L. 1855 (14 Feb.) 705. Canton Institute chartered; Pr. L. 1857 (14 Feb.) 705. Gas Light and Coke Co. chartered; 1 Pr. L. 1867 (12 Feb.) 971. Hotel Co. chartered; 2 Pr. L. 1867 (7 Mar.) 69. Driving Park Association chartered; Id. (21 Feb.) 471.

GALLATIN COUNTY.

County formed prior to the organization of the state. Court house established in Shawneetown on lots purchased for public square; L. 1819 (22 Mar.) 168. Late sheriff to collect state tax for 1816; Id. 168. Marmaduke S. Davenport to collect taxes for 1817-8; Id. (26 Mar.) 266. Sheriff discharged from liability for failing to collect taxes 1817-8; Id. (27 Mar.) 298. For building court house and jail; L. 1825 (17 Jan.) 165. Foregoing repealed; Pr. L. 1827 (11 Jan.) 10. Removal of county seat to geographical centre of county; L. 1826 (26 Jan.) 77. Commissioners carry provisions of foregoing into effect; Pr. L. 1827 (24 Jan.) 14. County clerk collect delinquent list for 1841; receive list from H. Bruce; L. 1843 (28 Jan.) 227. Jas. M. and Michael Jones released conditionally from judgment, by school commissioners; L. 1845 (28 Feb.) 149. Foregoing amended; Pr. L. 1847 (27 Feb.) 188. Line of Gallatin and Hardin located; L. 1845 (3 Mar.) 279. Assessments for 1846 by John Williamson, valid; L. 1847 (1 Mar.) 75. Part of Gallatin attached to Hardin; Pr. L. 1847 (20 Feb.) 30. County divided north and south; Eastern part still Gallatin. Western known as Saline; location of county seats and division of county debts and school funds; Id. (25 Feb.) 34. John E. Hall collector for 1846-7 released from interest; L. 1849 (30 Jan.) 114. Assessments in 1847, previous to division of Gallatin and Saline, legalized; also assessment by J. W. Trousdale; Id. (2 Feb.) 114. Division of school fund between Gallatin, Hardin and Saline; Id. 180. Vote on uniting Gallatin and Saline; L. 1851 (11 Feb.) 28. Foregoing amended; L. 1852 (21 June) 106. County collector for 1846-7 released from liability; Pr. L. 1851 (28 Jan.) 18. Line between Gallatin and White fixed; L. 1853 (12 Feb.) 265. Same subject; Pr. L. 1854 (28 Feb.) 143. Special tax for court house and clerks' office; Pr. L. 1855 (9 Feb.) 732. Removal of County seat from Shawneetown to New Market; vote thereon; L. 1857 (18 Feb.) 208. State lands granted the county under act 22 June 1852 for disposition of swamp and overflowed lands; Pr. L. 1857 (16 Feb.) 1071. Money for swamp lands $1,760. refunded the county; L. 1859 (23 Feb.) 148. Jurisdiction of county court extended; L. 1861 (21 Feb.) 106. J. R. Loomis complete records of circuit court; L. 1867 (6 Mar.) 68. Allowance to David Tade for taking care of Joseph Elliott, poor person; L. 1821 (19 Jan.) 18. Sheriff released from penalty for failing to pay over taxes; L. 1826 (19 Jan.) 58. John Lane sell lands of Christopher Robinson dec'd, and apply proceeds; Pr. L. 1827 (3 Jan.) 5. John Marshall allowed $36.31¼, cleaning 6 boxes U. S. arms; Id. (29 Jan.) 19. Robt. R. Funkhouser and others released from liability to state for metal; Id. (17 Feb.) 30. Potts and Robinett, toll bridge on Beaver creek, Ford's ferry and Equality road; L. 1831 (15 Jan.) 31. Alex. Kirkpatrick, toll bridge on Saline creek at Equality; Id. (22 Jan.) 32. John Crenshaw, toll bridge on north fork of Saline between Equality and Shawneetown; Id. (7 Jan.) 34. J. Braughton, toll bridge on north fork Saline, at old ferry between Carmi and Equality; Id. (22 Jan.) 36. David Potts, ferry across the Saline; Id. (7 Jan.) 78. Adm'r. and heirs of Saml. Marshall to sell real estate; Id. (1 Jan.) 118. Purchasers of lots at Equality allowed further time; Id. (9 Feb.) 121. Hampton Weed, floating bridge across the Saline; Pr. L. 1833 (2 Mar.) 8. Equality and Shawneetown Turnpike chartered; Id. 87. Election of additional justice and constable; Id. (28 Jan.) 103. Securities of Henry Boyer, late sheriff, collect taxes for 1824-5 by distress; Id. (26 Feb.) 120. Foregoing repealed; L. 1835 (7 Jan.) 77. Viola Ellis name changed to Potts; Id. (27 Feb.) 121. Sally Scroggins, widow of John Scroggins, sell real estate; Id. 124. Joseph Street discharged from payment of note for $540. held by state bank at Shawneetown; Id. (1 Mar.) 125. Guardian of heirs of Wm. P. Robinson, to sell real estate; Id. (20 Feb.) 143. Lands selected in lieu of sec. 16 town of Equality; L. 1835 (12 Feb.) 55. Rights of state, under Escheat act to estate of Edward Butler, transferred to Dan. Curtin; Id. (7 Jan.) 70. Robt. Richey, ferry right confirmed; Id. (6 Feb.) 73. Alex. Kirkpatrick and Wm. Hicks, toll bridge across the Saline at Equality; Id. (14 Jan.) 81. Willis Hargrave and others, saw and grist mill at Big Ripple; improvement of navigation; 1 L. 1837 (4 Mar.) 169. Equality Seminary chartered; Pr. L. 1837 (1 Mar.) 182. Gallatin Academy chartered; Id. (4 Mar.) 339. New Haven chartered; Pr. L. 1839 (15 Feb.) 59. Foregoing repealed; Pr. L. 1855 (6 Feb.) 708. Repeals act locating road from Vienna to Equality, in part; L. 1839 (2 Mar.) 255. Pisgah Academy chartered; L. 1841 (26 Jan.) 5. Bridge over Saline, on Golconda and McLeansboro road; Id. (7 Jan.) 42. Douglass and Vickers, mill dam on Rectors ford, Town 7—7; Id. (24 Feb.) 186. Benefit inhabitants of Town 9—8; deed for school lands; Id. (26 Feb.) 210. C. Gold paid for lands from which he was evicted; L. 1843 (3 Mar.) 224. Right of escheat in lands of Dan. Curtin released to his widow; L. 1845 (27 Feb.) 292. Act chartering Shawnee City, repealed (original act not printed); L. 1845 (1 Jan.) 185. Mary Ann Hicks and heirs, rebuild toll bridge across the Saline at Equality; Pr. L. 1847 (11 Feb.) 5. Guardian of Wm. Hicks' heirs, sell real estate; Id. (25 Feb.) 170. Tyler D. Hewitt's adm'r to pay $400.; Id. (20 Feb.)

179. Saline Coal and Manufacturing Co. chartered; repeals Saline river navigation improvement acts; Pr. L. 1851 (28 Jan.) 23. Foregoing amended and re-enacted for benefit of Hibbard Jewett and Joseph J. Castles; Pr. L. 1853 (10 Feb.) 512. Further amends charter; sell real estate; Pr. L. 1855 (15 Feb.) 656. Still further amends; stockholders entitled to certificates; Pr. L. 1857 (16 Feb.) 926. And again; purchasers of its property to form a corporation; 2 Pr. L. 1865 (16 Feb.) 86. Shawnee Coal Co. chartered; may build railroad to the Ohio; Pr. L. 1851 (12 Feb.) 102. Foregoing amended and extended; Pr. L. 1853 (18 Jan.) 483. Securities of John R. Smoot, late sheriff, conditionally released; Pr. L. 1851 (17 Feb.) 305. Same subject; L. 1857 (14 Feb.) 196. Further amends acts chartering Shawneetown and Equality plank road (see Part I. Ch. 82a., 26); tolls regulated; Pr. L. 1855 (13 Feb.) 521. Equality Salt Co. chartered; Id. (15 Feb.) 649. Shawnee Oil Co. chartered; Pr. L. 1857 (30 Jan.) 112. Southern Coal Co. chartered; Id. (7 Feb.) 300. Northern Coal Co. chartered; Id. (9 Feb.) 330. Right of escheat in estate of Barney Hargrave confirmed to Silenia and Joseph Hargrave; Id. (12 Feb.) 483. Shawneetown and Equality R. R. chartered; county take stock; Id. (16 Feb.) 974. Foregoing repealed; Pr. L. 1859 (24 Feb.) 501. Illinois Salt Co. chartered; Pr. L. 1857 (18 Feb.) 1408. South Illinois Salt Co. chartered; Pr. L. 1859 (24 Feb.) 412. Shawneetown and Eldorado R. R. chartered; Pr. L. 1861 (20 Feb.) 525. Town 10—9 allowed $1,400. payment for sec. 16 sold by state as saline lands; Id. (21 Feb.) 631. Saline River Bridge Co. chartered, at Ground Hog Landing; 1 Pr. L. 1865 (16 Feb.) 195. Bowlesville Mining Co. chartered; 2 Pr. L. 1865 (13 Feb.) 53. Ohio River Saline Coal Mining and Manufacturing Co.; changed to Arundin Manufacturing and Mining Co.; Id. 85. Joseph Reynolds allowed $300. in lieu of certificate of entry from Saline Commissioner; Id. (16 Feb.) 247.

Shawneetown.—Concerning the town; L. 1825 (10 Jan.) 75. Powers of town trustees extended; L. 1831 (22 Jan.) 176. Powers and duties of trustees; L. 1835 (12 Feb.) 40. Lots 1097-8, if escheated to state are granted to the town conditionally; application of proceeds; Pr. L. 1839 (27 Feb.) 128. Corporate powers extended; lease water power; tap grand rapids dam pool; Id. (23 Feb.) 129. Governor convey lots to E. J. Durbin; L. 1843 (23 Feb.) 172. Trustees macadamize Eddy street; L. 1841 (20 Feb.) 231. Supplemental to foregoing; Id. (27 Feb.) 355. Town chartered; boundary defined; vote thereon; Pr. L. 1847 (27 Feb.) 136. City chartered; Pr. L 1861 (22 Feb.) 259. Adm'r. of John Waggoner, sell town lots; L. 1821 (3 Jan.) 6. Town trustees, establish ferry across the Ohio; L. 1823 (14 Feb.) 142. President, directors and company of Bank of Illinois, chartered; L. 1835 (28 Dec. 1816) 15. Foregoing extended to 1 Jan. 1857; Id. (12 Feb.) 21. Said bank have branches at Jacksonville, Lawrenceville and Alton; capital increased; 1 L. 1837 (4 Mar.) 18. In relation to specie in said bank; L. 1843 (4 Mar.) 36. Shawneetown Insurance Co. chartered; L. 1836 (13 Jan.) 106. Shawneetown bank to borrow money; 1 L. 1837 (28 Feb.) 17. Lands of estate of John Cox escheated to John Logsdon and others; Id. (1 Mar.) 188. Shawneetown Academy chartered; Pr. L. 1839 (19 Feb.) 79. Shawneetown Coal Mining and Manufacturing Co. chartered; Pr. L. 1855 (9 Feb.) 617. Foregoing amended; Pr. L. 1857 (13 Feb.) 547.

GALLATIN SALINES.

See also Salines, Jackson, Gallatin, Bond and Vermilion Counties.

Governor lease Salines for 2 years to Jonathan Taylor and 5 others, upon the surrender to the state of their lease from the United States; L. 1819 (6 Feb.) 7. Governor to receive rent from August to December 1818; Id. (22 Mar.) 165. Superintendent elected by general assembly; L. 1821 (8 Feb.) 103. His duties, and those of the auditor; L. 1823 (3 Jan.) 76. Jonathan Taylor and securities released from payment of $1,511.11 on his lease; Id. (27 Dec. '22) 82. Relief of lessees; Id. (7 Feb.) 118. Same subject; L. 1825 (11 Dec. '24) 8. Regulating; L. 1826 (13 Jan.) 48. Same subject; superintendent's duties; lessees' liabilities; R. S. 1827 (2 Feb.) 360. Releasing John Henderson's lease to tavern lot; Pr. L. 1837 (6 Feb.) 23. Commissioners to select 30,000 acres; R. S. 1827 (15 Feb.) 353. Foregoing amended; R. S. 1833 (2 Mar.) 547. Further amended; §6 repealed; commissioners elected by general assembly; Id. (27 Feb.) 547. Sale of; proceeds applied to internal improvements; L. 1831 (16 Feb.) 13 §1. Foregoing amended; L. 1835 (11 Feb) 49. Disposition of proceeds; Id. (31 Jan.) 43. Respecting sale; Id. (13 Feb.) 145. H. M. Weed and V. Tite released from rents; L. 1831 (15 Feb.) 123. Right to dig for salt water; Id. (11 Jan.) 162. Superintendent's salary; Id. (25 Dec. '30) 165. Concerning Gallatin and Vermilion Salines; R. S. 1833 (2 Mar.) 548. Commissioners and state's attorney take account of improvements on lot leased to Andrew Frazier and held by H. M. Weed; Pr. L. 1833 (13 Feb.) 113. Commissioners to refund to Robt. G. Ormsby the purchase money for 40 acres previously entered by H. M. Weed; Pr. L. 1833 (28 Feb.) 122. Fixing rent; L. 1835 (13 Feb.) 40. Relating to, and the lands thereto belonging; L. 1836 (16 Jan.) 263. Foregoing amended; commissioners appointed; L. 1841 (27 Feb.) 294. Commissioner's duty under the two foregoing; L. 1845 (27 Feb.) 115. John L. Reynolds to have 80 acres; L. 1839 (2 Mar.) 285. Leased to J. Crenshaw; L. 1841 (9 Dec. '40) 291. Discharge judgment against T. D Hewitt, late commissioner; L. 1845 (25 Feb.) 289. Joseph Reynolds to have certain lands; Id. (3 Mar.) 300. Commissioners to prosecute certain writs; Id. 320. Rent due from John Crenshaw; L. 1847 (25 Feb.) 68. Crenshaw entitled to final acquittal upon payment of $129.; Pr. L. 1854 (27. Feb.) 77. Auditor to have books and papers; to sell lands; L. 1854 (28 Feb.) 17. Joseph Reynolds allowed $300. in leiu of certificate of entry; 2 Pr. L. 1865 (16 Feb.) 247.

GEOLOGICAL AND MINERALOGICAL SURVEY.

State geologist, appointment and duties; L.

1851 (17 Feb.) 154. Appropriating $5,000. annually for a survey; $500. for maps; L. 1853 (12 Feb.) 237. Efficiency of the survey increased; L. 1867 (28 Feb.) 10. Publication of 4th volume of report; salary for two years; L. 1869 (11 Mar.) 47.

GREEN COUNTY.

County formed; L. 1821 (20 Jan.) 26. Share in proceeds of Gallatin Salines; L. 1831 (16 Feb.) 14 §1. Justices and constables increased; Id. (14 Feb.) 49. Same subject; Pr. L. 1833 (27 Dec. '32) 102. Same subject; L. 1839 (24 Jan.) 51. White Hall justice's district; L. 1835 (12 Feb.) 30. Townships secure re-valuation of school lands, by three-fourths vote; Pr. L. 1833 (13 Feb.) 201. County commissioner's court construct certain roads; L. 1839 (2 Mar.) 257. Payment of taxes for 1839; L. 1841 (26 Feb.) 307. Records made by R. W. English legalized; L. 1843 (24 Jan.) 203. Records of sales of land for taxes transcribed etc.; L. 1847 (11 Feb.) 72. Swamp lands; L. 1857 (10 Feb.) 41. Game law of 1855 extended to said county; L. 1859 (24 Feb.) 120; Gross' Stat. 1868, 325. County issue bonds to encourage enlistments; 1 Pr. L. 1865 (16 Jan.) 125. Trustees of schools Town 10—12 to lease part of school lands; L. 1825 (3 Jan.) 52. Isaac Sinclair released from contract with school trustees Town 11—12; Id. (14 Jan.) 105. Leasing part of school section Town 9—12; L. 1826 (25 Jan.) 75. Sale of certain school lands; L. 1835 (17 Jan.) 31. Sale of school lands Towns 10—11 and 10—13 legalized; 1 L. 1837 (26 Feb.) 313. New patent issued to J. H. Weisner for part of school section Town 10—10; 2 L. 1837 (21 July) 9. Hamilton school house chartered; Pr. L. 1839 (28 Feb.) 139. Benj. King, school treasurer, Town 11—10 released from liability for $554. lost by robbery; 2 Pr. L. 1865 (16 Feb.) 241. James Turney discharged conditionally from judgment to the state; L. 1831 (27 Jan.) 120. Several streams examined—cost of making them navigable estimated; Id. (14 Feb.) 127. Bridge Macoupin creek; Id. (15 Feb.) 158 §6. Grafton Manufacturing Co. chartered; Pr. L. 1833 (22 Feb.) 67. Road, Vandalia to Atlas, a state road; L. 1836 (16 Jan.) 204. Jacob Fry, ferry at Guilford; 1 L. 1837 (7 Feb.) 118. Calvin's Slough navigable to Bluffdale; election of justices in Greenfield and White Hall; 2 L. 1837 (21 July.) 45. Carrollton and Bluffdale railroad and turnpike chartered; may substitute canal from Bluffdale to Illinois river; Pr. L. 1837 (27 Feb.) 118. Grand Pass Canal Co. chartered; Id. (28 Feb.) 129. Grafton chartered; Id. 132. Carrollton Seminary chartered; also, White Hall Seminary; Id. (1 Mar.) 182. Grafton and White Hall Hotel Co's.; Id. (3 Mar.) 267. White Hall and Greenfield chartered; Id. (4 Mar.) 307. Securities of Thos. Moore released; L. 1839 (6 Feb.) 89. Fayette chartered (under act 12 Feb., L. 1831, 82); Pr. L. 1839 (19 Feb.) 66. Green County Mutual Fire Insurance Co. chartered (organized under charter of Illinois Mutual Fire Ins. Co., Pr. L. 1839, 108); Id. (2 Mar.) 162. New Greenfield Hotel Co. chartered; Id. (1 Mar.) 180. Road, White Hall to the Illinois; L. 1840 (1 Feb.) 86. Bridge Macoupin creek; L. 1841 (31 Jan.) 42. Securities of Amos Merrott, indicted for adultery, released; Id. (24 Feb.) 209. Gives sheriff $100. and an office; Id. 210. Road, Newport to White Hall and Carrollton, re-located; Id. (27 Feb.) 253. Greenfield vacated in part; L. 1845 (28 Feb.) 287. Securities of Amos H. Squires, late treasurer, conditionally released; Pr. L. 1847 (24 Feb.) 182. Bluffdale plat vacated; Id. (26 Feb.) 204. Securities of Chas. Ketchens, agent internal improvement fund, liability defined; Id. (28 Feb.) 216. Bridge Macoupin creek at Randle's mill; L. 1851 (17 Feb.) 146. Wm. Lorton, state pedlar's license for life, conditionally; Pr. L. 1851 (12 Feb.) 85. Sam'l R. Perry and others, build pier wharf on the Illinois at Columbiana; Id. (14 Feb.) 131. Mary H. Beller name changed to Dewees; also her children, Louisa J., Wm. H., Julia A., Rachel T., Charlotte T. and Pernina L. to Dewees; Id. (15 Feb.) 242. Walnut Grove Literary Association chartered; Pr. L. 1853 (10 Feb.) 521. Benj. Doolittle name changed to Benj. F. Lyth; Pr. L. 1855 (14 Feb.) 704. Hugh Jackson, sheriff and collector, released from liability for $898.28 stolen; L. 1857 (14 Feb.) 177. Moneys arising from liquor licenses in White Hall paid to town treasury; Pr. L. 1861 (20 Feb.) 734. Apple Creek and Illinois River Hedging and Fencing Co. chartered; 1 Pr. L. 1865 (15 Feb.) 594. Greenfield chartered; 3 Pr. L. 1867 (26 Feb.) 403. Hollidaysburg changed to Kane; Id. (23 Feb.) 585.

Carrollton.—Town corporation dissolved; Pr. L. 1847 (28 Feb.) 210. Town chartered; Pr. L. 1861 (21 Feb.) 563. City chartered; 1 Pr. L. 1867 (28 Feb.) 625. Additional justice elected; 1 L. 1837 (3 Mar.) 176. Steam Mill Manufacturing Co. chartered; Pr. L. 1837 (4 Mar.) 329. Carrollton Lodge No. 50, F. and A. Masons; chartered; Pr. L. 1851 (8 Feb.) 56. City Hotel Co. chartered; 2 Pr. L. 1867 (8 Mar.) 72.

White Hall.—Town chartered; Pr. L. 1837 (19 Jan.) 6 Male and Female Academy and Orphan Institute; chartered; Pr. L. 1851 (17 Feb.) 279. Lodge No. 80, F. and A. Masons; chartered; Pr. L. 1853 (10 Mar.) 570. Town take stock in Rock Island and Alton R. R.; Pr. L. 1857 (13 Feb.) 552. Cemetery Association chartered; 1 Pr. L. 1865 (16 Feb.) 232.

GRUNDY COUNTY.

County created from LaSalle; boundary and organization; L. 1841 (17 Feb.) 74. Supplemental to foregoing; county seat and public buildings at Morris; L. 1853 (10 Feb.) 154. Assessment for 1842 legalized; L. 1843 (3 Feb.) 15. School commissioner of LaSalle to pay over part of school fund; L. 1845 (7 Feb.) 221. Borrow money to construct court house and jail; Pr. L. 1854 (4 Mar.) 153. Foregoing amended; part applied to court house fund; Pr. L. 1855 (14 Feb.) 733. Jurisdiction of county court extended (under act 27 Feb., Pr. L. 1854, 230); L. 1855 (15 Feb.) 160; also Pr. L. 1855 (15 Feb.) 656. Foregoing amended; terms of court changed; L. 1869 (30 Mar.) 146. Changes of venue from county court; L. 1857 (28 Jan.) 45. Supervisors dispose of swamp and overflowed lands; Pr. L. 1855 (14 Feb.) 702. Supervisors provide for transcribing certain records of La

Salle county; Id. (12 Feb.) 711. Illinois river a lawful fence; L. 1859 (22 Feb.) 112. Reform school established; 2 Pr. L. 1865 (16 Feb.) 237. Road law amended; L. 1869 (30 Mar.) 374. Wm. E. Armstrong, ferry across the Illinois Town 33—7; L. 1841 (27 Feb.) 110. Foregoing amended; build bridge at same place; Pr. L. 1847 (18 Feb.) 46. Dresden plat partly vacated Pr. L. 1849 (12 Feb.) 134. Securities of Wm. E. Armstrong, late sheriff, conditionally released; Pr. L. 1851 (20 Jan.) 4. Constructing bridge at Morris, vote thereon; L. 1852 (22 June) 171. Back taxes upon town lots of Kankakee relinquished; L. 1853 (12 Feb.) 227. Daniel Harrom, ferry across the Illinois, at Sec. 15, Town 33—6; Pr. L. 1853 (8 Feb.) 534. Will of Geo. Brown as proved, valid; Id. (10 Feb.) 578. Kankakee plat vacated; Pr. L. 1855 (12 Feb.) 619. Towns of Waponsa, Branville and Greenfield levy tax to bridge the Kankakee at Wilmington; Id. (15 Feb.) 667. Illinois bottom road, opposite Morris, improved; L. 1857 (18 Feb) 203. Towns of Greenfield, Braceville and Felix, and towns in Will and Kankakee counties, to vote for or against improving the Kankakee; Pr. L. 1861 (22 Feb.) 737. Wm. H. Underhill and others, ferry across the Illinois at Secs. 30 and 20, Town 33—6; 1 Pr. L. 1865 (16 Feb.) 560. School director's tax, district 3, Town 34, in 1858-9 legalized; 2 Pr. L. 1865 (16 Feb.) 321. Vote on repairing bridge at Wilmington; 1 Pr. L. 1867 (21 Feb.) 170. Gardner Coal Co. chartered; 2 Pr. L. 1867 (22 Feb.) 411. Towns of Ervenna and Norman established for school purposes; 3 L. 1867 (6 Mar.) 631.

Morris.—Certain town lots vacated; Pr. L. 1847 (17 Feb.) 204. Town chartered; Pr. L. 1853 (12 Feb.) 277. Vacates alleys; Id. 493. Town purchase of 80 acres canal lands legalized; Id. (11 Feb.) 533. Town charter amended; Pr. L. 1854 (1 Mar.) 195. City chartered; Pr. L. 1857 (18 Feb.) 1266. And again; Pr. L. 1861 (18 Feb.) 218. Boundary defined; Pr. L. 1863 (12 Feb.) 170. City sell part of block 3; 2 Pr. L. 1865 (16 Feb.) 660. City improve roads and bridges leading thereto; 1 Pr. L. 1867 (9 Feb.) 287. Fifth ward created; Id. (18 Feb.) 367. Cemetery Association chartered; Pr. L. 1853 (12 Feb.) 151. Morris Bridge Co. chartered; city and town take stock; Pr. L. 1855 (13 Feb.) 558. Foregoing amended; repeals §7; Pr. L. 1857 (13 Feb.) 537. Further amends; tolls regulated; 1 Pr. L. 1865 (13 Feb.) 193. Foregoing repealed; Id. (16 Feb.) 194. Gas Light and Coke Co. chartered; Pr. L. 1857 (16 Feb.) 1068. Foregoing revived; 1 Pr. L. 1867 (8 Mar.) 979. Grundy Academy chartered; 1 Pr. L. 1865 (16 Feb.) 3. Morris Coal Gas Light and Oil Co. chartered; Id. 587. National Insurance Co. chartered; Id. 724. Morris Coal and Oil Co. chartered; 2 Pr. L. 1865 (16 Feb.) 80.

HAMILTON COUNTY.

County formed from White; county seat located; L. 1821 (8 Feb.) 118. Land tax for 1826 applied to bridging Wheeler's creek; Pr. L. 1827 (17 Feb.) 20. Share in proceeds of Gallatin Salines; L. 1831 (16 Feb.) 15. County borrow money; L. 1839 (4 Mar.) 291. County indebtedness ascertained; Pr. L. 1849 (6 Feb.) 29. Line between Hamilton and Saline fixed; L. 1853 (10 Feb.) 265. Same subject; Pr. L. 1854 (28 Feb.) 143. Borrow $5,000. to feed the unfortunate; Pr. L. 1855 (14 Feb.) 704. Parts of townships organize as towns and divide funds; L. 1857 (16 Feb.) 199. Swamp and overflowed lands; L. 1859 (19 Feb.) 202. Transcribing public records; 2 Pr. L. 1867 (28 Feb.) 792. Fire-proof clerk's office; 3 Pr. L. 1867 (9 Feb.) 114. Ennis Moulding's mill on Skillett fork subject to general law; Pr. L. 1833 (15 Feb.) 106. Contract between Wm. Allen and Malina Rogers legalized; L. 1835 (31 Jan.) 69. Appropriations for improvement of roads; L. 1836 (13 Jan.) 186. Jonathan Harmeson, minor, to convey town lots in Independence; 1 L. 1837 (27 Feb.) 156. Rector Steam Mill Co. chartered; Pr. L. 1837 (4 Mar.) 308. Porter and Ghelson, mill dam on north fork of the Saline, Town 7—7; L. 1839 (4 Mar.) 291. David L. Erwin name changed to Bryant; Pr. L. 1855 (15 Feb.) 667. James M. Sneed restored to citizenship; Pr. L. 1857 (28 Jan.) 80. New Breman and Middletown, plats vacated; Id. (27 Jan.) 92. Jesse C. Duvalt name changed to Lockwood; Id. (16 Feb.) 891. John A. Wilson released from judgment; 2 Pr. L. 1865 (2 Feb.) 253. Defines a school district Town 4—6; 3 Pr. L. 1867 (20 Feb.) 25.

McLeansboro.—School money used for building a school house; 2 L. 1837 (21 July) 16. Foregoing repealed; L. 1839 (24 Jan.) 50. Town chartered; L. 1840 (31 Jan.) 36. Incorporation legalized; Pr. L. 1857 (18 Feb.) 1337. Surveyor to plant certain corner stone; plat partly vacated; Pr. L. 1855 (15 Feb.) 711. License moneys paid into town treasury; 3 Pr. L. 1867 (28 Feb.) 617.

HANCOCK COUNTY.

County formed, and boundary defined; L. 1823 (13 Jan.) 93 §3. County seat located; L. 1831 (1 Jan.) 63. Wm. Gilham and two others commissioners to locate county seat; meet at Montebello; Pr. L. 1833 (13 Feb.) 26. Supplemental to foregoing; Id. (22 Feb.) 20. The middle of the Mississippi the western boundary; 1 L. 1837 (3 Mar.) 91. Sales of school lands canceled; L. 1843 (25 Feb.) 278. Sheriff to collect taxes for 1845; assessments for 1846-7; auditor furnish list of lands subject to taxation; collection of assessments for 1846; tax sales in 1845 redeemable in four years; L. 1847 (26 Jan.) 76. Four years redemption under foregoing not allowed; Id. (28 Feb.) 78; and repeals §11 thereof; Id. (26 Jan.) 42. State pay for printing delinquent list for 1845; L. 1849 (9 Feb.) 37. Removal of county seat from Carthage to Warsaw; vote thereon; Id. (12 Feb.) 56. Ferry privilege across the Mississippi opposite Keokuk, vested in county; Pr. L. 1849 (9 Feb.) 36. Collection of taxes for 1852 regulated; L. 1853 (3 Feb.) 168. James McKee allowed $94. for publishing delinquent list for 1851; Pr. L. 1853 (10 Feb.) 439. Adoption of township organization, vote thereon; Id. (20 Jan.) 486. Assessment for 1853 legalized; L. 1855 (14 Feb.) 189. Same for 1857; L. 1859 (24 Feb.) 207. Reclaiming swamp lands; levee from Warsaw to Adams county line; L. 1861 (6 Feb.) 126. Assessments for

1859-60 legalized; L. 1861 (22 Feb.) 129. County, city or town appropriations, under act 2 May 1861 to encourage the formation of volunteer companies etc., must be authorized by a vote; Pr. L. 1865 (2 Feb.) 125. For the preservation of game; 1 Pr. L. 1867 (23 Feb.) 986. For the preservation of game and fish; Adams also included; Id. (21 Feb.) 989. County take stock in Carthage and Burlington R. R.; 2 Pr. L. 1867 (5 Mar.) 533. Also, in two other railroads; L. 1869 (9 Apr.) 202. James White, ferry across the Mississippi, at head of Des Moines rapids; Pr. L. 1833 (1 Mar.) 37. Venus plat vacated; L. 1835 (24 Jan.) 41. Thos. Moore released from certain recognizances; Id. (7 Feb.) 65. Lands of estate of James M. Mills conveyed; 1 L. 1837 (6 Dec. '36) 155. Mississippi Des Moines Rapids Bridge Co. chartered; Pr. L. 1837 (21 Feb.) 68. St. Mary's College chartered; may adopt manual labor system; Id. (1 Mar.) 187. Amzi Doolittle, ferry across the Mississippi Town 7—8; L. 1839 (22 Feb.) 159. Edward White, the same; Id. (12 Jan.) 195. Road Quincy to Macomb re-located in part; Id. (1 Mar.) 218. Des Moines Rapids Railroad chartered; Pr. L. 1839 (19 Feb.) 75. Commerce Hotel Co. chartered; ferry across the Mississippi; Id. (28 Feb.) 152. Road, Warsaw to Peoria, location confirmed; Id. (1 Feb.) 100. Montebello Manufacturing Co. chartered; Id. (10 Dec. '39) 151. Peoria road, between Carthage and Warsaw, vacated; L. 1841 (27 Jan.) 223. Gates and Higby, extend mill dam on rapids in Town 5—9; L. 1843 (6 Feb.) 175. Hannah Clark name changed to Bedell; Id. (24 Jan.) 179. Road, Carthage to Dorothy's on McDonough line; Id. (1 Feb.) 247. Macedonia chartered; Id. (3 Mar.) 304. Additional justice and constable in Fountain Green; Id. (6 Mar.) 307. Change part of the turnpike; Id. (1 Feb.) 313. Conveyances by Joseph Smith, as trustee for the Church of Latter Day Saints, legalized; L. 1845 (28 Feb.) 134. Additional justice and constable in Plymouth; Id. 154. Nauvoo and Warsaw R. R. chartered; Pr. L. 1847 (24 Feb.) 116. Rights and privileges under foregoing charter conditionally transferred to the Warsaw and Rockford R. R. Co.; Pr. L. 1849 (10 Feb.) 85. Charter amended; Pr. L. 1854 (3 Mar.) 160. Act 10 Feb. 1849 amended; may connect or consolidate with other roads; Pr. L. 1857 (10 Feb) 351. Original charter (24 Feb. '47) amended; borrow money; Pr. L. 1859 (11 Feb.) 483. Sale of lands and lots in Town 4—9; L. 1849 (10 Feb.) 181. Harmon T. Wilson allowed $235.53 as the damages and expenses defending the suit of Joseph Smith for illegal arrest; Pr. L. 1847 (19 Feb.) 178. Macedonia changed to Webster; Id. (17 Feb.) 202. Jo Duncan town plat vacated; Id (26 Feb.) 204. Yalrome plat vacated; Pr. L. 1849 (8 Feb.) 112. Accounts of school commissioner Michael Reckard audited; Pr. L. 1851 (12 Feb.) 104. Towns 5—9 and 5—8 united for school purposes; L. 1853 (10 Feb.) 185. Hancock Railroad and Bridge Co. chartered; Pr. L. 1853 (10 Feb.) 427. James Gray, ferry across the Mississippi at Appanoose; Id. (15 Jan.) 485. E. R. Clemens restored to citizenship; L. 1855 (14 Feb.) 111. Collection of school tax in district No. 2, Appanoose township; Id. 184. John Sellers, convicted of larceny, restored to citizenship; Pr. L. 1857 (14 Feb.) 615. Augusta chartered; Pr. L. 1859 (24 Feb.) 535. Foregoing amended, erect town jail; 3 Pr. L. 1867 (9 Mar.) 623. Niata Dyke and Ferry Co. chartered; Pr. L. 1861 (20 Feb.) 323. Prairieville plat vacated; Pr. L. 1863 (20 Feb.) 272. Town of Appanoose to pay bounties; money expended by citizens for war purposes refunded: 1 Pr. L. 1865 (16 Feb.) 153. Town of Fountain Green pay bounties to volunteers; Id. 159. Foregoing repealed; Jacob S. Ross, collector, to return money collected; 3 Pr. L. 1867 (13 Feb.) 116. Town of Hancock to pay bounties to volunteers; 1 Pr. L. 1865 (16 Feb.) 161. County Bridge Co. chartered; Id. (13 Feb.) 180. Plymouth town charter amended; commitment of offenders until payment of fine; 2 Pr. L. 1865 (15 Feb.) 548. Des Moines Rapids Improvement and Hydraulic Co. chartered; 2 Pr. L. 1867 (21 Feb.) 96. Hancock Stone Co. chartered; Id. (25 Feb.) 421. Hancock Branch R. R. chartered; Id. (12 June) 521. Nauvoo and La Harpe Extension of the Central Pacific R. R. chartered; Id. (20 Feb.) 692. Thos. Kelley and Adam Carpir, convicted of larceny, restored to citizenship; Id. (28 Feb.) 813. Road, Warsaw to Carthage re-located; Id. (7 Mar.) 843. Augusta School District chartered; 3 Pr. L. 1867 (5 Mar.) 29. Commerce City vacated in part; Id. 108. James W. Coon name changed to Jackson Kindsman; L. 1869 (29 Mar.) 263. Sutton changed to Bently and latter chartered; Id. (25 Mar.) 291.

Carthage.—Town chartered; Pr. L. 1837 (27 Feb.) 107. Town survey legalized; L. 1839 (26 Feb.) 118. Again chartered; officers failing to perform; Pr. L. 1854 (28 Feb.) 216. Amendment; 2 Pr. L. 1865 (16 Feb.) 421. Moneys received for licenses and forfeitures ennures to town; Pr. L. 1855 (14 Feb.) 44. Alleys vacated; Pr. L. 1857 (16 Feb.) 1067. The same; 2 Pr. L. 1865 (16 Feb.) 655. The same, in Hawley's addition; Id. 655. The same; 3 Pr. L. 1867 (28 Feb.) 100. The same; Id. (25 Feb.) 101. Town again chartered; Id. (27 Feb.) 429. Carthage Female High School and Teachers' Seminary chartered; Pr. L. 1837 (15 Feb.) 31. Hancock Lodge No. 20, F. and A. Masons chartered; Pr. L. 1855 (14 Feb.) 673. Carthage school district enlarged; L. 1861 (22 Feb.) 197. Foregoing amended: disposition of fines and licenses; 2 Pr. L. 1865 (16 Feb.) 272. Further amended and partly repealed; 3 Pr. L. 1867 (28 Feb.) 41. Carthage Hotel Co. chartered; 2 Pr. L. 1867 (23 Feb.) 56.

Warsaw.—Town chartered; Pr. L. 1837 (27 Feb.) 107. And again; Pr. L. 1839 (12 Feb.) 55. City chartered; Pr. L. 1853 (12 Feb.) 141. Foregoing amended; justices' jurisdiction under ordinances; Pr. L. 1854 (1 Mar.) 180. Further amends; Pr. L. 1855 (14 Feb.) 700. Still further amends; may take stock in railroads; limits extended; Pr. L. 1857 (7 Feb.) 269. Act chartering city with amendments reduced to one and amended; Pr. L. 1859 (14 Feb.) 281. Foregoing repealed; Pr. L. 1861 (22 Feb.) 736. Repeals original city charter (act 12 Feb., Pr. L. 1853, 141) and its amendments; Pr. L. 1863 (3 Feb. 167. For paying city indebtedness; 1 Pr. L. 1865 (16 Feb.) 523. A notary allowed; L. 1839 (12 Feb.) 88. Warsaw University chartered; Pr. L. 1839 (19 Feb.) 73. Warsaw Marine and Fire Insurance Co. chartered; Id. (28 Feb.) 141. Matthews and Aldrich, ferry; L. 1840 (18 Jan.) 48. Wm. English, ferry across the Mississippi; Pr. L. 1851 (17 Jan.) 3. Foregoing amended; may run to Keokuk; Pr. L. 1857 (14 Feb.) 616. First foregoing extended 25 years; 1 Pr. L. 1865 (14 Feb.) 566. John F. Charles lay off 25 acres as a cemetery; Pr. L 1855 (15 Feb.) 444. Library Association chartered; Id. (14 Feb.) 628. Gas Light and Coke Co. chartered; Pr. L. 1861 (20 Feb.) 339. Warsaw Bridge Co. chartered; 1 Pr. L. 1865 (16 Feb.) 201. City school lands sold, title confirmed; L. 1855 (14 Feb.) 94. System of graded schools established; 2 Pr. L. 1865 (16 Feb.) 287. Public school Library Society chartered; 2 Pr. L. 1867 (20 Feb.(244.

Nauvoo.—City chartered; L. 1841 (16 Dec. 1840) 52. Foregoing repealed, circuit court to appoint a receiver to sell property of corporation; L. 1845 (29 Jan.) 187. Town limits extended; Pr. L. 1847 (28 Feb.) 210. City to borrow money; organization legalized; take stock in rail or plank road; L. 1853 (10 Feb.) 188. Publication of city ordinances; Pr. L. 1855 (14 Feb.) 45 Erection of city hall; 1 Pr. L. 1865 (16 Feb.) 465. City provide a cemetery; 1 Pr. L. 1867 (28 Feb.) 839. Town plat partly vacated; 3 Pr. L. 1867 (5 Mar.) 108. System of graded schools established; Id. (28 Feb.) 58. Nauvoo House Association chartered; L. 1841 (23 Feb.) 131. Agricultural and Manufacturing Association; Id. (27 Feb.) 139. Citizens of county may join Nauvoo Legion; Id. (27 Jan.) 223. Conveyances by Joseph Smith, as trustee of the Latter Day Saints, legalized; L. 1845 (28 Feb.) 134. Repeals §2 of act 27 Jan. 1841 respecting a state road; Id. (29 Jan.) 187. Thos. H. Owens, ferry across the Mississippi; Pr. L. 1849 (8 Feb.) 35. Foregoing amended; Pr. L. 1853 (26 Jan.) 478. Geo. Heberting, ferry across the Mississippi; Pr. L. 1849 (10 Feb.) 36. Phineas Kimball jr, the same; 1 Pr. L. 1865 (14 Feb.) 562. United States Wine Co. chartered; 2 Pr. L. 1867 (8 Mar.) 320.

Hamilton.—City chartered; Pr. L. 1859 (24 Feb.) 160. Foregoing amended; publication of city ordinances; 1 Pr. L. 1865 (16 Feb.) 391. Ferry Co's Addition vacated; 2 Pr. L. 1865 (16 Feb.) 656. Vacates part of Reeves', Durkee's, Sanford's and Cox' addition to Oakwood and Hamilton; Id. 658. Incorporation of Hamilton Mill Co. confirmed; Pr. L. 1853 (3 Feb.) 593. Keokuk and Hamilton Bridge Co. chartered; Pr. L. 1857 (13 Feb.) 576. Keokuk and Hamilton Ferry and Manufacturing Co. chartered; Pr. L. 1857 (14 Feb.) 627. Supplemental to foregoing; extended 20 years; Id. 637. Further extension of 50 years; Pr. L. 1863 (13 Feb.) 189. Hamilton College chartered; Pr. L. 1857 (16 Feb.) 889. Town tax in 1859 for school house; L. 1859 (14 Feb.) 187.

Dallas City.—City chartered; Pr. L. 1859 (18 Feb.) 126. Foregoing amended; Pr. L. 1861 (22 Feb.) 190. First foregoing repealed; 1 Pr. L. 1865 (16 Feb.) 202. Wm. H. Rolloson, ferry across the Mississippi; Pr. L. 1853 (11 Feb.) 590. Foregoing amended; time extended 2 years; Pr. L. 1855 (15 Feb.) 606. Benj. F. Newton, ferry across the Mississippi; 1 Pr. L. 1865 (16 Feb.) 563.

La Harpe.—An additional justice; L. 1840 (8 Jan.) 41. City chartered; Pr. L. 1859 (24 Feb.) 169. Foregoing amended; Pr. L. 1861 (22 Feb.) 218. Trustees La Harpe Academy to convey property; Pr. L. 1863 (20 Feb.) 10. City charter again amended; rate of taxation; 1 Pr. L. 1867 (25 Feb.) 594.

HARDIN COUNTY.

County created; boundary and organization; L. 1839 (2 Mar.) 235. Foregoing amended; L. 1840 (8 Jan.) 38. Line of Hardin and Gallatin marked; L. 1845 (3 Mar.) 279. Attaching to the county a part of Gallatin; Pr. L. 1847 (20 Feb.) 30. Division of school fund between Hardin, Gallatin and Saline; L. 1849 (2 Feb.) 180. Borrow $10,000. to build court house; issue bonds therefor; Pr. L. 1854 (28 Feb.) 214. Fines paid into county treasury, except in towns; L. 1859 (14 Feb.) 34. Copying records in other counties; L. 1861 (21 Feb.) 166. Borrow $500. to bridge Big creek near Elizabethtown; 1 Pr. L. 1865 (16 Feb.) 540. Transcribing record books "A" and "B"; 2 Pr. L. 1865 (16 Feb.) 231. Hardin County Mining Co. chartered; Pr. L. 1847 (16 Jan.) 51. Election of school trustees Town 11—9; L. 1849 (25 Jan.) 182. Hardin Lodge No. 44, F. and A. Masons chartered; Pr. L. 1853 (10 Feb.) 570. Levi Mynes name changed to Levi Love; Pr. L. 1857 (16 Feb.) 918. Hardin Salt and Mining Co. chartered; 2 Pr. L. 1865 (16 Feb.) 64.

Elizabethtown.—Town chartered; Pr. L. 1857 (13 Feb.) 600. Foregoing amended; regulate assaults, batteries etc.; Pr. L. 1861 (20 Feb.) 617. James McFarlan, ferry across the Ohio; Pr. L. 1857 (18 Feb.) 1383.

HARRISON COUNTY.

County created from McLean, Champaign and Vermilion; vote thereon; L. 1855 (14 Feb.) 113.

HENDERSON COUNTY.

County created; boundary and organization; county seat at Oquawka; L. 1841 (20 Jan.) 67. Elect an additional county commissioner; Id. (19 Feb.) 92. Collection of taxes for 1840; Id. (20 Feb.) 306. Locate county seat; Pr. L. 1847 (26 Feb.) 33. Part of poor house used as jail; L. 1859 (24 Feb.) 35. Removal of county seat from Oquawka to Warren; Id. (19 Feb.) 44. Same subject; Oquawka to Sagetown; 1 Pr. L. 1865 (15 Feb.) 545. Same subject; Oquawka to Town 10—4; L. 1869 (4 Mar.) 155. Drainage law; Id. (8 Mar.) 171. Concerning county subscription to stock of Warsaw and Rockford R. R.; Id. (5 Apr.) 332. Lancaster plat vacated; L. 1841 (16 Dec. 1840) 315. Turnpike chartered; L. 1845 (1 Mar.) 155. Henry C. Anderson, ferry across the Mississippi opposite Burlington; Pr. L. 1849 (30 Jan.) 34. Securities of Solomon S. Leet, late collector, released from judgment for $765.50; Pr. L. 1853 (8 Feb.) 440. Peoria and Burlington Railroad Bridge Co.; Id. (12 Feb.) 553. John S. Pollock, ferry across the Missis-

sippi opposite Burlington; may land at Shokokon; Id. (27 Jan.) 596. Wm. Ray convicted of larceny, restored to citizenship; Pr. L. 1857 (14 Feb.) 615. East Burlington plat vacated; Id. (16 Feb.) 921. Benton plat vacated; Id. (18 Feb.) 1304. City of Dallas City chartere..; Pr. L. 1859 (18 Feb.) 126. Foregoing amended; Pr. L. 1861 (22 Feb.) 190. Tioga City annexed to Warsaw; Pr. L. 1859 (24 Feb.) 700. Jonathan Simpson, ferry across the Mississippi at East Burlington; Pr. L. 1867 (28 Feb.) 947. East Burlington Elevator and Stock Yard Co. chartered; 3 Pr. L. 1867 (6 Mar.) 674. Special tax for roads and bridges; 2 L. 1837 (13 June) 9.

Oquawka.—Town chartered; Pr. L. 1857 (11 Feb.) 472. Take stock in plank road and ferry; vote thereon; L. 1852 (21 June) 89. Same subject; Oquawka and Washington plank road and ferry; L. 1853 (8 Feb.) 252. A. and S. Phelps, ferry across the Mississippi; L. 1839 (19 Feb.) 131. Oquawka Lodge No. 123, A. F. and A. Masons; Pr. L. 1855 (14 Feb.) 634.

HENRY COUNTY.

County formed and boundary defined; L. 1825 (13 Jan.) 94 §6. Towns 12 to 18—5 attached thereto; L. 1831 (15 Jan.) 56 §12. Boundary defined; until organized, attached to Knox for judicial and other purposes; Id. (15 Jan.) 63 §3. County line so changed as not to include Towns 12—5 and 13—5; 1 L. 1837 (4 Mar.) 89. Organization of county; Id. (2 Mar.) 90. Appropriating $250. for internal improvements; L. 1839 (2 Mar.) 243. County seat at Geneseo instead of Richmond; L. 1840 (1 Feb.) 60. Removal of county seat from Morristown; L. 1843 (21 Feb.) 177. Adding Town 14—5 to Stark; vote thereon; L. 1849 (12 Feb.) 55. Sheep and swine not to run at large after 1 Mar. '53; L. 1853 (27 Jan.) 152. Section 2 general act 12 Feb. L. 1849, 152, regulating collection of road tax repealed as to said county; L. 1853 (10 Feb.) 168. Stephen Palmer to transcribe certain public records in other counties; Pr. L. 1857 (9 Feb.) 317. Township support of paupers; L. 1861 (20 Feb.) 131. Bounty tax; L. 1863 (21 Feb.) 51. Henry Hand, ferry at Cleveland across Rock River; L. 1841 (26 Feb.) 117. Cambridge Lodge No. 49, F. and A. Masons chartered; Pr. L. 1849 (8 Feb.) 45. Young, Stokes and others, ferry across Rock river at Cleveland; Pr. L. 1851 (15 Feb.) 220. Black Diamond Coal Co. chartered; Pr. L. 1857 (16 Feb.) 975. Andover Steam Mill chartered; Id. (18 Feb.) 1371. Henry County Mutual Fire Insurance Co. chartered; Id. 1389. Foregoing amended; name changed to Illinois Central Insurance Co.; office at Decatur; Pr. L. 1861 (21 Feb.) 389. Vacates old cemetery near Cambridge; Id. (20 Feb.) 65. Northwest Illinois Coal Co. chartered; in Henry and Rock Island counties; Id. (21 Feb.) 304. Cambridge chartered; Id. 557. Chas. Atkinson allowed $106.42 overpaid taxes; 2 Pr. L. 1865 (16 Feb.) 238. Geo. McHenry released from liability for cutting a ditch across the road in Phœnix; Id. 244. Securities of Julius A. Pratt, late collector, conditionally released; Id. 248. Same subject; time of payment extended; L. 1869 (27 Feb.) 338. Monroeville plat vacated; 2 Pr. L. 1865 (15 Feb.) 663. Susan N. Smith name changed to Jennings; 1 Pr. L. 1867 (19 Feb.) 233. School powers conferred upon township of Hanna; 3 Pr. L. 1867 (28 Feb.) 41. Atkinson chartered; Id. (7 Mar.) 269.

Geneseo.—Town chartered; Pr. L. 1855 (14 Feb.) 1. Foregoing amended; regulate sale of liquor; Pr. L. 1863 (16 Feb.) 205. City chartered; 1 Pr. L. 1865 (16 Feb.) 370. Geneseo Manual Labor High School chartered; Pr. L. 1839 (2 Mar.) 163. Foregoing amended; name changed to Geneseo Seminary; Pr. L. 1853 (11 Feb.) 488.

Galva.—Town chartered; 3 Pr. L. 1867 (16 Feb.) 570. School directors enabled to convey property; 2 Pr. L. 1865 (16 Feb.) 322. Collection of revenue for 1864 in the township postponed; Id. 334.

Kewanee.—Name of Berrian changed to Kewanee; Pr. L. 1855 (14 Feb.) 46. Town chartered; Pr. L. 1857 (14 Feb.) 765. Foregoing amended; offenders committed to callaboose; 2 Pr. L. 1865 (16 Feb.) 483. Vacates alleys; Pr. L. 1857 (16 Feb.) 857. Town issue bonds in aid of a Woolen mill; 3 Pr. L. 1867 (15 Feb.) 132.

Bishop Hill Colony.—Chartered; property held by trustees; conveyances heretofore to trustees of, confirmed; Pr. L. 1853 (17 Feb.) 328. Foregoing amended; members of, competent witnesses for or against; Pr. L. 1857 (29 Jan.) 93.

HIGHLAND COUNTY.

Name changed from Marquette, (which see) organization after vote thereon; L. 1847 (27 Feb.) 38.

HOLMES COUNTY.

Created from Champaign and Vermilion, after favorable vote thereon; L. 1857 (31 Jan.) 93. Vote being favorable, county judge to borrow $15,000. to erect public buildings; Pr. L. 1857 (18 Feb.) 1426.

ILLINOIS AND MICHIGAN CANAL.

Commissioners to consider, devise and adopt such measures as may be requisite to effect the communication by canal and locks, between the navigable waters of the Illinois river and Lake Michigan; L. 1823 (14 Feb.) 151. Incorporated; L. 1825 (17 Jan.) 160. Both foregoing repealed; L. 1826 (20 Jan.) 63. Memorializing Congress on the importance of the work; Id. 97. Provides for constructing; selection of lands granted by act of Congress 2 Mar. 1827 to aid the state in opening a canal to connect the Illinois with Lake Michigan; L. 1829 (22 Jan.) 14. Foregoing amended; L. 1831 (15 Feb.) 39 §§1—15. Office of canal commissioner abolished; auditor, attorney general and treasurer to adjust affairs; R. S. 1833 (1 Mar.) 113. Trespassing on canal lands; L. 1835 (9 Feb.) 34. Governor to borrow $500,000. to effect its construction; Id. (10 Feb.) 222. Foregoing repealed; governor to borrow $500,000. for its construction; L. 1836 (9 Jan.) 145. Foregoing amended;

commissioners elected; 1 L. 1837 (2 Mar.) 39. Protect canal lands against trespassers; Id. (4 Mar.) 44. Supplemental to foregoing; Id. 48. Amends two foregoing; L. 1839 (26 Feb.) 165. Repeals in part act 9 Jan. 1836; extension of time of payment to purchasers of canal lands; 2 Pr. L. 1837 (21 July) 9. Sale of canal lands; Id. 10. Repeals §10 of foregoing; L. 1839 (5 Jan.) 41. Fund commissioners to loan $390,000. to the Canal fund; Id. (21 Jan.) 41. Accounts between the state and the canal settled; Id. (12 Jan.) 42. Selling water lots and privileges; Id. (22 Feb.) 150. Further provisions for selling the canal lands; Id. 157. Loan of $4,000,000. for canal purposes; Id. (23 Feb.) 168. Supplemental to foregoing; Id. (1 Mar.) 238. Amends the several acts in relation to; Id. (26 Feb.) 177. Dedication of lots to public purposes; Id. (23 Feb.) 196. Foregoing amended; L. 1849 (31 Jan.) 30. Further amended; L. 1841 (17 Feb.) 48. Relief of purchasers of canal lots and lands; Id. (2 Mar.) 276. Amends the several acts in relation to; L. 1849 (1 Feb.) 79. J. W. Egan and others. contractors, settlement with; L. 1841 (27 Feb.) 212. Payment of canal debts, and provides for its completion; L. 1843 (21 Feb.) 54. Foregoing amended; L. 1847 (25 Feb.) 23. Further amended; penalties, how recovered: for injuring bank, bridge, dock etc.; re-appraisement of lands and lots; L. 1851 (14 Feb.) 90. Percentage on Section 187 returned by commissioners; L. 1843 (24 Feb.) 61. Number of officers reduced; Id. (2 Mar.) 62. To pay principal and interest due the contractors; Id. (3 Mar.) 62. Improvements on canal lands removed; Id. (25 Feb.) 220. James Ryan select canal lands in satisfaction of judgment for $8,000.; L. 1845 (1 Mar.) 137. Commissioners exchange lands in Town 33—5 with J. Crotty; Id. (26 Feb.) 183. Same, pay certain moneys to Crotty; Id. (21 Feb.) 348. Loan of $1,600 000. authorized; R. S. 1845 (21 Feb. 1843) 608. Canal lands taxed and sold for taxes; Id. (29 Jan.) 590. Loan of $1,600,000.; Id. (1 Mar.) 600. Protection against trespassers upon canal land timber, rock, materials or machinery thereon; Id. (27 Feb.) 602. Lot donated to any religious society, how used and sold; Id. (28 Feb.) 604. Foregoing amended; L. 1847 (26 Feb.) 25. Amends amendment; lots may be mortgaged; L. 1859 (24 Feb.) 123. Lot in Ottawa donated to Methodist E. Church for the erection of a house of worship; L. 1847 (18 Feb.) 21. American subscribers to the $1,600,000. loan upon same footing as foreign; Id. (27 Feb.) 22. Suits may be brought against the State Trustee; Id. (28 Feb.) 22. Pay balance due the contractors; Id. (16 Feb.) 24. Amends acts 4 Mar. 1837, 26 Feb. 1839 and 28 Feb. 1845, to protect canal lands against trespassers; Id. (1 Mar.) 24. W. W. Saltenstall assignee John K. Boyer, claim against commissioners settled; judge Cook county court appoint arbitrators; Pr. L. 1847 (1 Mar.) 191. Manner of proving claims before state trustee; L. 1847 (1 Mar) 32. Wm. E. Armstrong and others paid $151.50; Id. (27 Feb.) 49. Certificates to contractors whose bonds have one coupon detached; Id. (1 Mar.) 50. School directors in Will county to relinquish to the trustees certain lots; Id. (25 Feb.) 152. Canal indebtedness not funded with rest of state debt; Id. (23 Feb.) 161. John and Thomas Lonergan to receive $2,169. scrip for machinery on section 62—3; Pr. L. 1847 (18 Feb.) 176. Bonds issued to complete Northern Cross railroad paid out of canal fund; L. 1849 (10 Feb.) 45. Slip built on lot 3 block 2 Joliet; Id. (12 Feb.) 46. Payment to Geo. Steel for judgment in Cook county court; Id. (10 Feb.) 85. Scrip issued to James H. Collins and Hugh T. Dickey; Id. 85. Trustees settle with Wm. Whaley and others for lots in La Salle purchased in 1848; L. 1851 (28 Jan.) 11. Creating and leasing surplus water in Ottawa; Id. (14 Feb.) 91. State trustee refund to Adam Johnson and Wm. McGirr money erroneously paid; Pr. L. 1851 (17 Feb.) 276. H. T. Dickey, Abraham Lincoln and Noah Johnston to examine and adjust damages for right of way and injuries in construction of canal and feeders; L. 1852 (22 June) 152. Deeds by the trustees under seal valid without proof or acknowledgment; Id. (23 June) 200. Canal scrip issue to Judah W. Rathbun to replace lost bonds; Pr. L. 1855 (14 Feb.) 720. Trustees appropriate $1,500. for bridge at Seneca; L. 1855 (15 Feb.) 104. Contractor's claims settled; judges made commissioners; have an attorney and clerk; Id. (14 Feb.) 161. Certificate issue to widow of E. B. Hulbert for $875.; L. 1857 (16 Feb.) 32. R. M. Young allowed $2,500. for advances and losses sustained in New York 1840 paying interest on canal bonds; Id. (14 Feb.) 93. To indemnify the state against loss from scrip funded by Joel A. Matteson; L. 1859 (19 Feb.) 190. Police regulations on south branch of Chicago river at Bridgeport; L. 1861 (22 Feb.) 74. Trustees' contract for pumping water from Chicago river into canal; Pr. L. 1861 (20 Feb.) 742. James Michie allowed $1,383. 69 being amount of orders on canal commissioners; Id. (22 Feb.) 536. Completion of canal according to plans of 1836; L. 1865 (16 Feb.) 83. Trustees to sell tracts, lots and islands; Id. 85. To improve the present canal and secure its extension through the valleys of the Bureau and Green to the Mississippi; L. 1867 (28 Feb.) 81. Foregoing amended; L. 1869 (25 Feb.) 60. To improve the present canal from lock 15 to the Illinois; Id. (30 Mar.) 61. Redemption and sale of certain forfeited lands and lots; Id. (31 Mar.) 62.

INDUSTRIAL UNIVERSITY.

University located; L. 1867 (25 Jan.) 122. Appropriations for two years; L. 1869 (27 Mar.) 33.

INTERNAL IMPROVEMENT.

A general system established; 1 L. 1837 (27 Feb.) 121 §§1—56. Supplemental to foregoing; Id. (4 Mar.) 152. Further supplemental. Ibid. Survey, location and construction of railroads; 2 L. 1837 (21 July) 45. Memorial and resolution, relative to the duty of the United States to aid internal improvements; Id. (21 July) 110. General law amended; L. 1839 (1 Mar.) 89. Commissioners of public works, term of office; Id. (2 Mar.) 97. For the issue of bonds and certificates; Ibid. To bring into the state laborers for the public works; Id. 98. Also settle with

representatives of deceased contractors; Ibid. County commissioners' courts may recover moneys loaned; Id. (15 Feb.) 119. Regulated in Stephenson and nine other northern counties; Id. (2 Mar.) 201. Resolutions concerning a grant of land by Congress; Id. 293. Settlement of debts and liabilities incurred on account of; L. 1840 (1 Feb.) 93. Foregoing amended: L. 1841 (14 Dec. '40) 166. Boards of commissioners of Public Works and of Fund Commissioners abolished; L. 1840 (1 Feb.) 98. Relief of contractors upon public works; Id. (3 Feb.) 98. Edward Smith, late engineer, accounts audited and settled; Id. 112. Board of auditors for settling accounts of contractors, established; L. 1841 (26 Feb.) 38. Foregoing repealed; R. S. 1845, 467. Paying interest on the internal improvement debt; Id. (16 Dec. '40) 167. Settlers on lands purchased by the state; Id. (27 Feb.) 191. Concerning the Great Western mail route; Id. 247. Fund commissioners to compound for and adjust demands in favor of the state; Id. 300. Resolution that fund commissioners appoint an agent at New Orleans; Id. 359. Settle the accounts of R. F. Barret, late fund commissioner; L. 1843 (1 Mar.) 20. Also, of James W. Barrit; Id. (4 Mar.) 148. Settle the internal improvement fund between Clay and Richland; Id. (8 Feb.) 76. Office of fund commissioner abolished; Id. (4 Mar.) 117. Governor *ex officio* fund commissioner; Ibid. Payment to E. Willard, late member of board of public works; Id. 226. Resolution that the late fund commissioners be settled with; Id. 339.

IROQUOIS COUNTY.

County located and boundary defined; Pr. L. 1833 (26 Feb.) 19. County seat located and named; L. 1835 (10 Feb.) 46. Same subject; 1 L. 1837 (16 Jan.) 109. County seat removed from Montgomery; L. 1839 (23 Feb.) 185. Assessment for 1839 legalized; L. 1840 (30 Jan.) 70. Levy and collection of school tax and sale of lands; L. 1847 (28 Feb.) 146. John Wilson's assessment in 1846 legalized; Pr. L. 1847. (4 Feb.) 7. Borrow $1.000. to complete court house; Id. (16 Feb.) 27. Collection of taxes extended 3 months; Id. (28 Feb.) 201. Tax to improve the Kankakee and Iroquois rivers, vote thereon; L. 1849 (12 Feb.) 185. Special tax for building a jail; L. 1851 (15 Feb.) 125. Swamp lands selected; L. 1853 (3 Feb.) 93. Sheep and swine not to run at large; pound established; Id. (10 Feb.) 210. Foregoing repealed; L. 1861 (22 Feb.) 135. County court establish a thorough system of drainage; Pr. L. 1855 (14 Feb.) 623. Foregoing amended; Pr. L. 1857 (16 Feb.) 925. Further amended; L. 1859 (18 Feb.) 203. County issue $2,500. bonds to bridge the Iroquois on the Vincennes and Chicago road; Id. 724. Previous sales of school lands legalized; L. 1857 (16 Feb.) 235. Commissioners of highways acts in 1857 legalized, except in Loda; L. 1859 (21 Feb.) 36. Jurisdiction of county court extended; L. 1859 (24 Feb.) 96. Foregoing repealed; L. 1861 (18 Feb.) 109. Removal of county seat from Middleport to South Middleport; L. 1863 (11 Feb.) 51. Special annual tax to liquidate indebtedness incurred paying bounties; 1 Pr. L. 1865 (14 Feb.) 112. Conditional removal of county seat from Middleport to Watseka; Id. (6 Feb.) 546. To perpetuate evidence of the contents of records and papers destroyed by fire; 1 Pr. L. 1867 (28 Feb.) 902. Restoration of records of board of supervisors; 2 Pr. L. 1867 (30 Jan.) 786. Towns 29—10, 11, 12, 13 and 14 attached to Kankakee; 3 Pr. L. 1867 (8 Mar.) 632. Certain records of county court and board of Supervisors legalized; L. 1869 (9 Mar.) 151. Netting of fish prohibited; Id. (29 Mar.) 187. Organization of school district, Town 27—10; L. 1843 (21 Jan.) 279. John Nilson, pre-emption to certain lands; L. 1849 (12 Feb.) 102. Foregoing suspended; L. 1851 (17 Feb) 181. C. C. Venum and others, pre-emption to certain lands; L. 1849 (12 Feb. 104. Foregoing repealed; L. 1851 (17 Feb.) 181. Executor of John Nilson to settle with Robert Hill; Pr. L. 1851 (17 Feb.) 301. E. Dunning, certificate of indebtedness in lieu of $200. lost scrip; L. 1855 (14 Feb.) 191. Auditor to sell lands in towns 26—12 and 28—13; L. 1857 (13 Feb.) 89. A. B. Roff, stay of execution against for two years, upon confession of judgment; Id. (16 Feb.) 202. Grand Prairie Seminary and Commercial College chartered; at Onarga; Pr. L. 1865 (16 Feb) 23. Towns of Beaver and Papenea, levy tax for bridging the Kankakee at Aroma; Id. 188. Foregoing repealed; 3 Pr. L. 1867 (7 Mar.) 265, 627. Back taxes on Gilman lots reduced; 2 Pr. L. 1865 (15 Feb.) 335. Watseka boundary correctly defined; Id. (16 Feb.) 614. City of Watseka chartered; 1 Pr. L. 1867 (19 Feb.) 655. Ranges 10 and 11 united for school purposes; 3 Pr. L. 1867 (13 Feb.) 6. Onarga chartered; Id. (9 Mar.) 179. Gilman chartered; Id. (4 Mar.) 235. County Agricultural Society, powers extended; L. 1869 (13 Mar.) 10. Trustees I. and M. Canal to deed to J. Wadleigh lands in Town 29—10; Id. (5 Apr.) 345.

JACKSON COUNTY.

County formed prior to the organization of the state. County line between Randolph and Jackson; L. 1823 (10 Feb.) 122. Share in the proceeds of the Gallatin Salines; L. 1831 (16 Feb.) 13. Appropriation of $500. to improve the Big Muddy applied to the improvement of a road and bridge named; Pr. L. 1833 (25 Feb.) 4. County to borrow money to complete court house; L. 1843 (1 Mar.) 111. Removal of county seat from Brownsville; Id. (24 Feb.) 119. To restore the records burned at Brownsville; Id. (1 Feb.) 205. Certain returns under the school law legalized; Id. (3 Feb.) 280. Records of deeds to be made where former record was destroyed by fire; L. 1845 (1 Jan.) 186. Collection of taxes for 1842; loss of public records; Id. (21 Feb.) 324. Taxes of 1844 remitted to certain persons by reason of loss from high water; Id. 353. Muddy Saline Reservation sold for the benefit of the county; L. 1847 (28 Feb.) 113. Foregoing amended; agent to sell; Pr. L. 1849 (25 Jan.) 108. Erection of a jail; L. 1863 (20 Feb.) 53. For transcribing certain public records; 2 Pr. L. 1865 (15 Feb.) 232. Time of payment by J. H. Cully, sheriff and collector for 1867—8, extended; L. 1869 (31 Mar.) 334. Concerning town of Brownsville; trustees named; L. 1819 (25 Mar.) 239. John Ankeny, toll bridge across the Big Muddy near Brownsville; L. 1823 (12 Feb.) 129. Conrad Will allowed $2,200. for permanent improvement at the Muddy Saline; Id. (14 Feb.) 146. Conveyances by adm'r of Timothy Nash confirmed; L. 1825 (6 Jan.) 58. Bridges built by subscription; L. 1831 (14 Feb.) 20. Cashier Brownsville Bank convey certain lands to Benj. Henderson; Id. (7 Jan.) 119. Appropriates $200. to improve road, Brownsville to Gill's ferry; Pr. L. 1833 (25 Feb.) 4. Wm. Gill, toll bridge over Big Beaucoup creek near his ferry; Id. 9. Henry Dillenger, same, across the same; Id. (1 Mar.) 10. County court establish ferry across Big Muddy between Indian creek and Lick Branch; citizens of county pass free Wednesdays and Saturdays; Id. (18 Jan.) 30. Illinois Manufacturing Mining and Exporting Co. chartered; Id. (28 Jan.) 40. Foregoing amended; Pr. L. 1837 (4 Mar.) 293. Avanse River Navigation Co. chartered; Pr. L 1833 (27 Feb.) 71. Securities of Wm. Blocker released from certain recognizances; L. 1835 (7 Feb.) 66. Commission issue to Wm. Worthen as sheriff; Id. (20 Jan.) 76. Leasing the saline reserves; L. 1841 (26 Feb.) 292. Foregoing amended; L. 1843 (28 Jan.) 270. Mississippi Grand Tower Bridge Co. chartered; Pr. L. 1839 (6 Feb.) 39. Securities of James Willis, late sheriff, discharged from liability upon payment in state indebtedness; L. 1849 (8 Feb.) 117. Jackson County Coal and Railroad Co. chartered; Pr. L. 1853 (12 Feb.) 26. Securities of John Elmore, late sheriff, conditionally released; Id. (3 Feb.) 439. Carbondale Cemetery Association chartered; Pr. L. 1855 (6 Feb) 458. Isaac Dillinger name changed to Deason; Id. (9 Feb.) 687. Carbondale College chartered; Pr. L. 1857 (5 Feb.) 265. John Hooker restored to citizenship; Id. (13 Feb.) 551. Murphysboro and Carbondale Railroad and Coal Mining Co.; Id. (14 Feb.) 778. Stephen S. Hall and others, bridge Big Muddy near Marshall schools; Id. (18 Feb.) 1306. Fractional Town 7—5 to be a town for school purposes; L. 1857 (18 Feb.) 224. Foregoing amended; L. 1859 (24 Feb.) 183. Big Muddy navigable above east line of sec. 22, Town 9—3; act 28 Feb. 1839 respecting its navigation, partly repealed; Pr. L. 1861 (6 Feb.) 303. De Soto College chartered; 1 Pr. L. 1865 (16 Feb.) 6. Southern Illinois College at Carbondale chartered; 1 Pr. L. 1867 (8 Mar.) 32. City of Murphysboro chartered; Id. (5 Mar.) 681. Chalk Bank Ferry Co. chartered; Id. (18 Feb) 930.

Mt. Carbon Coal and Railroad Co.—Mt. Carbon Coal Co. chartered; L. 1835 (24 Jan.) 194. Supplemental to foregoing; L. 1841 (26 Feb.) 135. The foregoing acts declared in force; continue their line to Breeseville; Pr. L. 1851 (1 Feb.) 45. Amends foregoing; Id. (15 Feb.) 171. Supplemental to act 1 Feb. 1851; time to complete extended two years; Pr. L. 1853 (10 Feb) 536. Complete railroad in 5 years; Pr. L. 1857 (19 Jan.) 22. Name changed to Mt. Carbon Coal and Railroad Co.; Pr. L. 1861 (6 Feb.) 303. Powers extended; 2 Pr. L. 1865 (16 Feb.) 187. Consolidate and reissue its stock; 2 Pr. L. 1867 (25 Feb.) 779.

JASPER COUNTY.

County created, county seat at Newton; L. 1831 (15 Feb.) 50. County organization, county seat located; L. 1835 (19 Dec. '34) 154. Assessment for 1839 legalized; L. 1841 (26 Jan.) 93. County assessor appoint deputy; Pr. L. 1847 (11 Feb.) 8. County borrow $1,000. to complete court house; Id. (4 Feb.) 27. Swamp lands; L. 1855 (12 Feb.) 150. Jurisdiction of county court extended; L. 1863 (21 Feb.) 26. Foregoing repealed; L. 1865 (16 Feb.) 37. County expend $6,000. on bridges at Newton, St. Mary's and on Ewington road; Pr. L. 1865 (9 Feb.) 729. Wm. Lewis, mill dam on Little Wabash, Town 5—8; L. 1841 (27 Feb.) 188. Securities of H. Vanderhof released from penalty; L 1845 (3 Mar.) 298. A. S. Jeffries surity for Wm. A. Arnold, late collector, released; Pr. L. 1853 (22 Jan.) 481. Granville changed to Tenneytown, streets changed; Pr. L. 1855 (14 Feb.) 692. J. M. Buford released from liability on bond of J. Bridges, sheriff; L. 1855 (14 Feb.) 93.

JEFFERSON COUNTY.

County formed out of Edwards and White; Ambrose Maulding and 4 others to fix county seat; L. 1819 (26 Mar.) 267. Supplemental to foregoing; boundary extended; Id. (29 Mar.) 320. Election of a sheriff and coroner; L. 1821 (no date) 29. Share in the proceeds of the Gallatin Salines; L. 1831 (16 Feb.) 15. Respecting internal improvements; L. 1839 (2 Mar.) 252. For paying the county debt, borrow money; L. 1841 (19 Feb.) 91. Assessment in the northern division for 1840 legalized; Id. (7 Jan.) 302. Additional justices' district; L. 1845 (3 Mar.) 239. County take stock in Marion and Jefferson County Railroad; Pr. L. 1855 (15 Feb.) 228. County clerk execute deed to Robt. Nixon for swamp lands; Pr. L. 1857 (17 Feb) 1170. Road, Mt. Vernon to Fairfield, partly relocated; L. 1839 (28 Feb.) 207. Same, Mt. Vernon to Brownsville; L. 1841 (27 Feb.) 246. Wm. Pate, 4 years pedlar's license; Pr. L 1849 (12 Feb) 56. Plat and survey of Linchburg legalized; Pr. L. 1857 (17 Feb.) 1169. Relief of C. G. Vaughn, late collector; L. 1867 (15 Feb.) 148. Green Lawn Spring Co. chartered; 2 Pr. L. 1867 (6 Mar.) 440. Auditor convey lands in town 2—4 to B. T. Wood; L. 1869 (31 Mar.) 244.

Mt. Vernon.—Town may become incorporated; L. 1837 (10 Feb.) 331. Town resurveyed; L. 1839 (19 Feb.) 135. Survey by John Storms legalized; L. 1843 (21 Feb.) 300. Town chartered; Pr. L. 1861 (22 Feb.) 693. Width of Harrison street changed; 2 Pr. L. 1865 (16 Feb.) 513. Mt. Vernon Academy chartered; Pr. L. 1839 (15 Feb.) 67. To relieve said Academy; L. 1843 (24 Feb.) 6. Again chartered; patronage M. E. Church; Pr. L. 1855 (6 Feb.) 376. Illinois protection Insurance Co. chartered; Pr. L. 1857 (17 Feb.) 1156.

JERSEY COUNTY.

County formed; boundary and jurisdiction; L. 1839 (28 Feb.) 208. Foregoing amended; L. 1840 (1 Feb.) 104. Further amends; sales for taxes; bridge Macoupin creek; L. 1851 (17 Feb.) 145. Taxes of 1839, payment of; L. 1841 (26

Feb.) 307. Copying records of Green county; L. 1843 (1 Feb.) 204. County court to contract for improvement of roads; contractors incorporated; court fix amount of stock; Pr. L. 1854 (28 Feb.) 150. Concerning swamp lands; L. 1855 (15 Feb.) 148. Special tax to build jail and fire proof offices; Pr. L. 1857 (14 Feb.) 765. For erection of county jail; 3 Pr. L. 1867 (18 Feb.) 118. Construction of road, Jerseyville to the river; L. 1840 (8 Jan.) 40. Hamilton Primary School chartered; Id. (1 Feb.) 53. Foregoing amended; L. 1841 (7 Jan.) 259. Heirs of G. Finney, redeem lands Town 6—12, conditionally; L. 1845 (25 Feb.) 283. Marshall Myrick name changed to Cooper; Pr. L. 1853 (22 Jan.) 485. Pittsburg plat vacated; Id. (10 Feb.) 502. Randolph plat vacated; Id. 523. Fieldon chartered; Pr. L. 1857 (7 Feb.) 278. Foregoing amended; elect justice; Pr. L. 1859 (19 Feb.) 615. And again, same subject; 3 Pr. L. 1867 (9 Mar.) 600. Jersey County Manufacturing Co. chartered; Pr. L. 1857 (18 Feb.) 1412. Organization of Elza Building and Manufacturing Co. under general law, confirmed; Pr. L. 1859 (11 Feb.) 28. Rufus P. Blossom declared of full age; L. 1859 (16 Feb.) 124. Execution against C. H. Bowman, late collector, stayed; payments in instalments; L. 1861 (19 Feb.) 167. Judgment against said Bowman conditionally satisfied; L. 1863 (21 Feb.) 66. Jersey county Bank resume business; Pr. L. 1861 (22 Feb.) 38. Carrying into effect the nuncupative will of Geo. Washington, colored; 2 Pr. L. 1865 (16 Feb.) 251. Otterville chartered; 3 Pr. L. 1867 (7 Mar.) 155.

Jerseyville.—Town chartered; 2 L. 1837 (21 July) 102. And again; Pr. L. 1855 (14 Feb.) 33. Foregoing amended; Pr. L. 1857 (13 Feb.) 587. And again; fines satisfied by street labor; Pr. L. 1861 (22 Feb.) 660. Pott's addition partly vacated; 2 Pr L. 1865 (14 Feb.) 657. Same subject; 3 Pr. L. 1867 (28 Feb.) 608. City chartered; 1 Pr. L. 1867 (21 Feb.) 454. Jerseyville Academy chartered; Pr. L. 1837 (1 Mar.) 161. Hotel Co. chartered; Id. 197. And again; 2 Pr. L. 1867 (18 Feb.) 37. Sale of town lots to Samson Williams legalized; Pr. L. 1847 (17 Feb.) 202. Building Association chartered; L. 1852 (21 June) 62. County Farmer's Insurance Co. chartered; Pr. L. 1861 (21 Feb.) 402.

Grafton.—Town chartered; Pr. L. 1853 (12 Feb.) 239. Sale of town lots of estate of James Mason (under act 24 Jan., L. 1835, 140.); L. 1836 (16 Jan.) 259. Wm. H. Allen, ferry across the Mississippi; Pr. L. 1853 (26 Jan.) 478. Grafton Manufacturing Co. chartered; Pr. L. 1855 (15 Feb.) 613. J. L. Beirne Saw Mill and Dock Co. chartered; 3 Pr. L. 1867 (20 Feb.) 4. Stone and Transportation Co. chartered; Id. (6 Feb.) 643.

JO DAVIESS COUNTY.

County formed and boundary defined; R. S. 1827 (11 Feb.) 117. Special terms of circuit court; L. 1829 (25 Jan.) 52 §14. Extends §2 of act 22 Jan. L. 1831 33, concerning the erection of bridges; Pr. L. 1833 (22 Feb.) 13. County boundaries and organization; L. 1836 (16 Jan.) 273. County borrow money to complete court house; L. 1840 (18 Jan.) 22. Assessment of taxes for 1839; L. 1841 (27 Feb.) 307. School fund for 1845 apportioned; L. 1845 (7 Feb.) 195. County commissioners to appoint the assessors and collectors; Id. (21 Mar.) 324. Section 2 of the foregoing repealed; Pr. L. 1847 (1 Mar.) 39. And again; Pr. L. 1857 (13 Feb.) 512. Jurisdiction of county court extended; R. S. 1845 (1 Mar.) 576. Terms thereof; L. 1847 (22 Feb.) 28. Old county court cease after Sept. 1849; records transferred to circuit court; L. 1849 (8 Feb.) 67. Payment of B. B. Howard prosecuting attorney in said court; L. 1851 (14 Feb.) 89. Eight mill tax to pay R H. McGoon's mortgage; Pr. L. 1847 (17 Feb.) 30. County divided into 3 revenue districts; washing mineral dirt in Fevre river a misdemeanor; Id. (1 Mar.) 39. Distribution of the school fund; L. 1847 (20 Feb.) 155. County bonds issued in aid of the Galena and Chicago Union Railroad; L. 1851 (15 Feb.) 169. Duty of grand jury in liquor cases; L. 1855 (12 Feb.) 178. Acts of county and city of Galena issuing bonds in aid of Galena and Southern Wisconsin Railroad legalized; Pr. L. 1857 (23 Jan.) 26. Towns to support their own paupers; L. 1859 (24 Feb.) 130. Tax for erecting and maintaining bridges; Id. (18 Feb.) 210. Fees of county judge; L. 1869 (30 Mar.) 150. Compensation of county superintendent of schools; Id. 398. John Foley allowed $200. for recapturing Geo. Madeira charged with murder; Pr. L. 1833 (25 Feb.) 124. John Phelps, ferry across Rock river; L. 1835 (10 Feb.) 125 §3. John Bales and J. L. Kirkpatrick, toll bridge on Fevre river at Mecker's furnace; L. 1836 (12 Jan. 1835 [6]) 197. Jo Daviess Marine and Fire Insurance Co. chartered; Pr. L. 1837 (18 Feb.) 42. Charter amended; Pr. L. 1839 (19 Feb.) 92. Further amends; L. 1841 (17 Feb.) 150. Hanover Academy chartered; Pr. L. 1839 (12 Feb.) 42. Wapello Manufacturing Co. chartered; at Apple river falls; subscribers to stock of chartered as the Rockford Manufacturing Co.; Pr. L. 1839 (2 Mar.) 150. Jo Daviess Mining and Smelting Co., and Buncomb Mining and Smelting Co., chartered; Id. 187. Geo. W. Jones, ferry from Jordan's ferry to Dubuque; L. 1839 (2 Mar.) 270. Foregoing amended; Pr. L. 1854 (28 Feb.) 183. Further amends and time extended; Pr. L. 1857 (11 Feb.) 463. H. H. Gear, ferry across the Mississippi opposite Tete de Mort; L. 1840 (18 Jan.) 23. Letters of administration to R. W. Bush on estate of James Evans confirmed; L. 1841 (24 Feb.) 209. Payment for apprehending John Dormer, escaped convict; L. 1843 (17 Feb.) 214. Isaiah Cormack, convicted of larceny, restored to citizenship; L. 1849 (24 Jan.) 112. Wm. M. Young and others, ferry across the Mississippi at sec. 27, Town 28—1; Pr. L. 1849 (10 Feb.) 37. Wapello changed to Hanover; Id. (12 Feb.) 142. Thos. S. Parks, ferry across the Mississippi at Huntsville; Pr. L. 1851 (13 Feb.) 110. H. Marfield, ferry across the Mississippi; L. 1852 (21 June) 61. Name of Fevre river changed to Galena river; L. 1853 (12 Feb.) 96. Galena and Mississippi Intersection R. R. chartered; Pr. L. 1853 (10 Feb.) 42. Galena and Mineral Point plank road chartered; Id. 166. Amends foregoing; Pr. L. 1854 (1 Mar.) 162. And again; Pr. L. 1861 (21 Feb.) 479. Mississippi and Fevre River Portage Canal Co. chartered; Pr. L. 1853 (12 Feb.) 412. Sam'l Smith, ferry at mouth of Fevre River; Id. (9 Feb.) 528. Northwestern Insurance Co. chartered; Id. (10 Feb.) 583. James Robinson name changed to

James C. Johnson; Pr. L. 1857 (31 Jan.) 188. Mississippi Bridge Co. chartered; city of Galena and county take stock; Id. (4 Feb.) 234. Great Northwestern Railroad chartered; city of Galena and county take stock; Id. (7 Feb.) 247. Dunleith and Dubuque bridge Co. chartered; Id. (14 Feb.) 773. Amends foregoing; time of completion extended; 1 Pr. L. 1867 (8 Mar.) 188. Galena, Dunleith and Minnesota Packet Co. (organized under general act 23 June 1852) name changed to Galena, Dubuque, Dunleith and Minnesota Packet Co.; Pr. L. 1857 (18 Feb.) 1326. Union Agricultural Society of Jo Daviess, Stephenson, La Fayette (Wis) and Green (Wis.) counties chartered; Pr. L. 1861 (16 Feb.) 34. Foregoing amended; 1 Pr. L. 1865 (16 Feb.) 54. Special tax in Elizabeth to refund moneys used to pay bounties; Id. (15 Feb.) 126. Powers of County Agricultural Society extended; 1 Pr. L. 1867 (25 Feb.) 47.

Galena.—Town officers, if town is incorporated, need no property qualification; L. 1835 (7 Jan.) 140. Town corporate powers changed; boundary defined; Pr. L 1837 (26 Feb) 16. Several acts chartering amended; L. 1839 (15 Feb.) 25. Foregoing amended; Pr. L. 1853 (26 Jan.) 475. Repeals §43 of charter; one dollar poll tax for streets; L. 1845 (1 Mar.) 105. Same subject; Id. (28 Jan.) 183. The several acts chartering amended; L. 1852 (21 June) 77. City issue bonds in aid of Galena and Southern Wisconsin Railroad; L. 1853 (9 Feb.) 190. Jurisdiction ceded to the United States over the Marine Hospital, Custom House and Post Office; L. 1857 (9 Jan.) 39. The several city incorporation acts reduced to one and amended; Pr. L. 1857 (30 Jan.) 119. Foregoing amended; respecting schools and school funds; Pr. L 1861 (20 Feb.) 200. Further amends; each ward elect a supervisor; Id. (12 Feb.) 202. Still further amends; 1 Pr. L. 1865 (6 Feb.) 365. Foregoing amendment amended; 1 Pr. L. 1867 (20 Feb.) 472. Assistant supervisor elected in East and West Galena; L. 1861 (20 Feb.) 266 §11. Mechanic's Association and Benevolent Society chartered; Pr. L. 1839 (12 Jan.) 14. Chamber of Commerce chartered; Id. (1 Mar.) 147. Rose and Swan, ferry across the Fevre; L. 1840 (1 Feb.) 56. Wildy Lodge I. O. O. F.; Id. (3 Feb.) 184. Galena Manufacturing Co. chartered; L. 1843 (6 Mar.) 161. Franklin Literary and Medical College chartered; L. 1845 (7 Feb.) 219. City erect two bridges across the Fevre; free after tolls have paid building expenses; Pr. L. 1847 (16 Jan.) 8. Foregoing amended; L. 1851 (15 Feb.) 117. Galena Hydraulic Co. chartered; Pr. L. 1847 (27 Feb.) 143. Firemen exempt from jury duty; Id. (20 Feb.) 168. The control of Fevre river north of the city taken from the city; Pr. L. 1849 (25 Jan.) 28. Galena Insurance Co. chartered; Pr. L. 1851 (15 Feb.) 205. Galena Forum chartered; Id. 245. German Benevolent Society chartered; L. 1852 (23 June) 213. Galena Theological Seminary chartered; Pr. L. 1853 (9 Feb.) 274. Miner's Insurance Co. chartered; Id. (12 Feb.) 384. Galena Gas Light Co. chartered; Pr. L. 1857 (20 Jan.) 93. Hotel Co. chartered; Id. (31 Jan.) 232. De Soto White Lead Manufacturing Co. chartered; Id. (16 Feb.) 836. Galena Steam Engine and Machinery Manufacturing Co. chartered; Id. 1104. Upper Mississippi Transportation Co. chartered; Id. (18 Feb.) 1366. Galena Classical Institute chartered; Pr. L. 1859 (4 Feb.) 366. Library Association chartered; Pr. L. 1861 (22 Feb.) 550. Galena Mutual Fire Insurance Co. chartered; 1 Pr. L. 1865 (14 Feb.) 657. De Soto Hotel Co. chartered; 2 Pr. L. 1867 (16 Feb.) 45. Galena City Mining and Smelting Co. chartered; Id. (5 Mar.) 384.

Warren.—Town chartered; Pr. L. 1859 (24 Feb.) 700. Foregoing amended; Pr. L. 1861 (22 Feb.) 735. Town issue bonds for railroad purposes; 3 Pr. L. 1867 (25 Feb.) 134. Jo Daviess Insurance Co. chartered; 1 Pr. L. 1865 (16 Feb.) 685.

Dunleith.—Town chartered; Pr. L. 1857 (16 Feb.) 1091. Foregoing amended; Pr. L. 1861 (22 Feb.) 610. City chartered; 1 Pr. L. 1865 (16 Feb.) 335.

JOHNSON COUNTY.

County formed prior to the organization of the state. Copying county records; L. 1839 (12 Feb.) 84. Removal of county seat, vote thereon; L. 1845 (10 Jan.) 204. Borrow money to complete court house; L. 1852 (21 June) 88. For liquidating county indebtedness; 2 Pr. L. 1867 (7 Mar.) 798. Concerning costs due James S. Dorris, late sheriff; L. 1819 (27 Mar.) 297. Appropriates $200. to improve road from Wilcox's ferry to Vienna; Pr. L. 1833 (1 Mar.) 3. James Copeland allowed $100. for returning J. Solmon charged with kidnapping; L. 1836 (16 Jan.) 250. Ferries of Wilcox and Parker confirmed; L. 1839 (5 Mar.) 57. Road, Equality to Vienna relocated in part; Id. (23 Feb.) 187. Relief of A. Cochran and others settlers on section 16, Town 14—3; Id. (2 Mar.) 256. Town 14—2 attached to 13—2 for school purposes; Pr. L. 1855 (13 Feb.) 702. Emporium Real Estate and Manufacturing Co. chartered; Pr. L. 1857 (26 Jan.) 60. Wm. R., Joseph M. and Daniel M. Howell made heirs of Wm. Brill; Id. (10 Feb.) 361. Southern Illinois Seminary at Reynoldsborough chartered; 1 Pr. L. 1865 (16 Feb.) 28. D. Bauman released from a judgment; L. 1869 (9 Apr.) 339.

Vienna.—Town chartered; L. 1821 (14 Feb.) 160. Foregoing amended; L. 1823 (14 Feb.) 142. Again chartered; L. 1841 (27 Feb.) 340. Town incorporated under general act 12 Feb. 1831; Pr. L. 1837 (27 Feb.) 107. Again chartered; Pr. L. 1859 (22 Feb.) 694. Boundary defined; 2 Pr. L. 1865 (16 Feb.) 600. S. J. Chapman to lay off an addition; L. 1843 (2 Feb.) 208.

KANE COUNTY.

County formed; boundary and organization; L. 1836 (16 Jan.) 273. Extra tax in 1845 for county purposes; L. 1845 (10 Jan.) 187. School directors to raise money to build school houses; L. 1847 (28 Feb.) 158. Hogs not to run at large; L. 1849 (10 Jan.) 185. Assessment for 1849 legalized; 2 L. 1849 (6 Nov.) 51. Borrow $20,000. for erecting and repairing county buildings; L. 1853 (10 Feb.) 235. Towns support their own paupers, vote thereon; Id. (11 Feb.) 275. For the support of paupers; Id. (10 Feb.)

276. Repeals both the foregoing; Pr. L. 1855 (15 Feb.) 704. Annexing towns of Hanover, Barrington, Palatine and Schaumberg in Cook county, vote thereon; Id. (12 Feb.) 277. Commissioners of highways alter or vacate roads; Pr. L. 1854 (1 Mar.) 145. Borrow $30,000. to erect public buildings; Pr. L. 1857 (16 Feb.) 938. Union Agricultural Society chartered; Pr. L. 1839 (19 Feb.) 88. A. P. Hubbard, mill dam on Fox river, Town 39—8; L. 1840 (29 Jan.) 67. J. M. Strode, the same; Town 42—8; L. 1841 (17 Feb) 184. Barker and House, the same, at Big Woods; Id. (24 Feb.) 186. John Vanfleet, the same, Town 38—8; L. 1843 (2 Mar.) 176. Peck and Carpenter, the same, Town 42—8; L. 1845 (1 Mar.) 134. R. Fay, the same, Town 40—8; Id. (28 Jan.) 184. Benj. W. Raymond, the same, Town 41—8; Pr. L. 1847 (28 Feb.) 41. John P. Schneider, the same, Town 38—8; Pr. L. 1849 (12 Feb.) 46. Notice posted on Fox River bridge; fine for driving faster than walk; Pr. L. 1847 (27 Feb.) 15. Jefferson changed to Oak Park; Pr. L. 1849 (8 Feb) 112. Campton Cemetery Association chartered; L. 1852 (23 June) 267. Wm. Woodard, convicted of manslaughter, restored to citizenship; L. 1853 (10 Feb.) 92. Kate Bogart name changed to Eva Breek; Pr. L. 1857 (19 Jan.) 23. Belvidere chartered; Id. (5 Feb.) 252. Foregoing amended; Pr. L. 1859 (12 Feb.) 585. Towns and cities along Fox river borrow money to repair damages by the flood; Pr. L. 1857 (12 Feb.) 535. Big Rock Farmers Mutual Fire Insurance Co. chartered; Pr. L. 1863 (16 Feb.) 207. St. Charles and Geneva R. R. chartered; Id. 221. Construction of private ditches for drainage; 1 Pr. L. 1865 (16 Feb.) 555. Conservator for Sarah Minard, confirmed lunatic; 2 Pr. L. 1865 (13 Feb.) 244. School directors district No. 5, Town 38, borrow $50,000. to complete school house; Id. (15 Feb) 304. Globe manufacturing Co. chartered; 2 Pr. L. 1867 (7 Mar.) 816.

Geneva.—To alter or vacate town plat; R. J. Hamilton, dam across Fox river; 2 L. 1837 (21 July) 102. Wall street changed; Pr. L. 1847 (16 Jan.) 196. Constructing side walks; 3 Pr. L. 1867 (25 Feb.) 104. Town chartered; Id. 294. Vacates part of Harrington's addition; Id. (21 Feb.) 619. Kane College chartered; Pr. L. 1839 (21 Feb.) 96.

Aurora.—Correct mistakes in platting blocks 1, 8, 9, 16 and 23; L. 1845 (1 Mar.) 135. Town chartered; Pr. L. 1853 (8 Feb.) 355. Foregoing amended; Pr. L. 1854 (28 Feb.) 168. Further amends; general powers defined; Pr. L. 1855 (15 Feb.) 492. City chartered; court of common pleas established; Pr. L. 1857 (11 Feb.) 375. Foregoing amended; one judge for the Aurora and Elgin courts; L. 1859 (14 Feb.) 76. Further amends; powers generally extended; Pr. L. 1861 (16 Feb.) 89. Still further; times of holding court changed; L. 1863 (12 Feb.) 37. And, regulating practice therein; Id. (14 Feb.) 65. March term of; Id. (16 Feb.) 39. Further respecting said court; L. 1865 (16 Feb.) 38. The judge of, compensation; L. 1867 (8 Mar.) 76. Further amends act 11 Feb. 1857; city borrow money; powers extended; 1 Pr. L. 1865 (10 Feb.) 245. Charter again amended; 1 Pr. L. 1867 (28 Feb.) 680. Action taken April 2 1867 to secure the location of the C. B. & Q. R. R. shops, legalized; 2 L. 1867 (13 June) 9. Schools in district No. 5, Aurora township, supported by taxation; Pr. L. 1853 (24 Jan.) 481. Clark Seminary chartered; Pr. L. 1855 (15 Feb.) 384. Gas Light and Coke Co. chartered; Pr. L. 1857 (16 Feb.) 1126. Gas Light Co. chartered; Pr. L. 1861 (20 Feb.) 331. Foregoing amended; to borrow money; Pr. L. 1863 (20 Feb.) 213. Further amends; repeals §4 and clause granting exclusive privilege; 1 Pr. L. 1867 (9 Mar) 979. Farmer's Tornado Insurance Co. chartered; Pr. L. 1861 (22 Feb.) 378. People's Mutual Insurance Co. chartered; Id. 414. German Mutual Aid and Gymnastic Society; 1 Pr. L. 1865 (16 Feb.) 69. Aurora Cemetery Co. chartered; Id. (13 Feb.) 213. Aurora Fire Insurance Co. chartered; Id. (16 Feb.) 617. Aurora Library Association; 2 Pr. L. 1865 (16 Feb.) 15. West Aurora Cemetery Co. chartered; 1 Pr. L. 1867 (28 Feb.) 218. Aurora Hotel Co. chartered; 2 Pr. L. 1867 (9 Mar.) 38. Fox River Hydraulic and Manufacturing Co. chartered; Id. (16 Feb.) 91. Fox River Insurance Co. chartered; Id. (1 Mar.) 177. German Roman Catholic Benevolent Association chartered; Id. (21 Feb.) 264.

Elgin.—City chartered; revising and extending corporate powers; Pr. L. 1854 (28 Feb.) 88. Further amending town incorporation acts; acts of corporate authorities legalized; Pr. L. 1855 (15 Feb.) 185. Court of common pleas established; L. 1857 (16 Feb.) 173. Foregoing amended; one judge for the courts at Aurora and Elgin; L. 1859 (14 Feb.) 76. Changing time of holding said court; L. 1863 (12 Feb.) 37. Practice therein; Id. (14 Feb.) 65. Further respecting; L. 1865 (16 Feb.) 38. Compensation of judge; L. 1867 (8 Mar.) 76. Tax levied to pay bounties; 1 Pr. L. 1865 (6 Feb.) 148. Elgin Academy chartered; Pr. L. 1839 (22 Feb.) 97. Foregoing amended; Pr. L. 1855 (14 Feb.) 364. City take 80 shares of stock in said Academy; 1 Pr. L. 1865 (16 Feb.) 361. Gifford and Kimball's dam across Fox river; L. 1839 (15 Feb.) 108. Bridge Town 41—8 kept in repair; L. 1845 (28 Jan.) 260. Vacates cemetery lot; title thereto vested in school directors No. 1; Pr. L. 1847 (23 Feb) 21. Indebtedness for Fox river bridge built in 1849, discharged by town; Pr. L. 1851 (12 Feb.) 109. Geo. W. Renwick, build blacksmith shop at east end of the bridge; Pr. L. 1853 (24 Jan) 480. Waugonsha Mutual Insurance Co. chartered; Pr. L. 1855 (14 Feb.) 403. Elgin Gas Light and Coke Co. chartered; Pr. L. 1861 (21 Feb.) 333. Elgin Insurance Co. chartered; 1 Pr. L. 1865 (15 Feb.) 637. Kane County Savings, Loan and Trust Co. chartered; 2 Pr. L. 1855 (16 Feb.) 21. National Watch Co. chartered; Id. (15 Feb) 41. Elgin Hydraulic Co. chartered; 2 Pr L. 1867 (9 Mar.) 83.

St. Charles.—Charleston changed to St. Charles; L. 1839 (9 Feb.) 73. First street relocated; L. 1853 (24 Jan.) 297. Walnut street vacated in part; L. 1845 (18 Jan.) 194. Town chartered; Pr. L. 1853 (12 Feb.) 232. Foregoing amended, regulate the sale of liquor; Pr. L. 1863 (20 Feb.) 272. School district No. 7 to borrow money to build school house; L. 1857 (30 Jan.) 202. Town take stock in St. Charles R. R.; Pr. L. 1859 (21 Feb.) 684. Vacates part of Morrison's addition; 2 Pr. L. 1865 (16 Feb.) 658. Ira Minard and others, dam on Fox river; L. 1840 (1 Feb.) 76. St. Charles Academy chartered; L. 1843 (24 Jan.) 3. Literary and Medical College of Illinois chartered; Id. (6 Feb.) 60. St. Charles R. R. chartered; Pr. L. 1859 (18 Feb.) 506.

Batavia.—Cemetery Association chartered; L. 1845 (28 Feb.) 119. Alonzo T. Phillips, dam across Fox river, 18 inches high; Pr. L. 1847 (1 Mar.) 42. Van Buren street re-located; Id. (16 Jan.) 197. Batavia Institute chartered; Pr. L. 1853 (12 Feb.) 518. Wm. Coffin, dam on Fox river; 1 Pr. L. 1865 (16 Feb.) 552. Construction of sidewalks; 3 Pr. L. 1867 (25 Feb.) 104.

KANKAKEE COUNTY.

County formed; vote thereon; L. 1851 (11 Feb.) 30. Another vote thereon; boundary prescribed; L. 1853 (11 Feb.) 159. Title to swamp lands vested in the county; county judge settles with Will and Iroquois counties; Pr. L. 1854 (1 Mar.) 100. County borrow $10,000. to complete public buildings; Id. (22 Feb.) 102. Foregoing amended; powers of county court vested in board of supervisors; Pr. L. 1855 (15 Feb.) 43. Towns 30, 31 and the north ⅓ of 29 detached from Vermilion and attached to Kankakee conditionally; Id. (14 Feb.) 662. Sale of swamp lands; L. 1857 (16 Feb.) 122. Township support of paupers; L. 1861 (20 Feb.) 135. County orders issued to pay bounties legalized; 1 Pr. L. 1865 (16 Feb.) 127. County borrow money to pay war indebtedness and build fire proof vaults for records; 1 Pr. L. 1867 (25 Feb.) 887. Road and bridge tax legalized; 3 Pr. L. 1867 (19 Feb.) 120. Towns 29—10, 11, 12, 13 and 14 detached from Iroquois and attached to Kankakee; Id. (8 Mar.) 632. Prohibits the netting of fish; L. 1869 (29 Mar.) 187. Bloomfield Seminary of Learning chartered; Pr. L. 1839 (2 Mar.) 238. Kankakee Bridge Co. chartered; Pr. L. 1853 (12 Feb.) 399. Towns 30 and 31, 9 east levy tax to bridge the Kankakee at Wilmington (under foregoing charter); Pr. L. 1855 (15 Feb.) 667. Balance of $3,872.80 due said bridge company, to be levied on towns of Reid and Wilmington in Will county and Essex and Norton in this county; Pr. L. 1861 (22 Feb.) 537. Towns of Essex and Norton levy special tax to pay said bridge debt; 2 Pr. L. 1865 (16 Feb.) 339. Towns named vote for or against repairing said bridge; 1 Pr. L. 1867 (21 Feb.) 170. Momence Bridge Co. chartered; L. 1852 (18 June) 24. Towns of Momence and Ganeer borrow money to rebuild bridge at Momence (under foregoing charter); 1 Pr. L. 1867 (9 Mar.) 188. Auditor sell lands in Town 30—12 to G. Lambert; L. 1857 (13 Feb.) 89. Towns of Essex, Norton, Salina and Rockville, with towns in Will and Grundy, vote for or against tax to improve the Kankakee; Pr. L. 1861 (22 Feb.) 737. Bridge tax in town of Limestone Apr. 1862 legalized; Pr. L. 1863 (12 Feb.) 277. Kankakee University chartered; 1 Pr. L. 1865 (16 Feb.) 41. Towns of St. Anne and Aroma, special tax to bridge the Kankakee at Aroma; Id. 188. Kankakee Stone and Lime Co. chartered; 2 Pr. L. 1867 (23 Feb.) 415. Aroma and Kankakee R. R. chartered; Id. (8 Mar.) 642. New assessment for 1866 in Manteno; Id. (9 Mar.) 793. Union school district No. 5 in Manteno borrow money to build school house; 3 Pr. L. 1867 (9 Mar.) 28. Eli Hawkins adopt Adah M. Allen; L. 1869 (26 Mar.) 341.

Kankakee City.—Kankakee Depot and Bourbonnais changed to Kankakee City and chartered; Pr. L. 1855 (15 Feb.) 211. Foregoing generally amended after §3; Pr. L. 1861 (22 Feb.) 660. City chartered; 1 Pr. L. 1865 (16 Feb.) 393. Charter amended; limits and jurisdiction; 1 Pr. L. 1867 (7 Mar.) 710. Vacates part of River street; 3 Pr. L. 1867 (7 Mar.) 167. Kankakee School District chartered; 2 Pr. L. 1865 (16 Feb.) 295. Foregoing amended; 3 Pr. L. 1867 (22 Feb.) 25. Kankakee Male and Female Seminary chartered; 1 Pr. L. 1867 (4 Mar.) 25. Gas Light and Coke Co. chartered; Id. (23 Feb.) 985. Kankakee Insurance Co. chartered; 2 Pr. L. 1867 (25 Feb.) 135.

KENDALL COUNTY.

County created, boundary and organization; L. 1841 (19 Feb.) 75. La Salle county school commissioner pay over share school funds; L. 1845 (7 Feb.) 221. Monthly elections for locating county seat; Id. (25 Feb.) 306. Public records indexed; L. 1847 (16 Feb.) 71. County borrow $5,000. to pay county debts, vote thereon; Pr. L. 1849 (12 Feb.) 31. County take bonds of Ottawa, Oswego and Fox River R. R.; L. 1852 (21 Feb.) 64. Unpaid taxes for 1849 collected; Pr. L. 1853 (24 Jan.) 450. Records of La Salle affecting lands in Kendall transcribed; Pr. L. 1857 (16 Feb.) 877. Removal of county seat from Oswego, vote thereon; L. 1859 (24 Feb.) 45. Completing county buildings, time extended; L. 1861 (18 Feb.) 136. Township support of paupers, vote thereon; L. 1863 (13 Feb.) 46. County borrow $80,000. to redeem bounty orders—two acts; 1 Pr. L. 1865 (14 and 15 Feb.) 128. Foregoing amended; 1 Pr. L. 1867 (18 Feb.) 877. Action of towns paying bounties legalized; 1 Pr. L. 1865 (16 Feb.) 153. Town of Somonauk detached from De Kalb and attached to this county; 2 Pr. L. 1865 (16 Feb.) 579. T. Howe, mill dam across Fox river at Yorkville; L. 1845 (3 Mar.) 253. Michael C. Parker, the same, at Troy; Pr. L. 1857 (10 Feb.) 350. Frederick Post, the same, in Town 36—6; 2 Pr. L. 1867 (18 Feb.) 808. Towns and cities along Fox river borrow money to repair damages by the flood; Pr. L. 1857 (12 Feb.) 505. Oswego Branch R. R. chartered; Id. (16 Feb.) 862. Township of Big Grove pay bounties; 1 Pr. L. 1865 (16 Feb.) 156. Kendall County Mutual Fire Insurance Co at Yorkville chartered; Id. (15 Feb.) 638. Northwestern Farmers' Insurance Co. at Lisbon chartered; Id. (16 Feb.) 743. Plano chartered; 2 Pr. L. 1865 (16 Feb.) 542. Bristol R. R. chartered; 2 Pr. L. 1867 (6 Mar.) 572. Hector S. Humphrey, late treasurer, released from half the judgment against him; Id. 797.

Newark.—Georgetown changed to Newark; L. 1843 (28 Feb.) 301. Town corporate powers and jurisdiction extended; Pr. L. 1857 (18 Feb.) 1328. Town chartered; 3 Pr. L. 1867 (7 Mar.) 276. Fowler Female Institute chartered; Pr. L. 1857 (10 Feb.) 853. Charter amended; name changed to Fowler Institute; 1 Pr. L. 1867 (28 Feb.) 19.

Oswego.—Vacates certain alleys; Pr. L. 1849 (9 Feb.) 124; Pr. L. 1853 (11 Feb.) 503; and Pr. L. 1857 (7 Feb.) 287. Corporate powers and jurisdiction extended; Id. (18 Feb.) 1328. Oswego Manufacturing Co. chartered; L. 1845 (26 Feb.) 292. And again; 2 Pr. L. 1865 (15 Feb.) 44.

KNOX COUNTY.

County formed, boundary defined; L. 1825 (13 Jan.) 94 §8. Allowed $200. to bridge Spoon river; L. 1831 (22 Jan.) 37. Supplemental to foregoing; 1 L. 1837 (4 Mar.) 26. Formation of county of Coffee, vote thereon; Id. (1 Mar.) 86. Extends §2 of act 22 Jan. (L. 1831, 38) concerning the erection of bridges, to last Monday in Oct. 1833; Pr. L. 1833 (22 Feb.) 13. Same subject; L. 1839 (12 Feb.) 99. Revenue paid into county treasury; Id. (16 Feb.) 125. Removal county seat, Knoxville to Galesburg; L. 1863 (2 Feb.) 54; 1 Pr. L. 1865 (14 Feb.) 548; L. 1869 (10 Mar.) 152. Game law 1855 extended to; L. 1861 (21 Feb.) 126; Gross' Stat. 1868, 325. Collection of taxes, time extended; 2 Pr. L. 1865 (9 Feb.) 338. Supervisors appropriate $10,000. to build a soldiers' monument; 2 Pr. L. 1867 (21 Feb.) 449. Supervisors fix rate of commutation for road labor; also, determine what shall be a lawful fence; Id. (28 Feb.) 825. Additional justice and constable in Henderson; 1 L. 1837 (15 Feb.) 117. Henderson chartered; Id. (10 Feb.) 331. Sale of Sec. 16, Town 9—2 legalized; L. 1839 (15 Feb.) 102. Road, Knoxville and Peoria re-located; L. 1840 (1 Feb.) 59. Additional justice and constable in Cherry Grove L. 1841 (20 Feb.) 176. Cherry Grove Seminary chartered; L. 1845 (1 Mar.) 111. Harrisonville changed to Herman and chartered; L. 1852 (21 June) 108. Le Roy Wheeler and Adam Snyder, restored to citizenship; L. 1853 (8 Feb.) 96. Lapier and Walnut Grove name changed to Altona; Pr. L. 1857 (13 Feb.) 550. Township support of paupers; Id. (16 Feb.) 1090. Galesburg and Henderson plank road chartered; 2 Pr. L. 1865 (16 Feb.) 109. Wm. B. Mecham, convicted of larceny, restored to citizenship; 2 Pr. L. 1867 (28 Feb.) 813. Compensation of sheriff; L. 1867 (7 Mar.) 116.

Knoxville.—County seat located on S. W. 28 11—2, and called Henderson; L. 1831 (15 Jan.) 62. Name changed to Knoxville; Pr. L. 1833 (22 Dec. '32) 23. Vacates Heaton's addition; L. 1839 (18 Jan.) 49. Town chartered; L. 1845 (1 Mar.) 172. Amendment; repair roads leading thereto; Pr. L. 1849 (25 Jan.) 110. City chartered; no power to license sale of liquor; Pr. L. 1853 (10 Feb.) 222. Amendment; limits extended; council control common schools; Pr. L. 1854 (4 Mar.) 174. Foregoing amendment amended; special school tax; 1 Pr. L. 1865 (15 Feb.) 427. Charter further amended; powers extended; 1 Pr. L. 1867 (7 Mar.) 746. City take stock in Peoria and Oquawka R. R.; L. 1853 (11 Feb.) 146. Knoxville College chartered; Pr. L. 1853 (12 Feb.) 553. Masonic and Odd Fellows' Joint Stock Co. chartered; Pr. L. 1855 (6 Feb.) 683. Ewing Female University; Pr. L. 1859 (19 Feb.) 363.

Galesburg.—Town chartered; L. 1841 (27 Jan.) 321. Foregoing amended; Id. (24 Feb.) 339. City chartered; act 27 Feb. 1854, for the better government of towns and cities to form part of said charter; two police magistrates with extended jurisdiction to $500.; Pr. L. 1857 (14 Feb.) 673. Charter amended; grant licenses; adjust damages for opening streets; Pr. L. 1859 (19 Feb.) 150. Further amended; per diem of police magistrates; 1 Pr. L. 1867 (25 Feb.) 594. Divides Galesburg and West Galesburg; 3 Pr. L. 1867 (27 Feb.) 411. City borrow money to erect county buildings, when county seat is located there; Pr. L. 1863 (14 Feb.) 173. Same subject; 1 Pr. L. 1865 (15 Feb.) 369. Establish system of graded schools, vote thereon; L. 1859 (18 Feb.) 163. Foregoing amended; 2 Pr. L. 1865 (15 Feb.) 279. School tax Town 11—1; L. 1843 (4 Mar.) 292. Mutual Fire and Marine Insurance Co. chartered; Pr. L. 1857 (16 Feb.) 1132. Merchants' and Farmers' Home Insurance Co. chartered; Id. (18 Feb.) 1348. Merchants', Farmers' and Mechanics' Savings Bank; Pr. L. 1861 (22 Feb.) 42. Gas Light and Coke Co. chartered; Id. (18 Feb.) 334. Farmers' and Mechanics' Savings Bank of Knox Co. chartered; 1 Pr. L. 1865 (15 Feb.) 59. Travelers' Life and Health Insurance Co. chartered; Id. (16 Feb.) 703. Emmaritta Orcutt name changed to Brackett; 1 Pr. L. 1867 (7 Mar.) 237. Galesburg Horse Railway chartered; 2 Pr. L. 1867 (6 Mar.) 31. Galesburg Times Co. chartered; Id. (7 Mar.) 509.

Knox College.—Knox Manual Labor College chartered; located Sec. 15, 11—1; Pr. L. 1837 (15 Feb.) 33. Hold lands donated for 7 years; L. 1840 (18 Jan.) 23. Foregoing amended; time extended to 10 years; Pr. L. 1851 (15 Feb.) 38. Corporate name changed to Knox College; trustees establish a Female Collegiate Dep't; Pr. L. 1857 (16 Feb.) 834. Adelphi of said college chartered; Pr. L. 1847 (25 Feb.) 120.

Lombard University.—Illinois Liberal Institute chartered; Pr. L. 1851 (15 Feb.) 246. Foregoing amended; Pr. L. 1853 (26 Jan.) 477. Corporate name changed to Lombard University; original charter amended; Pr. L. 1857 (14 Feb.) 796. Conditions of grants, bequests, etc. strictly carried out; confer degrees etc.; Pr. L. 1861 (21 Feb.) 16.

Abingdon.—City chartered; Pr. L. 1857 (13 Feb.) 587. Foregoing amended; acts of officers legalized; powers extended; Pr. L. 1859 (19 Feb.) 34. Abingdon College chartered; Pr. L. 1855 (13 Feb.) 536. Philomathi of said College chartered; Pr. L. 1857 (9 Feb.) 315. Hedding Seminary and Central Illinois Female College chartered; Id. 315.

LAKE COUNTY.

County created, boundary and organization; L. 1839 (1 Mar.) 216. Collect tax levied by McHenry county; L. 1840 (18 Jan.) 47. Removal of county seat, Burlington to Little Fort; L. 1841 (17 Feb.) 95. Acts of county commissioner's court legalized; L. 1843 (19 Jan.) 109. County seat located at Little Fort; Id. 115. Roads laid out by county commissioners 1 June 1845 to 10 Sept. 1845 legalized; L. 1847 (17 Feb.) 104. Taxes for 1848 legalized; L. 1849 (12 Feb.)

186. County license in 1848 to Hiram Hugunin and others, to build plank road, continued; Pr. L. 1849 (8 Feb.) 30. Towns support their own paupers; L. 1851 (17 Feb.) 183. Vote in April whether towns shall support paupers; Pr. L. 1853 (26 Jan.) 464. Sheep and swine not to run at large; L. 1853 (27 Jan.) 152. Also, L. 1859 (19 Feb.) 200. And also; L. 1867 (28 Feb.) 97. Jurisdiction of county court extended to $500.; practice in and terms thereof; L. 1853 (12 Feb.) 263. Same subject; L. 1859 (19 Feb.) 101. Supervisors raise money for support of volunteers; L. 1863 (14 Feb) 56. Lake County Drainage Commissioners chartered; Pr. L. 1863 (21 Feb.) 185. Docket and jury fee; L. 1863 (15 Jan.) 49. County and towns pay a bounty of $300.; 1 Pr. L. 1865 (10 Feb.) 120. County aid in construction of a County Soldiers' Monument; 1 Pr. L. 1867 (13 Feb.) 874. Prohibits trapping of fur; Id. (25 Feb.) 993. Boundaries of townships changed; 3 Pr. L. 1867 (9 Mar.) 635. Middlesex Steam Mill Co. chartered, at Half Day P. O.; L. 1840 (31 Jan.) 31. Henry W. Dorsett take the oath as sheriff; Pr. L. 1849 (9 Jan.) 27. The same, credited with $3,603. of which he was robbed; Pr. L. 1851 (14 Feb.) 126. Payment to Chas. Gardner, as state's attorney; L. 1851 (15 Feb.) 126. Election of a justice in Avon legalized; L. 1853 (10 Feb.) 228. Waukegan and Antioch plank road chartered; Pr. L. 1853 (12 Feb.) 163. Foregoing amended; changed to a railroad; Pr. L. 1854 (1 Mar.) 181. Payment to Henry W. Blodgett, as state's attorney; Pr. L. 1853 (26 Jan.) 441. Tristram Vincent, dam on DesPlaines at Town 43—11; Id. (11 Feb.) 579. Jurisdiction ceded to the United States over light houses at Port Clinton, Taylorport and Waukegan; L. 1855 (13 Feb.) 139. Wauconda replatted; L. 1857 (12 Feb.) 57. Delia Murray name changed to Delia M. Ela; Pr. L. 1857 (9 Feb.) 304. Sale of swamp lands Towns 45 and 46—9 at private entry confirmed; Id. (10 Feb.) 363. Wauconda Academy chartered; Id. (14 Feb.) 759. Village of Antioch chartered; Id. (16 Feb.) 1014. And again; 2 Pr. L. 1865 (16 Feb.) 347. Refunding to R. Compton from school fund of Town 45—9; L. 1861 (20 Feb.) 203. Milburn Mutual Insurance Co. chartered; 1 Pr. L. 1865 (16 Feb.) 719. Vacates and relocates road Town 43—12; 2 Pr. L. 1865 (14 Feb.) 263. Streets in Cuba altered, etc.; Id. (16 Feb.) 661. Wauconda Mutual Insurance Co. chartered; 2 Pr. L. 1867 (4 Mar.) 162. Lake County Peat Co. chartered; Id. 386. Highland Park Building Co. chartered; Id. (23 Feb.) 845. Goodale changed to Grant; 3 Pr. L. 1867 (8 Mar.) 622. Old Milwaukee road, Town 45—12, partly re-located; L. 1869 (15 Mar.) 387. Chicago and Green Bay road, Town 43—12, partly re-located; Id. (31 Mar.) 388.

Waukegan.—State street in Little Fort resurveyed; L. 1845 (26 Feb.) 166. Town Little Fort chartered; Pr. L. 1849 (12 Feb.) 134. Charter amended; Pr. L. 1851 (15 Feb.) 210. Amending and supplementing town charter; name changed to Waukegan and substituted in all deeds; side walks and fire department; L. 1852 (15 June) 8. Three town constables elected; L. 1851 (15 Feb.) 117. Members of fire department exempt from jury duty; Id. 124. City chartered; Pr. L. 1853 (12 Feb.) 262. Again; Pr. L. 1859 (23 Jan.) 336. Amendment; firemen exempt from street labor tax; Pr. L. 1861 (22 Feb.) 330. Further amends; support of public schools; 1 Pr. L. 1865 (23 Jan.) 523. Issue of city bonds to pay bounties legalized; 1 Pr. L. 1865 (16 Feb.) 152. Borrow money to bridge Little Fort river; Pr. L. 1855 (14 Feb.) 690. Foregoing amended; Pr. L. 1857 (16 Feb.) 1090. Waukegan Mutual Insurance Co. chartered; Pr. L. 1853 (3 Feb.) 611. Charter amended; Pr. L. 1859 (19 Feb.) 399. Gas Light and Coke Co. chartered; Pr. L. 1855 (14 Feb.) 645. Waukegan Academy chartered; Pr. L. 1857 (18 Feb.) 1381. Waukegan Warehouse and Pier Co. chartered; Pr. L. 1859 (18 Feb.) 732. Union Insurance Co. chartered; 1 Pr. L. 1865 (16 Feb.) 802. Charter amended; office removed to Chicago; 2 Pr. L. 1867 (4 Mar.) 161. Waukegan Hotel Co. chartered; Id. (18 Feb.) 46. Illinois and Pah Ranagat Silver Mining Co. chartered; Id. (9 Mar.) 399.

Lake Forrest.—City chartered; Pr. L. 1861 (21 Feb.) 205. Lind University chartered; Pr. L. 1857 (13 Feb.) 514. Foregoing amended; medical department established; Pr. L. 1861 (18 Feb.) 18. Further amended; name changed to Lake Forrest University; 1 Pr. L. 1865 (16 Feb.) 49, 53. Hotel and Manufacturing Co. chartered; 2 Pr. L. 1867 (5 Mar.) 65.

Hainesville.—Town chartered; Pr. L. 1847 (26 Feb.) 207. Hainesville Academy chartered; Id. (28 Feb.) 4. Steam Mill Co. chartered; Id. (20 Feb.) 109.

LA SALLE COUNTY.

County formed, with county seat at Ottawa; L. 1831 (15 Feb.) 54 §2. Ferry across the Illinois at Ottawa, vested in the county; L. 1831 (15 Jan.) 56. Foregoing repealed; Pr. L. 1833 (28 Jan.) 32. County Commissioners account to auditor expenses of keeping the Pottawattamie Indians charged with the massacre on Indian creek; Pr. L. 1833 (22 Feb) 19. County and circuit clerks keep their offices at their residences; L. 1835 (27 Jan.) 70. County commissioners control court room; L. 1840 (29 Jan.) 65. School commissioners dispose of depreciated bank notes; L. 1843 (3 Mar.) 39. Assessment for 1841 legalized; Id. (6 Mar.) 23 §2. School commissioners pay trustees of school Towns 29 and 30—1, certain moneys; L. 1845 (28 Feb.) 102. County debt funded; Id. (1 Mar.) 125. Sale of certain school lands; L. 1847 (1 Mar.) 117. Proceeds of certain school lands paid to trustees of schools in Marshall county; L. 1849 (2 Feb) 180. Purchase of poor farm; Pr. L. 1853 (26 Jan.) 474. Records of county commissioners' court and probate court indexed; L. 1853 (10 Feb.) 167. Jurisdiction of county court extended; Pr. L. 1854 (27 Feb.) 239; also, L. 1865 (16 Feb.) 37. Changes of venue from county court; L. 1857 (28 Jan.) 45. Change the terms and regulate the practice therein; L. 1869 (6 Mar.) 146. Protection of fish in arm of the Illinois opposite Peru; L. 1861 (22 Feb.) 123. Action of supervisors paying bounties legalized; 1 Pr. L. 1865 (6 Feb.) 131. Prohibits seining of fish in certain places; L. 1867 (7 Mar.) 118. County take stock in railroads; 1 Pr. L. 1867 (6 Mar.) 866. Wm. Stadden, mill

dam on Fox river; Pr. L. 1833 (12 Feb.) 106. Foregoing amended; L. 1836 (14 Jan.) 196. David Walker confirmed in pre-emption of fractical quarter named; Pr. L. 1833 (5 Feb.) 113. Geo. E. Walker, sheriff, exact hostages from Pottawattamie nation; Id. (14 Jan.) 205. Marsellies Manufacturing Co. chartered; L. 1836 (7 Jan.) 138. Franklin Manual Labor College chartered; located in either Cook or La Salle counties; Id. (16 Jan.) 160. Wm. Seeley, toll bridge on the Big Vermilion; Id. (12 Jan.) 200. James Day, toll bridge across the Illinois; 1 L. 1837 (4 Mar.) 28. Green & Stadden, toll bridge on Fox river at Dayton; 2 L. 1837 (20 July) 8. D. F. Hitt, mill dam on a slough in Town 23—2; L. 1839 (2 Mar.) 236. Union Agricultural Society chartered; Pr. L. 1839 (19 Feb.) 88. Survey and plat of Dresden and Utica legalized; Id. (26 Feb.) 147. Kankakee Manuf. Co. chartered; L. 1840 (10 Dec. '39) 135. Payment on schedules kept in Town 33—3 in 1839; L. 1841 (14 [Dec.] 1840) 206. Certificates of purchase issued to assignee of Conrad Sebaugh; Id. (23 Feb.) 208. Index to records; Id. 311. Plat of Vermilionville vacated in part; Id. (14 Dec. '40) 315. LaSalle County Mutual Fire Insurance Co. chartered; L. 1843 (3 Mar.) 104. Charter amended; Pr. L. 1857 (11 Feb.) 453. Foregoing amendment amended; Pr. L. 1859 (23 Feb.) 395. Charter again amended; 1 Pr. L. 1865 (16 Feb.) 702. Trustees of schools Town 33—3, proceedings legalized; L. 1843 (23 Feb.) 273. Enterprise plat vacated; L. 1845 (3 Mar.) 266. Boyd and Twitchell, ferry across the Illinois Town 33—2; Id. (27 Feb.) 147. Foregoing extended; Pr. L. 1857 (18 Feb.) 1336. School trustees Town 33—1, lease lands; previous leases valid; L. 1849 (25 Jan.) 182. Henry L. Owens, toll bridge across the Illinois at Salisbury; Pr. L. 1849 (15 Feb.) 9. River Board for improvement of the Illinois from the Little Vermilion to Fox River; Pr. L. 1851 (12 Feb.) 80. Foregoing amended; L. 1852 (23 June) 206. Repeal of foregoing; L. 1853 (10 Feb.) 171. Jeremiah Crotty, ferry across the Illinois at Town 33—5; Pr. 1851 (12 Feb.) 85. Same, establish a toll gate; Pr. L. 1857 (13 Feb.) 579. Same, ferry privilege extended; Pr. L. 1861 (8 Feb.) 320. Boundaries of Earl and Meriden changed; east half Town 36—2 added to Earl; L. 1853 (12 Feb.) 67. Isaac R. Hitt and others, bridge the Big Vermilion Town 33—1; Pr. L. 1853 (11 Feb.) 601. David L. Hough and others, ferry across the Illinois Town 33—1; Pr. L. 1853 (11 Feb.) 607. School fund Town 34—5 divided between Manlius and Mission; Pr. L. 1854 (28 Feb.) 145. J. Strawn deed to lands Town 33—2; L. 1855 (3 Feb.) 113. Illinois and Wisconsin Mining and Manufacturing Co. chartered; Pr. L. 1855 (15 Feb.) 611. Title to lands Town 33—3 vested in heirs of D. Walker; L. 1857 (10 Feb.) 182. School trustees Town 33—1 borrow money to build school house; Id. (18 Feb.) 223. Diamond Coal Co. chartered; Pr. L. 1857 (13 Feb.) 508. Big Vermilion Coal Co. chartered; Id. 548. Eagle Coal Co. chartered, at Tonica; Id. (14 Feb.) 826. Charter amended; Pr. L. 1861 (22 Feb.) 301. And again; 2 Pr. L. 1865 (16 Feb.) 59. Starved Rock Manufacturing Co. chartered; Id. (16 Feb.) 878. Foregoing charter revived and continued; 2 Pr. L. 1867 (7 Mar.) 311. Little Rock Mining Co. chartered; Id. (18 Feb.) 1331. Boundary of school districts on Fox river changed; L. 1859 (22 Feb.) 188. David Strawn and others chartered as the Marseilles Bridge Co.; Pr. L. 1859 (21 Feb.) 18. And again; 1 Pr. L. 1865 (13 Feb.) 188. James Clark construct horse railroad on route named; Id. (24 Feb.) 532. Ottawa Northern Turnpike Co. chartered; any town take stock; Id. 720. Selah Robbins, ferry across the Illinois Town 33—2; Pr. L. 1861 (22 Feb.) 327. Northwestern Agricultural Manufacturing Co. chartered; Id. (16 Feb.) 470. Germantown plat vacated; Id. (22 Feb.) 631. Marseilles chartered; Id. (21 Feb.) 698. Charter amended; 3 Pr. L. 1867 (7 Mar.) 142. Ottawa and Vermilion Plank Road chartered; Pr. L. 1857 (14 Feb.) 669. Charter amended; Pr. L. 1863 (20 Feb.) 217. Town of Mission pay bounties; 1 Pr. L. 1865 (7 Feb.) 167. Seneca Bridge Co. chartered; across the Illinois Town 33—5; Id. (16 Feb.) 196. Town of Crotty chartered; 2 Pr. L. 1865 (16 Feb.) 433. Charter amended; 3 Pr. L. 1867 (6 Mar.) 177. Ellsworth changed to Lostant; 2 Pr. L. 1865 (16 Feb.) 440. LaSalle County Saving's Loan and Trust Co. chartered; 1 Pr. L. 1867 (5 Mar.) 65. County Dairy and Cheese Co. chartered; Id. 907. Highways town of Richland divided into repair sections; 2 Pr. L. 1867 (28 Feb.) 72. Valley Manufacturing Co. chartered; to dam Fox river; Id. (23 Feb.) 328. Illinois Excelsior Coal Co. chartered; Id. (5 Mar.) 383. Vermilion River Coal Co. chartered; Id. 389. Kentucky Coal Co. chartered; Id. (25 Feb.) 417. Vermilion Coal Co. chartered; Id. (19 Feb.) 435. Marseilles Land and Water Power Co. chartered; Id. (9 Mar.) 810. Whitford changed to Leland and latter chartered; 3 Pr. L. 1867 (23 Feb.) 606. M. Meeker name changed to M. M. Turner; L. 1869 (29 Mar.) 662.

Ottawa.—Canal commissioners alter town plat; county buildings on the square; L. 1831 (15 Feb.) 54, 56. Town chartered; 2 L. 1837 (21 July) 96. Amended; L. 1843 (4 Mar.) 296. Further amended; proof of town incorporation unnecessary; corporation deeds and leases prima facie regular; Pr. L. 1853 (12 Feb.) 572. Relief of purchasers of canal lots in 1839; L. 1841 (27 Feb.) 49. Sales in block 11 ratified; Id. (23 Feb.) 311. Leasing water power on the I. and M. Canal; L. 1843 (4 Mar.) 63. Day's addition vacated; L. 1845 (21 Feb.) 326. Streets vacated and grounds leased; Pr. L. 1849 (8 Feb.) 111. City chartered; Pr. L. 1853 (10 Feb.) 296. Alleys vacated in State's addition; Pr. L. 1853 (12 Feb.) 503. Amends charter; boundary corrected; Pr. L. 1854 (21 Feb.) 85. Further amends; take stock in Illinois Bridge Co.; Id. (1 Mar.) 201. Still further amends; 1 Pr. L. 1865 (16 Feb.) 466; 1 Pr. L. 1867 (5 Mar.) 691; Id. (7 Mar.) 745. City take stock in the Ottawa Manufacturing Co.; 2 Pr. L. 1867 (19 Feb.) 350. Vacates an alley in block 63 State's addition; Pr. L. 1855 (9 Feb.) 491. Ottawa Manufacturing Co. chartered; Pr. L. 1837 (1 Mar.) 145; again, may dam Fox river Town 33—3; Pr. L. 1851 (15 Feb.) 178; also, Pr. L. 1857 (13 Feb.) 580; may also dam the Illinois; 1 Pr. L. 1865 (16 Feb.) 551. Ottawa Central Bridge Co. chartered; across Fox River, Town 33—3; Pr. L. 1839 (2 Mar.) 178. Foregoing amended; proprietors chartered as Fox River Bridge Co.; Pr. L. 1849 (12 Feb.) 12. Wm. E. Armstrong, bridge Fox

LaSalle County.

river; L. 1839 (21 Feb.) 145. L. Leland, the same; L. 1845 (1 Mar.) 268. Geo. H. Norris, bridge the Illinois Town 33—3; failing in three years, town of Ottawa may; Pr. L. 1847 (1 Mar.) 16. Foregoing amended; time extended one year; Pr. L. 1849 (12 Feb.) 12. Both foregoing revived and extended to Henry Green; Pr. L. 1851 (15 Feb.) 250. Trustees I. and M. Canal to donate town lot to M. E. Church; Pr. L. 1847 (18 Feb.) 203. Town a road district; county court fix boundary; Id. (23 Feb.) 205. Rutland Bridge Co. chartered; Pr. L. 1853 (10 Feb.) 405. Ottawa Hydraulic Co. (organized under act 10 Feb. 1849) lease by trustees I. and M. Canal confirmed; same, extended to La Salle County Manufacturing Co.; Id. (11 Feb.) 427. Illinois River Bridge Co. chartered; town or city of Ottawa, county and any township may take stock; Id. (27 Jan.) 525; townships take stock in; Pr. L. 1854 (28 Feb.) 99; town subscriptions legalized; Pr. L. 1855 (15 Feb.) 557; town of Ottawa issue $10,000. bonds in aid of; other towns do the same; charter amended; Pr. L. 1857 (13 Feb.) 573; foregoing repealed; amends act 15 Feb. 1855; substitute "legalized" for "repeated"; Pr. L. 1861 (16 Feb.) 60. Ottawa school district established; Board of Education chartered; control common schools; Pr. L. 1855 (14 Feb.) 220. Foregoing amended; election of the board; Pr. L. 1861 (18 Feb.) 238. Further amends; 2 Pr. L. 1865 (16 Feb.) 303. Trustees First Baptist church sell and convey real estate; Pr. L. 1859 (4 Feb.) 33. Ottawa Water Works chartered; Pr. L. 1861 (20 Feb.) 239. Illinois Starch Co. chartered; Id. (7 Feb.) 469. City bank of Eames, Allen & Co. withdraw certificate; Pr. L. 1863 (14 Feb.) 37. German Benevolent Society chartered; 1 Pr. L. 1865 (16 Feb.) 70. Edward S. Leland and others to erect a hotel; Id. 607. Ottawa Petroleum and Mining Co. chartered; 2 Pr. L. 1865 (16 Feb.) 82. Ottawa Loan and Trust Co. chartered; 1 Pr. L. 1867 (7 Mar.) 83. Ottawa Savings Bank chartered; Id. 97. French Mutual Society chartered; Id. (5 Mar.) 146. Bridge Fox river within city limits; Id. (23 Feb.) 177. Town to bridge the I. and M. Canal; Id. (7 Mar.) 182. Ottawa Horse Railroad chartered; 2 Pr. L. 1867 (19 Feb.) 15. Ottawa Hotel Co. chartered; Id. (21 Feb.) 52. Mercy Hospital and School, and Orphan Asylum chartered; Id. (28 Feb.) 79. Agricultural Implement Manufacturing Co. chartered; Id. 294. Cotton Manufacturing Co. chartered; Id. (7 Mar.) 312. Paper Manufacturing Co. chartered; Id. (25 Feb.) 375. Woolen Manufacturing Co. chartered; Id. 376. Fox River Valley Coal and Mining Co. chartered; Id. (8 Mar) 393. Central Coal Co. chartered; Id. (21 Feb.) 438.

LaSalle.—City chartered; L. 1852 (23 June.) 242; amendment; borrow $15,000. for street improvement; Pr. L. 1853 (12 Feb.) 435; further amends; boundary defined; Pr. L. 1857 (18 Feb.) 1336; also, renew loan every 10 years; Pr. L. 1863 (20 Feb.) 166; corporate powers extended; 1 Pr. L. 1865 (15 Feb.) 427; boundary changed; 1 Pr. L. 1867 (5 Mar.) 693. Mining contracts between the city and Cody, Byrne & Duncan ratified; 2 Pr. L. 1867 (22 Feb.) 243. Re-appraisal and sale of so much of town as belongs to canal fund; Pr. L. 1849 (8 Feb.) 123. Township created out of that of Salisbury; L. 1851 (28 Jan.) 11. Vacates an alley; Pr. L. 1851 (28 Jan.) 32. Action of town for bridging the Illinois legalized; 2 Pr. L. 1865 (16 Feb.) 491. Recorder's court established; L. 1857 (18 Feb.) 168; also, jurisdiction and practice therein; L. 1859 (19 Feb.) 87. Both foregoing amended; L. 1861 (18 Feb.) 115. Repeals act 19 Feb. 1859 and foregoing amendment; L. 1865 (16 Feb.) 42. LaSalle Charity Hospital chartered; Pr. L. 1839 (23 Feb.) 115. Foregoing amended; L. 1840 (1 Feb.) 75. Wm. Byrne and others, ferry across the Illinois; Pr. L. 1847 (20 Feb.) 47. Foregoing continued; Pr. L. 1849 (31 Jan.) 34. Isaac Hardy and others, ferry across the Illinois; also chartered as La Salle Plank road; Pr. L. 1851 (28 Jan.) 32. Isaac Hardy and others, bridge the Illinois at crossing of I. C. Railroad; Pr. L. 1853 (12 Feb.) 558. LaSalle and Peru Gas Light and Coke Co. chartered; Pr. L. 1857 (30 Jan.) 182. And again; Pr. L. 1861 (18 Feb.) 335. LaSalle Bridge and Ferry Co. chartered; Pr. L. 1857 (11 Feb.) 459; amendment; time extended; Pr. L. 1859 (24 Feb.) 16. LaSalle Harbor Improvement Co. chartered; Pr. L. 1857 (14 Feb.) 782. Northern Illinois Coal and Iron Co. chartered; Id. (18 Feb.) 1252. Correct assessment against First National Bank; 2 Pr. L. 1865 (15 Feb.) 335. Collection of tolls on bridge over the Illinois; 1 Pr. L. 1867 (8 Mar.) 184. Union Gas Light and Coke Co. chartered; Id. (6 Mar.) 978. LaSalle and Peru Horse Railway chartered; 2 Pr. L. 1867 (6 Mar.) 29. LaSalle Glass Co. chartered; Id. (23 Feb.) 339.

Peru.—Town re-surveyed; L. 1839 (2 Mar.) 269. Mistake in recorded plat corrected; L. 1843 (23 Feb.) 295. Town corporate powers extended; L. 1845 (25 Feb.) 169. City chartered; Pr. L. 1851 (13 Feb.) 115. Amendment; power to license liquor revoked; L. 1852 (23 June) 219. Again amended; construct turnpike road; Pr. L. 1853 (3 Feb.) 398. Further amended; L. 1853 (12 Feb.) 92. Still further amended; limits extended; Pr. L. 1857 (18 Feb.) 1240. Town survey legalized; Pr. L. 1855 (15 Feb.) 201. Town pay bounties; 1 Pr. L. 1865 (7 Feb.) 173. Recorder's court established; L. 1857 (18 Feb.) 168. Again; jurisdiction and practice; L. 1859 (19 Feb.) 87. Two foregoing amended; L. 1861 (18 Feb.) 115. Freeman Mills, ferry across the Illinois; L. 1841 (24 Feb.) 115. Rights of Mills under foregoing transferred to Ettoine Boileau; Pr. L. 1855 (9 Feb.) 589. St. John's Lodge No. 13, F. and A. Masons chartered; Pr. L. 1849 (8 Feb.) 45. Zimri Lewis, ferry across the Illinois; town regulate tolls; Pr. L. 1851 (10 Feb.) 59. Foregoing amended; L. 1859 (24 Feb.) 114. LaSalle and Peru Gas Light and Coke Co. chartered; Pr. L. 1857 (30 Jan.) 182. Again, Pr. L. 1861 (18 Feb.) 335. Illinois River Bridge Co. chartered; Pr. L. 1857 (10 Feb.) 363. Amendment; may maintain a floating bridge; Pr. L. 1859 (24 Feb.) 22. Peru Coal Mining Co. chartered; Id. 356. Peru Coal Co. chartered; same powers as foregoing; 2 Pr. L. 1867 (23 Feb.) 416. Union Gas Light and Coke Co. chartered; 1 Pr. L. 1867 (6 Mar.) 978. LaSalle and Peru Horse Railway Co. chartered; 2 Pr. L. 1867 (6 Mar.) 29. Peru Sharpshooters Association chartered; 3 Pr. L. 1867 (7 Mar.) 95.

Mendota.—Town chartered; Pr. L. 1850 (19

Feb.) 647. Charter amended; 2 Pr. L. 1865 (16 Feb.) 512. City chartered; 1 Pr. L. 1867 (22 Feb.) 407. Mendota College chartered; Pr. L. 1857 (18 Feb.) 1398. German Benevolent Supporting Society chartered; 1 Pr. L. 1865 (16 Feb.) 71.

LAWRENCE COUNTY.

County formed out of Edwards and Crawford; L. 1821 (16 Jan.) 16. Deed by Jane Dubois and others, 15 Dec. 1821 to county commissioners legalized; Pr. L. 1827 (5 Feb.) 33. Application of Saline appropriation changed; L. 1839 (12 Feb.) 86. County put a stone pier under bridge at Lawrenceville; L. 1843 (3 Feb.) 44. Disposition of depreciated school money; Id. (3 Mar.) 153. Taxes for 1842 collected; L. 1845 (26 Feb.) 295. Acts of F. A. Thomas and Jack M. Morris circuit clerks legalized; L. 1849 (10 Feb.) 52. County orders issued; Id. 53. Vote on leveeing the Wabash; Id. (6 Feb.) 134. Money spent improving the navigation of the Wabash, building a jail or in public improvements; L. 1853 (12 Feb.) 183. Special tax to pay interest on railroad bonds; Id. (10 Feb.) 227. Swamp lands; Id. (12 Feb.) 150. Transcribing certain public records; Pr. L. 1857 (13 Feb.) 577. Removal of county seat, Lawrenceville to Bridgeport; L. 1861 (18 Feb.) 139. Record "A" of county commissioners copied; Id. (21 Feb.) 140. Election of circuit clerk; L. 1863 (17 Jan.) 55. Special tax to pay county indebtedness; 1 Pr. L. 1867 (25 Feb.) 888. Transcribing certain public records; Id. (22 Feb.) 900. Road, John McCawley's to Vincennes, relocated in part; L. 1825 (6 Jan.) 56. Allison Turnpike Co. chartered, Lawrenceville to Vincennes; Id. (13 Jan.) 88. Sheriff failing to pay over taxes, released from penalty; L. 1826 (19 Jan.) 58. Road, Vincennes to Danville, appropriates $600. for; same, Vincennes to Lawrenceville $500.; for bridge across Muddy creek $200.; L. 1829 (19 Jan.) 148 §12. Jacob Nabb, toll bridge across the Embarrass on Vincennes and St. Louis road; L. 1831 (16 Feb.) 28. Foregoing revived for 2 years; Pr. L. 1833 (26 Feb.) 12. John C. Reily, toll bridge across the Embarrass; Id. (28 Jan.) 5. G. W. Carrathers, security for McAlister indicted for polygamy, released; 1 L. 1837 (2 Mar.) 190. Road, Lawrenceville to Russellville, located; 2 L. 1837 (21 July) 71. Ferries across the Wabash at Vincennes may be forfeited; L. 1843 (1 Feb.) 143. Van Buren changed to Jackman's addition to St. Francisville; Id. (3 Mar.) 303. Survey of David Prince's addition to Russellville legalized; Pr. L. 1847 (26 Feb.) 211. Harrison Draw Bridge Co. chartered; across Wabash at Vincennes; Pr. L. 1853 (12 Feb.) 428. Bridgeport chartered; 2 Pr. L. 1865 (16 Feb.) 378. Board of directors for leveeing the Wabash and its tributaries on Allison Prairie chartered; 2 Pr. L. 1865 (16 Feb.) 10. Supplemental to foregoing; 2 Pr. L. 1867 (28 Feb.) 805. Charter amended, when work to begin; Id. (7 Mar.) 808. Indictment against John G. Long, nolle prosequi entered; L. 1861 (21 Feb.) 143.

Lawrenceville.—Town chartered; L. 1835 (12 Feb.) 214. Lawrenceville Manufacturing Co. chartered; Pr. L. 1837 (2 Mar.) 249. Bridge the Embarrass; L. 1840 (8 Jan.) 38. Lawrenceville Æsculapian Medical Society chartered; Pr. L. 1847 (17 Feb.) 94. Town boundaries altered; Pr. L. 1853 (12 Feb.) 580.

LEE COUNTY.

County formed, boundary and organization; L. 1839 (27 Feb.) 170. Rooms in court house leased; L. 1843 (20 Feb.) 127. County tax; Id. (2 Feb.) 201. Supervisors control swamp lands; sell or lease; L. 1853 (12 Feb.) 223. Proceeds of sale of swamp lands; Pr. L. 1857 (18 Feb.) 1346. Jurisdiction of county court extended; limit $1,500.; L. 1857 (18 Feb.) 128. Foregoing repealed; Id. 100. Loans in aid of volunteers legalized; L. 1863 (12 Feb.) 25. Towns pay bounties; 1 Pr. L. 1865 (14 Feb.) 132. Supervisors action paying bounties to volunteers legalized; Id. (15 Feb.) 132. Same subject; Id. (16 Feb.) 133. Swamp lands, fund to liquidate county indebtedness; 1 Pr. L. 1867 (28 Feb.) 889. Towns support their own paupers; 2 Pr. L. 1867 (21 Feb.) 481. County judge as justice, jurisdiction $600.; L. 1869 (4 Mar.) 150. Henry W. Cleaveland, toll bridge across the Winnebago swamp; L. 1839 (19 Feb.) 140. Supplemental to foregoing; L. 1843 (3 Feb.) 44. School directors district No. 4, Town 20—10, acts legalized; L. 1853 (11 Feb.) 187. Reuben Eastwood, restored to citizenship; Pr. L. 1853 (12 Feb.) 489. Oporto plat vacated; Id. (31 Jan.) 492. Lee Centre Cemetery Association chartered; Pr. L. 1855 (15 Feb.) 446. Shelburn Manufacturing Co. chartered; Id. (14 Feb.) 621. Hanna township changed to Sublette; Pr. L. 1857 (18 Feb.) 1208. Lee Centre Union Graded School and Union district No. 1, chartered; L. 1859 (21 Feb.) 168. Binghamton plat partly vacated; Pr. L. 1861 (18 Feb.) 557. Farmer's Mutual Fire Insurance Co. chartered at Plmyra; 1 Pr. L. 1865 (15 Feb.) 647. Franklin Grove chartered; 2 Pr. L. 1865 (13 Feb.) 450. Ogle station chartered; Id. (16 Feb.) 529; amendment; 3 Pr. L. 1867 (5 Mar.) 354.

Dixon.—Town chartered; P. L. 1853 (10 Feb.) 253; amendment, boundary defined; Pr. L. 1854 (28 Feb.) 138. City chartered; Pr. L. 1857 (14 Feb.) 656. And again; Pr. L. 1859 (19 Feb.) 135; amendment, election of officers; regulate sale of liquors; Pr. L. 1861 (22 Feb.) 197; further amends, powers extended; 1 Pr. L. 1865 (15 Feb.) 332. City Water commissioners chartered; Pr. L. 1857 (18 Feb.) 1191. Orders for a free bridge legalized; Pr. L. 1861 (22 Feb.) 199. City bridge Rock river; 1 Pr. L. 1867 (18 Feb.) 837. Dixon Hotel Co. chartered; Pr. L. 1837 (2 Mar.) 242. Lee Seminary of Learning chartered; Pr. L. 1839 (2 Mar.) 238. F. C. McKenny, toll bridge across Rock river; Pr. L. 1851 (15 Feb.) 230. Dixon Collegiate Institute chartered; Pr. L. 1857 (5 Feb.) 250. Star Insurance Co. chartered; 1 Pr. L. 1865 (16 Feb.) 778.

Amboy.—City chartered; Pr. L. 1857 (16 Feb.) 1080; amendment; grant licenses; 1 Pr. L. 1867 (1 Mar.) 622. Court of Common Pleas established; L. 1869 (11 Mar.) 120; amended by repealing §11; Id. 127. Amboy Academy chartered; Pr. L. 1855 (14 Feb.) 301.

LINCOLN COUNTY.

Provisions for creating the county, vote thereon; 1 Pr. L. 1867 (9 Mar.) 868.

LIVINGSTON COUNTY.

County formed, boundary and organization; 1 L. 1837 (27 Feb.) 83. Removal of county seat from Pontiac, vote thereon; L. 1839 (1 Mar.) 218. Sheep and swine not to run at large; L. 1853 (27 Jan.) 152. R. P. Breckenridge collector for 1846, time to redeem lands sold by the state extended; Pr. L. 1853 (12 Feb.) 513. Jurisdiction of county court extended; Pr. L. 1854 (27 Feb.) 239; same subject; Pr. L. 1855 (15 Feb.) 656. Change of venue from county court; L. 1857 (28 Jan.) 45. Sale of swamp lands; Id. (16 Feb.) 122. Additional tax to pay bounties; special tax to build jail; 1 Pr. L. 1865 (13 Feb.) 134. County take stock in Railroads; 2 Pr. L. 1867 (6 Mar.) 866. Daniel S. Ebersol, acts legalized; L. 1843 (3 Feb.) 170. Garret M. Blue, late sheriff, for conveying a convict; L. 1845 (1 Mar.) 122. Rock creek township, election of school trustees legalized; L. 1849 (10 Feb.) 183. Joseph Reynolds, bridge the Vermilion, Town 29—4; Pr. L. 1853 (12 Feb.) 531. Assessment for building school house district No. 2, Town 27—6, legalized; L. 1857 (29 Jan.) 207. Eureka Coal Co. chartered; lay out and sell town lots; Pr. L. 1857 (16 Feb.) 1046; amendment, include manufacture of coal oil, iron, etc., construct railroad, extend to LaSalle county; Pr. L. 1861 (22 Feb.) 302. Wm. M. Dustin, state refund $194.60 paid for lands Town 27—6, title thereto not being in the state; Id. 749. Empire Coal Co. chartered; 2 Pr. L. 1865 (16 Feb.) 59. Fairbury Union school district chartered; Id. 328. Town 28—5 and Pontiac, special tax for mining experiments; Id. 387. Dwight, special tax experimenting for coal; 3 Pr. L. 1867 (9 Mar.) 126. Chatsworth, corporate powers extended; Id. 206.

Pontiac.—Town chartered; Pr. L. 1857 (10 Feb.) 362; powers extended; 2 Pr. L. 1865 (14 Feb.) 550. Pontiac Coal Co. chartered; Pr. L. 1855 (15 Feb.) 590; 2 Pr. L. 1865 (16 Feb.) 83. Pontiac Woolen Manufacturing Co.; 2 Pr. L. 1867 (20 Feb.) 359. Pontiac Turn Verien chartered; 3 Pr. L. 1867 (28 Feb.) 645.

LOGAN COUNTY.

County formed, boundary and organization; L. 1839 (15 Feb.) 104. Supplemental to foregoing; Id. (28 Feb.) 205. Part of Tazewell attached to Logan; L. 1840 (27 Jan.) 29. County seat at Postville; L. 1841 (17 Feb.) 96. Postville changed to Camden; L. 1845 (3 Mar.) 179. Part of DeWitt added to Logan; Id. (26 Feb.) 189. Camden or Mt. Pulaski as county seat, vote thereon; Pr. L. 1847 (23 Feb.) 31. Removal of county seat from Mt. Pulaski to Sec. 31, Town 20—2, vote thereon; L. 1853 (14 Feb.) 153. Transcribing records of Sangamon, DeWitt, McLean and Tazewell counties; Pr. L. 1855 (12 Feb.) 723. Special tax to build jail and repair bridges; 3 Pr. L. 1867 (18 Feb.) 120. Acts of certain school directors legalized; L. 1847 (28 Feb.) 149. David G. Evans, family and neighborhood cemetery, 2 acres exempt from taxation; Pr. L. 1867 (18 Feb.) 1189. County Agricultural Society chartered; Id. (19 Feb.) 1378. G. Musick, late sheriff, discharged from liability by reason of loss by fire; L. 1859 (21 Feb.) 146. Elk Hart city chartered; Pr. L. 1861 (22 Feb.) 618. Thos. J. Larrison, late collector, securities conditionally released; 2 Pr. L. 1865 (13 Feb.) 242. County road through Elk Hart city partly vacated; Id. (16 Feb.) 257. Thos. Davis, restored to citizenship; L. 1869 (30 Mar.) 117.

Lincoln.—Town chartered; Pr. L. 1857 (18 Feb.) 1216; amendment, punish riots, routs, etc., offenders work the streets; Pr. L. 1861 (18 Feb.) 677. City chartered; 1 Pr. L. 1867 (21 Feb.) 302; supplemental; Id. (9 Mar.) 835. Camden changed to Postville, latter chartered; Pr. L. 1861 (21 Feb.) 569. Postville changed to Lincoln; city of Lincoln chartered; 1 Pr. L. 1865 (16 Feb.) 430. School district established; L. 1859 (24 Feb.) 172; amendment, limits curtailed; Pr. L. 1863 (21 Feb.) 258. System of Graded Schools established; 2 Pr. L. 1865 (16 Feb.) 280. Lincoln University chartered; 1 Pr. L. 1865 (6 Feb.) 44. Gas Light and Coke Co. chartered; Id. (16 Feb.) 285. Lincoln Mutual Insurance Co. chartered; Id. (15 Feb.) 706. Lincoln Coal, Wood and Lumber Co. chartered; 2 Pr. L. 1865 (16 Feb.) 76. Lincoln Horse Railway and Carrying Co. chartered; Id. (19 Feb.) 9.

Atlanta.—Name of Xenia changed to Atlanta; Pr. L. 1855 (14 Feb.) 194. Town chartered; Id. 163; amendment, boundary correctly defined; officers acts legalized; Pr. L. 1857 (7 Feb.) 271; further amends, build a jail; 2 Pr. L. 1865 (16 Feb.) 360. Atlanta Seminary chartered; Pr. L. 1855 (14 Feb.) 353. Atlanta Union Central Agricultural Society chartered; Pr. L. 1861 (15 Feb.) 30. Amends act 21 Feb. 1861, aiding and encouraging agricultural societies, provisions extended to said society (chartered in foregoing); L. 1869 (10 Mar.) 9. Farmer's Warehouse Association chartered; 2 Pr. L. 1865 (16 Feb.) 665. Union Hall Association chartered; 2 Pr. L. 1867 (25 Feb.) 86.

Mt. Pulaski.—Town corporate powers amended and extended; Pr. L. 1854 (4 Mar.) 146. Town to have the old court house for school purposes; Pr. L. 1857 (16 Feb.) 1071. Vacates an alley; 3 Pr. L. 1867 (21 Feb.) 110. Levy special tax; Id. (28 Feb.) 121.

LOTTERIES.

To raise not exceeding $10,000. for opening Grand Rapids in the Big Wabash near Palmyra; Joseph Kitchell and five others managers; L. 1819 (25 Mar.) 257. To raise not exceeding $50,000. to drain the American Bottom ponds; Hugh H. Maxwell and six others managers; Id. 27 Mar.) 310; amendment; L. 1839 (6 Feb.) 56.

MACALISTER AND STEBBINS BONDS.

Settlement authorized; L. 1843 (4 Mar.) 287; interest thereon not to be paid; R. S. 1845 (1

Mar.) 600; not to be received in payment for Northern Cross Railroad; L. 1847 (16 Feb.) 109; nor for Gallatin Salines; Id. (25 Feb.) 68; surrender the Kennedy bonds and scrip before settlement; Pr. L. 1847 (25 Feb.) 148; not to be funded with other indebtedness; L. 1847 (28 Feb.) 161; supplemental act, their history recited in preamble, new bonds issued; Id. (1 Mar.) 163; to prevent loss to the state upon said bonds; L. 1849 (10 Feb.) 43 foregoing amended; L. 1851 (6 Feb.) 22; must be surrendered by 1 Jan. 1865 and 1866; L. 1865 (16 Feb.) 89.

MACON COUNTY.

County formed, boundary defined; L. 1829 (19 Jan.) 28. Strip between Logan and Dane (Christian) attached to Macon; L. 1839 (2 Mar.) 265., Wm. Warnick, late collector, to collect taxes for 1840; L. 1843 (4 Mar.). 227. School funds transferred from Sangamon; L. 1845 (1 Mar.) 223. Copies of certain records legalized; L. 1859 (4 Feb.) 136. Official circuit court reporter; L. 1869 (31 Mar.) 350. Road, Decatur to Paris, re-located in part between Decatur and Wm. Martin's; Pr. L. 1833 (22 Feb.) 149. Lands of the estate of Christopher Whitman sold; L. 1836 (8 Dec. '35) 253. The same, estate of Mason Payne; also, estate of Michael Dillon; 1 L. 1837 (20 Feb.) 184. S. A. Smallwood purchase lands Town 19—3 at valuation; 2 L. 1837 (21 July) 56. Relief of John McMennaway; L. 1839 (2 Mar.) 286. Northwestern Agricultural Manufacturing Co. chartered; Pr. L. 1861 (16 Feb.) 470. Wm. Wheeler, sheriff in 1858–9 now file delinquent list; Id. (22 Feb.) 539. Mt. Zion male and Female Seminary chartered; 1 Pr. L. 1865 (16 Feb.) 25. Macon Agricultural Society chartered; Id. (15 Feb.) 53; amendement, powers extended; 1 Pr. L. 1867 (21 Feb.) 43. Geo. M. Filson, Emanuel Dyre, and Henry Hinds, convicted of manslaughter, restored; 2 Pr. L. 1867 (7 Mar.) 814. Plank or gravel road, Decatur to Marva, chartered; Id. (9 Mar.) 831. Marva chartered; 3 Pr. L. 1867 (7 Mar.) 247. John L. Foren restored to citizenship; L. 1869 (10 Mar.) 118. M. Phalon discharged from bail bond of James Meade; Id. (31 Mar.) 344. Resolution for relief of Jacob Shy, disabled soldier; Id. 423.

Decatur.—Town chartered; Pr. L. 1839 (2 Mar.) 243, powers extended; Pr. L. 1854 (4 Mar.) 185. Town trustees' acts legalized; Pr. L. 1855 (15 Feb.) 44. City chartered; Pr. L. 1855 (15 Feb.) 108. Re-chartered; foregoing repealed; Pr. L. 1857 (26 Jan.) 28; amendment, limits defined; Pr. L. 1861 (20 Feb.) 189; further amends; 1 Pr. L. 1865 (16 Feb.) 332. New city charter; 1 Pr. L. 1867 (21 Feb.) 419. Divided into election districts; 1 Pr. L. 1867 (6 Mar.) 921. Cemetery Association chartered; L. 1845 (3 Mar.) 265. Macon House Co. chartered; Pr. L. 1853 (12 Feb.) 458. Decatur Marine and Fire Insurance Co. chartered; Pr. L. 1855 (15 Feb.) 411. Decatur Gas Light and Coke Co. chartered; Pr. L. 1857 (18 Feb.) 1356; amendment; borrow money and issue bonds; Pr. L. 1861 (20 Feb.) 332; charter repealed; 1 Pr. L. 1865 (16 Feb.) 581; again chartered; Id. 581; foregoing amended; time to complete work extended; 1 Pr. L. 1867 (7 Mar.) 970. Decatur Seminary chartered; Pr. L. 1861 (22 Feb.) 13. Illinois Central Insurance Co.'s office located at; Id. (21 Feb.) 389; amendment, move office to Chicago; 2 Pr. L. 1867 (8 Mar.) 213. Masonic Hatl Stock Co. chartered; Pr. L. 1861 (18 Feb.) 473. Great Western Horse Insurance Co. chartered; 1 Pr. L. 1865 (16 Feb.) 663; amendment, powers extended; 2 Pr. L. 1867 (28 Feb.) 182. National Accident and Life Insurance Co. chartered; 1 Pr. L. 1865 (16 Feb.) 722; amendment, name changed to National Life, office moved to Chicago; 2 Pr. L. 1867 (21 Feb.) 152; another amendment, name changed to Lorillard Insurance Co.; Id. (1 Mar.) 185. School district created; 2 Pr. L. 1865 (16 Feb.) 314; amendment; 3 Pr. L. 1867 (23 Feb.) 64. Decatur Horse Railway and Carrying Co. chartered; 2 Pr. L. 1867 (9 Mar.) 33. Union Insurance Co. chartered; Id. (21 Feb.) 150.

MACOUPIN COUNTY.

County formed, boundary defined; L. 1829 (17 Jan.) 26. Share in proceeds of Saline lands; L. 1835 (13 Feb.) 155. Lagalizes records; L. 1849 (20 Jan.) 107. Assessment and sale of real estate for taxes of 1851 legalized; L. 1853 (12 Feb.) 218. Borrow $8,000. to construct a jail; Pr. L. 1854 (22 Feb.) 81. Special tax to erect fire proof offices; Pr. L. 1857 (13 Feb.) 550. Indexing and transcribing records; Pr. L. 1863 (21 Feb.) 214. Issue bonds to pay bounties; 1 Pr. L 1865 (6 Feb.) 134; amendment; apply to enlistments prior to act; 1 Pr. L. 1867 (23 Feb.) 888. Special game law; L. 1867 (19 Feb.) 120; Gross' Stat. 1868, 327. Building new court house; 1 Pr. L. 1867 (18 Feb.) 878. School tax limited to $1.50 per $100.; L. 1869 (29 Mar.) 394. Thos. Rattan, mill dam on Macoupin creek Town 9—11; L. 1835 (14 Jan.) 45. Lands of estate of Ezekiel Good sold in lots; 1 L. 1837 (10 Feb.) 180. Road out of Carlinville; Id. (7 Feb.) 258. Central Seminary of Illinois chartered; Pr. L. 1839 (15 Feb.) 71. Expenses of apprehending Aaron and Wm. Todd charged with murder of Larkin Scott; L. 1841 (17 Feb.) 207. Newburgh changed to Cummington; L. 1845 (7 Feb.) 216. Woodburn plat partly vacated; Pr. L. 1847 (26 Feb.) 207. Wm. R. Bishop, state pedlar's license for life; Pr. L. 1849 (9 Feb.) 56; also, Pr. L. 1851 (12 Feb.) 85. Wm. Welch released from recognizance in People *vs.* Geo. W. Scott; L. 1849 (10 Feb.) 118. Thomas Carr, security for James H Hall, released, Pr. L. 1851 (11 Feb.) 79. Farmers' College chartered; Id. (15 Feb.) 181. Blackburn Theological Seminary chartered; Pr. L. 1857 (13 Feb.) 584. New Hartford plat vacated; Id. (18 Feb.) 1244. Scottville chartered; Id. 1255. Carlinville and Chesterfield Coal Mining Railroad chartered; Id. 1321. Plat of Gillespie and Huggins addition thereto legalized; Pr. L. 1859 (12 Feb.) 616. Staunton chartered; Id. (23 Feb.) 680. J. G. Jarvis and four others, sureties for W. G. Jarvis, discharged; L. 1867 (6 Mar.) 154. Lyman L. Palmer, minor, sell lands; 2 Pr. L. 1867 (5 Mar.) 442. Edward F. Rice, the same; Id. (28 Feb.) 442. Andrew J. Henderson, minor, declared of full age; Id. (26 Feb.) 442. Macoupin Printing Co. chartered; Id. (5 Mar.) 517.

Shipman chartered; 3 Pr. L. 1867 (6 Mar.) 266. Nilwood chartered; Id. (9 Mar.) 448. O. W. and E. A. Engleman name changed to Bull; L. 1869 (11 Mar.) 264.

Carlinville.—Town chartered; Pr. L. 1837 (4 Mar.) 335; amendment; 2 L. 1837 (21 July) 101. Again chartered; Pr. L. 1853 (9 Feb.) 135; amendment, additional powers conferred; Pr. L. 1855 (15 Feb.) 226; further amends; sale of liquor; Pr. L. 1859 (19 Feb.) 591; and again, powers extended; Pr. L. 1863 (13 June) 274. City chartered; 2 Pr. L. 1865 (16 Feb.) 402; also, 1 Pr. L. 1867 (22 Feb.) 479. Cemetery Association chartered; Pr. L. 1853 (11 Feb.) 455; amendment, condemn lands; Pr. L. 1859 (24 Feb.) 28. Macoupin County Mutual Insurance Co. chartered; 1 Pr. L. 1865 (14 Feb.) 710. Anderson Female Seminary chartered; 1 Pr. L. 1867 (18 Feb.) 4. Henderson Loan and Real Estate Association; Id. (28 Feb.) 57. Catholic Aid Society chartered; Id. (23 Feb.) 126. Carlinville Horse Railway and Carrying Co. chartered; 2 Pr. L. 1867 (16 Feb.) 8. Carlinville Hotel Co. chartered; Id. 43.

Virden.—Town chartered; Pr. L. 1861 (22 Feb.) 733; and again; 2 Pr. L. 1865 (16 Feb.) 600; amendment; 3 Pr. L. 1867 (21 Feb.) 514.

Girard.—Town chartered; Pr. L. 1855 (14 Feb.) 194; amendment, town constitute school district No. 3; Pr. L. 1865 (16 Feb.) 459; further amends; powers extended; 3 Pr. L. 1867 (22 Feb.) 135, 467.

Brighton.—Town chartered; Pr. L. 1859 (23 Feb.) 586; and again; 3 Pr. L. 1867 (22 Feb.) 503. Trustees Methodist Church sell and convey real estate; Pr. L. 1855 (14 Feb.) 707.

Bunker Hill.—Town chartered; Pr. L. 1857 (17 Feb.) 1147; amendment, license insurance and express companies; 3 Pr. L. 1867 (22 Feb.) 608. Merchants' and Farmers' Savings Loan and Trust Co. chartered; Pr. L. 1857 (19 Feb.) 1386.

MADISON COUNTY.

County formed prior to the organization of the state. Conveyances recorded in Bond as valid as if recorded in Madison; L. 1821 (13 Jan.) 14. Part of Green attached to Madison; L. 1825 (3 Jan.) 53. Foregoing explained, not to affect Montgomery; L. 1826 (19 Jan.) 54. Circuit court appoint trustees to execute deed of trust made by John Todd and others; Id. (14 Jan.) 102. Share in proceeds of Gallatin Salines; L. 1831 (16 Feb.) 14. Fill vacancy by death of J. B. C. Canal; Id. (1 Jan.) 74. Election precincts increased; L. 1835 (31 Jan.) 58. Additional county surveyor; 1 L. 1837 (15 Feb.) 116. Re-location of county roads; 2 L. 1837 (22 July) 86. Pay for Milton bridge; L. 1839 (2 Mar.) 265. Certain public records rebound; L. 1829 (19 Feb.) 130. Any county copy Madison county records; L. 1841 (27 Feb.) 205. Collection of taxes for 1843 extended; L. 1845 (24 Jan.) 183. Certain taxes for 1844 remitted because of high water; Id. (21 Feb.) 353. Assessments for 1845-6-7 legalized; L. 1849 (5 Feb.) 187. Special tax to pay debts and build roads and bridges; Id. (10 Jan.) 187. State tax in certain towns to pay for levee on American bottom; L. 1861 (12 Feb.) 14. County bounties to volunteers; 1 Pr. L. 1865 (16 Feb.) 135. Pay of county judge and his associates; L. 1867 (8 Mar.) 78. Construct county jail; 1 Pr. L. 1867 (22 Feb.) 883. Evidence of marriages, its better preservation; Id. (7 Mar.) 926. Part of county take stock in certain railroads; 2 Pr. L. 1867 (8 Feb.) 681. Transcribing public records; Id. (28 Feb.) 790. Additional county tax; 2 Pr. L. 1867 (22 Feb.) 129. Jurisdiction over lands in Town 5—10 ceded to United States for a National Cemetery; L. 1869 (31 Mar.) 249. Road 100 feet wide from town of Illinois to Six Mile prairie; L. 1819 (27 Mar.) 297. Madison Steam Mill Co. chartered; L. 1821 (31 Jan.) 58. Nathaniel Buckmaster paid dieting prisoners, etc.; L. 1825 (15 Jan.) 108. Guardian of Olive Livermore's heirs sell real estate; Pr. L. 1833 (19 Feb.) 117. School trustees Town 3—7 re-value unsold lands; Id. (12 Feb.) 200. Guardian of heirs of James Mason sell real estate; L. 1835 (26 Jan.) 74. Illinois Exporting Co. chartered; L. 1836 (18 Jan.) 141. Lands of estate of Saml. Thurston sold; Id. (8 Dec. '35) 245. Road, Springfield to Alton, re-located between Foster's and Wood river bridge; 1 L. 1837 (15 Feb.) 215. Lands of estate of Wm. B. Collins sold; 2 L. 1837 (11 July) 57. Madison Mining and Manufacturing Co. chartered; pay county 2½ per cent. on employed capital; Pr. L. 1837 (1 Mar.) 202. Calhoun Coal Mining Co. chartered; Id. (2 Mar.) 238. Chippewa Dry Dock Co. chartered; Id. 251. Sales school land Town 6—8 legalized; L. 1839 (22 Feb.) 148. Madison County Ferry Co. chartered; L. 1840 (3 Feb.) 127; amendment, build road to ferry; L. 1841 (17 Feb.) 224; further amends, extended 20 years; Pr. L. 1847 (11 Feb.) 45; existence legally recognized (rendered desirable by loss of office and papers by flood of 1851); Pr. L. 1854 (25 Feb.) 101; charter further amended; 1 Pr. L. 1867 (20 Feb.) 932. John Cooper, collector, settle with state bank notes; L. 1845 (1 Mar.) 155. Wm. H. Berksdale and others, ferry across the Mississippi, Venice to St. Louis; Pr. L. 1849 (31 Jan.) 33. Mt. Auburn plat vacated; Id. (12 Feb.) 141. Certain state lands released to Matilda Powers; L. 1843 (2 Mar.) 221. Monticello Female Seminary chartered; Id. (23 Feb.) 282; amendment, regulate sale of liquor near; 3 Pr. L. 1867 (12 Feb.) 5. Wood River Coal Mining Co. chartered; Pr. L. 1851 (17 Feb.) 286; amendment; build railroad; Pr. L. 1854 (1 Mar.) 128. Andrew Miller, $50. for preventing violation of an injunction; Pr. L. 1851 (17 Feb.) 292. Joseph T. Gately name changed to Totten; Pr. L. 1853 (26 Jan.) 463. Collinsville plank road allowed 5 years to complete; Pr. L. 1855 (15 Feb.) 467. Madison County Coal Co. chartered; Pr. L. 1857 (13 Feb.) 506; amendment, extend railway; 2 Pr. L. 1865 (15 Feb.) 77. Madison county railroad chartered; Pr. L. 1857 (14 Feb.) 638; and again, 2 Pr. L. 1865 (15 Feb.) 165. Towns 3—9 and 3—10 unite for school purposes; Pr. L. 1857 (16 Feb.) 1136. Foregoing amended; 2 P. L. 1867 (7 Mar.) 797. Town of Troy chartered; Pr. L. 1857 (18 Feb.) 1334; part of Clay street vacated; Id. 1426. Sale of American Bottom Plank road to Frederick P. Kraft confirmed; Id. 1358; stock increased, may macadamize, Pr. L. 1859 (24 Feb.) 416. Trustees of Christian Society sell real estate at

Madison County.

Ridgely and build church at Litchfield; Id. 34. Highland and St. Louis Railroad chartered; Id. (12 Feb.) 443; charter amended; Pr. L. 1861 (21 Feb.) 496; further amendment, time extended; 2 Pr. L. 1865 (15 Feb.) 161. Acts of trustees Towns 4—7 and 5—7 legalized; L. 1861 (20 Feb.) 194. Thos. Judy, guardian heirs of Jacob J. Barnsback, invest in real estate; 2 Pr. L. 1865 (16 Feb.) 239. Towns 5 and 6—10 tax to Macadamize roads; Id. 258. State road, Town 5—8 re-located; Id. 265. Farmers' Exchange and Loan Co. chartered; 1 Pr. L. 1867 (9 Mar.) 115. Tyler J. Irish and others, ferry across the Mississippi near Venice; Id. (25 Feb.) 939. Julia Ann Avery, wife of Edward D. Avery, convey real estate; 2 Pr. L. 1867 (7 Mar.) 795. Collection of tolls on Collinsville and St. Louis plank road; Id. 799; time to repair said road extended; Id. (21 Feb.) 803. Alton and Edwardsville Macadamized road chartered; Id. (8 Mar.) 836. Illinois and Mississippi Stock Yard Co. chartered; 3 Pr. L. 1867 (28 Feb.) 97. Trumbull's sub-division of sec. 2, Town 5—10 vacated partly; Id. (23 Feb.) 110. Towns 5 and 6—10, outside Alton, levy special road tax; Id. (6 Mar.) 123. Marine chartered; Id. (8 Mar.) 479.

Edwardsville.—Chartering trustees of Madison Academy; town boundary defined; town trustees elected at general election; L. 1819 (23 Feb.) 48; so much of foregoing repealed as describes town boundaries; Id. (24 Mar.) 246; repeals part of first foregoing and all of amendment and amends; L. 1823 (7 Feb.) 116. Town chartered; Pr. L. 1853 (10 Feb.) 257; amended: acts of trustees legalized; Pr. L. 1854 (27 Feb.) 151; corporate powers extended; 2 Pr. L. 1865 (16 Feb.) 438; limits altered; 3 Pr. L. 1867 (22 Feb.) 515. Town take stock in Madison county railroad; Pr. L. 1859 (23 Feb.) 601; election 13 Oct. '66 authorizing said subscription legalized; 1 Pr. L. 1867 (22 Feb.) 918. Building sidewalks and street improvement; 3 Pr. L. 1867 (28 Feb.) 585. Edwardsville Library Association chartered; L. 1823 (31 Jan.) 100. Examination of Bank of Edwardsville; L 1826 (26 Jan.) 81. Edwardsville Steam Mill Co. chartered; Pr. L. 1839 (12 Feb.) 69. Illinois and Mississippi Transportation Co. chartered; 2 Pr. L. 1865 (15 Feb.) 674; amended, condemn lands in East St. Louis; 3 Pr. L. 1867 (28 Feb.) 639. Madison County Land and Loan Co. chartered; 1 Pr. L. 1867 (8 Mar.) 99. Edwardsville Hotel Co. chartered; 2 Pr. L. 1867 (5 Mar.) 63.

Alton.—Town trustees appointed; L. 1821 (30 Jan.) 39; town charter amended; L. 1823 (14 Feb.) 147. Town again chartered; Pr. L. 1833 (6 Feb.) 206; amendment; L. 1835 (13 Feb.) 172; further amended; trustees' acts legalized; Pr. L. 1837 (2 Mar.) 224. Additional notary and two justices; 1 L. 1837 (15 Feb.) 116. City chartered; 2 L. 1837 (21 July) 17 §§1—39; and again, Pr. L. 1839 (2 Mar.) 240; amendment; charter amended; L. 1845 (28 Feb.) 101; further amends, take census every five years; people accept or reject; Pr. L. 1847 (13 Feb.) 76; further amends; Id. (23 Feb.) 114; further amends; subscribe to Mt. Carmel and Alton Railroad; Pr. L. 1849 (8 Feb.) 15; boundary defined; Id. 16; issue bonds for improvement of river landing; Pr. L. 1851 (17 Feb.) 262; fines under liquor law of 1 Feb. '51 paid into city treasury; L. 1853 (12 Feb.) 219; re-enacts act 1 Feb. 1851 prohibiting retailing of liquor; Pr. L. 1853 (12 Feb.) 571; issue bonds to build city hall; Pr. L. 1854 (28 Feb.) 209; boundary extended and defined; Pr. L. 1855 (15 Feb.) 43; city re-issue bonds matured and held by St. Louis, Alton and Chicago, and Terre Haute and Alton railroads; Pr. L. 1857 (16 Feb.) 921; amends §13 of orginal city charter; Pr. L. 1859 (18 Jan.) 36. The several city incorporating acts reduced to one and amended; Id. (16 Feb.) 36; general amendment to charter; Pr. L. 1861 (18 Feb.) 100; levy tax to liquidate city indebtedness; 1 Pr. L. 1865 (16 Feb.) 242; foregoing repealed; 1 Pr. L. 1867 (28 Feb.) 625; establish and regulate markets, recovery of fines; 1 Pr. L. 1865 (16 Feb.) 244; §12 of charter amended respecting public schools; Id. (13 Feb.) 244; street commissioner's duty, corporate powers extended; 1 Pr. L. 1867 (25 Feb.) 577. City pay part of county election and court expenses; Pr. L. 1847 (27 Feb.) 38; amendment; L. 1851 (17 Feb.) 194. City court established, jurisdiction defined; L. 1859 (9 Feb.) 71; terms thereof; L. 1861 (21 Feb.) 117; times of holding; L. 1867 (8 Mar.) 77, and L. 1869 (10 Feb.) 119; salary of attorney $500.; Id. (1 Apr.) 50. Two justices and constables elected; L. 1835 (12 Feb.) 30. Partition of lands owned by Nathaniel Pope and others; 2 L. 1837 (21 July) 53; amendment; L. 1839 (18 Jan.) 37. Manning and Higham's addition vacated in part; Id. (20 July) 93. Alton Manufacturing Co. chartered; Pr. L. 1833 (1 Feb.) 48. Alton College of Illinois chartered; Id. (1 Mar.) 100; name changed to Shurtleff College; L. 1836 (12 Jan.) 181; trustees increased; Pr. L. 1851 (14 Feb.) 126, 250; vacancies in board of trustees filled by residents in other states; Pr. L. 1853 (11 Feb.) 500; sale of liquor within one mile of college buildings prohibited; Pr. L. 1861 (20 Feb.) 13. Alpha Zeta Society of said college chartered; 2 Pr. L. 1867 (20 Feb.) 263. Alton Marine and Fire Insurance Co. chartered; L. 1835 (7 Feb.) 186; amendment, investing capital stock; Pr. L. 1837 (27 Feb.) 109; powers extended, risks on lives, receive deposits, stock increased; Pr. L. 1839 (4 Mar.) 95; also, L. 1845 (20 Feb.) 328. Two justices and constables elected; L. 1835 (12 Feb.) 30. Alton Hotel Co. chartered; Id. 208; amendment; Pr. L. 1837 (4 Mar.) 286. Alton Shot and Lead Manufacturing Co. chartered; L. 1836 (16 Jan.) 143. Alton Female Institute chartered; Id. (9 Jan.) 178. Beet Sugar, Silk and Vegetable Oil Manufacturing Co. chartered; Pr. L. 1837 (27 Feb.) 150; amendment; L. 1840 (29 Jan.) 48. Alton Ferry Co. chartered; 2 L. 1837 (21 July) 40. Illinois Mutual Fire Insurance Co. chartered; report to Legislature; Pr. L. 1839 (23 Feb.) 108; amendment; L. 1843 (4 Mar.) 166; president administer oaths; Pr. L. 1847 (13 Feb.) 76; extended 20 years; Pr. L. 1855 (13 Feb.) 387; foregoing amendment amended; Pr. L. 1861 (20 Feb.) 395; charter extended 50 years; Pr. L. 1863 (13 Feb.) 202; amendment; 2 Pr. L. 1867 (7 Mar.) 197. Illinois and Missouri Bridge Co. chartered; L. 1841 (27 Feb.) 46. Ferry across the Mississippi established; L. 1841 (27 Feb.) 119; amendment, time extended 5 years; Pr. L. 1847 (27 Feb.) 48. Hardy & McElroy, ferry across the Mississippi; L. 1845 (27 Feb.) 164. Western Marine and Fire Insurance Co. chartered; L. 1841 (27 Feb.) 160.

Mechanics' Institute chartered; Pr. L. 1847 (25 Feb.) 121. Alton Cemetery chartered; Id. (1 Mar.) 122. Jurisdiction over cemetery for soldiers ceded to U. S.; L. 1867 (5 Mar.) 176. Cotton Manufacturing Co. chartered; L. 1845 (28 Feb.) 144. State taxes for 1839 on lots in Pope's addition remitted; Pr. L. 1847 (28 Feb.) 200. Franklin Marine and Fire Insurance Co. chartered; Pr. L. 1851 (17 Feb.) 281; name changed to Alton Savings Institution and Insurance Co.; Pr. L. 1859 (24 Feb.) 385. City Mutual Insurance Co. chartered; Pr. L. 1853 (12 Feb.) 362; name changed to Alton Mutual Insurance and Savings Co.; Pr. L. 1859 (19 Feb.) 384. Alton Gas Light and Coke Co. chartered; Pr. L. 1855 (14 Feb.) 644. Alton Hibernian Benevolent Society chartered; Pr. L. 1853 (10 Feb.) 518. Mississippi Bridge Co. chartered; Id. (12 Feb.) 577. Jacob Paul, ferry across the Mississippi; Pr. L. 1857 (16 Feb.) 924. Alton Water Works Co. chartered; city may purchase; Id. (18 Feb.) 1351. Alton Building and Savings Institution chartered; Pr. L. 1859 (24 Feb.) 24. Alton and St. Louis Packet Co. chartered; Id. (18 Feb.) 413. Alton Bank to resume business; Pr. L. 1861 (22 Feb.) 38. John Snowden and others, ferry across the Mississippi; Id. (20 Feb.) 318. Engine Co. No. 1 chartered; Id. (21 Feb.) 320. St. Joseph's Hospital chartered; 1 Pr. L. 1865 (16 Feb.) 94. Masonic Temple Association chartered; Id. (10 Feb.) 205. John and Thos. Lock, ferry across the Mississippi; Id. (13 Feb.) 566. Russell Manufacturing Co. chartered; 2 Pr. L. 1865 (16 Feb.) 46. Alton Horticultural Society chartered; 1 Pr. L. 1867 (18 Feb.) 42; 2 Pr. L. 1867, 36. Alton and St. Charles County Bridge Co. chartered; Id. (6 Mar.) 180. Alton Roman Catholic Ursuline Convent of the Holy Family chartered; Id. (9 Mar.) 250. Robert C. Berry, ferry across the Mississippi; Id. (28 Feb.) 946. Alton and Upper Alton Horse Railway and Carrying Co. chartered; 2 Pr. L. 1867 (20 Feb.) 10. Mutual Life Insurance Co. of the state chartered; Id. (7 Mar.) 107. Southern Horse Insurance Co. chartered; Id. (1 Mar.) 183. Alton Sharpshooter's Society chartered; 3 Pr. L. 1867 (22 Feb.) 93.

Upper Alton.—Town chartered; Pr. L. 1837 (18 Feb.) 57; foregoing repealed; L. 1839 (2 Mar.) 245. Again chartered; 3 Pr. L. 1865 (16 Feb.) 590; foregoing revived; 3 Pr. L. 1867 (5 Mar.) 620. Additional notary and two justices; L. 1837 (15 Feb.) 116. Salu attached to Upper Alton; L. 1836 (16 Jan.) 259. Plat of Salu addition changed; L. 1841 (17 Feb.) 309; further time under foregoing; L. 1843 (24 Feb.) 295. Vacates a certain street; 3 Pr. L. 1867 (19 Feb.) 106. Alton College chartered; L. 1835 (9 Feb.) 177. Upper Alton Manufacturing Co. chartered; Pr. L. 1839 (15 Feb.) 47. Alton Cemetery chartered; L. 1845 (28 Feb.) 118. Illinois Literary and Historical Society chartered; L. 1847 (11 Feb.) 51. Illinois Astronomical Society chartered, erect an Observatory; Pr. L. 1861 (22 Feb.) 546.

Highland.—Town chartered; Pr. L. 1863 (14 Feb.) 266; 2 Pr. L. 1865 (16 Feb.) 474. Governor re-convey certain town lots to Joseph Suppiger; Pr. L. 1847 (23 Feb.) 181. Helvetia Sharpshooters' Society chartered Pr. L. 1863 (16 Feb.) 191. Workman's Mutual Aid Society chartered; 1 Pr. L. 1867 (23 Feb.) 128. Highland Gymnastic Society chartered; 2 Pr. L. 1867 (13 Feb.) 202.

Collinsville.—Town chartered; Pr. L. 1855 (15 Feb.) 50; Pr. L. 1859 (24 Feb.) 591; charter amended; 3 Pr. L. 1867 (23 Feb.) 452. Cemetery Association chartered; 1 Pr. L. 1867 (28 Feb.) 211.

MAINE LIQUOR LAW.

Submitted to vote of the people; L. 1855 (12 Feb.) 3.

MARION COUNTY.

County formed and boundary established; L. 1823 (24 Jan.) 49. Share in proceeds of Gallatin Salines; L. 1831 (16 Feb.) 15 §1. Application of said Saline appropriation; L. 1835 (12 Feb.) 116; L. 1839 (2 Mar.) 278. County take stock in Marion and Jefferson county Railroad; Pr. L. 1851 (15 Feb.) 228. Issue $25,000. bonds to build court house; Pr. L. 1857 (14 Feb.) 623. Certain records copied; L. 1861 (20 Feb.) 106. Jurisdiction of county court extended; L. 1867 (9 Mar.) 73; foregoing repealed; L. 1869 (12 Mar.) 148. Road, Vandalia to Golconda, relocated *via* Salem; L. 1835 (12 Feb.) 116. Sam'l Witter, toll bridge across Skillet Fork on Fairfield and Salem road; L. 1836 (11 Jan.) 199. Auditor convey lands Town 2—1 to J. S. Martin and B. F. Marshall; L. 1855 (14 Feb.) 110. Marion County Fair Ground Association chartered; Pr. L. 1855 (15 Feb.) 618. Rantoul changed to Alma; Id. (6 Feb.) 602. Gainesville known as Halstlaw's addition to Central City; Pr. L. 1857 (10 Feb.) 338. Town Central City chartered; Id. (14 Feb.) 798. School lands Town 4—3 sold; L. 1859 (23 Feb.) 187. Sandoval chartered; Pr. L. 1859 (18 Feb.) 673. E. B. Green and 27 others discharged from liability as surities of H. Stanton; L. 1867 (6 Mar.) 153. Etta Belle Holt name changed to Turney; 1 Pr. L. 1867 (9 Mar.) 239. City of Kinmundy chartered; Id. (25 Feb.) 567. School directors district No. 1, Town 2—2 purchase real estate; 3 Pr. L. 1867 (25 Feb.) 79. Middleton changed to Iuka and latter chartered; Id. (9 Feb.) 524. Securites of James R. Waite discharged; L. 1869 (24 Mar.) 345.

Salem.—Town chartered; L. 1837 (10 Feb.) 331; Pr. L. 1855 (14 Feb.) 49. City chartered; 1 Pr. L. 1865 (16 Feb.) 507; amended; survey and plat of original town by Richard Atkins legalized; 1 Pr. L. 1867 (6 Mar.) 744. Salem Female Academy chartered; L. 1841 (26 Jan.) 3. Steam Mill Co. chartered; Id. (20 Feb.) 127. Southern Illinois Female College chartered; Pr. L. 1855 (14 Feb.) 517; amended, who to vote at elections; Pr. L. 1857 (18 Feb.) 1254; foregoing repealed; Pr. L. 1859 (19 Feb.) 377. Southern Illinois College chartered; 1 Pr. L. 1867 (7 Mar.) 29. Marion County Trust and Loan Co. chartered; Id. (8 Mar.) 117; 2 Pr. L. 1867 277.

Centralia.—City chartered; Pr. L. 1859 (18 Feb.) 114; amended, particularly §§1, 3, 4 and 12; 1 Pr. L. 1865 (16 Feb.) 256. Additional Police magistrate; L. 1861 (22 Feb.) 75. Literary

and Library Association chartered 2 Pr. L. 1867 (9 Mar.) 259.

Odin.—Town chartered; 2 Pr. L. 1865 (16 Feb.) 517; amendment; 3 Pr. L. 1867 (28 Feb.) 615.

Walnut Hill.—Resurvey of town legalized; Pr. L. 1849 (12 Feb.) 142. Part Smith's addition vacated; Pr. L. 1855 (14 Feb.) 691.

MARQUETTE COUNTY.

County created, boundary and organization; L. 1843 (11 Feb.) 77. Name changed to Highland; organized after favorable vote; L. 1847 (27 Feb.) 38.

MARSHALL COUNTY.

County formed, boundary and organization; L. 1839 (19 Jan.) 43. Vote on adding range 1 to said county; Id. (2 Mar.) 241. Part of La-Salle attached to Marshall; L. 1843 (1 Mar.) 93. Copy records from Putnam county, effect after certified and compared; L. 1845 (1 Mar.) 124. Tax to pay bonds issued to Western Air Line Railroad; Pr. L. 1861 (18 Feb.) 747. Issue bonds to pay bounties; Pr. L. 1865 (18 Jan.) 135. Probate records made by W. E. Cook and J. R. Chapman; L. 1869 (25 Mar.) 152. Plat of Bristol vacated; L. 1840 (3 Feb.) 108; also of Auburn; L. 1841 (27 Feb.) 315; also of Webster; Pr. L. 1847 (26 Feb.) 204. Benj. Lombard, ferry across the Illinois, Town 31—2; Pr. L. 1847 (1 Mar.) 50. North Illinois University chartered; Pr. L. 1855 (15 Feb.) 500; name changed to Marshall College; 1 Pr. L. 1867 (28 Feb.) 17. Wm. M. Davenport, ferry across the Illinois mouth Crow creek; Pr. L. 1855 (15 Feb.) 610. Sparland Mill and Coal Co. chartered; Pr. L. 1861 (22 Feb.) 305. Farmers Savings Association chartered; Id. 312. Wenona chartered; 3 Pr. L. 1867 (28 Feb.) 310. Sparland chartered; Id. (5 Mar.) 337.

Lacon—Town chartered; L. 1840 (10 Dec. '39) 123; limits defined; L. 1841 (27 Feb.) 315; further amends; Pr. L. 1849 (10 Feb.) 130; to purchase and fill up river front; Pr. L. 1853 (12 Feb.) 349; general amendment; Pr. L. 1855 (12 Feb.) 161. City chartered; Pr. L. 1854 (28 Feb.) 242; take stock in Lacon Bridge Co.; 1 Pr. L. 1867 (7 Mar.) 183. Lacon Manufacturing Co. chartered; Pr. L. 1837 (4 Mar.) 284. Wm. Fisher and others, ferry across the Illinois; Pr. L. 1849 (12 Feb.) 39. Silas Ramsay, ferry across the Illinois; city get 10 per cent net proceeds; Pr. L. 1855 (15 Feb.) 547. Lacon Union School District chartered; L. 1857 (16 Feb.) 188; amendment; 3 Pr. L. 1867 (25 Feb.) 77. Trustees Methodist E. Church to convey real estate; Pr. L. 1857 (9 Feb.) 309. Lacon Hotel Co. chartered; Id. (11 Feb.) 423. German Workingman's Association chartered; 1 Pr. L. 1867 (23 Feb.) 129. Lacon Bridge Co. chartered; Id. (21 Feb.) 171.

Henry.—City chartered; Pr. L. 1854 (1 Mar.) 226; amendment, powers extended; Pr. L. 1859 (24 Feb.) 619; regulate sale of liquor; 3 Pr. L. 1867 (28 Feb.) 625; take stock in Cotton Manufacturing Co.; 1 Pr. L. 1867 (28 Feb.) 840. School trustees, Town 13—10, ferry across the Illinois; Pr. L. 1847 (27 Feb.) 49; foregoing renewed and extended; 1 Pr. L. 1865 (16 Feb.) 559. Board of trustees of Perpetual Fund for Tuition of Indigent youths in Henry Female College chartered; Pr. L. 1857 (16 Feb.) 1063; amends §§1, 2 and 5 particularly; 1 Pr. L. 1865 (16 Feb.) 25. Henry City Bridge Co. chartered; Pr. L. 1857 (17 Feb.) 1170; amended, rates fixed, trestle extended to bluff; Pr. L. 1859 (18 Feb.) 16; complete by 10 Jan. 1867; Pr. L. 1861 (22 Feb.) 59; all foregoing amended; 1 Pr. L. 1867 (12 Feb.) 166.

MASON COUNTY.

County formed, boundary and organization; vote on county seat; L. 1841 (20 Jan.) 69; supplemental to foregoing; Id. 90. Removal of county seat Havana to Bath; L. 1843 (14 Jan.) 113. School funds transferred from Tazewell and Menard; L. 1845 (1 Mar.) 235. Collection of taxes extended 3 months; Pr. L. 1847 (28 Feb.) 201. Removal of county seat from Havana; L. 1851 (8 Feb.) 23. Draining and reclaiming certain lands, special tax therefore; L. 1853 (12 Feb.) 246. Transcribing public records in Sangamon, Menard and Tazewell; Pr. L. 1855 (9 Feb.) 718. Vote to take stock in Illinois River Railroad legalized; Pr. L. 1857 (29 Jan.) 105. Sheep and swine not to run at large after 1 Apr.; L. 1857 (14 Feb.) 200. Drainage of certain lands, special tax therefor, manner of collection and disbursement; L. 1859 (24 Feb.) 104; acts of commissioners legalized; L. 1861 (22 Feb.) 143; addition tax; 1 Pr. L. 1865 (16 Feb.) 557; survey of county perfected and road law modified; 2 Pr. L. 1867 (9 Mar.) 830. Smith Turner, ferry across the Sangamon at Myers' ford; L. 1843 (23 Feb.) 144. H. W. Wigginton, the same, across the Illinois at Matanzas; Id. (3 Mar.) 147. Thos. Cheney, the same, across same at Liverpool; Pr. L. 1847 (15 Feb.) 43. Sale of lots Town 20—9; Id. (2 Mar.) 172. Road, Bath to Matanzas, located; Id. (23 Feb.) 257 §5. Town 20—5, sell school section; Pr. L. 1847 (1 Mar.) 192. James M. Ruggles, bridge the Sangamon at Petersburg and Bath road; Mason and Cass counties keep in repair; Pr. L. 1849 (12 Feb.) 13. Alfred M. Wooley and Jackson Van Vranken, state pedlers, license for life; Pr. L. 1851 (12 Feb.) 85. Mason county Farmer's Railroad chartered; Pr. L. 1859 (24 Feb.) 477. Pennsylvania and other towns pay $500. bounty to volunteers; 1 Pr. L. 1865 (15 Feb.) 171. Sureties of Jacob West, late sheriff, released from judgment conditionally; 2 Pr. L. 1865 (16 Feb.) 253.

Bath.—Town chartered; Pr. L. 1857 (14 Feb.) 627; amendment; 3 Pr. L. 1867 (21 Feb.) 626. Joseph A. Phelps, ferry across the Illinois; L. 1845 (27 Feb.) 161.

MASSAC COUNTY.

County created, boundary and organization; L. 1843 (8 Feb.) 74. Erect armory at Fort Massac, consent therefor; R. S. 1845 (11 Dec. '44) 607. Copying records in Pope and Johnson, compared and certified, effect thereof; L. 1853 (10 Feb.) 225. Fines and forfeitures go to county treasury; Pr. L. 1857 (9 Feb.) 312. Construct turnpike across the Cache ponds on Metropolis and Vienna roads; Id. (16 Feb.) 1069. Swamp lands; L. 1857 (12 Feb.) 44. S. Copeland, ferry across the Ohio, Town 15—3; L. 1843 (28 Feb.) 146. John M. Robinson, the same, across the Mississippi at Massac; road from ferry to Wilcox, located; Id. (2 Mar.) 146. Thos. G. C. Davis, the same, across the Ohio at Brooklyn; Pr. L. 1851 (8 Feb.) 58. Adm'r of J. M. Robinson to deed property; L. 1845 (7 Jan.) 200. Robert Enders, adm'r John Hynes to join with proprietors of Massac in certain conveyances; Pr. L. 1847 (26 Feb.) 7. John W. Reed, sheriff, time to pay revenue for 1846 extended 3 months; Id. (1 Mar.) 192. Payment to Sam'l S. Marshall and others, for services in Massac troubles; L. 1849 (8 Feb.) 117. The same, to Anderson P. Corder, prosecuting attorney in Massac riots; L. 1851 (14 Feb.) 89. Brooklyn chartered; Pr. L. 1855 (15 Feb.) 170. Metropolitan Cemetery Association chartered; Id. 448. Emporium Real Estate and Manufacturing Co. chartered; Pr. L. 1857 (26 Jan.) 60.

Metropolis.—Plat altered; L. 1841 (24 Feb.) 313. Town chartered; L. 1845 (25 Feb.) 200; amendment; Pr. L. 1851 (15 Feb.) 242; further amends, license tippling houses etc., additions thereto; Pr. L. 1857 (16 Feb.) 876; further amends, and city chartered; Pr. L 1859 (18 Feb.) 214; foregoing amended, qualificanion of voters; Pr. L. 1861 (21 Feb.) 235; limits extended; 1 Pr. L. 1867 (22 Feb.) 496. Wm. J. Stephenson allowed $114.80 as clerk of District Court 19 Sept. 1849; Pr. L. 1851 (15 Feb.) 176. John M. Cunningham allowed $100. as Marshall of District Court; Pr. L. 1853 (3 Feb.) 494. Lots 407—8, block 33, deed to trustees Methodist E. Church; L. 1853 (10 Feb.) 261. Elect police justice with $150. jurisdiction; Pr. L. 1857 (16 Feb.) 924. Metropolis College chartered; Pr. L. 1861 (22 Feb.) 20. Library Association and Historical Society chartered; Id. 552. Jonathan C. Willis, ferry across the Ohio; 1 Pr. L. 1865 (15 Feb.) 565. Metropolis Seminary chartered; 1 Pr. L. 1867 (25 Feb.) 15.

McDONOUGH COUNTY.

County established, boundary defined; remain attached to Schuyler; L. 1826 (25 Jan.) 76. County seat located on S. E. 31. 6—2 and called Macomb; L 1831 (24 Dec. '30) 62. Sheriff allowed time to collect taxes; 1 L. 1837 (4 Mar.) 323. Payments in lieu of resident lands tax; 2 L. 1837 (21 July) 59. Records copied from Madison legalized; L. 1845 (1 Mar.) 143. Assessments for 1850 legalized; L. 1851 (28 Jan.) 8 Tax to pay bounties to soldiers and relieve their families; 1 Pr. L. 1865 (6 Feb.) 137. Index to circuit court records; sectional land index; 2 Pr. L. 1865 (16 Feb.) 233. Tax and issue bonds to build court house; Id. (15 Feb.) 336. County Aid Soldiers Monument Association; 1 Pr. L. 1867 (18 Feb.) 877. For erection of new court house and jail; 2 Pr. L. 1867 (7 Mar.) 126. Refund to Q. C. Ward the amount of county funds taken from his safe by burglars; L. 1869 (27 Mar.) 339. Section 2 act 22 Jan. 1831 [L. 1831, 38] concerning roads and bridges, to last Monday in Oct. 1833; Pr. L. 1833 (22 Feb.) 13; supplimental to said act; L. 1837 (4 Mar.) 26. Road, Macomb to Havana, changed in part; L. 1835 (27 Jan.) 124. Road, Troublesome creek *via* Bacons mill to Macomb and Burlington road; 1 L. 1837 (27 Feb.) 208. Road, Beardstown to Des Moines Rapids, re-locate in part; L. 1839 (24 Jan.) 51. Sewardsville plat vacated; Pr. L. 1847 (26 Feb.) 207. McDonough College chartered; Pr. L. 1849 (26 Jan.) 26; amendment; Pr. L. 1851 (23 Jan.) 11; appointment of trustees; Pr. L. 1855 (14 Feb.) 585; foregoing amended; act 1851 revived; Pr. L. 1859 (24 Feb.) 369. W. T. Head, late collector, allowed credits in 1850–1; L. 1855 (14 Feb.) 96. Prairie City Academy chartered; Pr. L. 1857 (30 Jan.) 117. Hill's Grove Academy chartered; Id. (16 Feb.) 880. Blandinsville Seminary and Joint Stock Education Society of the United Brethren in Christ; Pr. L. 1859 (24 Feb.) 358. Incorporation of Blandinsville confirmed and officers acts legalized; Id. 586. Middletown changed to Young; Id. 720. Creates additional voting precinct in Prairie City; 2 Pr. L. 1865 (16 Feb.) 560. School district of Bladinsville established; 3 Pr. L. 1867 (4 Mar.) 28. Colchester chartered; Id. (16 Feb.) 532. Industry chartered; Id. (19 Feb.) 611. Clarksville name changed to Sciota; L. 1869 (29 Mar.) 269. Sheridan name changed to Good Hope; Id. (31 Mar.) 290. Kate Lisk made heir of O. M. Lisk; Id. (29 Mar.) 341.

Macomb.—Town chartered; L. 1841 (27 Jan.) 317; vacates part of plat; Pr. L. 1847 (16 Feb.) 207; assessment and collection of taxes, sale of real estate for; L. 1853 (12 Feb.) 166. City chartered; Pr. L. 1855 (15 Feb.) 10; incorporating acts consolidated and amended; Pr. L. 1857 (14 Feb.) 713; foregoing amended; publish statement, penalty for neglect; take stock in any Railroad; Pr. L. 1859 (24 Feb.) 213; filling vacancies; Pr. L. 1861 (22 Feb.) 236; payment of fines; part of charter repealed; 1 Pr. L. 1865 (16 Feb.) 451; further amends, §4 repealed; 1 Pr. L. 1867 (21 Feb.) 392; election of supervisors and other officers; Id. (23 Feb.) 678. Additional judges of election; L. 1839 (15 Feb.) 120. McDonough College chartered; L. 1836 (12 Jan.) 164. Macomb Mutual Insurance Co. chartered; Pr. L. 1855 (14 Feb.) 407. Presbyter of Schuyler convey real estate to Macomb Lodge No. 17, A. F. and A. Masons; Pr. L. 1861 (21 Feb.) 89. McDonough Normal and Scientific College chartered; 1 Pr. L 1867 (1 Mar.) 18. McDonough Home Insurance Co. chartered; 2 Pr. L. 1867 (7 Mar.) 186.

Bushnell—Town chartered; 2 Pr. L. 1865 (16 Feb) 387; tax to pay Peoria and Warsaw Railway; 3 Pr. L. 1867 (5 Mar.) 127. Bushnell College chartered; Pr. L. 1857 (17 Feb.) 1175. National Brick Machine Co. chartered; 2 Pr. L. 1867 (28 Feb.) 299. Township established for school purposes; 3 Pr. L. 1867 (13 Feb.) 6.

McHENRY COUNTY.

County formed, boundary and organization; L. 1836 (16 Jan.) 273; to include Lake Michigan; 1 L. 1837 (1 Mar.) 89; assessment for 1839 legal-

ized; L. 1840 (1 Feb.) 77; boundary defined; L. 1843 (24 Feb.) 91; removal of county seat, vote thereon; Id. (6 Feb.) 115; part of county debt paid by Lake; Id. (24 Feb.) 218; county seat established at Certerville; L. 1845 (2 Jan.) 198. Voters elect school directors and raise money to build school houses; L. 1847 (11 Feb.) 157. Townships support their own paupers, vote thereon; L. 1853 (10 Feb.) 261. Borrow $15,000. to erect and repair county buildings, vote thereon; Pr. L. 1854 (22 Feb.) 81. Special tax to build court house and jail; Pr. L. 1855 (15 Feb.) 701. Removal of county seat to Algonquin, vote thereon; Id. (14 Feb.) 714; the same, to within one mile of Crystal Lake; Id. 736. Supporting county poor; vote thereon; L. 1859 (24 Feb.) 131. Additional justices and constables; L. 1861 (22 Feb.) 144. Netting of fish prohibited; L. 1869 (29 Mar.) 187. Jurisdiction of county court extended to $1,000.; Pr. L. 1854 (27 Feb.) 239; amendment, §4 repealed, §11 extended; L. 1857 (18 Feb.) 123. Wm. Jackson insert middle letters in his name; 1839 (1 Feb.) 48. Union Agricultural Society chartered; Pr. L. 1839 (19 Feb.) 88. H. Dodd and G. Early, dam Fox river, Town 43—8; L. 1845 (21 Jan.) 191. Crystal Lake Academy chartered; Id. (25 Feb.) 340; trustees to sell; Pr. L. 1857 (18 Feb.) 1223. Certain constables bonds legalized; L. 1845 (11 Feb.) 345. Sale of liquor regulated; Pr. L. 1847 (1 Mar,) 169. Thomas M. White and sureties allowed time to settle judgment; Pr. 1851 (14 Feb.) 128; further time; Pr. L. 1853 (14 Feb.) 490; auditor to settle with; L. 1857 (16 Feb.) 91. John Brink, $106. for recovering body of drowned convict; Id. (12 Feb.) 493. Wm. Sloan, dam Fox river at Algonquin; Id. (11 Feb.) 610. District No. 1, Town 43—5 to be known as Riley district, directors receive portion of school tax; Pr. L. 1854 (4 Mar.) 137. Union Manufacturing Co. chartered; Pr. L. 1857 (16 Feb.) 977. Charter of Crystal Lake Ice Co. amended; construct branch railroad; Pr. L. 1859 (24 Feb.) 381. Sumner plat vacated; Pr. L. 1861 (21 Feb.) 718. Assessment by school directors district No. 2, 19 Dec. 1862, legalized; Pr. L 1863 (17 Jan.) 257. Construction of private ditches for drainage; 1 Pr. L. 1865 (16 Feb.) 555. Clara Cook named changed to Gavitt; 2 Pr. L. 1865 (18 Jan.) 93. Triangle on the Josyln farm vacated; Id. (16 Feb.) 663. Sale of real estate by Thos. F. Johnson, guardian etc., legalized; 1 Pr. L. 1867 (20 Feb.) 900. McHenry County Manufacturing Co. chartered; 2 Pr. L. 1867 (28 Feb.) 288. Harrard chartered; 3 Pr. L. 1867 (28 Feb.) 397.

Woodstock.—Name of Centreville changed to Woodstock; part of plat vacated; Pr. L. 1851 (12 Feb.) 109; L. 1845 (3 Mar.) 179; town chartered; L. 1852 (23 June) 154; amendment, powers generally extended; Pr. L. 1857 (16 Feb.) 1073; charter conditionally repealed; Id. (17 Feb.) 1167; same subject, vote thereon; Pr. L. 1861 (22 Feb.) 740. Woodstock Insurance Co. chartered; Pr. L. 1853 (12 Feb.) 366; name changed to Western World Insurance and Trust Co.; Pr. L. 1859 (14 Feb.) 400. Conveyance by supervisors to Neill Donnelly legalized; Pr. L. 1857 (31 Jan.) 231. Woodstock University chartered; Pr. L. 1861 (22 Feb.) 26.

Marengo.—Town chartered; Pr. L. 1857 (9 Feb.) 331; amendment, establish a cemetery; Pr. L. 1861 (13 Feb.) 691. Maringo Collegiate Institute chartered, appointment of trustees; Pr. L. 1855 (14 Feb.) 503. Farmers and Mechanic's Savings Bank of McHenry County chartered; 1 Pr. L. 1865 (16 Feb.) 61.

McHenry.—Part of Elm street vacated; L. 1845 (3 Mar.) 267. Town chartered; Pr. L. 1855 (15 Feb.) 240; foregoing repealed; Pr. L. 1859 (19 Feb.) 646. John W. Smith and others, bridge Fox River; L. 1843 (3 Mar.) 177. McHenry Institute chartered; Pr. L. 1857 (18 Feb.) 1374. David S. Smith, dam Fox river; 2 Pr. L. 1867 (23 Feb.) 809.

Richmond.—Town chartered; 2 Pr. L. 1865 (16 Feb.) 563. Richmond Cemetery Association chartered; Pr. L. 1855 (14 Feb.) 438. Richmond Lodge No. 143, F. and A. Masons chartered; Id. 589.

McLEAN COUNTY.

County created, county seat to be located and called Bloomington; L. 1831 (25 Dec. '30) 57. Delinquent tax list for 1836; 1 L. 1 837 (3 Mar.) 95. Line between McLean and Woodford defined; L. 1843 (28 Feb.) 91. W. H. Hodge collect unpaid taxes of 1841, may sell lands; Id. (21 Feb.) 217. Sheep and swine not to run at large; L. 1855 (14 Feb.) 154. Sale of swamp lands; L. 1857 (16 Feb.) 122. Issue bonds to meet subscription to State Board of Education, vote thereon; L. 1859 (18 Feb.) 36. County attached to second grand division of supreme court; L. 1865 (16 Feb.) 25. Special tax to pay bounties; 1 Pr. L. 1867 (10 Feb.) 137; interest bearing bonds issued therefor legalized; 1 Pr. L. 1867 (21 Feb.) 883. For building a court house; 1 Pr. L. 1867 (18 Feb.) 878. Supervisors appropriate $15,000. to build soldiers' monument; 2 Pr. L. 1867 (13 Feb.) 454. The several towns enabled to raise money for war purposes; 3 Pr. L. 1867 (21 Jan.) 134. Official circuit court reporter; L. 1869 (31 Mar.) 350. Road, Bloomington to Danville, re-located in part; L. 1835 (6 Feb.) 121. State road, Waynesville to Herbert's; 2 L. 1837 (21 July) 82. Waynesville Seminary chartered; Pr. L. 1837 (2 Mar.) 222. Peru plat vacated; L. 1839 (18 Jan.) 48. Road, Bloomington to Lexington, re-location; Id. (2 Mar.) 240. State road east from Bloomington; Id. 268. Draining mill dams on Mackinaw creek; L. 1841 (19 Feb.) 185. LeRoy Manual Labor University chartered; Id. (25 Feb.) 298 Livingston plat vacated; Id. (7 Jan.) 315. McLean County Agricultural Society chartered; Pr. L. 1853 (12 Feb.) 423; amendment, annual meeting; Pr. L. 1861 (13 Feb.) 37; election and duties of officers; 1 Pr. L. 1867 (21 Feb) 43. H. C. Dickerson restored to citizenship; Pr. L. 1853 (12 Feb.) 494. Littleville plat vacated; Id. 518. LeRoy Seminary chartered; appointment of trustees; Id. 547. Oneida plat vacated; Pr. L. 1855 (13 Feb.) 46. LeRoy chartered; Pr. L. 1857 (18 Feb.) 1244. Execution against sureties of J. H. Moore stayed; L. 1859 (17 Feb.) 150. Levy school tax district No. 1, in Chenoa; Id. (24 Feb.) 178. Town 22—2, division into school districts legalized; L. 1861 (18 Feb.) 202. John J. Erwin name changed to Mitchell; Pr. L. 1861 (7 Feb.) 308. McLean County Central Branch Railroad chartered; Id.

(22 Feb.) 506. Moneys recovered from sureties of Julius and Rachel Talbert indicted for inhumanity to their child Frank, held in trust for said child; Id. (20 Feb.) 538. Towns of Towanda and Danvers, tax to meet obligations for war purposes; 1 Pr. L. 1865 (16 Feb.) 173. Towns 24—2 re-surveyed; 2 Pr. L. 1865 (16 Feb.) 254. Incorporation of Chenoa legalized; Id. 430. Bloomington and Normal Horse Railway chartered; 2 Pr. L. 1867 (19 Feb.) 12. Assessment in school district No. 4, Old Town, for 1866 legalized; 3 Pr. L. 1867, 14. Heyworth School District chartered; Id. (5 Mar.) 33. Padua, special bounty tax levied; Id. (1 Mar.) 122. Saybrook chartered; Id. (7 Mar.) 148. Lexington, corporate powers extended; Id. (25 Feb.) 542. Town 25—2 re surveyed; Id. (16 Feb.) 628. Part of Town 21 attached to 22; Id. (7 Mar.) 632. Allin name changed to Stanford; L. 1869 (30 Mar.) 268. Concord name changed to Danvers; Id. 273.

Bloomington.—Town chartered; Pr. L. 1839 (2 Mar.) 172; supplemental to foregoing; L. 1840 (31 Jan.) 33. Incorporation under general law 10 Feb. 1849 legalized; fines and penalties paid to city treasury; L. 1852 (19 June) 45. Alley vacated; Pr. L. 1853 (12 Feb.) 489; also, in Morton's addition; Id. 502. City charter amended, limits extended; Pr. L. 1854 (1 Mar.) 170; incorporation and acts of city council legalized; disposition of fines and forfeitures; Pr. L. 1855 (9 Feb.) 52; special tax to improve streets; Pr. L. 1857 (9 Feb.) 313; part of 2nd and 3rd streets vacated; Id. (13 Feb.) 509; charter amended and limits extended; Id. (16 Feb.) 1063; the several acts chartering amended; Pr. L. 1859 (24 Feb.) 112; city again chartered; Pr. L. 1861 (13 Feb.) 104; general amendment; 1 Pr. L. 1867 (7 Mar.) 639; divided into two voting precincts; 3 Pr. L. 1867 (5 Mar.) 619. Bloomington Female Seminary chartered; L. 1836 (9 Jan.) 175. Roads in town limits vacated; 1 L. 1837 (27 Feb.) 201. Wesleyan University chartered; Pr. L. 1853 (12 Feb.) 324; amendment; Pr. L. 1857 (30 Jan.) 116. City Hotel Co. chartered; Pr. L. 1853 (10 Feb.) 437. Gas Light and Coke Co. chartered; Pr. L. 1855 (14 Feb.) 650. Bloomington Cemetery Association chartered; Pr. L. 1857 (16 Feb.) 1023. Establishing a system of public schools; L. 1857 (16 Feb.) 226; amendment; 2 Pr. L. 1865 (16 Feb.) 271; powers of Board of Education extended; 3 Pr. L. 1867 (22 Feb.) 26. Phœnix Savings, Loan and Trust Co. chartered; Pr. L. 1859 (24 Feb.) 404. Northwestern Normal Academy of Music chartered; 1 Pr. L. 1865 (16 Feb.) 4. German Benevolent Society chartered; Id. (15 Feb.) 71. Bloomington Turn Verein chartered; Id. (16 Feb.) 97. Odd Fellows' Library Association chartered; 2 Pr. L. 1865 (15 Feb.) 17. McLean County Banking institution chartered; 1 Pr. L. 1867 (6 Mar.) 79. Hotel Co. chartered; 2 L. 1867 (19 Feb.) 48. Bloomington Insurance Co. chartered; Id. (7 Mar.) 192, 198. Library Association chartered; Id. (23 Feb.) 249. Young Men's Christian Association chartered; Id. (25 Feb.) 271.

Normal.—North Bloomington changed to Normal; 2 Pr. L. 1865 (16 Feb.) 517. Town chartered; 3 Pr. L. 1867 (25 Feb.) 321. Wrightonian Society chartered; 2 Pr. L. 1867 (28 Feb.) 273.

MENARD COUNTY.

County formed, boundary and organization; L. 1839 (15 Feb.) 104; supplemental to foregoing; Id. (28 Feb.) 205; boundaries defined; L. 1843 (2 Mar.) 94. Assessment for 1844 legalized; L. 1845 (10 Feb.) 233. County school fund transferred to Mason; Id. (1 Mar.) 235. Part of Sangamon attached to Menard; Pr. L. 1847 (28 Feb.) 39. Copy records in Sangamon; L. 1851 (12 Feb.) 80. Special tax to bridge the Sangamon at Petersburg; L. 1853 (12 Feb.) 226; said bridge legalized; Pr. L. 1853 (10 Feb.) 534. Action in offering bounties to volunteers legalized; 1 Pr. L. 1865 (15 Feb.) 138. Special tax to pay bounties; Id. 138. Additional justice and constable in Athens, then in Sangamon; L. 1835 (24 Dec. '34) 139. Athens Female Academy chartered; Pr. L. 1837 (27 Feb.) 110. Old plat of Athens vacated and J. B. Watson's legalized; L. 1840 (10 Dec. '39) 155. Greensburg plat vacated; L. 1845 (28 Feb.) 287; Pr. L. 1849 (6 Feb.) 111. Levi W. Riley, convicted of larceny restored; Pr. L. 1847 (16 Feb.) 174. Vote of school district No. 1 Town 18—7, 20 July 1850, levying tax, confirmed; Pr. L. 1853 (26 Jan.) 442; boundary of said district extended; 3 Pr. L. 1867 (5 Mar.) 32. Official acts of Wm. Armstrong J. P. legalized; Pr. L. 1855 (15 Feb.) 695. Hamilton Nation, convicted of larceny, restored; 2 Pr. L. 1867 (27 Feb.) 813.

Petersburg—Town plat partly vacated; alleys may be closed; L. 1841 (26 Jan.) 316. Town chartered; Id. (23 Feb.) 330; amendment; Pr. L. 1851 (17 Feb.) 261; also, 3 Pr. L. 1867 (23 Feb.) 565; part of plat vacated; Id. (7 Mar.) 111. Clinton Lodge No. 19, F. and A. Masons chartered; Pr. L. 1855 (9 Feb.) 675.

MERCER COUNTY.

County formed, boundary defined; L. 1825 (13 Jan.) 93 §5; attached to Peoria; L. 1826 (25 Jan.) 76; attached to Warren; L. 1831 (27 Jan.) 68 §5; organization of county, election of officers; New Boston temporary county seat; L. 1835 (31 Jan.) 156; western boundary the middle of the Mississippi; 1 L. 1837 (3 Mar.) 91; location of county seat; Id. (4 Mar.) 107; vote on its removal from Millersburg; L. 1839 (26 Feb.) 188; also, L. 1843 (28 Feb.) 124; its relocation; Pr. L. 1847 (26 Feb.) 37; venue of certain county seat cases changed to Rock Island; L. 1849 (12 Feb.) 220; removal from Keithsburg to Aledo, vote thereon; L. 1857 (20 Feb.) 91. Pay of recorder for transcribing indexes; Pr. L. 1847 (16 Jan.) 24. Part of territory detached from and added to Rock Island, vote thereon; L. 1849 (8 Feb.) 51. Sheep and swine not to run at large after 1 March; L. 1857 (18 Feb.) 194; foregoing repealed, not to run after 1 May 1859; L. 1859 (19 Feb.) 199; foregoing also repealed; L. 1861 (20 Feb.) 145. Additional tax to pay interest, vote thereon; Id. (22 Feb.) 144. Erection of court house and other buildings; Id. (21 Feb.) 145. Equalization of taxes; L. 1869 (25 Mar.) 406. Millersburg Seminary of Learning chartered; Pr. L. 1839 (2 Mar.) 238. Robt. Burns Lodge No. 113, F. and A. Masons chartered; Pr. L. 1855 (14 Feb.) 673. Aledo Colle-

giate Institute chartered; Pr. L. 1857 (16 Feb.) 1010. Mercer Collegiate Institute at Aledo chartered; 1 Pr. L. 1865 (6 Feb.) 10. Banner Coal and Coal Oil Co. chartered; 2 Pr. L. 1865 (16 Feb.) 50. Towns of Rivoli and Richland Grove levy tax to pay bounties; Id. (15 Feb.) 337. Windsor plat partly vacated; Id. (16 Feb.) 664. Minnie A. Miller name changed to Dihel, heir of Robt. M. Dihel; 1 Pr. L. 1867 (28 Feb.) 233. Wm. Kile, convicted of larceny, restored; 2 Pr. L. 1867 (5 Mar.) 814.

Keithsburg.—Town chartered; Pr. L. 1857 (16 Feb.) 868; amendment, subscription to Warsaw and Rockford Railroad legalized; establish a house of correction; Pr. L. 1861 (22 Feb.) 675. Robt. Keith, ferry across the Mississippi; Pr. L. 1847 (28 Feb.) 50. Green Mound Cemetery Association chartered; Pr. L. 1853 (10 Feb.) 545. Northwestern Masonic University chartered; Pr. L. 1855 (14 Feb.) 486. Seth H. Rodman, ferry across the Mississippi; Pr. L. 1857 (16 Feb.) 1021.

New Boston.—City chartered; Pr. L. 1859 (21 Feb.) 239; amendment, elect police magistrate; wharves, docks and ferries; Pr. L. 1861 (22 Feb.) 236. Election additional justice; Pr. L. 1847 (26 Feb.) 168. Harley Ives, ferry across the Mississippi; Id. (13 Feb.) 42; T. P. Willets succeeds Ives; Pr. L. 1854 (28 Feb.) 213.

MICHIGAN COUNTY.

To be formed from Cook, upon favorable vote; 1 L. 1837 (2 Mar.) 82.

MILITARY TRACT.

State recorder's books removed to Rushville, deeds in Military Tract transcribed; L. 1835 (9 Feb.) 157. Counties in Military Tract to transcribe deeds recorded elsewhere; Id. (12 Feb.) 159 §8; amendment, compensation for work done; L. 1836 (16 Jan.) 226; meaning as to Madison county; Id. (18 Jan.) 247; further amends, manner of transcribing said records; L. 1843 (4 Mar.) 212; compared and certified; R. S. 1845 (1 Mar.) 587. Resolution concerning bounty to soldiers in late war; L. 1839, 295. Any county authorized to copy records in Madison; L. 1841 (27 Feb.) 205.

MILTON COUNTY.

County formed; boundary and jurisdiction; vote thereon; L. 1843 (21 Feb.) 88.

MONROE COUNTY.

County formed prior to the organization of the state. Milton Moore and Jno. Messenger commissioners to establish line St. Clair and Monroe; L. 1821 (3 Jan.) 57; further respecting boundaries, removing county seat; L. 1825 (15 Jan.) 109; county seat permanently established; L. 1826 (20 Jan.) 59; boundary extended to embrace territory west of the Kaskaskia; Pr. L. 1827 (9 Jan.) 8; establishing line between Monroe and Randolph; L. 1829 (20 Jan.) 31; share in proceeds of Gallatin Salines; L. 1831 (16 Feb.) 13 §1; county seat permanently located; Id. (15 Jan.) 66; borrow money to pay for public buildings; L. 1841 (17 Feb.) 91; collect unpaid taxes for 1839; L. 1843 (21 Feb.) 229; assessment for 1850 legalized; L. 1851 (15 Feb.) 126; borrow money and levy tax to build court house; Id. (12 Feb.) 84; restoration of record book "C" of deeds; Pr. L. 1855 (15 Feb.) 528; indexes to records copied and perfected; L. 1861 (21 Feb.) 146; foregoing amended, §2 rate changed; 2 Pr. L. 1865 (15 Feb.) 234; take stock in Waterloo and Carondelet turnpike and ferry; Pr. L. 1861 (16 Feb.) 746; borrow $10,000, for construction and repairs of county buildings; Id. (21 Feb.) 747; pay of county and associate judges; L. 1867 (5 Mar.) 77. Leasing school section Town 3—9; L. 1821 (2 Feb.) 70. Elizabeth Whaley, to contract herself in marriage; Pr. L. 1827 (26 Dec. '26) 4. Road, Harrisonville to the Kaskaskia located; L. 1829 (22 Jan.) 134; also, Columbia to the Mississippi opposite Jefferson Barracks; Id. 135. Sale of school section Town 3—8; L. 1836 (16 Jan.) 239. Monroe Mining, Manufacturing and Exporting Co.; Pr. L. 1837 (11 Feb.) 26, 283. Mordock precinct established; L. 1845 (26 Feb.) 179. Columbia plat re-surveyed; Id. (3 Mar.) 278. Taxes of certain persons for 1844 remitted because of loss by high water; Id. (21 Feb.) 353. Acts of Bradly Rust, as justice under estray law legalized; L. 1849 (2 Jan.) 75. Bluff precinct established; L. 1853 (11 Feb.) 222; amendment; Pr. L. 1855 (15 Feb.) 703. Towns 3—8 2—9 and 3—9 pay Mary A. Ames for teaching; L. 1857 (16 Feb.) 207. Harlow Ferry Co. chartered; Pr. L. 1857 (9 Feb.) 302. Construction of Levee, Prairie du Pont to Harrisonville; L. 1859 (24 Feb.) 110. Columbia chartered; Pr. L. 1859 (19 Feb.) 597; amendment; property taken for streets; 2 Pr. L. 1865 (16 Feb.) 431; formation of school district in Towns 2 and 3—10; L. 1861 (21 Feb.) 195; foregoing repealed; boundary of district in Town 2—9 defined; 2 Pr. L. 1865 (16 Feb.) 313. Harrisonville Levee and Drainage Co. chartered; Pr. L. 1861 (21 Feb.) 436; amendment; 2 Pr. L. 1867 (28 Feb.) 807. Tax in Town 2—11 to replace township funds used for school houses; Id. (20 Feb.) 692.

Waterloo.—Town chartered; L. 1849 (12 Feb.) 226; plat changed; Pr. L. 1849, 131; re-surveyed; L. 1845 (3 Mar.) 278; again chartered; election of town trustees 18 Dec. '54 legalized; Pr. L. 1855 (15 Feb.) 192; general amendment, officers' acts legalized; Pr. L. 1857 (9 Feb.) 319; consolidating and amending incorporating acts; Pr. L. 1859 (18 Feb.) 705; town elections; Pr. L. 1861 (22 Feb.) 737. Monroe Academy chartered; Pr. L. 1827 (17 Feb.) 30; trustees appointed; Pr. L. 1833 (26 Feb.) 111. Waterloo Gas Light and Coke Co. chartered; Pr. L. 1857 (17 Feb.) 1158. Waterloo Saengerbund Society chartered; Id. (18 Feb.) 1307. School districts changed; L. 1861 (21 Feb.) 195.

MONTGOMERY COUNTY.

County formed out of Bond; L. 1821 (12 Feb.) 142; removal of county seat from Hamilton; L. 1823 (31 Jan.) 110; appropriation from Saline lands for internal improvement; L. 1835 (13 Feb.) 155; school commissioner settle demand of Daniel Scherer; L. 1845 (28 Feb.) 102; collection of unpaid revenue for 1835—7843; Id. (21 Jan.) 194; special tax to meet interest on bonds subscribed to Terre Haute and Alton R. R.; Pr. L. 1855 (15 Feb.) 720; foregoing amended; rate of taxation specified; Pr. L. 1857 (13 Jan.) 25; county court pay expenses of amputating Wm. M. Weatherspoon's arm, and compensation for lost time; 2 Pr. L. 1867 (18 Feb.) 802; increase county revenue; Id. (25 Feb.) 812. Joel Smith and sureties released from judgment as lessee Shoal Creek Saline; L. 1823 (17 Feb.) 155. Road, Hillsboro to Carlinville, partly changed; L. 1835 (6 Feb.) 126; same, Hillsboro to Honey Point, re-located in part; foregoing act repealed; L. 1836 (9 Jan.) 204; same, the Greenville and Sangamon re-located; 1 L. 1837 (7 Feb.) 255. Estate of Pleasant Sheapheard sold; Id. (6 Dec. '36) 192. Leesburg name changed to Zanesville; L. 1839 (22 Feb.) 156. Guardian of Louiza Buzan to make settlement; Pr. L. 1851 (1 Feb.) 40. Securities of Meredith J. Blockberger, late collector, allowed two years to make settlement; Pr. L. 1851 (15 Feb.) 234. Vacates lots named in plat of Van Burensburg; Pr. L. 1857 (16 Feb.) 850. Expenses of posse commitatus summoned by sheriff Wm. N. Stephenson July and Aug. 1864; 1 Pr. L. 1865 (16 Feb.) 541. Nokomis chartered; 3 Pr. L. 1867 (9 Mar.) 602.

Hillsboro.—Concerning Hamilton, Armstrong, Winter and Summer streets; L. 1831 (28 Jan.) 80; sale of streets; L. 1841 (23 Feb.) 313; town chartered; Pr. L. 1855 (14 Feb.) 180; amendment; 3 Pr. L. 1867 (7 Mar.) 275. Oak Grove Cemetery Association chartered; L. 1843 (23 Feb.) 15. Charter of Hillsboro Academy amended; L. 1852 (21 June) 97. Literary and Theological Institute of the Far West chartered; Pr. L. 1847 (22 Jan.) 57; amendment, new corporation formed, Illiinois State University located at Springfield; Pr. L. 1853 (3 Feb.) 425. Hillsboro Building Association chartered; Pr. L. 1855 (15 Feb.) 600.

Litchfield.—City chartered; Pr. L. 1859 (16 Feb.) 181; amendment, election of magistrate, marshall and constable; Pr. L. 1861 (18 Feb.) 204; limits extended; Pr. L. 1867 (5 Mar.) 638. Tax levied in 1857 in school district No. 1, Town 9—5, to belong to Litchfield; Pr. L. 1861 (21 Feb) 748. Elmwood Cemetery Association chartered; 1 Pr. L. 1867 (21 Feb.) 209. Litchfield Hotel Co. chartered; 2 Pr. L. 1867 (23 Feb.) 55. Montgomery County Fire Insurance Co. chartered; Id. (5 Mar.) 154.

MORGAN COUNTY.

County formed out of the attached part of Greene; L. 1823 (31 Jan.) 108; fix county seat; Id. (17 Feb.) 163 §8; permanent location of county seat; L. 1825 (6 Jan.) 57; increase justices and constables; L. 1831 (14 Feb.) 49; increase justices districts; Pr. L. 1833 (27 Dec. '32) 102; survey of public roads; L. 1831 (7 Jan.) 140; election precincts increased; L. 1835 (31 Jan.) 58; line between Morgan and Sangamon determined; Id. (12 Feb.) 62; money paid on recognizances to the auditor in mistake refunded; L. 1849 (9 Feb.) 37; vote to take stock in Illinois River Railroad legalized; Pr. L. 1857 (29 Jan.) 105; to secure the State Agricultural College; 1 Pr. L 1867 (29 Jan.) 875; for building court house; Id. (28 Feb.) 891; official circuit court reporter; L. 1869 (31 Mar.) 350. Sale of sec. 16, Town 13—9, claim of Wm. Spencer for damages; L. 1835 (13 Feb.) 71. Manchester a justices' district; Pr. L. 1833 (1 Feb.) 104. State roads, location of certain; L. 1836 (18 Jan.) 184. Road, Springfield and Beardstown, relocation in part; Id. (15 Jan.) 205. Estate of Jas. Evans sold; Id. (2 Jan.) 234. Lynnville chartered under general law irrespective of number of inhabitants; Pr. L. 1837 (27 Feb.) 107; foregoing repealed; L. 1839 (19 Feb.) 132. Grand Pass Canal Co. chartered; Pr. L. 1837 (28 Feb.) 129. The Waverly, the Sylvan Grove and the Manchester Seminaries chartered; Id. (1 Mar.) 182. Justices and constable in Appalonia; 1 L. 1837 (27 Jan.) 115; same subject; Id. (2 Mar.) 118. Beardstown notaries public, election of justices and constables; Id. (15 Feb.) 116. Watson J. Philley name changed to Cyrus; Id. (16 Jan.) 174. Wm. Lock name changed to Wm. W. Hobbs; Id. (18 Feb.) 175. Franklin chartered; 2 L. 1837 (21 July) 101. Road, Jacksonville to Naples, relocated in part; L. 1839 (9 Feb.) 83. Jarboe & Jarboe, ferry at Bridgeport; Id. (16 Feb.) 100. The Mauvaise-terre navigable to Oxville bridge; Id. 122. Manchester a justices' district; Id. (19 Feb.) 130. Road, Springfield and Jacksonville, relocation in part; Id. 136. Phillips Ferry road changed in part; Id. (26 Feb.) 156. School fund Town 13—8; Id. (2 Mar.) 273. Certain Railroads issue policies of insurance; L. 1840 (27 Jan.) 24; amendment; Id. 52. Illinois Agricultural and Stock Association chartered; L. 1841 (26 Feb.) 137. Mary E. Brown, name changed to Stribling; Id. (26 Jan.) 206; Catharine Marshall to Van Wagener and Adelia A. Scott to Trumble; Id. 211. Meredosia plat partly vacated; Id. (19 Feb.) 310. Estate of Edward Mlodzianowski disposed of; L. 1843 (4 Mar.) 138. Road, Jacksonville to Vandalia, relocated in part; Id. (24 Feb.) 260. Levying school tax in Town 17—11; Id. (4 Mar.) 294 §8. Levying tax in Lynnville; Id. (3 Mar.) 301. School Commissioner pay over funds of Town 13—9; L. 1845 (23 Jan.) 193. Liberty and Williamsburgh town plats vacated; Id. (28 Feb.) 287. Bethel Methodist Church name changed to Hebron; Id. (15 Jan.) 177. Trenton and Appalonia plats vacated; Pr. L. 1847 (26 Feb.) 204. Road, through sec. 16, Town 15—8, vacated; same, through Liberty changed; L. 1849 (12 Feb.) 148. Liberty plat vacated; Pr. L. 1851 (28 Jan.) 28. New Lexington, name changed to Arcadia; Pr. L. 1853 (12 Feb.) 491. Morgan County Agricultural and Mechanical Association chartered; Pr. L. 1855 (14 Feb.) 612; Pr. L. 1861 (13 Feb.) 37; grounds exempt from taxation; 1 Pr. L. 1867 (25 Feb.) 48. Illinois Agricultural Implement Manufacturing Co. chartered; Pr. L. 1861 (22 Feb.) 465. Northwestern Agricultural Manufacturing Co. chartered; Id. (16 Feb.) 470. Lynnville chartered; 2 Pr. L. 1865 (15 Feb.) 493. Grayson S. Middleton, founding, heir of Grayson F. Middleton; 2 Pr. L. 1867 (21 Feb.) 85. Murrayville chartered; 3 Pr. L. 1867 (22 Feb.) 289. Mere-

dosia chartered; Id. (25 Feb.) 303. Waverly chartered; Id. 371. Two children of J. H. Alderman kept in insane hospital at expense of county; L. 1869. (31 Mar.) 52.

Jacksonville.—Public Square enclosed, street 100 feet wide around it; L. 1836 (16 Jan.) 228; town chartered; L. 1840 (3 Feb.) 106; amendment; L. 1841 (17 Feb.) 328; supplemental to act chartering, officers acts legalized; Pr. L. 1847 (16 Feb.) 94; re-chartered; Pr. L. 1849 (10 Feb.) 124; foregoing amended, limits extended; Pr. L. 1851 (13 Feb.) 111; repeals §3 of foregoing; Pr. L. 1855 (14 Feb.) 47; 1 Pr. L. 1867 (21 Feb.) 392; building court house at, town trustees build Illinois Hall conditionally; Pr. L. 1853 (14 Feb.) 444; part of Morgan street vacated; Id. (12 Feb.) 489; road through Bibb's addition vacated; Pr. L. 1854 (1 Mar.) 198; vacates part of Court street; Pr. L. 1855 (14 Feb.) 193. City chartered; Pr. L. 1857 (10 Feb.) 344; corporate limits extended half mile each way; Id. (18 Feb.) 1188; charter amended, assessment for 1857 legalized; L. 1859 (21 Feb.) 208; Duncan's addition legalized; 2 Pr. L. 1865 (15 Feb.) 483; city re-chartered; 1 Pr. L. 1867 (15 Feb.) 336. Illinois College chartered; L. 1835 (9 Feb.) 177; governor, secretary of state and senator from Morgan county district ex-officio trustees; Pr. L. 1853 (12 Feb.) 575. Jacksonville Female Academy chartered; L. 1835 (27 Jan.) 192; §7 repealed; Pr. L. 1837 (4 Mar.) 286. Morgan County Mutual Fire Insurance Co. chartered; L. 1836 (18 Jan.) 102. Additional notary public; 1 L. 1837 (15 Feb.) 116. Jacksonville Mechanics Union chartered; Pr. L. 1837 (28 Feb.) 131. Jacksonville Seminary chartered; Id. (1 Mar.) 182. Jacksonville Hotel Co. chartered; Id. (4 Mar.) 286; 2 Pr. L. 1867 (28 Feb.) 58. Morgan Institute chartered; L. 1843 (6 Mar.) 163. Illinois Conference Female Academy chartered; Pr. L. 1847 (16 Jan.) 52; named changed to Illinois Conference Female College; Pr. L. 1851 (29 Jan.) 35. Jacksonville Mutual Life Insurance Co. chartered; Pr. L. 1849 (12 Feb.) 54. School district of West Jacksonville levy tax to extinguish interest of Harmony Lodge No. 3 in school house; L. 1853 (10 Feb.) 168. Berean College chartered; Pr. L. 1855 (12 Feb.) 513. Jacksonville Gas Light and Coke Co. chartered; Id. (14 Feb.) 646; clause restricting price repealed; 1 Pr. L. 1865 (13 Feb.) 585. Ridgely Encampment No. 9, I. O. O. F. chartered; Pr. L. 1857 (14 Feb.) 655. Jacksonville Hydraulic Co. chartered; Id. 803. Illinois Female College chartered; Pr. L. 1863 (13 June) 18. Union Fire Co. chartered; 1 Pr. L. 1867 (22 Feb.) 953. Jacksonville Railway Co. chartered; 2 Pr. L. 1867 (25 Feb.) 4. Young Ladies Atheneum chartered; Id. 257. Home Manufacturing Co. chartered; Id. (5 Mar.) 302. Jacksonville Mining Co. chartered; Id. (12 Feb.) 432; amendment; Id. (7 Mar.) 420.

MOULTRIE COUNTY.

County created, boundary and organization; L. 1843 (16 Feb.) 83; assessment for 1844 legalized; L. 1845 (15 Jan.) 178; probate justice hold his office at his residence; Id. 191; county seat located in Town 13—5 conditionally; Id. (29 Jan.) 202. Sullivan Academy chartered; Pr. L. 1853 (12 Feb.) 459. Moultrie County Academy at Sullivan chartered; Pr. L. 1855 (14 Feb.) 882.

NORMAL UNIVERSITY.

Establishment and maintenance; L. 1857 (18 Feb.) 298. Appropriation of the interest on the college fund; L. 1861 (14 Feb.) 147; supplemental to foregoing; Id. (20 Feb.) 149. Accounts for labor and material in the building; L. 1865 (4 Feb.) 53. Declared a State institution, property held in trust for the state; L. 1867 (28 Feb.) 21. Supplemental to former acts—further appropriations for; L. 1869 (10 Mar.) 32. Illinois Natural History Society chartered; museum established, property exempt from taxation; Pr. L. 1861 (22 Feb.) 551; Philadelphia Society of, chartered; 2 Pr. L. 1867 (28 Feb.) 274.

NORMAL UNIVERSITY—SOUTHERN.

Establishment and maintenance; L. 1869 (9 Mar.) 34. Cities and towns to secure its location; Id. (19 Apr.) 297.

OGLE COUNTY.

County created, boundary and organization; L. 1836 (16 Jan.) 274 §5; acts of S. C. McClure, probate justice, legalized; L. 1841 (18 Feb.) 175; school fund for 1846 apportioned; L. 1847 (16 Feb.) 116; hogs not to run at large; L. 1849 (10 Jan.) 185; towns support their own paupers; Pr. L. 1857 (16 Feb.) 1090. Rock River Seminary chartered; L. 1841 (18 Feb.) 295; amendments; L. 1843 (3 Feb.) 282; L. 1845 (21 Feb.) 347; chartering Rock River University in connection therewith; Pr. L. 1853 (14 Feb.) 507. St. Marion name changed to Buffalo; L. 1843 (20 Feb.) 299. Hosea Hathaway, state pedlers license for life; Pr. L. 1851 (12 Feb.) 85. Securities Elisha W. Dutcher, late sheriff, released from judgment conditionally; Pr. L. 1853 (10 Feb.) 492. Town of Scott purchase school libraries; L. 1857 (14 Feb.) 195. Mt. Morris chartered; Pr. L. 1857 (13 Feb.) 563. Rock River Seminary and Collegiate Institute at Mt. Morris charter; Id. (16 Feb.) 1136. School district formed, Town 23—11; L. 1861 (12 Feb.) 193. Forreston Cemetery Association chartered; Pr. L. 1861 (14 Feb.) 69. Lots in Haldam vacated, town changed to Campus; Id. (21 Feb.) 586. Release Lucinda Noe's right of dower in certain lands; 2 Pr L. 1865 (16 Feb.) 246; relief of J. C. Noe—wife insane; L. 1869 (9 Apr.) 342. Dement levy special tax to build soldiers Monument; 2 Pr. L. 1867 (21 Feb.) 449; town chartered; 3 Pr. L. 1867 (7 Mar.) 142; name changed to Creston and latter chartered; L. 1869 (1 Apr.) 274.

Oregon.—Florence name changed to Oregon; L. 1843 (21 Feb.) 300; vacates certain streets; Pr. L. 1851 (13 Feb.) 113. Oregon Seminary of Learning chartered; Pr. L. 1839 (2 Mar.) 238. Oregon Bridge Co. chartered; bridge Rock river, voters and jurymen pass free; Pr. L. 1847 (15

Feb.) 10. James H. Hanchete, bridge Rock river; Pr. L. 1851 (17 Feb.) 311. Oregon Union Institute chartered; Pr. L. 1853 (12 Feb.) 497. Protection of Rock River bridge; Pr. L. 1861 (21 Feb.) 61.

Byron.—Vacates certain streets; Pr. L. 1851 (1 Feb.) 46; block 17 vacated; 2 Pr. L. 1865 (16 Feb.) 658. Byron Hydraulic Co. chartered; L. 1845 (28 Feb.) 347. Byron Bridge Co. chartered; Pr. L. 1861 (22 Feb.) 57. Soldiers Monument, location at legalized; 2 Pr. L. 1867 (21 Feb.) 448.

Grand de Tour.—Town plat and additions thereto legalized; Pr. L. 1859 (24 Feb.) 616. Rock River Bridge Co. chartered; L. 1843 (3 Mar.) 48. Grand de Tour Manufacturing Co. chartered; Id. (4 Mar.) 158. Grand de Tour Bridge Co. chartered; Pr. L. 1855 (15 Feb.) 607.

Polo.—Town chartered; Pr. L. 1857 (16 Feb.) 1095; amendment, powers generally extended; Pr. L. 1859 (18 Feb.) 654; further extended; 2 Pr. L. 1865 (16 Feb.) 548. Polo school district chartered; 3 Pr. L. 1867 (14 Feb.) 7.

Rochelle.—Town chartered; Pr. L. 1861 (22 Feb.) 678. Town of Lane name changed to Rochelle, corporate powers extended; 2 Pr. L. 1865 (15 Feb.) 488. Augus Bain and others chartered to build a Hotel; 1 Pr. L. 1865 (16 Feb.) 607.

OKAW COUNTY.

County created, boundary and organization, vote thereon; L. 1841 (24 Feb.) 80.

OREGON COUNTY.

County formed from Sangamon, Morgan and Macoupin, vote thereon; L. 1851 (15 Feb.) 131.

PEDLING.

John Bross, one armed, license for life; L. 1849 (17 Jun.) 111. Name of Roderick R. Lorton inserted in act 12 Feb. 1851, privileges thereof also extended to Edward Kiernan, Jacob Whitmore and Wm. H. Hartley; L. 1852 (22 June) 121. Archibald Adams, license for life; L. 1853 (12 Feb.) 170.

PEORIA COUNTY.

County formed out of country in vicinity of Ft. Clark; L. 1825 (13 Jan.) 85; respecting revenue; L. 1826 (27 Jan.) 89; payment in lieu of resident land tax; 2 L. 1837 (21 July) 59; assessment for 1838 legalized; L. 1839 (12 Jan.) 38; county may tax the Pekin ferry; Pr. L. 1839 (23 Feb.) 24; lost land, the "gore", attached to Peoria and Fulton; L. 1845 (28 Feb.) 267; special tax for 1846-7, 8 and 9, for building jail; Id. (21 Feb.) 352; public records copied; L. 1847 (16 Feb.) 71; collection of back taxes for 1847-8 and 9; L. 1851 (15 Feb.) 105; jurisdiction of magistrates extended to $300; L. 1855 (14 Feb.) 154; special tax to build court house; Pr. L. 1855 (12 Feb.) 670; jurisdiction of county court, concurrent with circuit court in civil causes; also in Misdemeanors, the fine not exceeding $100.; L. 1855 (9 Feb.) 194; foregoing repealed; L. 1861 (18 Feb.) 109; road, Brimfield to Rochester, highway commissioners to alter or discontinue; L. 1857 (18 Feb.) 198; issue bonds for court house and jail; Pr. L. 1856 (9 Feb.) 319; foregoing amended; L. 1859 (21 Feb.) 37; for abstracting records of tax sales; 2 Pr. L. 1865 (13 Feb.) 235; present system of indexing records maintained; Id. (16 Feb.) 234; fees of officers; L. 1867 (23 Feb.) 111; official circuit court reporter; L. 1869 (31 Mar.) 350. James Latham's adm'r convey real estate; Pr. L. 1827 (31 Jan.) 19. Road, Peoria and Galena, relocated in part; L. 1836 (18 Jan.) 218. Cambridge plat partly vacated; 2 L. 1837 (20 July) 93. Illinois Manufacturing Co. chartered, located in Fulton or Peoria; Pr. L. 1837 (4 Mar.) 331. Commission the sheriff lately elected; L. 1839 (12 Jan.) 40. Hudson plat vacated; Id. (18 Jan.) 49. Road, Peoria to Stephenson, change in part; Id. (19 Feb.) 131. Re-valuation of sec. 16, Town 7—7; Id. (22 Feb.) 149. Justices district, Town 7—7; Id. (1 Mar.) 211. Caledonia plat and first addition to Rome vacated; Id. 239. LaSalle Prairie Co. chartered, drain part of Town 11—8; Pr. L. 1839 (16 Feb.) 65. Wm. L. May, ferry at outlet of Lake Peoria; L. 1840 (1 Feb.) 49; also L. 1841 (23 Feb.) 113; same, bridge the Illinois, at same; L. 1845 (3 Mar.) 237; also Pr. L. 1847 (26 Jan.) 9; foregoing amended; L. 1852 (19 June) 98; run a ferry when bridge is out of order; Pr. L. 1853 (17 Jan.) 487. Money paid for school lands Town 8—5 refunded; L. 1840 (1 Feb.) 131. Farmers Exporting Co. chartered; L. 1841 (23 Feb.) 129. Wm. Mitchell, witness in contested election case, payment to; Id. (7 Feb.) 206. Peoria road near Chillicothe relocated; L. 1843 (24 Feb.) 259. Charleston plat corrected, name changed to Brimfield; Id. (2 Mar.) 296; town chartered; Pr. L. 1857 (18 Feb.) 1297. Kingston plat vacated; L. 1845 (26 Feb.) 165. Jubilee College chartered; Id. (28 Jan.) 207; re-chartered, qualifications of officers, foregoing act repealed; Pr. L. 1847 (22 Jan.) 54; amends charter, three additional trustees; Pr. L. 1859 (23 Feb.) 367. Sale of school lands Town 7—6; L. 1845 (26 Feb.) 346. Victoria Polly Herod Ann Green name changed to Hamlin; Pr. L. 1847 (27 Feb.) 21. Andrew Gray use Peoria and Warsaw Railroad west of Peoria city; Id. (1 Mar.) 195. Kickapoo Mills plat vacated; Id. (27 Feb.) 210. Sale of counterfeiting presses, tools, etc. taken from Rufus Webb and others; Pr. L. 1849 (12 Feb.) 31. Sureties of Wm. Compher, absconding sheriff, conditionally released; Pr. L. 1851 (14 Feb.) 130; same released from judgment; Pr. L. 1853 (11 Feb.) 440. Ira T. Munn and others chartered as the Spring Bay Ferry and Dyke Co.; Id. (12 Feb.) 538. Springdale Cemetery Association chartered; Pr. L. 1855 (14 Feb.) 460; repeals §§7 and 9; Pr. L. 1857 (28 Jan.) 81. Smith Frye, ferry across the Illinois Town 9—8; Pr. L. 1855 (15 Feb.) 549. Wm. P. Bryant and others, ferry across the Illinois, Town 8—8; Peoria and Tazewell counties improve roads leading thereto; Pr. L. 1857 (14 Feb.) 753. Assessment in Rome school district for 1858 legalized; L. 1859 (24 Feb.) 175. Ela H. Clapp, ferry across the Illinois at Rome; 1 Pr. L. 1865 (16 Feb.) 559.

Peoria County.

Geo. W. Andrews, foundling, heir of Edward A. Andrews; 2 Pr. L. 1865 (16 Feb.) 93. Union school districts in Akron and Hallock established; Id. (15 Feb.) 323. Refunding to estate of J. R. Thompson taxes paid in error; L. 1867 (28 Feb.) 166. Thief Detective and Mutual Aid Association of Princeville chartered; 1 Pr. L. 1867 (5 Mar.) 150. Schools in Town 8—8; 3 Pr. L. 1867 (6 Mar.) 36. School district No. 1, Town of Hallock, limits extended; Id. (28 Feb.) 43. Peoria and Kickapoo Turnpike chartered; Id. (23 Feb.) 654. Peoria and Limestone Turnpike chartered; Id. (28 Feb) 660. P. Lahargonette name changed to P. L. Mars; L. 1869 (10 Mar.) 266. Glascoe name changed to Glasford; Id. (30 Mar.) 278.

Peoria.—Town chartered; Pr. L. 1837 (21 Feb.) 64; amendment; 2 L. 1837 (20 July) 92; further amends, trustees elected in November; Pr. L. 1839 (26 Feb.) 13; Garrit's addition vacated; L. 1839 (18 Jan.) 49; general amendment to charter; L. 1841 (27 Feb.) 347. City chartered; L. 1845 (2 Dec. '44) 224; town trustees construct water works; Id. (3 Mar.) 252; foregoing repealed; city to construct water works; Pr. L. 1849 (12 Feb.) 16; repeals §§2 and 3 of city charter, officers acts legalized, limits extended, Mayor to act as justice; Pr. L. 1847 (13 Feb.) 79; city to take stock in Wm. L. May's bridge; Id. (25 Feb.) 120; city issue bonds to Peoria and Oquawka Railroad; L. 1852 (21 June) 98; said bonds not to exceed $300,000., vote thereon; L. 1853 (3 Feb.) 191; city charter amended, recorder's office established, corporate powers extended; Pr L. 1853 (12 Feb.) 589; further amended and boundary defined; Pr. L. 1854 (25 Feb.) 74; general charter amendment; Pr. L. 1855 (12 Feb.) 118; vacates alley running through block 91 Voris and Lavielle's addition; Id. (15 Feb.) 193; system of public schools established; L. 1855 (14 Feb.) 195; also, L. 1857 (29 Jan.) 231; foregoing amended; L. 1859 (18 Feb.) 174; further amends; 1 Pr. L. 1865 (16 Feb.) 467; board of city school inspectors levy tax; 3 Pr. L. 1867 (6 Mar.) 123; city issue $100,000. bonds in aid of Peoria City Hydraulic Works, jurisdiction over vagrants, prostitutes etc.; Pr. L. 1857 (4 Feb.) 233; city charter (3 Dec. '44) and amendatory acts amended, change in time of city election; Pr. L. 1861 (20 Feb.) 244; recorder's court established; L. 1861 (22 Feb.) 110; foregoing repealed; L. 1863 (20 Feb.) 39; each ward elect an additional supervisor; L. 1861 (20 Feb.) 265 §3; city charter amended, issue $10,000. bonds, city officers term of office, time of elections, boundary; Pr. L. 1863 (12 Feb.) 167; payment of bounties; L. 1865 (16 Feb.) 149; repeals §8 of original charter (3 Dec. '44); also, act 3 Feb. [12 Feb.] 1863; 1 Pr. L. 1865 (16 Feb.) 469; charter further amended, limits defined; 1 Pr. L. 1867 (1 Mar.) 622. Town of Peoria divided into election precincts; L. 1863 (21 Feb.) 64; regulates holding of elections; 1 Pr. L. 1867 (7 Mar.) 922. Peoria Bridge Co. chartered; L. 1835 (10 Feb.) 181. Peoria Academy chartered; Pr. L. 1837 (11 Feb.) 27; also, Pr. L. 1855 (6 Feb.) 368. Peoria Manufacturing and Exporting Co.; Pr. L. 1837 (2 Mar.) 241. Peoria Hotel Co. chartered; Id. 253; also, 1 Pr. L. 1865 (16 Feb.) 608; and, 2 Pr. L. 1867 (22 Feb.) 51. Peoria Commercial Insurance Co. chartered; Pr. L. 1837 (18 Feb.) 36; amendment; L. 1840 (3 Feb.) 112. Peoria Marine and Fire Insurance Co. chartered; L. 1841 (20 Feb.) 151; amendment; Pr. L. 1857 (15 Jan.) 22. State road in Hale's second addition vacated; L. 1843 (2 Mar.) 262. Peoria Water Co. chartered; Id. (1 Feb.) 314. Musical Association chartered; L. 1845 (7 Feb.) 273. Peoria Lodge No. 15, F. and A. Masons chartered; Pr. L. 1847 (18 Feb.) 105. Peoria Female Seminary chartered; Id. (1 Mar.) 166. Acting members of fire companies exempt from jury duty; L. 1849 (12 Feb.) 84. Wesleyan Seminary chartered; Pr. L. 1851 (17 Feb.) 277. School trustees Town 8—8 to sell lots in Monson and Sandford's addition; Pr. L. 1853 (24 Jan.) 449. Stockholders Peoria Female School Association chartered as Peoria Female Academy; Id. (11 Feb) 506. Peoria Gas Light and Coke Co. chartered; Id. (12 Feb.) 516. Peoria Mutual Fire and Marine Insurance Co. chartered; Pr. L. 1855 (15 Feb.) 426; name changed to Peoria City Fire and Marine Insurance Co.; Pr. L. 1859 (24 Feb.) 395. Peoria University chartered; appointment of trustees; Pr. L. 1855 (14 Feb.) 484. Germania Fire Co. No. 3 chartered; Id. 699. Peoria city Hydraulic Co. chartered; Pr. L 1857 (11 Feb.) 426. Peoria Starch Manufacturing Co. chartered; Id. 449. Peoria Mutual Fire Insurance Co. chartered; Id 468. People's Express Co. chartered; Id. (19 Feb.) 1362. Peoria Drainage Co. chartered; Id. (18 Feb.) 1409. American Pottery Co. chartered; Pr. L. 1859 (19 Feb.) 407. German Savings Bank chartered; Pr. L. 1861 (20 Feb.) 39. Preacher's Aid Society of the Central Illinois Annual Conference of M. E. Church chartered; Id. (18 Feb.) 51. New Peoria Fire Co. No. 4 chartered; Id. 329. Peoria City Railway Co. chartered; Id. (21 Feb.) 342. Central City Trust Co. chartered; Id. 453. Peoria Savings Loan and Trust Co. chartered; Id. (20 Feb.) 456. German Library Association chartered; Id. (18 Feb.) 553. Peoria German School Association chartered; 1 Pr. L. 1865 (16 Feb.) 36. Illinois River Bridge Co. chartered; Id. 184. Waterworks established; Id. 469. Peoria Horse Railway Co. chartered; Id. 600. Illinois Mutual Life Insurance Co. chartered; Id. 677. Peoria Mercantile Library Association chartered; 2 Pr. L. 1865 (15 Feb.) 18. Peoria Gazette Co. chartered; Id. (16 Feb.) 121. Peoria Savings Bank chartered; 1 Pr. L. 1867 (8 Mar.) 110. German Workingmen's Mutual Relief and Insurance Co. chartered; Id. (7 Mar.) 151. Union Brewery and Coopering Co. chartered; Id. (28 Feb.) 199. Peoria Hebrew Congregation Anshai Emeth chartered; Id. (7 Mar.) 243. Central City Horse Railway Co. chartered; 2 Pr. L. 1867 (21 Feb.) 16. Mutual Health Assurance Association chartered; Id. (9 Mar.) 228. Peoria Manufacturing Co. chartered; Id. 374. Peoria and Langdon Coal and Coke Co. chartered; Id. (5 Mar.) 406. St. Louis and Peoria Plow Co. chartered; Id. (18 Feb.) 482. Peoria Transcript Co. chartered; Id. (25 Feb.) 505. Peoria Turn Verein chartered; 3 Pr. L. 1867 (23 Feb.) 649.

Chillicothe.—Town chartered; Pr. L. 1861 (22 Feb.) 577. John H. Batchelder and others, ferry across the Illinois; Id. (20 Feb.) 319. Acts of trustees Methodist E. Church legalized; 1 Pr. L. 1867 (8 Mar.) 244. Chillicothe Ferry

Road and Bridge Co. chartered; Id. (4 Mar.) 935.

Elmwood.—Town chartered; 3 Pr. L. 1867 (27 Feb.) 412. Elmwood Mining and Manufacturing Co. chartered; Pr. L. 1861 (18 Feb.) 467. Elmwood Building Co. chartered; 1 Pr. L. 1867 (20 Feb.) 201.

PERRY COUNTY.

County formed and limits defined; R. S. 1827 (29 Jan.) 110; share in proceeds of Gallatin Salines; L. 1831 (16 Feb.) 15 §1; line between Perry and Franklin determined; L. 1835 (6 Feb.) 36; assessments for 1843–4 legalized; L. 1845 (11 Feb.) 348; taxes for 1843, how collected; Id. 349; building jail; 1 Pr. L. 1865 (15 Feb.) 542; foregoing amended, expend $10,000. working road from Pinckneyville to Tamaroa and to DuQuoin; 1 Pr. L. 1867 (28 Feb.) 890; pay of county judge and associates; L. 1867 (5 Mar.) 77; transcribing certain public records; 2 Pr. L. 1867 (28 Feb.) 791; county estray law; L. 1869 (4 Mar.) 173. Refunds taxes erroneously paid; L. 1835 (31 Jan.) 142. Lands of estate of Robt. B. Murphy sold; L. 1836 (8 Dec. '35) 234; his contract for sale of lands in Tennessee to be performed; 1 L. 1837 (6 Dec. '36) 156. Lands of James Woodside's estate sold; Id. (28 Feb.) 185. Elizabeth Buxton, prosecution for bigamy dismissed and divorced from Monroe Rice; Id. (6 Mar.) 189. Road, Pinckneyville to Grand Coat Prairie, and Shawnectown to Kaskaskia changed; Id. (28 Feb.) 286; same, DuQuoin to Denmark relocated; 2 Pr. L. 1867 (4 Mar.) 842; same, Pinckneyville to Mt. Vernon, partly relocated; L. 1869 (31 Mar.) 386. Payton Brown, fine for fireing prairie remitted; L. 1841 (26 Feb.) 211. Iowa plat vacated; Id. (24 Feb.) 313. Pinckneyville chartered; Pr. L. 1861 (21 Feb.) 716. Wall's Mining and Manufacturing Co. chartered; 2 Pr. L. 1867 (28 Feb.) 425.

DuQuoin.—Town plat partly vacated; Pr. L. 1861 (22 Feb.) 589; town chartered; Id. 590. City chartered; 1 Pr. L. 1865 (10 Feb.) 341; location of Southern Normal University, vote thereon; L. 1869 (19 Apr.) 298 §§5, 6. DuQuoin Female Seminary chartered; Pr. L. 1855 (13 Feb.) 370. Illinois Central Coal Mining Co. chartered; Id. 628. DuQuoin Coal Mining and Manufacturing Co. chartered; Pr. L. 1861 (20 Feb.) 299.

Tamaroa.—Appleton town plat partly vacated; Pr. L. 1857 (14 Feb.) 615; name changed to Smith's addition to Tamaroa and latter chartered; Pr. L. 1859 (17 Feb.) 534; foregoing amended; 3 Pr. L. 1867 (5 Feb.) 598; vacates streets and alleys; Pr. L. 1861 (14 Feb.) 723.

PIATT COUNTY.

County formed, boundary and organization, temporary county seat at Monticello; L. 1841 (27 Feb.) 71; supplemental provisions; Id. 91; sale of swamp lands; L. 1857 (16 Feb) 122. Edgar R Robins name changed to Monroe, heir of Wm. Monroe; Pr. L. 1857 (31 Jan.) 188. Monticello and Bement Railway chartered; 1 Pr. L. 1865 (15 Feb.) 598.

PIKE COUNTY.

County formed including territory north and west of the Illinois river; L. 1821 (3 Jan.) 59; boundaries defined; L 1823 (30 Dec. '22) 84; penalty against sheriff released, collection of taxes for 1824; L. 1825 (10 Jan.) 80; record in Pike of deeds to lands in Fulton legalized; Ibid; county revenue; L. 1826 (27 Jan.) 89; removal of county seat; Pr. L. 1827 (16 Jan.) 34; extends §2 of act 29 Jan. 1831 concerning the erection of bridges, to first Monday in October; Pr. L. 1833 (22 Feb.) 13; Sam'l Alexander and others relocate county seat; Id. 21; the Snicarty navigable to Atlas Mills; L. 1835 (31 Jan.) 50; county town lots and buildings in Atlas sold; Id. (7 Jan.) 149; revenue law as to said county partly repealed; L 1836 (15 Jan.) 231; McKee's creek navigable to Chambersburg; 1 L. 1837 (1 Mar.) 168; sale of school lands legalized; Id. (2 Mar.) 313; for internal improvements; L. 1839 (9 Feb.) 81; fine for contempt imposed by circuit court upon county commissioners released; L. 1849 (12 Feb.) 121; ferry licenses worked out upon the roads leading thereto; Pr. L. 1851 (12 Feb.) 104; levee from Millville along the river into Calhoun, for reclaiming overflowed lands; L. 1857 (10 Feb.) 255; special tax for bridge purposes; Pr. L. 1857 (18 Feb.) 1188; for payment of bounties; 1 Pr. L. 1865 (10 Feb.) 140; county and towns take stock in any railroad; 1 Pr. L. 1867 (25 Feb.) 884; exempt from game laws; L. 1867 (5 Mar.) 121; Gross' Stat. 1868, 327; county take stock in two Railroads; L. 1869 (9 Apr.) 209; school law of (28 Feb. '67) as to county repealed; Id. (30 Mar) 398. Road, Breman's ferry to Atlas, relocated; Pr. L. 1833 (22 Feb.) 150; same, Gilead and Rushville, in Town 3—3 relocated; 1 L. 1837 (15 Feb.) 213; same, Carrollton and Atlas, partly relocated; 2 L. 1837 (21 July) 82; same, Griggsville to the Mississippi, located; L. 1839 (28 Feb.) 204; same, Phillips ferry to Pittsfield, and Perry to the Illinois, $500. to each; Id. (2 Mar) 283; same, Griggsville to Quincy, changed in part; L 1840 (27 Jan.) 20; vacates road located under §50 act 2 Mar. 1839; L. 1840 (1 Feb.) 52; same, new Philadelphia and Kinderhook, vacated; Id. 129. Boonville plat vacated; L. 1836 (15 Jan.) 189. Tree Frank name changed to Frank McWorter; 1 L. 1837 (19 Jan.) 175. New Canton and Piketown Railroad chartered; Pr. L. 1837 (3 Mar.) 255. James Davis late county clerk, execution against stayed; L. 1839 (1 Feb.) 52. Augusta name changed to Florence; Id. (16 Feb.) 119. Certain railroads issue insurance policies; L. 1840 (27 Jan.) 24; foregoing amended; Id. (1 Feb.) 52. Credit on judgment against R. Davis surity for James Davis; Id. (27 Jan.) 28. Worcester name changed to Barry; Id. (15 Jan.) 44. Glascock and Hawkins, ferry across the Missippi opposite Hannibal; L. 1841 (27 Feb.) 123. Additional justice and constable in Florence; Id. (17 Feb.) 174. Reedfield plat vated; L. 1843 (23 Feb.) 295. Perry plat partly vacated; L. 1845 (1 Mar.) 122. Fairfield name changed to Pleasant Hill; Id. 135. Isaac G. Israel, build turnpike, New Canton Cincinnati; Pr. L. 1847 (27 Feb.) 194. Velasco plat vacated; Id. (28 Feb.) 211. Sale of parks and squares in Barry, proceeds applied; L. 1851 (17 Feb.) 186. Griggsville and Illinois River Plank Road chartered;

Pr. L. 1851 (17 Feb.) 306. Pike County Railroad chartered under act 5 Nov. 1849, condemn private property; Pr. L. 1854 (22 Feb.) 75; again chartered; Pr. L. 1857 (14 Feb.) 624; time of completion extended, bridge the Illinois at Naples; Pr. L. 1859 (12 Feb.) 491; time to complete further extended; Pr. L. 1861 (14 Feb.) 509. School house erected district 3, Town 6—4; L. 1855 (13 Feb.) 110. St. Louis plat vacated; Pr. L. 1855 (15 Feb.) 195; also of Franklin; Id. (13 Feb.) 603; Pr. L 1857 (14 Feb.) 713. O. M. Hatch and others ferry across the Mississippi, Town 4—8; Id. (14 Feb.) 606. Stephen S. Taylor, state pedler's license for two years; Id. 655. Barry, alley vacated; Id. 688. School land Town 5—6 part patented to L. Gard; L. 1857 (18 Feb.) 171. Ross, Gay & Co. refunded $49.34 tax collected in 1854 in error; Id. (16 Feb.) 192. Pittsfield Central Railroad chartered; Pr. L. 1857 (16 Feb.) 1056. County Agricultural Society, incorporation under general act 15 Feb. 1855 legalized; Id. (18 Feb.) 1837. Pike and Scott County Bridge Co. chartered, bridge the Illinois at Naples; Pr. L. 1859 (4 Feb.) 23; again chartered; 1 Pr. L. 1867 (13 Feb.) 166. Barry chartered; Pr. L 1859 (19 Feb.) 548. Abbey Stafford and others, ferry across the Illinois at Flint; Pr. L. 1861 (22 Feb.) 325. Milton chartered; Id. (21 Feb.) 697. Chartering turnpike or macadamized road, Perry to the Illinois opposite Naples; Id. (20 Feb.) 743. Hannibal and Naples Railroad chartered; Pr. L. 1863 (12 Feb.) 232. Wm. Ross, allowed amount of coupons lost by robbery; 2 Pr. L. 1865 (16 Feb.) 248 Great Western Warehouse and Transportation Co. at Douglasville chartered; Id. (13 Feb.) 668. Pike County Bridge Co. chartered; 1 Pr. L. 1867 (1 Mar.) 179. W. & T. Burnett's ferry (under act 19 Feb. '59), transfer of to Jas. B. Thurman confirmed; Id. (6 Feb.) 928. Geo. W. Babbitt, ferry across the Illinois at Florence; Id. (9 Feb.) 929. Cincinnati Ferry Co. chartered; Id. (27 Feb.) 943. Perry Springs' Hotel and Railroad Co. chartered; 2 Pr. L. 1867 (7 Mar.) 66. Louisiana and Pike County Railroad chartered; Id. (9 Mar.) 640. Barry, New Canton and Mississippi River Macademized Road Co. chartered; 3 Pr. L. 1867 (23 Feb.) 657.

Pittsfield.—Town may incorporate with less than 150 inhabitants; L. 1835 (7 Jan.) 150; vacates certain streets; Pr. L. 1847 (1 Mar.) 198; part of plat vacated; Pr. L. 1851 (12 Feb.) 105; part of Mississippi street vacated; Pr. L. 1855 (15 Feb.) 195. Pittsfield school district formed, school house built; L. 1861 (18 Feb.) 201; supplemental to foregoing; Id. 202; purchase of grounds and erection of school buildings; Pr. L. 1863 (21 Feb.) 259; the three foregoing acts amended; 2 Pr. L. 1865 (16 Feb.) 303. County and William Ross convey lot to Presbyterian Church; L. 1841 (27 Feb.) 92. Pittsfield Academy chartered; Pr. L. 1837 (24 Feb.) 82; trustees of to sell buildings and grounds and pay debts; Pr. L. 1847 (22 Feb.) 3. Pittsfield Hotel Co. chartered; Pr. L. 1857 (14 Feb.) 791.

Griggsville.—Levying taxes for school purposes; L. 1841 (27 Feb.) 288; town plat partly vacated; Id. 326; vacates part of Jones & Puckit's addition; 3 Pr. L. 1867 (26 Feb.) 617. Griggsville Female Academy chartered; Pr. L. 1837 (7 Feb.) 20. Pike County Mutual Fire Insurance Co. chartered; Id. (24 Feb.) 88. Griggsville Cemetery chartered; Pr. L. 1847 (15 Feb.) 80.

POPE COUNTY.

County formed prior to the organization of the state. County share in proceeds of Gallatin Salines; L. 1831 (16 Feb.) 13 §1. Seven mile creek navigable to John McIntier's; 1 L. 1837 (1 Mar.) 168; Lusk Creek, the same, to Ritt's mill; L. 1840 (29 Jan.) 67. Boundaries of county fixed; L. 1843 (3 Mar.) 101; collector for 1841 to collect unpaid taxes for 1840–1; Id. (1 Mar.) 220; certain sales by school commissioner legalized; Id. (3 Mar.) 222; purchase of poor farm and erection of county buildings; 1 Pr. L. 1867 (18 Feb.) 865. Amos Chipps, late sheriff, allowed $44.38 being the one per cent per day penalty for not paying over taxes; L. 1823 (24 Jan.) 51; time for him to pay over extended; L. 1825 (10 Jan.) 85. Bridge Lusk creek; R. S. 1827 (15 Feb. '27) 360 §27. Road, Belgrade to the State road near Massac or Paletto's Bluff, located; L. 1829 (20 Jan.) 128 §§1—3. Ferry at sec. 16, Town 16—7 legalized; L. 1831 (27 Jan.) 76. H. C. Shouse, convicted of murder, payment for apprehending; L. 1835 (24 Dec. 1835 [1834]) 72. W. T. Reed, ferry across the Ohio at Newport; 1 L. 1837 (3 Mar.) 119. Wm. G. W. Fitch, collector, released from payment of $30.; L. 1841 (23 Feb.) 208. T. W. Tanner's adm'r deed lands in Town 14—6; L. 1845 (21 Feb.) 323. Erection of tomb stone over grave of Wm. Rhodes, late representative; Pr. L. 1847 (24 Feb.) 213. Election of school trustees Town 12—6, 10 Apr. '52, legalized; Pr. L. 1853 (26 Jan.) 447. Thos. P. Blair name changed to Warwick; Id. 480. John Raum and others, toll bridge over Will Creek; Id. (12 Feb.) 581. Sureties of Wm. M. Finney, late collector, released from liability for amount of which he was robbed; L. 1853 (12 Feb.) 96. Newton Clark and others, toll bridge over Lusk creek; Id. 182. Illinois Iron, Lead and Coal Co. chartered; Pr. L. 1855 (14 Feb.) 539. Wabash Mining Co. chartered; Id. 631. Jonathan C. Willis, toll bridge across Mill creek; Pr. L. 1855 (14 Feb.) 660; two years to complete; Pr. L. 1857 (19 Jan.) 24; Philip Vineyard assignee of Willis allowed two years to complete; Pr. L. 1859 (24 Feb.) 21; further extension to Sept. 1861; Pr. L. 1861 (22 Feb.) 59.

Golconda.—Town chartered; L. 1845 (1 Mar.) 128; justice of the peace elected; Pr. L. 1855 (13 Feb.) 198; again chartered; 2 Pr. L. 1865 (16 Feb.) 460; amendment; 3 Pr. L. 1867 (25 Feb.) 621. Golconda Seminary chartered; Pr. L. 1839 (2 Mar.) 203. Golconda Lodge No. 131, A. F. and A. Masons; Pr. L. 1857 (11 Feb.) 464. Philip Vineyard and others, bridge Lusk creek; Pr. L. 1859 (19 Feb.) 17. J. Field, ferry across the Ohio; L. 1859 (24 Feb.) 118. Golconda Cemetery Association chartered; 1 Pr. L. 1867 (25 Feb.) 231.

PULASKI COUNTY.

County formed, boundary and organization; L. 1843 (3 Mar.) 99; assessment for 1843 legalized; L. 1845 (25 Feb.) 299; acts of officers not keeping their offices at county seat, legalized; Id. (21 Feb.) 326; records in Johnson and Alexander transcribed and certified; L. 1847 (11 Feb.) 73; borrow $600. to complete court house; Pr. L. 1847 (16 Jan.) 24; tax to build jail; L. 1861 (13 Feb.) 161; removal of county seat, Caledonia to Mound City, vote thereon; 1 Pr. L. 1865 (16 Feb.) 549; pay of county judge and associates; L. 1867 (5 Mar.) 77; special assessment of real estate for 1866; 1 Pr. L. 1867 (7 Mar.) 904; erection of new county buildings; 3 Pr. L. 1867 (9 Mar.) 115. Caledonia chartered; 2 L 1837 (21 July) 31. Caledonia Railroad chartered; Id. 36; amendment, name changed to the Caledonia Railroad and Manufacturing Co.; Pr. L. 1839 (6 Feb.) 3. James D. Southard, ferry across the Ohio, Town 16—1; Pr. L. 1853 (12 Feb.) 598. Mound City Railroad chartered; Pr. L. 1855 (12 Feb.) 281. Sale of liquors in Pulaski prohibited; Pr. L. 1857 (16 Feb.) 1078 James M. Davidge and others, ferry across the Ohio at North Caledonia; Id. (18 Feb.) 1334. Bridge across the Cache at sec. 1, Town 17—1 legalized; Pr. L. 1859 (24 Feb.) 15. Title to sec. 1, Town 14—1, confirmed to Edmund Sowers; Pr. L. 1861 (21 Feb.) 536. America plat vacated; Id. (13 Feb.) 556. Old Caledonia plat vacated; Id. 715. Villa Ridge Horticultural Society chartered; 1 Pr. L. 1867 (23 Feb.) 46. Special tax in 1866, Town 16—1, legalized; 3 Pr. L. 1867 (9 Mar.) 40.

Mound City.—Emporium City name changed to Mound City and latter chartered; Pr. L. 1857 (29 Jan.) 86; towns of Emporium City and Mound City consolidated, city of Mound City chartered; Pr. L. 1859 (24 Feb.) 226; foregoing amended, powers extended; 1 Pr. L. 1865 (16 Feb.) 362; further amends; 1 Pr. L. 1867 (28 Feb.) 835. Emporium Real Estate and Manufacturing Co. chartered; Pr. L. 1857 (26 Jan.) 60. Emporium Hotel Co. chartered; Id. (16 Feb.) 824. Police magistrate's jurisdiction extended to $300.; L. 1859 (24 Feb.) 132. Mound City Gas Light and Coke Co. chartered; 1 Pr. L. 1865 (15 Feb.) 588. Pulaski County Insurance and Loan Co. chartered; 2 Pr. L. 1867 (8 Mar.) 214. Appropriates $12,500. to build a Soldiers' Monument; L. 1869 (29 Mar.) 45; resolution concerning; Id. 423. Resolution respecting a Naval Station; Id. 420.

PUTNAM COUNTY.

County formed, boundary and organization; L. 1825 (13 Jan.) 94 §7; again established, county seat called Hennepin; L. 1831 (15 Feb.) 54 §3; range 1 added to county, vote thereon; L. 1839 (2 Mar.) 241; school funds of Marshall and Stark paid over by commissioner; L. 1840 (27 Jan.) 92; Towns 31 and 32—1 taken from LaSalle and added to Putnam, vote thereon; L. 1851 (15 Feb.) 111; index to public records kept up; Id. 130; sheep and swine not to run at large; L. 1855 (14 Feb.) 154. Isaac B. Essex execute deeds for sec. 16, Town 12—6; Robt. Bird, the same for Town 29—2; Pr. L. 1833 (1 Mar.) 202. Concord and West Windsor plats vacated; 1 L. 1837 (28 Feb.) 328. Columbia name changed to Lacon; Id. (19 Jan.) 336. Lacon Academy chartered; Pr. L. 1837 (19 Jan.) 4. Caledonia plat vacated; L. 1841 (7 Jan.) 316. Mt. Palestine Academy Town 31—1 chartered; L. 1845 (3 Mar.) 263; Judson College chartered, in connection with said Academy; Pr. L. 1851 (17 Feb.) 299. Hennepin ferry leased by counties of Putnam and Bureau; L. 1845 (28 Feb.) 109. Hugh Teeny's lease of Hennepin ferry, county may extend 10 years; Pr. L. 1847 (17 Feb.) 44. Northern Illinois Agricultural College chartered; Pr. L. 1853 (12 Feb.) 407. Buel Institute chartered; Pr. L. 1855 (9 Feb.) 505. Benj. Newell, ferry across the Illinois at Trenton; Id. (15 Feb.) 655.

Hennepin.—Town chartered; Pr. L. 1839 (2 Mar.) 1 5; limits extended; L. 184 (3 Feb.) 108; amends charter; Pr. L 1851 (17 Feb.) 315; acts of incorporation reduced to one and amended; L. 1852 (22 June) 131; Hennepin Bridge Co. chartered; Pr. L. 1837 (2 Mar.) 227. Vacates Water street in West addition; Pr L. 1853 (15 Feb.) 501; limits defined; Pr. L 1854 (1 Mar.) 175; town trustees, ferry across the Illinois at Leefertown, former acts amended; L. 1857 (17 Feb.) 90; plat partly vacated, boundary defined; Pr. L. 1857 (13 Feb.) 510; act 22 June 52 chartering amended, town trustees not to be school directors; L. 1857 (16 Feb.) 259; charter further amended, license sale of liquor, ink artesian well; Pr. L. 1863 (14 Feb.) 263; and again; 3 Pr. L. 1867 (7 Mar.) 167. Hennepin Union Seminary chartered; Pr. L. 1851 (17 Feb.) 312. Hennepin Union Hall chartered; Pr. L. 1857 (16 Feb.) 841.

Granville.—Town chartered; Pr. L. 1861 (21 Feb.) 631. Granville Academy chartered; Pr. L. 1837 (31 Jan.) 14; re-chartered and foregoing repealed; Pr. L. 1851 (12 Feb.) 106. Putnam County Mutual Insurance Co. chartered; Pr. L. 1855 (15 Feb.) 430; name changed to American Insurance Co., office removed to Freeport; Pr. L. 1859 (19 Feb.) 396.

RANDOLPH COUNTY.

The division of the Illinois Territory into the counties of Randolph and St. Clair, was officially recognized by Gov. Pope in April 1809; MS Records, Sec'y State. Non-residents' land sold by sheriff for taxes; L. 1819 (10 Feb.) 12; county recorder made custodian of ancient books, papers etc., dated prior to 13 July 1787; L. 1821 (30 Jan.) 46; R. S. 1833, 502; for running line between Randolph and Jackson; L. 1823 (10 Feb.) 122; same, between Randolph and Monroe; L. 1829 (20 Jan.) 31; share in proceeds of Gallatin Salines; L. 1831 (16 Feb.) 14 §1; removal of county seat, Kaskaskia to Miller's farm; L. 1835 (12 Feb.) 58; appropriation from avails of saline lands for roads and bridges; Id. (6 Feb.) 155; county commissioners alter state roads; L. 1839 (12 Feb.) 101; taxes for 1844 remitted to certain persons account of loss by high water; L. 1845 (21 Feb.) 353; re-location of county seat, vote thereon, three elections if necessary; Pr. L. 1847 (30 Jan.) 25; borrow money to pay county indebtedness, vote thereon; L. 1852 (21 June) 109; record books "A" to "C" transcribed; Wm. Henry to translate those in French; Pr. L. 1855 (14 Feb.) 677; foregoing repealed; Pr. L. 1857 (16 Feb.) 1070; removal of county seat, Chester to Evansville, vote thereon; L. 1861 (21 Feb.) 163; build fire proof recor-

Randolph County.

der's office; 1 Pr. L. 1865 (16 Feb.) 543; pay of county judge and associates; L. 1867 (5 Mar.) 77; issue bonds to complete jail now building; 1 Pr. L. 1867 (5 Mar.) 801; county estray law; L. 1869 (4 Mar.) 173; manner of giving legal notice; Id. (27 Mar.) 253; special collector for the delinquent personal tax; Id. (17 Apr.) 353. Michael Jones paid $30. for certain abstracts; L. 1821 (6 Feb.) 93. Union College of Illinois chartered; Pr. L. 1833 (22 Feb.) 37. James Thompson allowed $54.12½ for viewing road Vandalia to Kaskaskia; Id. (25 Feb.) 121. Taxes erroneously paid refunded; L. 1835 (31 Jan.) 142. Randolph Manufacturing Co. chartered; L. 1836 (16 Jan.) 136; foregoing revived; Pr. L. 1839 (2 Mar.) 237. Moneys of estate of John Thompson invested in wild lands; 1 L. 1837 (27 Feb.) 186; same subject, foregoing repealed; L. 1839 (9 Feb.) 75. Illinois Female Institute chartered, at Flat Prairie; 2 L. 1837 (20 July) 87. Liberty chartered; 1 L. 1837 (10 Feb.) 331; powers increased; L. 1839 (19 Feb.) 133. Liberty Steam Mill Co. chartered; Pr. L. 1839 (23 Feb.) 170. Georgetown chartered; L. 1840 (31 Jan.) 32. Kaskaskia Beet Sugar and the Randolph Silk Co's chartered; Id. (1 Feb.) 57. James Hughes Exec'r sell lands; L. 1841 (19 Feb.) 23. Additional justice in Plumb creek precinct; Pr. L. 1847 (26 Feb.) 169. Additional constable elected; L. 1851 (17 Feb.) 162. Georgetown changed to Steeleville; Pr. L. 1851 (17 Feb.) 265. Randolph Plank Road Co. chartered; Pr. L. 1853 (11 Feb.) 161; amendment, borrow $30,000. and mortgage road; Pr. L. 1854 (28 Feb.) 236; directors may sell and county may purchase; Pr. L. 1859 (24 Feb.) 417. Part of Front St. in Menard vacated; Pr. L. 1853 (12 Feb.) 501. Wm. Henry, ferry across the Mississippi at Town 6—8; Pr. L. 1855 (14 Feb.) 604; foregoing repealed; Pr. L. 1861 (22 Feb.) 325. James Walsh, ferry across the Kaskaskia at Evansville; Pr. L. 1857 (13 Feb.) 546; Michael Walsh, the same; 1 Pr. L. 1867 (23 Feb.) 933. Randolph Coal Railroad and Manufacturing Co. chartered, construct railroad; Id. (14 Feb.) 754; name changed to Chester and Chicago Branch Junction Railroad; Pr. L. 1859 (24 Feb.) 492; further amends; 2 Pr. L. 1865 (16 Feb.) 208. Mary's River Bridge Co. chartered; Id. (22 Feb.) 20. John W. Brewer, ferry across the Mississippi at Town 6—8; Pr. L. 1861 (22 Feb.) 325. Union Fire Aid Insurance Co. at Red Bud chartered; 1 Pr. L. 1865 (16 Feb.) 706. Liberty name changed to Rockwood; 2 Pr. L. 1865 (16 Feb.) 493; latter chartered; Id. 572. Stuben name changed to Shiloh Hill; Id. 562. Randolph County Library and Historical Association chartered; 2 Pr. L. 1867 (28 Feb.) 256. Rockwood Manufacturing Co. chartered; Id. 293. Red Bud chartered; 3 Pr. L. 1867 (25 Feb.) 376. Coulterville name changed to Grand Cote; L. 1869 (30 Mar.) 278. School district Town 5—5 chartered; Id. (29 Mar.) 343.

Chester.—Town may be incorporated with less than 150 inhabitants; L. 1835 (7 Jan.) 150; increase annual tax on lots; Pr. L. 1837 (16 Jan.) 8; town chartered; Pr. L. 1839 (12 Feb.) 50; foregoing amended; L. 1840 (18 Jan.) 46; former chartering acts repealed; L. 1843 (16 Feb.) 299; Cole's and Erskine's addition name changed to Menard; L. 1845 (28 Feb.) 101; acts of trustees respecting taxes legalized; Id. (3 Mar.) 130; two recesses in plat vacated and sold; Pr. L. 1847 (28 Feb.) 211; special tax to improve streets; L. 1853 (10 Feb.) 216. City chartered; Pr. L. 1855 (13 Feb.) 144; amendment, repair streets, etc.; Pr. L. 1859 (23 Feb.) 124; additional tax and bonds issued; 1 Pr. L. 1865 (13 Feb.) 274; disposition of fines, forfeitures, etc.; 1 Pr. L. 1867 (9 Feb.) 286. Chester Insurance Co. chartered; Pr. L. 1839 (19 Feb.) 81. Thos. S. Bond, ferry across the Mississippi; Pr. L. 1849 (17 Jan.) 32; amendment, run a ferry flat or horse ferry; Pr. L. 1851 (17 Feb.) 289; fares regulated; 1 Pr. L. 1867 (12 Feb.) 929. Williams & Nevill, ferry across the Mississippi; L. 1859 (21 Feb.) 115. City Hotel Co. chartered; 1 Pr. L. 1865 (13 Feb.) 603. Evergreen Cemetery chartered; 1 Pr. L. 1867 (9 Mar.) 229. Foundry and Machine Shop Co. chartered; 2 Pr. L. 1867 (14 Feb.) 361.

Kaskaskia.—Town trustees, ferry across the Kaskaskia; L. 1831 (14 Feb.) 79; amends act 6 Jan. 1818 (territorial) chartering town; L. 1841 (20 Feb.) 328. President and trustees of Kaskaskia Common chartered, may lease; Pr. L. 1851 (23 Jan.) 5. Kaskaskia Bridge Co. chartered; county regulate tolls, citizens of county pass free; Pr. L. 1837 (31 Jan.) 6; supplemental to foregoing, citizens not pass free, county take stock; Id. (4 Mar.) 331; amends charter; 2 L. 1837 (20 July) 7; repeals §15 of charter; Pr. L. 1839 (24 Jan.) 38. Wm. Morrison and E. C. Hickox, take toll at their bridge; L. 1823 (24 Jan.) 52. Menard Academy chartered; Pr. L. 1839 (24 Jan.) 15. Kaskaskia Insurance Co. chartered; Id. (1 Mar.) 193; name changed to Insurance and Trust Co. of Illinois; L. 1840 (31 Jan.) 29; adopt mutual plan; Pr. L. 1855 (14 Feb.) 386.

Sparta.—Town chartered; 1 L. 1837 (10 Feb.) 331; additional justice; 2 L. 1837 (20 July) 46; concerning additional justice; L. 1839 (9 Feb.) 72; town name of Columbus changed to Sparta; L. 1840 (8 Jan.) 37; town again chartered; Pr. L. 1847 (28 Feb.) 155. City chartered; Pr. L. 1859 (24 Feb.) 255; amendment, boundary defined, city recorder; Pr. L. 1861 (20 Feb.) 258; further amendment, subscription to railroads; 1 Pr. L. 1867 (8 Mar.) 790; common pleas court established; L. 1869 (20 Apr.) 138. Union Academy chartered; Pr. L. 1855 (13 Feb.) 373. Sparta Cemetery Association chartered; Id. (14 Feb.) 452. Board of Education of Public Schools chartered; 2 Pr. L. 1865 (16 Feb.) 307; amendment; 1 Pr. L. 1867 (28 Feb.) 916. Odd Fellows and Masonic Hall and Orphan Asylum Association chartered; 2 Pr. L. 1867 (25 Feb.) 467. Randolph Hotel Co. chartered; 2 Pr. L. 1867 (28 Feb.) 60.

Prairie du Rocher.—Town chartered; L. 1821 (14 Feb.) 160; amendment; L. 1823 (14 Feb.) 142; trespasses on Common, how punished; L. 1845 (25 Feb.) 307; for leasing Common; Pr. L. 1851 (8 Feb.) 51; foregoing partly repealed, school organization confirmed; L. 1852 (21 June) 98; for draining wet lands in Common field; L. 1853 (9 Feb.) 249; amends act 8 Feb. '51; L. 1855 (14 Feb.) 112; supplemental to said act; application of proceeds; Pr. L. 1863 (16 Feb.) 273; town plat vacated; Pr. L. 1857 (14 Feb.) 619.

RELIEF.

Joel Wright and John Tillson, taxes paid in error refunded; L. 1823 (10 Feb.) 120; Cornelius Lafferty and sureties discharged from rents due; L. 1826 (28 Jan.) 92 §7; Ephraim Hubbard, late territorial sheriff; R. S. 1827 (24 Jan.) 370 §2; Richard M. Young; Pr. L. 1827 (22 Jan.) 11; Wm. Plant and Benj. Johnson; Id. (10 Feb.) 20; James Ratcliff, credit at Shawneetown Bank for $264.; L. 1831 (9 Feb.) 121; Rachel and Sylvia Hall, late captives with hostile Indians, 80 acres each canal lands; J. B. Campbell and G. E. Walker, pre-empt each 80 acres canal lands; Pr. L. 1833 (2 Mar.) 111; Wilson Lagow and Allen McGahey, each $18.; Id. (18 Jan.) 112; John Taylor, $553.23; Id. (14 Jan.) 112; act for relief of Thos. Redmond extended two years; Id. (5 Feb.) 112; guardian of heirs Willis Snyder invest in real estate; L. 1835 (17 Dec. '34) 73; James Mason's administrator make deeds; Id. (24 Jan.) 140; lands of T. G. B. S. Kirkman, minor, conveyed by Thos. C. Kirkman; 1 L. 1837 (6 Dec. '36) 181; Benj. A. Clark's administrator make collections; Id. (11 Feb.) 186; J. T. Cyrus, heir of Matthew Cyrus, upon petition; L. 1839 (4 Dec. '38) 78; C. J. Wood, further time to build mill dam; L. 1841 (17 Feb.) 207; D. B. Bush refunds taxes paid in error; L. 1843 (23 Feb.) 217; Robert Davis' administrator pay judgments; L. 1845 (1 Mar.) 122; marriage of Joseph L. and Margaret Ruddick; Id. (3 Mar.) 239; repeals act 6 Feb. '35 for relief of R. Richey; Id. 346; Edward B. Tinney, $211.75; Pr. L. 1837 (20 Feb.) 178; Isaac Demint, $94. state scrip; S. J. Sherwood, $98.66 same, for a leveling instrument; Id. (23 Feb.) 179; issue patent to Geo. W. Cassiday; refund to Eben Conant; Id. (24 Feb.) 181; Michael Kennedy, $38,215.44 in scrip, upon assignment of certain bonds; Id. (25 Feb.) 184; Francis Hannegan, a pedlar's license for life; Id. (27 Feb.) 187; heirs of Justus Post allowed $1,000.; Id. (27 Feb.) 188; Patrick Strachan and Wm. D. Scott, for certain bonds; Id. (28 Feb.) 189; John Van Horn, $135. for making sectional state map; Id. (17 Feb.) 212; Don Alonzo Cushman and others, certificate state indebtedness for lost bonds; L. 1849 (30 Jan.) 113; M. Brayman, adm'r of Milton Carpenter, $500. for distributing constitution 1848; Id. (8 Feb.) 117; Archibald Job, as state house comm'r; Id. (10 Feb.) 118; Thos. H. Owens and Thos. Wells, for provisions used in Morman war; Ibid; Arenton J. Douglass, lost bonds replaced; Id. (12 Feb.) 119; Tweed and Freeman, lost warrant duplicated; same to Matthew Stokes; Id. 120; Henry H. Snow, $30.; Pr. L. 1851 (28 Jan.) 18; for services and supplies in Hancock county troubles, Arch. Q. Brown $50., Benj. M. Prentice $252.40, Stephen Banning and Robert Todd each $75., Chauncey Robinson $20., John E. Johnson $70.25, P. M. Lockwood $40.38, E. A. Bedell $115.69 and Jonathan Clark $31.59; Id. (12 Feb.) 101; E. B. Rose, for arm lost in Hancock 1845; Id. (17 Feb.) 290; Tuthill King, certificate of state indebtedness in lieu of lost bonds; L. 1852 (21 June) 63; state claim against estate of Wm. Kinney, time of payment extended, when paid lands held as security conveyed to Wm. C. Kinney; Pr. L. 1853 (10 Feb.) 441; Noah Johnson $278.50 and Abraham Lincoln $149. as comm'rs on canal claims; R. E. Goodell $161.; Id. (17 Jan.) 448; Sarah B. Prentice, $400. as damages by Northern Cross Railroad; Id. (10 Feb.) 490; Hart L. Stewart $768. for funding state scrip; Id. (4 Feb.) 491; W. and M. Osman $2., and Scripps and Bross $5. for printing notices to canal claimants; Id. (12 Feb.) 522; M. Peck, new certificate in lieu of lost coupons; L. 1855 (15 Feb.) 96; Jos. and Wm. Harvey, certificate in lieu of stolen scrip; Id. 106; heirs of P. Redmond, $310. in lieu of Shawneetown lots; Id. 117; James A. Barrett, settle for judgment rendered in 1841 against James Shields then auditor; Pr. L. 1855 (15 Feb.) 695; Moses Turner discharged from liability for cavalry arms; Id. (14 Feb.) 717; S. B. Opdycke, $295.87 taxes paid in error refunded; L. 1857 (16 Feb.) 153; Wm. Zeigler, lost canal bond duplicated; Id. (12 Feb.) 160; taxes for 1858 remitted to residents of American Bottom account of loss by high water; L. 1859 (24 Feb.) 144; G. W. Cassidy, for land where title failed; Id. (22 Feb.) 145; John Crenshaw, discharged from judgment account of loss by fire; Id. (5 Feb.) 145; W. C. Kinney, time to redeem estate of extended; Id. (24 Feb.) 149; Mrs. E. K. Bissell, widow of the governor, allowed his salary for unexpired term; Pr. L. 1861 (30 Jan.) 535; John G. Offner, new certificate for lost one; L. 1863 (12 Feb.) 68; H. F. McClosky, allowed for lost coupons upon proof; 2 Pr. L. 1865 (16 Feb.) 243; heirs of E. Bement, duplicate of lost bond; L. 1867 (7 Mar.) 151, and 2 Pr. L. 1867, 793; John Welsh, warrant for lost scrip; Id. (6 Mar.) 151; Elizabeth Lane adm'x of Samuel Horine, new bond conditionally; 2 Pr. L. 1867 (21 Feb.) 803.

RESOLUTIONS.

Approving of gradual emancipation; L. 1823, 185. To increase trade with the Indians; Id. 186. Fine by Judge Hall on Gen. Jackson in 1814 refunded; L. 1843, 322. For the reduction of postage, with a memorial; Id. 326. Settlement of Oregon Territory; Id. 332. Settlement of Oregon boundary; Id. 333. Oppose renewal of patents to Cyrus H. McCormick, Moore & Haskell and Obed Hussey, for reaping and mowing machines; Pr. L. 1855, 739. Members and officers have bound copy of journals and laws of 19th general assembly; Id. 739. Legal proceedings instituted against Julius Wadsworth and Wadsworth & Shelden, for balances due the state; Id. 740. Secure pensions to soldiers of 1812; Id. 741. Oppose disturbing compromise measures of 1850 and fugitive slave law; Id. 744. General incorporation laws for banking, cities and towns, insurance companies, companies for mining and working minerals, manufactures, railroads, ferries, colleges, schools, churches, libraries and benevolent societies; Pr. L. 1857, 1453. Ratification of an amendment to the Constitution of the United States, forbidding Congress to interfere with domestic institutions; L. 1863 (2 June) 41. To adjourn in honor of Lincoln; L. 1869, 412. To investigate charges of corruption; Id. 416. To adopt the 15th amendment to the Constitution of the United States; Id. 417. Official reporting for the session of 1869; Id. 422.

RICHLAND COUNTY.

County formed, boundary and organization; L. 1841 (24 Feb.) 77; share in internal improvement appropriation; L. 1843 (21 Feb.) 215; assessment and collection of taxes; Pr. L. 1847 (11 Feb.) 8; commissioners' court issue 6 per cent. county orders; L. 1849 (10 Feb.) 53; special tax to pay interest on bonds issued to Ohio and Mississippi railroad; L. 1853 (10 Feb.) 227; swamp lands; L. 1855 (12 Feb.) 150; John Wolf transcribe certain records of Lawrence and Clay; Pr. L. 1857 (18 Feb.) 1327; boundaries of certain school districts; L. 1859 (23 Feb.) 188; provisions for payment of bounties legalized; 1 Pr. L. 1867 (20 Feb.) 157; erection of court house; Id. (9 Feb.) 874. Creation of school districts, Towns 3 and 4—10, boundary of other districts changed; L. 1855 (14 Feb.) 50. Southern Illinois Christian University at Claremont chartered; 1 Pr. L. 1867 (8 Mar.) 35.

Olney.—Alleys in certain additions vacated; L. 1843 (2 Feb.) 298; part of Morgan street vacated; Pr. L. 1857 (18 Feb.) 1202. City chartered; 1 Pr. L. 1867 (9 Mar.) 824; system of Public Graded Schools in town of; 3 Pr. L. 1867 (8 Mar.) 39; same, in city; Id. (9 Mar.) 39. Olney Male and Female College chartered; Pr. L. 1859 (19 Feb.) 371

ROCK ISLAND COUNTY.

County formed from Jo Daviess, county seat temporarily located; L. 1831 (9 Feb.) 52; John Dixon and others, comm'rs to locate county seat; Pr. L. 1833 (1 Mar.) 17; county seat located and named Stephenson; L. 1835 (12 Feb.) 159; collection of taxes for 1839; L. 1841 (18 Feb.) 306; county bridge Rock river near its mouth; L. 1843 (23 Feb.) 46; adding part of Mercer to Rock Island, vote thereon; L. 1849 (8 Feb.) 51; borrow $10,000. to liquidate county debt; Pr. 1849 (6 Feb.) 29; amends act creating county, establish line between Rock Island and Whiteside; Pr. L. 1853 (26 Jan.) 462; foregoing amended, action of single comm'r and citizens confirmed; Pr. L. 1854 (4 Mar.) 161; foregoing repealed; L. 1869 (29 Mar.) 161; further defining said line; Id. (16 Apr.) 94; build jail and fire proof office; Pr. L. 1855 (13 Feb.) 660; sheep and swine not to run at large; L. 1859 (19 Feb.) 199; foregoing repealed; L. 1861 (20 Feb.) 145; for the protection of fish; Id. (22 Feb.) 122; foregoing repealed; L. 1863 (20 Feb.) 47; action of supervisors in sale of lands for taxes legalized; L. 1861 (22 Feb.) 183; jurisdiction over lands for arsenal and armory ceded to the U. S.; L. 1867 (1 Feb.) 175; townships consolidated for school purposes; 2 Pr. L. 1867 (30 Jan.) 261, and 3 Pr. L. 1867 (30 Jan.) 627; tax levy in 1866 legalized; Id. 118. Spencer and Shears, mill dam on Rock Island slough; 1 L. 1837 (11 Feb.) 161; build in 3 years; L. 1839 (26 Feb.) 189. Mississippi and Rock River Canal Co. chartered; Pr. L. 1837 (21 Feb.) 72. Road from Hampton vacated; L. 1839 (2 Mar.) 64. Additional lots in Stephenson; Id. (6 Feb.) 78; foregoing repealed; L. 1841 (27 Feb.) 309. N. C. Wilcox, ferry opposite Bloomington; L. 1839 (26 Feb.) 202; foregoing amended; Pr. L. 1849 (10 Feb.) 87. J. Vandruff, ferry across Rock river at his island; L. 1839 (2 Mar.) 268. Rock Island Mutual Fire Insurance Co. chartered; Pr. L. 1839 (2 Mar.) 149; amendment, take risks on personal property; L. 1840 (18 Jan.) 23. Stephenson Seminary of Learning chartered; Pr. L. 1839 (2 Mar.) 238. Rock River University, at Hampton, chartered; L. 1840 (18 Jan.) 17. John Wilson, ferry across the Mississippi at Stephenson; L. 1841 (26 Feb.) 116; renewed for 10 years; L. 1849 (2 Feb.) 114; privileges of foregoing extended to John W. Spencer, Thos. J. Robinson and James Grant; Pr. L. 1857 (28 Jan.) 81; supplemental to foregoing, county regulate tolls; Id. (18 Feb.) 1328; provisions of act 28 Jan. 1857 continued 14 years; 2 Pr. L. 1867 (25 Feb.) 804. S. Prentice, ferry across the Mississippi, Town 16—6; L. 1841 (27 Feb.) 120. L. Wells, ferry across the Mississippi at Hampton; L. 1845 (25 Feb.) 356; foregoing extended for 10 years; Pr. L. 1854 (4 Mar.) 136. Acknowledgements by Wm. E. Franklin, notary public, legalized; L. 1845 (1 Mar.) 135. J. Foster and others, wing mill dam in the Mississippi, Town 18—1; Id. (28 Feb.) 286. J. Cox and others, the same; Ibid. Illinois City plat partly vacated; Quebec plat vacated; Id. 287. John Baxter, murderer of Geo. Davenport, imprisoned for life instead of hung; Pr. L. 1847 (24 Feb.) 212. Towns of Milan and Hampton united; Pr. L. 1849 (10 Feb.) 130. Truman R. Barlow, state pedlar's license for life; Pr. L. 1851 (12 Feb.) 85. Wm. Dickson, bridge Rock river at Camden; Id. (15 Feb.) 189. A. J. Brown, ferry across the Mississippi at Port Byron; Id. (17 Feb.) 303; L. 1859 (21 Feb.) 117. Rock Island and Moline Plank road chartered; Pr. L. 1853 (12 Feb.) 280. Moline and Rock River Plank and Macadamized Road and Bridge Co. chartered; Pr. L. 1855 (14 Feb.) 488; name changed to Moline Bridge Co.; Pr. L. 1857 (16 Feb.) 999; again changed to Moline and Rock River Bridge Co.; Pr. L. 1859 (16 Feb.) 22. Black Diamond Coal Co. chartered; Pr. L. 1857 (16 Feb.) 975. Rock Island Coal and Coke Co. chartered; Pr. L. 1857 (16 Feb.) 1061. Rock River Coal Mining Co. chartered; Id. 1077. Cheppeaunock Cemetery Co. chartered; Id. (18 Feb.) 1199. John Warren, bridge Rock river, Town 17—2; Id. 1202. Upper Mississippi Bridge Co. chartered; Id. 1308. Wm. Marshall Sr. and others, ferry across the Mississippi, Town 19—1; Id. (19 Feb.) 1354. Northwest Illinois Coal Co. chartered, hold lands in this and Henry counties; Pr. L. 1861 (21 Feb.) 304. Randall W. Smith, ferry across the Mississippi, Town 20—2; 1 Pr. L. 1865 (16 Feb.) 562. Philoman L. Mitchell, same, across same at Hampton; Id. 564. Coal Valley Mining Co., organized under general law, powers defined; 2 Pr. L. 1865 (15 Feb.) 57. Rock Island Petroleum and Mining Co. chartered; Id. (16 Feb.) 84. Muscatine and Camden Railroad chartered; Id. 180. Town Camden Mills chartered; Id. (13 Feb.) 393. Moline and Rock Island Horse Railroad chartered; 2 Pr. L. 1867 (21 Feb.) 18. Rock Island Woolen Manufacturing Co. chartered; Id. (25 Feb.) 346. Towns 20 and 21—2 united for school purposes; 3 Pr. L. 1867 (19 Feb.) 25.

Rock Island.—Town chartered; L. 1841 (27 Feb.) 348; city plat vacated; L. 1843 (20 Feb.)

299; town again chartered; L. 1845 (17 Jan.) 203. City chartered; Pr. L. 1849 (12 Feb.) 18; annual tax to meet interest of city bonds subscribed to Chicago and Rock Island Railroad; L. 1852 (14 June) 7; city charter amended; Pr. L. 1854 (28 Feb.) 199; action of council 22 Aug. 1853, regulating depot grounds, legalized; Id. (1 Mar.) 200; city incorporating acts reduced to one and amended; Pr. L. 1857 (16 Feb.) 939; foregoing amended, municipal government defined; Pr. L. 1861 (22 Feb.) 257; further amendment, city not to hold railroad stock; 1 Pr. L. 1865 (16 Feb.) 506; provide for additonal depot grounds; 1 Pr. L. 1867 (3 Mar.) 693; Western addition partly vacated; Pr. L. 1861 (18 Feb.) 257; Briggs Place, partly vacated; 2 Pr. L. 1865 (16 Feb.) 656. Rock Island City Bridge Co. chartered; Pr. L. 1837 (11 Feb.) 29. Rock Island City Hydraulic and Manufacturing Co. chartered; improve Rock River at Vanduffs Island; Pr. L. 1847 (22 Feb.) 110. St. John's Academy chartered; Pr. L. 1849 (12 Feb.) 3. Free Lodge No. 57, F. and A. Masons chartered; Id. (8 Feb.) 45. Rock Island Bank, report for Oct. 1852 filed; L. 1853 (1 Feb.) 228. Railroad Bridge Co. chartered, across the Mississippi; Pr. L. 1853 (17 Feb.) 329. Rock Island and Camden Plank road, sale of franchises to city legalized; Pr. L. 1859 (23 Feb.) 418; foregoing amended; 1 Pr. L. 1867 (25 Feb.) 178. Rock Island Insurance Co. chartered; Pr. L. 1861 (22 Feb.) 423; name changed to Mississippi Valley Insurance Co.; 1 Pr. L. 1865 (16 Feb.) 770; further amends; Id. 775. Rock Island Mutual Insurance Co. chartered; Id. 771. Rock Island School District chartered; L. 1857 (18 Feb.) 248; amendment; L. 1859 (22 Feb.) 173; further amends; L. 1861 (18 Feb.) 194, and 3 Pr. L. 1867 (18 Feb.) 23. Rock Island German and English School Society; Id. (25 Feb.) 77. Rock Island Turn Gemeinde chartered; Id. (22 Feb.) 648.

Moline.—Town chartered; Pr. L. 1855 (14 Feb.) 76; amendment, §9 to read $12,000.; Pr. L. 1857 (18 Feb.) 1215; further amends, regulate street labor; 2 Pr. L. 1865 (16 Feb.) 512; town establish ferry across the Mississippi; Pr. L. 1857 (18 Feb.) 1365; same, borrow money, vote thereon; Pr. L. 1863 (20 Feb.) 273. Moline Manufacturing Co. chartered; Pr. L. 1847 (25 Feb.) 122. Moline Cemetery Association chartered; Pr. L. 1851 (17 Feb.) 304. Harvey P. Jones, ferry across the Mississippi; Id. 316. Moline Water Power and Manufacturing Co. chartered; Pr. L. 1855 (14 Feb.) 651. Trustees Town 18—1 to sell certain town lots; L. 1855 (14 Feb.) 120. Moline Water Power Co. chartered; 2 Pr. L. 1865 (16 Feb.) 685. Illinois Soap Stone Stove Co. chartered; 2 Pr. L. 1867 (5 Mar.) 303.

Cordova.—Acts of highway commissioners legalized; 2 Pr. L. 1865 (16 Feb.) 257. System of Graded Schools established; Id. 274. John Marshall, ferry across the Mississippi; Pr. L. 1853 (10 Feb.) 580.

SALINE COUNTY.

County formed out of Gallatin, location of county seat, debts of Gallatin divided; Pr. L. 1847 (25 Feb.) 34; assessments in 1847 before the division legalized; L. 1849 (2 Feb.) 115; Saline river navigable; Id. (25 Jan.) 133; school fund divided between Saline, Hardin and Gallatin; Id. (2 Feb.) 180; union of Gallatin and Saline, vote thereon; L. 1851 (11 Feb.) 28; removal of county seat from Raleigh, vote thereon; L. 1853 (10 Feb.) 213; line between Saline and Hamilton settled; Id. 205; same subject; Pr. L. 1854 (28 Feb.) 143; removal of county seat, Raleigh to Harrisburg, vote thereon; L. 1657 (7 Feb.) 204; borrow money to erect public buildings; L. 1859 (14 Feb.) 38; records in Gallatin copied; L. 1861 (21 Feb.) 184; swamp land fund; Id. (20 Feb.) 185. Saline river, improvement of navigation; 1 L. 1837 (4 Mar.) 169; amendment, contracts of John Crenshaw, comm'r confirmed; L. 1851 (13 Feb.) 94. Stephen F. Michel, to dam the Big Saline at Independence; Pr. L. 1853 (12 Feb.) 579. Saline and Ohio River Railroad and Coal Mining Co. chartered; Pr. L. 1857 (16 Feb.) 1055. Shawneetown and Eldorado Railroad chartered; Pr. L. 1861 (20 Feb.) 525. Galatia may incorporate under general law; Id. (21 Feb.) 630. Harrisburg chartered; Id. 636. Raleigh chartered; 2 Pr. L. 1865 (16 Feb.) 562. Relief of Union District No. 7; 2 Pr. L. 1867 (18 Feb.) 801.

SALINES.

See also the Gallatin Salines, and the counties of Gallatin, Saline, Jackson, Bond and Vermilion.

Governor lease the Muddy Salines near Brownsville; L. 1819 (24 Mar.) 238; same to James Pearce; L. 1825 (3 Jan.) 49; same to Conrad Will; L. 1831 (11 Jan.) 162; encourage the discovery of salt water; L. 1819 (4 Mar.) 114; Elijah Creal and sureties released from contract for Muddy Salines; L. 1823 (7 Feb.) 115; prevent cattle from being injured at Salines; L. 1825 (14 Dec. '24) 10; L. 1829, 142 and R. S. 1833, 546. A general law concerning the saline reserves; comm'rs to sell 30,000 acres saline lands; R. S. 1827 (15 Feb.'27) 353; foregoing amended and continued in force; L. 1829 (19 Dec. '28) 142; foregoing amendment amended; L. 1831 (4 Jan.) 165; further amends act 15 Feb. 1827 as to Gallatin and Saline; R. S. 1833 (2 Mar. '33) 547; further amending said act and partly repealing it; Id. 550; pay of comm'rs re-selecting 5000 acres of land under above act 19 Dec. '28; R. S. 1833 (5 Feb. '33) 114. Persons discovering salt water; L. 1831 (11 Jan.) 162. Part of proceeds of saline lands in Gallatin' appropriated for internal improvements; Id. (16 Feb.) 12; foregoing amended; L. 1835 (11 Feb.) 49; further respecting this sale; L. 1831 (15 Feb.) 167. Leonard White to be commissioner; L. 1831, 166. Commissioner of Salines elected; former section repealed; R. S. 1833 (27 Feb. '33) 547. Concerning Gallatin and Vermilion Salines; Id. (2 Mar. '33) 548. Future discovery of salt water, encourage the manufacture of salt; Id. (28 Jan.) 552. Proceeds of Gallatin Salines expended in Champaign, Vermilion, Green and Wabash; L. 1835 (31 Jan.) 43. Superintendent of Gallatin and Receiver of Vermilion Salines settle with auditor; Id. (13 Feb.) 48. Receiver of Vermilion and comm'r of Gallatin Salines pay money into state treasury; Id. (7 Feb.) 51. The $2,000. proceeds of Vermilion Salines appropriated for improvement of Kaskaskia river,

divided among 9 counties; Id. (13 Feb.) 75. Timothy Guard and others, released from rents; L. 1836 (16 Jan.) 236. Certificates for purchasers of saline lands; 1 L. 1837 (16 Jan.) 309. Sureties of T. D. Hewitt, late comm'r, pay over moneys; Id. (3 Mar.) 310; suit brought against his sureties; 2 L. 1837 (21 July) 86. Application of proceeds of salines; 1 L. 1837 (31 Jan.) 340. Residue of proceeds of Vermilion Salines—how disposed of; 2 L. 1837 (22 July) 86. Sale of Vermilion and Iroquois Salines; L. 1843 (25 Feb.) 270. Resolution respecting duty on foreign salt; Id. 325. Sale of Saline reserve; L. 1847 (23 Feb.) 114. Legislative memorial to congress for the sale of lands reserved for the Ohio Salines; Pr. L. 1847, 219.

SANGAMON COUNTY.

County established and boundary defined; L. 1821 (30 Jan.) 45; first election held at the house of John Kelly on Spring Creek; Id. (6 Feb.) 99; Robert Hamilton paid $80.75 for building a jail; L. 1825 (7 Dec. '24) 4; boundary established and county seat located; Id. (23 Dec. '24) 20; tax to improve navigation of the Sangamon; Id. (29 Dec. '24) 48; county comm'rs license mill dams on the Sangamon; Pr. L. 1827 (14 Feb.) 27, and L. 1831 (22 Jan.) 99; justices and constables increased; Id. (14 Feb.) 49; comm'rs to report on the removal of obstructions to the navigation of the Sangamon; expenses paid from the proceeds of Saline lands under act 19 Jan. 1829 (L. 1829 148, appropriating $1,000. to Sangamon); Pr. L. 1833 (1 Mar.) 127; line between Sangamon and Morgan determined; L. 1835 (12 Feb.) 62; county to bridge the Sangamon on the Peoria road; L. 1836 (14 Jan.) 189; completion of said bridge; L. 1843 (3 Mar.) 52; erection of fire proof recorder's office north east corner of the square; 1 L. 1837 (15 Feb.) 180; certain school funds paid over to Menard, Logan and Dane (Christian); L. 1840 (27 Jan.) 91; supplemental to foregoing; Id. (3 Feb.) 92; James Shepherd collect unpaid taxes of 1840; L. 1843 (24 Feb.) 230; settlement of said Shepherd's accounts; L. 1845 (28 Feb.) 117; school funds transferred to Macon county; Id. (Mar.) 223; public records copied; Id. (10 Feb.) 234; sale of certain school lands legalized; L. 1847 (26 Feb.) 117; a part of county territory attach to Menard; Pr. L. 1847 (28 Feb.) 39; county court to have certain records transcribed, force and effect; L. 1853 (10 Feb.) 167; record books "C.", "D.", "E." and "F." transcribed; Pr. L. 1857 (14 Feb.) 614; supervisors action for payment bounties legalized; 1 Pr. L. 1865 (2 Feb.) 142; official circuit court reporter; L. 1869 (31 Mar.) 350; the county to constitute the 30th judicial circuit; Id. (11 Mar.) 90. Sangamo Milling Co. chartered; L. 1821 (14 Feb.) 151. Jas. Adams, toll bridge across the Sangamon mouth of Fancy creek; L. 1823 (24 Jan.) 47. Road, Springfield to Quincy, comm'rs to stake out; Pr. L. 1827 (11 Jan.) 9; same, Springfield to Paris, re-location far as David Owens' house; L. 1829 (26 Dec. '28) 126; certain state roads changed; L. 1831 (14 Feb.) 152; road, Springfield to Paris, relocation far as Judd's ferry; Pr. L. 1833 (2 Mar.) 171; same, Springfield to Decatur; 1 L. 1837 (27 Feb.) 304, Id. (16 Feb.) 217, 2 L. 1837 (20 July) 63, L. 1839 (22 Feb.) 154; same, Springfield to Jacksonville, relocation in part; 1 L. 1837 (21 Feb.) 212; Peoria road, between Springfield and the Sangamon, re-located; L. 1843 (25 Feb.) 260; same, from north end of Sixth street to H. Converse's house, located; L. 1857 (18 Feb.) 198; same, Springfield to Beardstown, far as Pleasant Plains located; 2 Pr. L. 1865 (15 Feb.) 267; same, Springfield to Bloomington, re-location in part; L. 1869 (29 Mar.) 391. John Cameron and others, mill dam on Sangamon at Fish Trap ford, not to obstruct navigation; L. 1829 (22 Jan.) 132. Sam'l Music, toll bridge over Salt creek; L. 1831 (7 Jan.) 35. Same, build toll bridge; L. 1835 (7 Jan.) 84. Salome Enos adm'rx, sell lands; Pr. L. 1833 (20 Feb.) 115. John Fletcher Sr., adm'r to execute deeds to John S. Wilson of Kentucky; Id. (2 Mar.) 126. Bridge over the Sangamon on Springfield and Peoria road, not to obstruct navigation; Id. (20 Feb.) 210. Election of senator in place Geo. Forquer dec'd; L. 1835 (12 Feb.) 29. Chatham Manual Labor School Town 14—6 chartered; L. 1836 (9 Jan.) 167. John Donovan, toll bridge over Salt creek; 1 L. 1837 (4 Mar.) 25. Sam'l Evans, same over same, Town 19—3; Id. (1 Mar.) 33. Stonington College of Illinois chartered; Pr. L. 1837 (18 Feb.) 54. Edinburgh Manufacturing Co. chartered; Id. (4 Mar.) 299. Sangamon Coal Bank Bridge Co. chartered; L. 1840 (3 Feb.) 102. John Primm Sr., mill dam on Sangamon at Fisher's ford; Wm. Carpenter, same at his ferry; L. 1841 (27 Feb.) 189. Relief of creditors of late Wm. Wernway, bridge builder; Id. 212. Cicero plat vacated; Id. (7 Jan.) 316, L. 1845 (28 Feb.) 288. J. F. Reed, finish bridge at Jamestown; L. 1843 (3 Mar.) 51. A. J. and T. H. Vandegriff, securities of James Hume released; Id. (25 Feb.) 220. Taxes in Rochester school district, pay for school house; L. 1845 (3 Mar.) 266. Sangamon town plat vacated; Id. 267. Jesse Florney Jennett named changed to Gray; Robert J. Jeppiers to Stringfield; Pr. L. 1847 (27 Feb.) 21. Election of justices in Athens, law authorizing modified; Id. (26 Feb.) 169. Geo. Passfield, recognized for appearance of Love S. Cornwell, conditionally released; Id. (16 Feb.) 174. Nicholas A. Garland, defaulter, released on payment by James L. Lamb of $283.64; Id. (18 Feb.) 175. Cornelius Ludlam, $198.57 for labor; Id. (28 Feb.) 189. Rienze plat vacated; Pr. L. 1851 (17 Feb.) 297. Springfield and Richland plank road chartered; Pr. L. 1853 (11 Feb.) 181. Sangamon Agricultural and Mechanical Association chartered; Id. 422. Leanna Knox, colored, one half lot 6 block 30 escheated to the state by death of her husband; Id. 443. Tax assessment for school house district No. 1, Town 13—5 legalized; L. 1853 (12 Feb.) 95. A. Elliott, on recognizance for Thos. Elliott, released; L. 1855 (12 Feb.) 51. Sangamon Mineral Co. chartered; Pr. L. 1857 (16 Feb.) 936. Auburn chartered; 2 Pr. L. 1865 (16 Feb.) 362. Benton changed to Williamsville and latter chartered; Id. 373. Sangamon Coal and Manufacturing Co. at Howlett chartered; 2 Pr. L. 1867 (5 Feb.) 404. Illinois Soldiers Capital Monumental Home Association chartered; Id. (25 Feb.) 453. Wilson changed to Illiopolis; 3 Pr. L. 1867 (6 Mar.) 266; Illiopolis school district established; Id. (7 Mar.) 35. Jamestown changed to Howlett; Id. (28 Feb.) 336. Dawson chartered; Id. (9 Mar.) 473. Bates plat vacated; Id. (8 Mar.) 601. George L. Huntington and J. S. Vredenburg securities of E. P. Clover released; L. 1867 (28 Feb) 150. John Jackson, discharged from recognizance for Jas. Freeman; L. 1869 (29 Mar.) 341.

Springfield.—Street superintendent clear the streets of trees and stumps; Pr. L. 1827 (9 Feb.) 23; plat of Calhoun made part of Springfield and deeds legalized; Pr. L. 1833 (20 Feb.) 210; powers of town trustees extended; 2 L. 1837 (20 July) 94; foregoing repealed; L. 1839 (15 Feb.) 104. City chartered; L. 1840 (3 Feb.) 6; charter amended; L. 1841 (27 Feb.) 61; tax to pay city bonds; L. 1843 (23 Feb.) 65; new orders issued to persons for moneys paid to state bank; L. 1845 (1 Mar.) 105; charter amendment, power to borrow money limited, jurisdiction of Mayor; Id. (26 Feb.) 285; charter amendment, grand jury take cognizance of criminal offenses; Pr. L. 1849 (26 Jan.) 15; charter acts reduced to one and amended; Pr. L. 1854 (2 Mar.) 35; charter amendment, limits extended, city pay county annually $800.; Pr. L. 1855 (14 Feb.) 75; amendment, county help keep up roads and bridges; Pr. L. 1857 (16 Feb.) 1050; amendment, limits extended, councilmen compensated, negotiate city bonds; Id. (18 Feb.) 1229; amendment, limits and jurisdiction extended; Pr. L. 1859 (18 Feb.) 269; foregoing amendment amended, charter election, treasury department established; Pr. L. 1861 (21 Feb.) 277; amends §3 Art. 8 of charter, council discretion as to sewers; 1 Pr. L. 1865 (16 Feb.) 522; charter amendment, managers Oak Ridge Cemetery as to nuisances; Id. 522; charter construed as to jurisdiction of circuit court over criminal cases; Id. 523. Circuit court fines collected of city residents paid to city treasury; L. 1851 (15 Feb.) 123. Jurisdiction over post office, corner 6th and Monroe, ceded to U. S.; L. 1857 (12 Jan.) 40; other lots ceded for same purpose; Id. (16 Feb.) 2. Each ward elect supervisor with powers of township supervisors; Pr. L. 1863 (16 Feb.) 170; town divided into election districts corresponding with city wards and one more; 1 Pr. L. 1867 (19 Feb.) 917. Vacates a street and alley; 2 Pr. L. 1865 (16 Feb.) 654. Sangamon Insurance Co. chartered; L. 1836 (7 Jan.) 71. Springfield Academy chartered; Pr. L. 1839 (1 Mar.) 145. Springfield Marine and Fire Insurance Co. chartered; L. 1841 (23 Feb.) 152; re-chartered; buy and sell exchange; Pr. L. 1851 (28 Jan.) 13. Obligors on a certain bond pay in scrip; Id. (27 Feb.) 300. Auditor and J. Whitney exchange lots; Id. 308. Springfield Lodge No. 4, A. and F. Masons chartered; L 1845 (3 Mar.) 137. Springfield Hotel Co. chartered; Pr. L. 1847 (1 Mar.) 164, 1 Pr. L. 1865 (3 Feb.) 610. Literary and Theological Institution of the Evangelical Lutheran Church, changed from Hillsboro to Springfield, name changed to Illinois University; L. 1852 (21 June) 49; foregoing amended and partly repealed; Pr. L. 1853 (3 Feb.) 425. Sangamon House Co chartered; Pr. L. 1853 (27 Jan.) 456. Central Lodge No. 71, F. and A. Masons chartered; Id. (12 Feb.) 521. Springfield Gas Light Co. chartered; Pr. L. 1854 (27 Feb.) 189; amendment; Pr. L. 1855 (13 Feb.) 648. Illinois Military Institute chartered, counties purchase scholarships, use of state arms etc.; Id. (14 Feb.) 509. Springfield Water Works Co. chartered, sink artesian well; Id. 544. Masonic Hall Stock Co. chartered; Id. (6 Feb.) 678. Literary Association chartered; Pr. L. 1857 (16 Feb.). 1012. Sangamo Insurance Co. chartered; Id. 1033; amendment, failure to pay installments; 1 Pr. L. 1865 (15 Feb.) 777. Springfield Water Works Co. chartered; city take stock; Pr. L. 1857 (16 Feb.) 1129. Ursuline Convent of St. Joseph chartered; Pr. L. 1859 (24 Feb.) 376; name changed to Springfield Roman Catholic Ursuline Convent of St. Joseph; 1 Pr. L. 1867 (22 Feb.) 249. Hutchinson Cemetery Association chartered; Pr. L. 1861 (18 Feb.) 74. Board of Water Commissioners chartered; Id. (21 Feb.) 285; foregoing submitted to vote; Id. 295; amendment; Pr. L. 1863 (21 Feb.) 165; further, borrow money and dam the Sangamon; 3 Pr. L. 1867 (19 Feb.) 679. City Railway Co. chartered; Pr. L. 1861 (18 Feb.) 343. Illinois Central Mutual Insurance Co. chartered; Id. 390; name changed to Springfield Insurance Co.; 1 Pr. L. 1865 (16 Feb.) 673. Illinois Railroad and Steamboat Passenger and Live Stock Insurance Co. chartered; Pr. L. 1861 (21 Feb.) 395. Morris Lindsay, interest on postage advanced to general assembly; Id. (5 Feb.) 535. Home for the Friendless chartered; Pr. L. 1863 (12 Feb.) 27; $1,000. appropriated for; 1 Pr. L. 1865 (7 Feb.) 81. Illinois Journal Co. chartered; Pr. L. 1863 (16 Feb.) 211. Watchman for the public buildings; L. 1865 (9 Feb.) 133. Pioneer Fire Co. No. 1 chartered; 1 Pr. L. 1865 (16 Feb.) 575. Phœnix Fire and Bucket Co. chartered; Id. 576. Phœnix Fire Co. No. 2 chartered; 577. Young America Fire Co. chartered; Id. (15 Feb.) 578. Illinois State Insurance Co. chartered; Id. (16 Feb.) 680; office moved from Springfield to Lena, Stephenson Co.; 2 Pr. L. 1867 (9 Mar.) 215. Planters Insurance Co. chartered; 1 Pr. L. 1865 (16 Feb.) 755. Travelers Insurance Co. chartered, office at Springfield or Chicago; Id. 790. German Reading Association chartered; 2 Pr. L. 1865 (16 Feb.) 16. Caroline A. Smith name changed to Gorman, heir of Thos. G. Gorman; Id. 96. Susan Keedy, $200. for a barn removed from near the Arsenal; Id. 241. Springfield Saving's Bank chartered; 1 Pr. L. 1867 (28 Feb.) 62. Journeymen Plasterers' Benevolent and Protective Society chartered; Id. (21 Feb.) 123. Firemen's Benevolent Association chartered; Id. (28 Feb.) 143. Springfield Hebrew Congregation chartered; Id. (25 Feb.) 242. Red Rover Hook and Ladder Co. No. 2 chartered; Id. (9 Mar.) 954. Carson Consistory of Free Masons chartered; Id. (20 Feb.) 961. Capital Railway Co., incorporation of confirmed; 2 Pr. L. 1867 (25 Feb.) 27. American Standard Life Insurance Co. chartered; Id. 126. Dubois Insurance Co. chartered; Id. (20 Feb.) 143. Union Investment Co. chartered; Id. (12 June) 235. Emes Lodge No. 67, Independent order of Bnai Brith chartered; Id. (21 Feb.) 268. Illinois Nevada Silver Mining Co. chartered; Id. (6 Mar.) 395. Junction Coal Co. chartered; Id. 396. Northwestern News Association chartered; Id. (8 Mar.) 495. Springfield Turn Verein chartered; 3 Pr. L. 1867 (25 Feb.) 650. A. B. Gilmore name changed to McIntire; L. 1869 (29 Mar.) 265.

SCHUYLER COUNTY

County formed and boundary defined; L. 1825 (13 Jan.) 92; county seat permanently located; L. 1826 (23 Jan.) 64; county revenue; Id. (27 Jan.) 89; revenue law as to county partly repealed; L. 1836 (15 Jan.) 231; commissioners' court change state roads; L. 1839 (2 Mar.) 289; school comm'rs pay funds to Brown county; L. 1840 (27 Jan.) 92; Sheriff settle with county, time allowed; L. 1841 (18 Feb) 207; school comm'rs dispose of depreciated funds; L. 1843 (4 Mar.) 40; J. D. Maulove collect tax for 1841; Id. (19 Jan.) 213; John G. McHatton, collect unpaid taxes; Id. (4 Mar.) 226; taxes of 1844, collection extended; L. 1845 (21 Feb.) 325; records of land titles transcribed, effect; L. 1849 (20 Jan.) 108; foregoing amended; L. 1851 (1 Feb.) 18; assessment for 1850 legalized; Id. (28 Jan.) 10; county borrow $10.000. to pay its debts; L. 1853 (12 Feb.) 145; supervisors bridge crooked creek at Birmingham; Pr. L. 1857 (13 Feb) 586; county bonds purchased with township funds; L. 1859 (21 Feb.) 39; county's subscription to Peoria and Hannibal Railroad expended within the county; Pr. L. 1863 (11 June) 235; issue bonds to pay bounties; 1 Pr. L. 1867 (15 Feb.) 142; towns levy tax to pay same; Id. (16 Feb.) 143; duties of county supt. of schools; L. 1869 (16 Apr.) 395. Sugar creek navigable to sec. 5, Town 1—1; Pr. L. 1833 (13 Feb.) 128; same, up to Henly's mill; L. 1835 (11 Feb.) 143. Road, Beards ferry to Quincy; L. 1829 (22 Jan.) 133; repealed; Pr. L. 1833, 178; same, Meredosia to Rushville; Id. (2 Mar.) 170. Rushville Railroad chartered; L. 1836 (16 Jan.) 85. Road, Rushville to Macomb, also Rushville to Commerce; 1 L. 1837 (2 Mar.) 307. Sheriff commissioned; L. 1839 (2 Mar.) 277. Schuyler County Mutual Fire Insurance Co. chartered; Pr. L. 1839 (4 Feb.) 33. J. G. McHatton, $58. for apprehending Wm. Frame charged with murder; L. 1840 (1 Feb.) 99. Cedar Mill Co. chartered; L. 1841 (24 Feb.) 134. Elvira Pease name changed to Horney; L. 1843 (1 Mar.) 179. R. Dougherty, $174.75 for copying records of Madison county; Id. (24 Feb.) 219. Erie plat vacated; L. 1845 (3 Mar.) 234. Securities of T. Hayden released from judgment; Id. (25 Feb.) 352. Acts of justices holding commissions declared valid; L. 1851 (12 Feb.) 85. Frederick Ferry, Dyke and Plank Road chartered; Pr. L. 1851 (17 Feb.) 271; amendment; Pr. L. 1854 (1 Mar.) 171. Glenwood Presbyterian Academy chartered; Pr. L. 1855 (14 Feb.) 367. Huntsville public square vacated; Pr. L. 1861 (21 Feb.) 732. J. Dyson, late sheriff, relief; L. 1867 (25 Feb.) 149. Buena Vista surplus war fund transferred to school fund; 3 Pr. L. 1867 (25 Feb.) 628.

Rushville.—Town chartered; Pr. L. 1839 (2 Mar.) 196; amendment, concerning road tax; L. 1845 (25 Feb.) 285; further amends, tax to pay debts; Pr. L. 1854 (4 Mar.) 154. Vacates an alley; Pr. 1847 (26 Feb.) 200. Same, Pr. L. 1851 (17 Feb.) 250. Same, McCreery's addition; L. 1855 (15 Feb.) 108. State Recorder's books removed to, also records of deeds in Military Tract; L. 1835 (9 Feb.) 157. Lots of estate of Alex. McAlister sold; 2 L. 1837 (21 July) 51. Rushville Seminary chartered; Pr. L. 1837 (24 Feb.) 93. Rushville Insurance Co. chartered; Id. (2 Mar.) 230. Rushville Female Seminary chartered; Pr. L. 1839 (1 Mar.) 191. Schuyler City Manuf. Co. chartered; L. 1841 (17 Feb.) 182. High School Association chartered; L. 1845 (3 Mar.) 311. Rushville Lodge No. 9, F. and A. Masons chartered; Pr. L. 1853 (12 Feb.) 520.

SCOTT COUNTY.

County formed, county seat at Winchester; L. 1839 (16 Feb.) 126; foregoing amended; L. 1845 (28 Feb.) 116; records in Morgan county transcribed; L. 1847 (28 Feb.) 70; special tax for building jail; L. 1852 (18 June) 15; Exeter replatted; 1 L. 1837 (19 Jan.) 320. Additional justices and constables in Naples; L. 1839 (1 Feb.) 55. Exeter Manuf. Co. chartered; Pr. L. 1839 (1 Mar.) 189; amendment; L. 1841 (17 Feb.) 184. Certain railroads issue policies of insurance; L. 1840 (27 Jan.) 24; amended; Id. (1 Feb.) 52. Manchester, road labor therein; L. 1843 (23 Feb.) 300. Geneva plat vacated; L. 1845 (28 Feb.) 287. Manchester additions vacated; Id. (26 Feb.) 295. Francis G. Murray, $249.50 for labor; Pr. L. 1847 (28 Feb.) 190. Brussels plat vacated; Id. 211. Scott County Canal Co. chartered; Pr. L. 1853 (11 Feb.) 495. Pike and Scott County Bridge Co. chartered; Pr. L. 1859 (4 Feb.) 23; 1 Pr. L. 1867 (13 Feb.) 166. M. J. Read name changed to Foashee; L. 1869 (25 Mar.) 267.

Winchester.—Town chartered; L. 1843 (4 Mar.) 307; jurisdiction for road purposes; Pr. L. 1847 (1 Feb.) 201; town re-chartered; Pr. L. 1861 (21 Feb) 706; limits extended; Id. (22 Feb.) 739; town charter amended; 3 Pr. L. 1867 (18 Feb.) 609. Town a justices district; Pr. L. 1837 (27 Feb.) 108. Winchester Seminary chartered; Id. (1 Mar.) 182. Winchester Common and Preparatory school chartered; L. 1841 (27 Feb.) 289. Winchester Female Seminary chartered; Ibid. Town constables collect delinquent taxes; L. 1845 (28 Feb.) 116. Union Insurance Co. chartered; Pr. L. 1851 (15 Feb.) 223; foregoing amended; Pr. L. 1855 (15 Feb.) 386. Winchester school district issue bonds to build school house; 2 Pr. L. 1865 (16 Feb.) 333. Winchester Cemetery Association chartered; 1 Pr. L. 1867 (20 Feb.) 208.

Naples.—Murray McConnel, ferry across the Illinois; Pr. L. 1851 (13 Feb.) 125. Protection Association chartered, for building levee; L. 1852 (21 June) 93; foregoing amended; Pr. L. 1859 (19 Feb.) 419. Hotel Co. chartered; 2 Pr. L. 1867 (23 Feb.) 54.

SECRET SOCIETIES.

Masonic.—Grand Lodge chartered; Pr. L. 1847 (20 Feb.) 108; foregoing amended; Pr. L. 1855 (14 Feb.) 681. General Law for chartering regularly constituted Lodges; Pr. L. 1849 (8 Feb.) 45. Subordinate Lodges chartered; Piasa No. 27; Pr. L. 1847 (28 Feb.) 159; Temple No. 46; L. 1852 (18 June) 23; Mt. Nebo No. 76; Id. (21 June) 99. Grand Royal Arch Chapter chartered; Pr. L. 1853 (10 Feb.) 402. Grand Commandery of Knights Templar chartered; 1 Pr. L. 1867 (7 Mar.) 963.

Odd Fellows.—Grand Lodge chartered; Pr. L. 1849 (8 Feb.) 46; foregoing amended; 1 Pr. L. 1865 (16 Feb.) 83. Grand Encampment chartered; Pr. L. 1857 (18 Feb.) 1207.

Temperance.—Grand Division of the Sons chartered; Pr. L. 1849 (8 Feb.) 109. Grand Union of the Daughters chartered; L. 1852 (19 June) 34. Grand Lodge of Good Templars chartered; 2 Pr. L. 1865 (16 Feb.) 340.

Sons of Herman.—Grand Lodge chartered; Pr. L. 1863 (21 Feb.) 33.

SHELBY COUNTY.

County formed; R. S. 1827 (23 Jan.) 115; share in proceeds of Gallatin Salines; L. 1831 (16 Feb.) 15; county erect bridge across the Kaskaskia on Paris road; Id. (10 Feb.) 23; foregoing repealed; Pr. L. 1833 (2 Jan.) 24; D. Harriss make assessment for 1842; L. 1843 (3 Mar.) 225; sale of non-residents lands for taxes; Ibid.; collector sell lands for taxes 1842–3; L. 1845 (28 Feb.) 108; part of Christian added to this county, vote thereon; L. 1851 (15 Feb.) 118; county issue bonds to pay bounties; 1 Pr. L. 1865 (15 Feb.) 144. Geo. H. Beeler, ferry across the Kaskaskia; Pr. L. 1833 (28 Jan.) 32. Asa Ledbetter's widow, sell real estate; Id. (20 Feb.) 118; other lands sold; 1 L. 1837 (20 Feb.) 183. Heirs of John Scroggins, guardian appointed; Id. (27 Feb.) 125. Dan. Francisco, mill dam on the Kaskaskia, Town 12—4; L. 1835 (14 Jan.) 45. Securities Solomon Story released; L. 1836 (16 Jan.) 248. Reese & Fergason, mill dam on Robinson creek; 1 L. 1837 (15 Feb.) 162. Road, Shelbyville to Fayette county line; 1 L. 1837 (31 Jan.) 244. Sheriff allowed time to pay over tax of 1836; Id. (21 Feb.) 323. Road, Maysville to Shelbyville, re-location; 2 L. 1837 (20 July) 66. Essex Steam Mill Co. chartered; Pr. L. 1837 (27 Feb.) 115. Shelby Steam Mill Co. chartered; Id. (4 Mar.) 319. Vesta A. Martin, declared full age; L. 1840 (10 Dec. '39) 136. Nathan Lowe, fine $25. for fireing prairie remitted; L. 1841 (26 Feb.) 211. Relief of Jordan's district, Town 10—4; L. 1845 (20 Dec. '44) 202. Peter Warren and others, sureties of J. L. Fleming, late sheriff; Id. (28 Feb.) 271. Wm. Nichols, J. P., to solemnize marriages; Pr. L. 1857 (18 Feb.) 1188. Jesse York, refunding for land sold without title; L. 1859 (24 Feb.) 152. W. M. K. Eaton, schedules for 1855 at Moweaqua legalized; Id. (18 Feb.) 176. Windsor chartered; 2 Pr. L. 1865 (16 Feb.) 634. Sale of state lands; L. 1867 (28 Feb.) 131. Sigel chartered; 3 Pr. L. 1867 (7 Mar.) 158. Oconee, same; Id. (25 Feb.) 358. Road, Mattoon to the Shelbyville and Sullivan, relocated; L. 1869 (26 Mar.) 376.

Shelbyville.—Town chartered; Pr. L. 1839 (2 Mar.) 17; charter amendment; Pr. L. 1851 (17 Feb.) 305; further amendment, boundary corrected; Pr. L. 1857 (14 Feb.) 704; limits extended, use debtors room in county jail; Pr. L. 1861 (20 Feb.) 717. City chartered; Pr. L. 1863 (16 Feb.) 157; charter amendment, powers extended; 1 Pr. L. 1865 (16 Feb.) 521; further amends charter, vacates streets and alleys; 1 Pr. L. 1867 (19 Feb.) 389. Elect additional justice; Pr. L 1833 (27 Feb.) 105. School district elect directors; L. 1847 (26 Feb.) 152. Jackson Lodge No. 53, F. and A. Masons chartered; Pr. L. 1849 (8 Feb.) 45. Vacates streets and alleys; Pr. L. 1857 (9 Feb.) 310. Same; Pr. L. 1861 (21 Feb.) 717. Shelbyville Seminary chartered; 1 Pr. L. 1867 (15 Feb.) 3. Cemetery Association chartered; Id. (5 Mar.) 222. Hotel Co. chartered; 2 Pr. L. 1867 (7 Mar.) 67.

SILK.

Culture of encouraged; L. 1839 (1 Mar.) 212.

SOLDIERS COLLEGE.

Soldiers College at Fulton, $20,000. annually for two years, in aid; L. 1869 (10 Mar.) 40.

SOLDIERS ORPHAN HOME.

Chartered; L. 1865 (16 Feb.) 76; amendment; L. 1867 (5 Mar.) 29; further amends and appropriations for; L. 1869 (1 Mar.) 39.

STARK COUNTY.

County formed, boundary and organization; L. 1839 (2 Mar.) 229; locate county seat and extend county limits, after vote; L. 1840 (1 Feb.) 62; share in internal improvement fund; Id. (29 Jan.) 65; assessments for 1839 legalized; Id. (1 Feb.) 77; Toulon to be county seat; L. 1841 (27 Feb.) 98; records made by B. Turner, deputy of B. M. Jackson, legalized; L. 1845 (18 Feb.) 364; township from Henry and added to this county, vote thereon; L. 1849 (12 Feb.) 55; sheep and swine not to run at large; L. 1855 (14 Feb.) 154. School lands Town 12—6, sold by Isaac B. Essex, deeded by governor; L. 1853 (8 Feb.) 151. Osceola plat vacated; Pr. L. 1855 (14 Feb.) 46. Wyoming chartered; 2 Pr. L. 1865 (16 Feb.) 642.

Toulon.—Town chartered; Pr. L. 1859 (11 Feb.) 688; amendment, offenders committed; 2 Pr. L. 1865 (16 Feb.) 583. Washington street partly vacated; Pr. L. 1847 (26 Feb.) 204; same; Pr. L. 1851 (28 Jan.) 18. County to sell town lots; Pr. L. 1849 (12 Feb.) 133; and Pr. L. 1855 (14 Feb.) 526. Toulon Lodge No. 93, A. and F. Masons chartered; Pr. L. 1853 (10 Feb.) 569. Trustees First Baptist Church, acts legalized; Pr. L. 1859 (12 Feb.) 33. Supervisors sell Seminary; 1 Pr. L. 1867 (18 Feb.) 4.

STATE AGRICULTURAL SOCIETY.

Chartered; L. 1853 (8 Feb.) 230. Resolutions, printing and distributing reports; Pr. L. 1855, 741; same, 8000 copies; Pr. L. 1857 (13 Feb.) 1454; same; L. 1869, 414.

STATE ARMS.

Preserved by Quartermaster General; L. 1847 (1 Mar.) 18. Principal and sureties on bonds of J. J. Hardin and John Henry, and H. New-

ton and H. P. Crawford, conditionally discharged; L. 1849 (3 Feb.) 115. Appropriation, $7,000. to purchase lot and build arsenal; L. 1855 (14 Feb.) 150. Purchase arms, construct magazine and repair arsenal; 2 L. 1861 (2 May) 10; foregoing repealed; L. 1863 (14 Feb.) 56.

STATE BANK OF ILLINOIS.

Chartered; L. 1819 (22 Mar.) 151; subscriptions not paid in gold or silver; Id. (27 Mar.) 209; re-chartered, both foregoing repealed; L. 1821 (no date, probably 3 Feb.) 80; foregoing amended, president's salary; Id. (12 Feb.) 144; further amends, notes on hand burned, no more interest bearing issued; L. 1825 (10 Jan.) 82; and, defaulters renew notes, stay of executions in favor of bank; R. S. 1827 (15 Feb. '27) 376; and again; Id. (13 Feb. '27) 377; part of §3, act 10 Jan. 1825 repealed; L. 1829 (2 Jan.) 164; amending further said act 1825; Id. (23 Jan.) 166; foregoing amendment amended; for finally closing the bank; L. 1831 (15 Feb.) 182; supplemental to foregoing; R. S. 1833 (25 Feb.) 683. Subscribers to, re-chartered; L. 1835 (12 Feb.) 7; supplemental to foregoing; L. 1836 (16 Jan.) 237; state take $100,000. stock; 1 L. 1837 (2 Mar.) 18; capital increased by $2,000,000., further respecting; Id. (4 Mar.) 18; stock taken by state alienated; 2 L. 1837 (21 July) 5; further respecting; L. 1840 (31 Jan.) 15; foregoing amended; L. 1841 (27 Feb.) 40; further concerning; Ibid.; put into liquidation; L. 1843 (24 Jan.) 21; supplemental to foregoing; Id. 27; treasurer's duty with fund comm'r; Id. (4 Mar.) 288; resolution, state disconnected from banks; L. 1843 (12 Dec. '42) 321; same, bank's accounts investigated; Id. 323; bank to pay comm'r; L. 1845 (3 Mar.) 144; affairs closed by 1 Nov '48; L. 1847 (1 Mar.) 20; trustees of, maintain suits; L. 1849 (10 Feb.) 38; relief of assignees, time of liquidation extended to 1 Jan. '51, assignees sue, suits how maintained; Ibid.; assignees' successors appointed, sales of real estate, compromises, etc.; L. 1851 (15 Feb.) 120; settlement with trustees, of certain account; L. 1855 (15 Feb.) 141. Resolution, notes of state bank received at land office; L. 1821, 188. Mortgages to, recorded; L. 1823 (18 Feb.) 179. Branch banks reports, officers' salaries, former acts concerning partly repealed; Id. 181. Shawneetown branch, examination of; L. 1825 (16 Dec. '24) 16; salary of examiners; Id. (15 Jan.) 120; resolution concerning examination; Id. 185. Defaulting officers' salaries withheld; L. 1826 (25 Jan.) 72. Attorney general and circuit attorneys prosecute for bank; Id. (27 Jan.) 88 §3. Debts due to not sealed, how enforced; Id. (28 Jan.) 92 §5. Bank debtors not paid by state; L. 1829 (19 Jan.) 114; the same subject; R. S. 1833 (12 Feb.) 588; foregoing repealed; R. S. 1845, 464. Cashiers, duty with notes for collection; L. 1829 (22 Jan.) 115. Claims due bank at Shawneetown; Id. (23 Jan.) 165. Banking house at Vandalia repaired; Id. 170. Accounts of James M. Duncan settled; L. 1831 (16 Feb.) 19, and Id. (1 Feb.) 178; two foregoing amended; Id. (15 Feb.) 179. Notes of burned; Id. (1 Feb.) 180. Paper of funded; Id. 181. Accounts and notes in attorneys' hands for collection; R. S. 1833 (22 Jan. '29) 505. Auditor and treasurer settle with the banks' collectors; L. 1835 (7 Feb.) 59; foregoing repealed; R. S. 1845, 455. Depositories of public money; 1 L. 1837 (4 Mar.) 23. Duty, while specie payment is suspended; 2 L. 1837 (21 July) 6. Interest on auditor's warrants; L. 1839 (21 Feb.) 145. Directors' appointment by governor; Id. (2 Mar.) 233. Resolution to secure national deposits; Id. 294. Clerks of Sangamon and other counties, relief in bank cases; L. 1840 (10 Dec. '39) 156. Payment, bank claims against state; L. 1841 (26 Feb.) 39. Receive payment in bills; L. 1843 (22 Dec. '42) 21. Treasurer, pay bank's bills on auditor's warrants; Id. (25 Feb.) 231. Outstanding bills and notes received as revenue; L. 1851 (15 Feb.) 119. Bank of Illinois, governor appoint directors; L. 1839 (2 Mar.) 233; said bank establish two branches; Id. 272; put into liquidation; L. 1843 (3 Mar.) 27; and Id. (25 Feb.) 30; supplemental to two foregoing; L. 1845 (28 Feb.) 246.

STATE CLAIMS.

Settlement with John Tillson, conveyance of Quincy House, settlement with other debtors of the estate; L. 1847 (23 Feb.) 68. John Crenshaw, rent of Gallatin salt mills; Id. (25 Feb.) 68. A. Starne, trustee of claims against Joel A. Matteson; L. 1863 (14 Feb.) 77. State agent to collect war claims against the United States; L. 1869 (10 Mar.) 42.

STATE ENTOMOLOGIST.

Appointment and duties; L. 1867 (9 Mar.) 35. B. D. Walsh, salary from 11 June 1867; L. 1869 (25 Mar.) 53.

STATE HORTICULTURAL SOCIETY.

Chartered; L. 1857 (11 Feb.) 201.

STATE INSTITUTIONS.

See Agricultural Colleges, Blind Asylum, Deaf and Dumb Asylum, Industrial University, Insane Hospital, Normal University, Normal University—Southern, Soldiers' College, Soldiers' and Orphans' Home, Penitentiary and State Bank of Illinois.

Resolution, legislative committee visit and examine; Pr. L. 1855, 742.

STATE INDEBTEDNESS.

See also Internal Improvement.

Governor borrow $25,000., proceeds Ohio Salines pledged; L. 1819 (19 Feb.) 16. Same, borrow $100,000.; L. 1831 (27 Jan.) 92. Same, borrow $128,000.; L. 1839 (1 Mar.) 219. Sale of public property, and payment of debt; L. 1843 (4 Mar.) 191. Canceling state indebtedness; Id. (2 Mar.) 42. Unsigned bonds destroyed; Id. (3 Mar.) 43. Resolution respecting the origin and nature of public debt; Id. 335. Plate from which state bonds are printed destroyed; Id.

839. Interest fund created; R. S. 1845 (1 Mar.) 599. Counties loan at interest their internal improvement fund; Id. (28 Feb.) 605. Unliquidated state claims barred after 1 Jan. 1849; L. 1847 (1 Mar.) 32. Scrip issue to Lyon and Howard on Illinois river improvement; Id. (4 Feb.) 50. State debt (except canal, and Macalister and Stebbins' bonds) re-funded; Id (28 Feb.) 161. Funding state scrip; Id. (22 Feb.) 165. Govern or invest annual dividend on surplus revenue, time for funding claims extended, annual dividend 1 Jan., expense of agency in New York; L. 1849 (12 Feb.) 70; amendment; L. 1852 (23 June) 198. Bonds for completion of Northern Cross railroad funded; L. 1851 (14 Feb.(88. Certificate of Internal Improvement stock issue to Nevins, Townsend & Co.; L. 1853 (12 Feb.) 185. Reduction of state debt; Id. 200. Interest due 1 Jan. 1855 paid; L. 1855 (15 Feb.) 153. Bonds or scrip issued to J. J. and J. McKillips account of public works; Id. (14 Feb.) 179. Interest payments in New York and London; Id. (15 Feb.) 180. Disposition of surplus funds arising from the 2 mill tax; L. 1857 (19 Feb.) 100. Funding arrears of interest accrued and unpaid; Id. (18 Feb.) 104. Payment, if just, of Magniac, Jardine & Co's claims; L. 1859 (16 Feb.) 18. Claim, Thompson & Foremen adjusted and paid; Id. 19. Payment of principal and interest, certain acts repealed; Id. (22 Feb.) 192; foregoing amended; L. 1863 (5 Jan.) 76. Three bonds, issued to P. O. Strang, not to be paid; Pr. L. 1861 (22 Feb.) 72. Payment of claims under the Thornton loan; Id. (21 Feb.) 212; foregoing amended; L. 1863 (20 Feb.) 84. Payment of interest on certain bonds resumed; L. 1865 (16 Feb.) 21. Interest on Sterling bonds; Id. 22. Bonds issued in lieu of unregistered canal bonds; Ibid. New internal improvement bonds issued to Murray Forbes' executors; L. 1869 (1 Apr.) 340.

STATE SEAL.

To be renewed; L. 1867 (7 Mar.) 36.

ST. CLAIR COUNTY.

The division of the Illinois Territory into the counties of Randolph and St. Clair was officially recognized by Gov. Pope in April 1809; MS Records, Sec'y State. Special term circuit court to try prisoners charged with homicide; L. 1819 (24 Feb.) 64; supplemental act, new sheriff to act; Id. (2 Mar.) 102; line between St. Clair and Monroe established; L. 1821 (31 Jan.) 67; county share in proceeds of Gallatin Salines; L. 1831 (16 Feb.) 14; revenue for 1829 collected; Id. (1 Jan) 121; present sheriff to collect said tax; L. 1835 (7 Jan.) 60; county establish ferry across the Mississippi at St. Louis; L. 1839 (2 Mar.) 175; foregoing amended, clause respecting payments to the state repealed; Pr. L. 1851 (14 Feb.) 130; commissioners' court change state roads; L. 1839 (26 Feb.) 109; taxes of certain persons for 1844 remitted account of loss by high water; L. 1845 (21 Feb.) 353; assessments for 1845–6 legalized, how collected; L. 1847 (26 Jan.) 76; records in Book 1 transcribed, force and effect thereof; L. 1849 (12 Feb.) 110; assessments for 1847–8 legalized, excess in 1847 retained in 1849; Id. 186; borrow money to build court house and improve roads; L. 1851 (29 Jan.) 12; lands forfeited to state for taxes, clerk receive redemption money; Id. (17 Feb.) 163; issue bonds in aid of plank roads and to build court house; L. 1853 (10 Feb.) 219; islands in the Mississippi, title conveyed to county; Id. (12 Feb.) 223; borrow money to complete court house; L. 1859 (3 Feb.) 39; same subject; L. 1861 (5 Feb.) 204; school district created from several towns; L. 1859 (14 Feb.) 182; weight and measurement of coal; L. 1861 (20 Feb.) 83; prevent stock running at large; 1 Pr. L. 1865 (16 Feb.) 55; transcribing old public records; 2 Pr. L. 1865 (16 Feb.) 235; fees of county officers; L. 1867 (18 Feb.) 110; pay of sheriff for dieting prisoners; Id. (7 Mar.) 114; fees of county and circuit clerks; Id. 115; facilitate the assessments of real estate; L. 1869 (8 Mar.) 162; amends act 14 Feb. '59 concerning swamp lands; Id. (11 Mar.) 243. Wm. A. Beaird, payment of $101.23; L. 1819 (25 Mar.) 253. Road, 100 feet wide from town of Illinois to Six Mile Prairie; Id. (27 Mar.) 297. Same, from Illinois town to Highland; L. 1825 (6 Jan.) 60; foregoing amended; L. 1826 (19 Jan.) 57 §3. Same, from Vandalia to St. Louis partly re-located, also from opposite St. Louis to Jacksonville, also Vandalia to Lebanon; Pr. L. 1833 (22 Feb.) 148. Same, Belleville to Pulliam's ferry; L. 1836 (15 Jan.) 214. Same, Lebanon to Wiggins' ferry; 1 L. 1837 (27 Feb.) 233. Wm. D. Noble, confined for forgery, released; L. 1823 (30 Jan.) 96. Joseph Frotier, toll bridge across Cahokia creek opposite St. Louis; Id. (18 Feb.) 200. John McKnight's administrator sell real estate; Pr. L. 1827 (15 Feb.) 28. Canal or railroad, route surveyed across American Bottom; L. 1831 (28 Jan.) 44. St. Clair Turnpike Road Co. chartered; Pr. L. 1833 (15 Feb.) 53; charter amended; L. 1835 (12 Feb.) 172. Thos. W. Talbott, grist mill on middle fork of Prairie de Long creek, may dig canal; Pr. L. 1833 (22 Feb.) 116. McKendreean College chartered; L. 1835 (9 Feb.) 177. McKendree College chartered; Pr. L. 1839 (26 Jan.) 4. Eli Pain, sale of lands of estate; L. 1836 (8 Dec. '35) 252. Reuben Goddard, the same; Id. 260; Wm. G. Rogers, a minor, the same; 1 L. 1837 (21 Feb.) 138. Reynolds and Seymour, toll bridge over Kaskaskia at Farmington; Id. (27 Jan.) 32, and Pr. L. 1839 (24 Jan.) 38. German Library Society of said county chartered; Id. (22 Feb.) 101; said Society and the Belleville Saengerbund consolidated under name of Belleville Saengerbund and Library Society; Pr. L. 1861 (18 Feb.) 548. Lebanon Female Academy chartered, department attached to constitute the district common school; Pr. L. 1839 (2 Mar.) 247. St. Clair railroad chartered; L. 1841 (26 Feb.) 195; charter amended; Pr. L. 1849 (9 Feb.) 81; further amends, name changed to St. Clair Railroad and Coal Co.; Pr. L. 1853 (11 Feb.) 91; again changed to Pittsburg Railroad and Coal Co.; Pr. L. 1859 (19 Feb.) 511; and again to Illinois and St. Louis Railroad and Coal Co.; 2 Pr. L. 1865 (16 Feb.) 203. J. P. Morris, remove drift wood from Cahokia creek; L. 1841 (25 Feb.) 214. Shiloh Meeting house tract exempt from taxation; L. 1843 (17 Feb.) 214. Brooklyn plat vacated; L. 1845 (25 Feb.) 325. St. Clair County Turnpike Co. chartered; may lease ferry Pr. L. 1847 (13 Feb.) 71; charter amended;

western terminus fixed; Pr. L. 1849 (26 Feb.) 103; hold 10 acres land at each toll gate; Pr. L. 1851 (15 Feb.) 192; further amends; Pr. L. 1853 (11 Feb.) 573; connect in one year with St. Louis Dyke; Pr. L. 1857 (14 Feb.) 752; increase stock; Pr. L. 1859 (4 Feb.) 726; charter and amendments amended; Pr. L. 1861 (16 Feb.) 745; may use Nicholson pavement; 2 Pr. L. 1865 (16 Feb.) 653. Wm. Kinney's executor redeem lands; Pr. L. 1847 (11 Feb.) 173. Heirs of James M. Reynolds, guardian sell real estate; Id. (25 Feb.) 184. St. Louis and Illinois Wire Suspension Bridge Co. chartered; Pr. L. 1849 (10 Feb.) 7. James M. Needles and others, ferry across the Mississippi opposite Carondelet, plank road across American Bottom; Id. (12 Feb.) 38; amendment, stone dyke; Pr. L. 1851 (12 Feb.) 99. Belleville and Illinoistown Railroad chartered; Pr. L. 1849 (12 Feb.) 93, and L. 1852 (21 June) 114; charter amended; 2 Pr. L. 1865 (16 Feb.) 154. [See Part 1 Chap. 86*a*, 28.] Illinois Coal Co. chartered railroad from coal lands to Brooklyn ferry across the Mississippi; Pr. L. 1849 (12 Feb.) 42; amendment repeals ferry grant; Pr. L. 1851 (29 Jan.) 33. Real estate of Wm. C. Kinney discharged from lien by state; Pr. L. 1851 (10 Feb.) 75. David W. Hopkins, late sheriff, securities released conditionally; Id. (14 Feb.) 132. Walnut Hill Cemetery exempt from taxation; Id. (17 Feb.) 289; foregoing amended; provisions extended to Thos. Harrison's Cemetery; Pr. L. 1853 (26 Jan.) 465; use of Harrison's Cemetery legalized; Pr. L. 1861 (22 Feb.) 77. Conrad Madler restored to citizenship; Pr. L. 1853 (12 Feb.) 494. Ohio and Mississippi Railroad, location of mail route at Big Silver creek changed; Id. (31 Jan.) 537. Narsisse Pensoneau and others, ferry and toll bridge across the Kaskaskia, Town 1—6; Id. (12 Feb.) 540; amendment, limit as to completion repealed; Pr. L. 1857 (18 Feb.) 1339. Centreville and Illinoistown plank road chartered; Pr. L. 1853 (12 Feb.) 567. Resolution, granting J. M. Peck duplicates of laws, reports, etc.; Id. (31 Jan.) 619. Belleville and Westfield, and Belleville and Mascoutah plank roads, organized under general act 12 Feb. '49, borrow money, issue bonds and hold real estate; Pr. L. 1854 (1 Mar.) 166; sale of Belleville and Mascoutah; Pr. L. 1861 (22 Feb.) 479. Caseyville Steam Mill Co. chartered; Pr. L. 1855 (15 Feb.) 634. Sheriff collect school tax, Town 2—6 for 1853; L. 1855 (15 Feb.) 109. St. Clair Green name changed to Forrester; Pr. L. 1857 (19 Jan.) 22. Phœnix Coal and Iron Co. chartered; Pr. L. 1855 (14 Feb.) 550. St. Louis and Illinois Bridge Co. chartered, bridge the Mississippi at St. Louis; Id. (15 Feb.) 601; charter amendment, quality of material and capacity; Pr. L. 1857 (5 Feb.) 267. Lebanon chartered; Id. (16 Feb.) 1116. Philip B. Fouke, ferry across the Mississippi 2 miles above the Wiggins; Id. (17 Feb.) 1180. American Bottom Lime, Marble and Coal Co. chartered; Id. (18 Feb.) 1209; foregoing revived; 2 Pr. L. 1867 (8 Mar.) 419. St. Louis and Belleville Manuf. and Coal Mining Co.; Pr. L. 1857 (18 Feb.) 1413. Levee, Prairie du Pont to Harrisonville; L. 1859 (24 Feb.) 110; amendment, commissioners of chartered as St. Clair and Monroe Levee and Drainage Co.; 2 Pr. L. 1865 (16 Feb.) 2; foregoing amendment amended; 2 Pr. L. 1867 (22 Feb.) 806. Urbanna name changed to Freeburg; Pr. L. 1859 (21 Feb.) 616; Freeburg charter amended; 3 Pr. L. 1867 (4 Mar.) 201. Mississippi Warehouse Co. chartered, on Bloody Island; Pr. L. 1863 (13 Feb.) 215. Corporators named in act 5 Feb. '64 under laws of Missouri, to organize in this state as the St. Louis and Illinois Bridge Co.; 1 Pr. L. 1865 (16 Feb.) 191. School district No. 3, Town 2—10, boundary defined; 2 Pr. L. 1865 (16 Feb.) 322. O'Fallon chartered; Id. (15 Feb.) 524. Illinois and St. Louis Bridge Co. chartered; 1 Pr. L. 1867 (21 Feb.) 168. Centreville Railroad chartered; 2 Pr. L. 1867 (7 Mar.) 566. Mascoutah and Lebanon Railroad chartered; Id. (1 Mar.) 594. Old Town of St. Clair, useless streets vacated; 3 Pr. L. 1867 (25 Feb.) 103. Centreville, streets vacated; Id. 107.

Belleville.—Town trustees appointed; L. 1819 (27 Mar.) 305; town charter amended; L. 1823 (14 Feb.) 147; [town incorporated under general acts 12 Feb. '31, and 31 Jan. '35]; corporate powers extended; Pr. L. 1839 (26 Feb.) 115; charter amended; L. 1841 (23 Feb.) 334. City chartered; L. 1845 (26 Feb.) 359; foregoing declared in force; Pr. L. 1847 (24 Feb.) 119; incorporation under act 10 Feb. '49 legalized; Pr. L. 1851 (13 Feb.) 111; fines and forfeitures paid into city treasury; L. 1851 (17 Feb.) 156; issue $10,000. bonds for market house; L. 1853 (10 Feb.) 279; corporate powers extended, act 3 Feb. '40 chartering Springfield, extend over this city; Pr. L. 1853 (10 Feb.) 566; general charter amendment; Pr. L. 1854 (1 Mar.) 223, and Pr. L. 1855 (15 Feb.) 53; moneys from licenses and fines in West Belleville paid into town treasury; Pr. L. 1857 (5 Feb.) 264; city incorporation acts reduced to one and amended; Pr. L. 1859 (18 Feb.) 80; West Belleville to borrow money; Id. (24 Feb.) 719; city charter amendment, cemeteries, additions, etc.; Pr. L. 1861 (22 Feb.) 115; corporate powers extended; 1 Pr. L. 1865 (15 Feb.) 254; general amendment; 1 Pr. L. 1867 (22 Feb.) 530; to take stock in plank roads etc.; Id. (5 Mar.) 841. Trustees Belleville Academy appointed; L. 1819 (27 Mar.) 305; lease for 10 years sec. 16, Town 1—8; L. 1821 (27 Jan.) 34. Debating and Library Association chartered; Id. 35. Election of trustees of Literary Society and School Association legalized; Pr. L. 1851 (28 Jan.) 19. Belleville Water Co. chartered; Pr. L. 1853 (3 Feb.) 206. Belleville Mutual Fire Insurance Co. chartered; Pr. L. 1855 (14 Feb.) 388; charter extended 50 years; Pr. L. 1857 (17 Feb.) 1174. Belleville Fire Co. chartered; Pr. L. 1855 (15 Feb.) 591; name changed to St. Clair Fire Co.; 1 Pr. L. 1865 (16 Feb.) 573. Belleville Mutual Aid Society chartered; Pr. L. 1855 (6 Feb.) 657. Belleville Gymnastic Society chartered; Pr. L. 1857 (5 Feb.) 301. Illinois Grove No. 1, U. A. Order of Druids; Id. (10 Feb.) 366; foregoing repealed, and charters United Brethren at Belleville; Pr. L. 1861 (12 Feb.) 54. Hotel Co. chartered; Pr. L. 1857 (18 Feb.) 1253. St. Clair Savings and Insurance Co. chartered; Pr. L. 1859 (24 Feb.) 396. Oakwoods Cemetery Association chartered; Pr. L. 1861 (22 Feb.) 63. South Belleville Fire Co. chartered; 1 Pr. L. 1865 (16 Feb.) 574. Belleville Water Works Co. chartered; 2 Pr. L. 1865 (16 Feb.) 687. Board of Trade chartered; 1 Pr. L. 1867 (28 Feb.) 852. City Railway Co. chartered; 2 Pr. L. 1867 (25 Feb.) 25. Sharpshooters'

Society chartered; 3 Pr. L. 1867 (20 Feb.) 90.

Cohokia.—Village plat re-surveyed; Pr. L. 1855 (14 Feb.) 199. Common confirmed to inhabitants of town; L. 1819 (5 Mar.) 122; supplemental act; Id. (25 Mar.) 255; further supplemental; L. 1823 (7 Feb.) 117; first foregoing (5 Mar. '19) repealed; Pr. L. 1827 (9 Feb.) 22; leasing part of said common; L. 1841 (17 Feb.) 65; foregoing amended; L. 1843 (1 Mar.) 71; amends act 17 Feb. '41, further concerning leasing; Pr. L. 1857 (18 Feb.) 1203; supplemental to foregoing; 3 Pr. L. 1867 (5 Mar.) 621. For raising a levee opposite town; Pr. L. 1827 (24 Jan.) 17; supplemental act; L. 1840 (1 Feb.) 99; amendment, supervisor bring action of trespass; Pr. L. 1857 (16 Feb.) 1079.

East St. Louis.—Illinoistown chartered; Pr. L. 1859 (19 Feb.) 621, and again, may adopt name of East St. Louis; Pr. L. 1861 (21 Feb.) 646. City chartered; 1 Pr. L. 1865 (13 Feb.) 844; charter amendment, city court created; 1 Pr. L. 1867 (22 Feb.) 473; city police force established; 2 Pr. L. 1867 (23 Feb.) 483. St. Clair Steam Mill chartered; L. 1840 (1 Feb.) 100. East St. Louis Real Estate. Loan and Trust Co. chartered; 1 Pr. L. 1865 (16 Feb.) 57. East St. Louis Gas Light and Coke Co., two charters; Id. 582, 584. Rail Mill chartered; 2 Pr. L. 1865 (16 Feb.) 33. Board of Trade chartered; 1 Pr. L. 1867 (21 Feb.) 852. Hotel Co. chartered; 2 Pr. L. 1867 (1 Mar.) 61. Tribune Co. chartered; Id. (7 Mar.) 512. Broadway and Dyke Railroad chartered; Id. 556. Transfer Co. chartered; 3 Pr. L. 1867 (28 Feb.) 640. East St. Louis Turn Verein chartered; Id. 652. Elevator Warehouse Co. chartered; Id. (6 Mar.) 670.

Fayetteville.—Thos. Pulliam and others, bridge the Kaskaskia; Pr. L. 1855 (14 Feb.) 599; foregoing amended; Pr. L. 1857 (15 Jan.) 24. James A. Knight and others, bridge the Kaskaskia; Pr. L. 1855 (15 Feb.) 698; amendment, chartered as Kaskaskia Floating Bridge Co.; Pr. L. 1857 (30 Jan.) 104. James W. Hughes and others, ferry across the Kaskaskia; Pr. L. 1863 (13 Feb.) 190.

Mascoutah.—Mechanicsburg name changed to Mascoutah; L. 1839 (16 Feb.) 126; tax for sidewalks, vote thereon; Pr. L. 1853 (10 Feb.) 605; town chartered; Pr. L. 1857 (4 Feb.) 236; charter amendment, limits defined; Pr. L. 1859 (24 Feb.) 646; town take stock in plank roads, etc.; 1 Pr. L. 1867 (5 Mar.) 841. German School Association chartered; Pr. L. 1855 (9 Feb.) 514. Mascoutah Savings and Insurance Co. chartered; Pr. L. 1861 (20 Feb.) 407. Real Estate and Savings Bank chartered; Id. (7 Mar.) 81. Mascoutah Turn Verein chartered; 3 Pr. L. 1867 (19 Feb.) 647.

New Athens.—Town name of Athens changed to New Athens; 3 Pr. L. 1867 (25 Feb.) 601. N. Pensaneau, bridge the Kaskaskia; L. 1839 (1 Mar.) 237. D. Anderson, ferry across the Kaskaskia; L. 1845 (20 Feb.) 357; foregoing extended 10 years; Pr. L. 1855 (15 Feb.) 603. Athens Bridge Co. chartered; Pr. L. 1853 (8 Feb.) 606. James W. Hughs and others, ferry across the Kaskaskia; Pr. L. 1855 (15 Feb.) 597. Wm. H. Burnett, the same; Pr. L. 1857 (16 Feb.) 842; foregoing amended; 1 Pr. L. 1867 (8 Mar.) 935.

Prairie du Pont.—A Common confirmed to the inhabitants of; L. 1819 (5 Mar.) 122; supplemental acts; Id. (25 Mar.) 255, and L. 1823 (7 Feb.) 117. Village erected into a school district; L. 1847 (20 Feb.) 155; foregoing amended; L. 1849 (8 Feb.) 152. Village plat re-surveyed; Pr. L. 1855 (15 Feb.) 199.

ST. LOUIS.

City of.—Allowed until 17 Feb. 1853 to complete works for protection of harbor, works above and below Bloody Island; L. 1851 (17 Feb.) 150.

STEPHENSON COUNTY.

County created, boundary and organization; L. 1837 (4 Mar.) 96; taxes of 1839, collection; L. 1841 (18 Feb.) 306; extra tax levied for 1845–6 and 7; L. 1845 (3 Mar.) 251; the sick in 1846 released from road labor; Pr L. 1847 (18 Feb.) 27; borrow $50,000. to complete county buildings; Pr. L. 1857 (30 Jan.) 108; borrow money to rebuild poor house; L. 1859 (9 Feb.) 40; township support of paupers; L. 1861 (18 Feb.) 206, and 2 Pr. L. 1867 (25 Feb.) 490; tax to meet county indebtedness, vote thereon; L. 1861 (18 Feb.) 208; special bounty tax levied 20 Jan. '65 legalized; 1 Pr. L. 1865 (9 Feb.) 145; time for collection of taxes extended; 2 Pr. L. 1865 (9 Feb.) 338. Winslow Bridge Co. chartered; Pr. L. 1839 (2 Mar.) 184; tolls fixed; L. 1843 (4 Mar.) 51. Bridge the Pecatonica in town of Pennsylvania; Id. (1 Mar.) 47. Guardian of D'Kyle Stephenson, sell and convey lands; L. 1845 (27 Feb.) 149. Harrison, name changed to Cedarville; Pr. L. 1849 (12 Feb.) 132, and Pr. L. 1851 (17 Feb.) 277. Acts of John Howe as probate justice, and Isaac Bectel, Philip Fowler, Julius Smith and Jas. J. Rogers as justices, legalized; L. 1849 (25 Feb.) 100. West half Town 28—6 added to West Point; L. 1851 (17 Feb.) 187. Sam'l H. Fischer, to dam the Pecatonica, Town 28—6; Pr. L. 1853 (3 Feb.) 583. Trustees Bolander's school district, Towns 28 and 29—9, convey lands; L. 1853 (12 Feb.) 179. Cedarville Cemetery Association chartered; Pr. L. 1855 (14 Feb.) 456. Freeport and Monroe Railroad chartered; Pr. L. 1857 (29 Jan.) 95, and 2 Pr. L. 1867 (25 Feb.) 781. Trustees Town 28—9, acts in 1858 legalized; L. 1859 (14 Feb.) 177. Union Agricultural Society of JoDaviess, Stephenson, LaFayette Wis. and Greene Wis. counties chartered; Pr. L. 1861 (16 Feb.) 34; foregoing amended, same powers as granted County Agricultural Societies under act 21 Feb. '61; 1 Pr. L. 1865 (16 Feb.) 54. Vacates alley in Davis; Pr. L. 1861 (20 Feb.) 38. W. S. Gray, late sheriff, conditionally released from judgment; L. 1863 (13 Feb.) 67. Caleb W. Brown, to dam the Pecatonica; Pr. L. 1863 (2 Feb.) 213. Place of holding elections in Silver Creek; 1 Pr. L. 1867 (19 Feb.) 917. Davis Union School District, Town 28—9; 3 Pr. L. 1867 (28 Feb.) 52. Orangeville chartered; Id. (7 Mar.) 536. Buckeye Insurance Co., charter amended, also, other township insurance co's

organized under act 20 Feb. '67; L. 1869 (19 Feb.) 236.

Freeport.—Plat partly vacated, town re-surveyed; Pr. L. 1851 (12 Feb.) 86; Rice's addition re-surveyed; Pr. L. 1855 (14 Feb.) 48. City chartered; Id. 122; charter amendment, powers extended; Pr. L. 1857 (11 Feb.) 465; issue $4,000. city bonds to cancel floating debt; Pr. L. 1861 (20 Feb.) 199; omissions in assessment lists, corporate powers extended; 1 Pr. L. 1865 (16 Feb.) 363; further extended; 1 Pr. L. 1867 (9 Mar.) 747. Freeport Seminary of Learning chartered; Pr. L. 1839 (2 Mar.) 238. J. A. Clark, bridge the Pecatonica; L. 1840 (27 Jan.) 26. Stephenson County Hydraulic and Manuf. Co. chartered, may dam the Pecatonica; Pr. L. 1847 (18 Feb.) 100. Young Men's Association chartered; Pr. L. 1855 (15 Feb.) 533. Hotel Co. chartered; Id. (14 Feb.) 595. Gas Light and Coke Co. chartered; Id. 643. Freeport Manuf. Co. chartered; Pr. L. 1857 (10 Feb.) 347. Freeporter Saengerbund chartered; Id. (17 Feb.) 1185. Savings Institute chartered; Pr. L. 1861 (22 Feb.) 315. City Railway chartered; 2 Pr. L. 1867 (25 Feb.) 22. Notaries public; L. 1867 (28 Feb.) 135. City Market chartered; 2 Pr. L. 1867 (7 Mar.) 415. Freeport School District chartered; 3 Pr. L. 1867 (25 Feb.) 65. Freeport Turn Verein chartered; Id. 651. Freeport Insurance Companies: The Stephenson County Mutual Fire, chartered; Pr. L. 1853 (12 Feb.) 376; general amendment; Pr. L. 1861 (20 Feb.) 425. The Farmers, chartered; Pr. L. 1857 (16 Feb.) 996; corporate powers extended; 1 Pr. L. 1865 (15 Feb.) 643; accept installment notes; 2 Pr. L. 1867 (28 Feb.) 181. The American, home office removed from Granville Putnam Co.; Pr. L. 1859 (19 Feb.) 396; take lightning risks, assessments on premium notes; Pr. L. 1863 (13 Feb.) 196; take premium notes and receive guaranteed capital; 1 Pr. L. 1865 (16 Feb.) 615; office may be taken to Chicago; 2 Pr. L. 1867 (25 Feb.) 125. The Columbian, chartered; Pr. L. 1861 (20 Feb.) 350; may have branch office in Chicago, classification of business; Pr. L. 1863 (13 Feb.) 203; invest in U. S. securities; 2 Pr. L. 1867 (28 Feb.) 161. The Tornado, chartered; Pr. L. 1861 (22 Feb.) 429; name changed to Fire and Tornado; Pr. L. 1863 (12 Feb.) 197; general amendment; Pr. L. 1865 (16 Feb.) 653; name again changed to the Continental; 2 Pr. L. 1867 (7 Mar.) 229. The Winneshiek, chartered; Pr. L. 1861 (18 Feb.) 433; guaranteed capital increased; 1 Pr. L. 1865 (16 Feb.) 824. The Adams, transferred from Greenville; Pr. L. 1863 (21 Feb.) 192; may remove to Aurora; 1 Pr. L. 1865 (16 Feb.) 613; also, to Chicago; 2 Pr. L. 1867 (28 Feb.) 180. The State, chartered, must organize within a year; Pr. L. 1863 (10 June) 194. The Accident, chartered; 1 Pr. L. 1865 (16 Feb.) 612. The Citizens' Life, chartered; Id. 628; amendment, time of organization extended; 2 Pr. L. 1867 (9 Mar.) 200. The Citizens' Health, chartered; 1 Pr. L. 1865 (16 Feb.) 630. The National, chartered; Id. (15 Feb.) 728. The Freeport, chartered; Id. (16 Feb.) 735; name changed to the German; 2 Pr. L. 1867 (25 Feb.) 124. The Relief, chartered; 1 Pr. L. 1865 (16 Feb.) 766. The Stephenson, [act chartering not found] general charter amendment; Id. 781. The Union, chartered; Id. (15 Feb.) 799. The Western World, chartered; Id. (16 Feb.) 821. The Protection Life, chartered; 2 Pr. L. 1867 (7 Mar.) 171. The Mokena, chartered; Id. (8 Mar.) 204.

TAZEWELL COUNTY.

County formed and limits defined; R. S. 1827 (31 Jan. '27) 113; boundaries defined; L. 1829 (22 Jan.) 32; county seat located; L. 1831 (16 Feb.) 69, and L. 1835 (12 Feb.) 53; lease offices in court house; L. 1841 (26 Feb.) 92; records A to D transcribed; Id. (18 Feb.) 204; county agent to make certain purchases; L. 1843 (3 Feb.) 109; school funds transferred to Mason and Woodford; L. 1845 (1 Mar.) 235; census return 9 Apr. 1846 true enumeration, distribution of school fund; L. 1847 (26 Jan.) 41; relocation of county seat, erection of county buildings; L. 1849 (2 Feb.) 47; foregoing amended; L. 1850 (22 Feb.) 46; tax to build jail; L. 1851 (8 Feb.) 24; township support of paupers; Id. (17 Feb.) 194; paupers chargeable, on what towns; construction of §§14, 15 and 16, Chap. 8, R. S.; L. 1852 (21 June) 113; jurisdiction of county court extended; L. 1857 (16 Feb.) 36; foregoing repealed; L. 1859 (15 Jan.) 67; tax to pay bounties; 1 Pr. L. 1865 (2 Feb.) 145; tax levies to pay bounties legalized; Id. 146; secure the location of Agricultural and Mechanical College; Id. (16 Feb.) 543; fees of county judge; L. 1869 (25 Mar.) 149. Springfield and Peoria road changed; Pr. L. 1833 (22 Feb.) 147. Road, Pekin and Danville, re-located; L. 1835 (6 Feb.) 107. Same, Liberty to Tremont; L. 1836 (16 Jan.) 220. Same, Wesley City to Mackinaw, located; 1 L. 1837 (27 Feb.) 205. Same, Springfield and Ottawa, re-location; Id. (18 Feb.) 216. Same, Peoria to Indiana line, report of location received; Id. (4 Mar.) 259. Same, Tremont to Washington, also to Dillon, located; L. 1839 (2 Mar.) 60. Same, Pekin to Crane creek, located; Id. 246. State road, between Pekin and Washington, legalized; L. 1840 (3 Feb.) 112. Road, Oliver's Grove to Pekin, pay of locating, comm'rs; L. 1843 (6 Feb.) 250. Pekin and Tremont Railroad chartered; L. 1836 (13 Jan.) 90. School lands, Towns 28—2 and 25—2; Id. (8 Dec. '35) 228. Benj. Kellogg, Jr., toll bridge over the Mackinaw; 1 L. 1837 (2 Mar.) 36. Liberty changed to Dillon; Id. (19 Jan.) 330. Hanover College chartered; Pr. L. 1837 (27 Feb.) 101. Mackinaw and Illinois Canal Co. chartered; Id. 112. R. and S. Haines, mill dam on the Mackinaw, Town 24—2; L. 1839 (15 Feb.) 108. Auburn plat vacated; Id. (23 Feb.) 176. Tremont chartered; L. 1841 (27 Feb.) 344. J. C. & G. L. Gibson, ferry at Wesley City; L. 1843 (3 Feb.) 143. Wm. L. May, ferry across the Illinois at outlet of Lake Peoria; L. 1841 (23 Feb.) 113, [see also Peoria county] foregoing amended, double rates; L. 1843 (10 Feb.) 144. Farmer's and Mechanic's Co. chartered; Id. (3 Mar.) 155. Wesley City plat plartly vacated; Id. 294. J. O'Brien, pay treasurer state bank notes; L. 1845 (18 Feb.) 327. Heirs Timothy Losey, guardian invest in real estate; Pr. L. 1847 (27 Feb.) 187. James B. Worley, coroner elect, give bond by 1 Apr.; Pr. 1853 (26 Jan.) 463. County Agricultural Society chartered; Pr. L. 1855 (9 Feb.) 665. Peoria and Fon du Lac Coal Mining Co. chartered; Pr. L. 1857 (14 Feb.)

809. Fon du Lac Cemetery Association chartered; Id. (17 Feb.) 1167 Tazewell County Coal Mining Co. chartered; Id. 1178. Drain lands, Towns 22—4 and 5; L. 1861 (21 Feb.) 209. Wm. S. Maus, late collector, released from sales of land on execution; 2 Pr. L. 1865 (16 Feb.) 242. School directors district No. 1, Town 25, borrow money to complete school house; Id. 305. Danforth changed to Tullamore; Id. 437. John Davenport, taxes for 1863; L. 1867 (28 Feb.) 165. Mackinaw chartered; 3 Pr. L. 1867 (7 Mar.) 167. Blue Town changed to Hilton; L. 1869 (25 Mar.) 269.

Pekin.—Town incorporation 2 July 1835, legalized; Pr. L. 1837 (19 Jan.) 3; town chartered, establish ferry across the Illinois; Pr. L. 1839 (23 Feb.) 24; rates of ferriage; L. 1840 (1 Feb.) 51 §14; charter amendment, additional justice; L. 1843 (1 Mar.) 302; town grant of ferry to Benj. S. Prettyman confirmed; Pr. L. 1849 (10 Feb.) 129; acts of town authorities organizing under general Law of 1849 legalized; Pr. L. 1851 (24 Jan.) 12; charter amendment; L. 1852 (19 June) 41; construct plank road across the bottom; Pr. L. 1853 (12 Feb.) 570; city expend $5,000. open road to river, sale of ferry to Railroad; Pr. L. 1854 (27 Feb.) 157; take stock in Illinois River Railroad, vote thereon legalized; Pr. L. 1857 (29 Jan.) 105; limits of city and town extended; Pr. L. 1859 (14 Feb.) 250; city charter amendment; Pr. L. 1861 (20 Feb.) 240. Hotel Co. chartered; Pr. L. 1837 (18 Feb.) 51. Tazewell Commercial and Fire Insurance Co. chartered; Pr. L. 1839 (2 Mar.) 21. Tazewell County Commercial and Fire Insurance Co. name changed to Pekin Insurance Co.; L. 1841 (18 Feb.) 151. Election of James Harriott as justice, and Wm. Stanberry Jr. as collector, legalized; L. 1851 (11 Feb.) 79. Pekin Plank Road chartered; Pr. L. 1853 (12 Feb.) 178. Pekin Water Co. chartered; Id. 417. Pekin Gas Light Co. chartered; Pr. L. 1861 (18 Feb.) 336; amendment; 1 Pr. L. 1867 (25 Feb.) 974. German Workingmen's Association chartered; Id. (8 Mar.) 137. German Turner Association chartered; 3 Pr. L. 1867 (9 Feb.) 646.

Washington.—Town chartered; Pr. L. 1857 (10 Feb.) 355; amendment, license sale of liquor; Pr. L. 1859 (24 Feb.) 704; election and jurisdiction of police magistrate; 2 Pr. L. 1865 (16 Feb.) 611, same, Id. (10 Feb.) 612. Washington Academy chartered; Pr. L. 1837 (4 Mar.) 296. Washington Seminary chartered; Pr. L. 1859 (23 Feb.) 377.

TURNPIKES.

Embarrass.—Incorporated; from Yellowbanks Crawford county to Gifford's sign post opposite Vincennes; L. 1819 (4 Mar.) 116.

Carrollton and Alton.—Incorporated; Pr. L. 1833 (28 Feb.) 64.

Springfield and Alton.—Incorporated; Pr. L. 1833 (1 Mar.) 77. Additional commissioners; L. 1836 (28 Dec. '35) 181. Charter amended; Alton the terminus; L. 1836 (19 Dec. '35) 182. Charter further amended; extend from Springfield to Bloomington; Pr. L. 1837 (2 Mar.) 248. Time of completion extended; not to compete with the state work from Alton to Carlinville; Pr. L. 1839 (2 Mar.) 162. Supplemental to charter; L. 1841 (27 Feb.) 353.

Rushville and Beardstown.—Incorporated; Pr. L. 1833 (2 Mar.) 82. Charter amended; L. 1835 (12 Feb.) 180.

Alton, Jacksonville and Galena.—Incorporated; L. 1836 (14 Jan.) 115.

Wabash and Mississippi.—Incorporated; L. 1836 (13 Jan.) 120.

Chicago and Fox River.—Incorporated; via. Berry's Point and Naperville to Aurora; Pr. L. 1837 (1 Mar.) 165. Section 13 of the foregoing repealed; 2 L. 1837 (21 July) 39.

White Hall and Albany.—Incorporated; Pr. L. 1837 (31 Jan.) 11.

Grafton and Carrollton.—Incorporated; via. Carrollton, Whitehall and Manchester to Jacksonville; extend to Springfield and branch to Jerseyville; Pr. L. 1837 (2 Mar.) 207.

Darwin and Charleston.—Incorporated; Laws 1839 (2 Mar.) 229. Extended to Springfield; L. 1841 (27 Feb.) 352. Supplemental to the foregoing; Id. 177. Relocation in part; L. 1843 (6 Mar.) 311.

Quincy, Jacksonville and Springfield.—Incorporated; state may purchase after 10 years; Pr. L. 1837 (1 Mar.) 143. Foregoing amended; Pr. L. 1839 (28 Feb.) 148. Time of completion extended 5 years; Pr. L. 1839 (1 Mar.) 193.

Vandalia and Alton.—Incorporated; condemn lands, timber, etc.; state may purchase; Pr. L. 1839 (2 Mar.) 165. May borrow money to amount of capital; Pr. L. 1839 (28 Feb.) 196.

Vandalia and Mississippi.—Incorporated; L. 1840 (10 Dec. '39.) 139. May Borrow money to amount of capital; Pr. L. 1839 (28 Feb.) 196.

Springfield and Quincy, and Beardstown and Warsaw.—Incorporated; L. 1841 (1 Mar.) 356.

Fulton.—Incorporated; Pr. L. 1839 (2 Mar.) 200.

Metropolis and Vienna.—Incorporated; $20' 000. of stock exempt from taxation; sell roadbed to any railroad company; Pr. L. 1855 (14 Feb.) 470.

Waterloo and Carondelet.—Incorporated; state may purchase; establish a ferry across the Missisippi; Pr. L. 1855 (14 Feb.) 521. Charter amended; repeals part of § 8; legalizes acts of commissioners; Pr. L. 1857 (14 Feb.) 774. Charter further amended; counties, cities and towns to take stock; 3 Pr. L. 1867 (5 Mar.) 653.

Prairie du Rocher and St. Charles Landing.—Incorporated; Pr. L. 1859 (21 Feb.) 723.

Illinois and Indiana.—Incorporated; 2 Pr. L. 1865 (16 Feb.) 650. Charter amended; location in and near Chicago changed; 3 Pr. L. 1867 (5 Mar.) 664.

Waterloo, Columbia and Mississippi.—Incorporated; establish ferry; 3 Pr. L. 1867 (6 Mar.) 665.

UNION COUNTY.

County formed prior to the organization of the state. County share in proceeds of Gallatin

Salines; L. 1831 (16 Feb.) 14; borrow money to complete county buildings; L. 1840 (1 Feb.) 75; A. Deardorff, acts as county clerk legalized; L. 1845 (26 Feb.) 295; management of school fund; Id. (3 Mar.) 321; taxes of 1844 remitted in part, account of loss by high water; Id. (21 Feb.) 353; borrow $1,000. to repair court house; L. 1853 (11 Feb.) 234; borrow $2,500. to build jail; Pr. L. 1854 (4 Mar.) 167; borrow $5,000. to build court house; Pr. L. 1857 (19 Jan.) 25. Sheriff discharged from liability for failing to collect land tax; L. 1819 (27 Mar.) 300. Isaac Worley, indicted for murder, change of venue; Pr. Laws 1827 (24 Jan.) 17. Road, America to Vandalia, relocation; L. 1831 (7 Jan.) 141; examination of said road between Jonesboro and county line south; Pr. L. 1833 (20 Dec. '32) 199. Same, Jonesboro to Snider's ferry, a state road; L. 1835 (13 Feb.) 122. Same, Mauville's mills to Saratoga, and Jonesboro to Fredonia, locations; L. 1843 (20 Feb.) 252. Champion Anderson, $28.17 for selling bank property; L. 1835 (7 Feb.) 78. School lands, Town 12—3, sale of; L. 1836 (19 Dec. '35) 230. Saratoga changed to Western Saratoga; L. 1843 (21 Jan.) 297. Hygean Spring at W. Saratoga chartered; L. 1845 (1 Mar.) 113. County Charcoal Road chartered; Pr. L. 1847 (28 Feb. 160. Andrew Dearduff, $32.67 overpaid; Id. (24 Feb.) 181. Union Turnpike Co., chartered; Pr. L. 1849 (12 Feb.) 104. Jonesboro Plank Road chartered; Pr. L. 1851 (13 Feb.) 112; amendment; Pr. L. 1855 (14 Feb.) 467. County Agricultural and Mechanical Society chartered; Pr. L. 1857 (22 Jan.) 27. Union Insurance and Trust Co. chartered; Id. (30 Jan.) 110; may be moved to Chicago; Pr. L. 1861 (22 Feb.) 433. Peru plat vacated; Pr. L. 1857 (9 Feb.) 310. R. and J. Slay, convicted of larceny, restored; L. 1859 (24 Feb.) 18. Jos. G. Webb, restored to citizenship; 2 Pr. L. 1867 (21 Feb.) 812. J. H. McElhany robbed of $9,303.68, time of payment extended; L. 1869 (13 Mar.) 337. D. Grow; released from judgment on recognisance; Id. (7 Apr.) 340.

Jonesboro.—Town chartered; L. 1821 (14 Feb.) 160; amendment; L. 1823 (14 Feb.) 142; Hancock's addition vacated; Pr. L. 1849 (8 Feb.) 112; vacates alley in Grammar's donation; L. 1852 (18 June) 29; foregoing repealed; L. 1855 (12 Feb.) 93. City Chartered; Pr. L. 1857 (28 Jan.) 74. Jonesboro College chartered; L. 1835 (9 Feb.) 178; regulating; L. 1840 (3 Feb.) 131; charter amendment; Pr. L. 1857 (16 Feb.) 875. Election of trustees Methodist E. Church legalized; Pr. L. 1851 (15 Feb.) 200. Jonesboro Lodge No. 111, F. and A. Masons chartered; Pr. L. 1855 (14 Feb.) 734.

Anna.—Town chartered; 2 Pr. L. 1865 (16 Feb.) 342; amendment; 3 Pr. L. 1867 (8 Mar.) 216; vacates an alley; Id. (6 Mar.) 107.

VERMILION COUNTY.

County formed and boundary defined; L. 1826 (18 Jan.) 50; foregoing amended, county seat fixed; Pr. L. 1827 (26 Dec. '26) 3; share in proceeds of Gallatin Salines; L. 1831 (16 Feb.) 14; sale of certain school lands; L. 1839 (2 Mar.) 232; special election for circuit clerk; Pr. L. 1849 (11 Jan.) 28; township organization avoided after adoption; L. 1851 (17 Feb.) 135; detach towns 30, 31, and 2-6 of 29 and attach them to Kankakee, conditionally; Pr. L. 1855 (14 Feb.) 662; county court jurisdiction extended and practice therein; L. 1859 (24 Feb.) 96; foregoing amended; L. 1861 (18 Feb.) 108; terms in said court; L. 1867 (7 Mar.) 72; sale of swamp lands; L. 1857 (16 Feb.) 122; sheriff's fees, L. 1869 (20 Mar.) 183. Road, Vincennes and Chicago, relocation; L. 1835 (10 Feb.) 119. Same, Danville to County line, located; 2 L. 1837 (20 July) 62. Improve navigation of Big Vermilion; 1 L. 1837 (3 Mar.) 171. John Rearson, elected county judge, discharged as ad'mr of Francis Prince; Id. (2 Mar.) 187. Additional judges of election at county seat; L. 1839 (15 Feb.) 120. Bridge the Big and Little Vermilion; Id. (19 Feb.) 137. Sheperdstown plat vacated; L. 1840 (8 Jan.) 44. School district Town 19—10; L. 1841 (19 Feb.) 258. Same, Town 20—10, and sale of school lands; L. 1843 (6 Feb.) 274, and L. 1855 (15 Feb.) 106. Same, Towns 17—10 and 11; Id. (28 Jan.) 280. Same, Town 18—10; L. 1845 (26 Feb.) 161. Thos. Short, $100. lost in settlement; L. 1845 (28 Feb.) 107. G. Richards, convicted of perjury, restored; Id. (1 Jan.) 184. Trustees Town 19—11, received deed from Wm. Moss; Id. (17 Jan.) 193. Georgetown Seminary chartered; Id. (7 Feb.) 209. Estate of Stephen S. Collett of Indiana, partition of; Pr. L. 1847 (16 Jan.) 22. Isaac Lodowsky, surety for Wm. O'Neil, released; Id. (18 Feb.) 175. Trustees Schools, Town 20—12, execute release to Salomon Davis; Id. (1 Mar.) 191. Georgetown and Perryville Plank Road to bridge Big Vermilion; Pr. L. 1851 (18 Jan.) 4. Hiram Hickman, late collector, settlement; L. 1851 (11 Feb.) 79. Essex established and organized; Pr. L. 1853 (8 Feb.) 160. Streets in Vermilion vacated; Pr. L. 1855 (15 Feb.) 47. Champaign and Vermilion Rail-Road and Coal Mining Co., chartered; Id. (14 Feb.) 336. Vermilion Coal Mining Co. chartered; Pr. L. 1857 (16 Feb.) 999. Assessments district 1, Town 19—11, legalized; L. 1859 (14 Feb.) 176. Part of Town 19—12; attached to 18—12; Id. (21 Feb.) 211. Farmer' Steam Wagon Road chartered; Pr. L. 1861 (22 Feb.) 310. Fractional sections Town 22—10 attached to 22—11, and the same, Town 23—10 to 23—11; Pr. L. 1863 (2 Feb.) 277. Wm Holden name changed to Alvan Gilbert; 2 Pr. L. 1865 (16 Feb.) 94. Ary J. Huffman name changed to Yapp; 1 Pr. L. 1867 (5 Mar.) 236. Chillicothe, town incorporation legalized; Id. (19 Feb.) 897. Danville and Indianapolis Railway chartered; 2 Pr. L. 1867 (7 Mar.) 658. Druzilla Lacock name changed to Gilbert; L. 1869 (15 Mar.) 265.

Danville.—Town chartered; Pr. L. 1839 (3 Feb.) 8, and Pr. L. 1855 (15 Feb.) 22; last foregoing revived; Pr. L. 1857 (16 Feb.) 1127; charter amendment, additions, sale of liquor; Pr. L. 1861 (21 Feb.) 588; vacates part of McRobert's and Walker's addition; 1 L. 1837 (1 Mar.) 329, and Pr. L. 1857 (7 Feb.) 272; moneys from licenses paid to town treasury; Pr. L. 1863 (20 Feb.) 273; township issue $20.000. to bridge Big Vermilion; Id. (12 Feb.) 263. City chartered; 1 Pr. L. 1865 (16 Feb.) 294 and 1 Pr. L. 1867 (7 Mar.) 711. Danville Academy chartered; L. 1836 (15 Jan.) 154. John Parmer and five others, commr's to bridge the Big Vermilion; Pr L. 1833 (2 Mar.) 14. Danville

Coal Mining Co. chartered; Pr. L. 1855 (14 Feb.) 587. Danville Coal and Coke Co. chartered; Pr. L. 1857 (14 Feb.) 775. Illinois Insurance Co. chartered; 1 Pr. L. 1865 (16 Feb.) 674. Merchants' and Mechanics' Savings Bank chartered; Pr. L. 1867 (5 Mar.) 68. Savings Loan and Trust Co. chartered; Id. (7 Mar.) 87. Danville Gas Light Co. chartered; Id. (21 Feb.) 983. Horse Railway Co. chartered; 2 Pr. L. 1867 (21 Feb.) 19.

VERMILION SALINES.

Relating to; L. 1823 (12 Feb.) 133; foregoing amended; L. 1825 (15 Jan.) 118; sale of Saline reserve, use of funds; R. S. 1827 (15 Feb. '27) 358 §21; lease of Salines extended to16 Dec. '32; Pr. L. 1827 (10 Jan.) 9; proceeds from sale to improve Kaskaskia river; L. 1829 (23 Jan.) 125 § 7; further respecting sale, disposition of proceeds, bridge the Big and Little Vermilion; Id. (19 Jan.) 143; respecting occupants of Saline lands; L. 1831 (28 Jan.) 163. Concerning the Vermilion and Gallatin Salines; R. S. 1833 (2 Mar '33.) 348. John Powell and others, right of pre-emption; L. 1831 (25 Dec. '30.) 117.

WABASH COUNTY.

County formed from Edwards; L. 1825 (27 Dec. '24) 25; claims against Edwards devided; L. 1826 (19 Jan.) 53; payment of revenue collected in Edwards; Id. 28 Jan.) 95 § 19; com'r to adjust debts of Edwards when Wabash was formed; Pr. L. 1827 (12 Jan.) 11; share in proceeds of Gallatin Salines; L. 1831 (16 Feb.) 15; for removal of county seat [this act only appears in a list of private acts of session of 1829, L. 1829, 240]; foregoing amended; L. 1831 (15 Jan.) 65; concerning school funds; L. 1839 (2 Mar.) 233; disposition of depreciated school money; L. 1843 (3 Mar.) 153; restoration of public records; L. 1859 (16 Feb.) 187; foregoing amended; L. 1861 (22 Feb.) 270; bonds issued to Illinois Southern Rail Road, action of county court redeeming legalized; 2 Pr. L. 1867 (30 Jan.) 801; seining of fish in the Wabash prohibited; L. 1867 (5 Mar.) 117. August Tugaw, dam across channel west of Coffe Island; Pr. L. 1833 (25 Feb.) 107. Road, Mt. Carmel to Dr. Ezra Baker's, vacated and relocated; Id. (7 Jan.) 178. School fund, Town 2—14, interest thereon; L. 1843 (3 Mar.) 168. Heirs Moses Bedell, mill dam on great Wabash, Town 1—12; L. 1845 (28 Feb.) 116. Bon Pass Bridge Co. chartered; Pr. L. 1857 (16 Feb.) 858. County Agricultural and Mechanical Society chartered; Id. 1103. C. Cuqua, late sheriff, discharged from liability; L. 1859 (21 Feb.) 146. School districts 1 and 2, Town 1—12 consolidated; 2 Pr. L. 1865 (16 Feb.) 312. Vincennes Draw Bridge Co. hold real estate and bridge the Wabash; 1 Pr. L. 1867 (5 Feb.) 163. G. W. Lucas and E. Baines, restored to citizenship; L. 1869 (13 Mar.) 117.

Mt. Carmel.—Town chartered; L. 1825 (10 Jan.) 72; amendment; L. 1831 (10 Feb.) 87; further amends; Pr. L. 1833 (27 Feb.) 211; again chartered; L. 1835 (31 Jan.) 210; charter amendment; Pr. L. 1847 (11 Feb.) 71; and Pr. L. 1851 (17 Feb.) 323; sale of town commons; Pr. L. 1853 (12 Feb.) 595; take $50,000. stock in Ohio River and Wabash Rail Road; Pr. L. 1854 (28 Feb.) 164. City Chartered; 1 Pr. L. 1865 (15 Feb.) 453. Mt. Carmel Academy chartered; L. 1836 (16 Jan.) 170. Selma town name changed to Mt. Carmel, Hiram Bell keep ferry there, road to Fox River changed; 1 L. 1837 (24 Feb.) 327. Marine and Fire Insurance Co chartered; Pr. L. 1837 (2 Mar.) 216. Female Seminary chartered; Pr. L. 1839 (23 Feb.) 93. Grimke Literary Association chartered; Id. (1 Mar.) 148. Mt. Carmel Manufacturing, Co. (2 charters) chartered; Id. (2 Mar.) 215, and Pr. L. 1853 (14 Feb.) 432. Philomathean Society chartered; L. 1841 (18 Feb.) 126. Rights and franchises conveyed by deed 7 May 1846 by Thos. H. Hindes executor to Abraham Russell, confirmed; Pr. L. 1861 (22 Feb.) 545.

WABANSIE.

James Kenzie to amend town plat to conform to survey; Laws 1835 (26 Jan.) 41.

WARREN COUNTY.

County formed and boundary defined; L. 1825 (13 Jan.) 93 § 4; attached to Peoria; L. 1826 (25 Jan.) 76; county seat located and named; L. 1831 (27 Jan.) 67; extends act 22 Jan. 1831 concerning bridges, to Oct. '33; Pr. L. 1833 (22 Feb.) 13; county allowed $187.40 expenses capturing 4 Sac and Fox Indians charged with murdering Wm. Martin; L. 1835 (7 Feb.) 76; middle of the Mississippi the western boundary; 1 L. 1837 (3 Mar.) 91; sheriff pay county tax into county treasury; Id. (2 Mar.) 194; D. McNeil, settled with for building court house; L. 1845 (3 Mar.) 238; bonds subscribed to Peoria and Oquawka Rail Road, tax to pay interest; L. 1853 (11 Feb.) 171; complete numerical index to records; Pr. L. 1855 (15 Feb.) 719; jurisdiction of county court extended; L. 1859 (24 Feb.) 96; fees of circuit and county clerks; L. 1867 (7 Mar.) 115; so much of act 16 Feb. 1865, exempting this county from the game law, repealed; Id. (5 Mar.) 120; Gross' Stat. 1868, 327; for building court house and jail; 1 Pr. L. 1867 (7 Mar.) 881; take stock in two Rail Roads; L. 1869, (9 Apr.) 202. Geneva changed to Bedford; L. 1839 (12 Jan.) 40. School Land, Town 2—8, valuation revoked; Id. (9 Feb.) 85. Savannah changed to Cold Brook; Id. (15 Feb.) 119. Peoria and Burlington road legalized; L. 1840 (18 Jan.) 46. Greenfield changed to Greenbush; L. 1843 (23 Feb.) 300. Bowling Green changed to Berwick; Id. (3 Mar.) 303. Carroll plat vacated; L. 1845 (3 Mar.) 266. Greenbush Union Academy chartered; Pr. L. 1853 (12 Feb.) 519. Greenbush School district established; 3 Pr. L. 1867 (25 Feb.) 73. Auditor assign certificate of purchase for 50 acres, Town 9—2; L. 1869 (31 Mar.) 58.

Monmouth.—Blocks re-numbered; 1 L. 1837 (2 Mar.) 332; survey in 1836 legalized; Id. (2 Mar.) 333; G. H. Wright's plat of block 41 vacated; L. 1839 (12 Feb.) 103; lot numbers, block 53 changed; Pr. L. 1847 (17 Feb.) 208.

City chartered, vote thereon; L. 1852 (21 June) 68; city limits altered and defined; Pr. L. 1859 (16 Feb.) 226; charter amendment, reorganization of city schools; Pr. L. 1863 (21 Feb.) 165; corporate powers extended; 1 Pr. L. 1865 (14 Feb.) 452, and 1 Pr. L. 1867 (5 Mar.) 638. Additional justice and constable; 1 L. 1837 (15 Feb.) 117. County Male and Female Seiminary chartered; Pr. L. 1839 (2 Mar.) 205. Monmouth Lodge No. 37, F. and A. Masons chartered; Pr. L. 1853 (12 Feb.) 522. Monmouth College chartered; Pr. L. 1857 (16 Feb.) 883; amendment; Pr. L. 1859 (18 Feb.) 369. Monmouth Insurance and Loan Co. chartered; Pr. L. 1857 (16 Feb.) 1198. Excelsior Insurance Co. chartered; 1 Pr. L. 1865 (16 Feb.) 640. Prairie State Live Stock Insurance Co. chartered; Id. (15 Feb.) 758. County Home Insurance Co. chartered; Id. 814. Eccritian Literary Society chartered; 2 Pr. L. 1865 (16 Feb.) 15. Black Hawk Mining Co. chartered; Id (15 Feb.) 52. Gas Light and Coke Co. chartered; 1 Pr. L. 1867 (5 Mar.) 970. Union Hall Association chartered; 2 Pr. L. 1867 (9 Feb.) 87. Farmers' and Mechanics' Mutual Life Insurance Co. chartered; Id. (8 Mar.) 221.

WASHINGTON COUNTY.

County formed prior to the organization of the state. Location of county seat, named Georgetown, sale of county buildings at Covington; Pr. L. 1827 (10 Jan.) 7; removal of county seat 19 Jan. 1829 [this act appears only in a list of private acts in L. 1829, 240]; said act amended, court held at Nashville instead of Covington; L. 1831 (9 Feb) 66; Washington county debts on 27 Dec. '24 divided with Clinton; Pr. L. 1833 (2 Mar.) 16; borrow money to build a court house and jail; L. 1839 (16 Feb.) 110; assessments and collections for 1836–7–8 and 1841–2–3 legalized; L. 1845 (4 Feb.) 199; revenue for 1844, how collected; L. 1847 (26 Feb.) 75; school funds paid to comm'r of Clinton; Id. (28 Feb.) 116; county court hold sessions in lower rooms of jail and control them; L. 1853 (11 Feb.) 225; borrow $100,000. to pay bounties; 1 Pr. L. 1865 (15 Feb.) 115; county estray law; L. 1869 (4 Mar.) 173. Trustees Washington Academy and town of Carlisle appointed; L. 1819 (30 Mar.) 368. Wm. Morrison, further time to build toll bridge over Kaskaskia; L. 1823 (10 Feb.) 121. John Row, grist mill on the Kaskaskia; Pr. L. 1833 (1 Mar.) 12. Tabley, ferry across the Kaskaskia; Id. (28 Jan.) 35. Road, Nashville to Middleton's old ferry, located; L. 1840 (3 Feb.) 110. Public roads all confirmed and kept in repair; L. 1843 (24 Feb.) 253. Concerning sec. 16, Town 1—5; Id. (28 Feb.) 276, and L. 1845 (26 Feb.) 168. Heirs of J. Moore, guardian, sell lands Town 1—3; Id. (28 Feb.) 262. Thos. A. Nichols, convicted of perjury, restored; Id. (25 Feb.) 279. Securities of John H. McElhanon, late collector, pay in state scrip; L. 1849 (9 Feb.) 116. Wm. Pate, 4 years pedlar's license; Pr. L. 1849 (12 Feb.) 56. Ferry across the Kaskaskia established 9 June 1841 legalized; Pr. L. 1851 (15 Feb.) 231; foregoing amended, county court regulate rates; Pr. L. 1853 (12 Feb.) 605. Nelson, ferry road partly vacated; Pr. L. 1854 (1 Mar.) 199. Andrew Eisenmayer, plank road across Kaskaskia bottom, with associates chartered as Okaw Ferry Co.; Pr. L. 1855 (14 Feb.) 468. James Ingraham restored to citizenship; Id. 686. Ashley town chartered; Pr. L. 1857 (16 Feb.) 1013, and Pr. L. 1861 (22 Feb.) 557. Ferry across Kaskaskia near Wertenberg regulated; 1 Pr. L. 1865 (16 Feb.) 559. Coloma changed to Dubois and latter chartered; L. 1869 (1 Apr.) 270.

Nashville.—Town chartered; Pr. L. 1853 (11 Feb.) 351, and 2 Pr. L. 1865 (16 Feb.) 513. Nashville Academy chartered; Pr. L. 1855 (14 Feb.) 658. Washington Lodge No. 55, F. and A. Masons chartered; Id. (9 Feb.) 685. Male and Female Seminary chartered; Pr. L. 1859 (23 Feb.) 370.

Covington.—Town trustees appointed; L. 1821 (14 Feb.) 160. William Morrison to build a toll bridge across the Kaskaskia; L. 1821 (12 Feb.) 145. Town charter amended; L. 1823 (14 Feb.) 142.

Richview.—Richmond name changed to Richview; Pr. L. 1855 (9 Feb.) 47; town chartered; 2 Pr. L. 1865 (16 Feb.) 569. Washington Seminary chartered; 1 Pr. L. 1865 (16 Feb.) 32.

WAYNE COUNTY.

County formed out of Edwards, commissioners locate county seat; L. 1819 (26 Mar.) 268; southern line of Wayne and Edwards defined; L. 1829 (22 Jan.) 32; share in proceeds of Gallatin Salines; L. 1831 (16 Feb.) 15; application of Saline appropriation changed; 1 L. 1837 (2 Mar.) 93, and Id. (4 Mar.) 100; county borrow $5,000. to purchase breadstuffs for the unfortunate; Pr. L. 1855 (14 Feb.) 704; territory taken from Wayne and added to Clay; L. 1863 (12 Feb.) 84; board of supervisors; L. 1867 (28 Feb.) 102. A. C. Mackey and others, leases on school section Town 2—8, released; L. 1826 (26 Jan.) 76 §2. Benj. Sumpter, toll bridge on Little Wabash; L. 1833 (20 Feb.) 13. Eunis Maulding, ferry across Skillett Fork; Id. (28 Feb.) 35. E. W. Jones, mill dam at Harris' Shoals; L. 1831 (1 Jan.) 98; amendment, Benj. Sumpter raise his dam; Pr. L. 1833 (22 Feb.) 107. Sam. Leech, mill dam at Harris' Shoals; L. 1835 (14 Jan.) 45. Burnt Prairie Manual Labor Seminary, in Town 3—8 (partly in Wayne); L. 1836 (15 Jan.) 163. Fairfield Library Co. chartered; 2 L. 1837 (2 Mar.) 41. Proprietors selling town lots without recording plat, released; L. 1839 (2 Mar.) 268. Fairfield Institute chartered, Library Co. merged into; Pr. L. 1839 (27 Feb.) 124. Methodist Parsonage lot in Fairfield, transfer of; L. 1843 (23 Feb.) 171. Ewing Seminary chartered; L. 1845 (21 Feb.) 354. Johnson M. Owen, convicted of larceny, restored; L. 1849 (19 Jan.) 112. Wiley Webb, toll bridge at New Massillon; Pr. L. 1851 (17 Feb.) 290. Concerning Carmi Mill, to be approved by county courts of Wayne and Clay; L. 1853 (12 Feb.) 246. John D. Walters, convicted of larceny, restored; 2 Pr. L. 1867 (8 Mar.) 815. Road, Fairfield to Albion, located; Id. (23 Feb.) 819. Same, Fairfield to Noble; Id. (25 Feb.) 821. Fairfield chartered; 3 Pr. L. 1867 (25 Feb.) 494.

WHITE COUNTY.

County formed prior to the organization of the state. County share in proceeds of Gallatin Salines; L. 1831 (16 Feb.) 15; re-location of state roads; L. 1835 (24 Jan.) 79; county take $5,000. stock in Carmi Bridge Co.; Pr. L. 1837 (4 Mar.) 331; taxes for 1846-7 collected by J. B. Blackford, delinquent list for 1846, settlement with said collector; L. 1851 (17 Feb.) 101; line between White and Gallatin settled; L. 1853 (10 Feb.) 265; same subject; Pr. L. 1854 (28 Feb.) 143; auditor pay interest on county school fund; L. 1855 (15 Feb.) 103, 178. Wm. McHenry retain part of sec. 16, Town 5—10; L. 1819 (26 Feb.) 69. Benj. R. Smith, discharged from liability as sheriff; Id. (24 Mar.) 235. Cumberland Presbyterians lease part of school section Town 5—8; L. 1821 (14 Feb.) 153; foregoing amended; L. 1823 (18 Feb.) 180. Road, Caleb Ridgeway's to Carmi; L. 1825 (18 Jan.) 92 §2; same, Joseph Patton's to Caleb Ridgeway's; L. 1826 (23 Jan.) 67. Same, Carmi to Collins' ferry; L. 1829 (26 Dec. '28) 127. Same, Carmi to Fairfield, comm'rs report; Pr. L. 1833 (28 Jan.) 129. Same, Carmi to Shawneetown, in part; Id. (22 Feb.) 145; Charles Slocumb change said road on his land; Id. (27 Dec. '32) 195. Same, Logan's to Tecumseh; 2 L. 1837 (20 July) 67. Same, Carmi to Mt. Carmel, re-located near Grayville; L. 1841 (27 Feb.) 254. John Funkhouser, toll bridge over Skillett Fork; Pr. L. 1833 (28 Jan.) 6. David Ridgeway, released from payment of $500. note at Shawneetown State Bank; Id. (1 Mar.) 126. Sale of school lands, Town 5—14; L. 1835 (6 Feb.) 26. C. J. Wilman and C. J. Weed, ferry on Little Wabash; Id. (7 Jan.) 80. Burnt Prairie Manual Labor Seminary chartered; located Town 3—8; L. 1836 (15 Jan.) 163. Towns in Range 11 attached to Range 14 for school purposes; Id. (13 Jan.) 231. John Haynes, toll bridge across Skillet Fork; 1 L. 1837 (27 Feb.) 26. James Jessup, same across same; Id. (10 Feb.) 30. C. J. Weed, mill dam on Skillet Fork; Id. (27 Jan.) 182. Fox river, navigable to Town 4—14; L. 1839 (21 Feb.) 150. New Haven chartered; Pr. L. 1839 (15 Feb.) 59. Victoria changed to Philadelphia; L. 1840 (29 Jan.) 65. Remove a dam from Little Wabash; Id. (3 Feb.) 130. Additional justice's district created; L. 1841 (24 Feb.) 175. Howell & Hodges, dam the Little Wabash, Town 3—10; L. 1843 (3 Mar.) 177. Construction of dams for mills at Carmi and New Haven; L. 1845 (1 Mar.) 99; said mills sold; L. 1847 (27 Feb.) 59; foregoing amended; L. 1853 (12 Feb.) 246; and L. 1859 (24 Feb.) 40. Ewing Seminary chartered; L. 1845 (21 Feb.) 354. Reuben Emerson and securities released from rent of Carmi mills; L. 1849 (27 Jan.) 113. Wabash election precinct abolished and new one formed; Pr. L. 1849 (12 Feb.) 30. Lemuel Corwin, convicted of larceny, restored; L. 1857 (18 Feb.) 219. Elizabeth Smith name changed to Hudson; Pr. L. 1857 (31 Jan.) 228. Jane N. Brockett, name changed to Rice; Id. (10 Feb.) 352. C. L. Perigo, surety for H. W. Bompas, released; L. 1869 (30 Mar.) 344.

Carmi.—Town chartered; L. 1819 (24 Mar.) 240; amendment; L. 1823 (14 Feb.) 147; again chartered; L. 1840 (30 Jan.) 70; foregoing amended; L. 1841 (8 Feb.) 327; again chartered; Pr. L. 1857 (9 Feb.) 304; foregoing repealed; Pr. L. 1859 (24 Feb.) 591; again chartered; 3 Pr. L. 1867 (13 Feb.) 530. Public road Fackney's addition vacated; L. 1869 (30 Mar.) 392. Toll bridge over Little Wabash; L. 1819 (2 Mar.) 103. Allen Rudolph, toll bridge over Little Wabash; L. 1829 (20 Jan.) 12. Carmi Bridge Co. chartered; L. 1835 (6 Feb.) 218; amendment; Pr. L. 1839 (18 Jan.) 15; further amends; L. 1841 (8 Feb.) 327. Carmi Academy chartered; L. 1836 (16 Jan.) 158.

Grayville.—Florence name changed to Grayville; L. 1839 (2 Mar.) 273; additional justice L. 1845 (28 Jan.) 182; town chartered; Pr. L. 1851 (15 Feb.) 237, and Pr. L. 1855 (13 Feb.) 203; license money paid to town treasury; Id. (6 Feb.) 689; charter amended, town prison; 2 Pr. L. 1865 (16 Feb.) 471. Martin Doyle, ferry across Great Wabash; L. 1850 (21 Feb.) 113.

WHITESIDE COUNTY.

County created, boundary and organization; L. 1836 (16 Jan.) 274; vote on location of county seat; L. 1839 (21 Feb.) 143; same subject; L. 1843 (28 Feb.) 121; same subject, Lyndon voted for, §§3 and 4 of foregoing revived; L. 1849 (8 Feb.) 48; certain moneys added to school fund for 1846; L. 1847 (16 Jan.) 119; perfecting dividing line between Whiteside and Rock Island; Pr. L. 1853 (26 Jan.) 462; foregoing amended, action of single comm'r and citizens; Pr. L. 1854 (4 Mar.) 161; foregoing repealed; L. 1869 (29 Mar.) 161; further defining said line; Id. (16 Apr.) 94; jurisdiction of county court extended to $1,500.; L. 1857 (18 Feb.) 128; foregoing repealed; L. 1859 (19 Feb.) 103 §7; removal of county seat, Sterling to Morrison; L. 1857 (7 Feb.) 236; towns and cities on Fox river, rebuild bridges lost by flood; Pr. L. 1857 (12 Feb.) 505; sales of swamp lands legalized; L. 1859 (14 Feb.) 41; swamp land school fund apportioned; Id. (24 Feb.) 189; tax for bounties legalized; L. 1863 (12 Feb.) 85; county assist Young Men's Soldiers' Monument Association; 2 Pr. L. 1867 (8 Mar.) 454. Little Rock Academy chartered; Pr. L. 1837 (27 Feb.) 125. Illinois City plat partly vacated, name changed to Uniontown; L. 1840 (10 Dec. '39) 154. H. B. Cone, pre-empt lands Town 22—5, and J. W. Nobles, in Town 21—5; L. 1843 (4 Mar.) 170. Daniel Halse name changed to Winfield D. M. Cone; Pr. L. 1849 (12 Feb.) 14. Lyndon and Como, new entry of plats; Id. 132. Public lots in Como vacated; Pr. L 1851 (14 Feb.) 127. Mississippi Railroad Bridge Co. chartered, near Fulton City; Pr. L. 1853 (11 Feb.) 575; amendment; Pr. L. 1855 (14 Feb.) 286. J. Dow and A. Adams, acts as school trustees, Town 19—4, legalized; L. 1855 (9 Feb.) 122. Geo. H. and Alice A. Clark, name changed to Dubridge; Pr. L. 1857 (9 Feb.) 314. Wm. Murray name changed to M. Ustick; Id. (16 Feb.) 891. Rock River Coal Mining Co. chartered; Id. 1077. Albany, town taxes for 1860 remitted, account of tornado; L. 1861 (22 Jan.) 12. Erie Bridge Co. chartered; 1 Pr. L. 1865 (16 Feb.) 176. Whiteside Central Bridge Co. chartered, Town 20—5; Id. 202. Henry G. Pulnam and L. E. Rice, dam Rock river Town 20—5; Id. 553. Whiteside Peat and Mining Co.

chartered; 2 Pr. L. 1867 (14 Feb.) 427. Osceola Gold and Silver Mining Co. chartered; Id. (13 Feb.) 433. Tampico and Jordan, special bounty tax; 3 Pr. L. 1867 (18 Feb.) 119.

Morrison.—City chartered; 1 Pr. L. 1867 (27 Feb.) 595. Northwestern Insurance Co. chartered; 1 Pr. L. 1865 (16 Feb.) 740. Baptist Church of Union Grove changed to First Baptist Church of Morrison; 1 Pr. L. 1867 (21 Feb.) 241.

Prophetstown.—New entry of town plat; Pr. L. 1849 (12 Feb.) 132; re-survey of town plat; Pr. L. 1835 (15 Feb.) 184; town chartered; Pr. L. 1859 (22 Feb.) 665. Alexander & Young, ferry across Rock river; Pr. L. 1833 (28 Jan.) 33.

Sterling.—Chatham town name changed to Sterling; L. 1841 (17 Feb.) 327; Harrisburg changed to Sterling; L. 1843 (23 Feb.) 301; town to remain county seat until the $3,700. expended on court house is refunded; Pr. L. 1847 (16 Feb.) 29; town plat partly vacated; Pr. L. 1853 (24 Jan.) 480. City chartered; Pr. L. 1857 (16 Feb.) 980; charter amendment, borrow money; Pr. L. 1859 (24 Feb.) 279; general amendment; 1 Pr. L. 1867 (5 Mar.) 695; city and certain towns erect free bridge over Rock river; Id. (9 Mar.) 843. Sterling Hydraulic and Manuf. Co., to improve Rock river; Pr. L. 1847 (18 Feb.) 97; amendment; L. 1852 (21 June) 90; both foregoing amended; L. 1861 (21 Feb.) 183. Sterling Academy chartered; Pr. L. 1849 (12 Feb.) 5. Western Union Insurance Co. chartered; Pr. L. 1857 (11 Feb.) 367. Sterling Bridge Co. chartered; Pr. L. 1857 (11 Feb.) 480, and 1 Pr. L. 1865 (13 Feb.) 199. Sterling Cemetery Association chartered; Id. (16 Feb.) 226. Sterling Navigation Co. chartered; 2 Pr. L. 1865 (16 Feb.) 98. Union Printing Association chartered; Id. 125. Sterling Bank chartered; 1 Pr. L. 1867 (9 Mar.) 113. Sterling Literary Society chartered; 2 Pr. L. 1867 (21 Feb.) 268

Fulton.—City chartered; Pr. L. 1859 (14 Feb.) 150; special tax to pay city bonds; 1 Pr. L. 1865 (16 Feb.) 364. Augustine Phelps' ferry privilege confirmed to Wm. H. Knight; Pr. L. 1853 (11 Feb.) 581. Geo. W. Sayre, ferry across the Mississippi; Pr. L. 1857 (28 Feb.) 1340. Galena and Chicago Union R. R. Bridge Co. bridge the Mississippi; Pr. L. 1859 (18 Feb.) 15. Fulton Foundry Manuf. Co. chartered; 2 Pr. L. 1865 (15 Feb.) 35. Illinois Soldiers' College chartered; 1 Pr. L.) 1867 (25 Feb.) 6. Home Insurance Co. chartered; 2 Pr. L. 1867 (6 Mar.) 189.

Albany.—New entry of town plat; Pr. L. 1849 (12 Feb.) 132. D. & S. Mitchell, ferry across the Mississippi; L. 1841 (26 Feb.) 118; foregoing amended and extended; Pr. L. 1851 (14 Feb.) 126. Albany R. R. Bridge Co. chartered; Pr. L. 1857 (14 Feb.) 668.

Rapid City.—New entry of town plat; Pr. L. 1849 (12 Feb.) 132; partly vacates plat; Pr. L. 1853 (11 Feb.) 503, and Pr. L. 1855 (14 Feb.) 48; plat vacated; Pr. L. 1857 (18 Feb.) 1336.

WIGGINS' FERRY.

Samuel Wiggins, ferry across the Mississippi, near town of Illinois; L. 1819 (2 Mar.) 104; same, turnpike road 100 feet wide from opposite St. Louis to the Bluff, move ferry to avoid sand-bar; L. 1821 (6 Feb.) 94; concerning rates; L. 1831 (15 Feb.) 78; redemption of the Wiggins loan; L. 1841 (27 Feb.) 246. Wiggins' Ferry Co. chartered, purchase franchises of Samuel Wiggins; Pr. L. 1853 (11 Feb.) 193; charter amendment, repeals all after §6; Pr. L. 1857 (17 Feb.) 1146; repeals §1 of foregoing, and re-enacts sections repealed; 1 Pr. L. 1867 (12 June) 938.

WILL COUNTY.

County formed with county seat at Juliet; L. 1836 (12 Jan.) 262; funds from sale of school lands by Cook county paid over; 1 L. 1837 (31 Jan.) 314; apportionment of school fund for 1841–2 corrected; L. 1845 (26 Feb.) 167; Cook county records transcribed; L. 1847 (11 Feb.) 72; certain school directors relinquish lots to trustees I. and M. canal; Id. (25 Feb.) 152; records of judgments in circuit court indexed; Id. (1 Mar.) 70; regulates sale of liquor; Pr. L. 1847 (1 Mar.) 169; sheep and swine not to run at large after 1 Mar.; L. 1853 (27 Jan.) 152; jurisdiction of county court extended; L. 1857 (16 Feb.) 145; jurisdiction of county judge as a justice; L. 1867 (7 Mar.) 78; foregoing amended; L. 1869 (13 Mar.) 151; township support of paupers, vote thereon; L. 1861 (21 Feb.) 271; drainage of lands; Id. (22 Feb.) 271; action of county and towns levying tax to pay bounties legalized; 1 Pr. L. 1865 (6 Feb.) 147; same as to towns; Id. (16 Feb.) 153; time of holding town meetings changed; 1 Pr. L. 1867 (7 Mar.) 924; county estray law; L. 1869 (27 Mar.) 176; netting of fish prohibited; Id. (16 Apr.) 188. Wooster & Holmes, mill dam on Kankakee, Town 31—14; 1 L. 1837 (10 Feb.) 162. Vienna changed to East Buffaloa; Id. (3 Mar.) 328. Franklin Manual Labor College chartered; L. 1836 (16 Jan.) 160; amendment, may locate in Will; Pr. L. 1837 (27 Feb.) 111. Middletown plat vacated; L. 1839 (21 Feb.) 145; foregoing amended; L. 1840 (18 Jan.) 47. Union Agricultural Society chartered; Pr. L. 1839 (19 Feb.) 88. Kankakee chartered, borrow $10,000. for bridges etc.; Id. (27 Feb.) 121. Proceedings concerning schools. Town 35—10 legalized; L. 1841 (26 Feb.) 287; same, Town 35—12; L. 1843 (4 Mar.) 282. Rockville Academy chartered, Town 32—11; Id. (24 Feb.) 5. Plainfield public square vacated; L. 1845 (1 Mar.) 121. Romeo plat vacated; Id. (3 Mar.) 138. Erection of school house, Town 35—10; L. 1847 (16 Jan.) 159. County Literary and Historical Society; Pr. L. 1847 (27 Feb.) 149. Chas. W. Dodd, convicted of larceny, restored; Id. (22 Jan.) 172. David Bloom released from recognizance for Thos. Hendricks; Id. (15 Feb.) 174. Robert Stephens, patent for tract of land; L. 1849 (12 Feb.) 102; foregoing amended; L. 1851 (13 Feb.) 87. Florence and Wesley, towns established; Id. (15 Feb.) 113. Town 35—12, incorporation of for school purposes legalized; Pr. L. 1849 (12 Feb.) 40. Jos. Campbell, vacates street running through his property; Id. 131. Jos. McCoy, state pedlar's license for life; Pr. L. 1851 (12 Feb.) 85. Troy, town established; L. 1852 (23 June) 207 Trenton abolished, Manhattan and Green Garden created; L. 1853 (10 Feb.) 206. Alonzo Leach, late sheriff, allowed $350.; Pr. L. 1853 (12 Feb.) 492. Willard Grove Cemetery Association chartered; Pr. L. 1855 (14 Feb.) 440. Mound Cemetery Association chartered; Id. 454. Oakwood Cemetery chartered; Id. (12 Feb.) 473. Plainfield Methodist E. Church, acts legalized; Id. 680. Road, Town 37—9, proceedings as to legalized; L. 1857 (18 Feb.) 197. Town 36—9, acts of school trustees, and directors district 1, legalized; L. 1859 (19 Feb.) 177. Manhattan, parish of sell real estate; Pr. L. 1859 (24 Feb.) 34. Crete Farmers' Mutual Insurance Co. chartered; Pr. L. 1861 (20 Feb.) 353. Wilmington, Reed, Wesley and Florence, with towns in Kankakee and Grundy vote on tax to improve the Kankakee; Id. (22 Feb.) 737. Plainfield College of Evangelical Association of North America changed to Northwestern College of etc.; 1 Pr. L. 1865 (15 Feb.) 12. DuPage, action of town re-imbursing advances to pay recruits legalized; Id. (16 Feb.) 156. Wheatland Cemetery Association chartered; Id. 230. Wilmington and Monee Railroad chartered 2 Pr. L. 1865 (16 Feb.) 227; amendment; 2 Pr. L. 1867 (7 Mar.) 585. Union Mining and Manuf. Co. chartered; Id. (6 Mar.) 377. Allandale Coal Mining and Manuf. Co. chartered, at Joliet or Wilmington; Id. (19 Feb.) 428. Monee, Crete and Dyer Railroad chartered; Id. (7 Mar.) 588. Chicago and Wilmington Coal Co. to build a railroad; Id. (21 Feb.) 707. Fred. D. S. Stewart late treasurer, $3,000. lost by bank failures; Id. (12 June) 794. DuPage and Wilton, town bounty tax legalized; 3 Pr. L. 1867 (30 Jan.) 117. Frankfort, Holden's addition partly vacated; Id. (28 Feb.) 234.

Joliet.—Town of Juliet chartered; Pr. L. 1837 (1 Mar.) 194; foregoing repealed; L. 1841 (27 Jan.) 317; tax to pay town liabilities; Id. (17 Feb.) 305; sell lots for burying grounds; Id. (27 Feb.) 49; Juliet name changed to Joliet; L. 1845 (26 Feb.) 166; bridging the Des Plaines, vote thereon; Pr. L. 1847 (1 Mar.) 17; Des Plaines street re-located; Id. (16 Jan.) 196; Joliet street partly vacated; L. 1849 (12 Feb.) 46; certain streets changed; Pr. L. 1851 (28 Jan.) 31, and Id. (17 Feb.) 274; building sidewalks; Id. 263; Michigan street partly vacated; Id. 277. City chartered; L. 1852 (22 June) 161; amendment, control of common schools; Pr. L. 1853 (10 Feb.) 275; water works and gas; Pr. L. 1854 (4 Mar.) 187; incorporating acts reduced to one and amended; Pr. L. 1857 (31 Jan.) 188; parts of streets vacated; Id. (18 Feb.) 1432; grounds vacated; Pr. L. 1861 (21 Feb.) 203; charter amendment, elect police magistrate; Id. (22 Feb.) 204; city jurisdiction for school purposes; 1 Pr. L. 1865 (16 Feb.) 302; charter amendment, tenure of office police magistrate two years, repeals laws named; Ibid.; boundary defined; 1 Pr. L. 1867 (1 Mar.) 619; town two election precincts; Id. (7 Mar.) 924. Juliet Academy chartered; L. 1841 (27 Feb.) 14. Juliet Seminary chartered; L. 1843 (4 Mar.) 284. Purports to change name of First Congregational Society; L. 1852 (23 June) 267; acts of said society legalized; 2 Pr. L. 1867 (21 Feb.) 266. James Lyon name changed to Lewis James, heir of Royal Reed; Pr. L. 1855 (9 Feb.) 694; Wm. W. Field name changed to Wm. Field Reed, heir of same; Id. (14 Feb.) 738. Joliet Insurance Co. chartered; Pr. L. 1857 (12 Feb.) 484. Joliet Gas Light Co. chartered; Pr. L. 1859 (11 Feb.) 381. Des Plaines Cemetery Association chartered; 1 Pr. L. 1865 (16 Feb.) 217. Joliet Manuf. Co. chartered; 2 Pr. L. 1865 (25 Feb.) 343. Sharpshooters' Association chartered; 3 Pr. L. 1867 (21 Feb.) 92.

Lockport.—Archer's addition chartered: L. 1839 (2 Mar.) 260; village chartered; Pr. L. 1853 (12 Feb.) 216: town plat of West Lockport vacated; 3 Pr. L. 1867 (7 Mar.) 259. Bridge the Des Plaines; Pr. L. 1849 (12 Feb.) 12. School lots sold; application of proceeds; L. 1851 (17 Feb.) 185. Lockport Cemetery Association chartered; Pr. L. 1853 (12 Feb.) 548. Baptist church convey real estate; Pr. L. 1855 (6 Feb.) 687; foregoing amended, description corrected; Pr. L. 1857 (30 Jan.) 116. Lockport Seminary chartered; Pr. L. 1861 (22 Feb.) 17. Public School District chartered; 2 Pr. L. 1865 (16 Feb.) 301.

Wilmington.—Winchester town name changed to Wilmington; 2 L. 1837 (21 July) 102; tax in aid of Kankakee and Iroquois Navigation and Manuf. Co.; L. 1852 (15 June) 10; build sidewalks; Pr. L. 1853 (11 Feb.) 561; town charter generally amended; 2 Pr. L. 1865 (15 Feb.) 623. Wilmington Coal Mining and Manuf. Co. chartered; Id. (16 Feb.) 88; foregoing amended; 2 Pr. L. 1867 (25 Feb.) 416. Wilmington Manuf. Co. chartered; Id. (23 Feb.) 331.

Wilmington Bridge.—Towns of Wilmington and Reed, tax to improve the Kankakee and bridge the same; Pr. L. 1851 (15 Feb.) 232. Wilmington Bridge Co. chartered; Pr. L. 1853 (12 Feb.) 347, and 1 Pr. L. 1867 (8 Mar.) 189. Towns of Wilmington and Reed, tax in aid of, Wilmington failing to make levy renders act void; Pr. L. 1855 (15 Feb.) 667; balance of $3,872.80 due under foregoing, levied upon towns of Reed and Wilmington, and Essex and Norton, Kankakee county; Pr. L. 1861 (22 Feb.) 537. Wilmington levy special tax to pay bridge debts; 2 Pr. L. 1865 (16 Feb.) 339. Towns in county to repair, vote for or against; 1 Pr. L. 1867 (21 Feb.) 170.

WILLIAMSON COUNTY.

County created, boundary and organization; L. 1839 (28 Feb.) 110; foregoing amended; L. 1840 (18 Jan.) 88; said act to be sent to circuit clerk; Id. 87; John Bainbridge as probate justice, and E. McIntosh as county clerk, acts legalized; L. 1843 (2 Feb.) 185; John R. Miller deputy recorder, acts legalized; Pr. L. 1847 (28 Feb.) 217; transcribing records books "A," "C," "D," "E," "F" and "G"; Pr. L. 1855 (6 Feb.) 688; transcribing probate records; Pr. L. 1857 (30 Jan.) 115; additional tax to pay county orders; L. 1863 (13 Jan.) 86. H. H. Singleton, mill dam on Crab Orchard creek; L. 1843 (1 Feb.) 174. John T. Davis and others, mill dam on Saline creek; Id. (23 Feb.) 175. W. T. Ryburn, mill dam on the Big Muddy; Id. (4 Mar.) 178. Bainbridge plat vacated; Pr. L. 1847 (20 Feb.) 205. Jas. F. Chinneworth and others, bridge the Big Muddy; Pr. L. 1849 (10 Feb.) 11. Thos. D. Davis and others, dam the Big Saline Town 10—4; Pr. L. 1851 (15 Feb.) 244. Lucilla

Dean name changed to Mary A. Scurlock; Pr. L. 1857 (13 Feb.) 585.

Marion.—Town chartered; L. 1841 (24 Feb.) 334; foregoing repealed; Pr. L. 1847 (15 Feb.) 81; again chartered; 2 Pr. L. 1865 (16 Feb.) 498. Marion Academy chartered; L. 1841 (17 Feb.) 7. School district established: L. 1857 (16 Feb.) 187; foregoing amended; 3 Pr. L. 1867 (9 Feb.) 23.

WINNEBAGO COUNTY.

County formed; L. 1836 (16 Jan.) 278; boundary defined; 1 L. 1837 (4 Mar.) 95; removal of county seat from Winnebago; L. 1839 (2 Mar.) 264; its location at Rockford; L. 1843 (25 Feb.) 121; special tax for county purposes 1845–6; L. 1845 (28 Feb.) 115; records in book "A" confirmed, copying of records in Boone county; Id. (26 Feb.) 160; jurisdiction of county court extended; Pr. L. 1854 (27 Feb.) 239, and L. 1857 (18 Feb.) 150; both foregoing repealed; L. 1863 (12 Feb.) 28; supervisors appoint their own clerk; Pr. L. 1855 (9 Feb.) 715; borrow money to build court house and jail; Pr. L. 1857 (29 Jan.) 91; loan of school money to C. A. Huntington legalized; L. 1861 (12 Feb.) 193; transcribing public records; 2 Pr. L. 1865 (14 Feb.) 236; and 2 Pr. L. 1867 (25 Feb.) 789; county estray law; L. 1869 (27 Mar.) 176. Belvidere College chartered; Pr. L. 1837 (1 Mar.) 200. Peckatonica Bridge Co. chartered; Pr. L. 1839 (2 Mar.) 234. Rock River Seminary of Learning at Pecatonica chartered; Kishwaukee Seminary chartered; Id. 238. S. L. Hall and others, ferry across Rock River; L. 1840 (1 Feb.) 110. Kishwaukee Ferry Co. chartered; L. 1841 (27 Feb.) 121. S. Jenks and others, bridge Fox river Town 45—2; L. 1843 (6 Feb.) 45. J. B. Thayer and others, free bridge over Rock river, Town 46; Id. (1 Mar.) 47. F. Van Volkenburg, preemption right Town 27—10; Id. (4 Mar.) 171 §2. Wm. Talcott and others, mill dam on Rock river Town 46—1; Id. (3 Mar.) 177. A. Durbin, pre-emption Town 26—10; B. Van Etten; same, Town 27—10; L. 1845 (1 Mar.) 212. Roscoe Cemetery Association chartered; Id. (3 Mar.) 301. Certain school district levy tax; L. 1847 (17 Feb.) 157. Trustees of schools, acts legalized; Id. 156. Albert Ellis, pre-emption right; Pr. L. 1847 (19 Feb.) 177. Owen Miller Jr., security for Lewis and Shedrick Crane, discharged; Pr. L. 1851 (17 Feb.) 303. Agricultural Society chartered; L. 1852 (21 June) 52. Howard Cemetery Association chartered; Pr. L. 1853 (11 Feb.) 453. Union Cemetery Association at Butler chartered; Id. (26 Jan.) 475. James H. Hanchett, toll bridge at Roscoe; Id. (8 Feb.) 561. Willow Creek Cemetery Association chartered; Pr. L. 1855 (15 Feb.) 451. Winnebago Swamp Drainage Co. chartered, acts relating to said swamps repealed; Id. (14 Feb.) 592. Butler changed to Cherry Valley; Id. (31 Jan.) 228. New Milford Cemetery Association chartered; Pr. L. 1857 (16 Feb.) 902. S. Talcott, dam on the Pecatonica; Id. 1073. Branch Railroad chartered; Pr. L. 1863 (16 Feb.) 229. David Jewitt, dam on Pecatonica at Harrison; 1 Pr. L. 1865 (16 Feb.) 552. Franklin Blair and D. Reed Jr., the same, in Lysander; 2 Pr. L. 1867 (7 Mar.) 810. Howard changed to Durand; L. 1869 (no date) 279. Lysander changed to Pecatonica; Id. (29 Mar.) 279.

Rockford.— Acknowledgement of town plat legalized; L. 1845 (3 Mar.) 271; tax to repair Rock river bridge, bridge comm'rs chartered; Pr. L. 1847 (25 Feb.) 14; re-location of streets; Id. (22 Feb.) 198; borrow money to build bridge; L. 1852 (18 June) 33; foregoing repealed, same subject; L. 1853 (3 Feb.) 189; additional justice, etc.; Id. (12 Feb.) 169; width of River street; Id. (11 Feb.) 528. Incorporation of city 3 Jan. 1852 under general law, legalized; Pr. L. 1853 (8 Feb.) 565. City chartered; Pr. L. 1854 (4 Mar.) 103; amendment; Pr. L. 1855 (14 Feb.) 43; alley in block 11 vacated; Pr. L. 1857 (31 Jan.) 227; amends §175 of charter; Pr. L. 1859 (24 Feb.) 255; Roberts' addition vacated; Pr. L. 1861 (13 Feb.) 253; laying of railroad tracts, sidewalks etc., regulated; Id. (22 Feb.) 254; acts incorporating reduced to one and revised; 1 Pr. L. 1855 (15 Feb.) 472. G. W. Brinkerhoof and others ferry across Rock river; L. 1839 (2 Mar.) 284. Rockford Manuf. Co. chartered; Pr. L. 1839 (2 Mar.) 159. Rockford Seminary of Learning chartered; Id. 238. Free Bridge over Rock river; L. 1843 (27 Feb.) 47. Cemetery Asssociation chartered; L. 1845 (28 Feb.) 174. Improve navigation of Rock river, Rockford Hydraulic and Manuf. Co. chartered; Pr. L. 1843 (28 Feb.) 240; amendment; L. 1845 (11 Feb.) 237; comm'rs from other counties constitute special board; Pr. L. 1847 (18 Feb.) 95. Cedar Bluff Cemetery Association chartered; Pr. L. 1847 (18 Feb.) 103. Rockford Female Seminary chartered; Id. (25 Feb.) 124; amendment, borrow money; Pr. L. 1857 (30 Jan.) 112. Organization of First Congregational Society conditionally legalized; Pr. L. 1847 (28 Feb.) 150. Cemetery Association chartered; L. 1852 (23 June) 220. Rock River Mutual Fire Insurance Co. chartered; Id. (21 June) 80; name changed to Rock River Insurance Co.; Pr. L. 1861 (15 Feb.) 422; further amendment; Pr. L. 1863 (10 June) 195. Rockford Water Power Co. declared chartered; Pr. L. 1853 (10 Feb.) 405; to determine width of chute; Pr. L. 1863 (13 Feb.) 213. John A. Holland and others chartered to erect buildings; Pr. L. 1853 (12 Feb.) 524. Gas Light and Coke Co. chartered; Pr. L. 1855 (15 Feb.) 653, and Pr. L. 1861 (22 Feb.) 338. Hotel Co. borrow money; Pr. L. 1857 (30 Jan.) 114. Forest City Hotel Co. chartered; Id. (11 Feb.) 450. Commercial and Mathematical Institute chartered; Id. (13 Feb.) 511. Loan and Trust Association chartered; Id. (15 Feb.) 647. Wesleyan Seminary chartered, confer degrees Master of Theoretical Agriculture and Lady of Liberal Learning; Id. (14 Feb.) 792. Rockford Insurance and Savings Co. chartered; Id. (19 Feb.) 1384; name changed to Rockford Insurance Co.; 2 Pr. L. 1867 (23 Feb.) 121. Building Association chartered; 1 Pr. L. 1867 (28 Feb.) 202. Horse Railway Co. chartered; 2 Pr. L. 1867 (28 Feb.) 6. Rockford Library chartered; Id. (22 Feb.) 251.

Rockton.— Pecatonica changed to Rockton, plat partly vacated; Pr. L. 1847 (26 Feb.) 206; alley located; Pr. L. 1851 (17 Feb.) 265; take stock in railroad, vote thereon; L. 1853 (12 Feb.) 169; borrow $10,000. to build bridges, vote thereon; Id. (10 Feb.) 191; boundary defined;

Id. (11 Feb.) 201; location of a state road; L. 1857 (11 Feb.) 66. Rockton Water Power Co. chartered; Pr. L. 1853 (10 Feb.) 504; contribution of owners towards its maintenance; 2 Pr. L. 1865 (16 Feb.) 686.

Winnebago.—Vacates alleys; L. 1840 (10 Dec. '39) 134; plat vacated; Pr. L. 1847 (17 Feb.) 202; Elydatown name changed to Winnebago; Pr. L. 1855 (9 Feb.) 692; vacates streets; 3 Pr. L. 1867 (25 Feb.) 102.

WOODFORD COUNTY.

County formed, county seat at Versailles; L. 1841 (27 Feb.) 84; repeals §9 of foregoing; L. 1843 (1 Mar.) 93; part of Tazewell attached to Woodford, vote thereon; Id. (17 Feb.) 86; line between McLean and Woodford; Id. (28 Feb.) 91; locate county seat; Id. 123; supplemental; Id. (6 Mar.) 127; school fund of Tazewell transferred to Woodford and Mason; L. 1845 (1 Mar.) 235; location of county seat at Hanover legalized; Hanover changed to Metamora; Id. (21 Feb.) 345; transcribing records of Tazewell and McLean; Pr. L. 1857 (18 Feb.) 1333; copying records; L. 1861 (21 Feb.) 274; auditor's sale of real estate; L. 1865 (16 Feb.) 86; fees of officers; L. 1867 (28 Feb.) 112; take stock in railroads; 1 Pr. L. 1867 (6 Mar.) 866; purchase county poor farm; Id. (9 Feb.) 875; removal of county seat, Metamora to El Paso, vote thereon; Id. (27 Feb.) 897, and Metamora to Eureka; L. 1869 (9 Feb.) 157. Tazewell changed to Spring Bay; Pr. L. 1849 (9 Feb.) 124. County Plank Road Co. chartered; Pr. L. 1853 (12 Feb.) 249. Spring Bay Ferry and Dyke Co. chartered; Id. 538. Uniontown changed to Mantua; Pr. L. 1855 (15 Feb.) 195, and Mantua changed to Washburne; Pr. L. 1857 (7 Feb.) 272. Assessment district No. 5, Cazenovia; L. 1861 (21 Feb.) 192. Metamora chartered, officers' acts legalized; Pr. L. 1861 (13 Feb.) 690. Kappa, Cook's addition partly vacated; 2 Pr. L. 1865 (15 Feb.) 657. Spring Bay partly vacated; 3 Pr. L. 1867 (21 Feb.) 109. Minonk chartered; Id. (7 Mar.) 259. Secor chartered; Id. (21 Feb.) 586; alley vacated; Id. 109. Panola chartered; Id. (28 Feb.) 618.

El Paso.—Town chartered; Pr. L. 1861 (22 Feb.) 625. City chartered; 1 Pr. L. 1867 (27 Feb.) 792; establishing recorder's court; L. 1869 (6 Mar.) 128, supplemental Id. 132. El Paso Academy chartered; Pr. L. 1851 (20 Feb.) 14. Cemetery Association chartered; Id. (18 Feb.) 66. Gas Light and Coke Co. chartered; 1 Pr. L. 1867 (5 Mar.) 974. Horse Railway and Carrying Co. chartered; 2 Pr. L. 1867 (9 Mar.) 34. Mining and Manuf. Co. chartered; Id. (28 Feb.) 422.

Eureka.—Town chartered; Pr. L. 1859 (23 Feb.) 603; amendment; Pr. L. 1861 (20 Feb.) 617; further amendment; 1 Pr. L. 1867 (22 Feb.) 919. Eureka College chartered; near to and succeed the Walnut Grove Academy; Pr. L. 1855 (6 Feb.) 540; amendment, portion of school fund; Id. (9 Feb.) 585. Pereclesian Society chartered; Pr. L. 1857 (16 Feb.) 1032. Simpson Seminary and Collegiate Institute chartered; 1 Pr. L. 1867 (25 Feb.) 10.

NOTE.—An act chartering the town of Belvidere (Pr. L. 1857, 252) and an amendment thereto (Pr. L. 1859, 585) appear under the head Kane County, and an act chartering Belvidere College (Pr. L. 1837, 200), under Winnebago County. They should all have appeared under BOONE COUNTY, *Belvidere*. An act for the organization and government of the Militia, approved 2 Mar. 1833 and taking effect 2 July 1833, was not published with the Laws of 1833 but in a volume by itself. This was not observed until Part I had gone to press. The act is found Gale's Stat. 469. An act amending Union College charter, L. 1839 (22 Feb.) 50, should have appeared Chap. 25, Div. 2.

www.ingramcontent.com/pod-product-compliance
Lightning Source LLC
Chambersburg PA
CBHW021947220326
41599CB00012BA/1225

* 9 7 8 3 7 4 2 8 1 3 9 0 9 *